D0619336

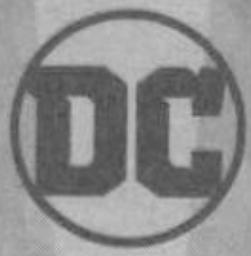

WONDER WOMAN

THE COMPLETE COVERS

VOL. 2

INSIGHT EDITIONS
San Rafael, California

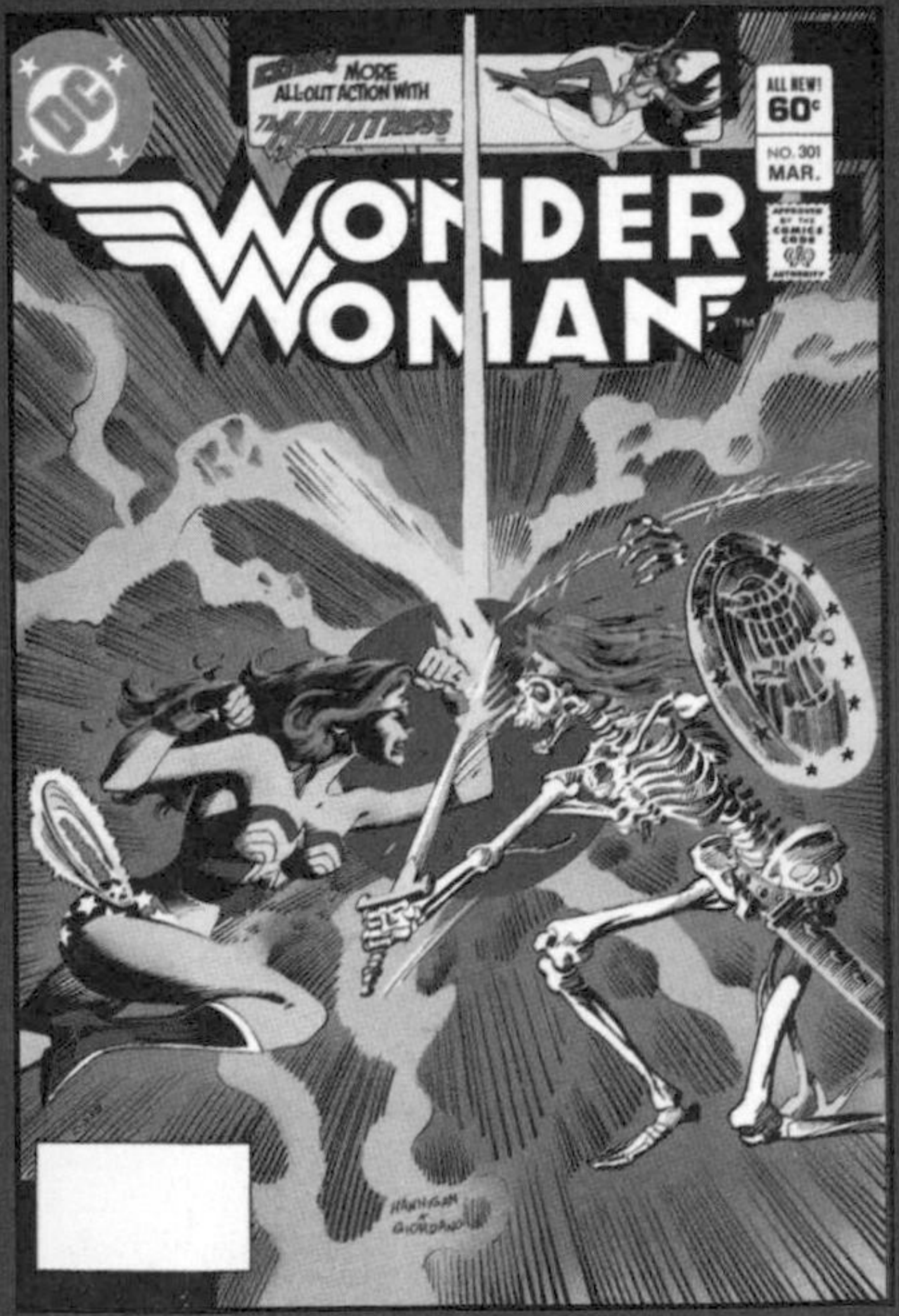
DC
MORE ALL-OUT ACTION WITH THE HUNTRESS
ALL NEW!
60¢
NO. 301
MAR.
WONDER WOMAN
HANNIGAN & GIORDANO

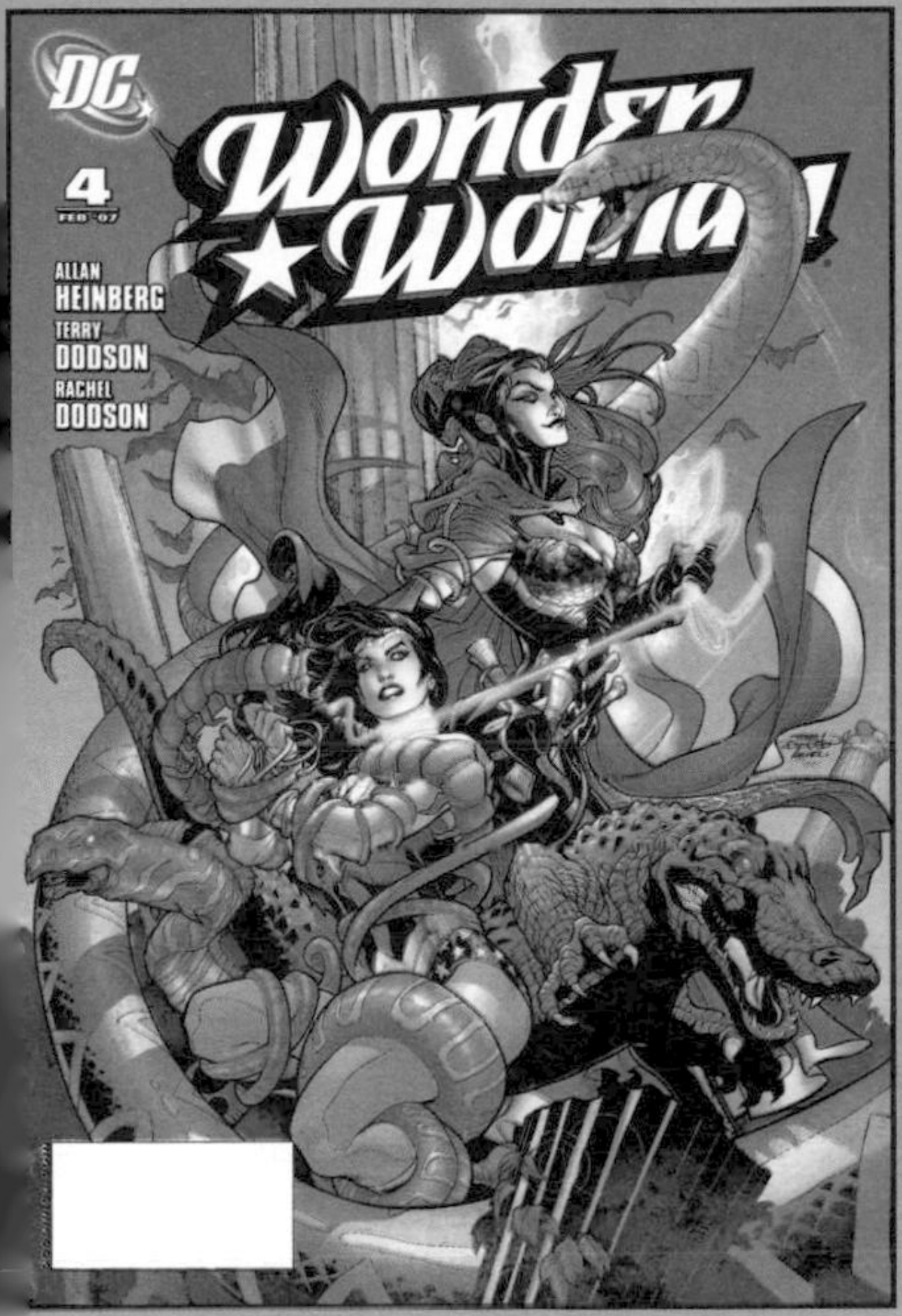
DC
Wonder Woman
4
FEB '07
ALLAN HEINBERG
TERRY DODSON
RACHEL DODSON

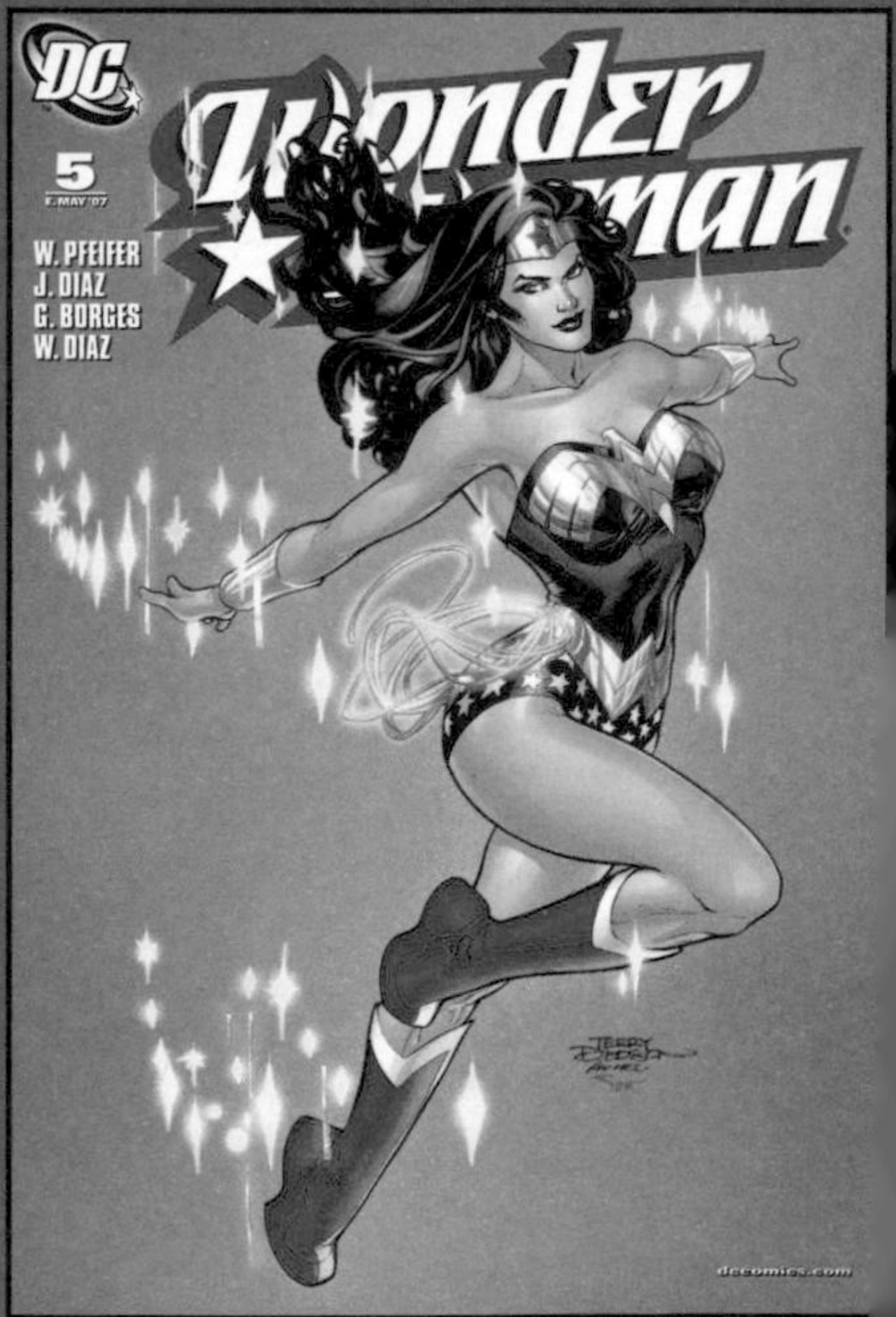
DC
Wonder Woman
5
E. MAY '07
W. PFEIFER
J. DIAZ
G. BORGES
W. DIAZ
dccomics.com

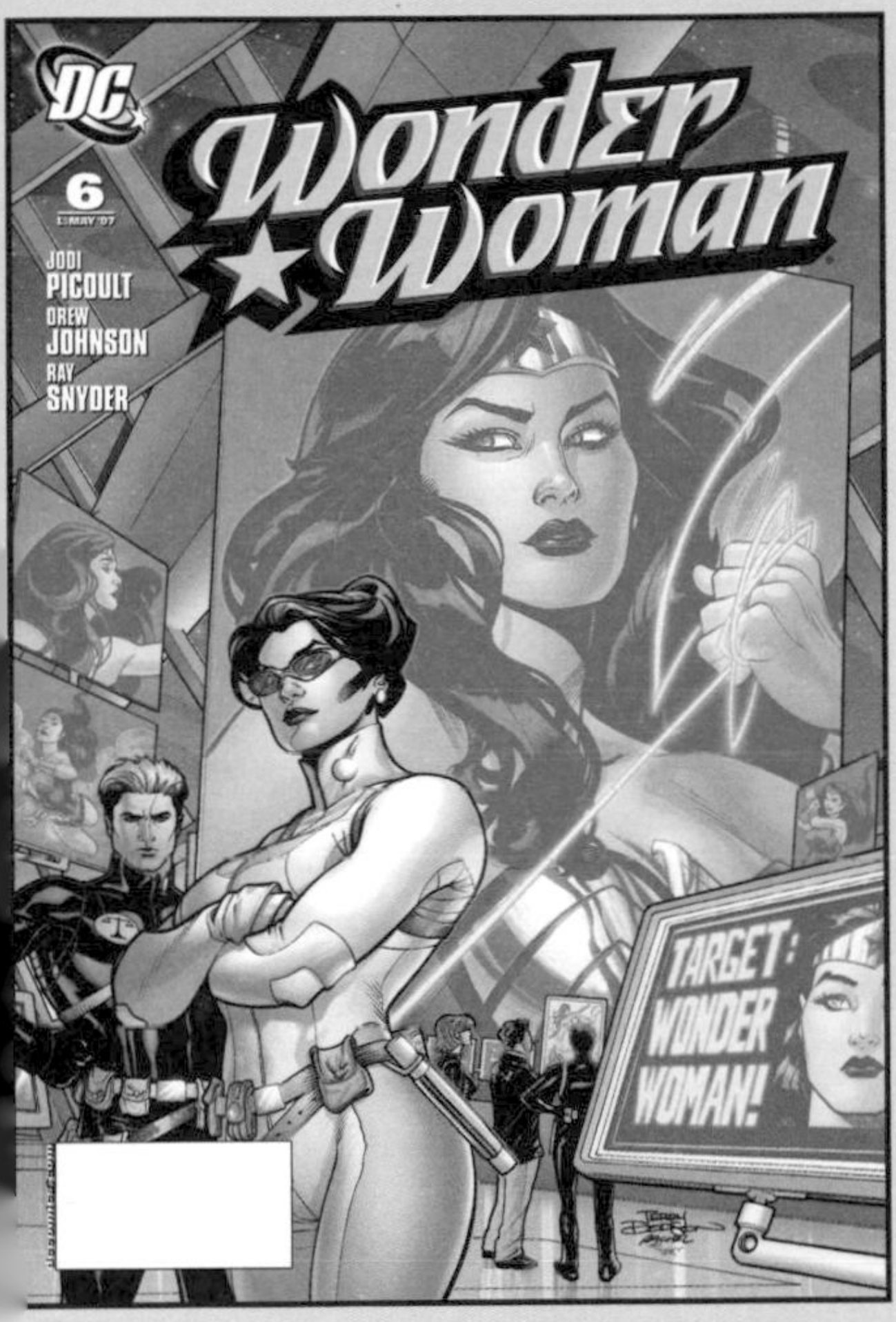
DC
Wonder Woman
6
JODI PICOULT
DREW JOHNSON
RAY SNYDER
TARGET: WONDER WOMAN!

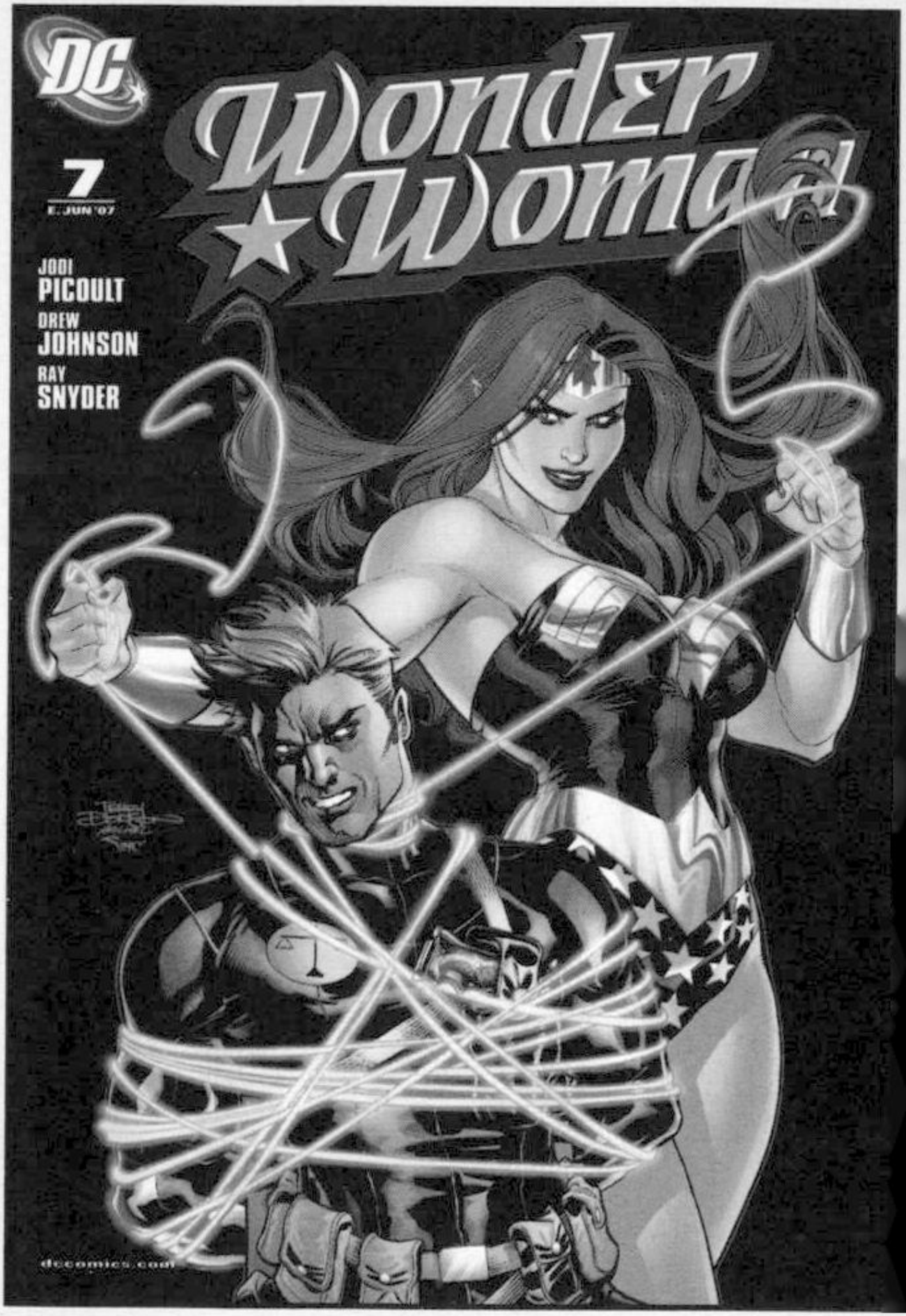
DC
Wonder Woman
7
E: JUN '07
JODI PICOULT
DREW JOHNSON
RAY SNYDER
dccomics.com

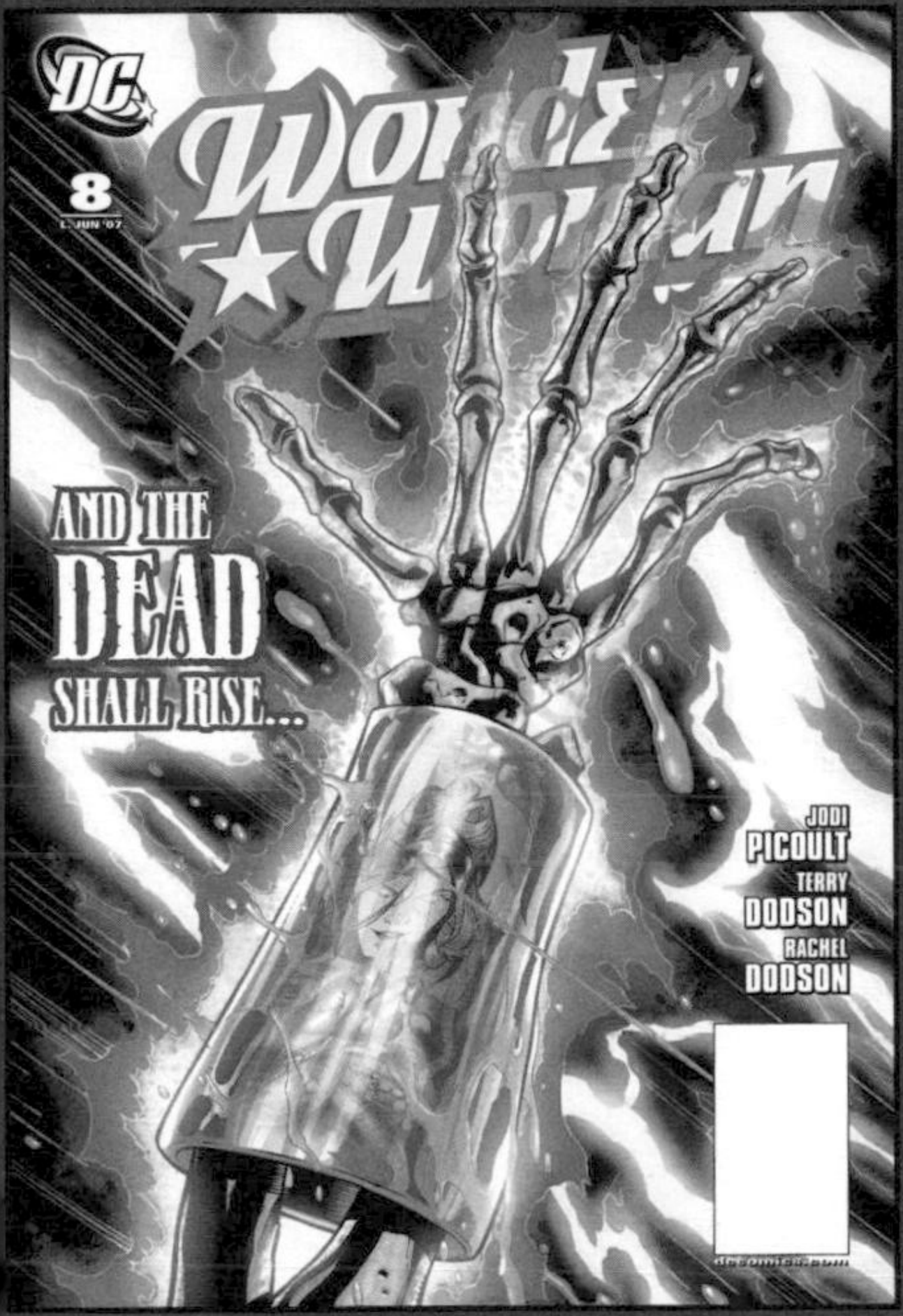
DC
Wonder Woman
8
JUN '07
AND THE
DEAD
SHALL RISE...
JODI
PICOULT
TERRY
DODSON
RACHEL
DODSON

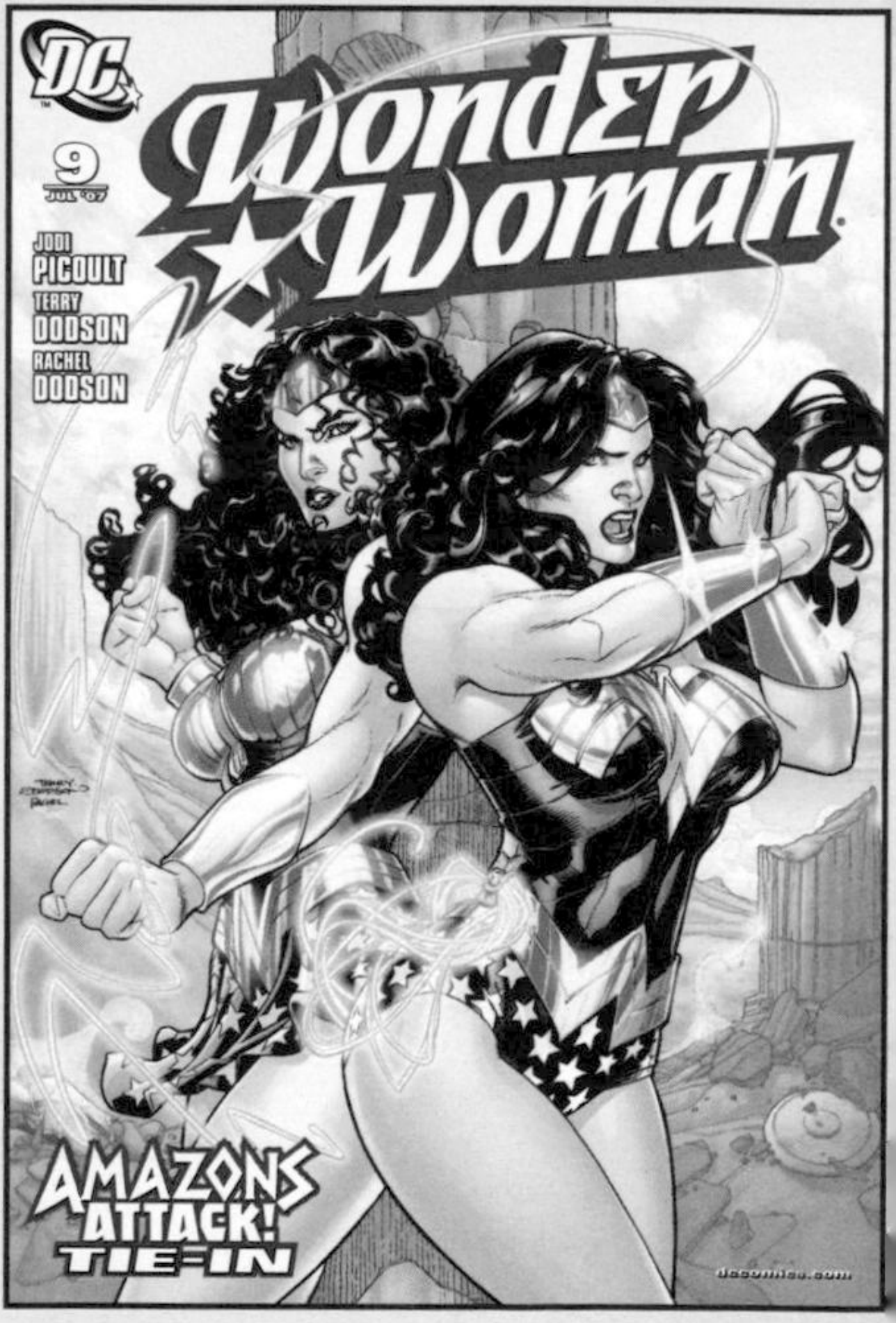
DC
9
JUL '07
Wonder Woman
JODI PICOULT
TERRY DODSON
RACHEL DODSON
AMAZONS ATTACK! TIE-IN

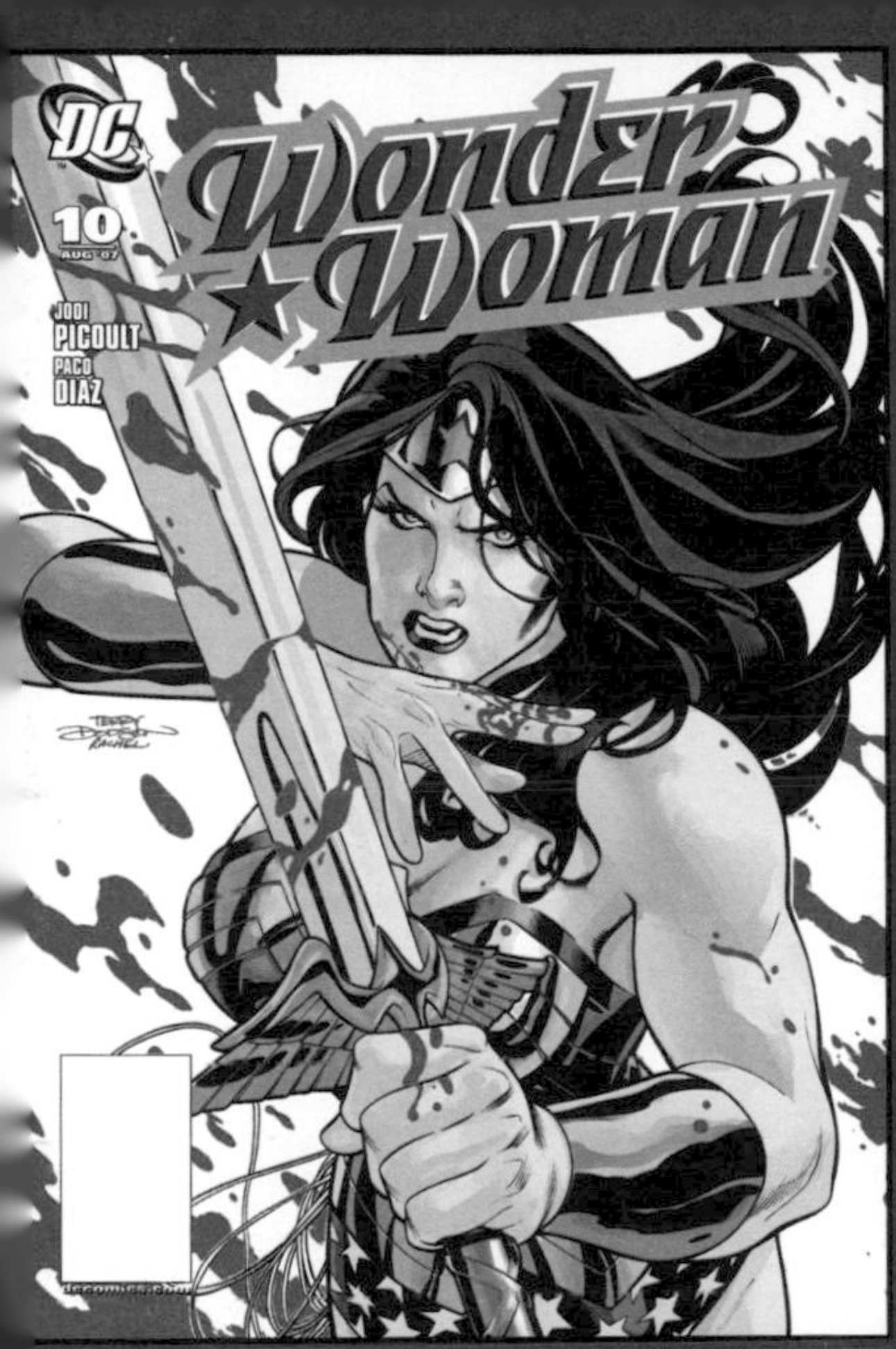
DC
Wonder Woman
10
AUG '07
JODI PICOULT
PACO DIAZ

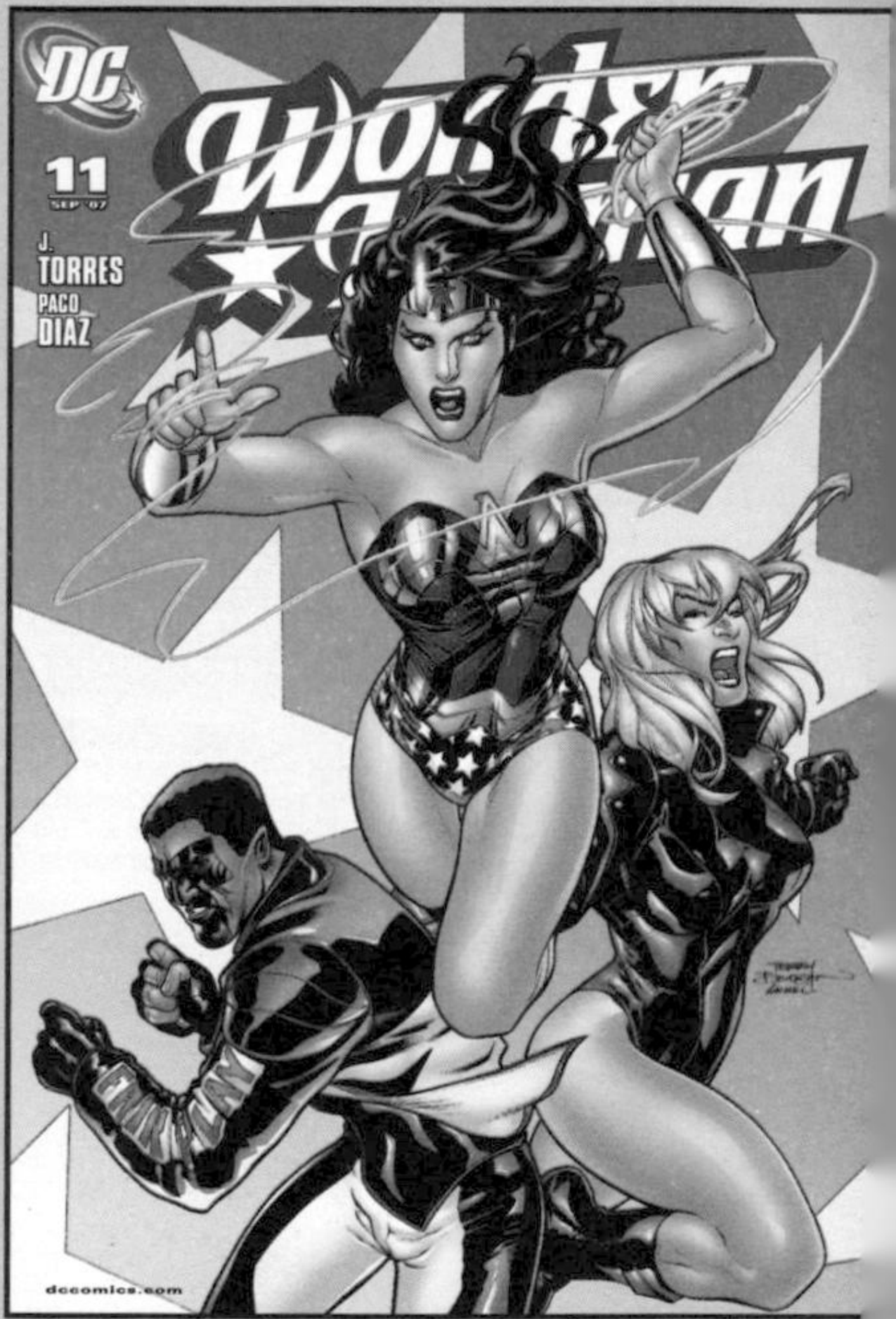
DC
Wonder Woman
11
SEP '07
J. TORRES
PACO DIAZ
dccomics.com

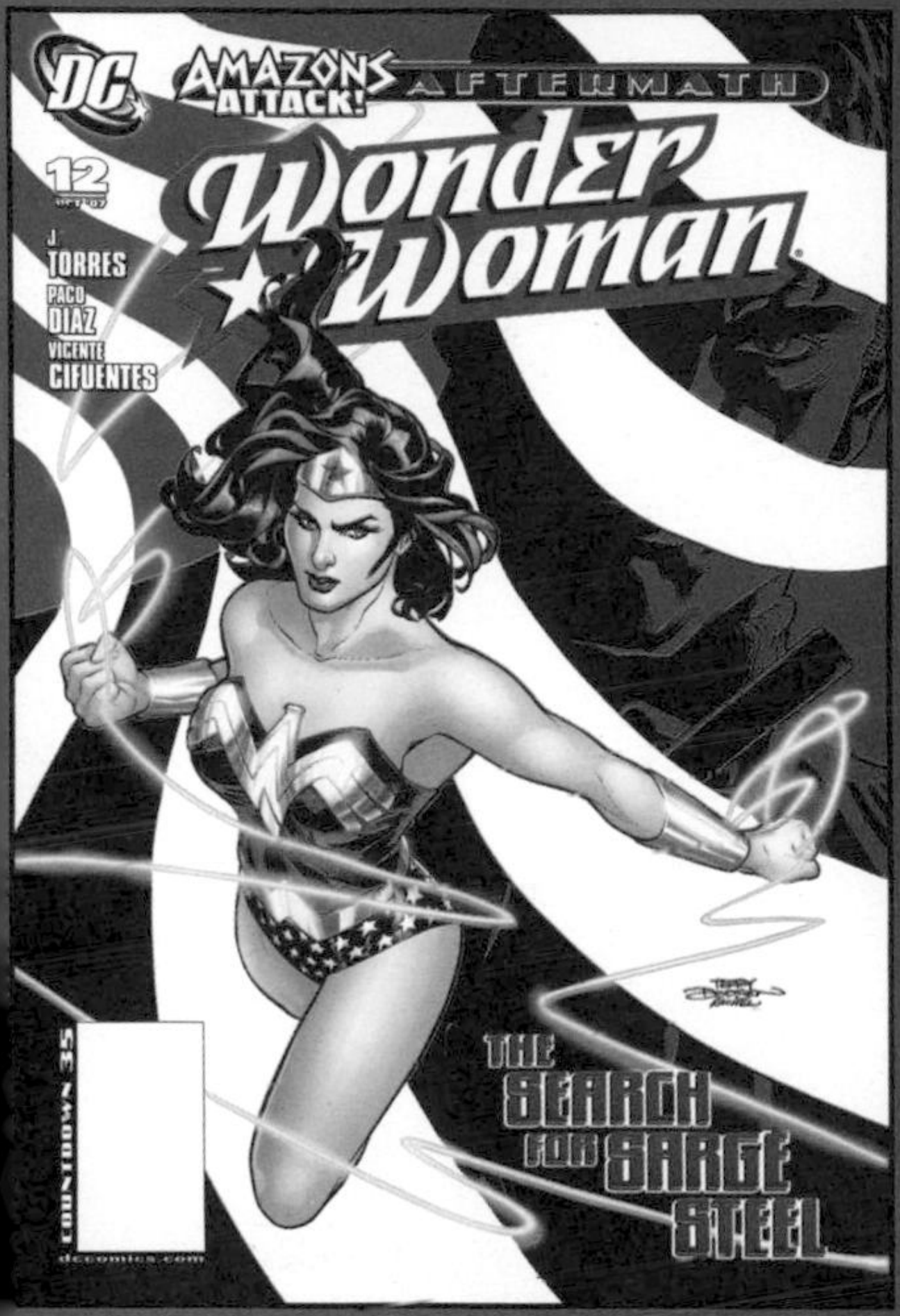
DC
AMAZONS ATTACK!
AFTERMATH
12
Wonder Woman
J. TORRES
PACO DIAZ
VICENTE CIFUENTES
THE SEARCH FOR SARGE STEEL
COUNTDOWN 35 NOW
dccomics.com

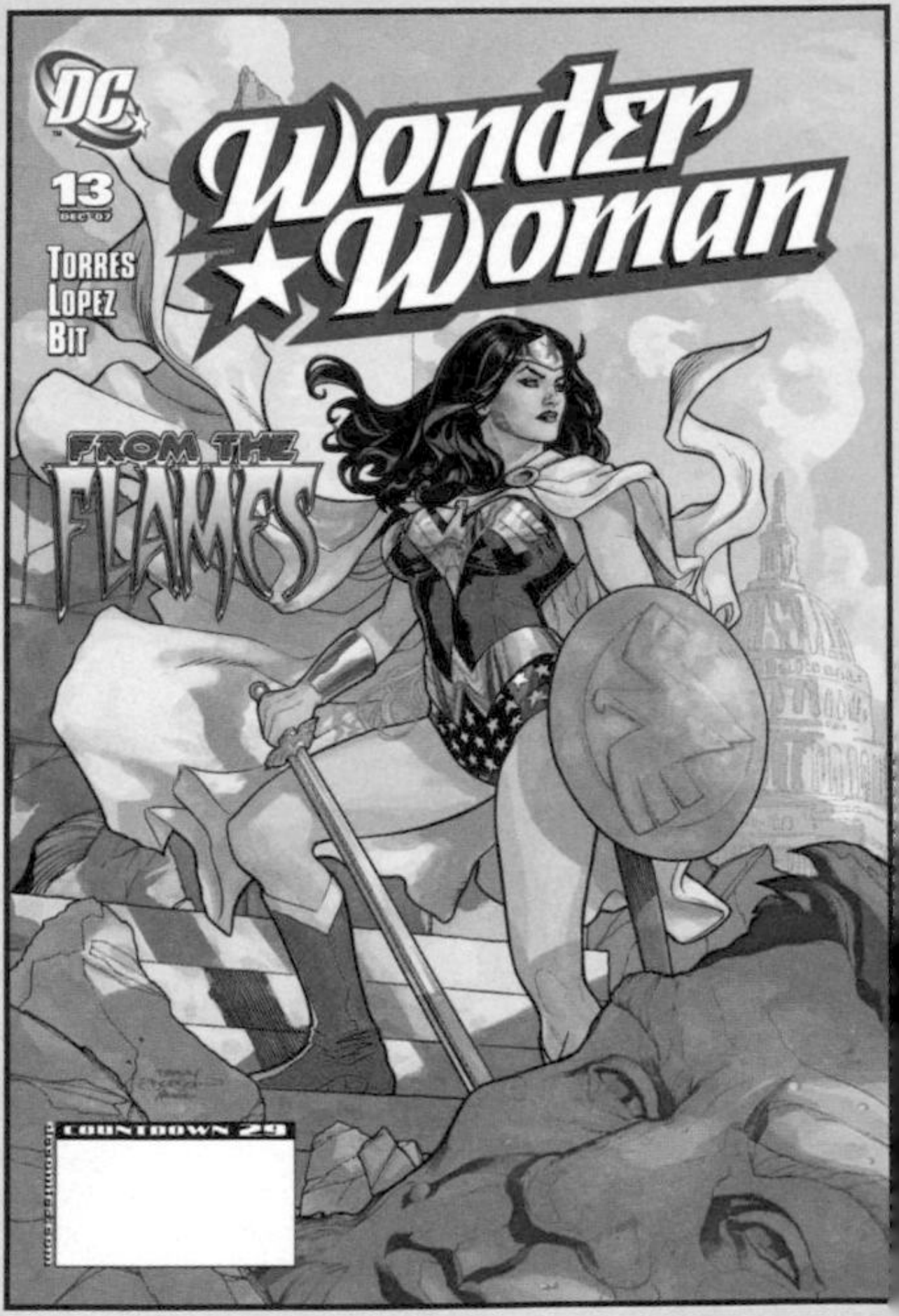
DC
13
DEC '07
Wonder Woman
TORRES
LOPEZ
BIT
FROM THE
FLAMES
COUNTDOWN 29

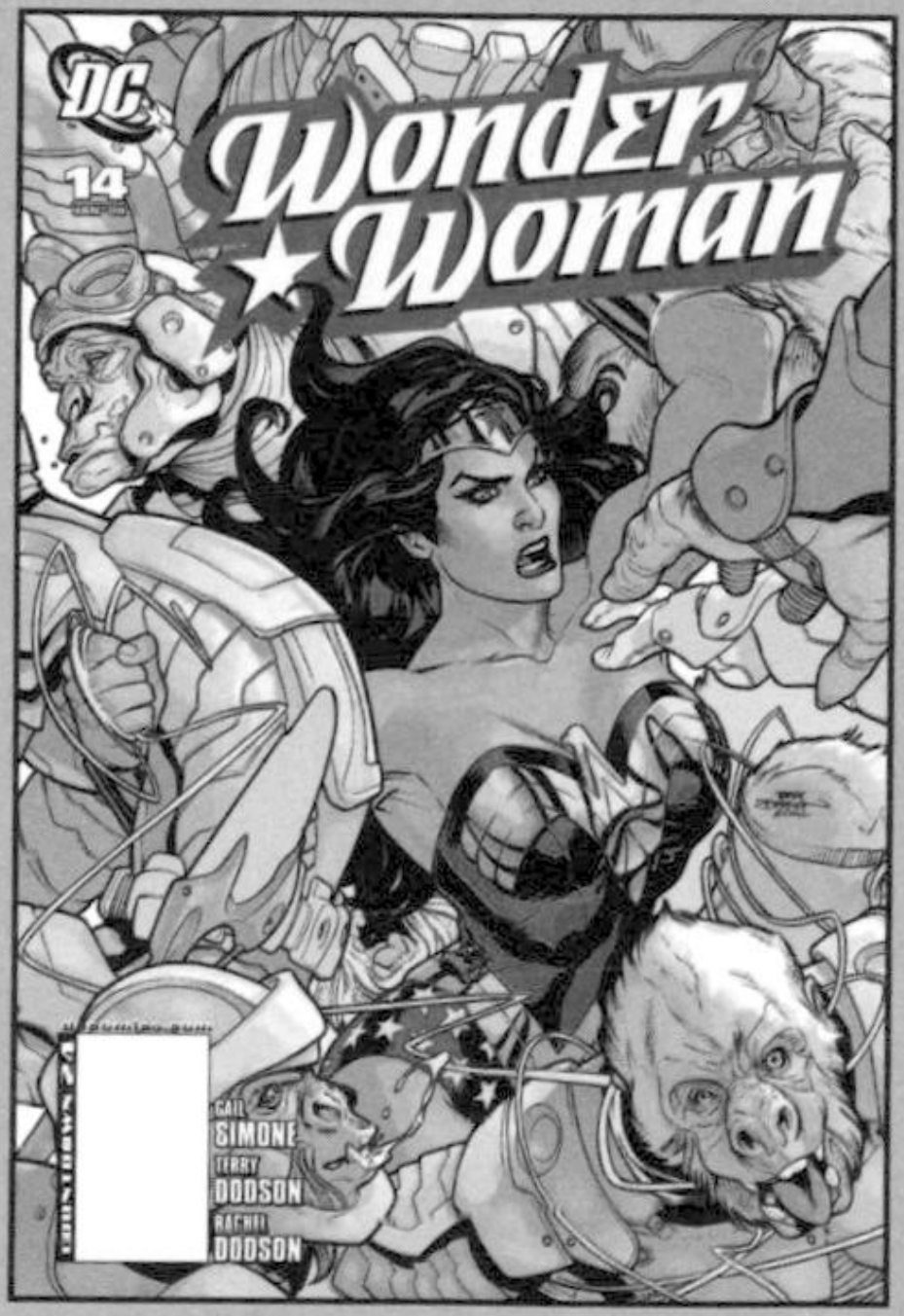

Wonder Woman (Vol. 3) #14

Issue #14 in the third volume of *Wonder Woman* marks the debut of Gail Simone's ake on the character. Simone would go on to become the longest-running female writer in *Wonder Woman*'s history.

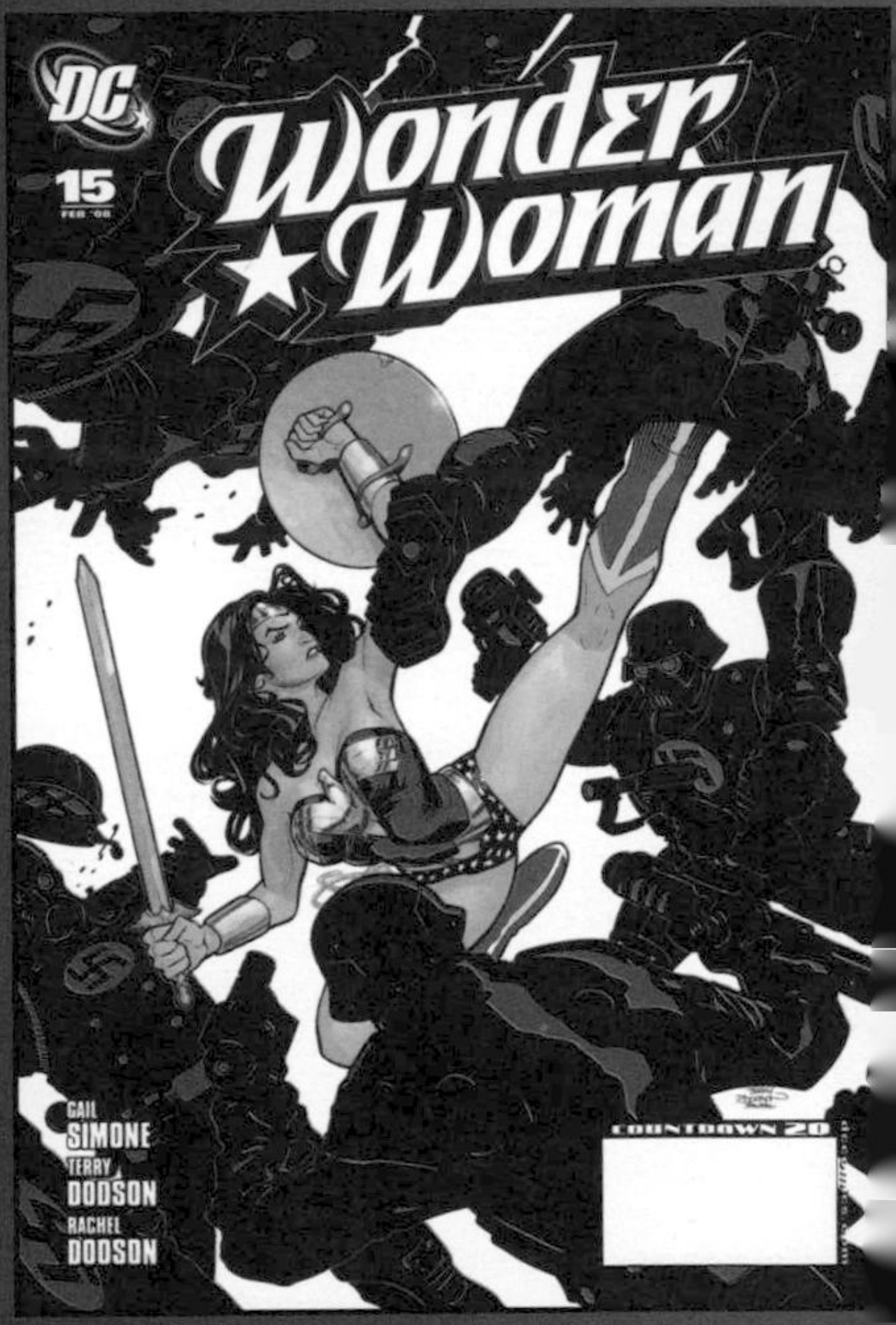
DC
15
FEB '06
Wonder Woman
GAIL SIMONE
TERRY DODSON
RACHEL DODSON
COUNTDOWN 20

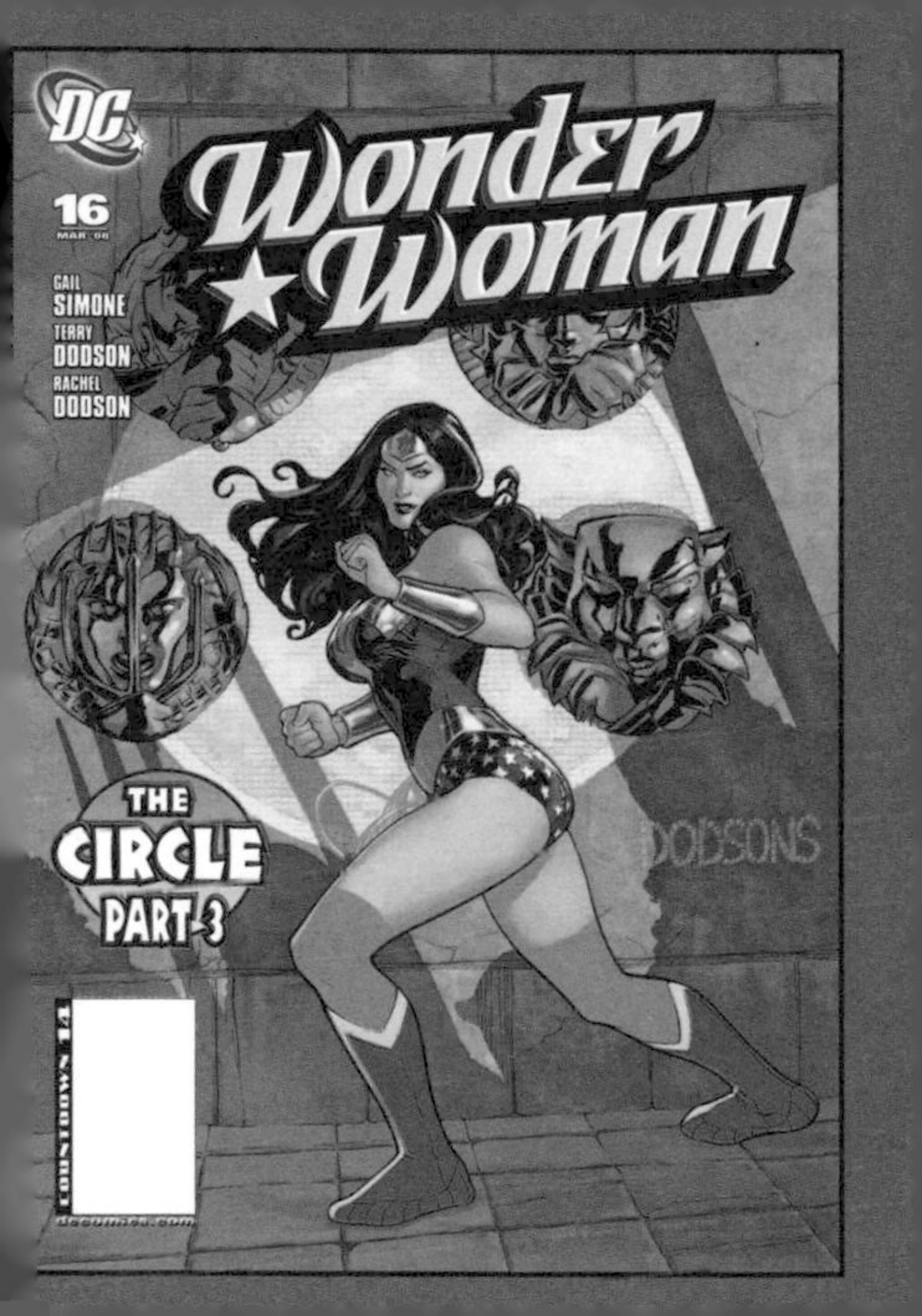
DC
Wonder Woman
16
MAR 08
GAIL SIMONE
TERRY DODSON
RACHEL DODSON
THE CIRCLE PART 3
DODSONS
COUNTDOWN 14
dccomics.com

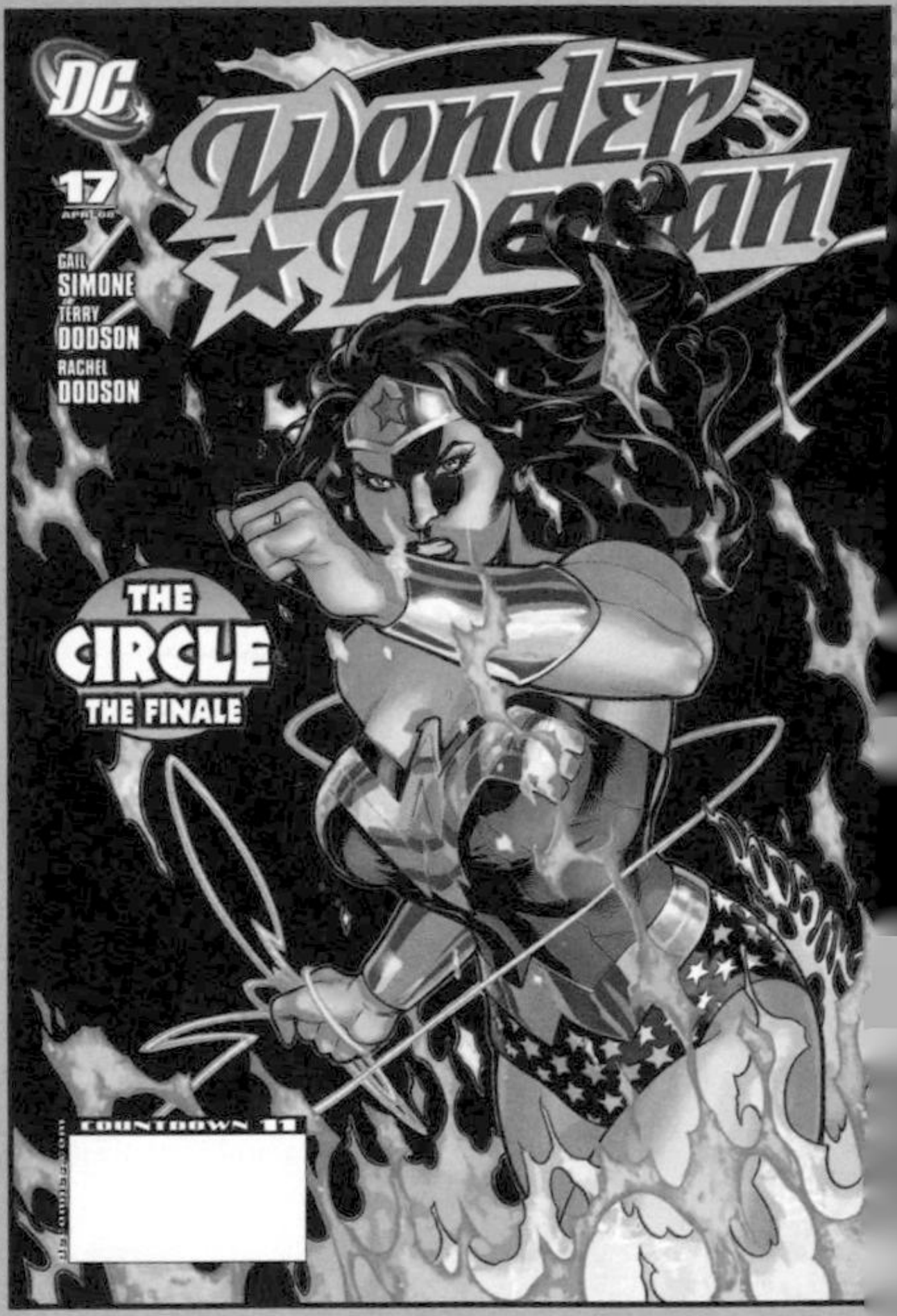
DC
Wonder Woman
17
GAIL SIMONE
TERRY DODSON
RACHEL DODSON
THE CIRCLE
THE FINALE
COUNTDOWN 11

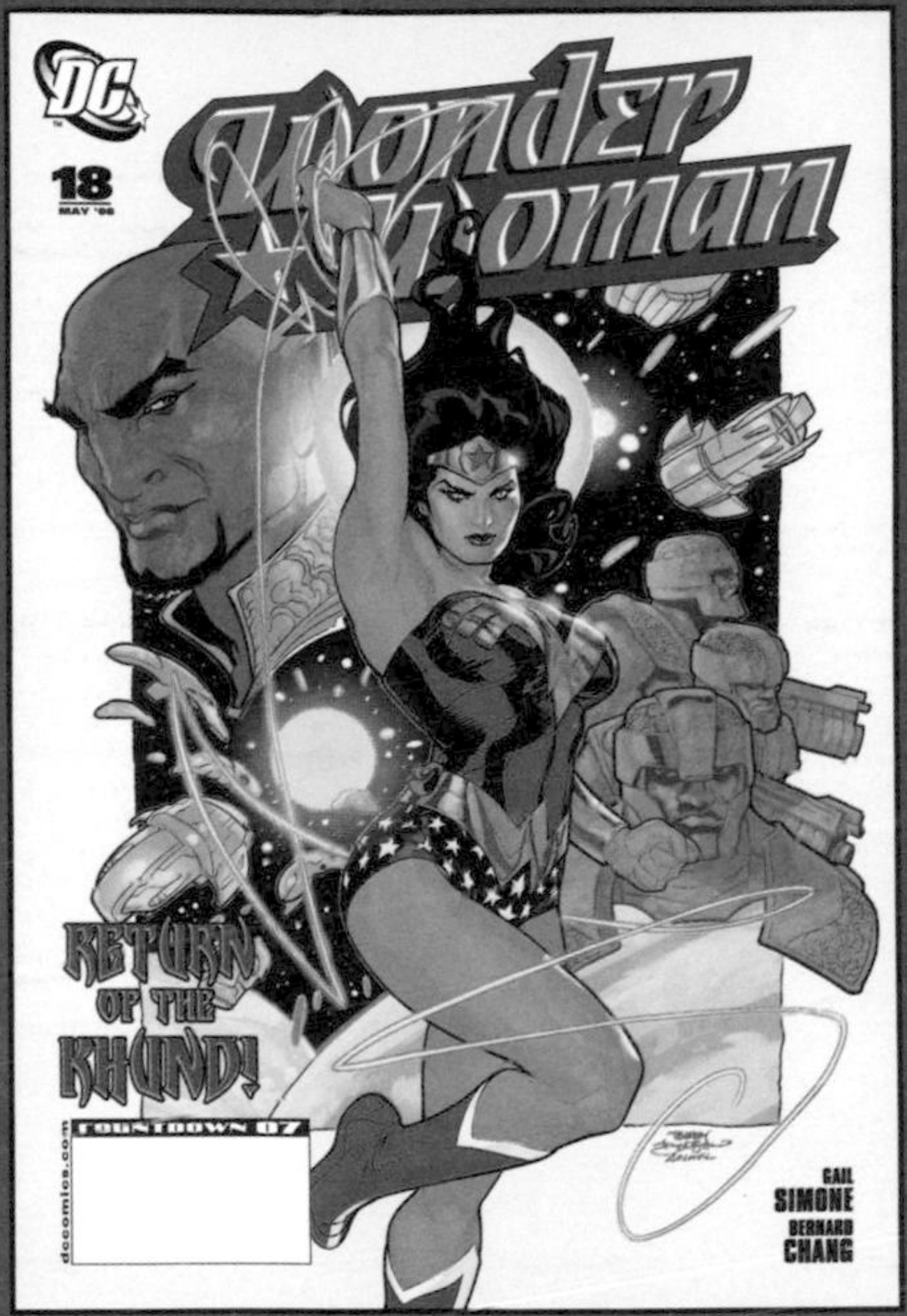
DC
Wonder Woman
18
MAY '06
RETURN OF THE KHUND!
COUNTDOWN 07
dccomics.com
GAIL SIMONE
BERNARD CHANG

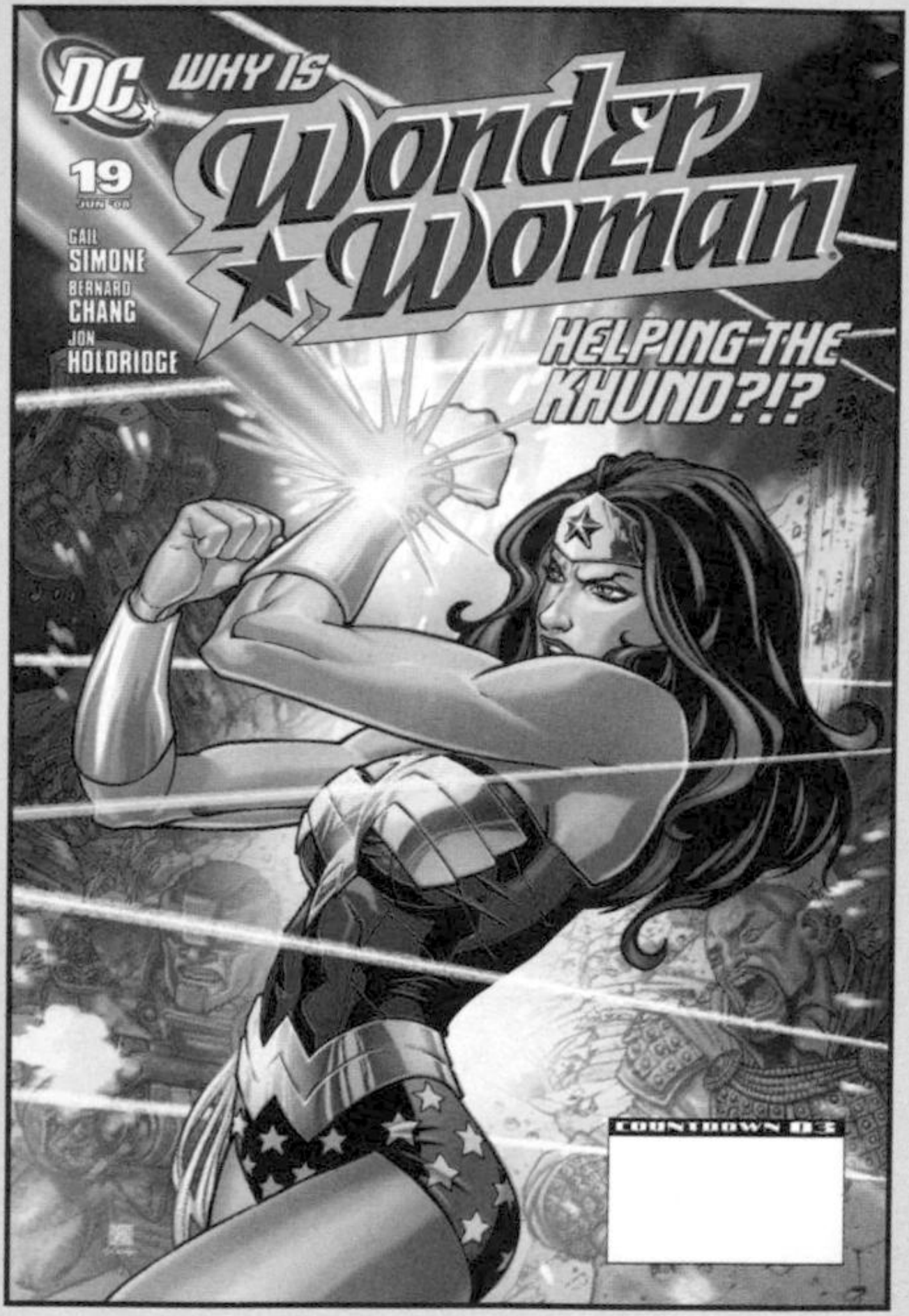
DC
WHY IS
Wonder Woman
19
JUN '08
GAIL SIMONE
BERNARD CHANG
JON HOLDRIDGE
HELPING THE KHUND?!?
COUNTDOWN 0:3

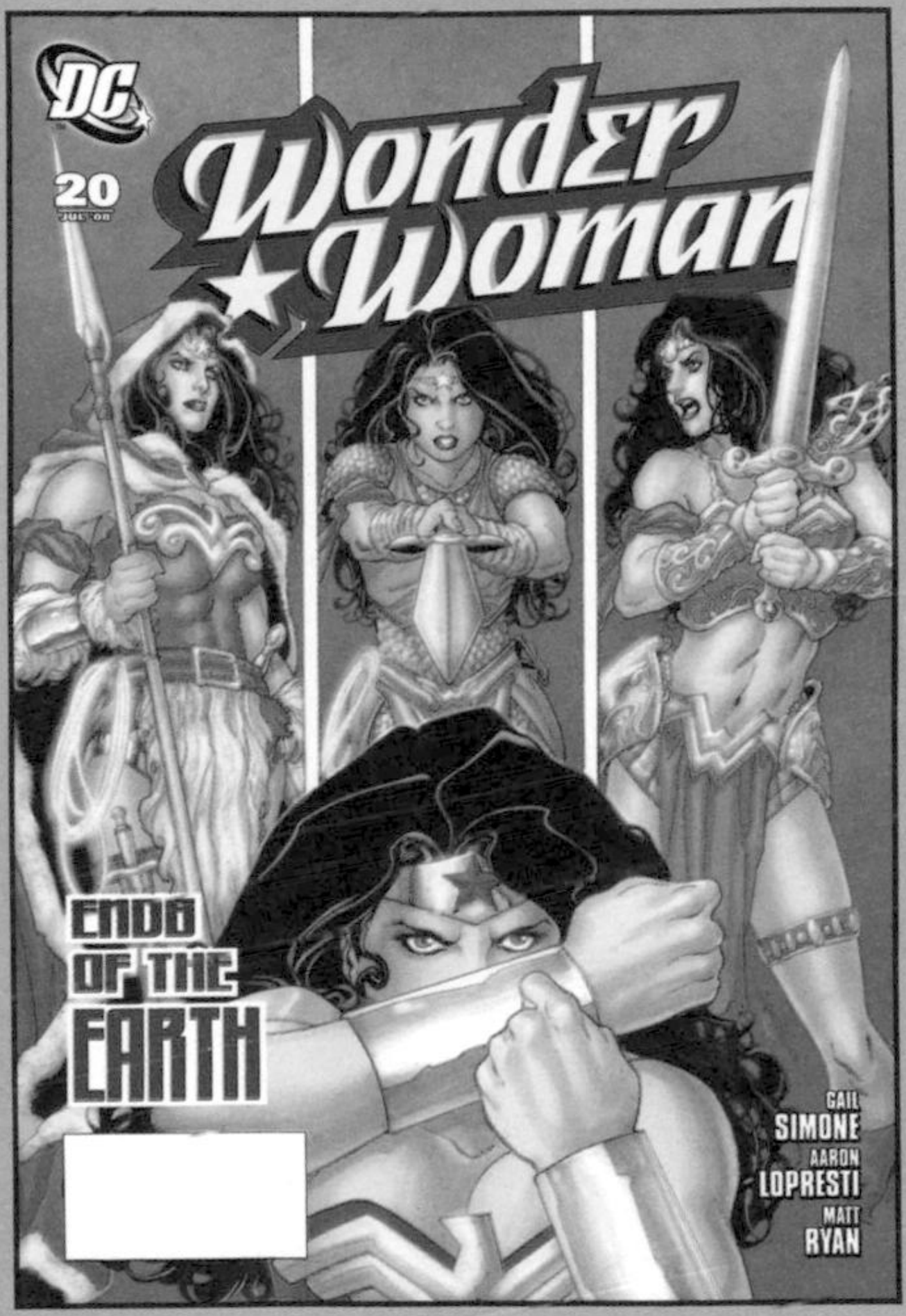
DC
20
JUL '08
Wonder Woman
ENDS OF THE EARTH
GAIL SIMONE
AARON LOPRESTI
MATT RYAN

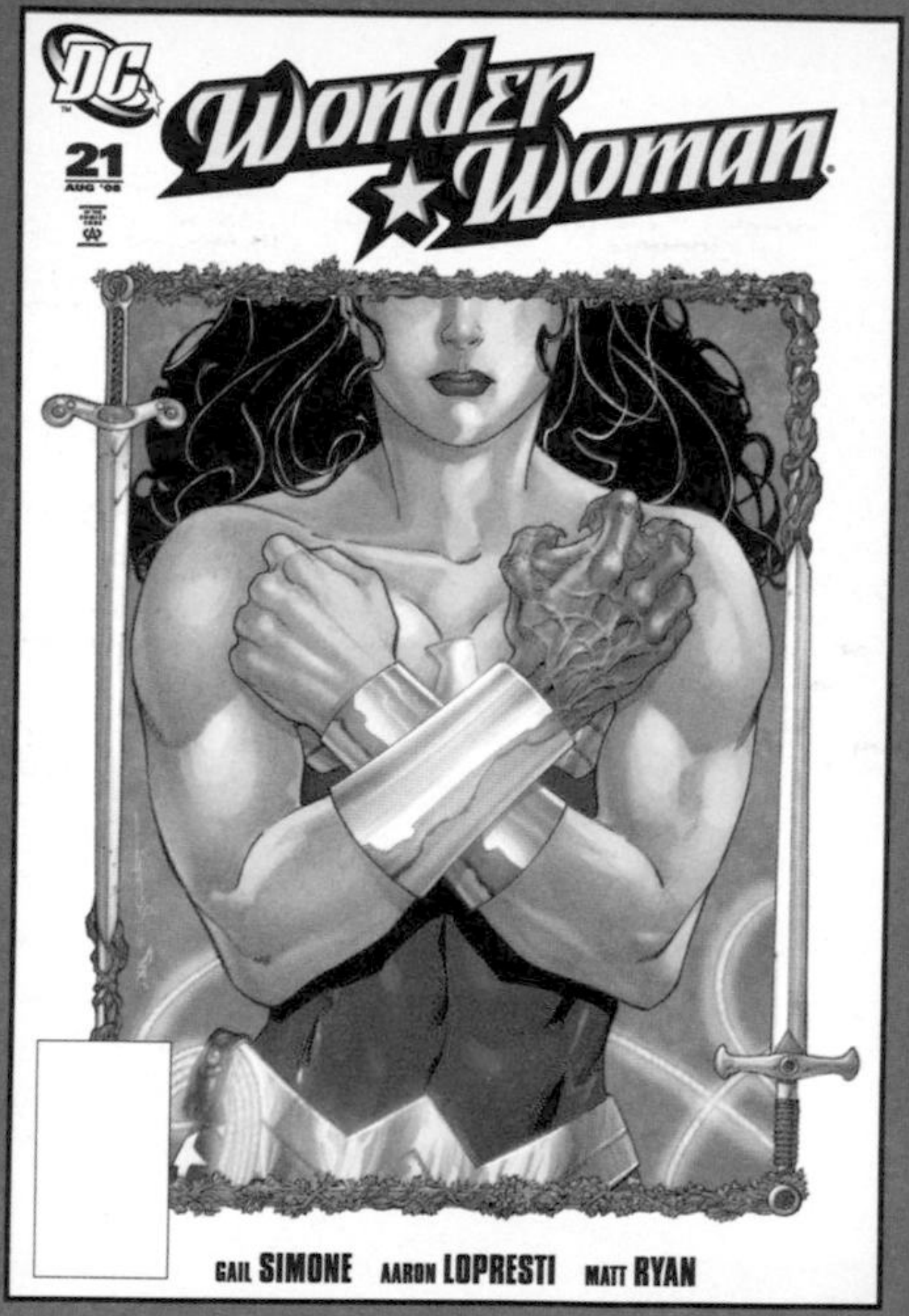
DC
Wonder Woman
21
AUG '08
GAIL SIMONE
AARON LOPRESTI
MATT RYAN

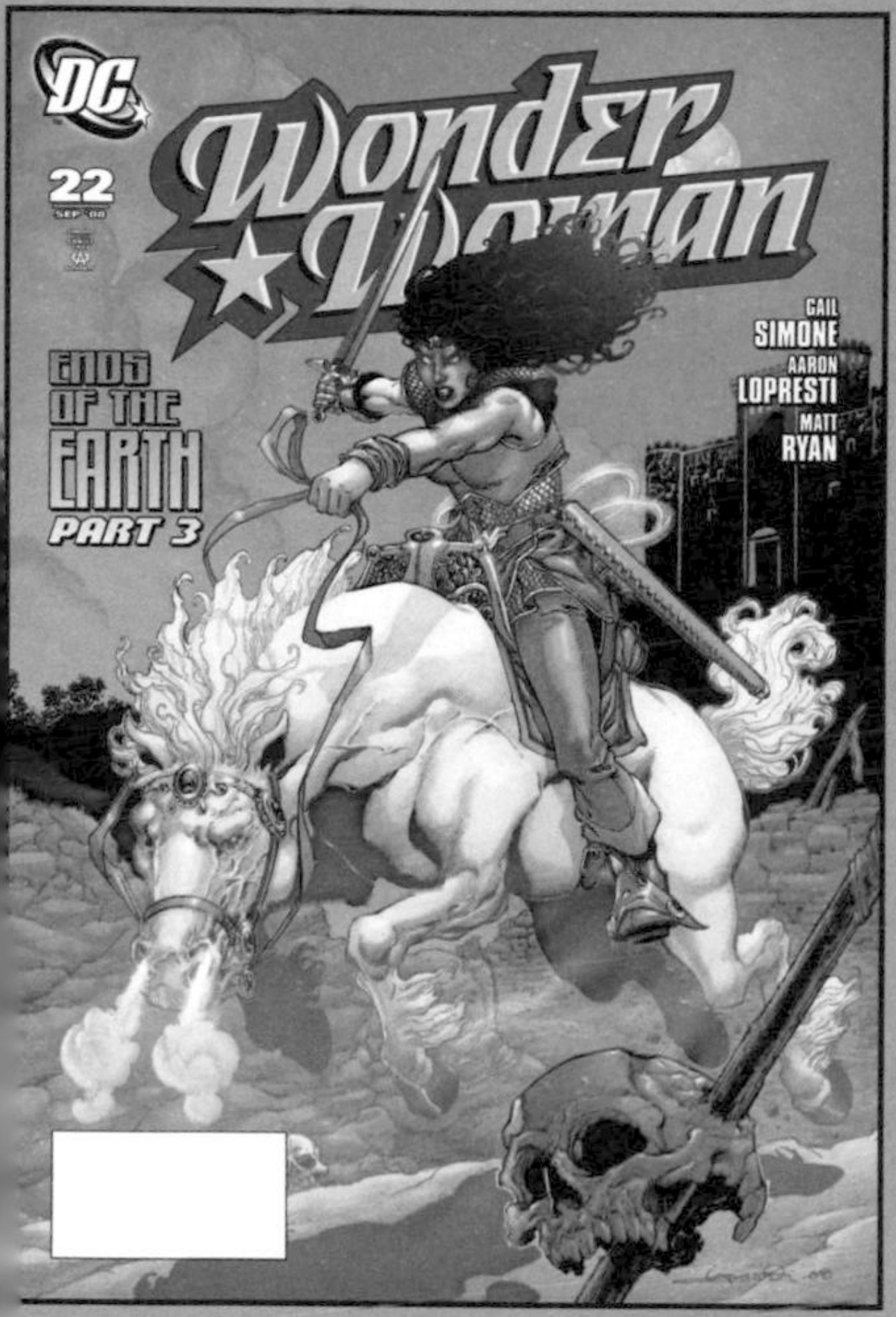
DC
Wonder Woman
22
SEP '08
GAIL SIMONE
AARON LOPRESTI
MATT RYAN
ENDS OF THE EARTH
PART 3

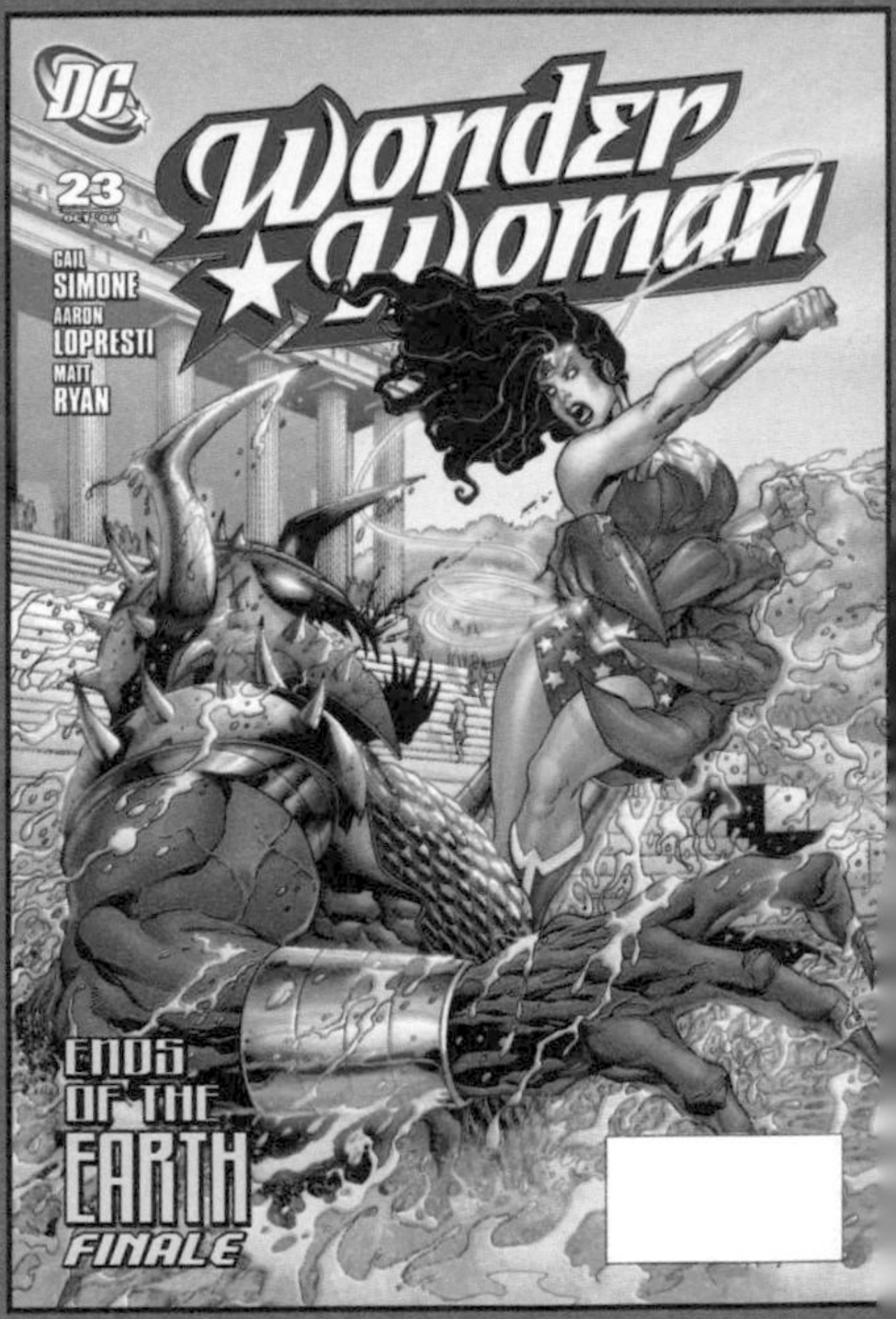
DC
Wonder Woman
23
GAIL SIMONE
AARON LOPRESTI
MATT RYAN
ENDS OF THE EARTH
FINALE

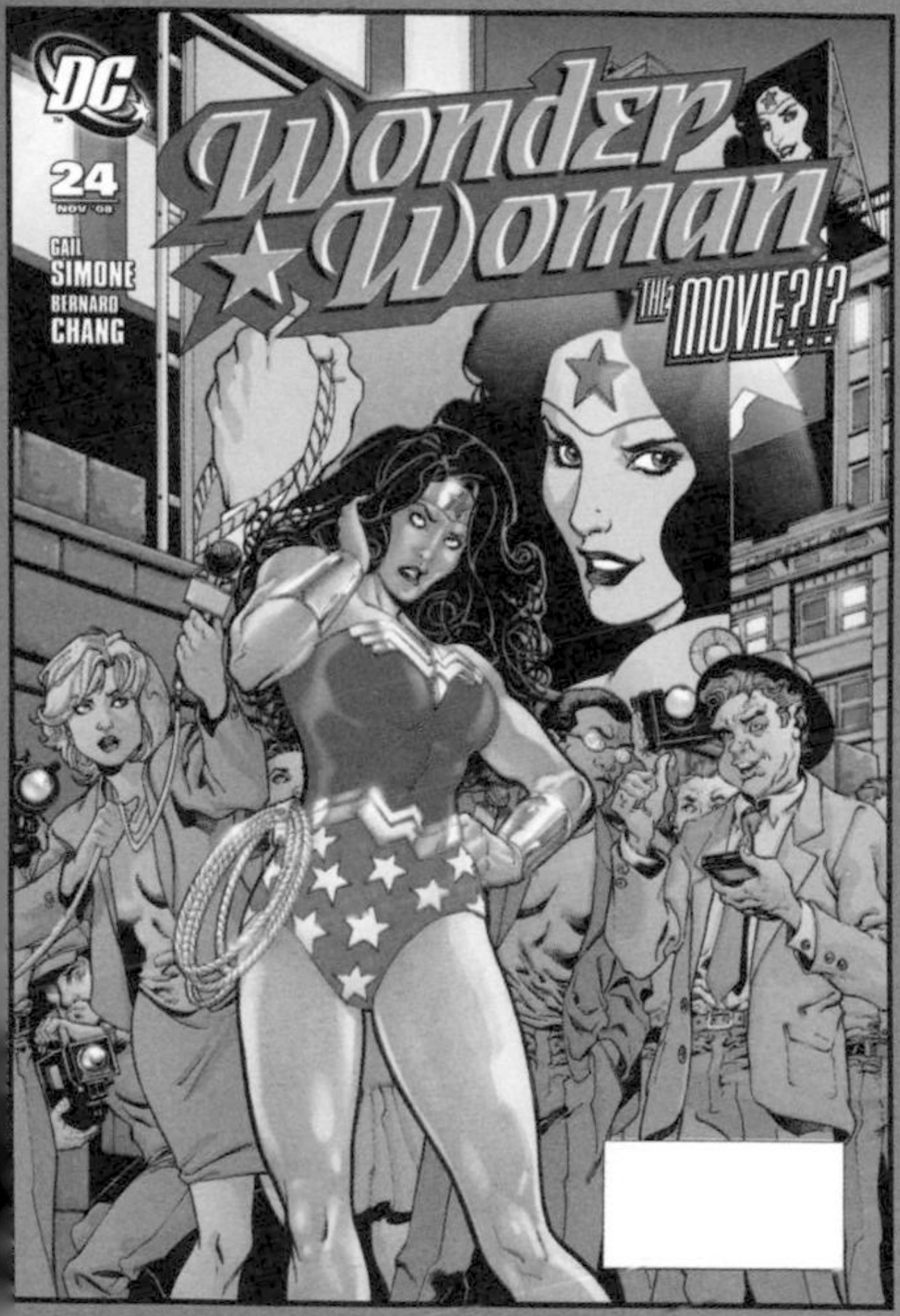
DC
24
NOV '08
GAIL SIMONE
BERNARD CHANG
Wonder Woman
THE MOVIE?!?

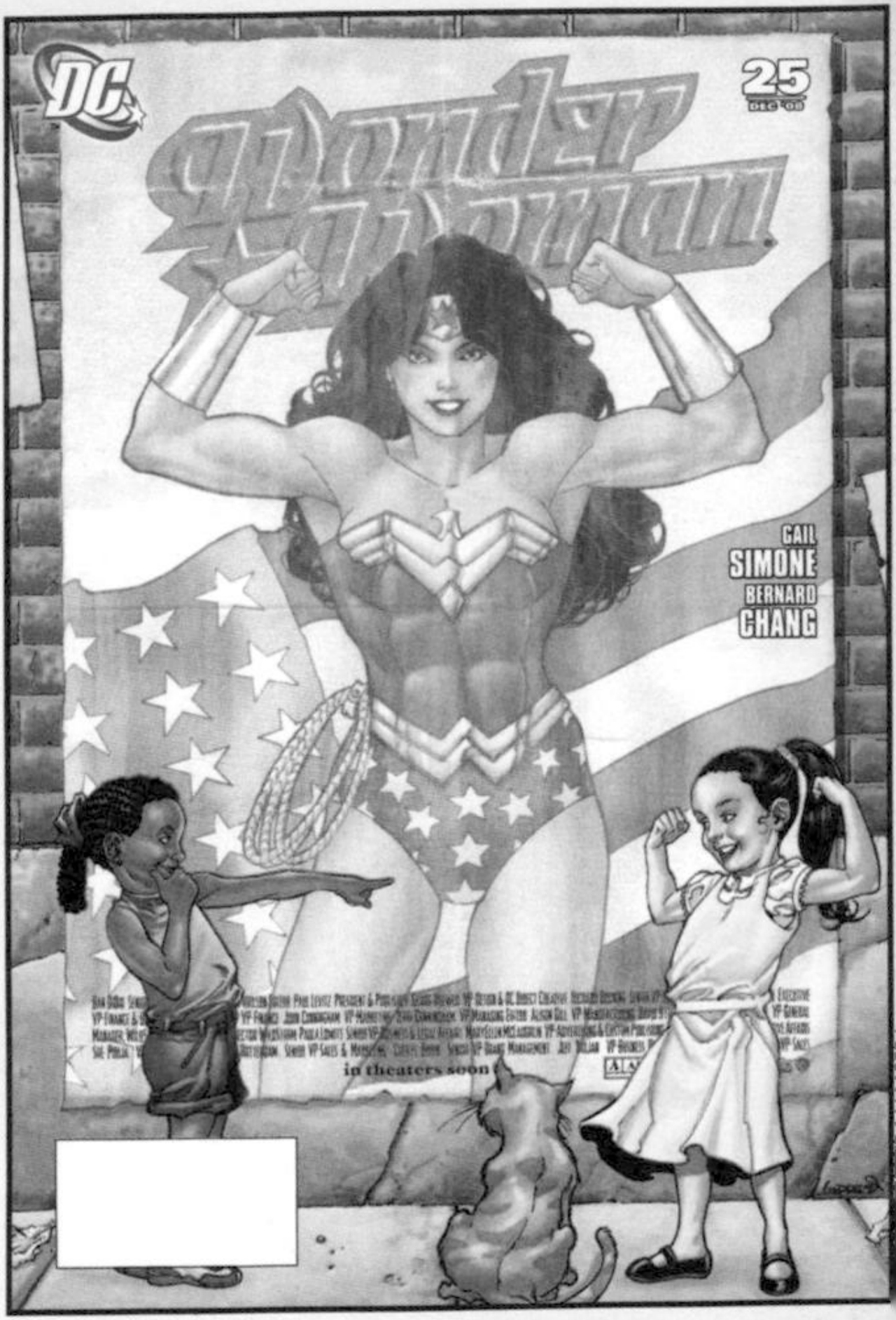
DC
25
DEC '08
WONDER WOMAN
GAIL
SIMONE
BERNARD
CHANG
in theaters soon

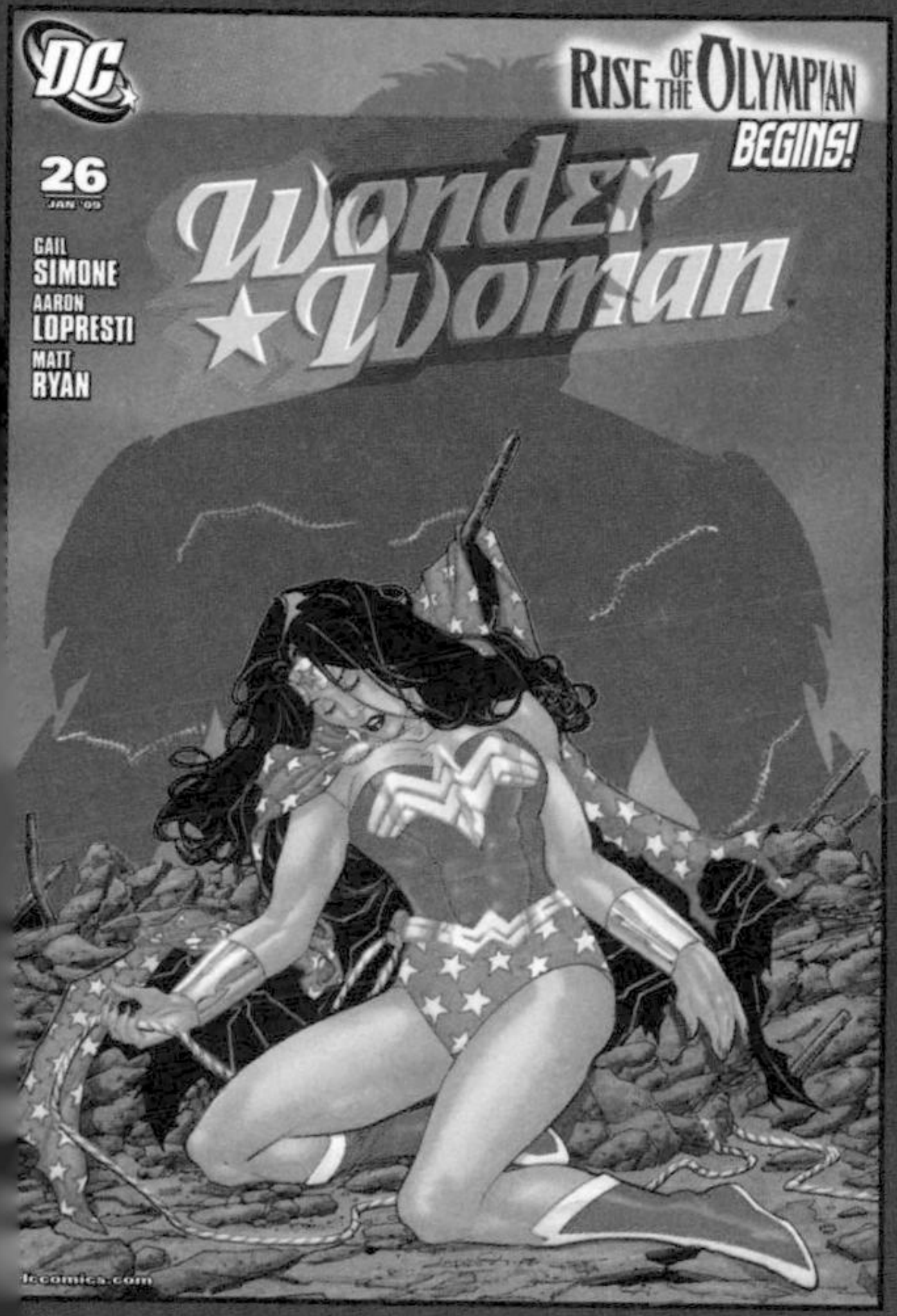
DC
RISE OF THE OLYMPIAN
BEGINS!
26
JAN '09
Wonder Woman
GAIL SIMONE
AARON LOPRESTI
MATT RYAN
dccomics.com

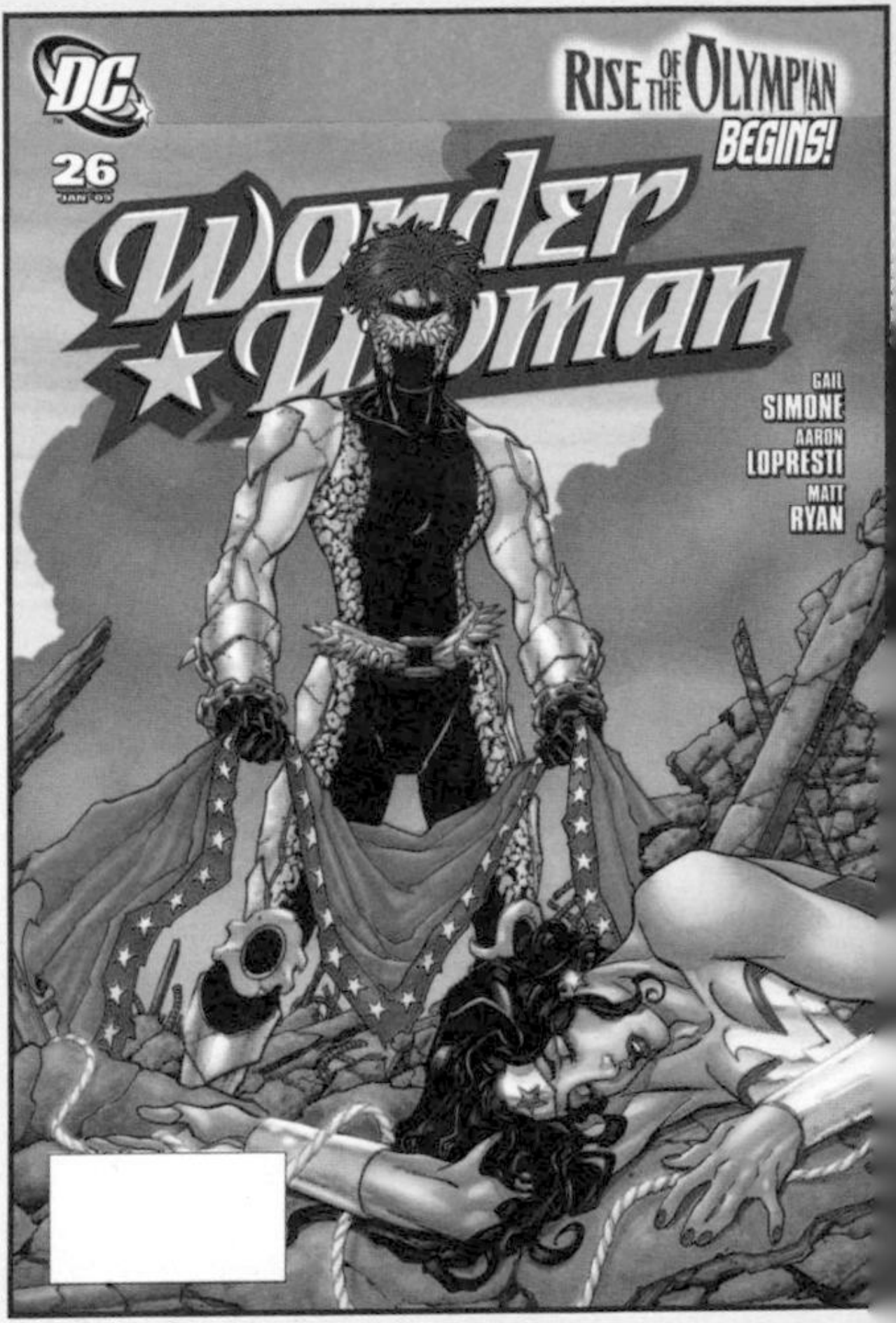
DC
RISE OF THE OLYMPIAN
BEGINS!
26
JAN '09
Wonder Woman
GAIL
SIMONE
AARON
LOPRESTI
MATT
RYAN

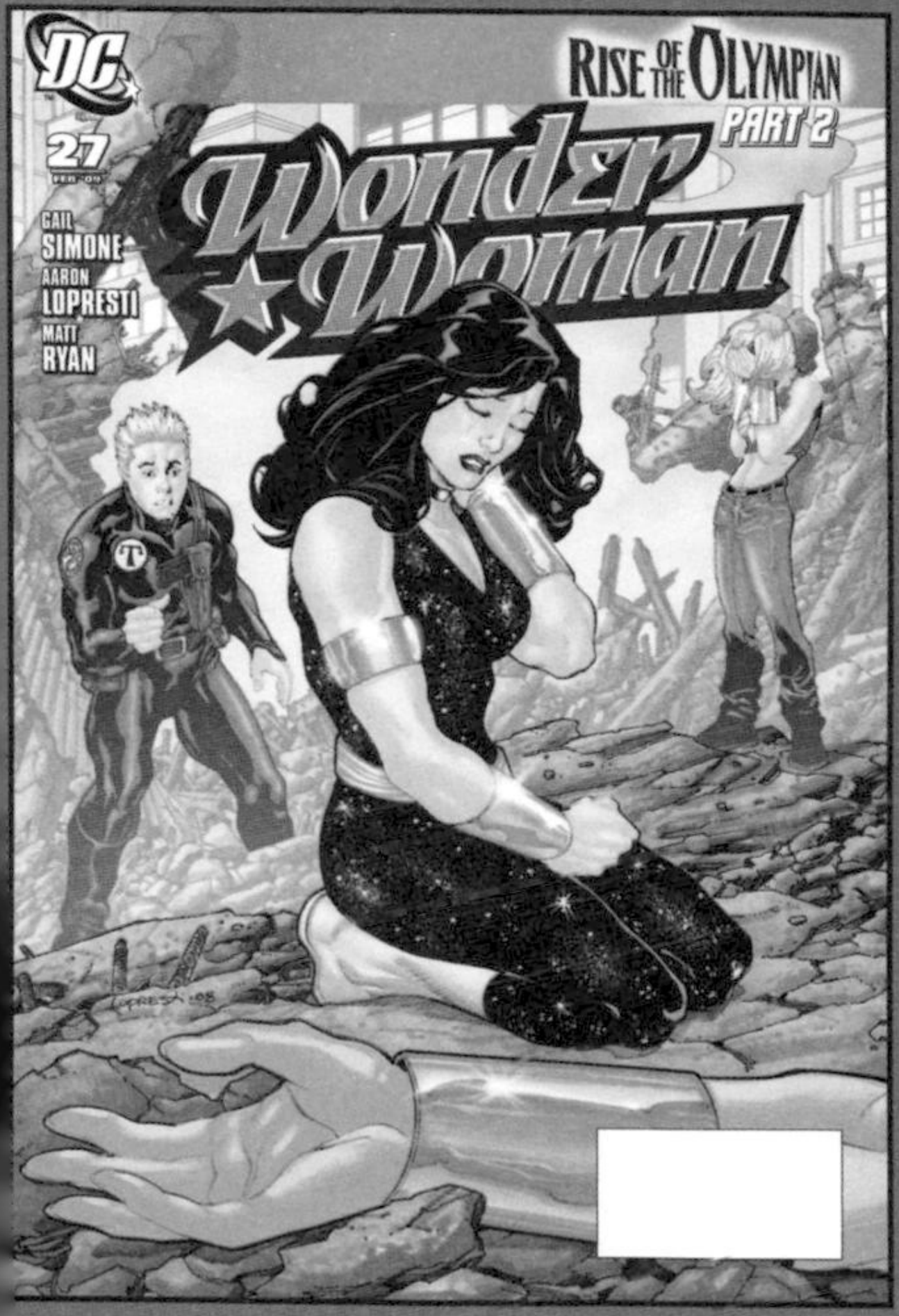
DC
RISE OF THE OLYMPIAN
PART 2
27
FEB '09
Wonder Woman
GAIL SIMONE
AARON LOPRESTI
MATT RYAN

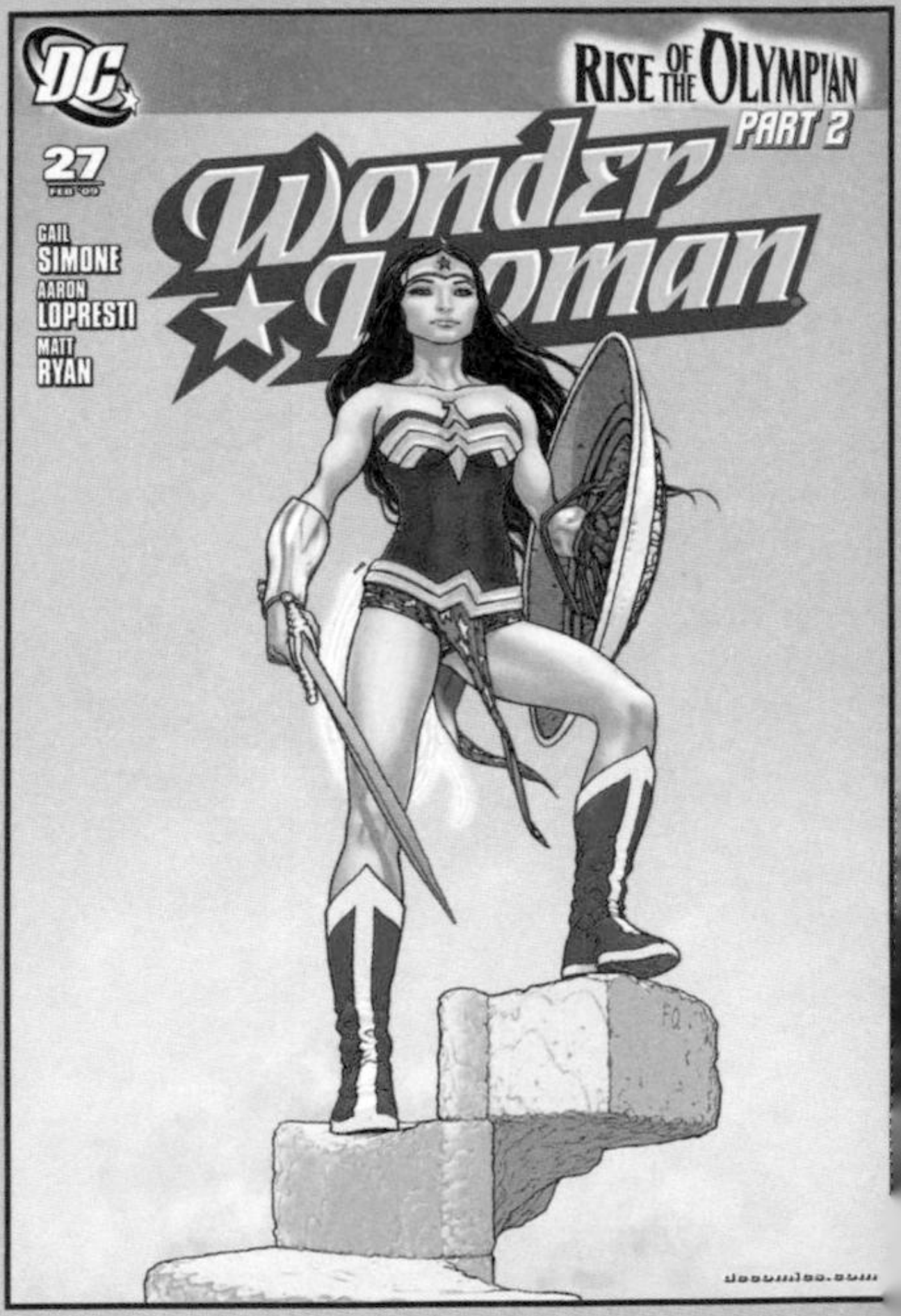
DC
RISE OF THE OLYMPIAN
PART 2
27
FEB '09
Wonder Woman
GAIL SIMONE
AARON LOPRESTI
MATT RYAN

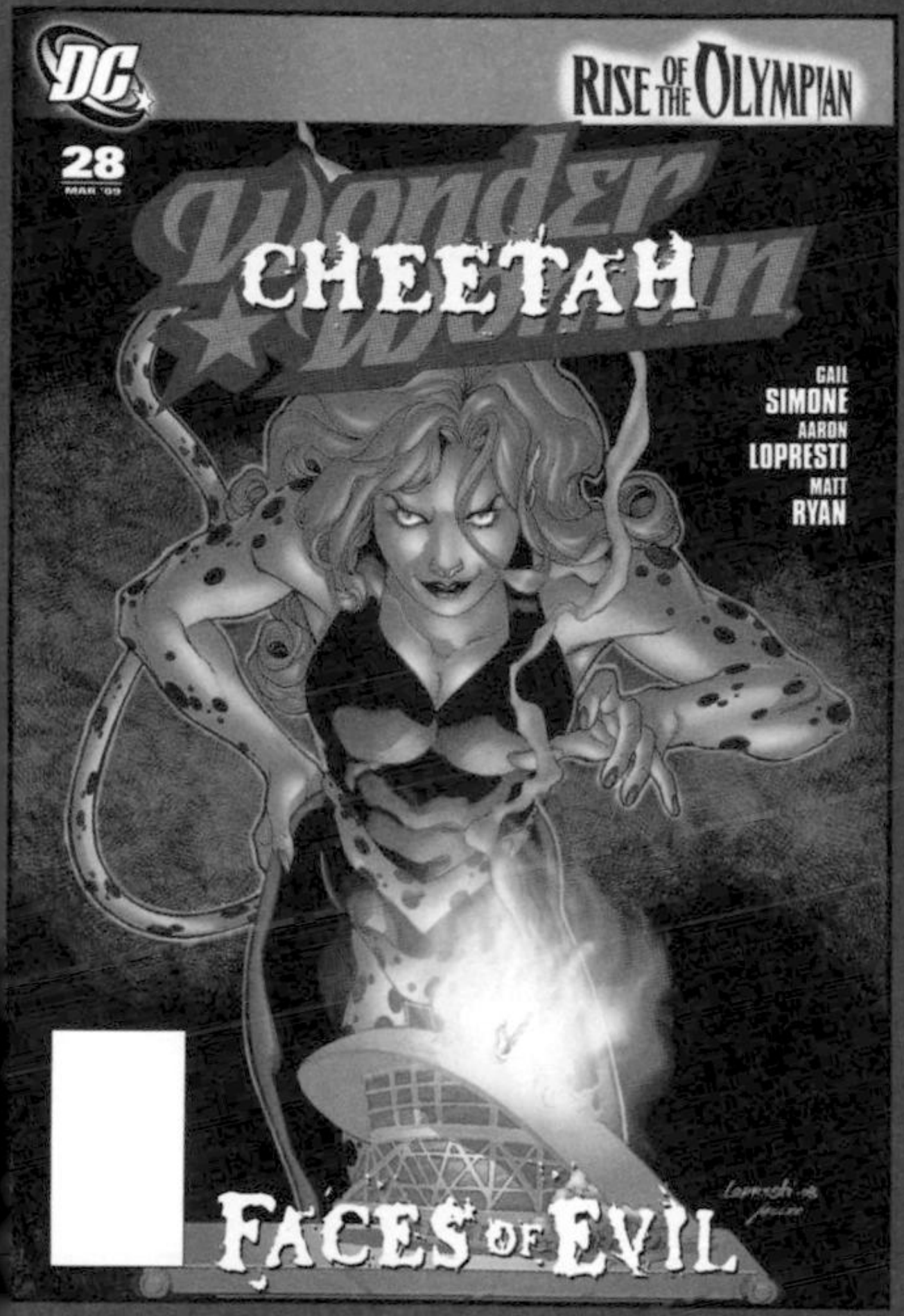
DC
RISE OF THE OLYMPIAN
28
MAR '09
Wonder Woman
CHEETAH
GAIL SIMONE
AARON LOPRESTI
MATT RYAN
FACES OF EVIL

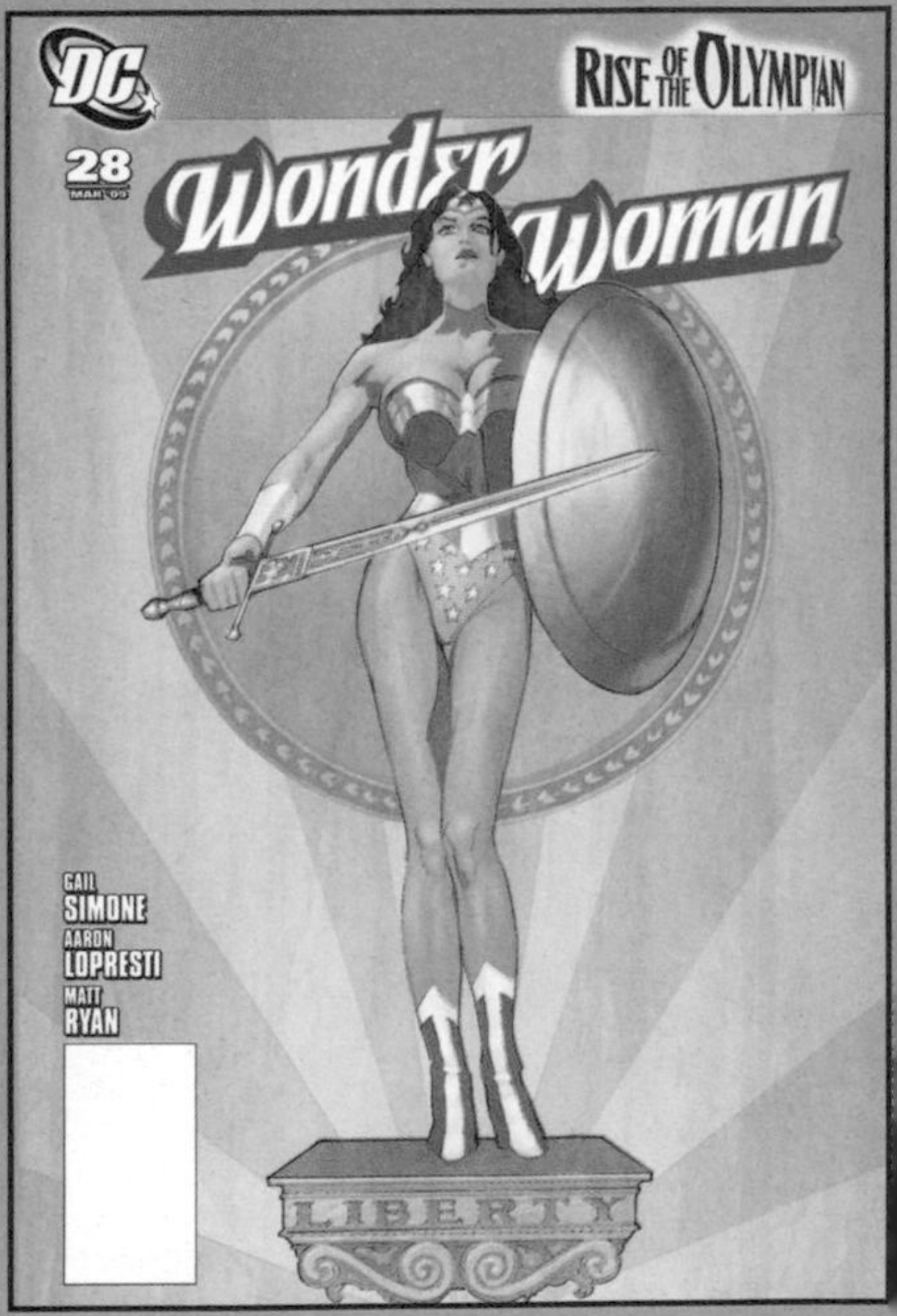
DC
RISE OF THE OLYMPIAN
28
MAR '05
Wonder Woman
GAIL SIMONE
AARON LOPRESTI
MATT RYAN
LIBERTY

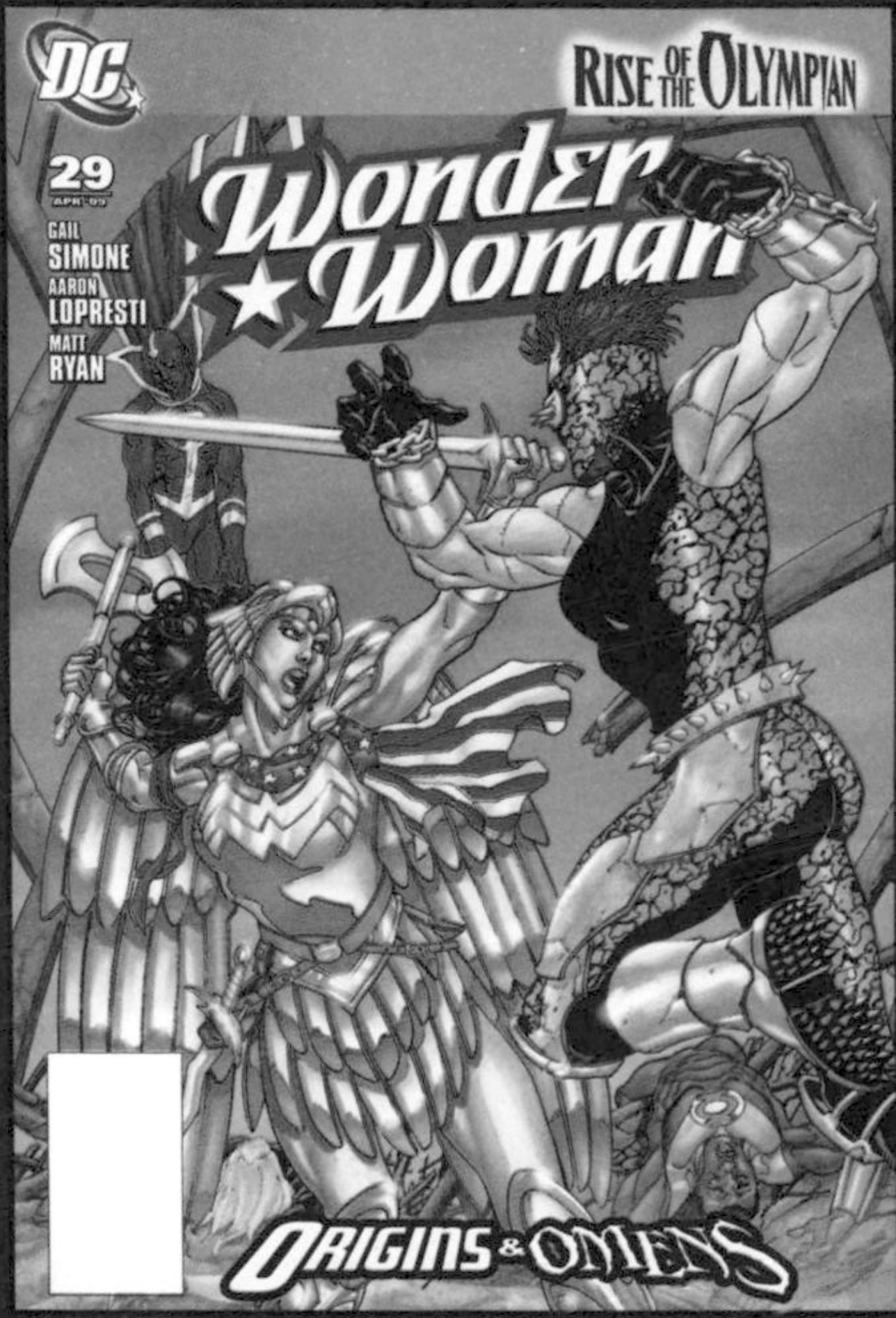
DC
RISE OF THE OLYMPIAN
29
APR '09
GAIL SIMONE
AARON LOPRESTI
MATT RYAN
Wonder Woman
ORIGINS & OMENS

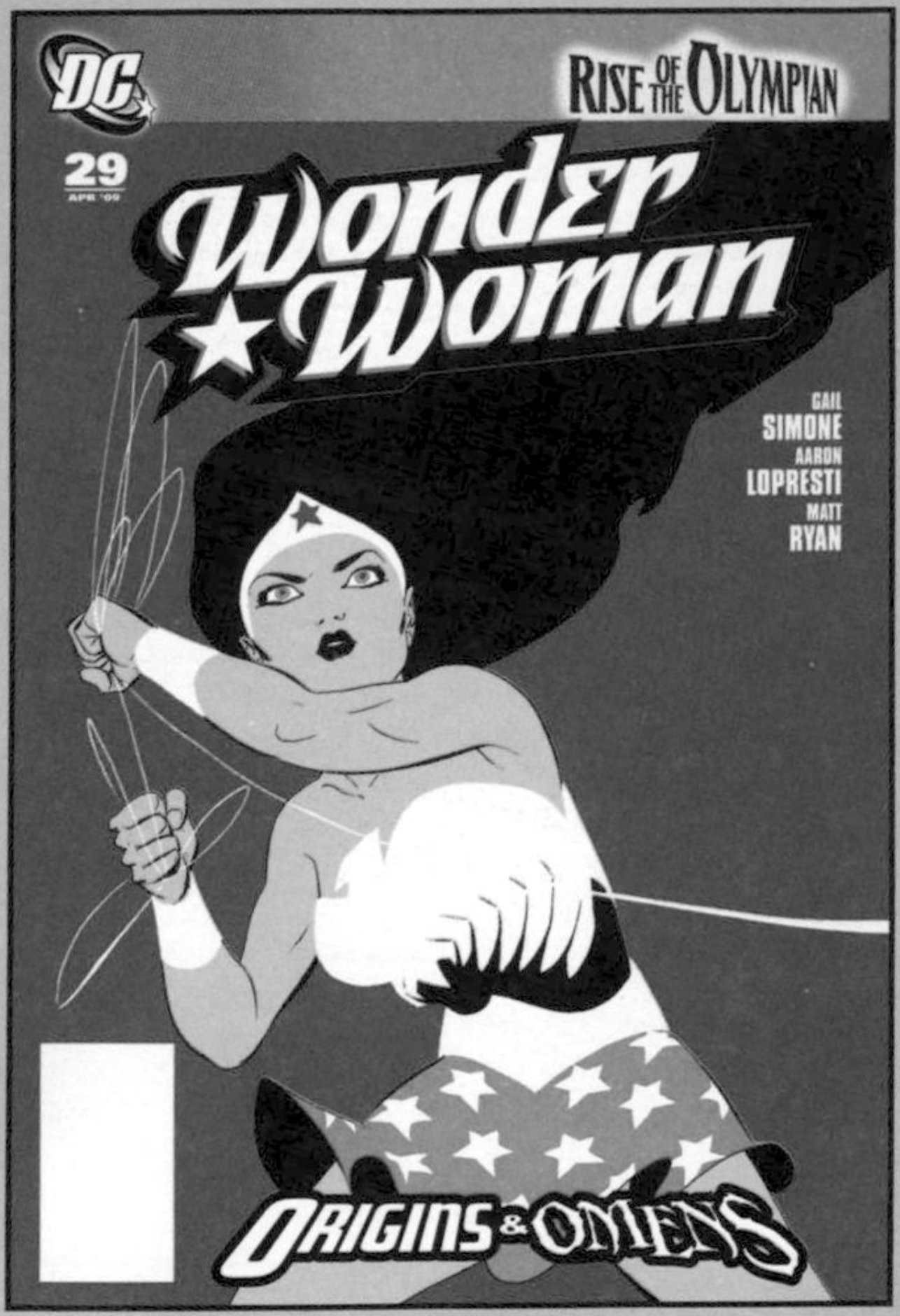
DC
RISE OF THE OLYMPIAN
29
APR '09
Wonder Woman
GAIL SIMONE
AARON LOPRESTI
MATT RYAN
ORIGINS & OMENS

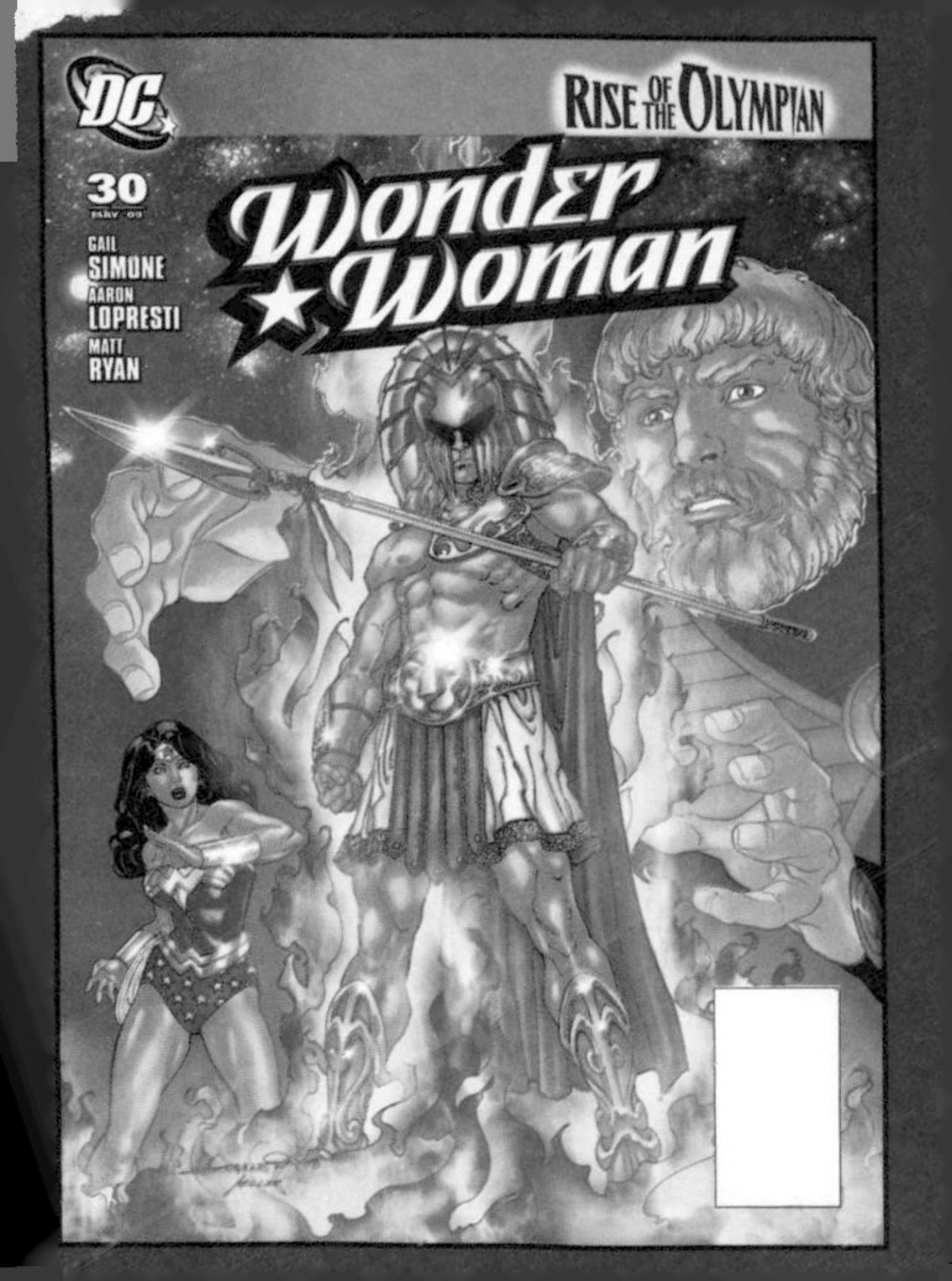
DC
RISE OF THE OLYMPIAN
30
MAY '09
Wonder Woman
GAIL SIMONE
AARON LOPRESTI
MATT RYAN

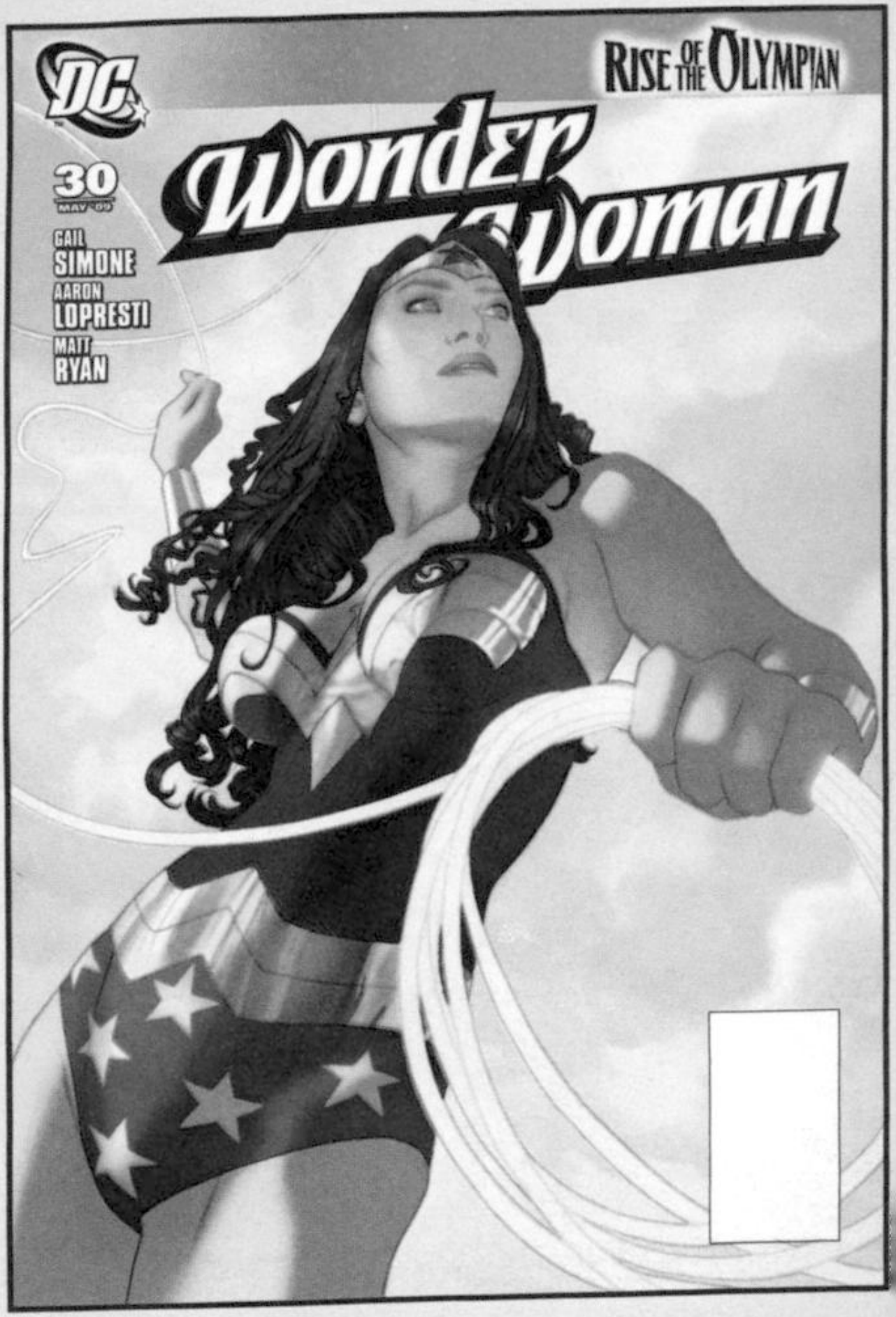
DC
RISE OF THE OLYMPIAN
Wonder Woman
30
MAY '09
GAIL SIMONE
AARON LOPRESTI
MATT RYAN

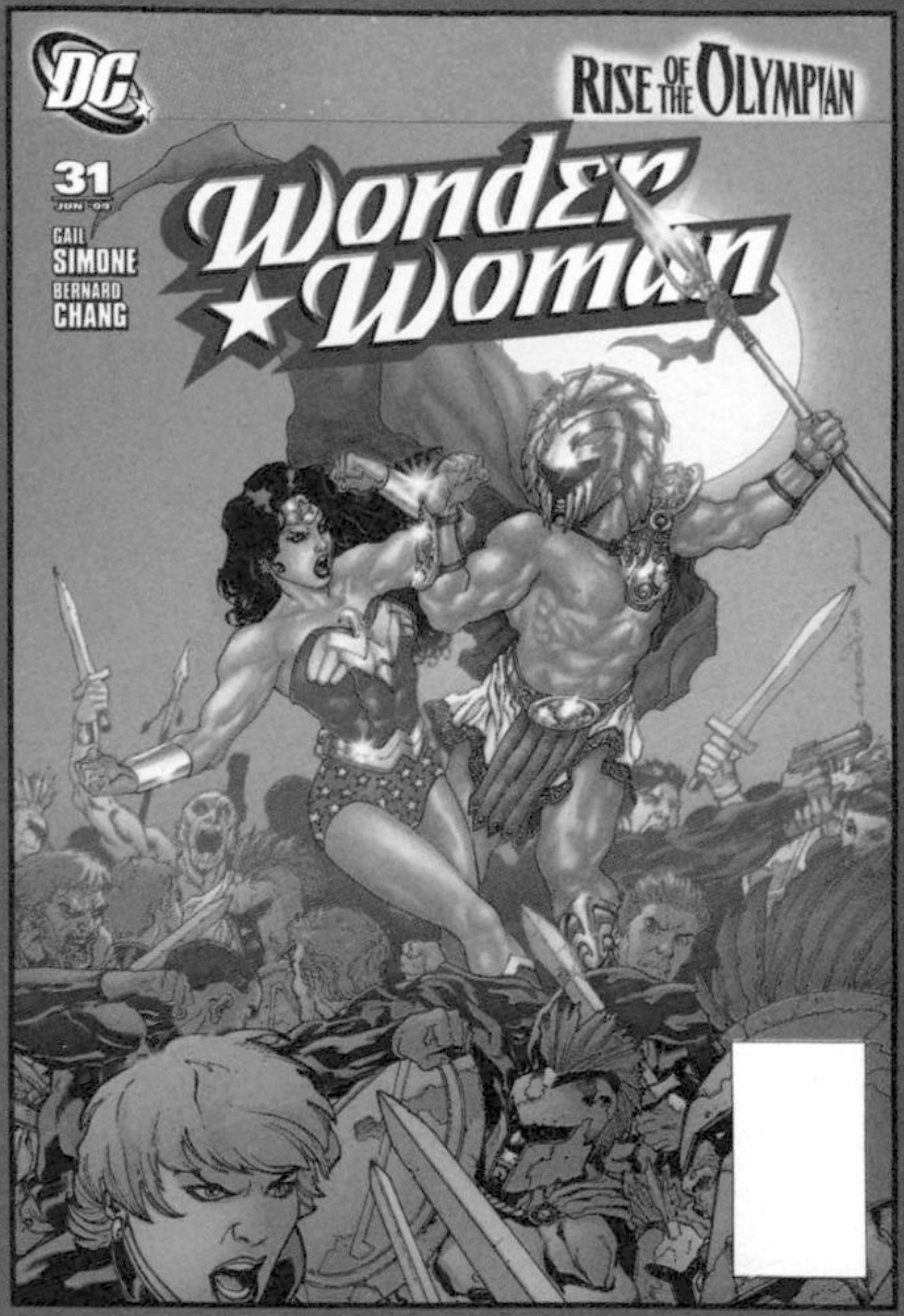
DC
RISE OF THE OLYMPIAN
31
JUN 09
GAIL SIMONE
BERNARD CHANG
Wonder Woman

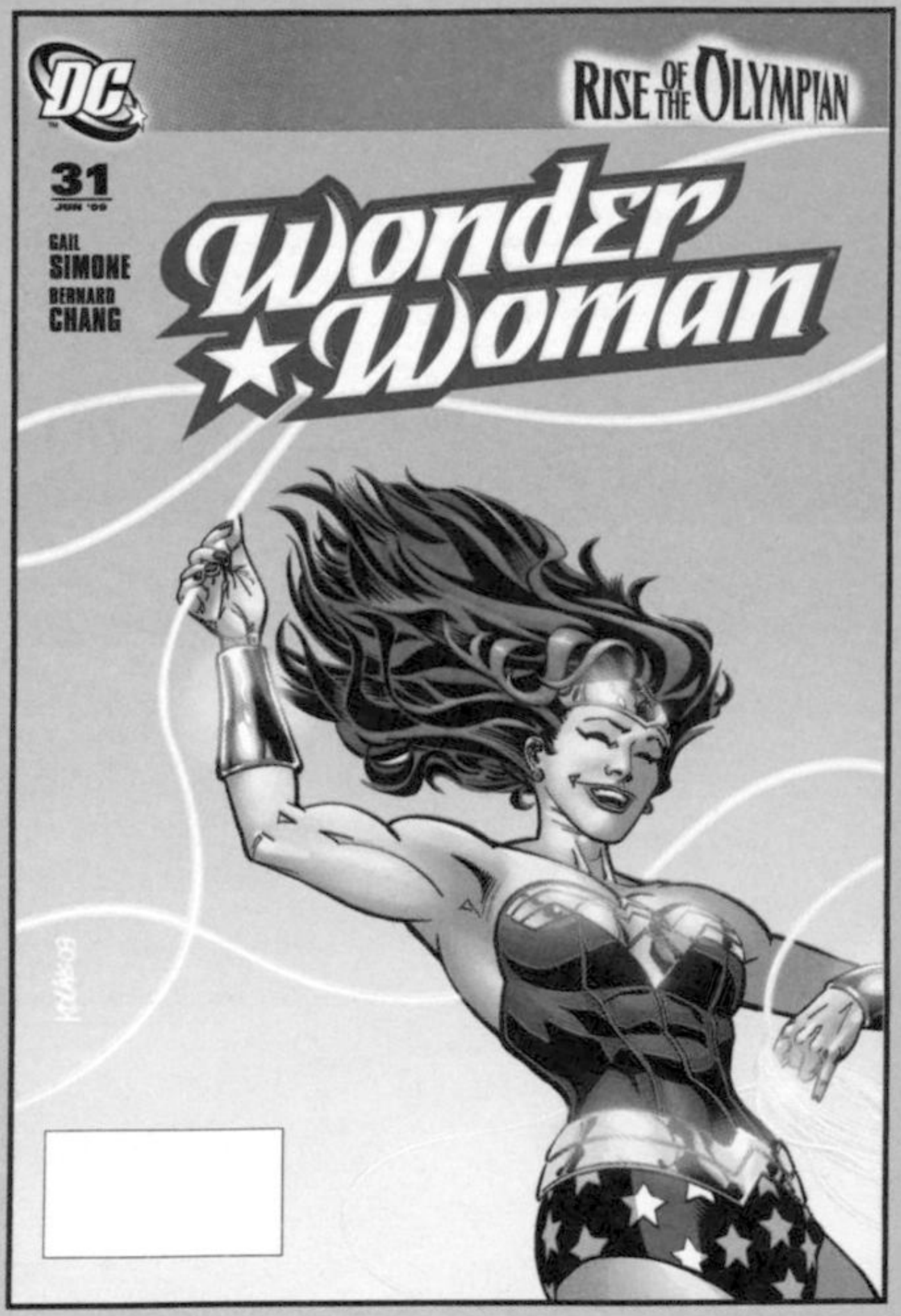
DC
RISE OF THE OLYMPIAN
31
JUN '09
GAIL SIMONE
BERNARD CHANG
Wonder Woman

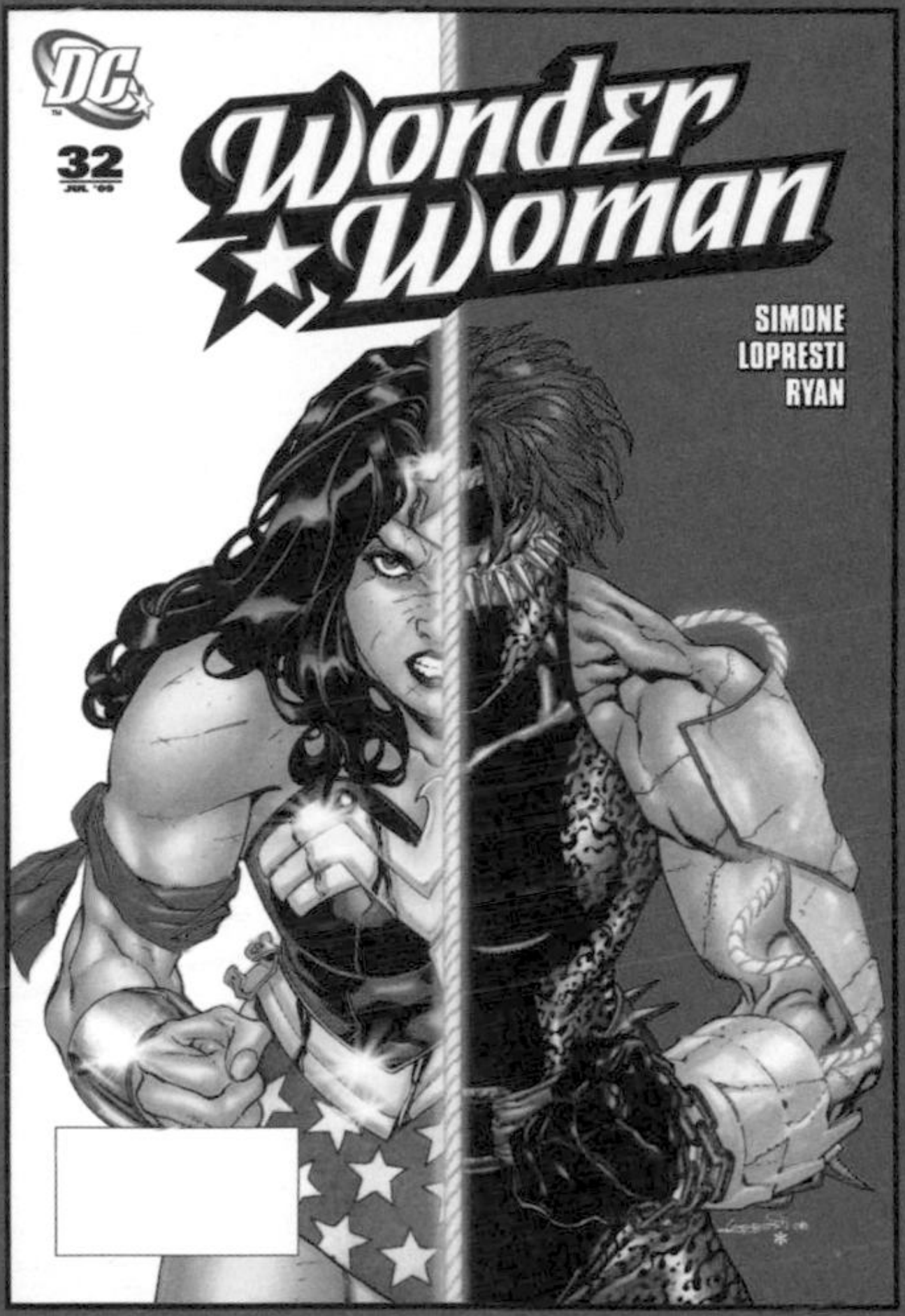
DC
32
JUL '09
Wonder Woman
SIMONE
LOPRESTI
RYAN

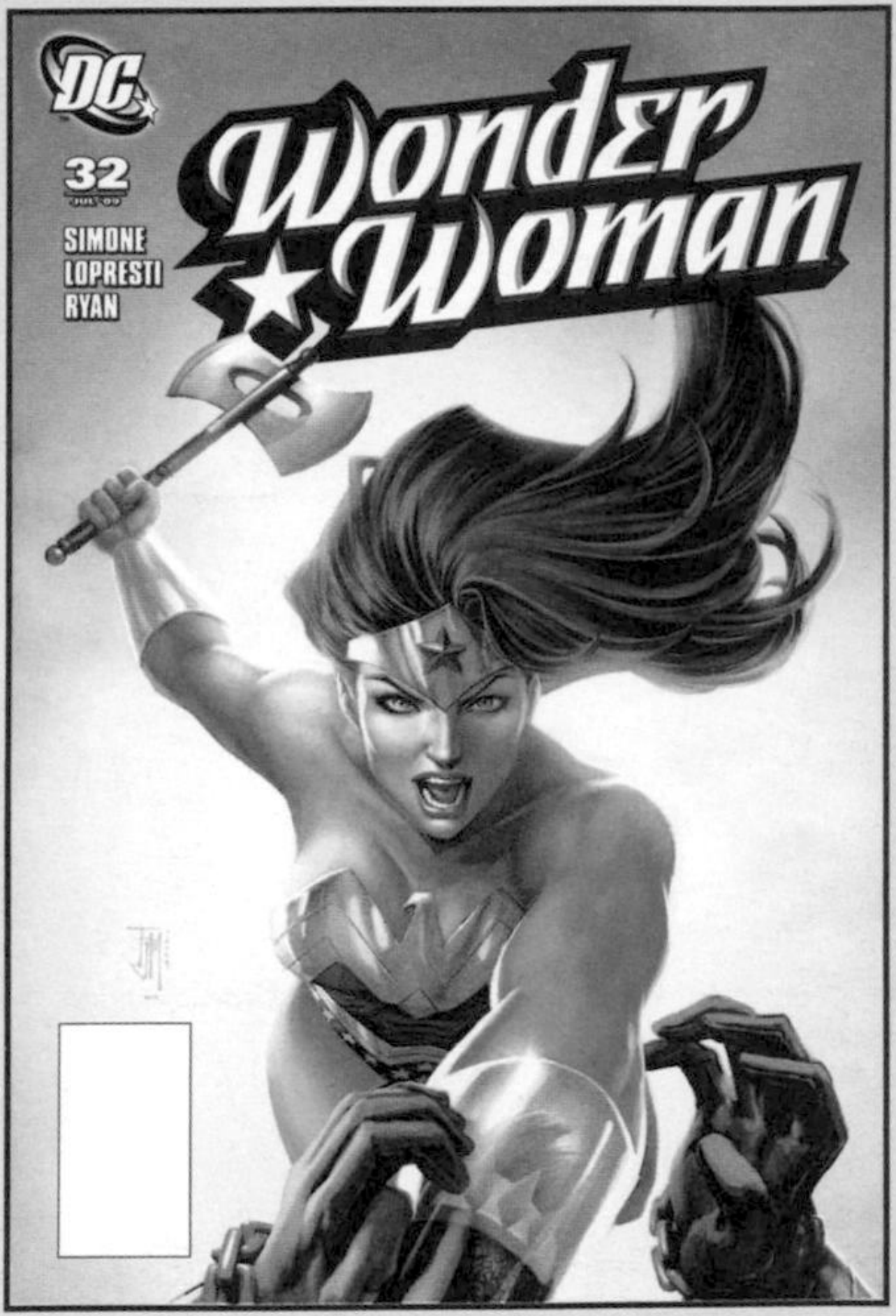
DC
32
JUL '09
SIMONE
LOPRESTI
RYAN
Wonder Woman

THE MODERN AGE OF AN ICON

Wonder Woman has been ever-present in comics since her debut in 1941 and continues to be one of the most popular characters of all time. This second collection celebrates *Wonder Woman* covers beginning from *Wonder Woman* #301 (Vol. 1, March 1983) and features notable issues by famed comic book artists such as George Pérez, Phil Jimenez, Adam Hughes, and José Luis García-López.

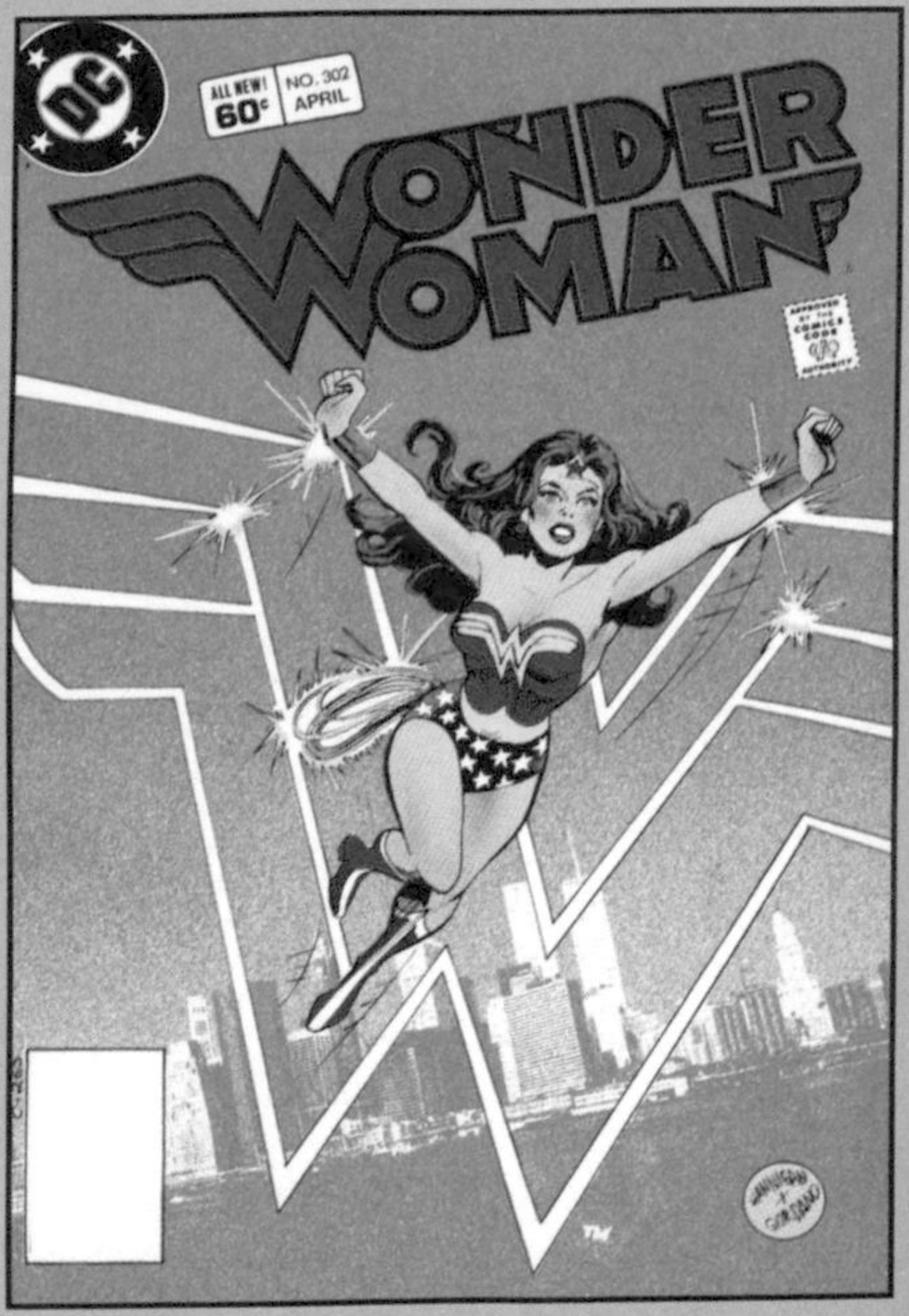
DC
ALL NEW!
60¢
NO. 302
APRIL
WONDER WOMAN
TM

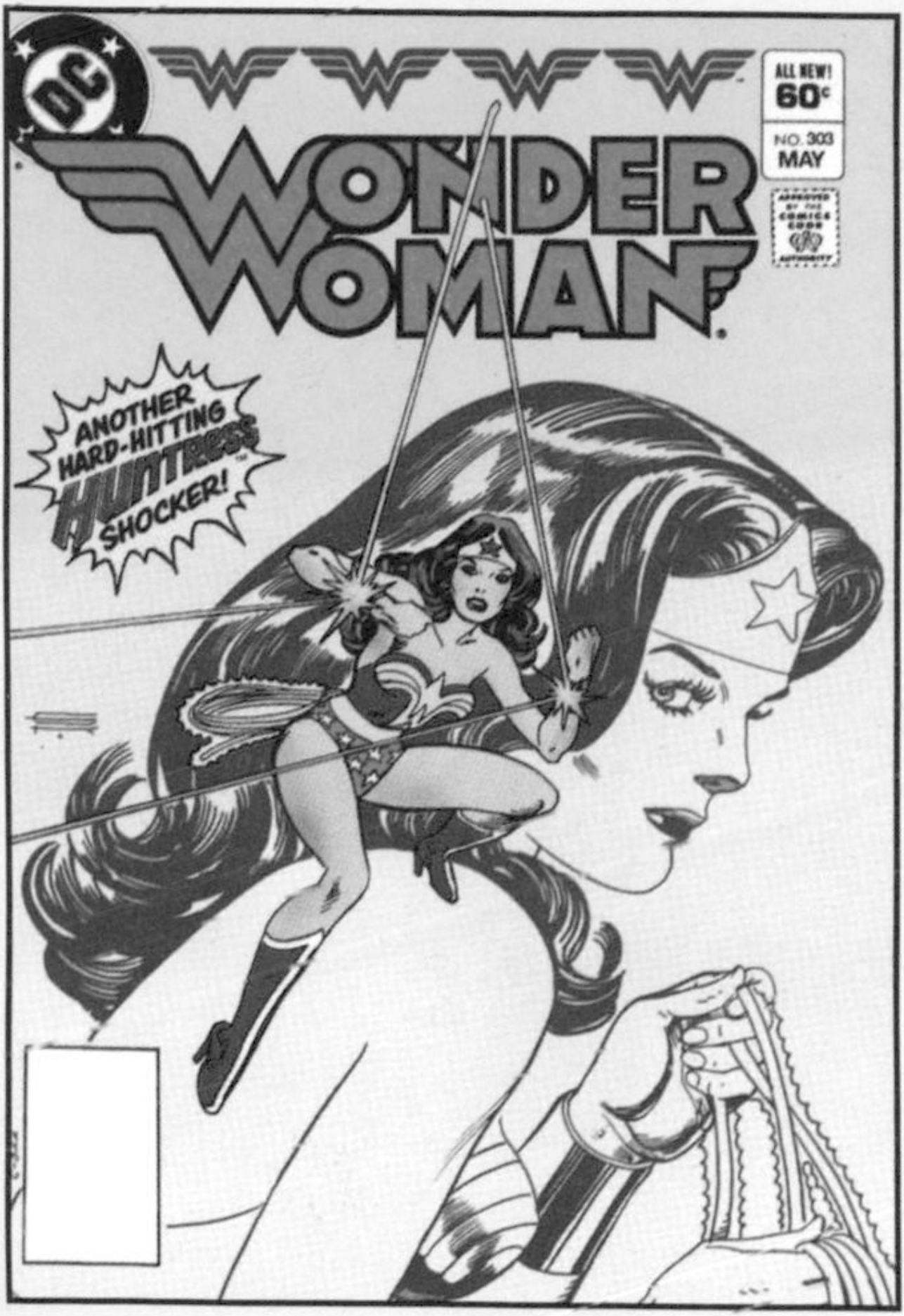
DC
WONDER WOMAN
ALL NEW!
60¢
NO. 303
MAY
ANOTHER HARD-HITTING HUNTRESS SHOCKER!

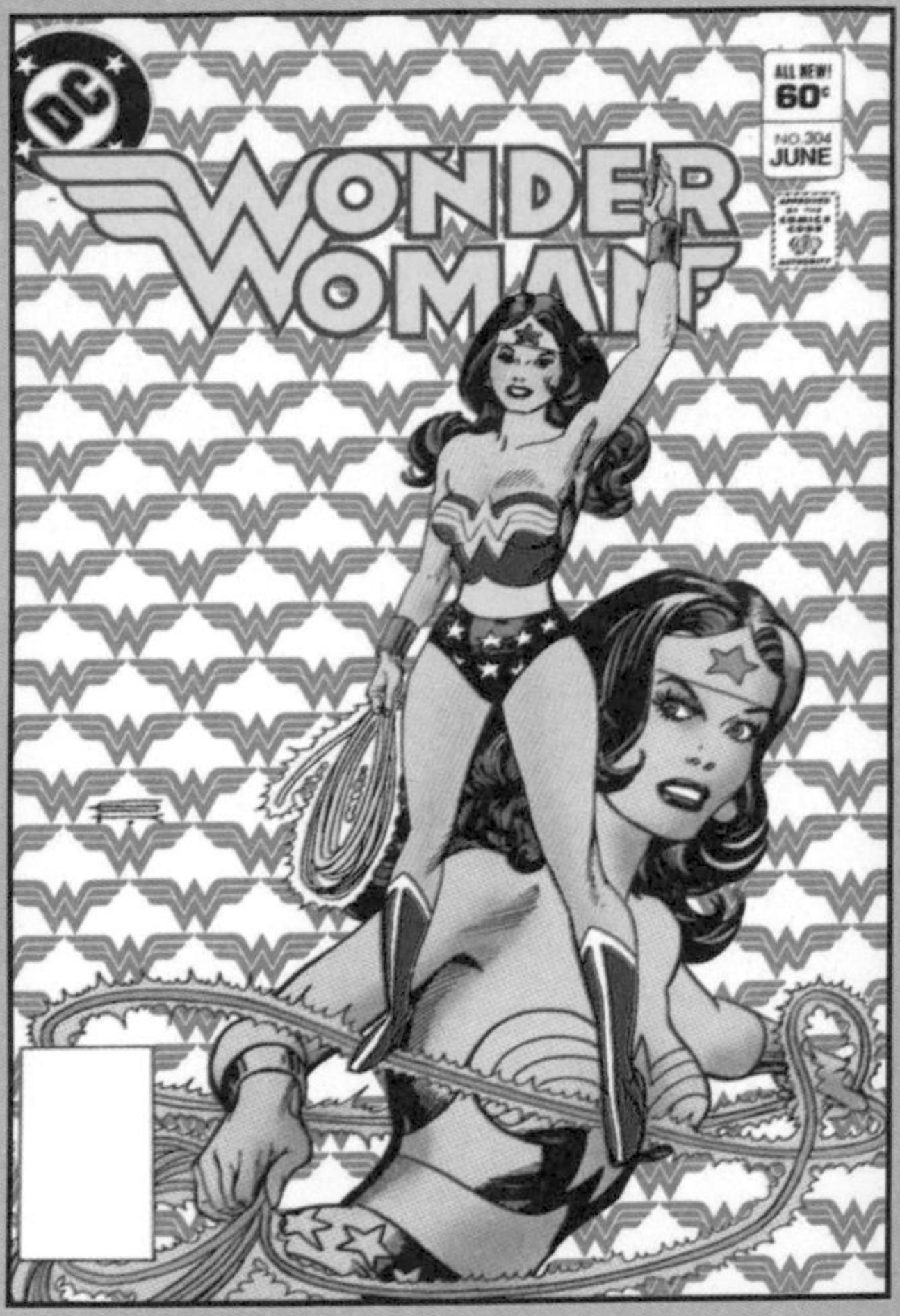
DC
ALL NEW!
60¢
NO. 304
JUNE
WONDER WOMAN

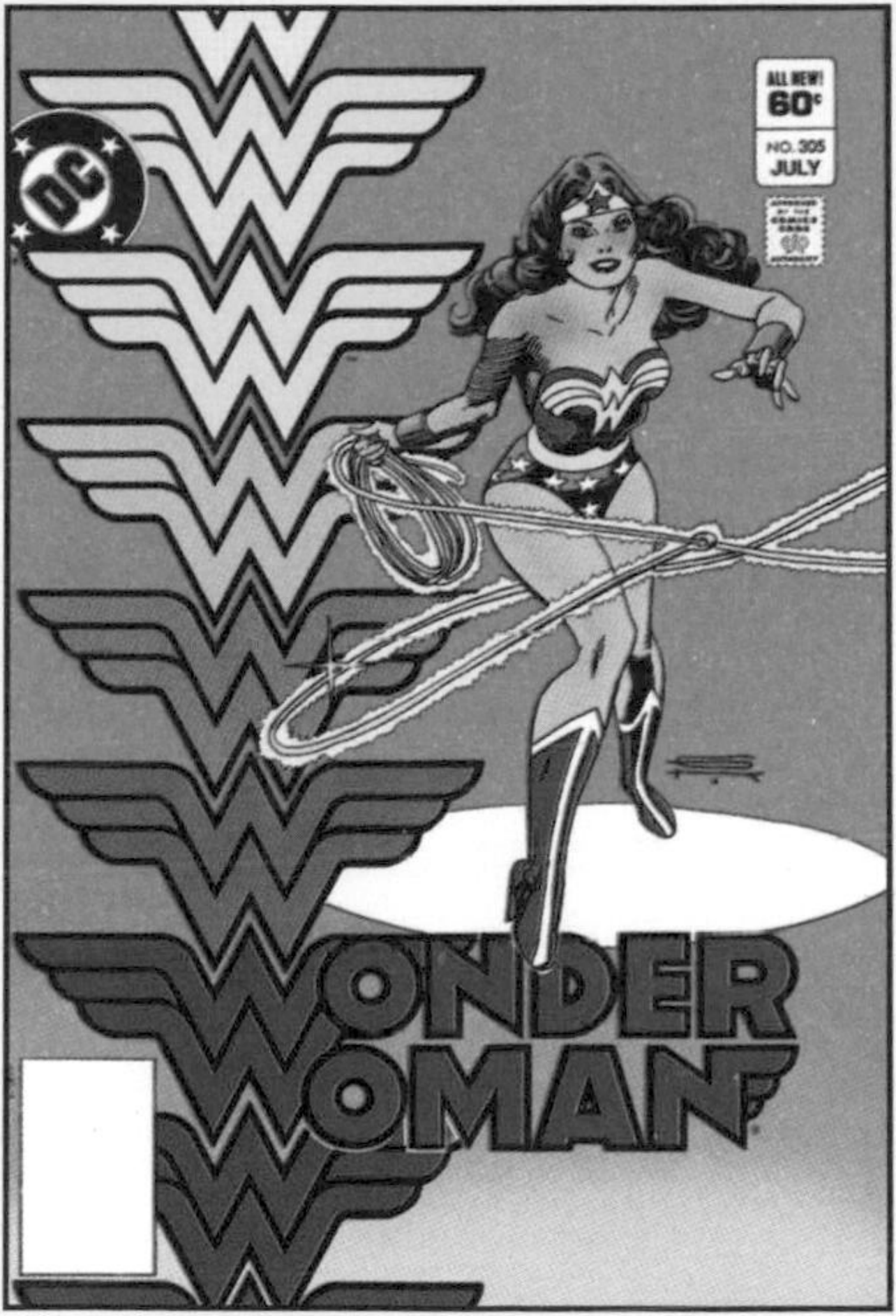
DC
ALL NEW!
60¢
NO. 305
JULY
WONDER
WOMAN

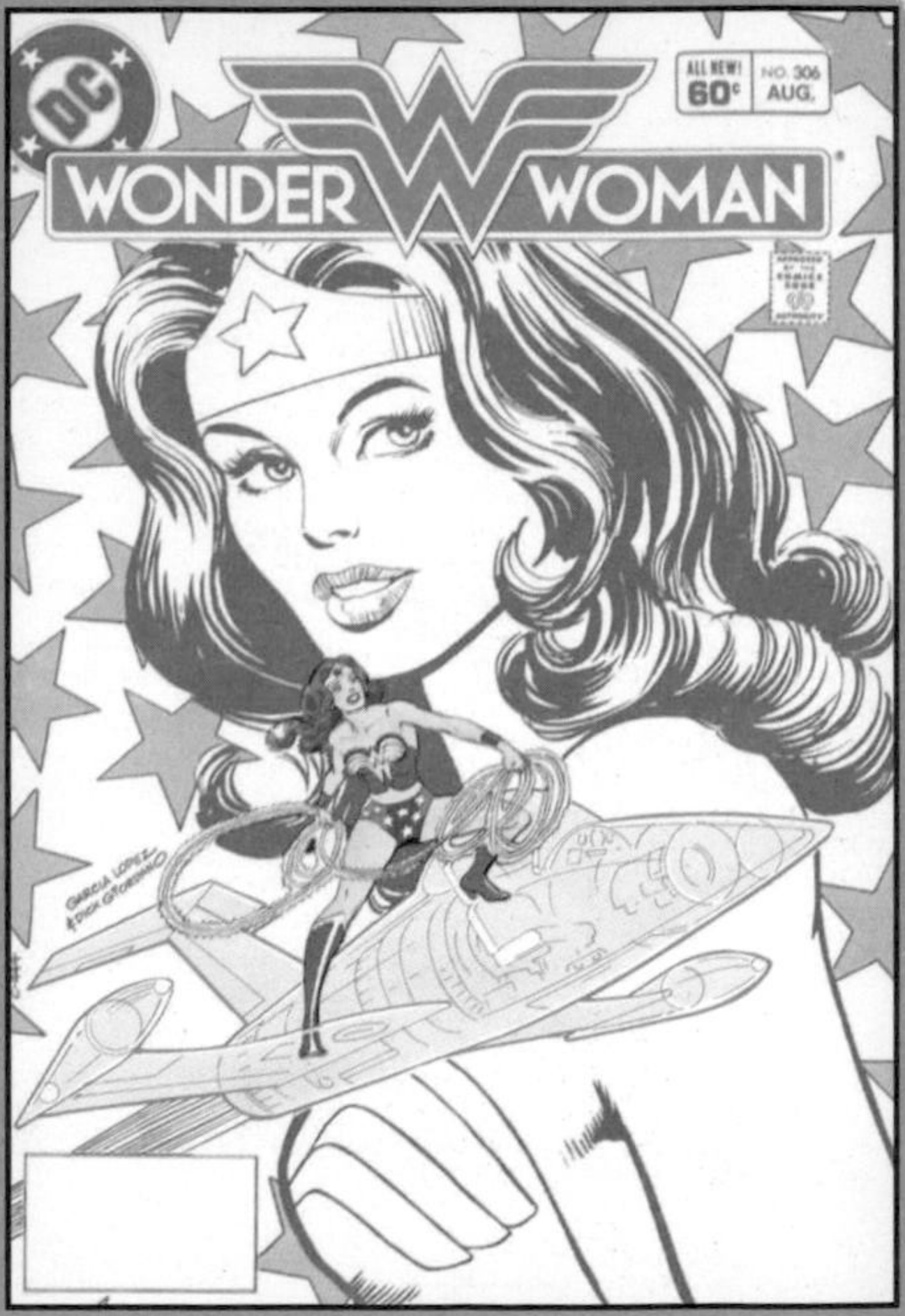
DC
ALL NEW!
60¢
NO. 306
AUG.
WONDER WOMAN
GARCIA LOPEZ
& DICK GIORDANO

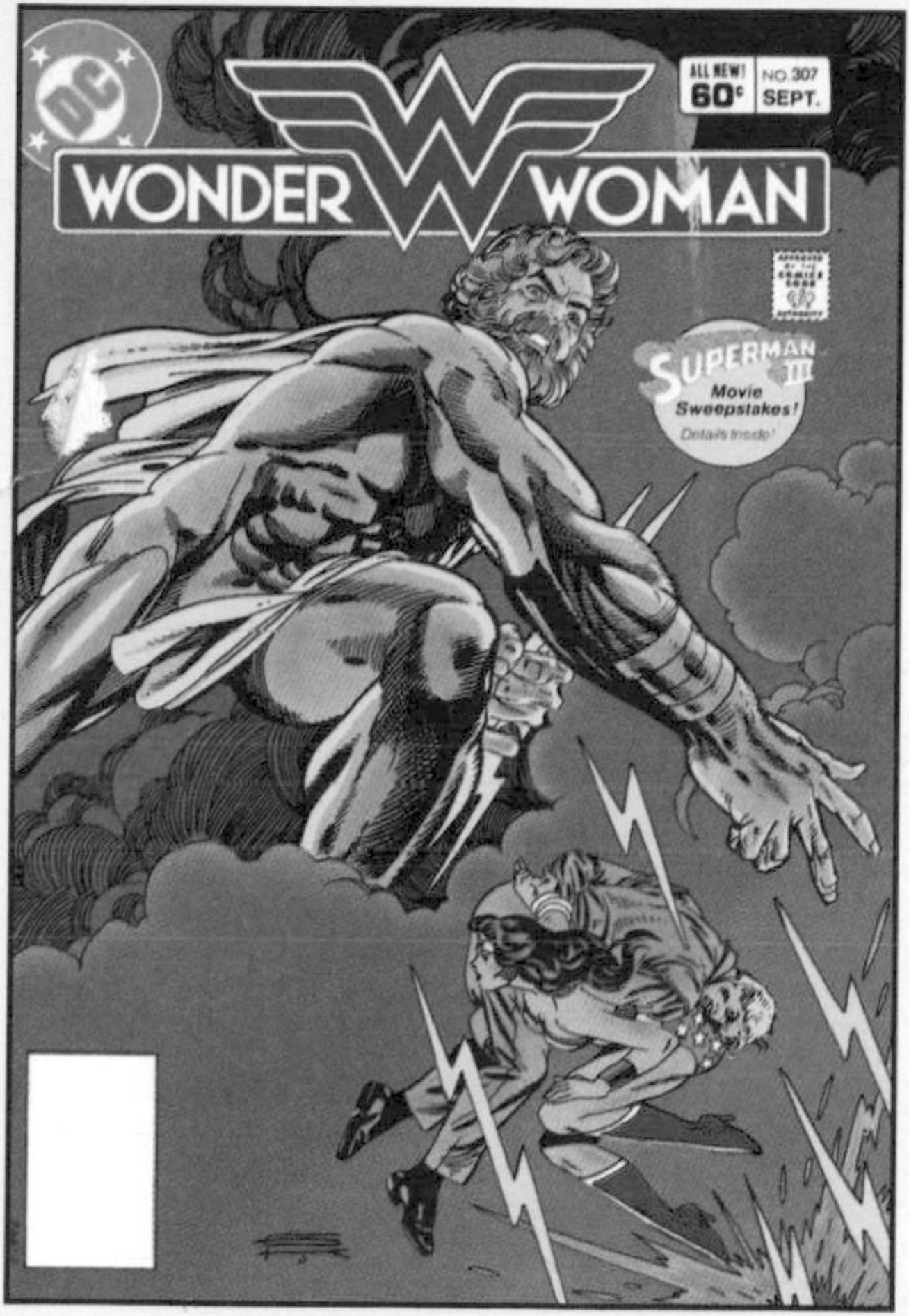
DC
WONDER WOMAN
ALL NEW!
60¢
NO. 307
SEPT.
SUPERMAN III
Movie Sweepstakes!
Details inside!

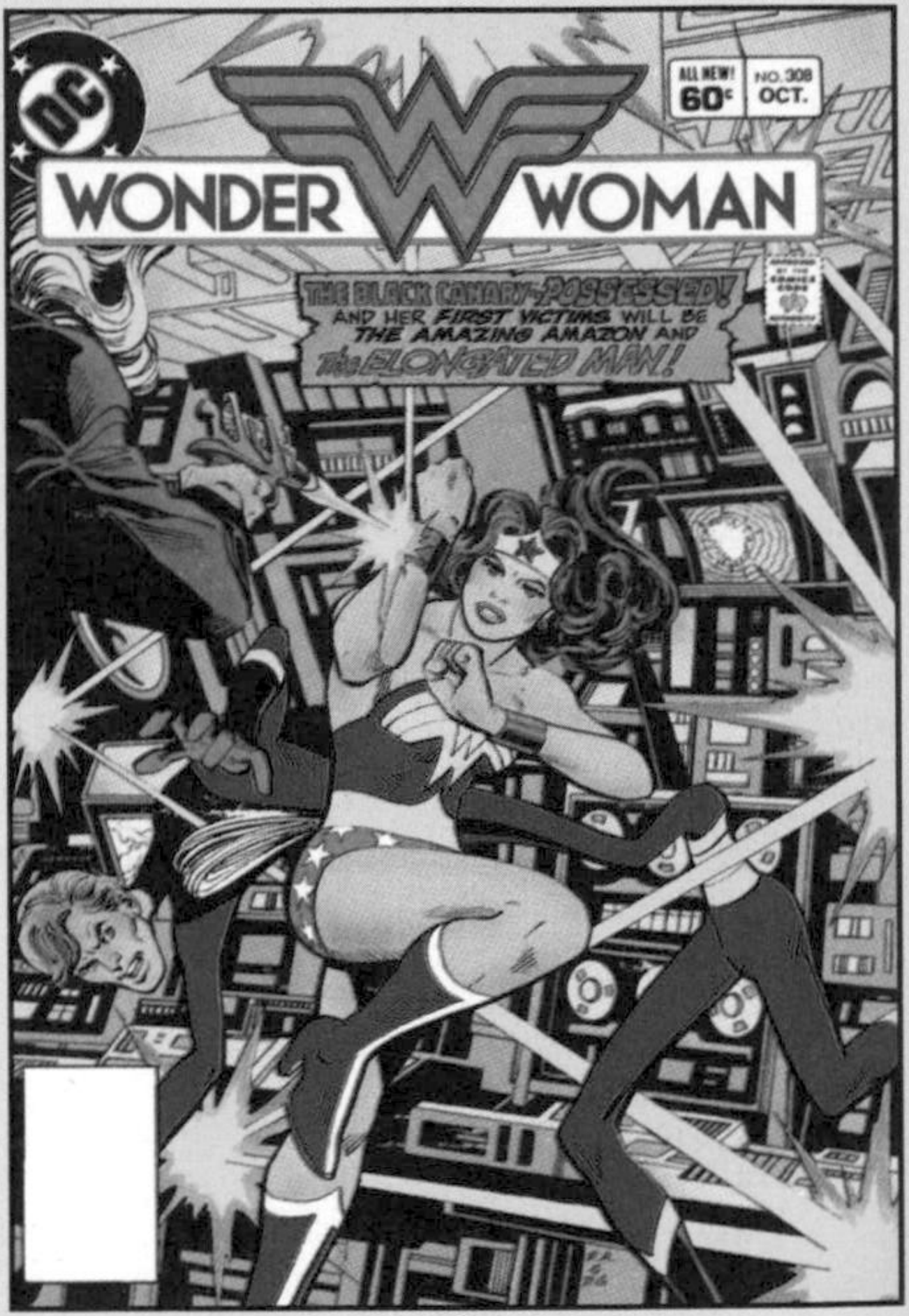
DC
ALL NEW!
60¢
NO. 308
OCT.
WONDER WOMAN
THE BLACK CANARY—POSSESSED!
AND HER FIRST VICTIMS WILL BE
THE AMAZING AMAZON AND
THE ELONGATED MAN!

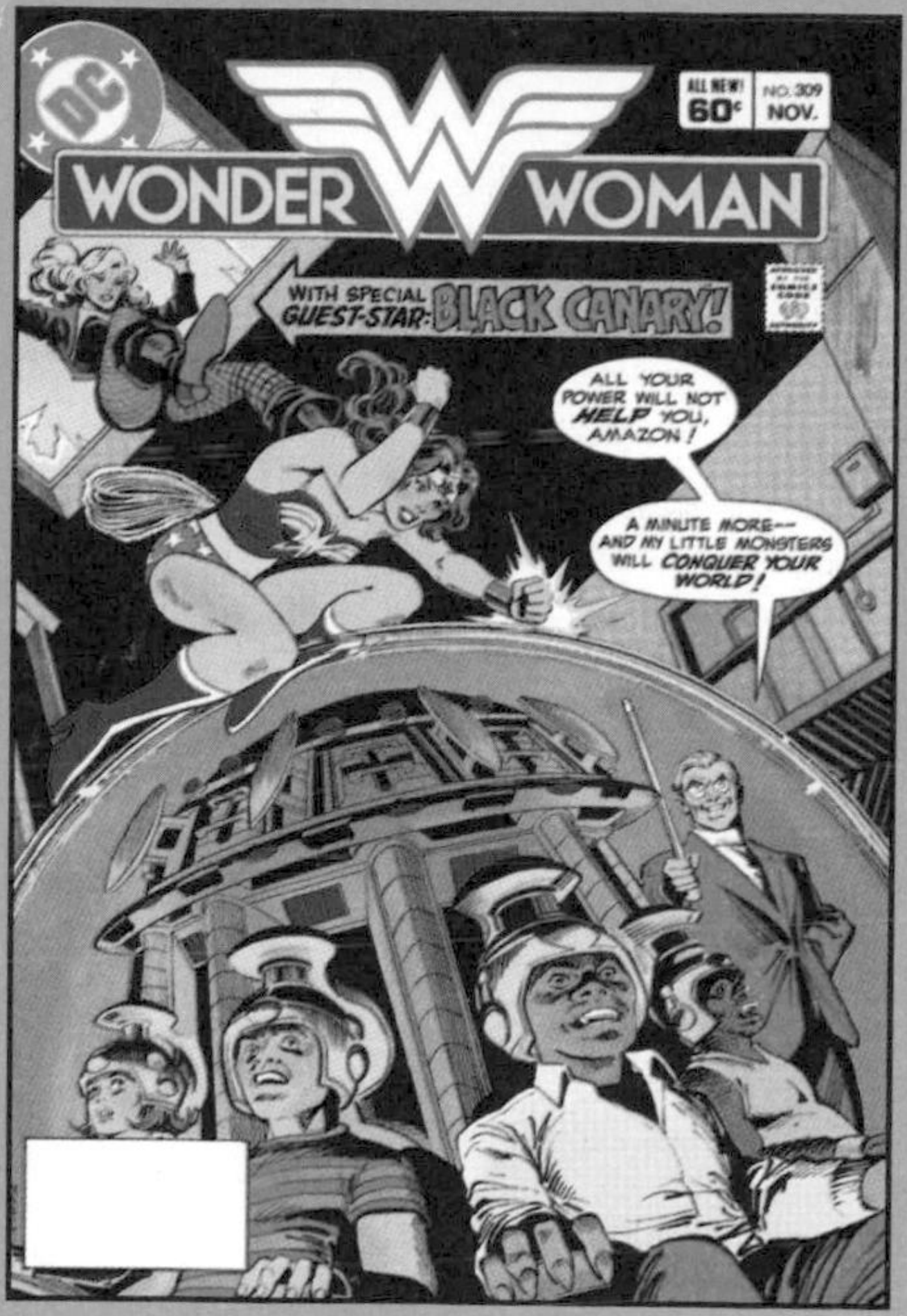
DC
WONDER WOMAN
ALL NEW!
60¢
NO. 309
NOV.
WITH SPECIAL GUEST-STAR: BLACK CANARY!
ALL YOUR POWER WILL NOT HELP YOU, AMAZON!
A MINUTE MORE— AND MY LITTLE MONSTERS WILL CONQUER YOUR WORLD!

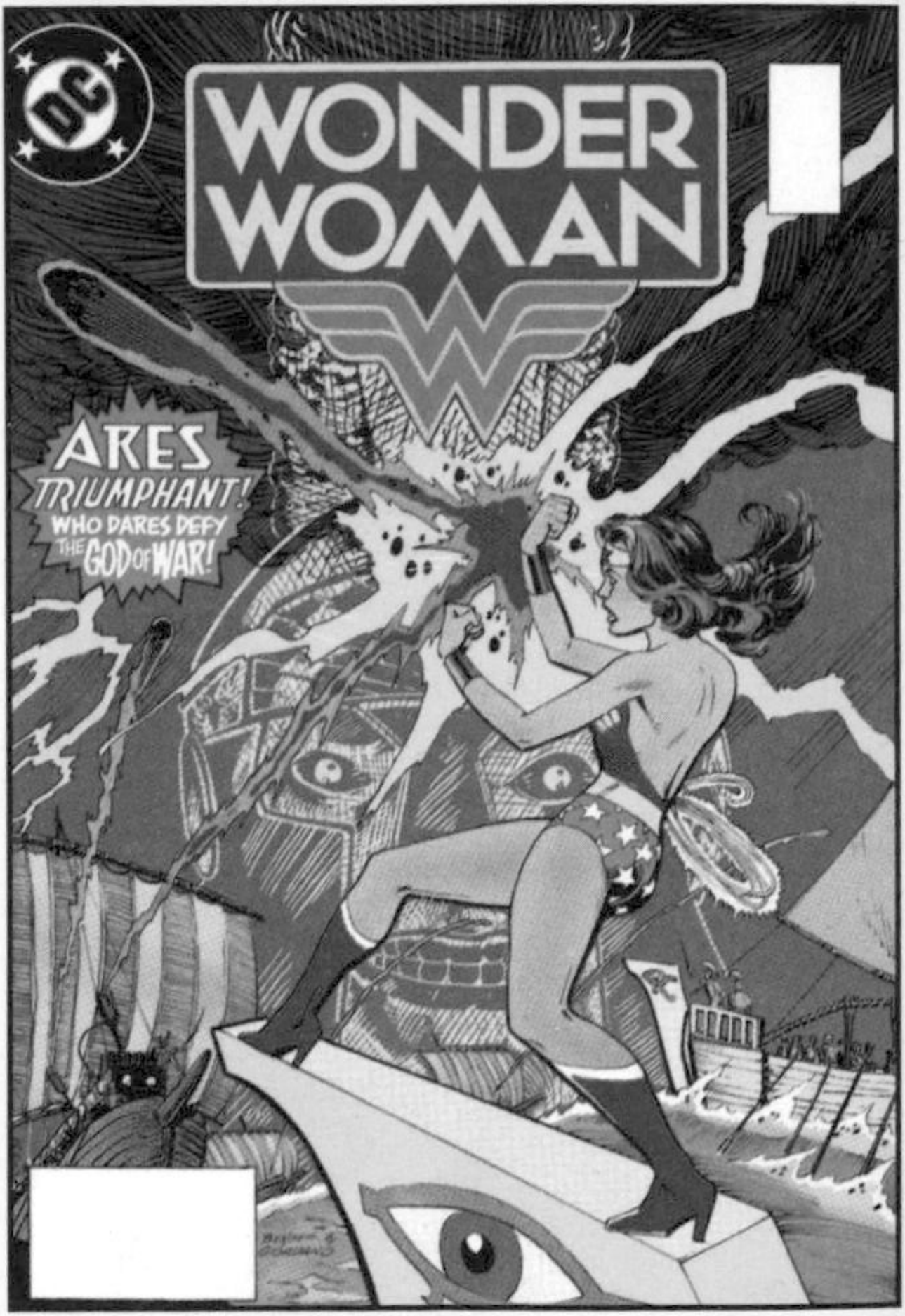
DC
WONDER WOMAN
ARES TRIUMPHANT!
WHO DARES DEFY THE GOD OF WAR!

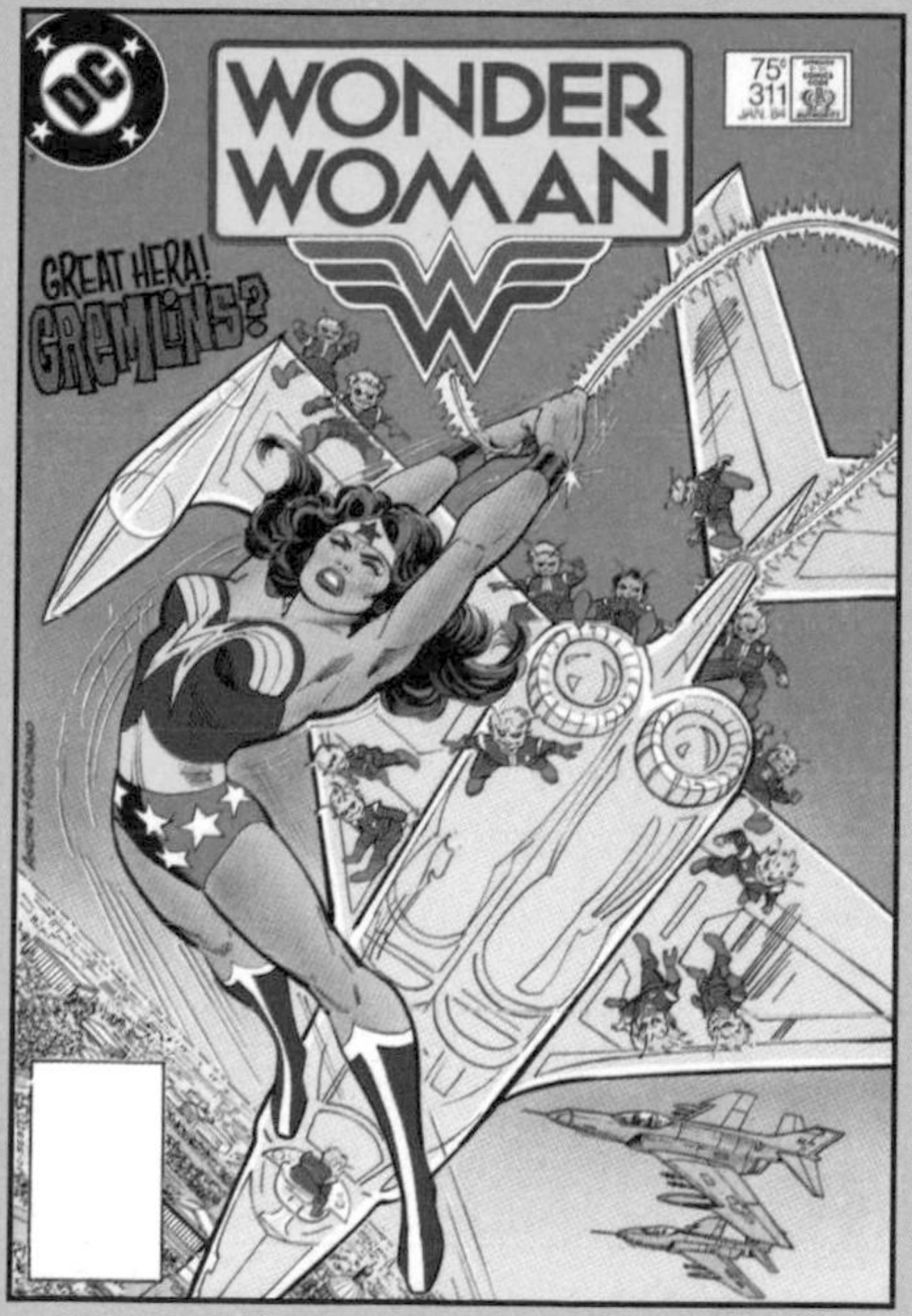
DC
WONDER WOMAN
75¢
311
GREAT HERA!
GREMLINS?

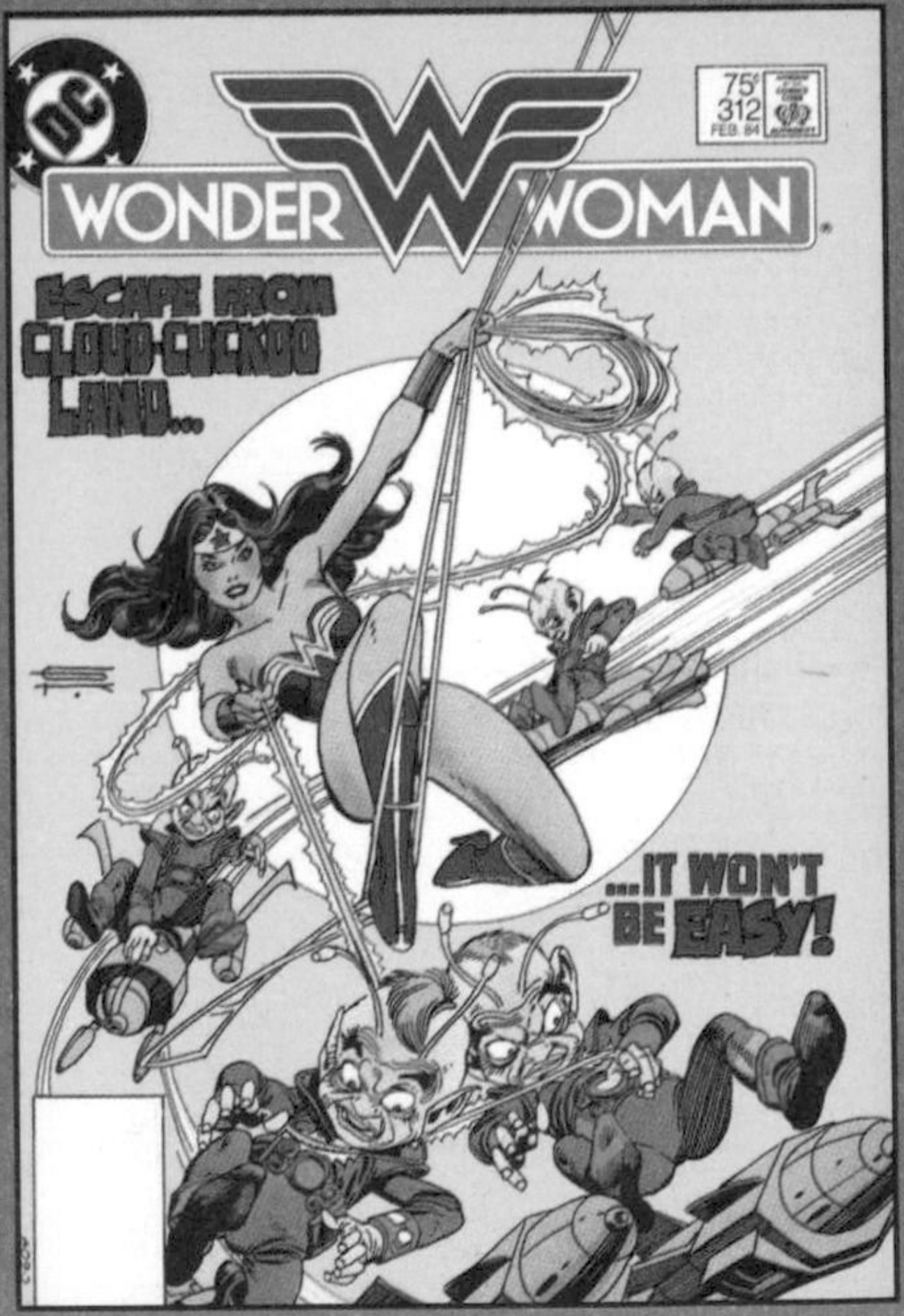
DC
WONDER WOMAN
75¢
312
FEB. 84
ESCAPE FROM CLOUD-CUCKOO LAND...
...IT WON'T BE EASY!

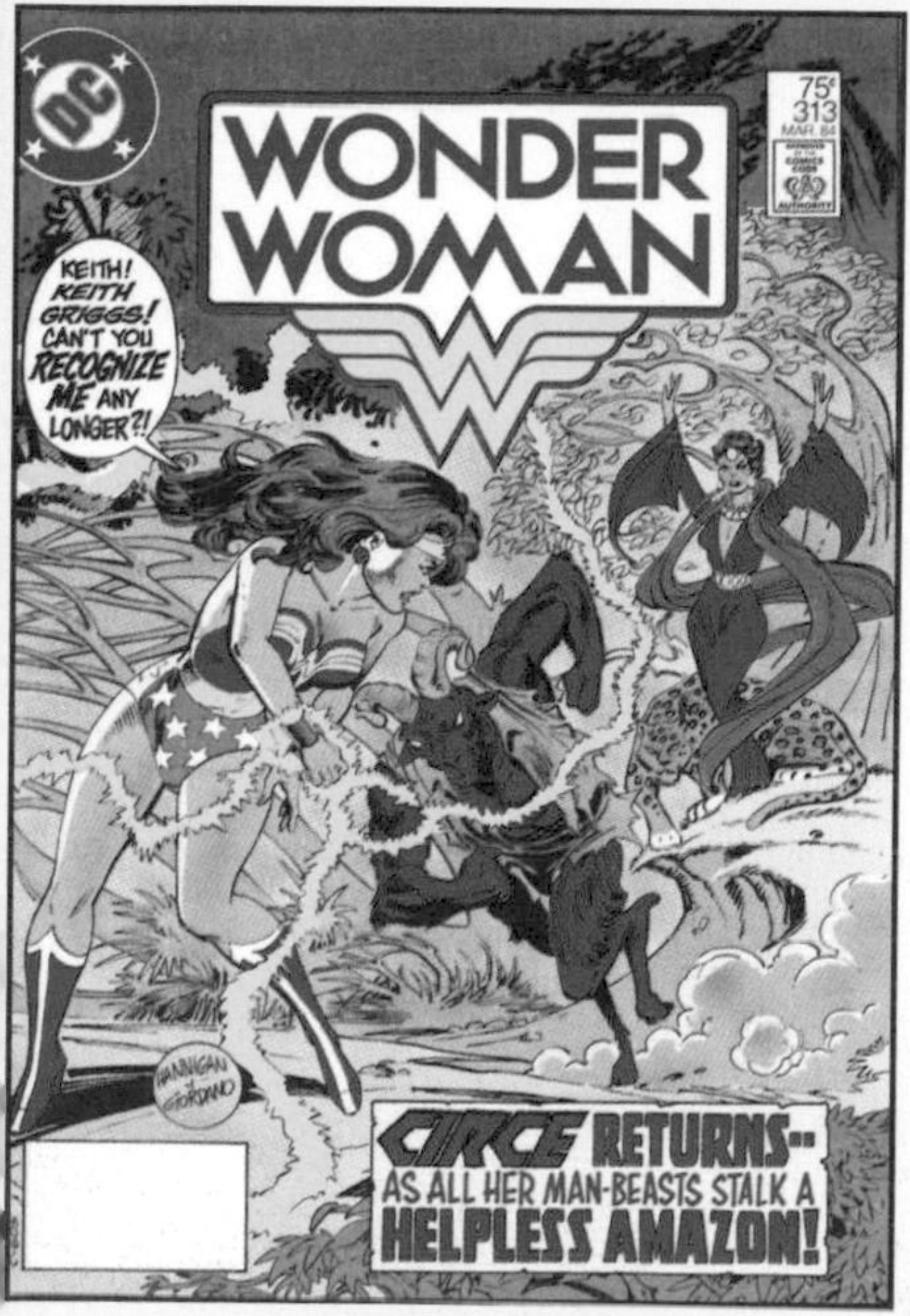
DC
WONDER WOMAN
75¢
313
MAR. 84
KEITH! KEITH GRIGGS! CAN'T YOU RECOGNIZE ME ANY LONGER?!
HANNIGAN & GIORDANO
CIRCE RETURNS--
AS ALL HER MAN-BEASTS STALK A
HELPLESS AMAZON!

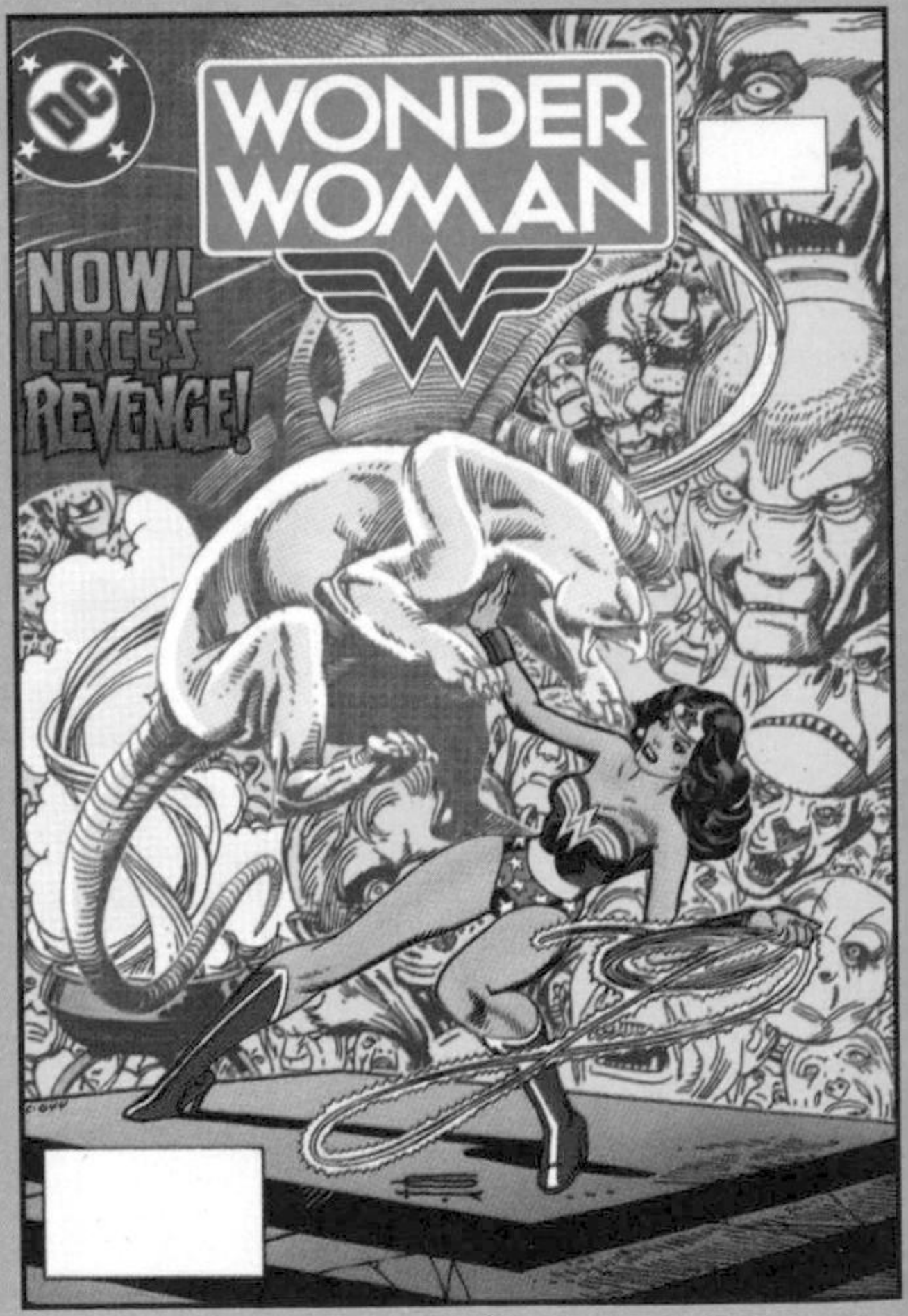
DC
WONDER WOMAN
NOW! CIRCE'S REVENGE!

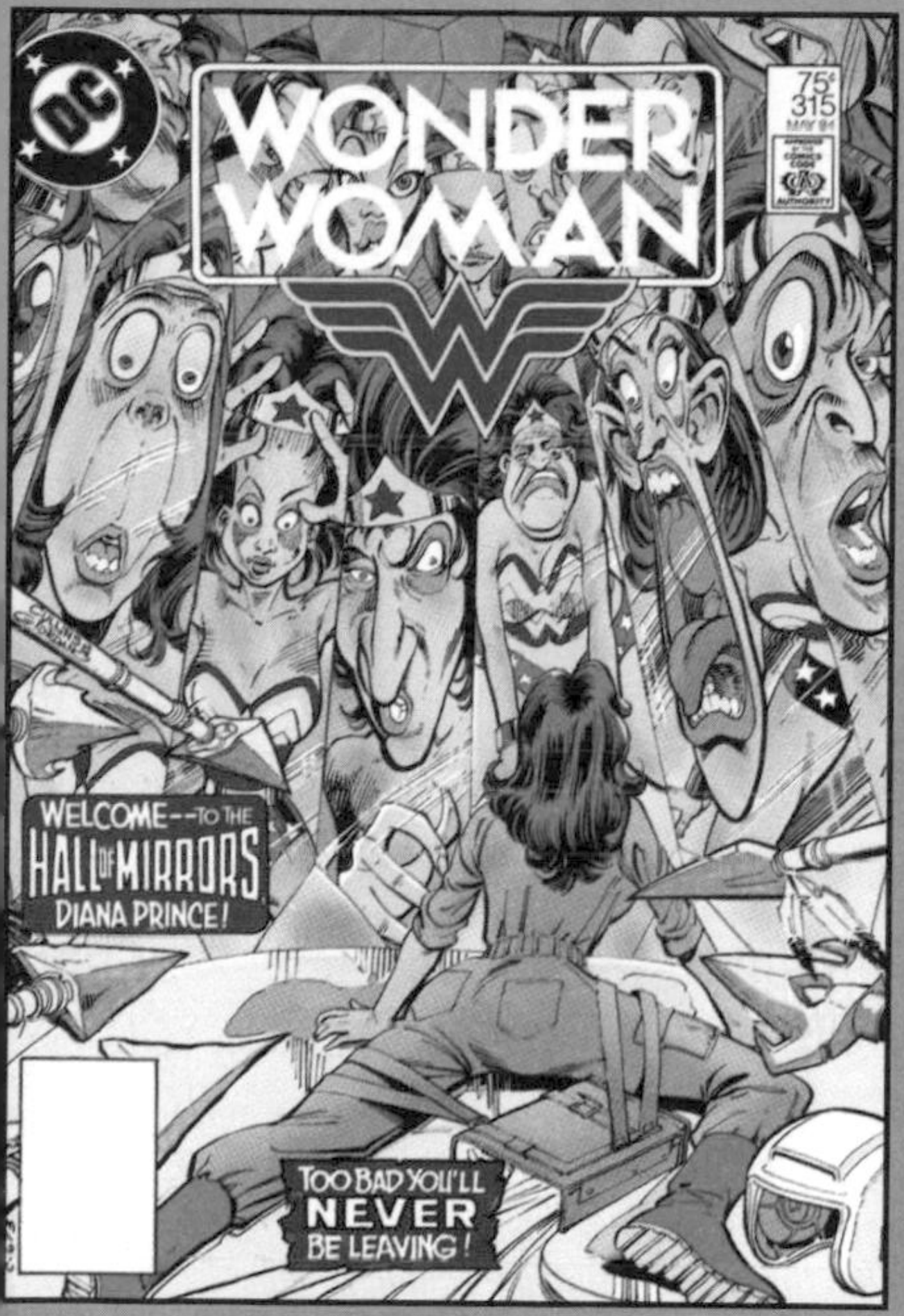
DC
WONDER WOMAN
75¢
315
MAY 84
WELCOME--TO THE HALL OF MIRRORS DIANA PRINCE!
TOO BAD YOU'LL NEVER BE LEAVING!

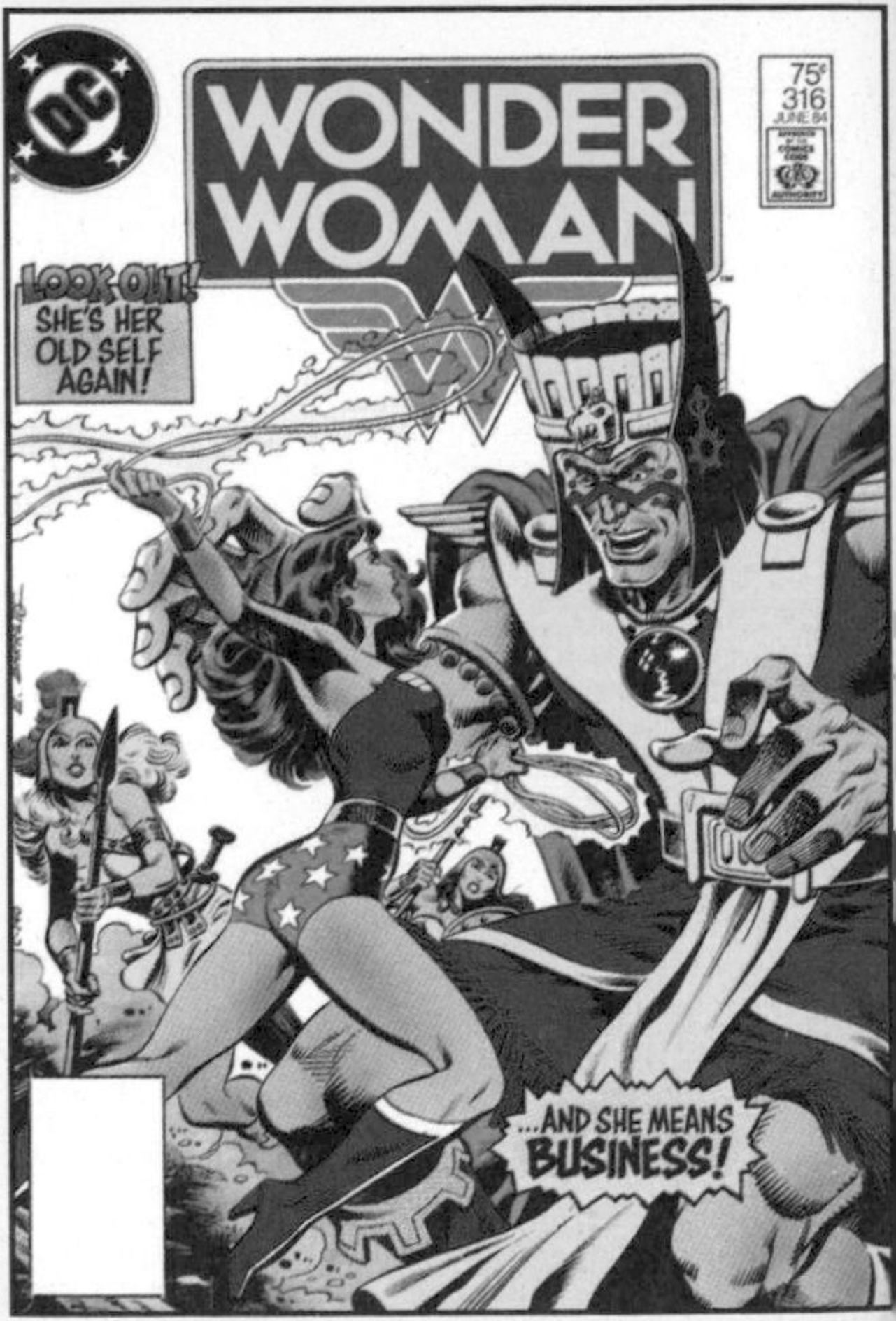
DC
WONDER WOMAN
75¢
316
JUNE 84
LOOK OUT!
SHE'S HER OLD SELF AGAIN!
...AND SHE MEANS BUSINESS!

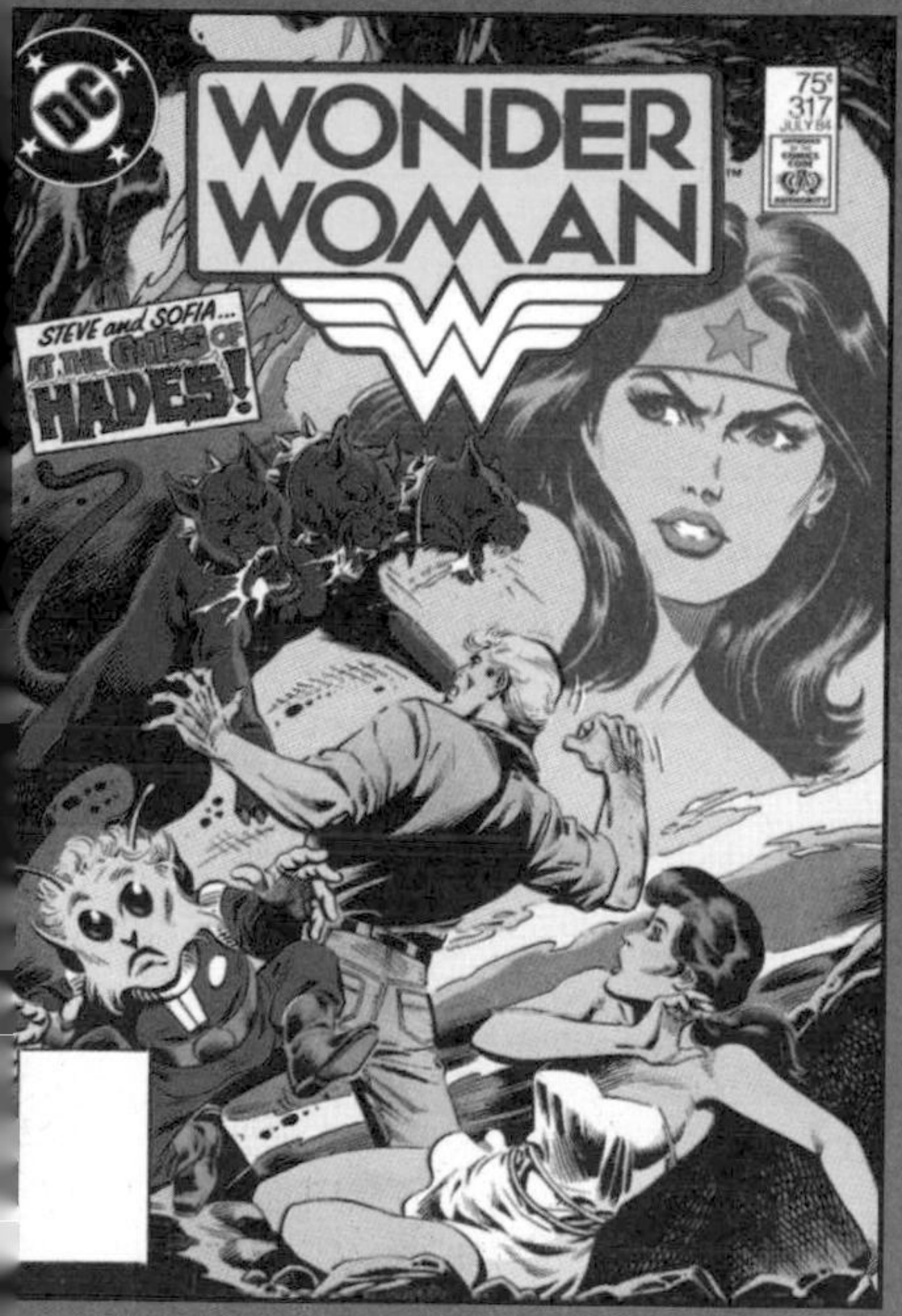
DC
WONDER WOMAN
75¢
317
JULY 84
STEVE and SOFIA...
AT THE GATES OF HADES!

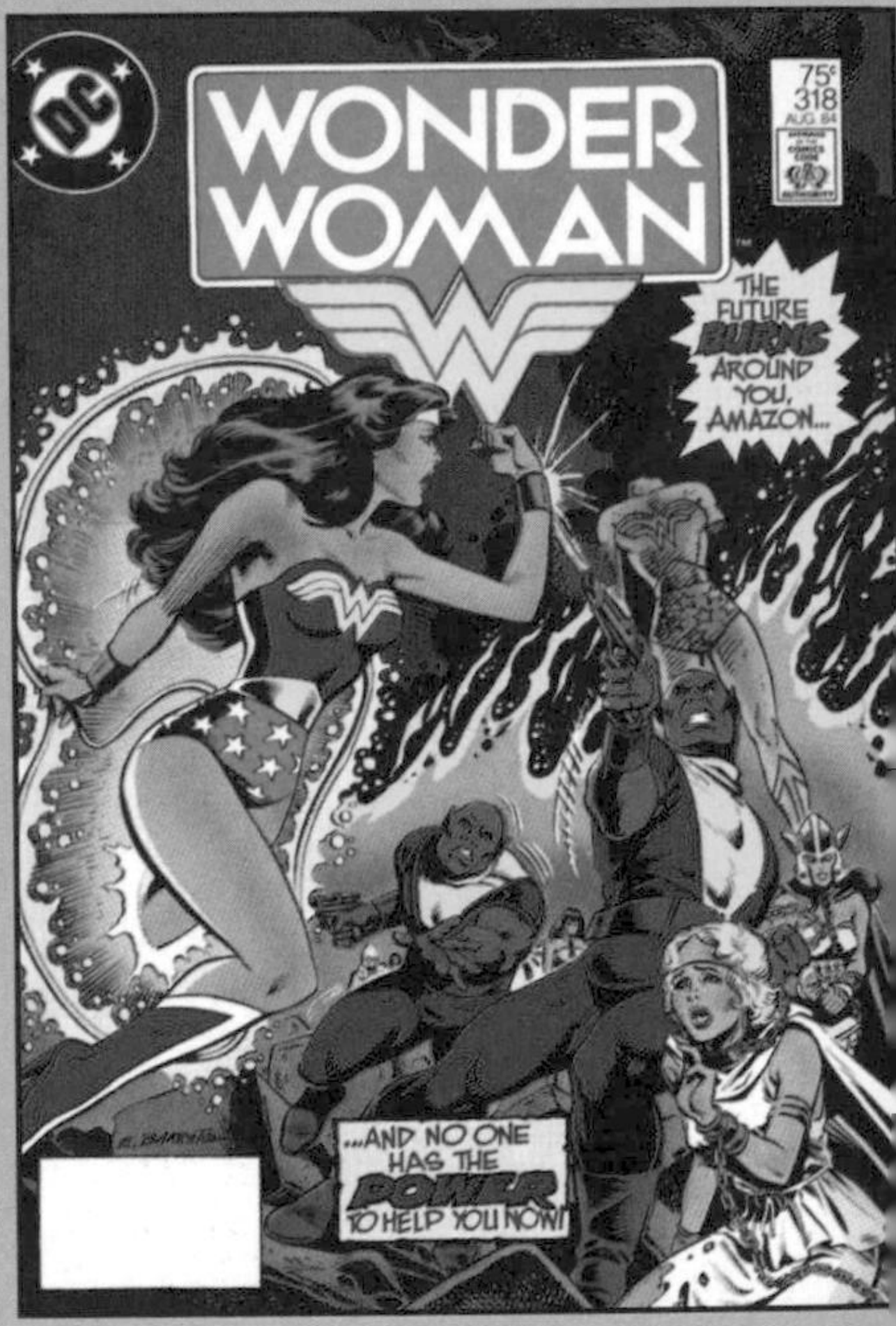
DC
WONDER WOMAN
75¢
318
AUG 84
THE FUTURE BURNS AROUND YOU, AMAZON...
...AND NO ONE HAS THE POWER TO HELP YOU NOW!

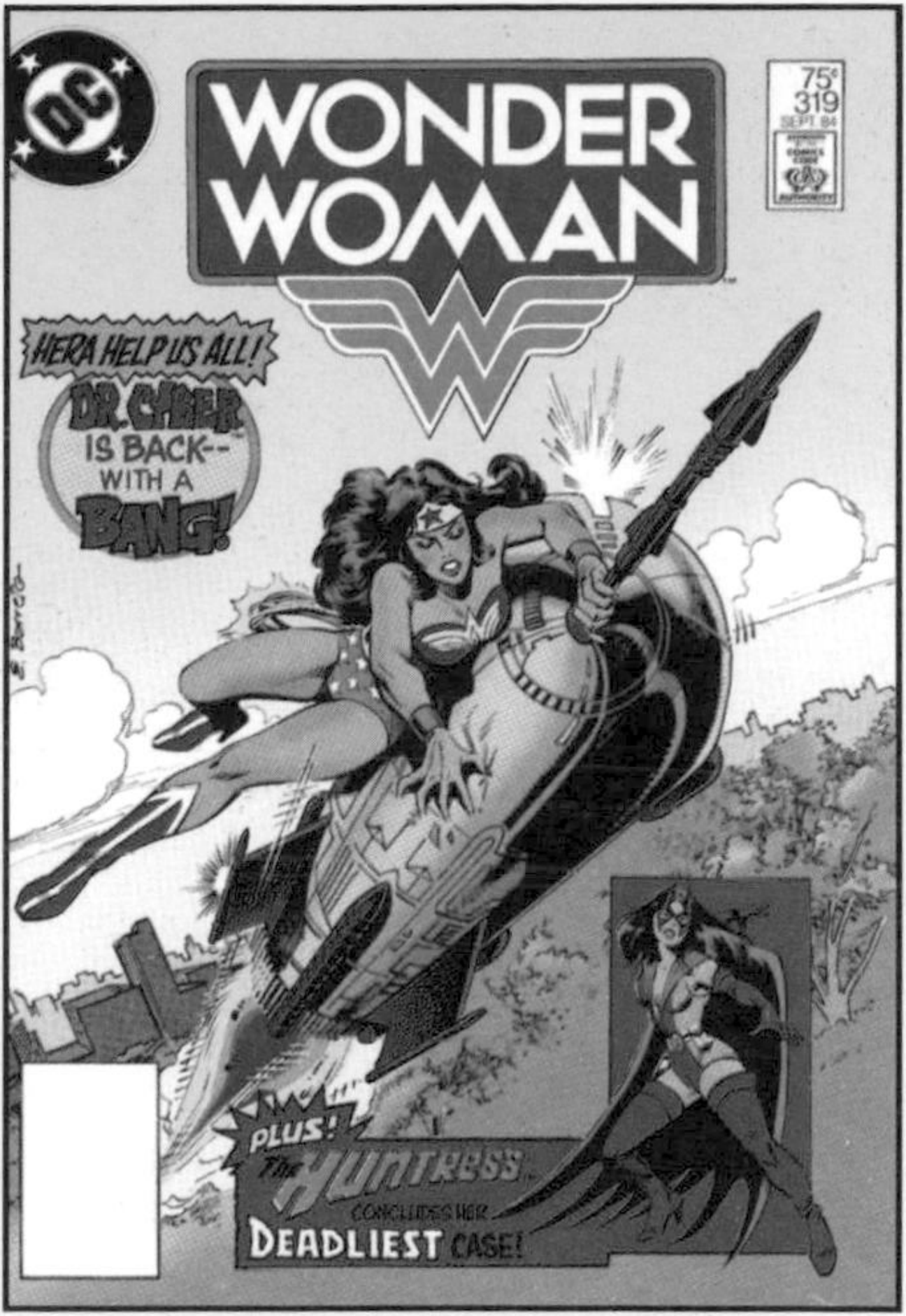
DC
WONDER WOMAN
75¢
319
SEPT 84
HERA HELP US ALL!
DR. CHEER IS BACK-- WITH A BANG!
PLUS! THE HUNTRESS CONCLUDES HER DEADLIEST CASE!

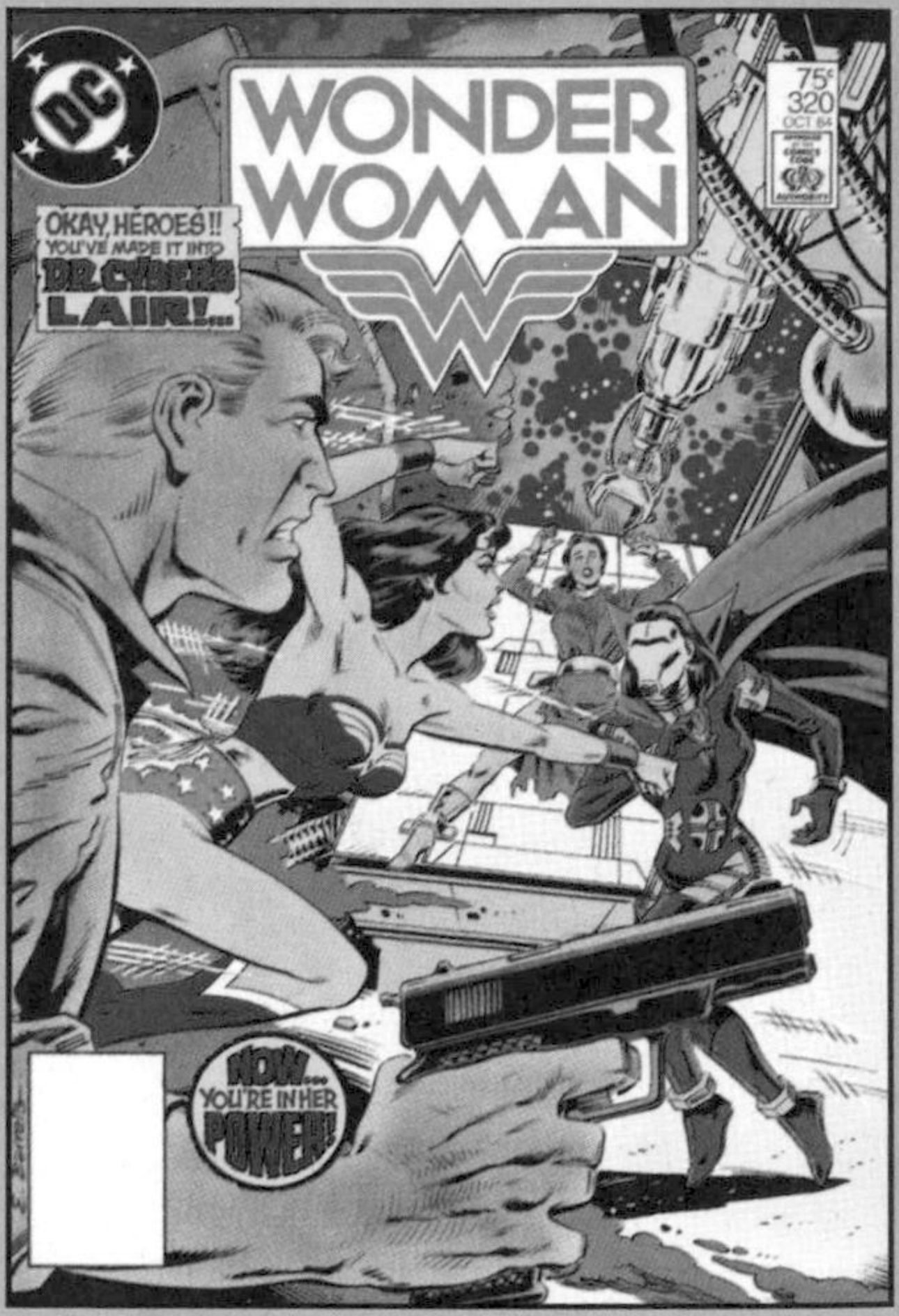
DC
WONDER WOMAN
75¢
320
OCT 84
OKAY, HEROES!! YOU'VE MADE IT INTO DR. CYBER'S LAIR!...
NOW... YOU'RE IN HER POWER!

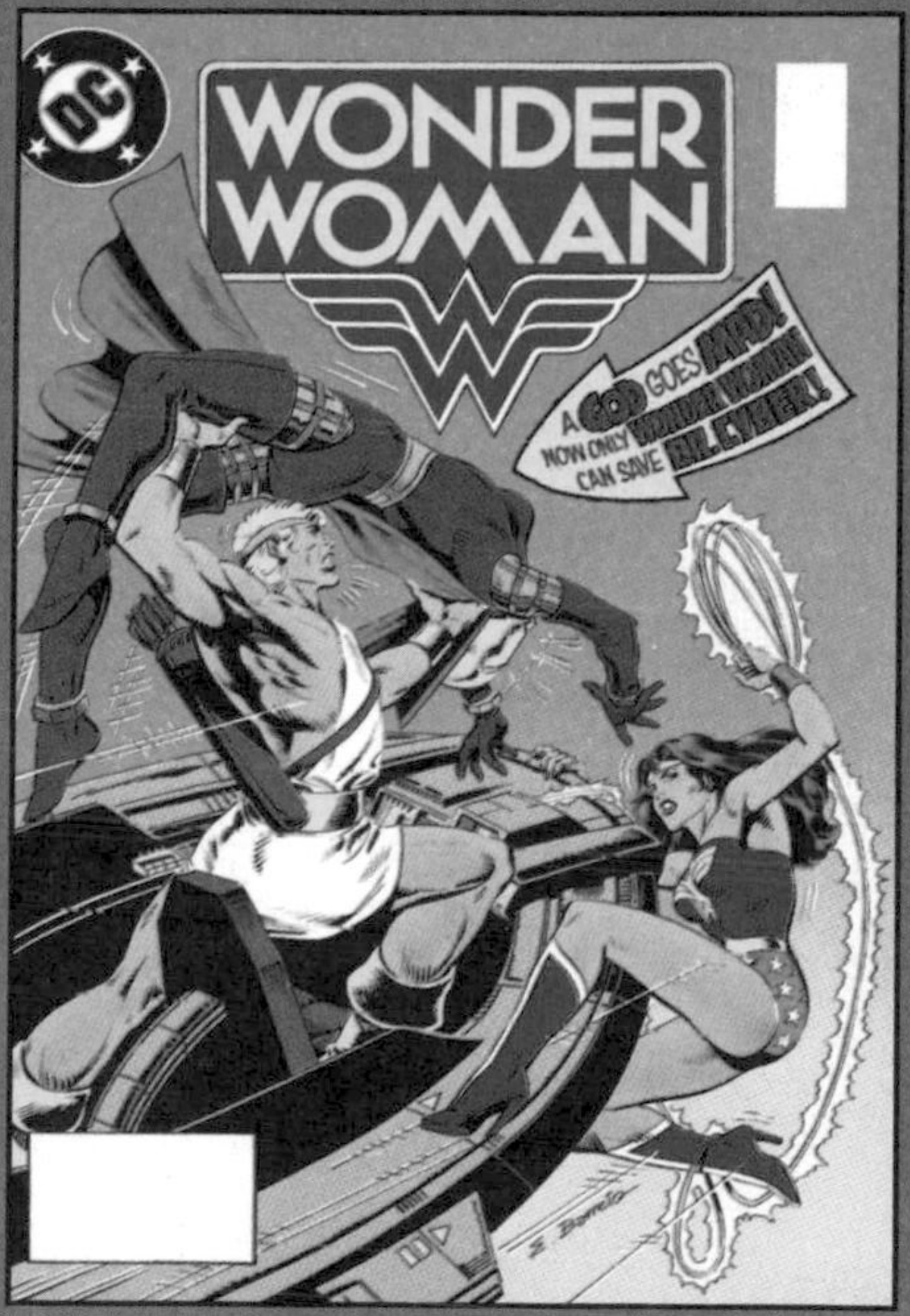
DC
WONDER WOMAN
A COP GOES MAD!
NOW ONLY WONDER WOMAN CAN SAVE MR. EVER!

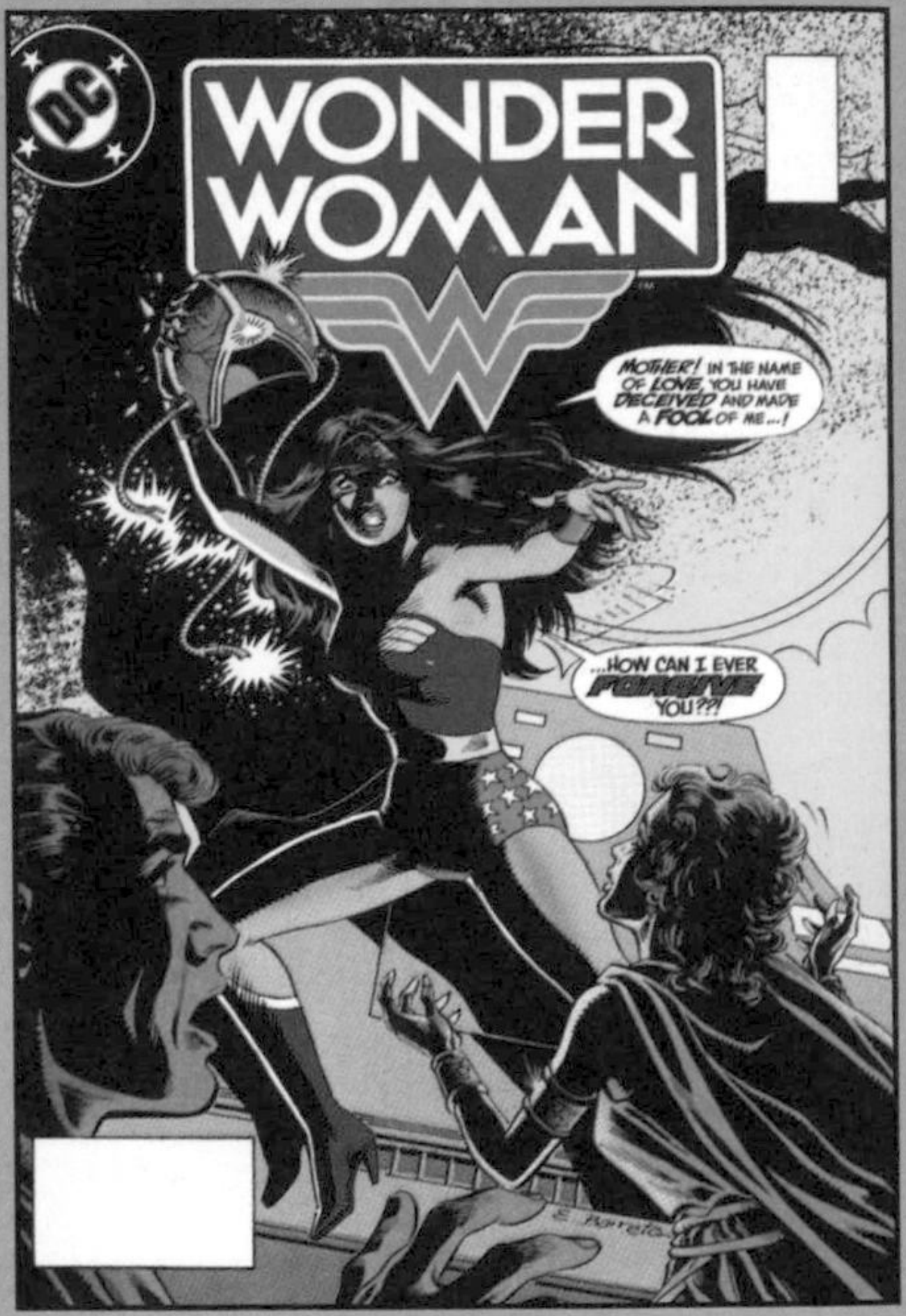
WONDER WOMAN
MOTHER! IN THE NAME OF LOVE, YOU HAVE DECEIVED AND MADE A FOOL OF ME...!
...HOW CAN I EVER FORGIVE YOU???

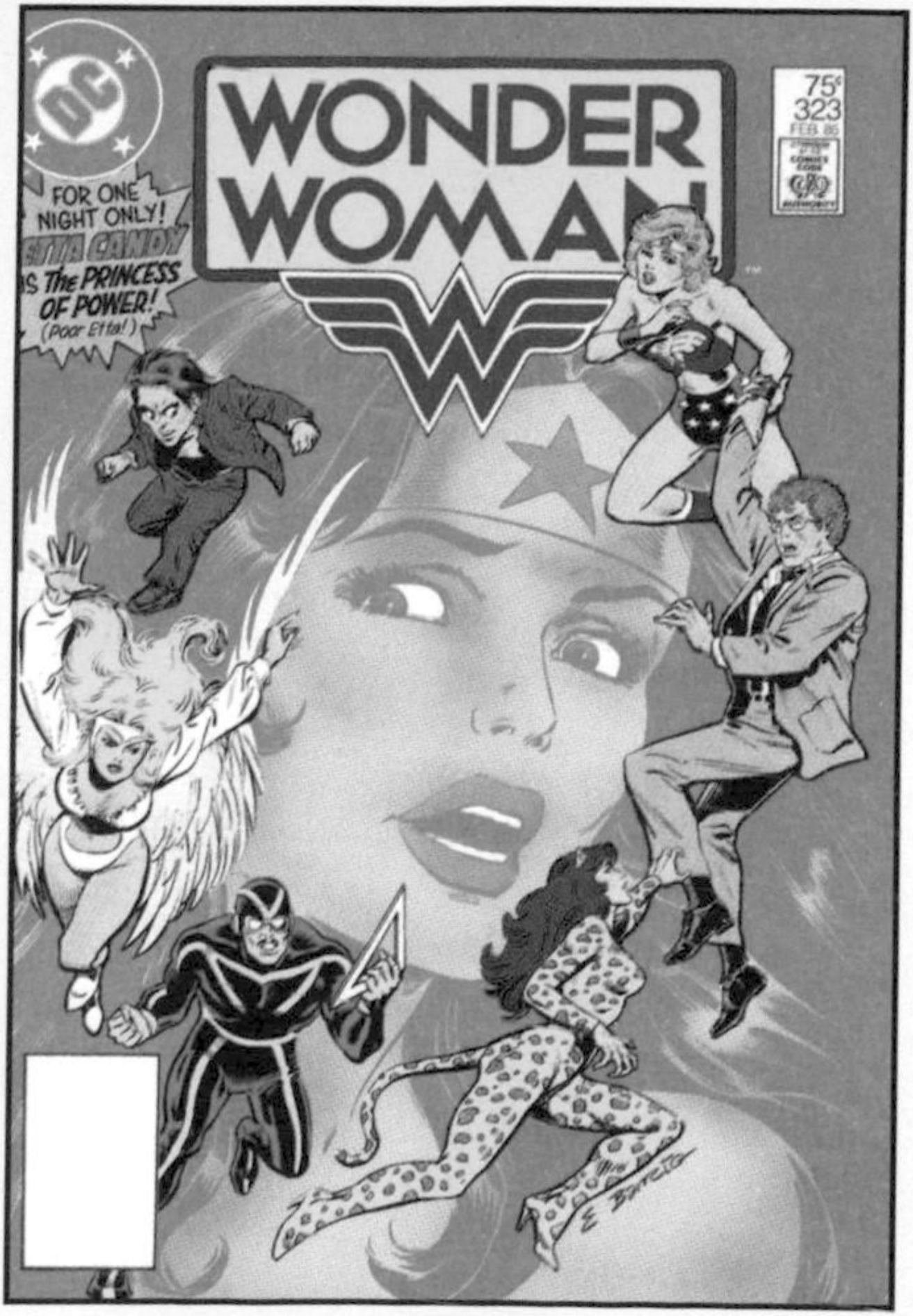
DC
WONDER WOMAN
75¢
323
FEB 85
FOR ONE NIGHT ONLY!
ETTA CANDY
AS The PRINCESS OF POWER!
(Poor Etta!)
E. Barreto

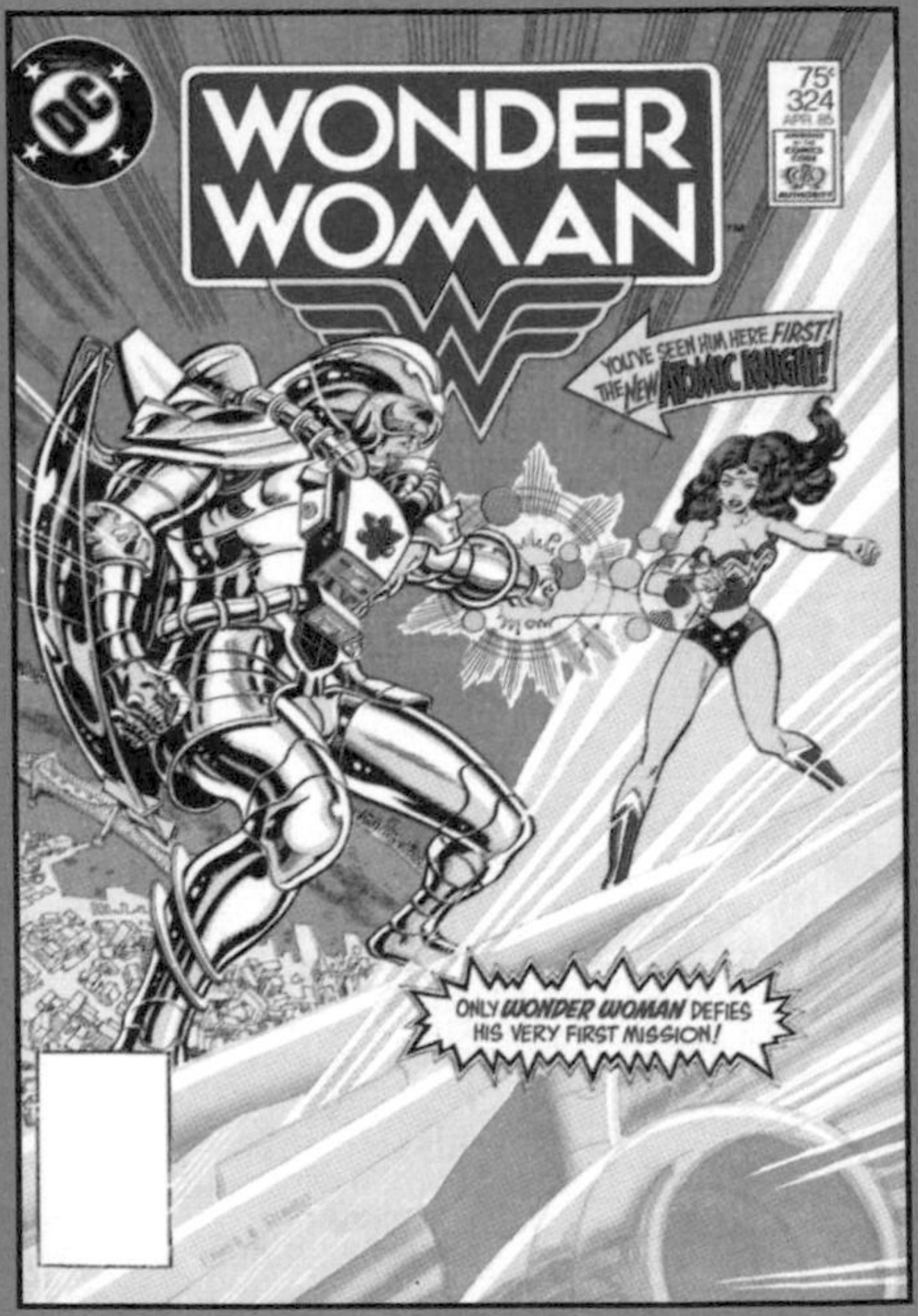
DC
WONDER WOMAN
75¢
324
APR. 85
YOU'VE SEEN HIM HERE FIRST!
THE NEW ATOMIC KNIGHT!
ONLY WONDER WOMAN DEFIES HIS VERY FIRST MISSION!

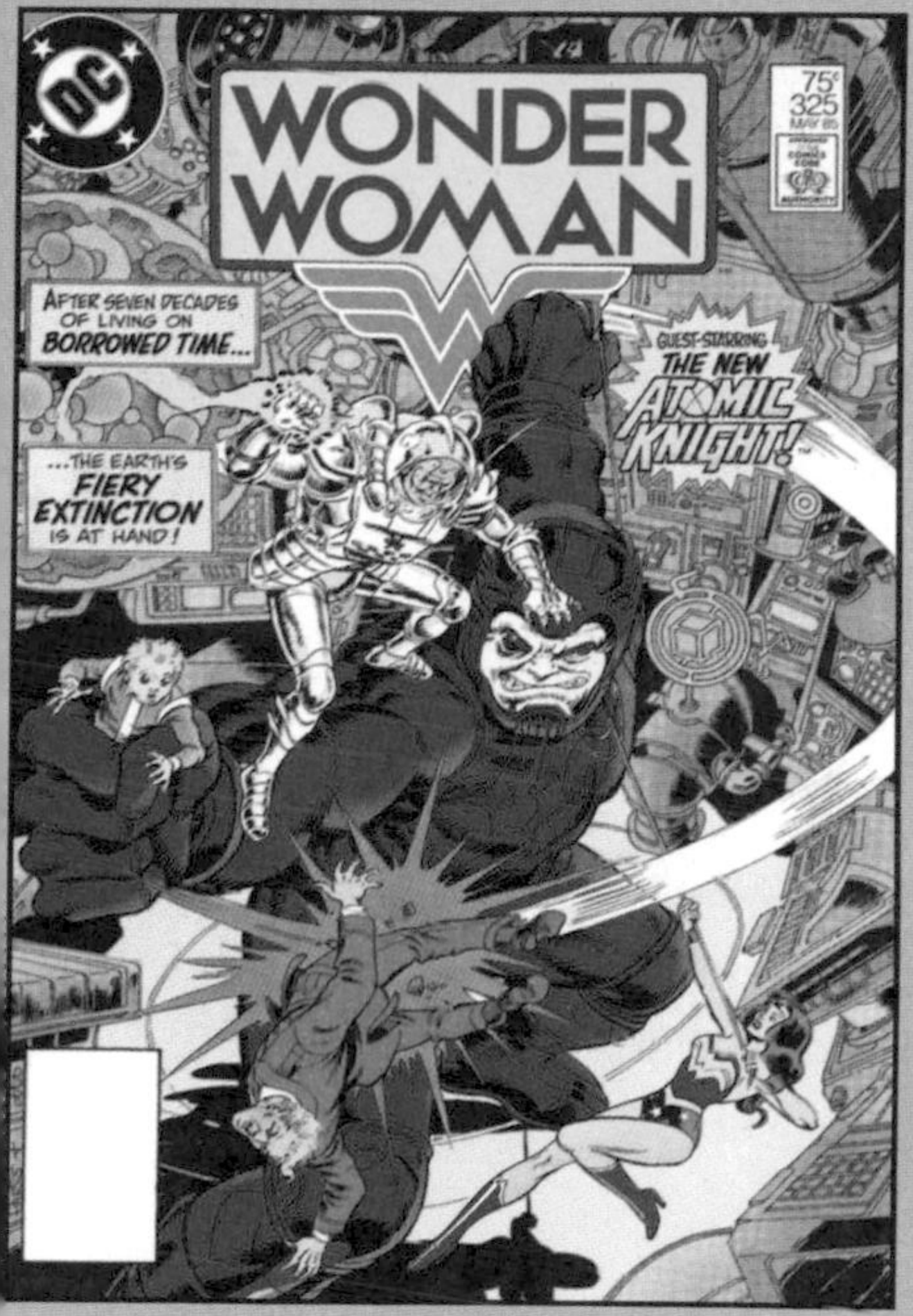
DC
WONDER WOMAN
75¢
325
MAY 85
AFTER SEVEN DECADES OF LIVING ON BORROWED TIME...
...THE EARTH'S FIERY EXTINCTION IS AT HAND!
GUEST-STARRING THE NEW ATOMIC KNIGHT!

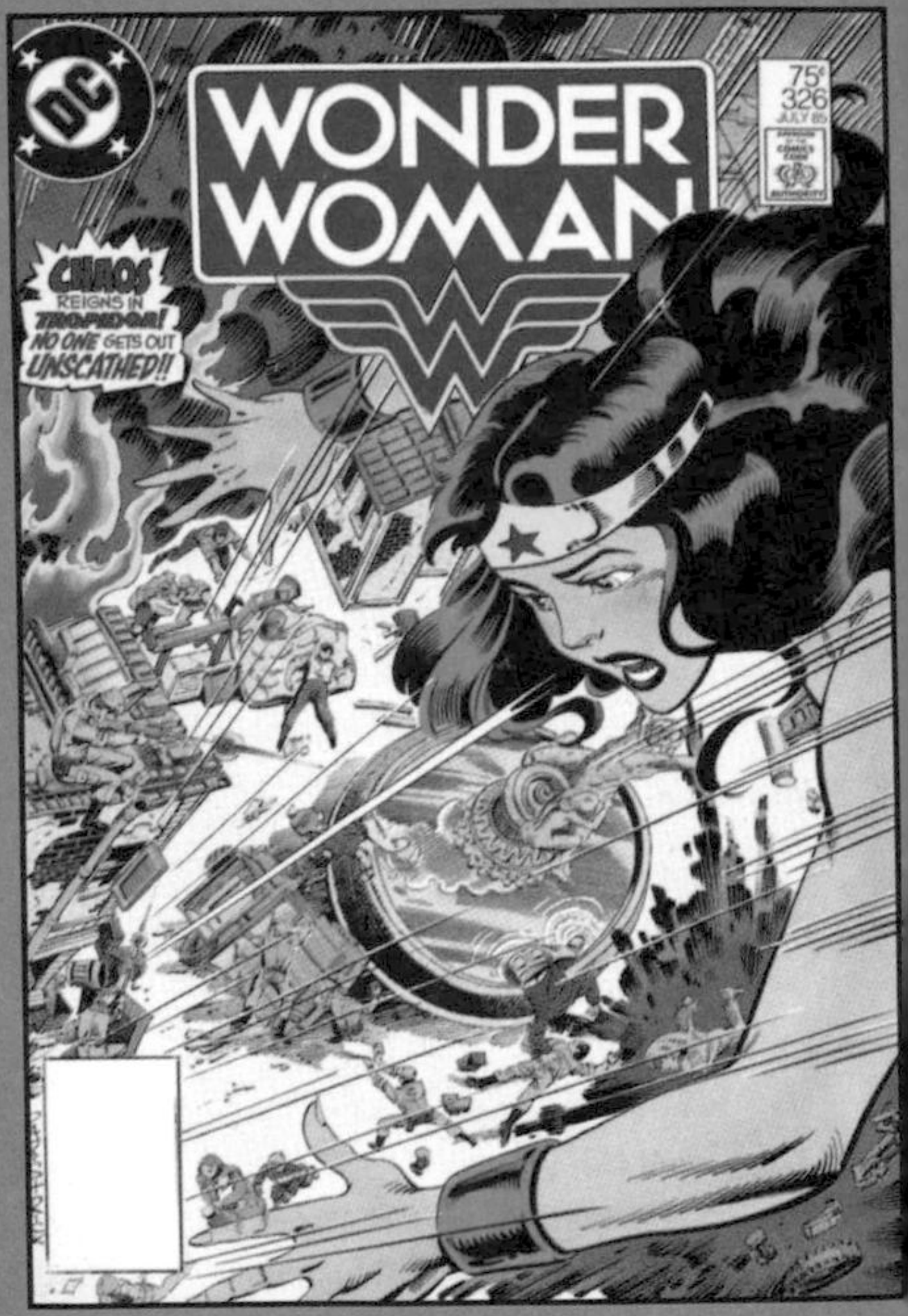
DC
WONDER WOMAN
75¢
326
JULY 85
CHAOS REIGNS IN TROMPEDOM! NO ONE GETS OUT UNSCATHED!!

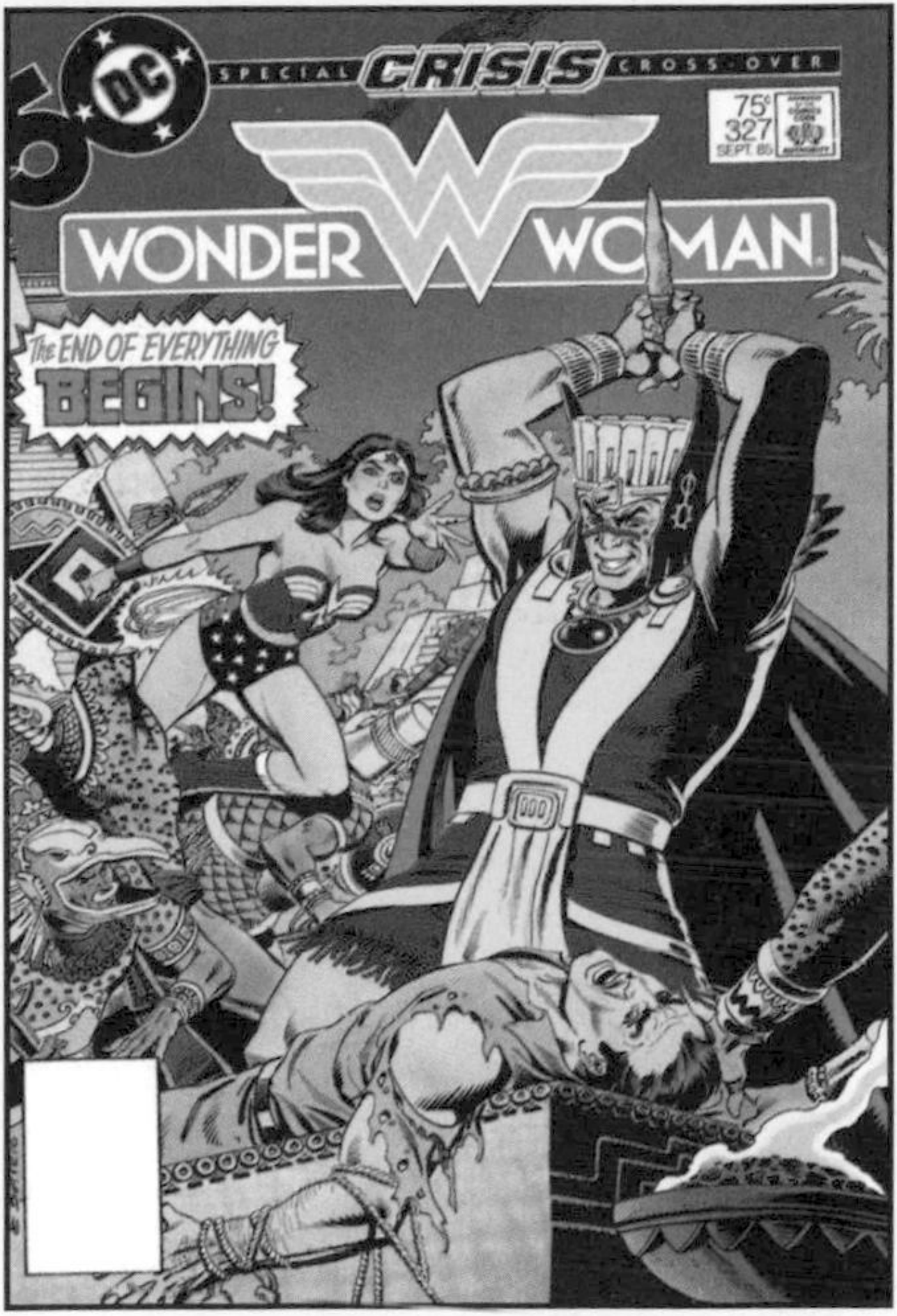
DC
SPECIAL CRISIS CROSS-OVER
75¢
327
SEPT. 85
WONDER WOMAN
The END OF EVERYTHING
BEGINS!

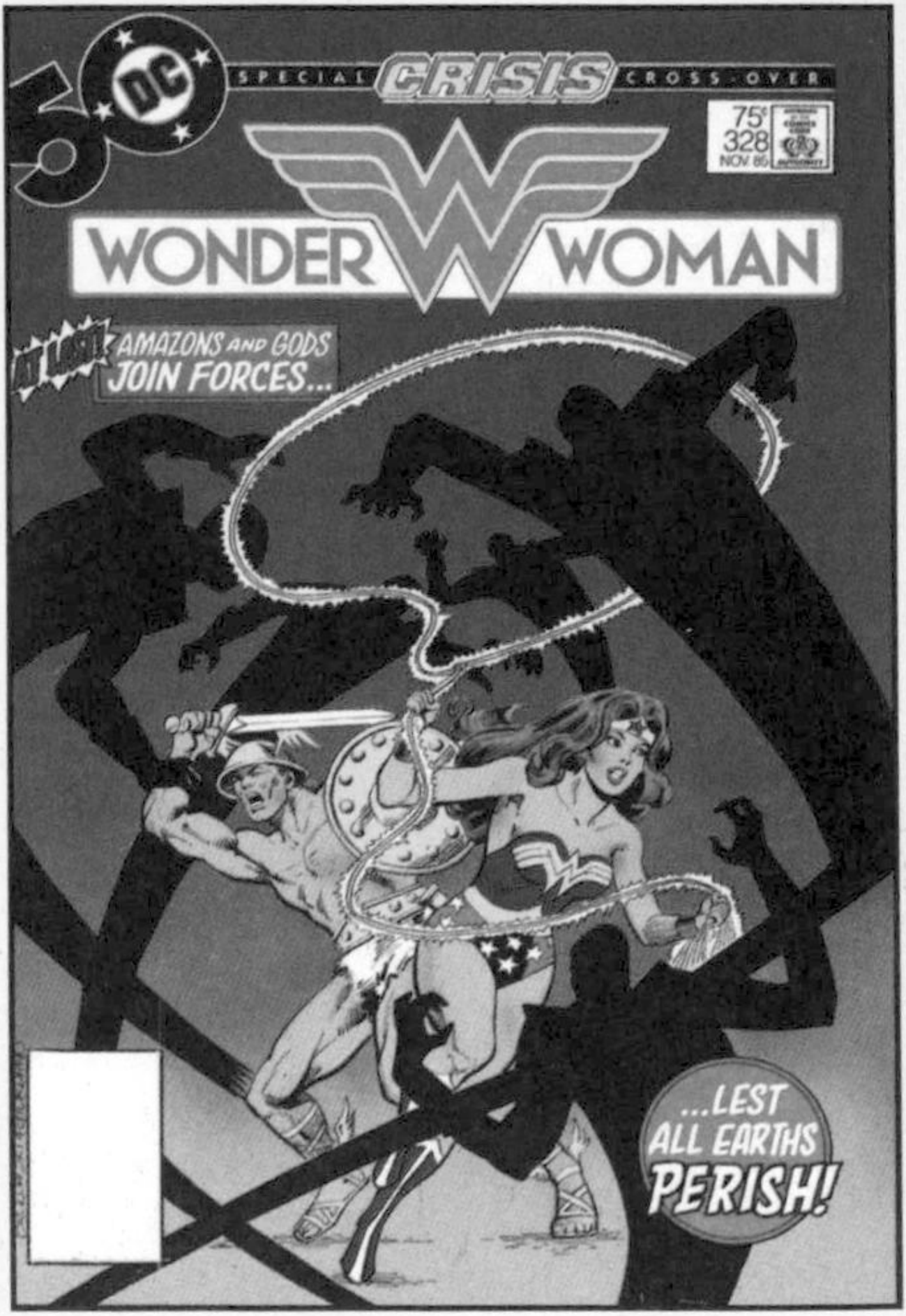
DC
SPECIAL CRISIS CROSS OVER
75¢
328
NOV 86
WONDER WOMAN
AMAZONS AND GODS JOIN FORCES...
...LEST ALL EARTHS PERISH!

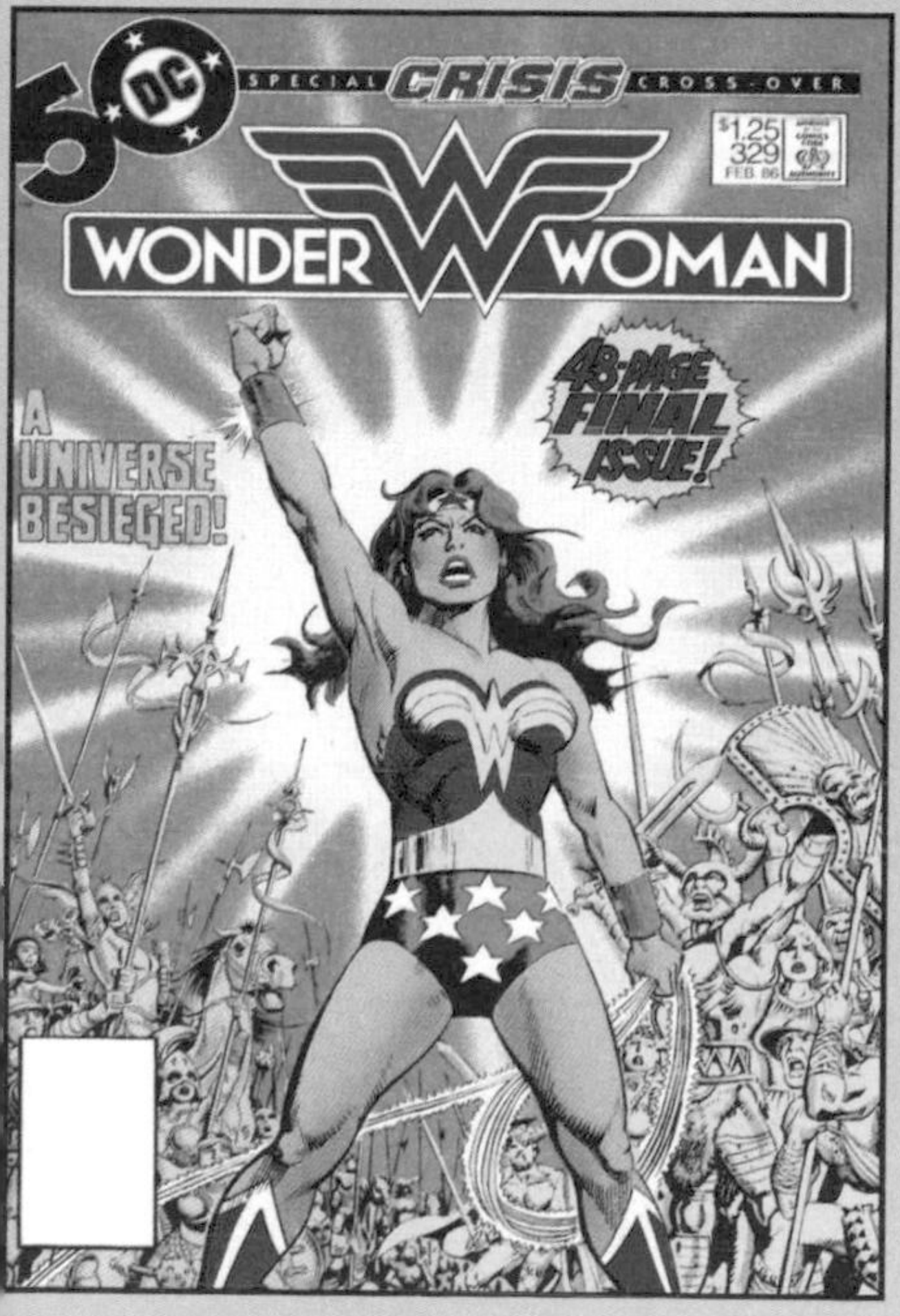
DC
SPECIAL CRISIS CROSS-OVER
$1.25
329
FEB. 86
WONDER WOMAN
48-PAGE FINAL ISSUE!
A UNIVERSE BESIEGED!

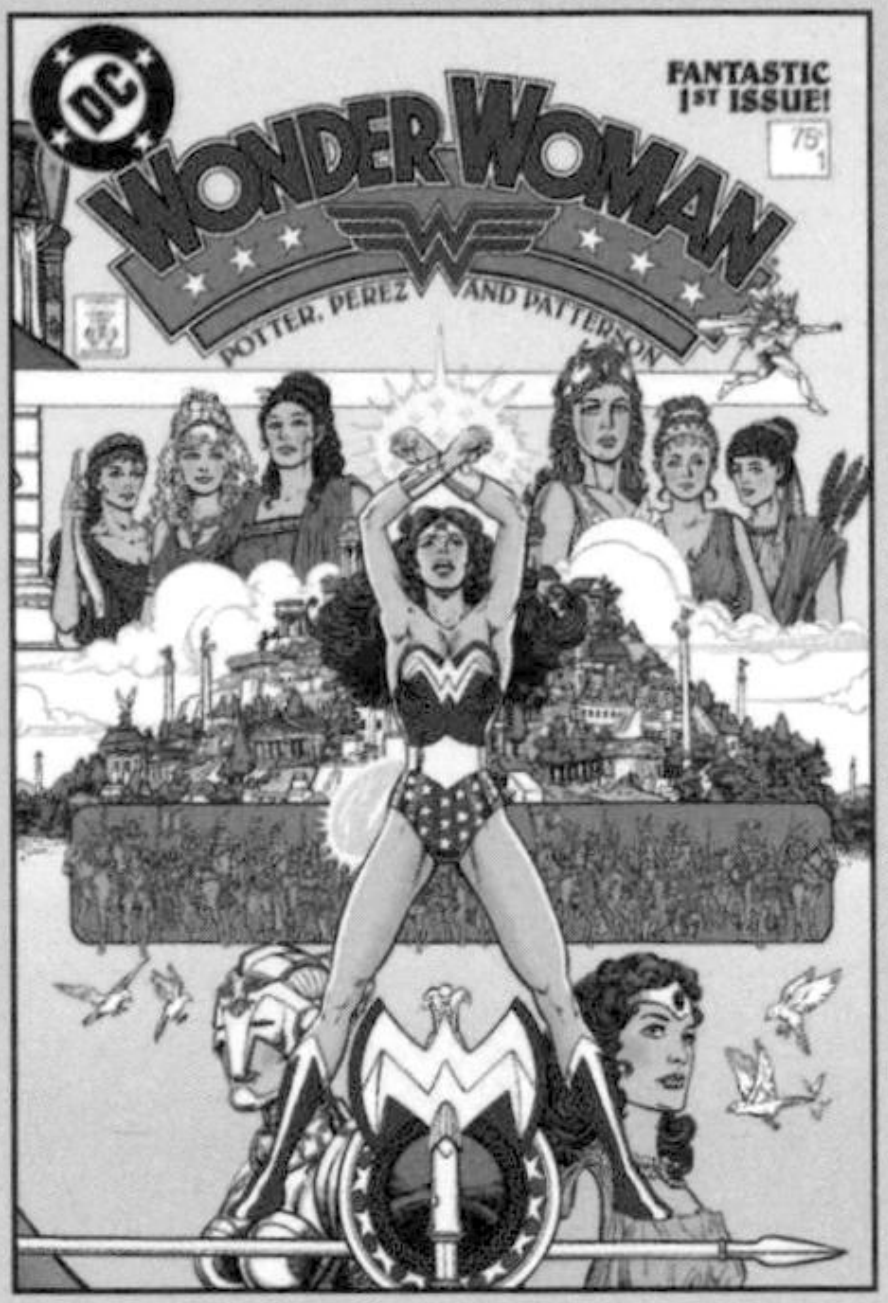

Wonder Woman (Vol. 2) #1

In the first issue of *Wonder Woman* (Vol. 2, 1987) writer George Pérez expanded on Wonder Woman's origin story and emphasized her Amazonian upbringing, in addition to doubling down on the character's association with Greek mythology.

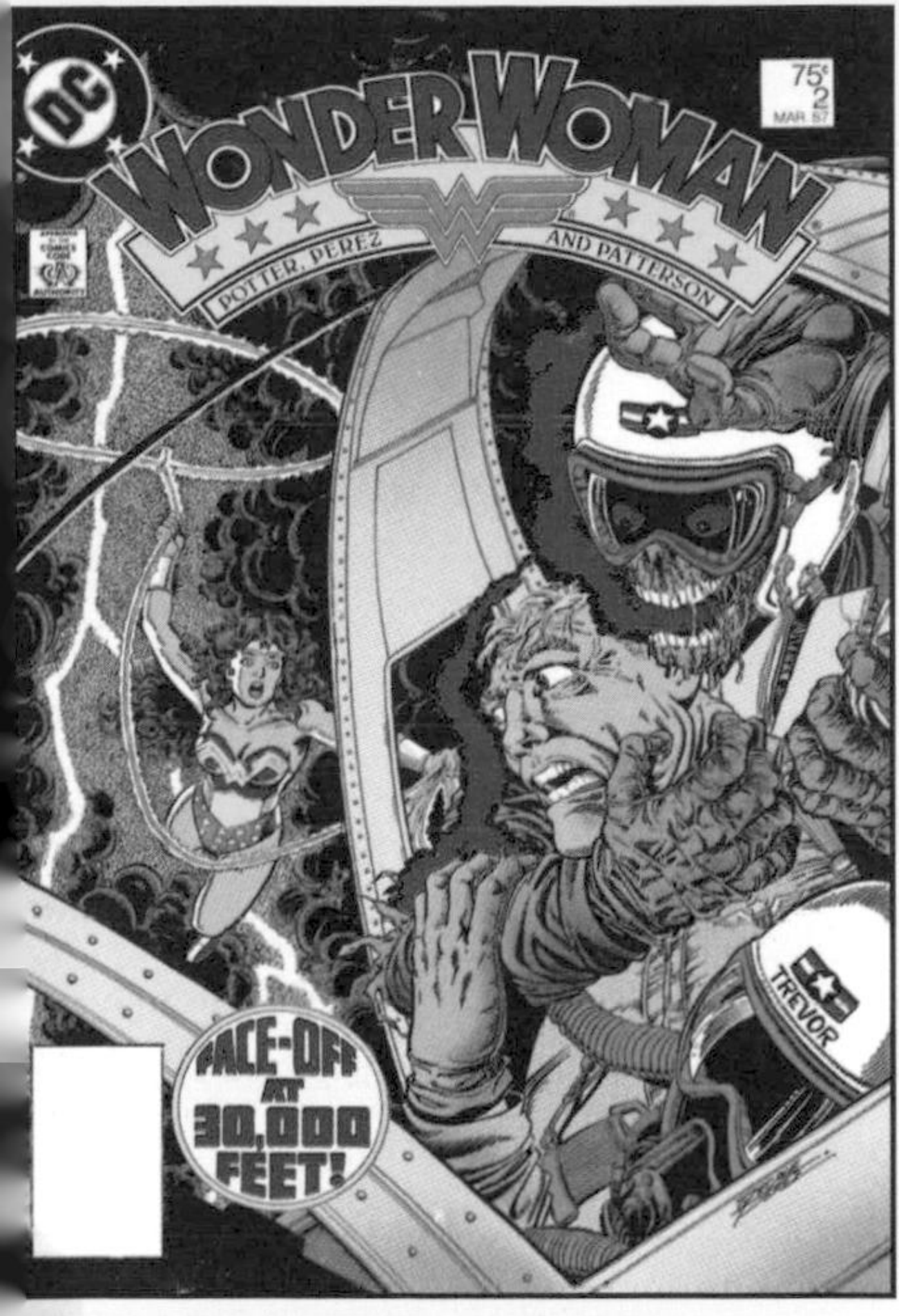
DC
WONDER WOMAN
POTTER, PEREZ AND PATTERSON
75¢
2
MAR. 87
FACE-OFF AT 30,000 FEET!
TREVOR

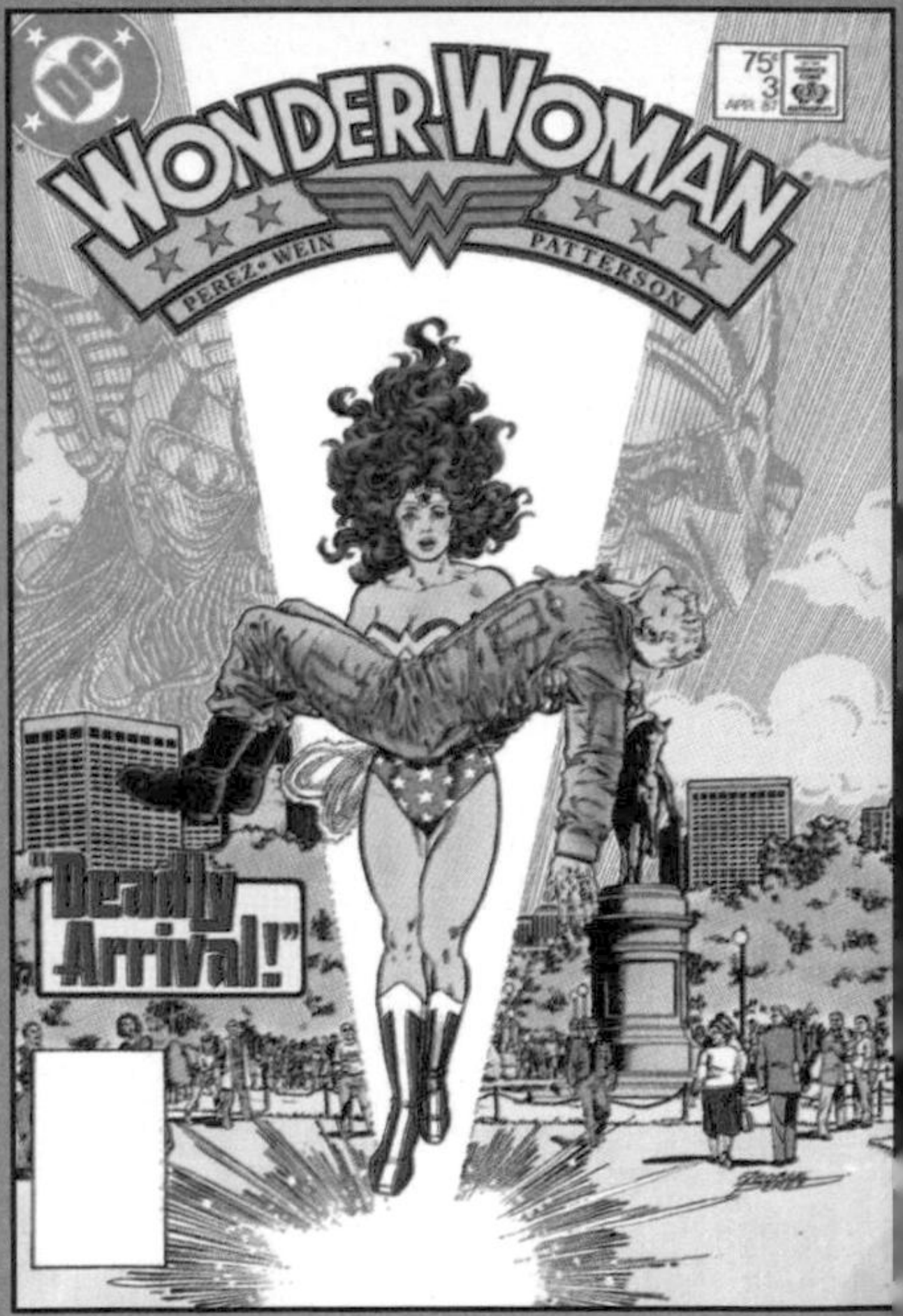
DC
WONDER WOMAN
PEREZ • WEIN
PATTERSON
75¢
3
APRIL 81
"Deadly Arrival!"

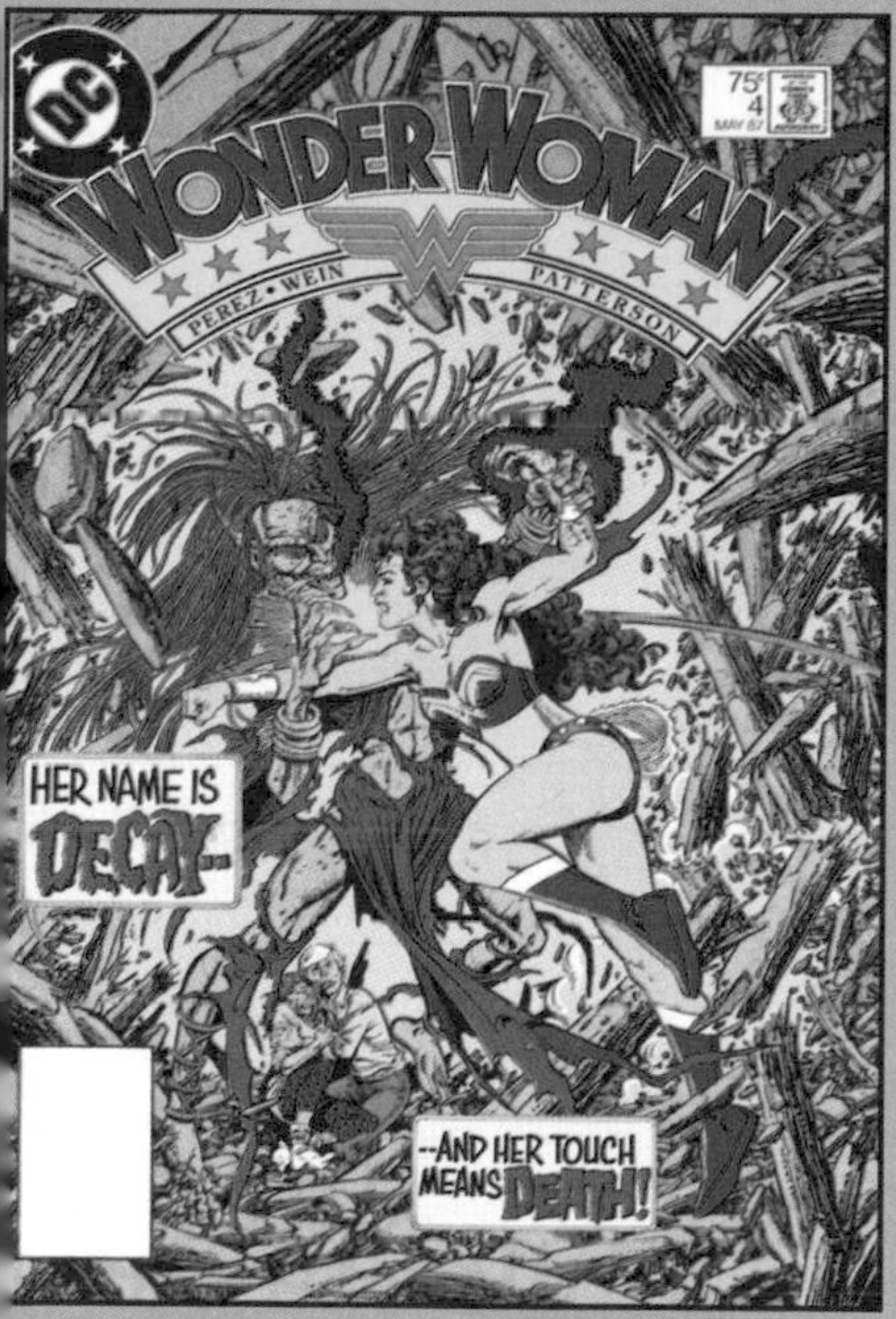
DC
WONDER WOMAN
PEREZ • WEIN
PATTERSON
75¢
4
MAY 87
HER NAME IS DECAY--
--AND HER TOUCH MEANS DEATH!

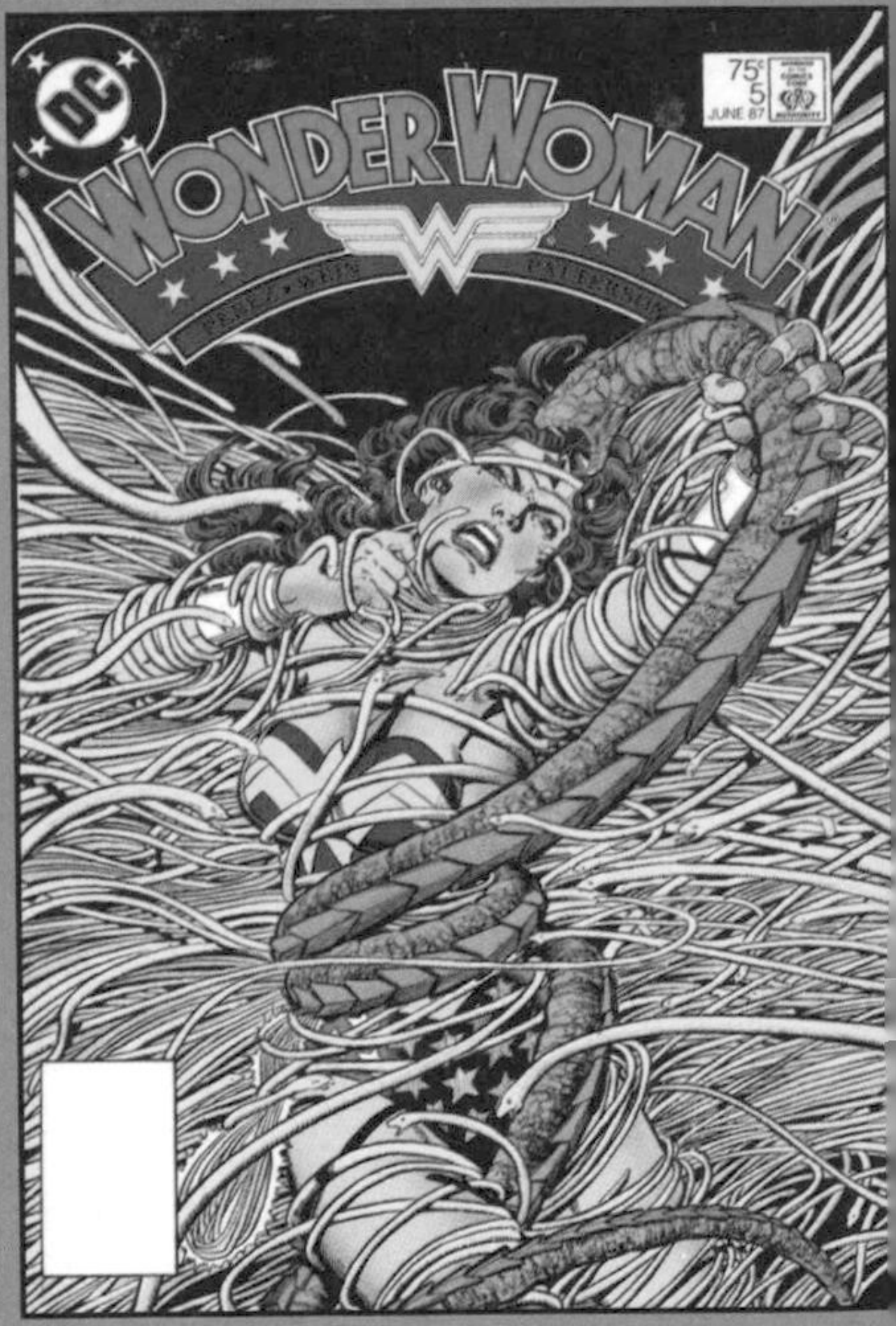
DC
WONDER WOMAN
75¢
5
JUNE 87

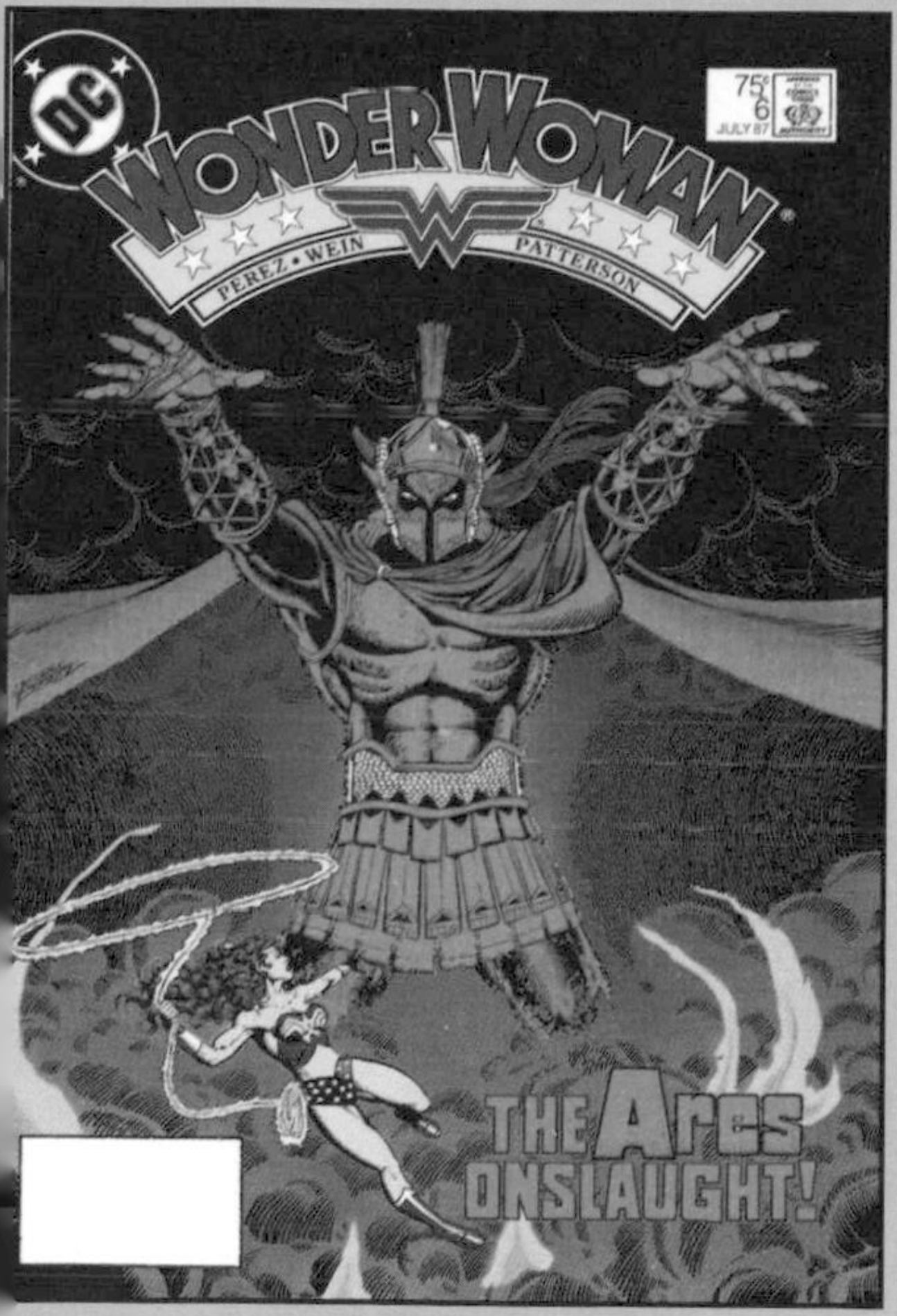
DC
WONDER WOMAN
PEREZ • WEIN
PATTERSON
75¢
6
JULY 87
THE ARES ONSLAUGHT!

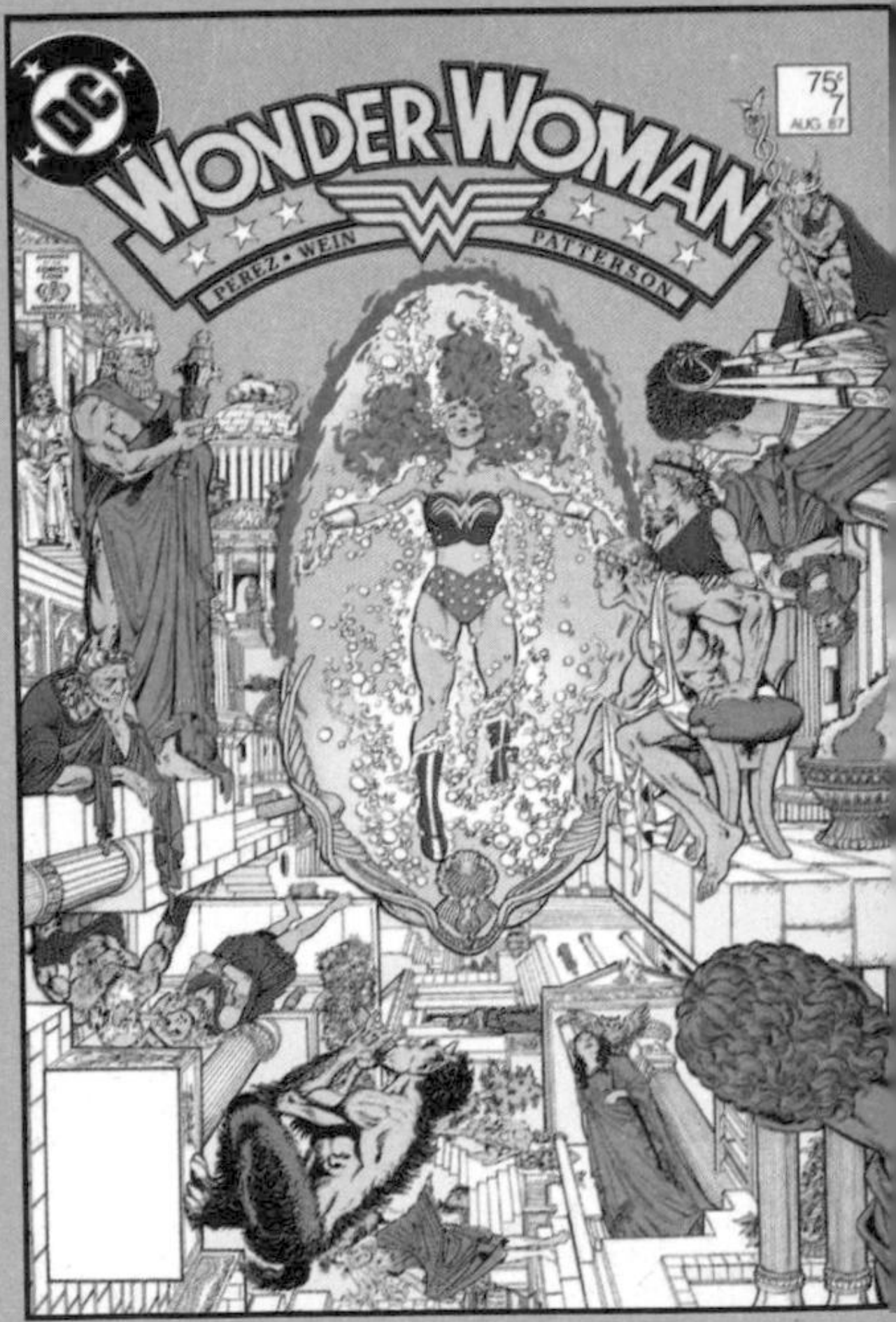
DC
WONDER WOMAN
PEREZ • WEIN
PATTERSON
75¢
7
AUG 87

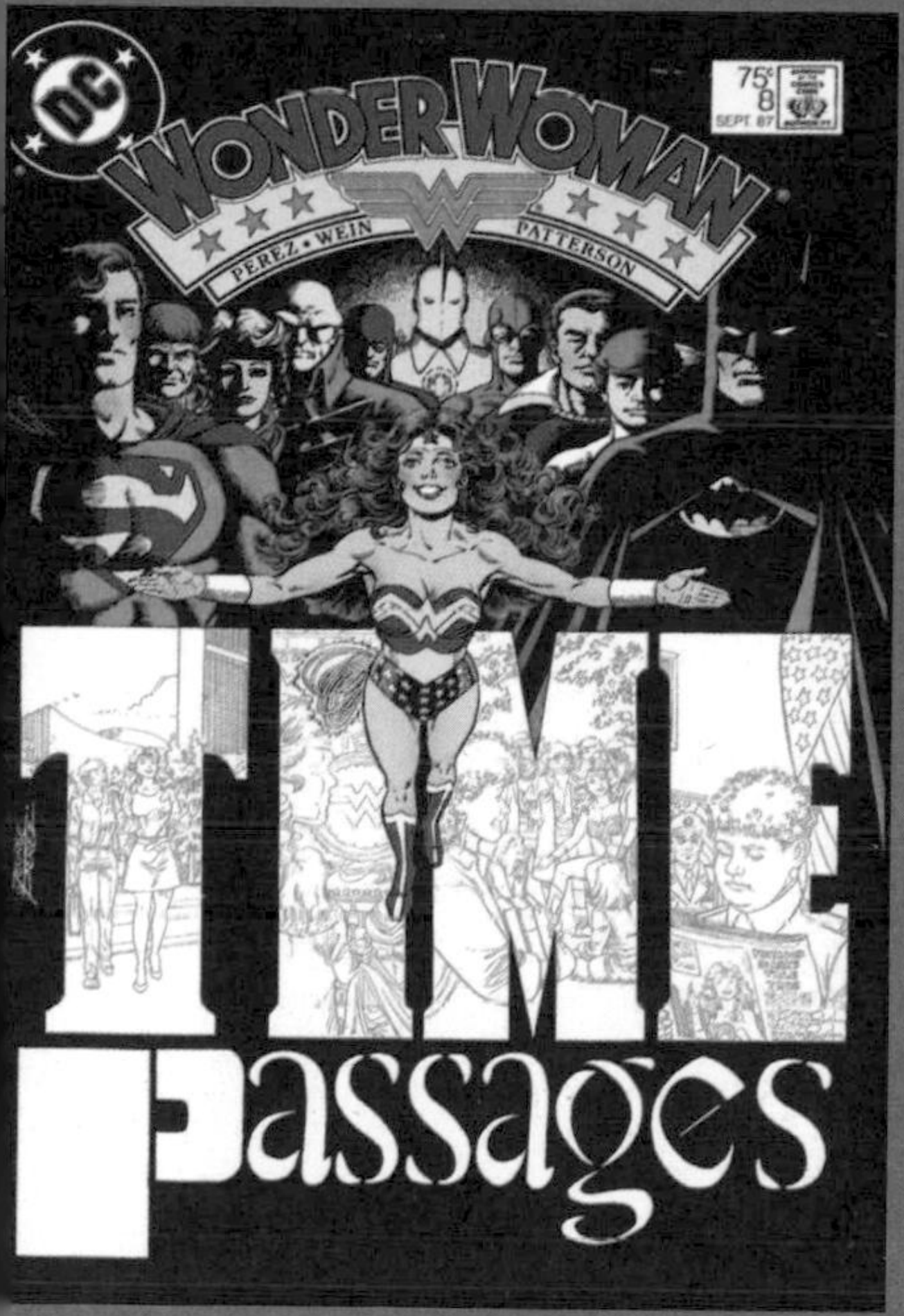
DC
WONDER WOMAN
PEREZ • WEIN
PATTERSON
75¢
8
SEPT. 87
TIME
Passages

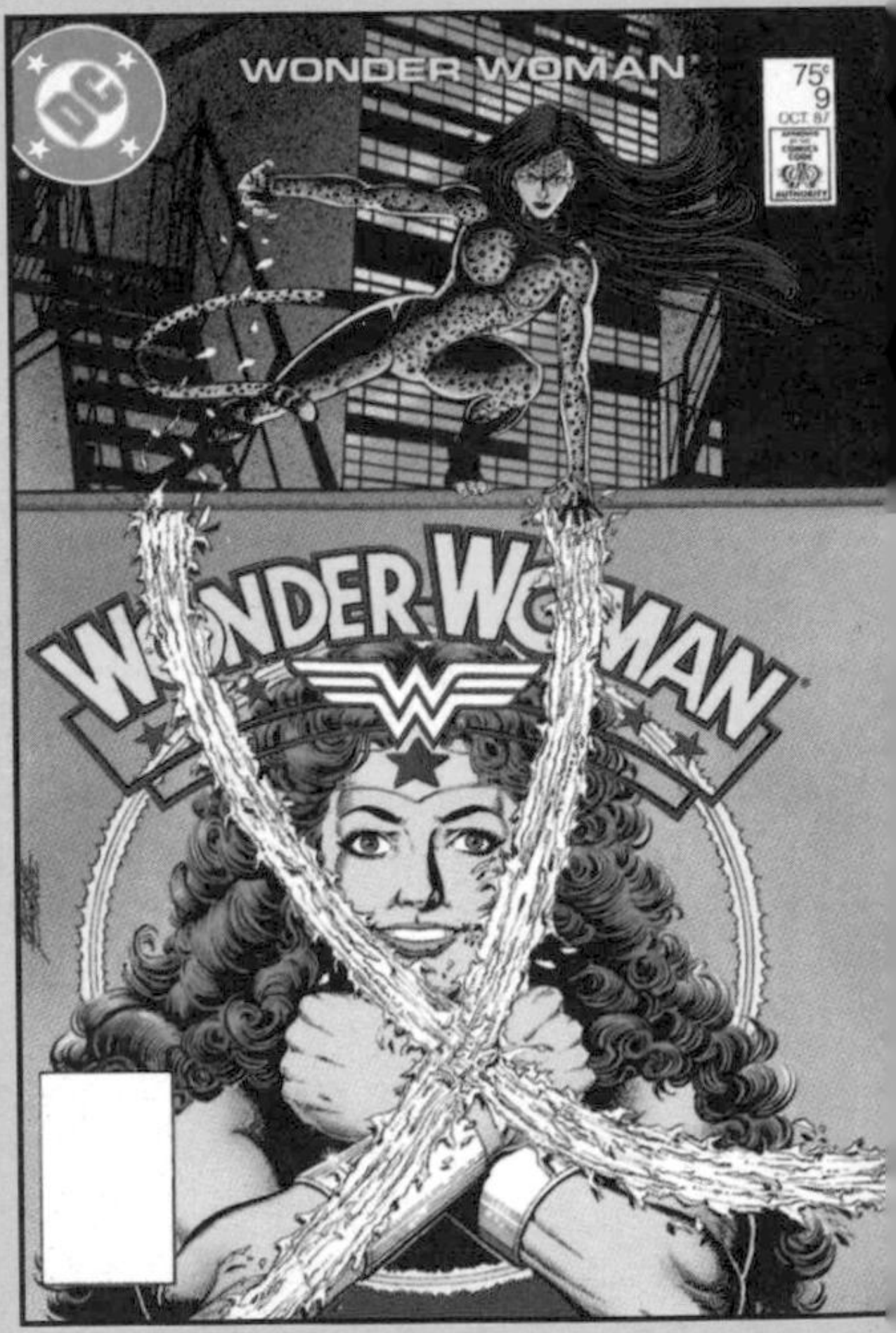
WONDER WOMAN
75¢
9
OCT. 87
WONDER WOMAN

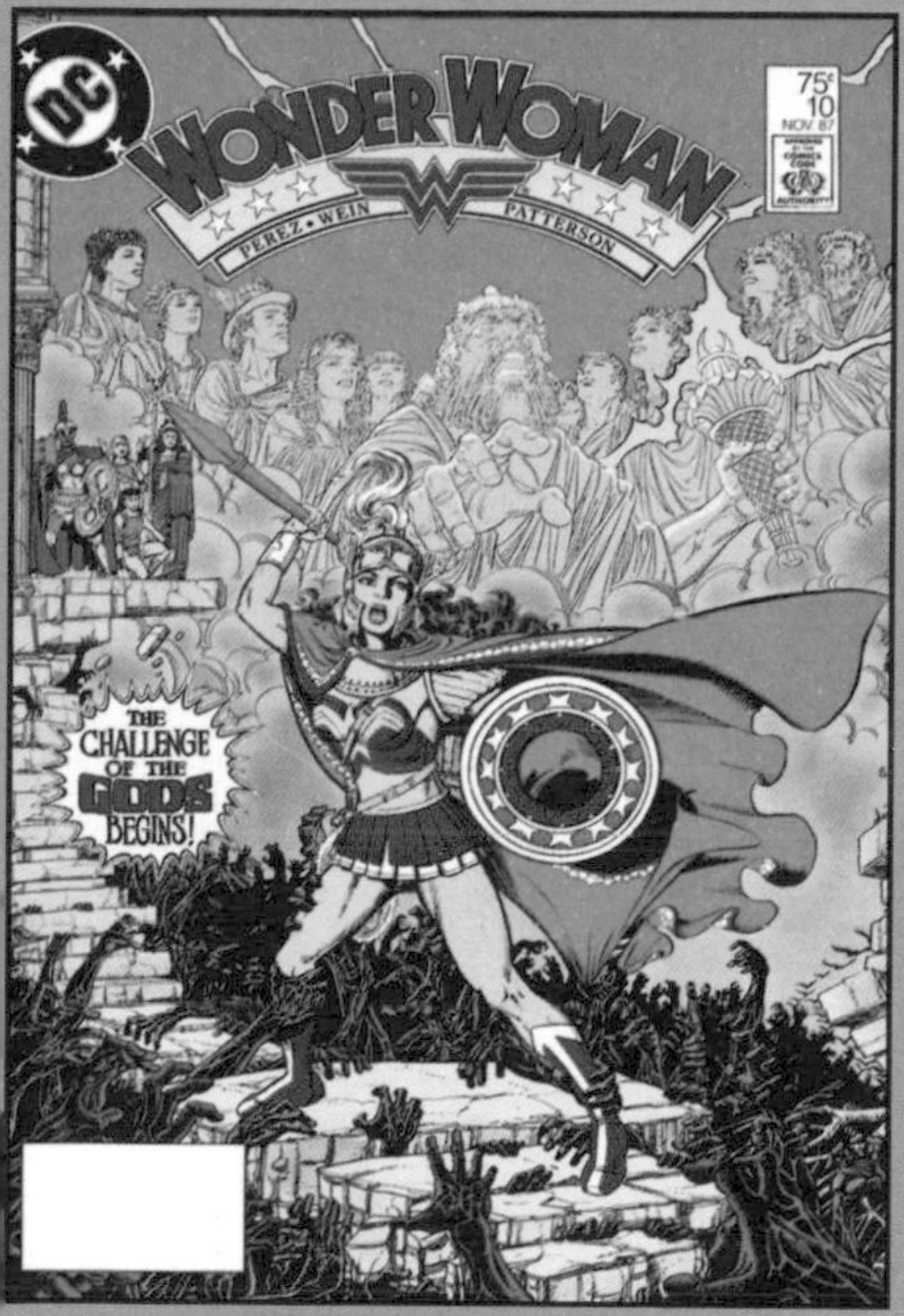
DC
WONDER WOMAN
PEREZ • WEIN
PATTERSON
75¢
10
NOV 87
THE CHALLENGE OF THE GODS BEGINS!

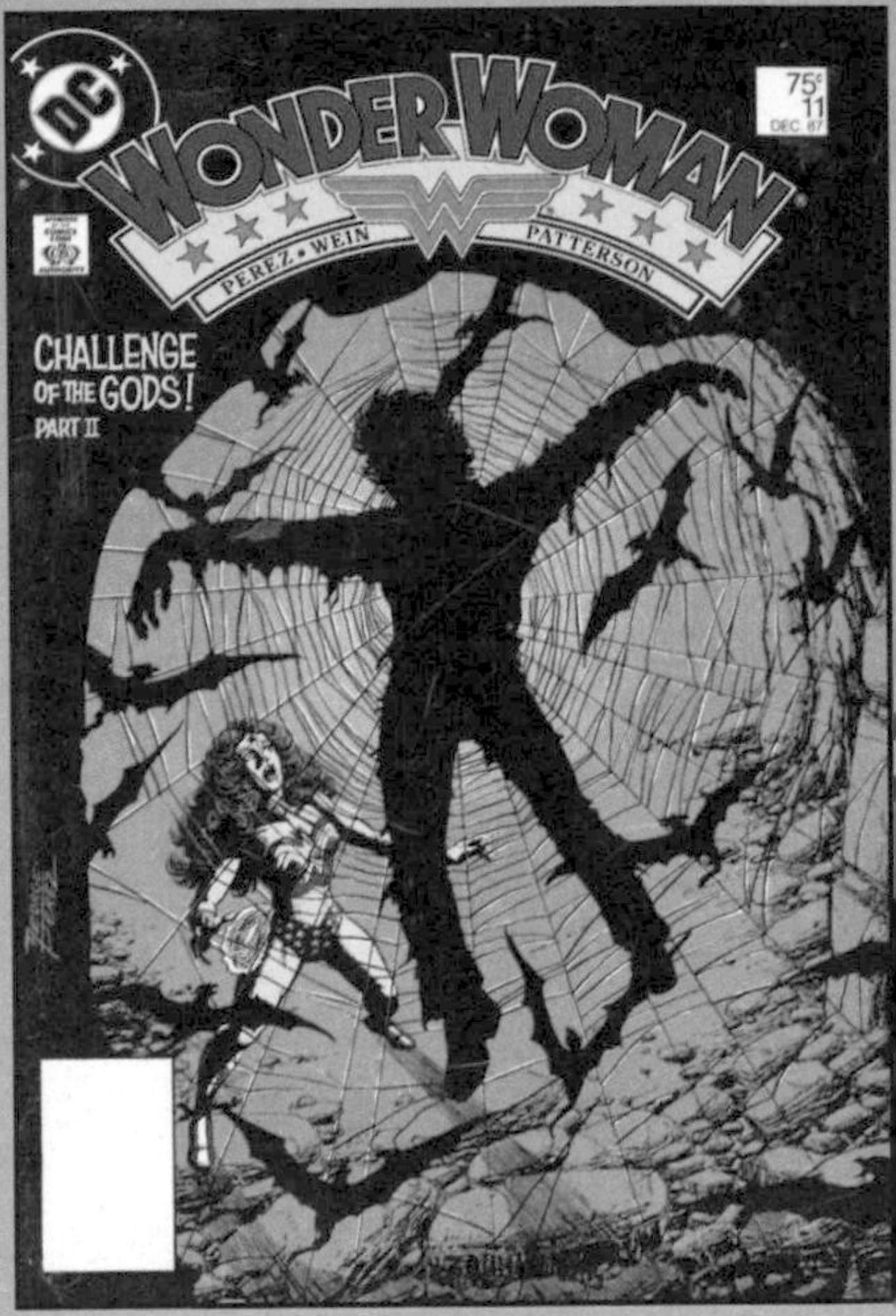
DC
WONDER WOMAN
PEREZ • WEIN
PATTERSON
75¢
11
DEC 87
CHALLENGE
OF THE GODS!
PART II

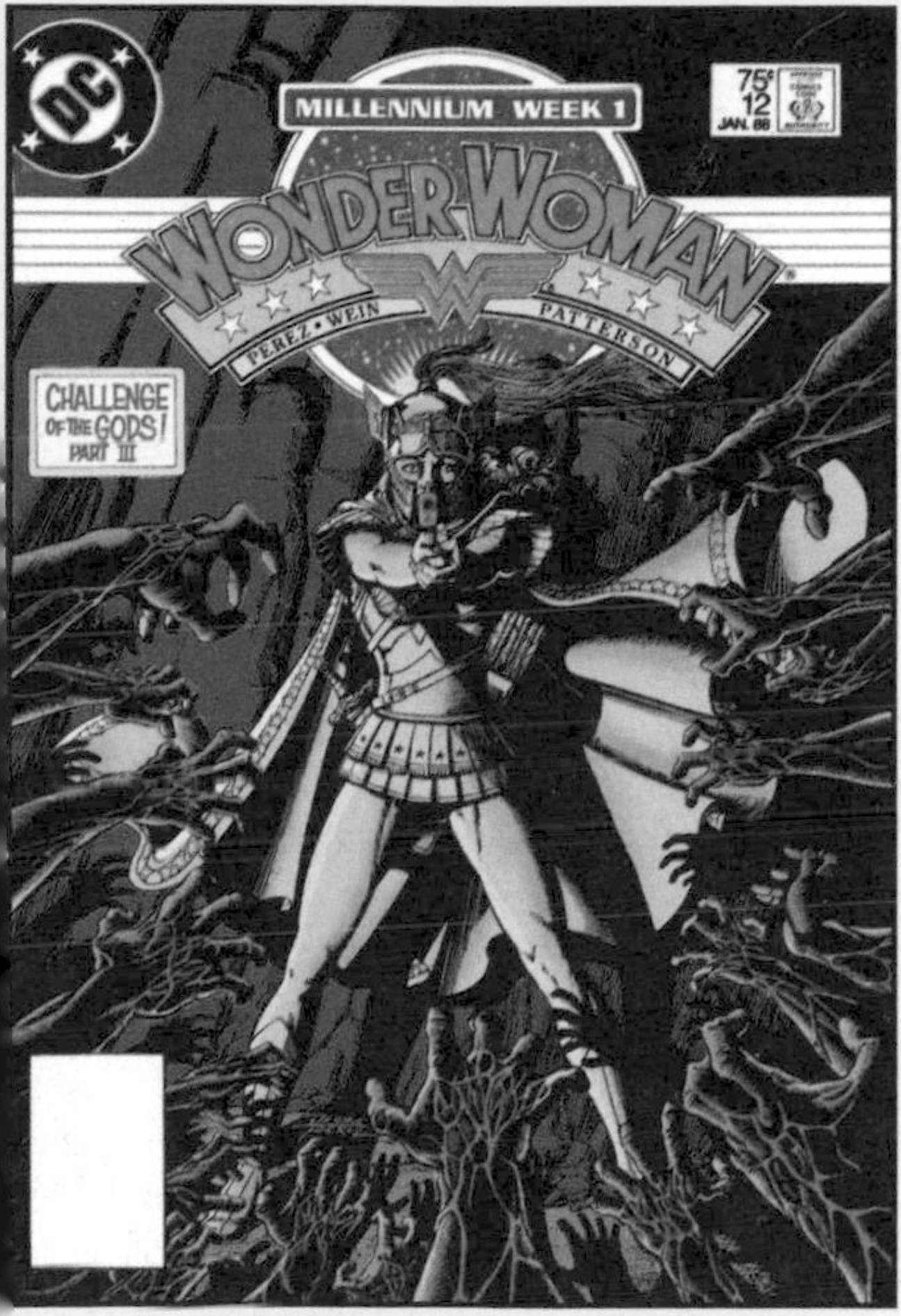
DC
MILLENNIUM WEEK 1
75¢
12
JAN. 86
WONDER WOMAN
PEREZ • WEIN
PATTERSON
CHALLENGE OF THE GODS! PART III

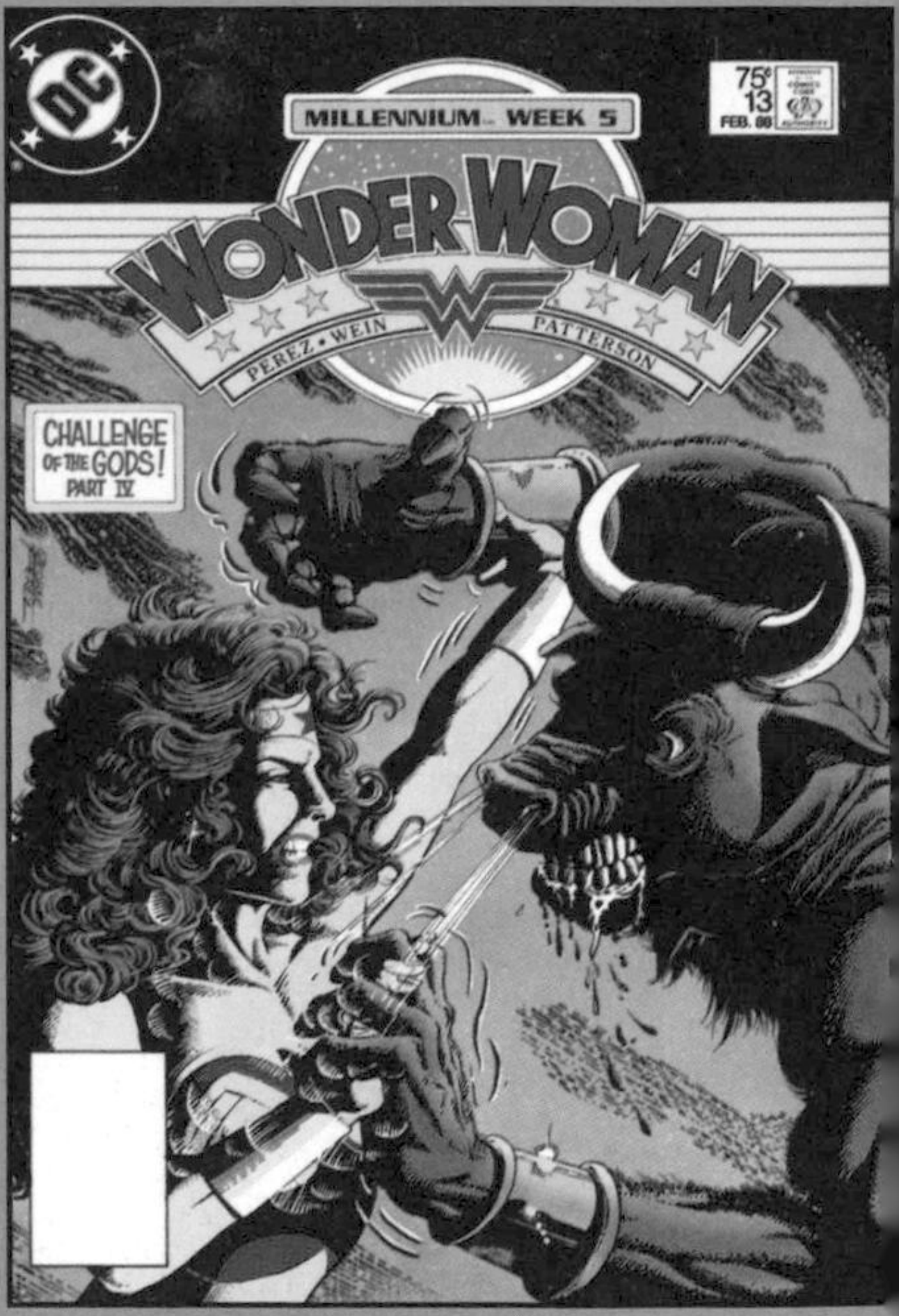
DC
MILLENNIUM — WEEK 5
75¢
13
FEB. 88
WONDER WOMAN
PEREZ • WEIN
PATTERSON
CHALLENGE OF THE GODS! PART IV

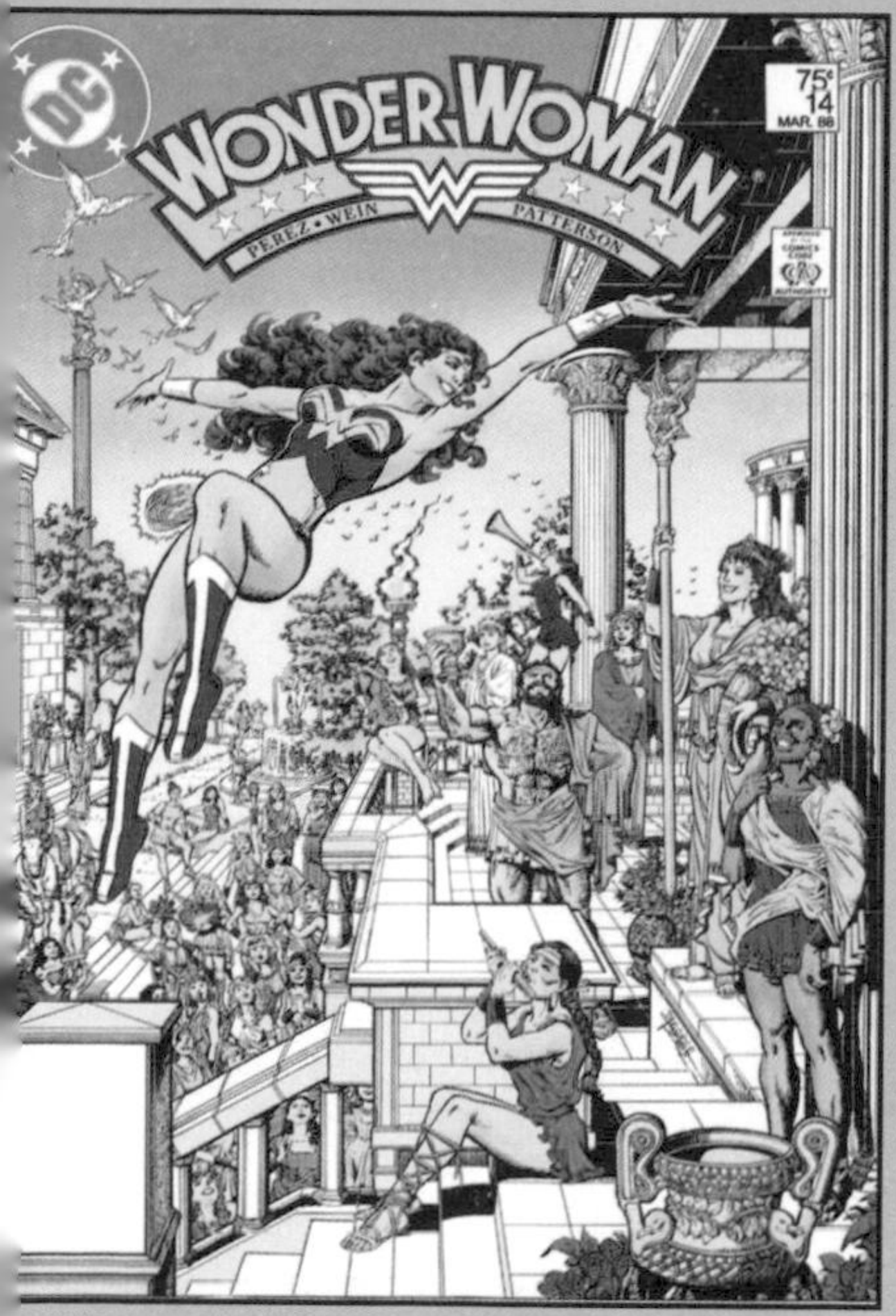
DC
WONDER WOMAN
PEREZ • WEIN
PATTERSON
75¢
14
MAR. 86

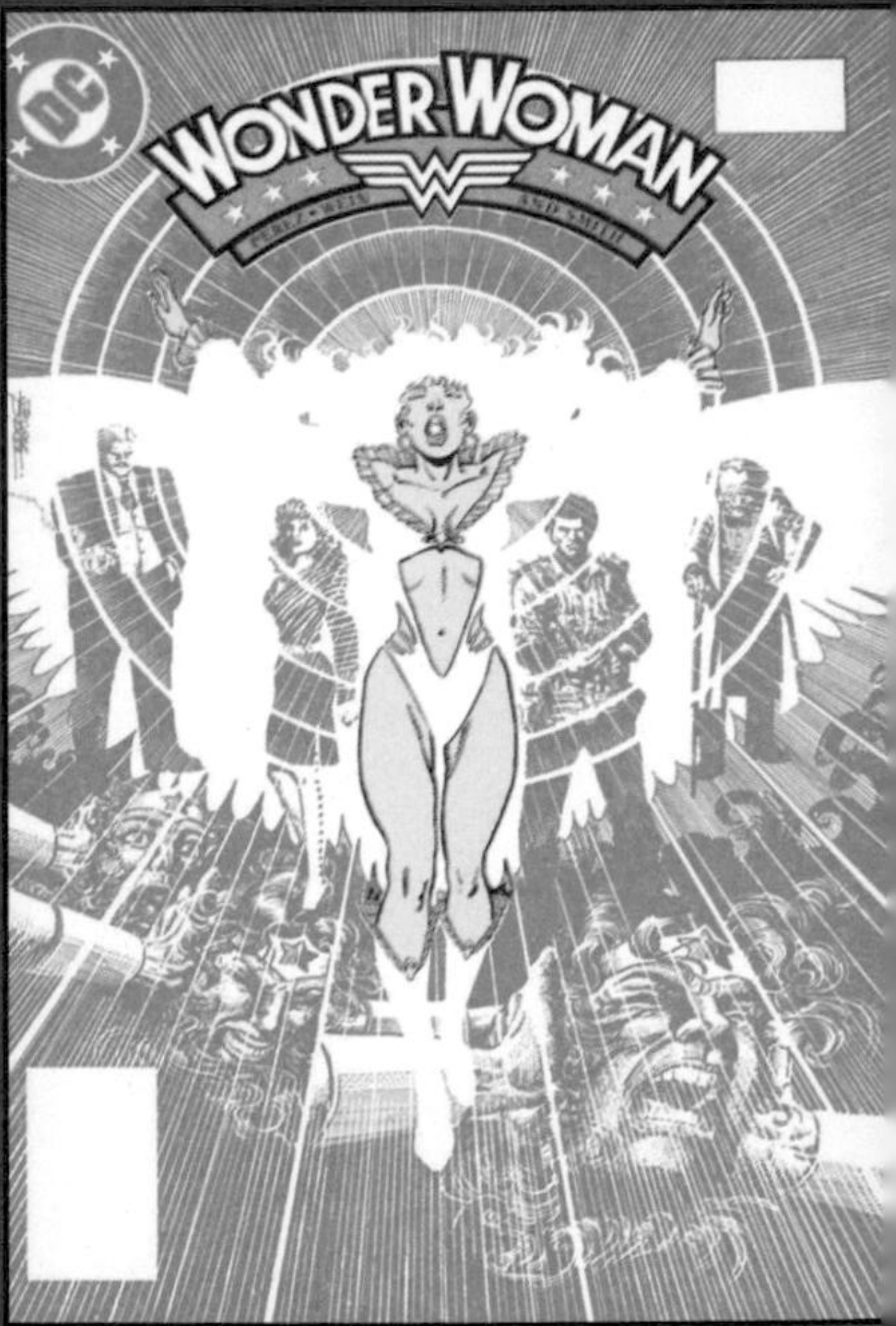
DC
WONDER WOMAN

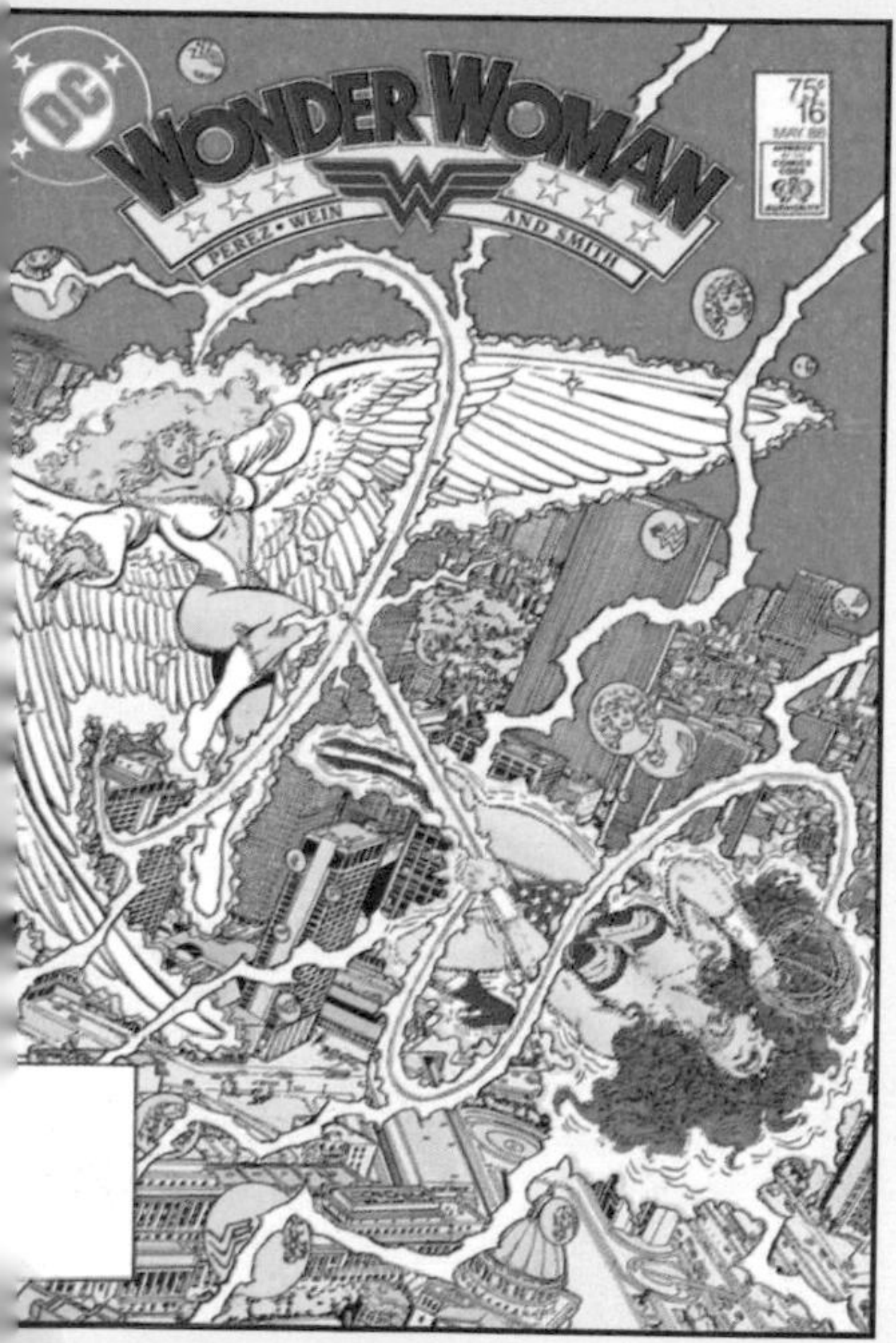
DC
WONDER WOMAN
PEREZ • WEIN AND SMITH
75¢
16

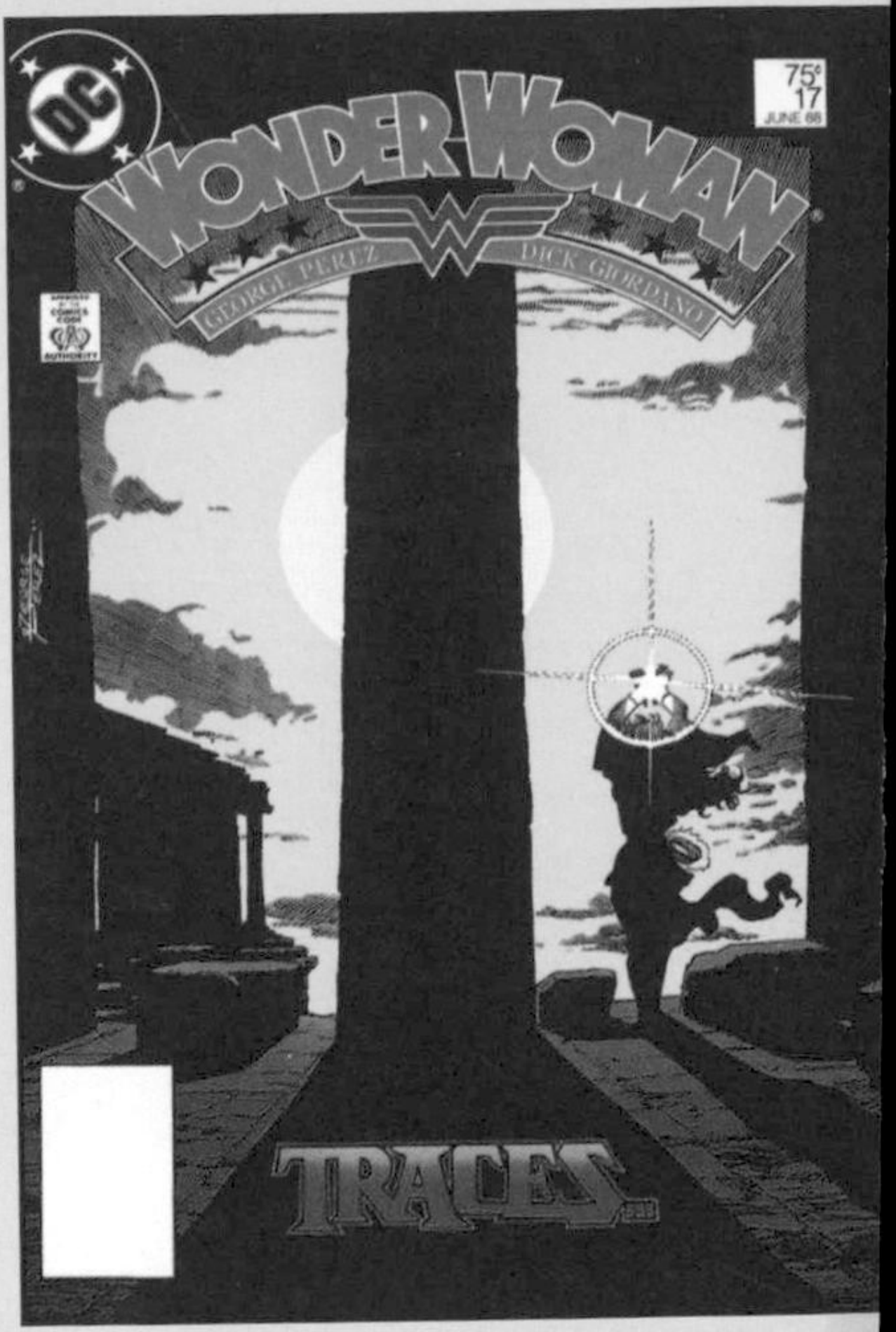
DC
75¢
17
JUNE 88
WONDER WOMAN
GEORGE PEREZ
DICK GIORDANO
TRACES

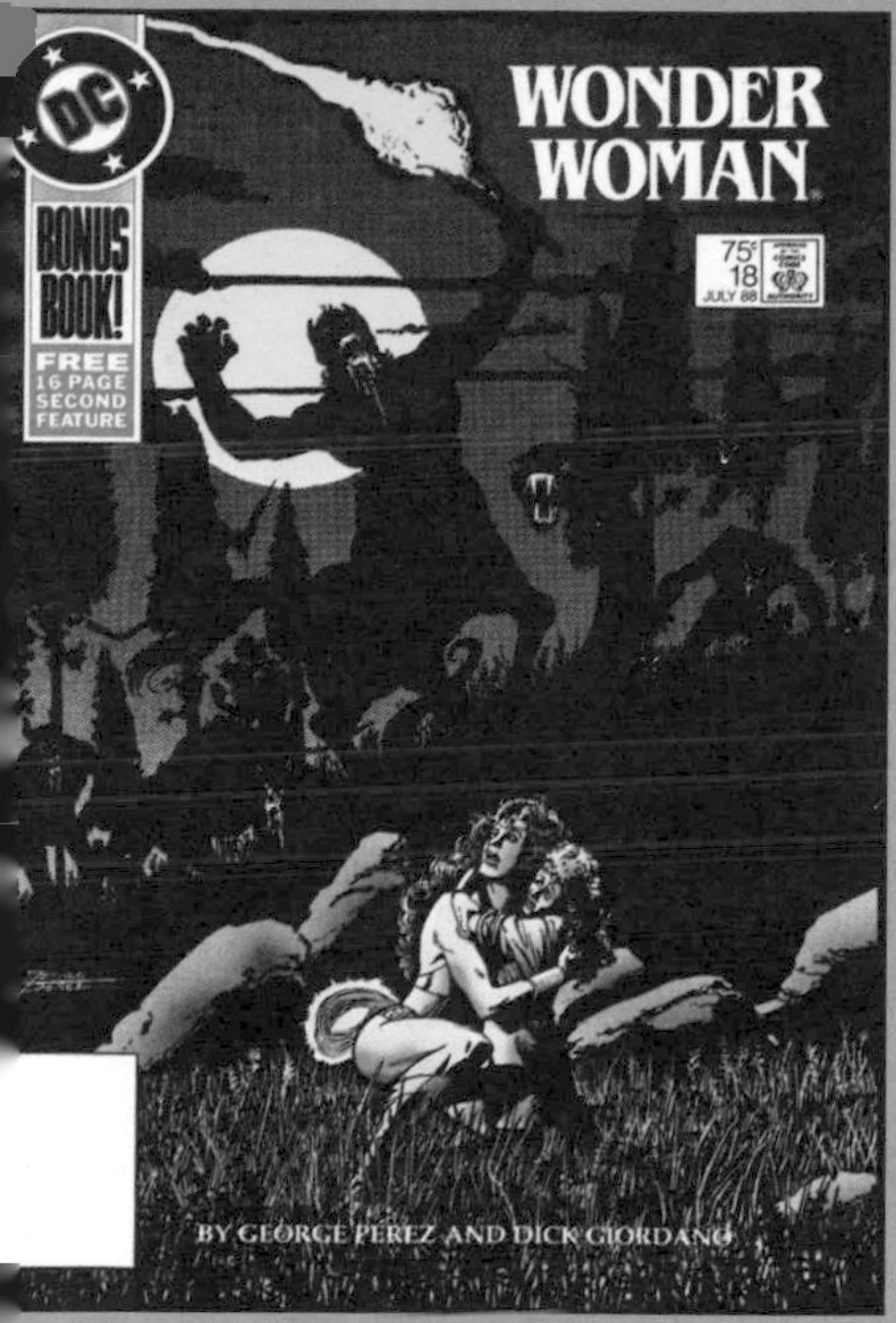
DC
BONUS BOOK!
FREE 16 PAGE SECOND FEATURE
WONDER WOMAN
75¢
18
JULY 88
BY GEORGE PEREZ AND DICK GIORDANO

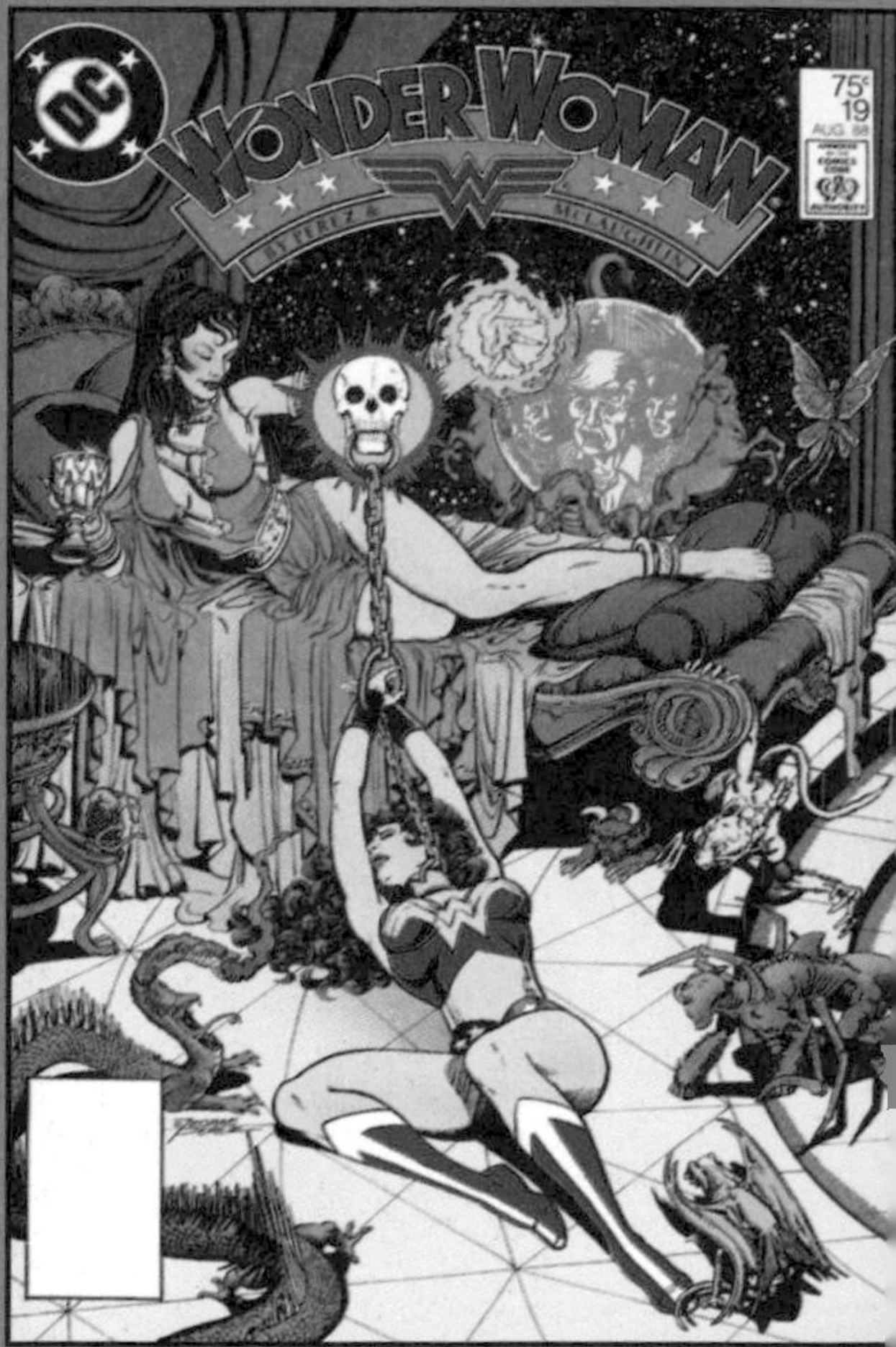
DC
WONDER WOMAN
75¢
19
AUG. 88
BY PEREZ & McLAUGHLIN

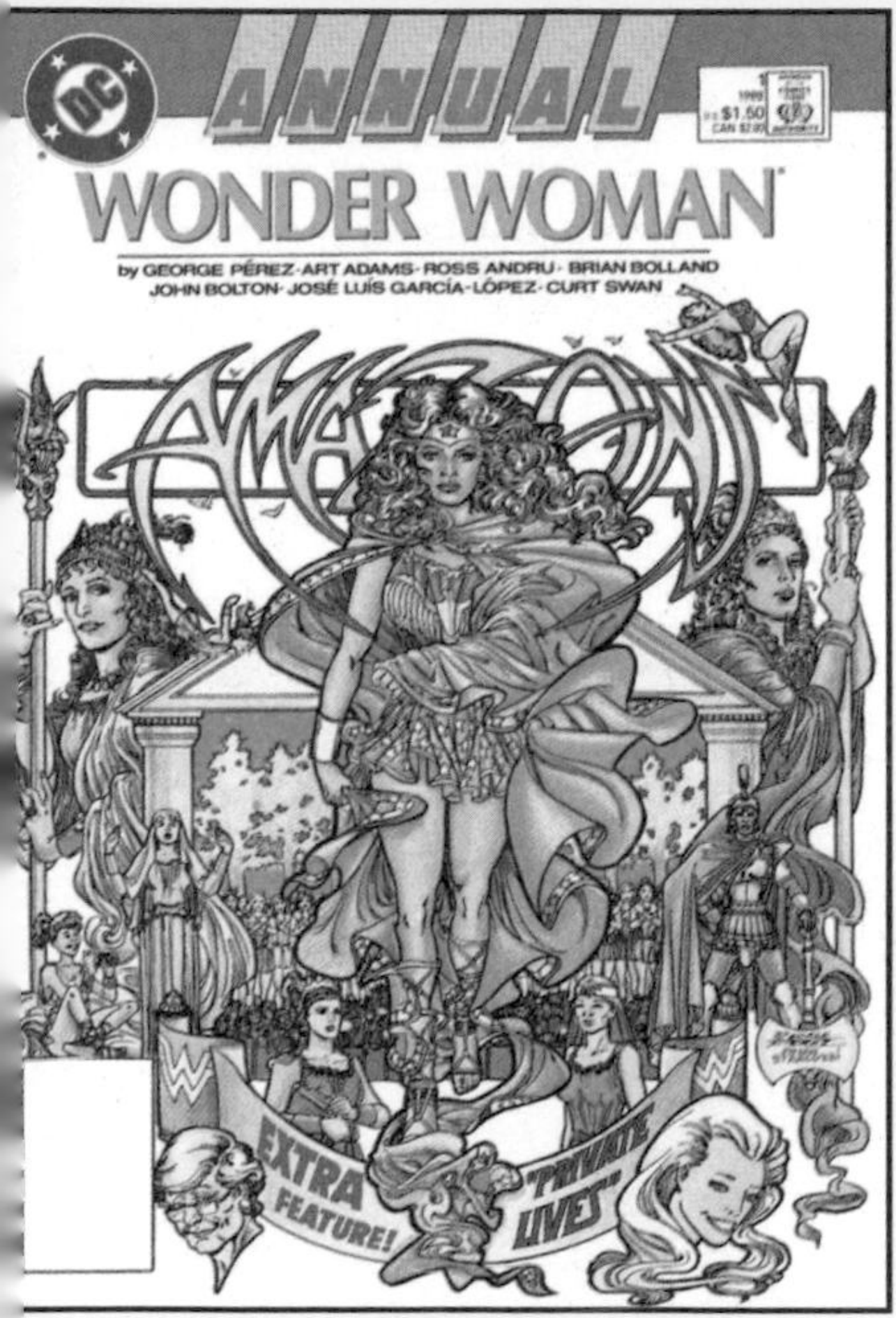
DC
ANNUAL
1
1985
U.S. $1.50
CAN $2.00
WONDER WOMAN
by GEORGE PÉREZ · ART ADAMS · ROSS ANDRU · BRIAN BOLLAND
JOHN BOLTON · JOSÉ LUIS GARCÍA-LÓPEZ · CURT SWAN
AMAZON
EXTRA FEATURE!
"PRIVATE LIVES"

★ ★ ★ EXTRA ★ ★ ★

WONDER WOMAN

75¢ 20 SEPT. 88

GEORGE PÉREZ and BOB Mc LEOD

WHO KILLED MYNDI MAYER?

MURDERED 'STAR PUBLICIST' HAD MANY ENEMIES

BOSTON—Police investigating the brutal death of controversial publicist Myndi Mayer have found no shortage of suspects among her clientele and acquaintances, according to Detectives Ed Indelicato and (Continued on Page 2)

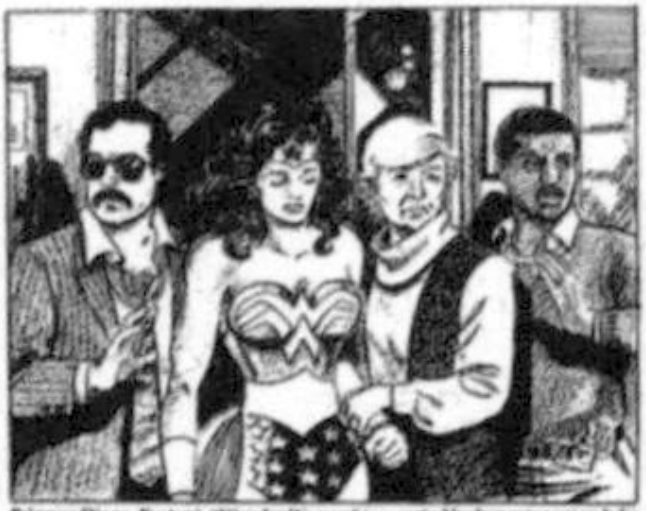

Princess Diana, Boston's "Wonder Woman," is escorted by her companion Julia Kapatelis and police detectives after learning of the apparent murder of her

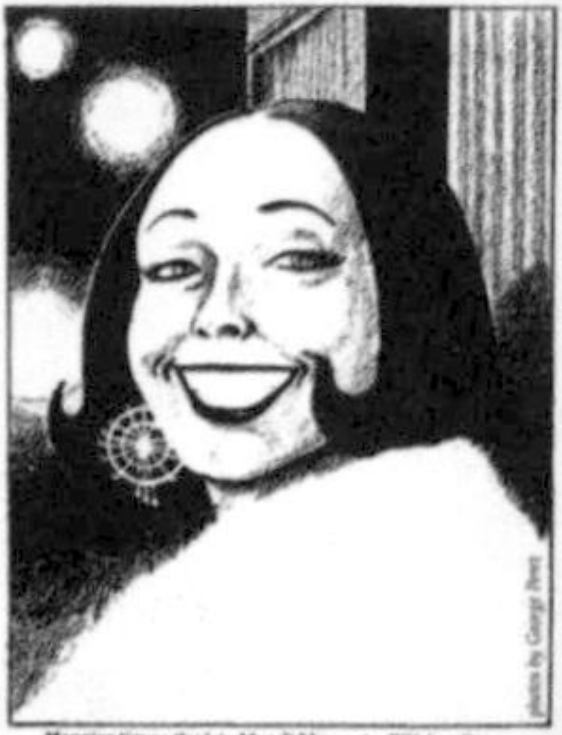

photos by George Perez

Happier times: the late Myndi Mayer at a 1986 function.

TUESDAY 'BOARD MEETING MASSACRE' NETS MAIN SUSPECT—Story on page 3

A FACE OF A KILLER?

Suspects: Art Director Steve London, Secretary Christine Fenton, PR Manager Mike "Skeeter" Boyd, Art Asst. Deni Hayes.

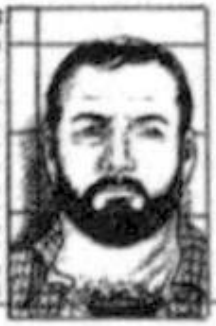

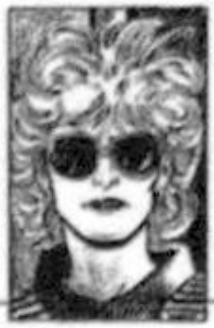

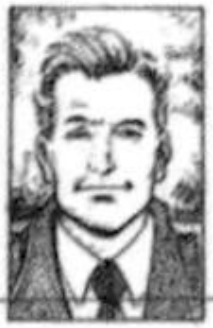

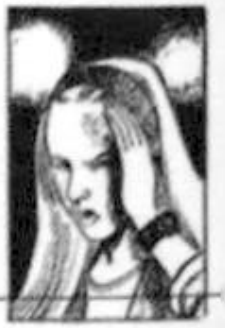

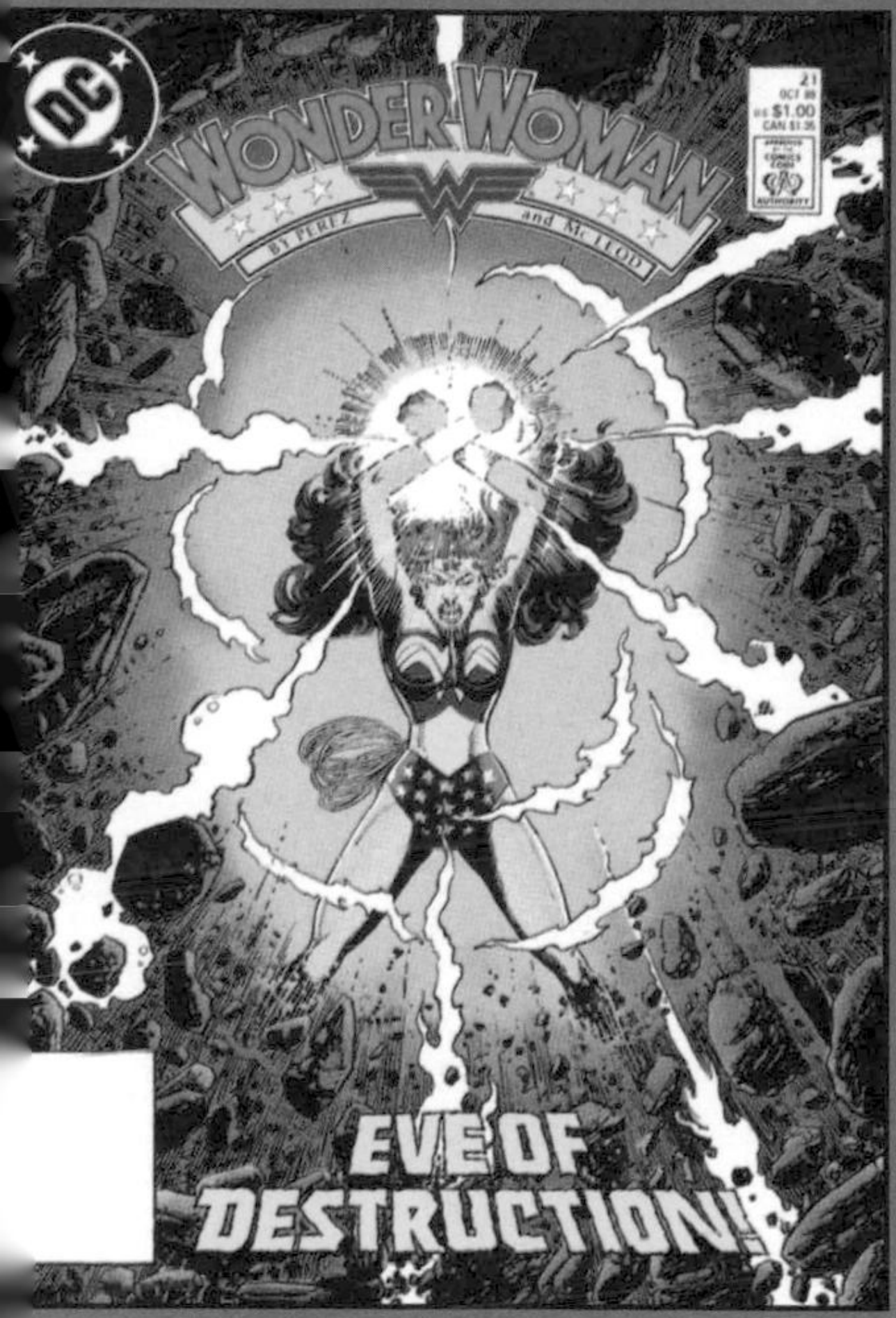
DC
WONDER WOMAN
BY PEREZ and McLEOD
21
OCT 89
US $1.00
CAN $1.35
EVE OF DESTRUCTION!

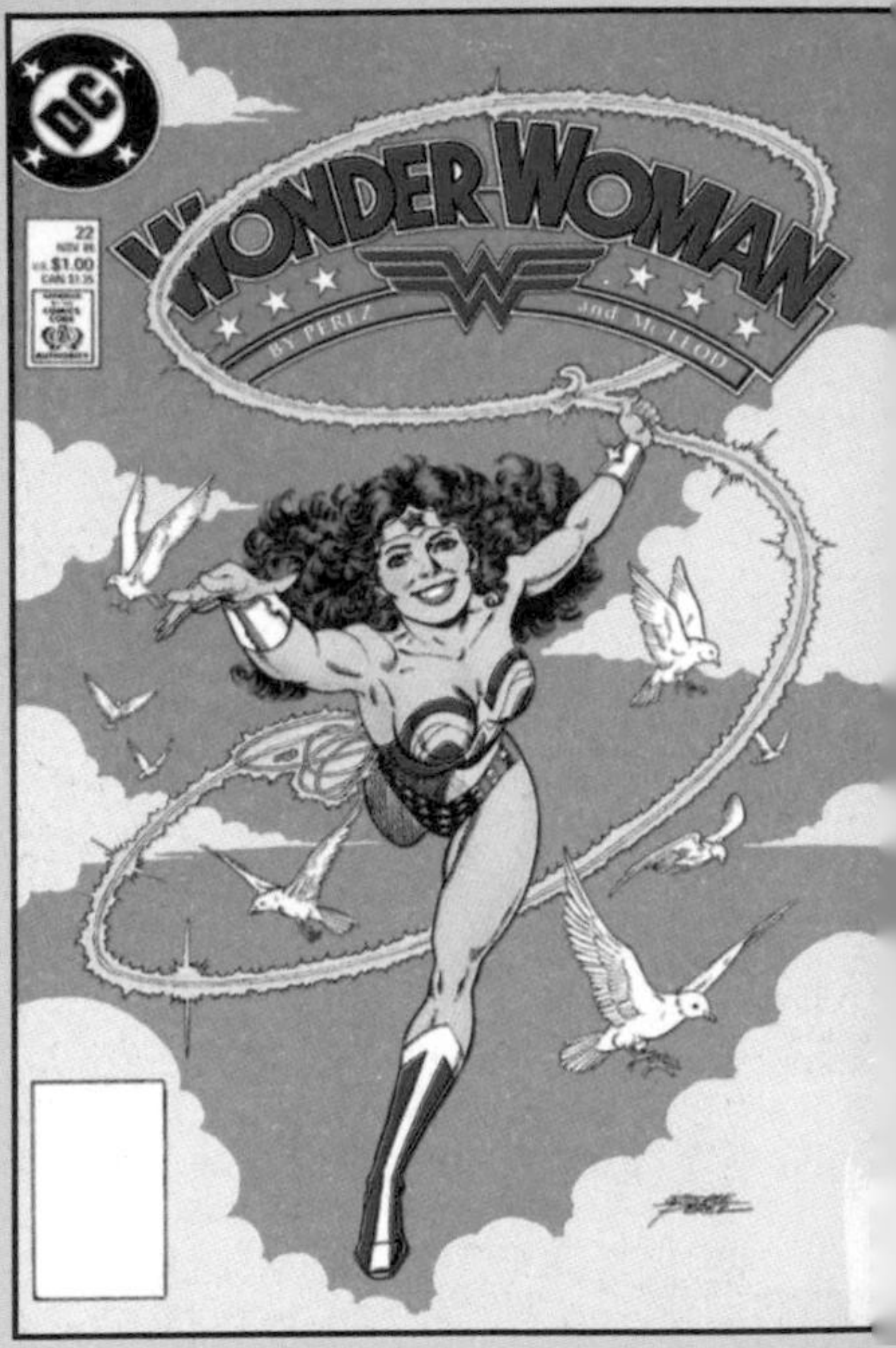
DC
WONDER WOMAN
BY PEREZ and McLEOD
22
U.S. $1.00
CAN $1.35

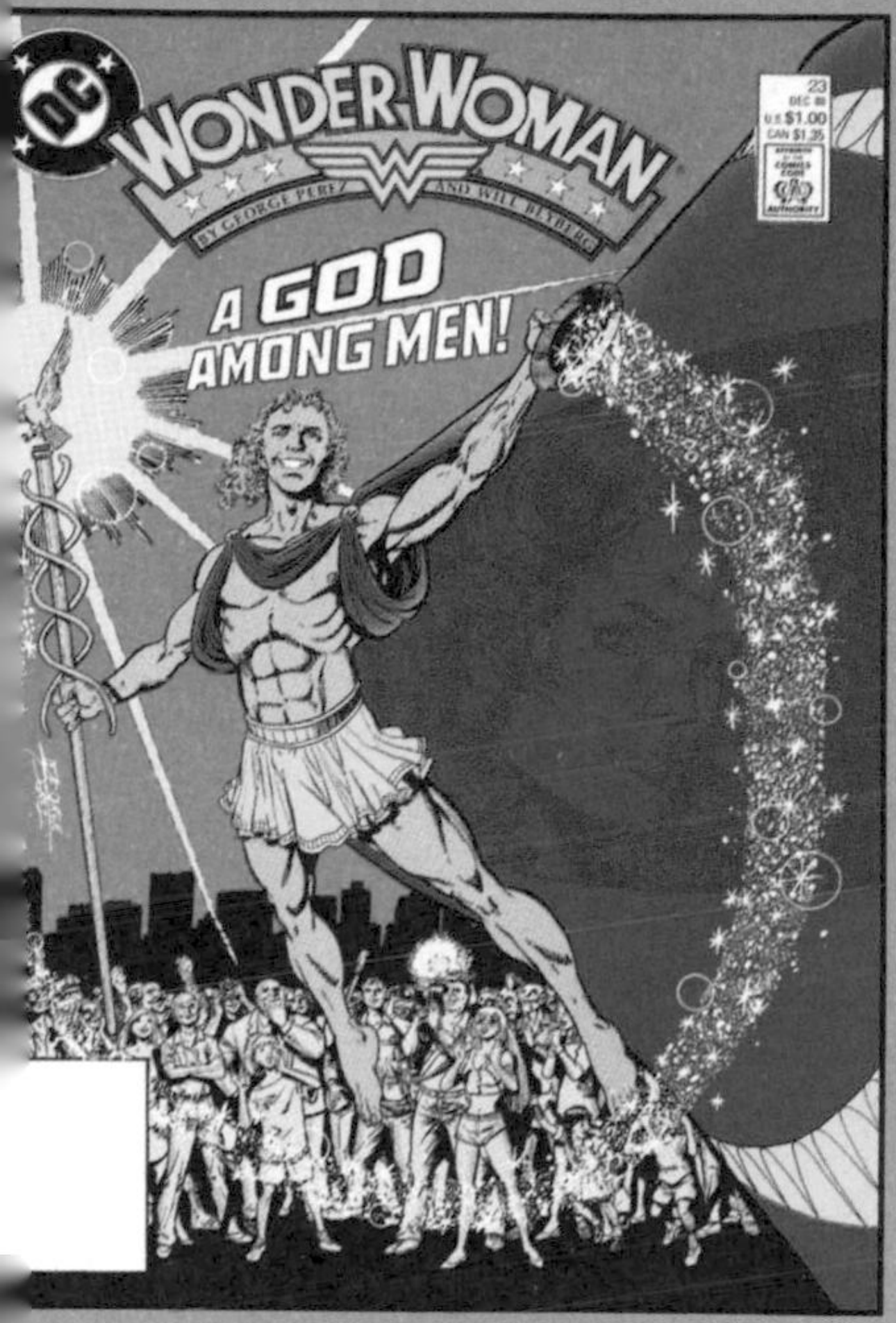
DC
WONDER WOMAN
BY GEORGE PEREZ AND WILL DEMPSTER
23
DEC 86
U.S. $1.00
CAN $1.35
A GOD AMONG MEN!

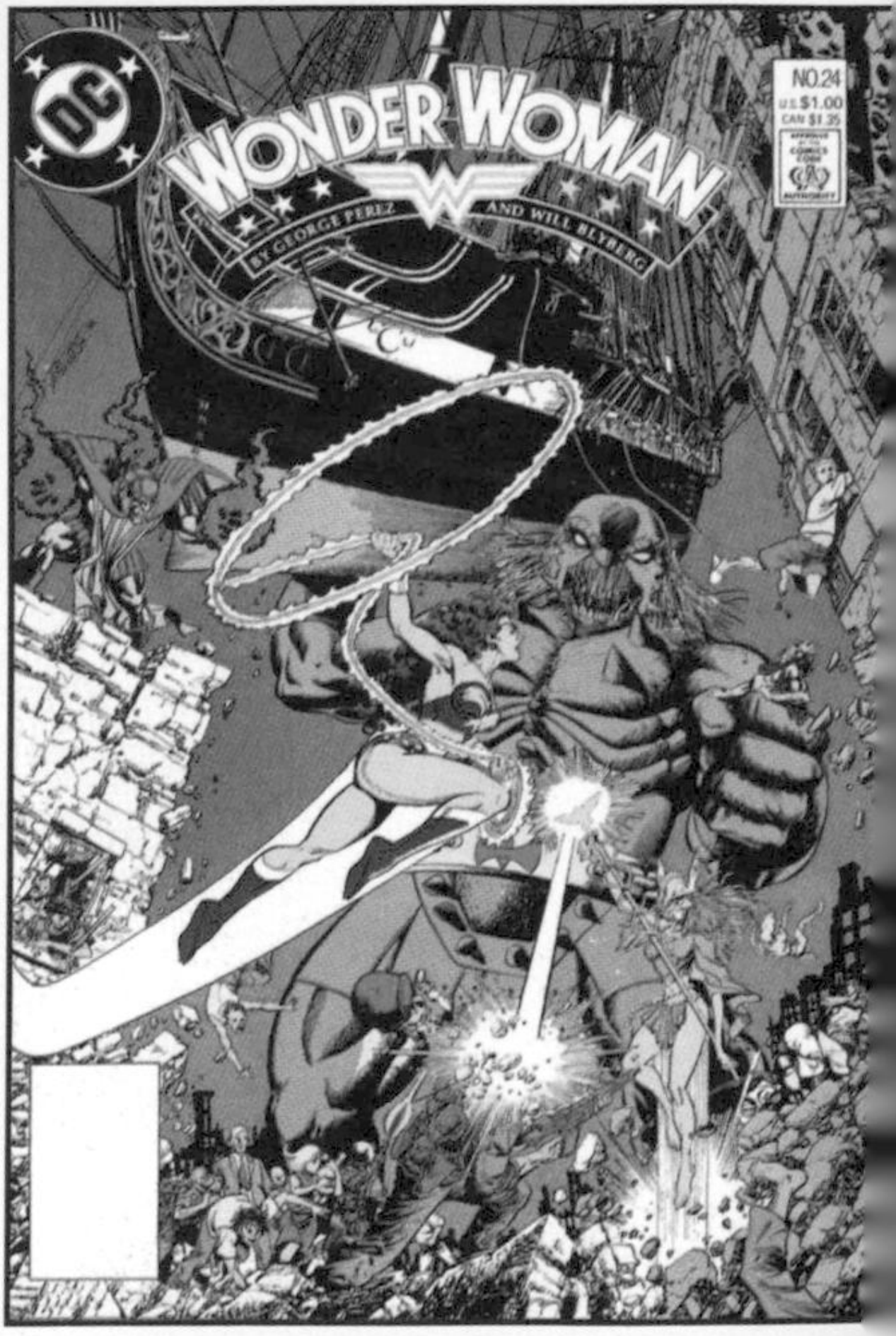
DC
WONDER WOMAN
BY GEORGE PEREZ AND WILL BLYBERG
NO.24
U.S. $1.00
CAN $1.35

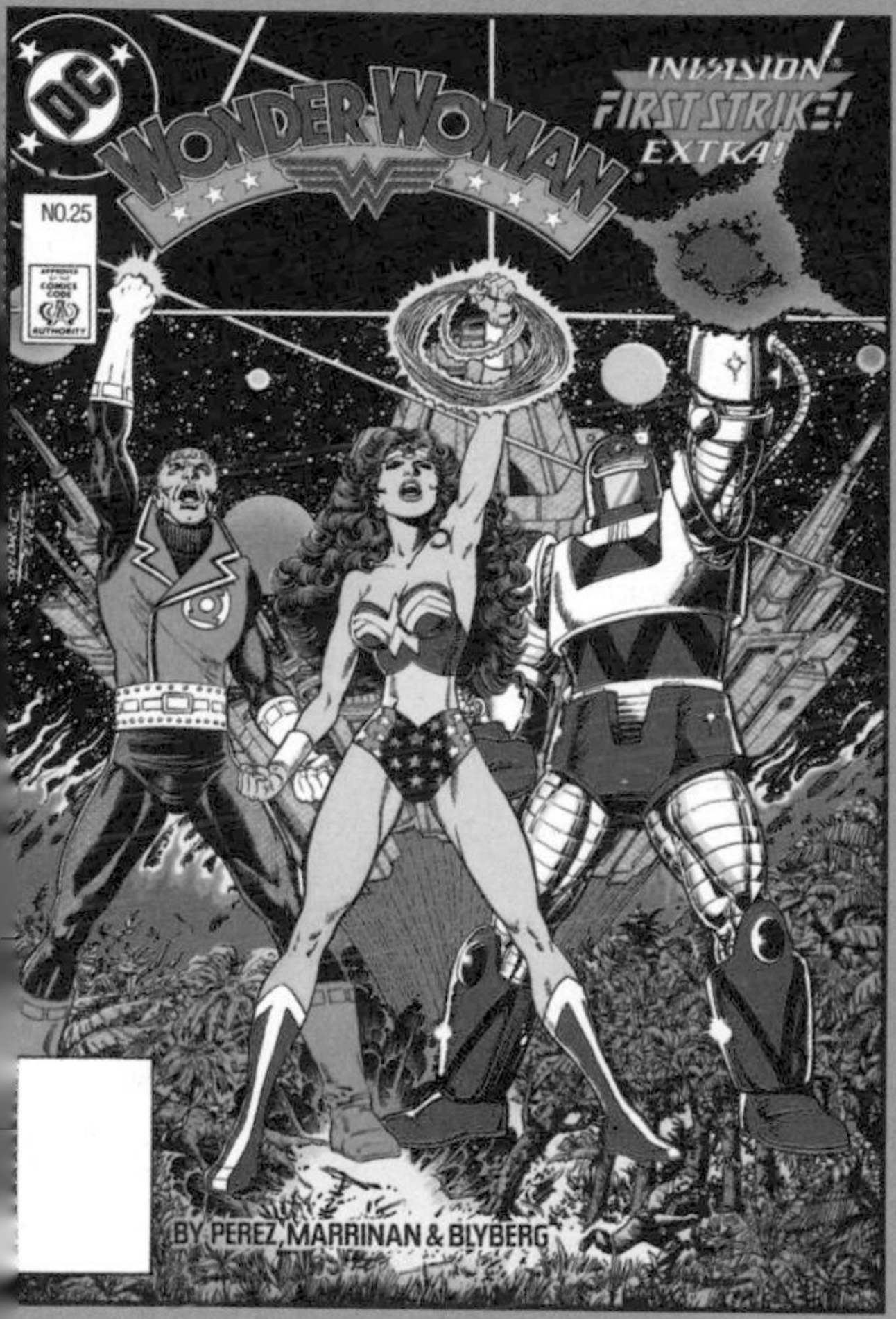
DC
WONDER WOMAN
INVASION!
FIRST STRIKE!
EXTRA!
NO.25
APPROVED BY THE COMICS CODE AUTHORITY
BY PEREZ, MARRINAN & BLYBERG

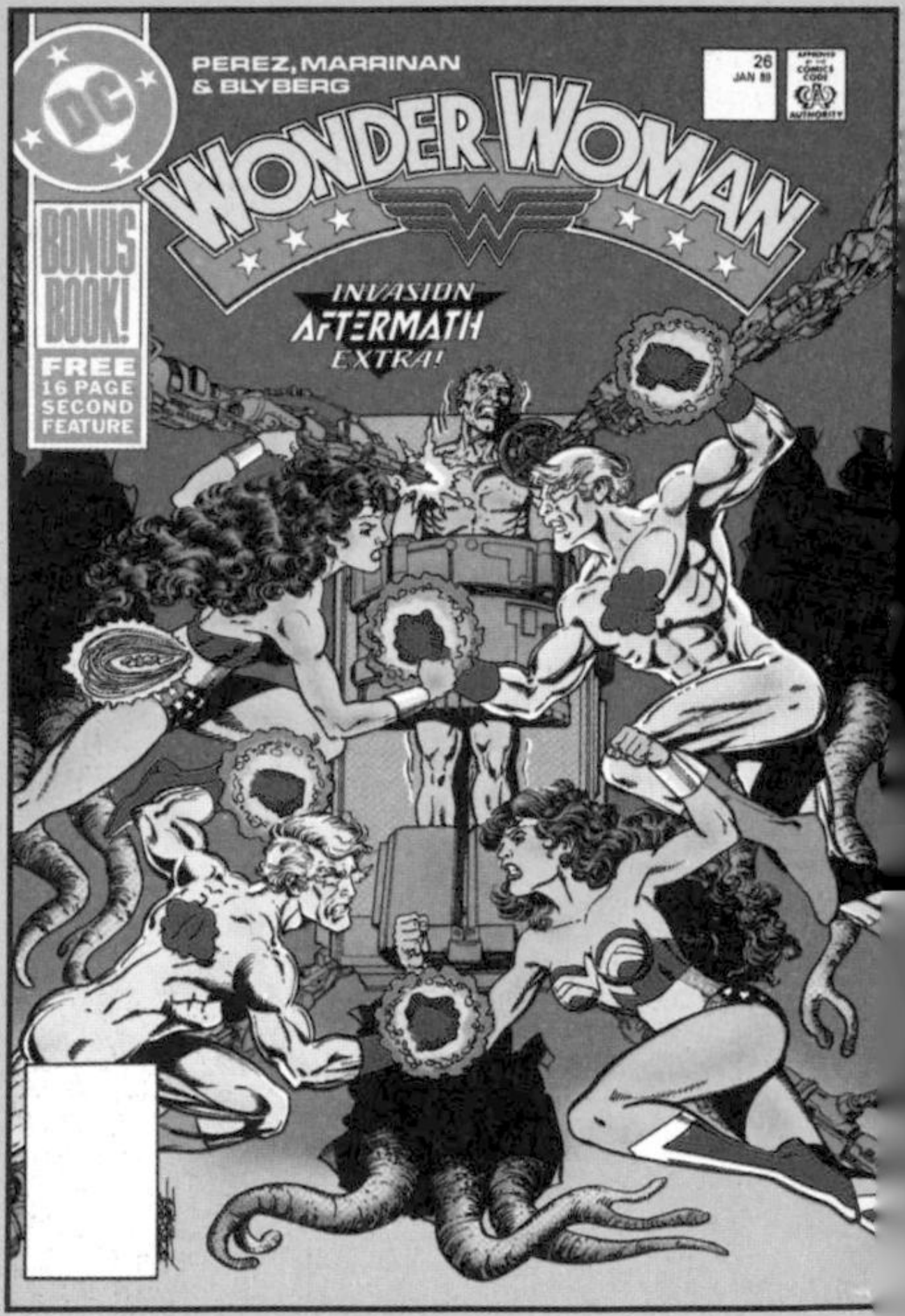
PEREZ, MARRINAN
& BLYBERG
26
JAN 88
WONDER WOMAN
INVASION
AFTERMATH
EXTRA!
BONUS
BOOK!
FREE
16 PAGE
SECOND
FEATURE

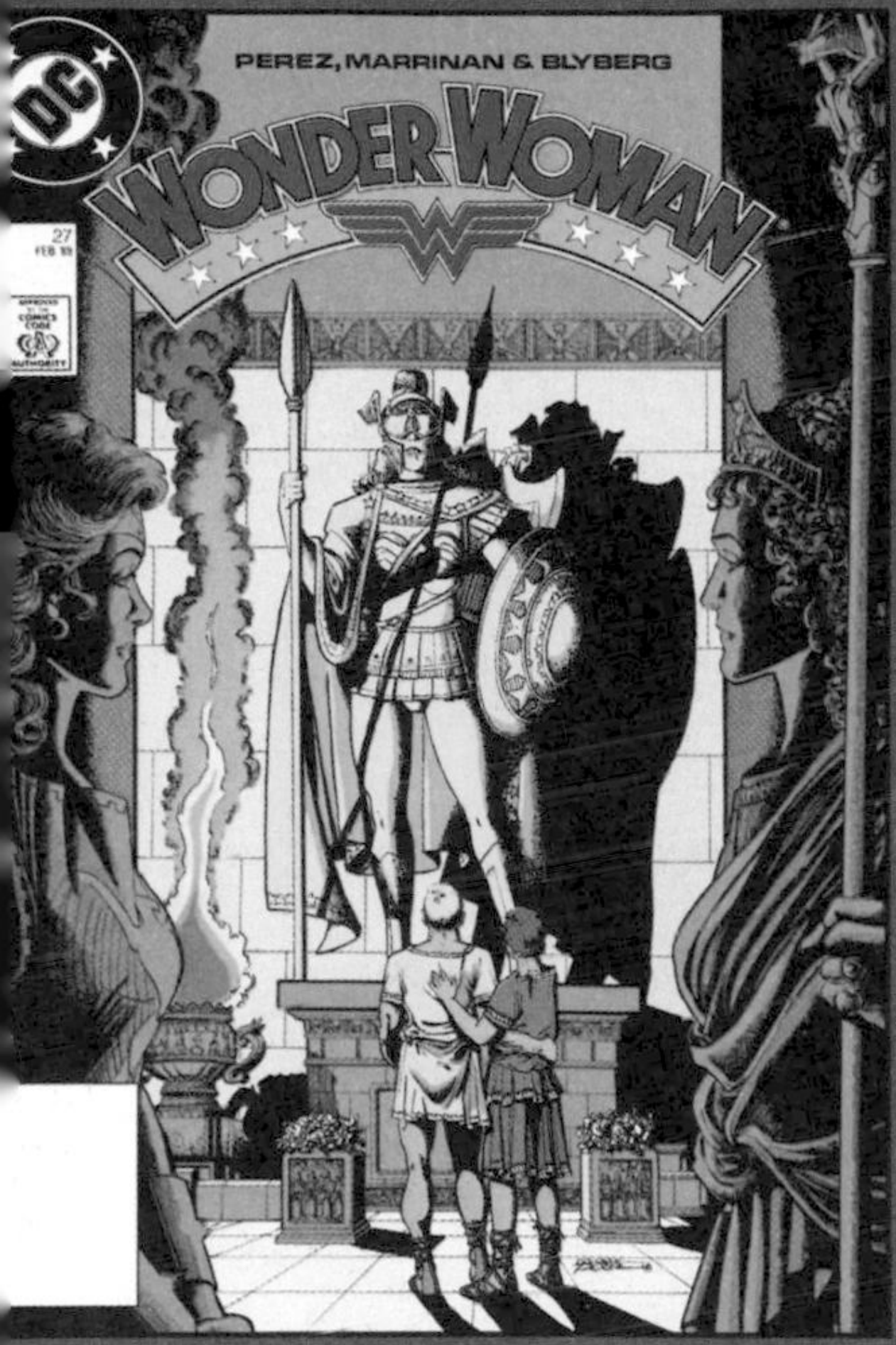
PEREZ, MARRINAN & BLYBERG
WONDER WOMAN
27
FEB '89
APPROVED BY THE COMICS CODE AUTHORITY

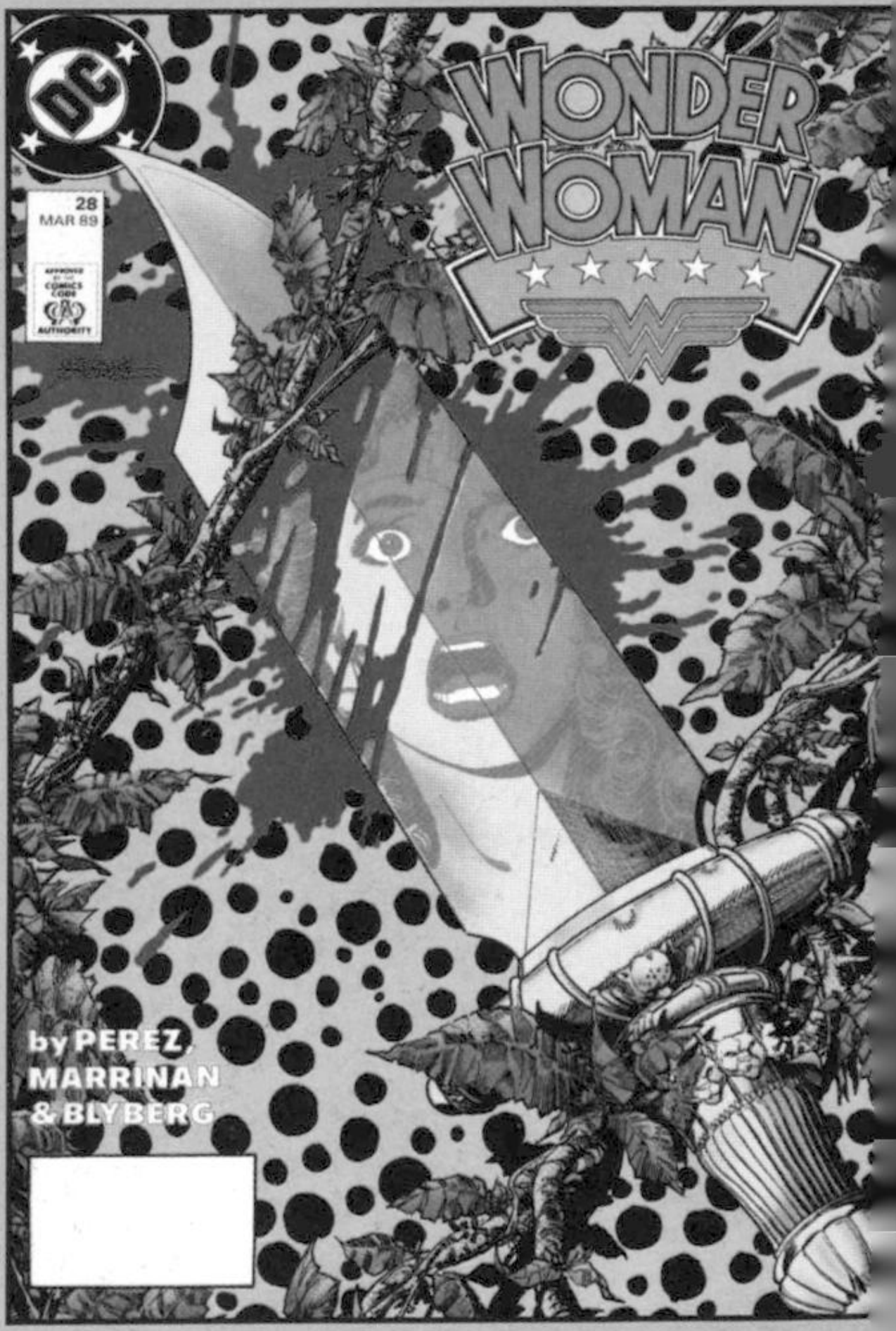
DC
28
MAR 89
APPROVED BY THE CODE AUTHORITY
WONDER WOMAN
by PEREZ, MARRINAN & BLYBERG

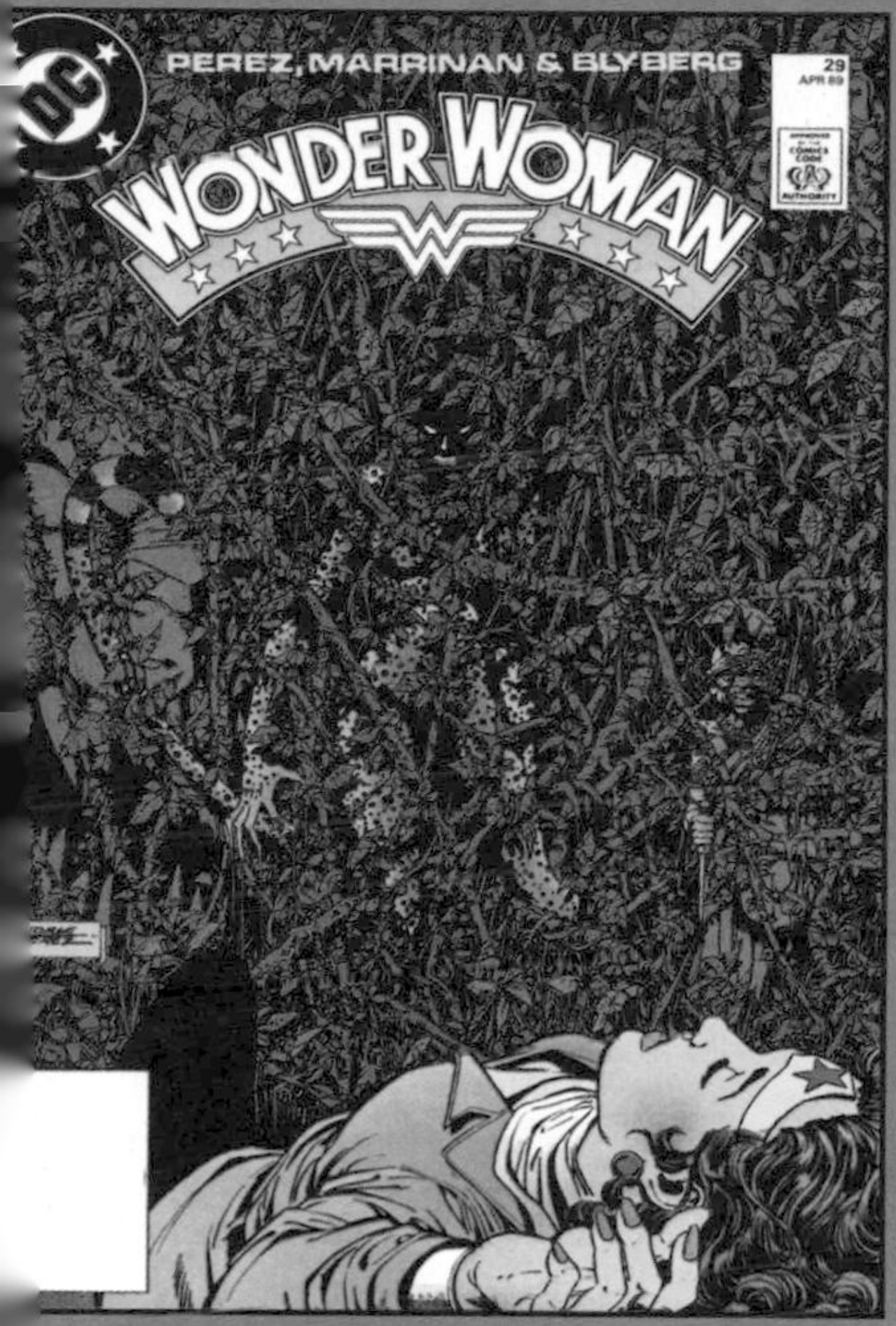
PEREZ, MARRINAN & BLYBERG
29
APR 89
WONDER WOMAN

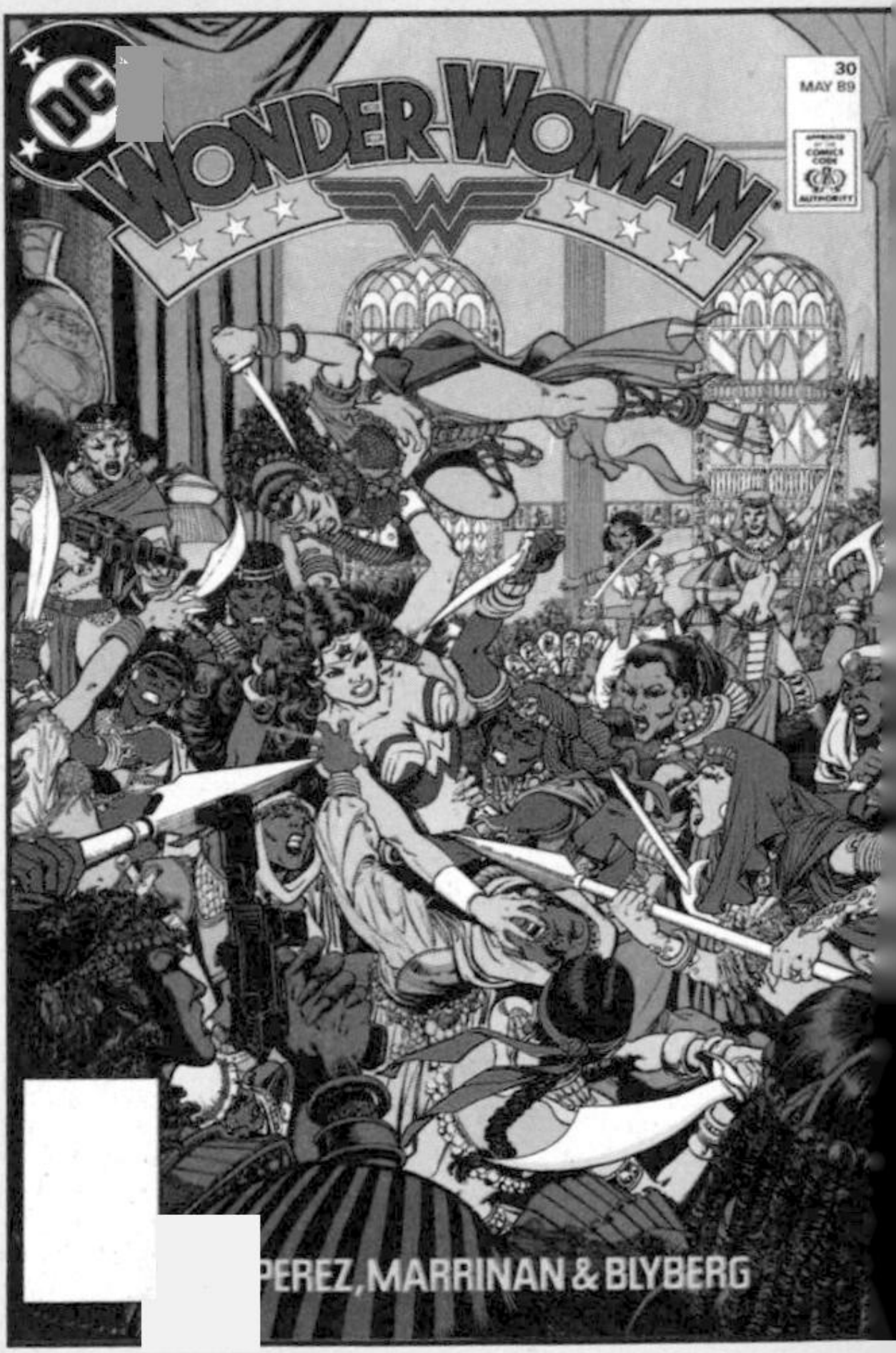
DC
WONDER WOMAN
30
MAY 89
APPROVED BY THE COMICS CODE AUTHORITY
PEREZ, MARRINAN & BLYBERG

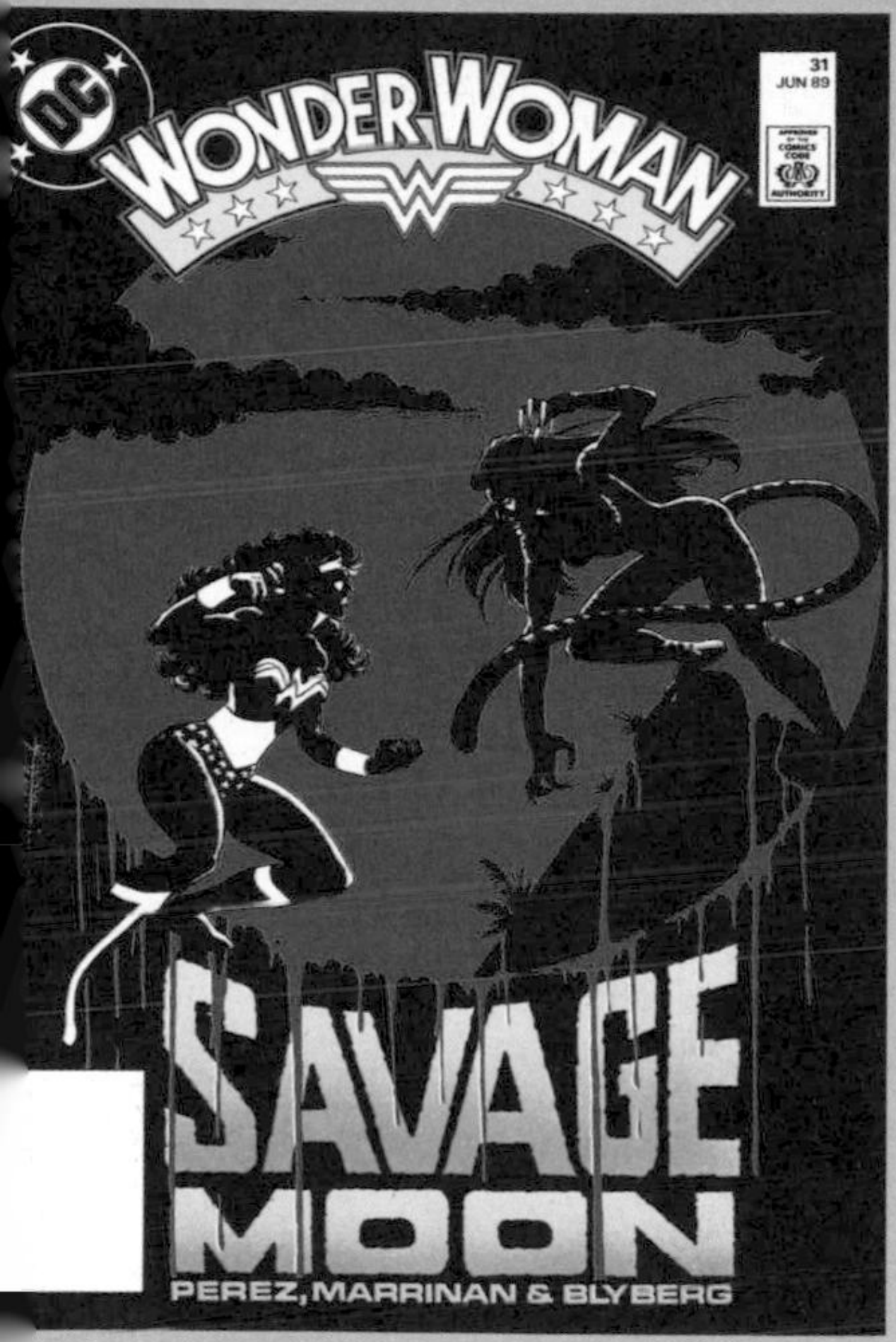
DC
WONDER WOMAN
31
JUN 89
APPROVED BY THE COMICS CODE AUTHORITY
SAVAGE MOON
PEREZ, MARRINAN & BLYBERG

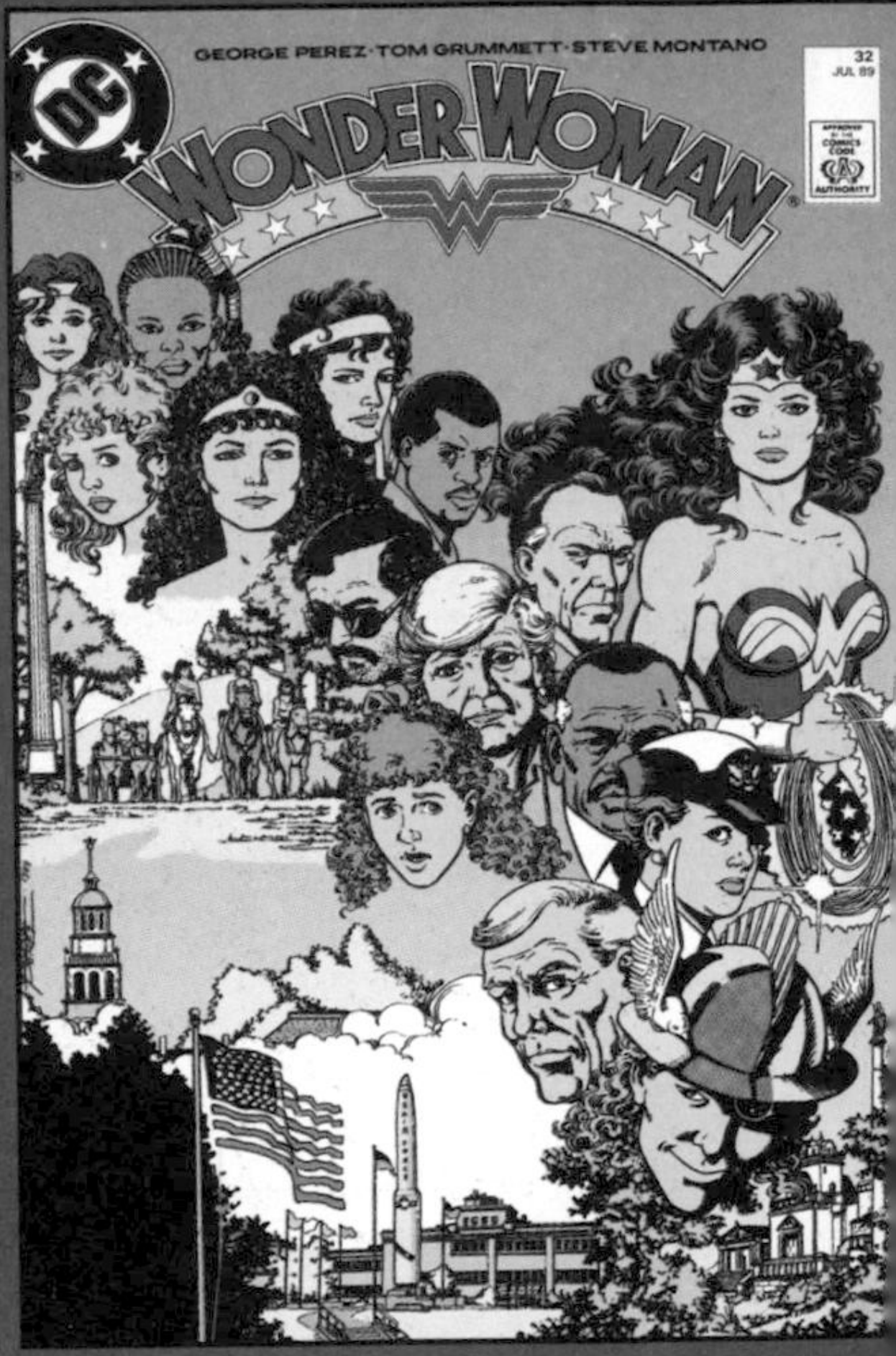
GEORGE PEREZ · TOM GRUMMETT · STEVE MONTANO
DC
WONDER WOMAN
32
JUL 89
APPROVED BY THE COMICS CODE AUTHORITY

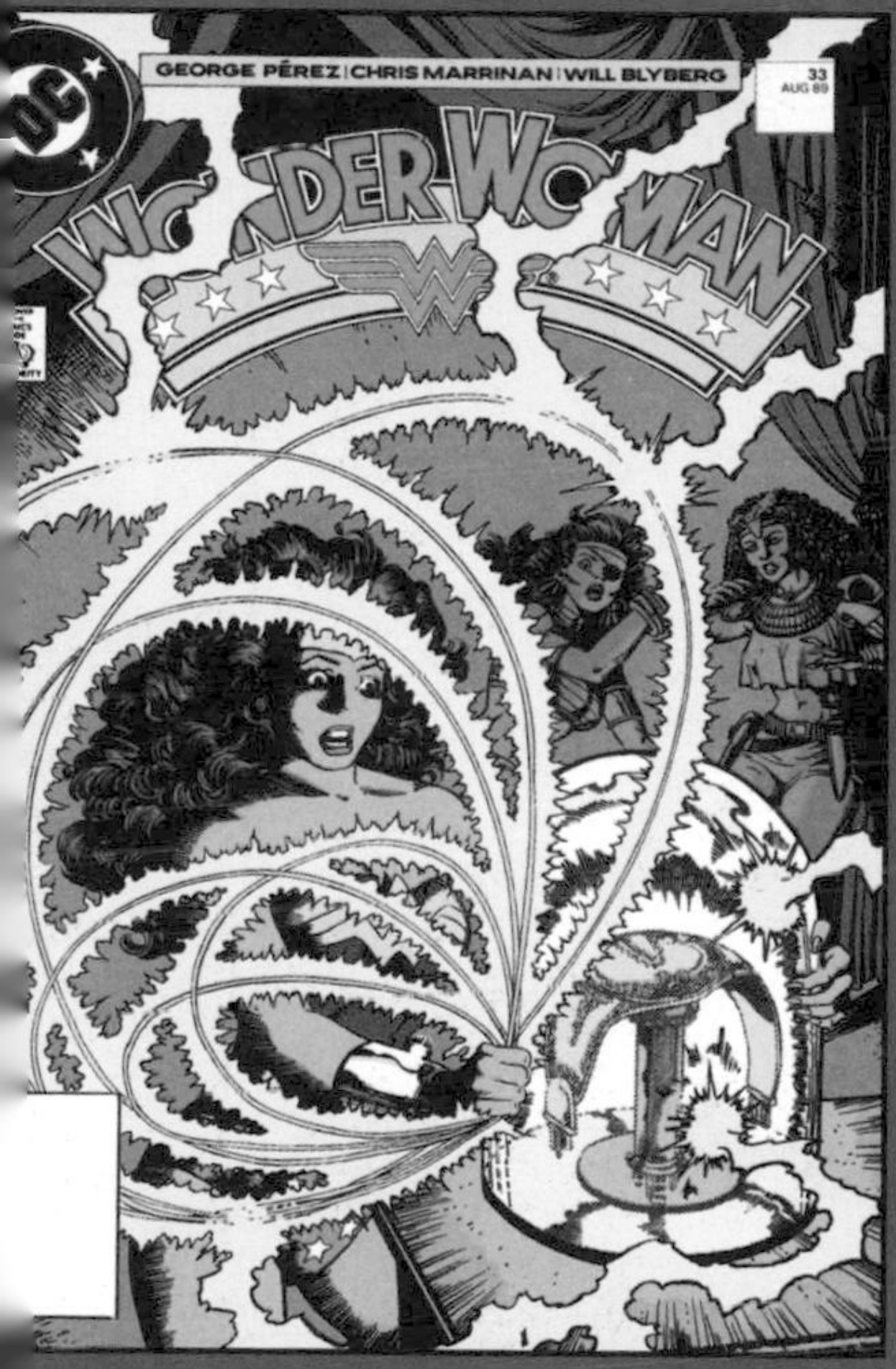
GEORGE PÉREZ | CHRIS MARRINAN | WILL BLYBERG
33
AUG 89
WONDER WOMAN

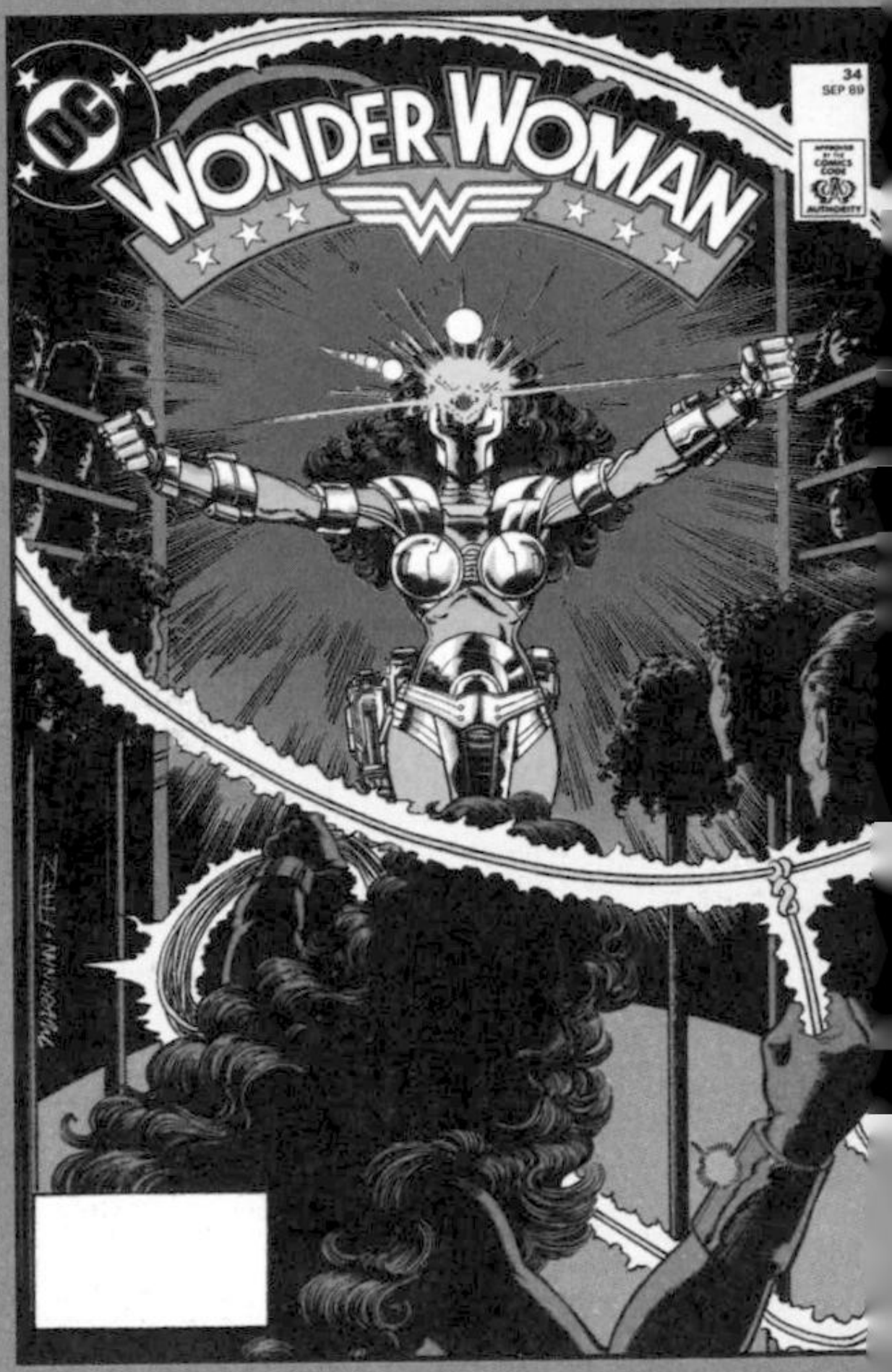
DC
WONDER WOMAN
34
SEP 89
APPROVED BY THE COMICS CODE AUTHORITY

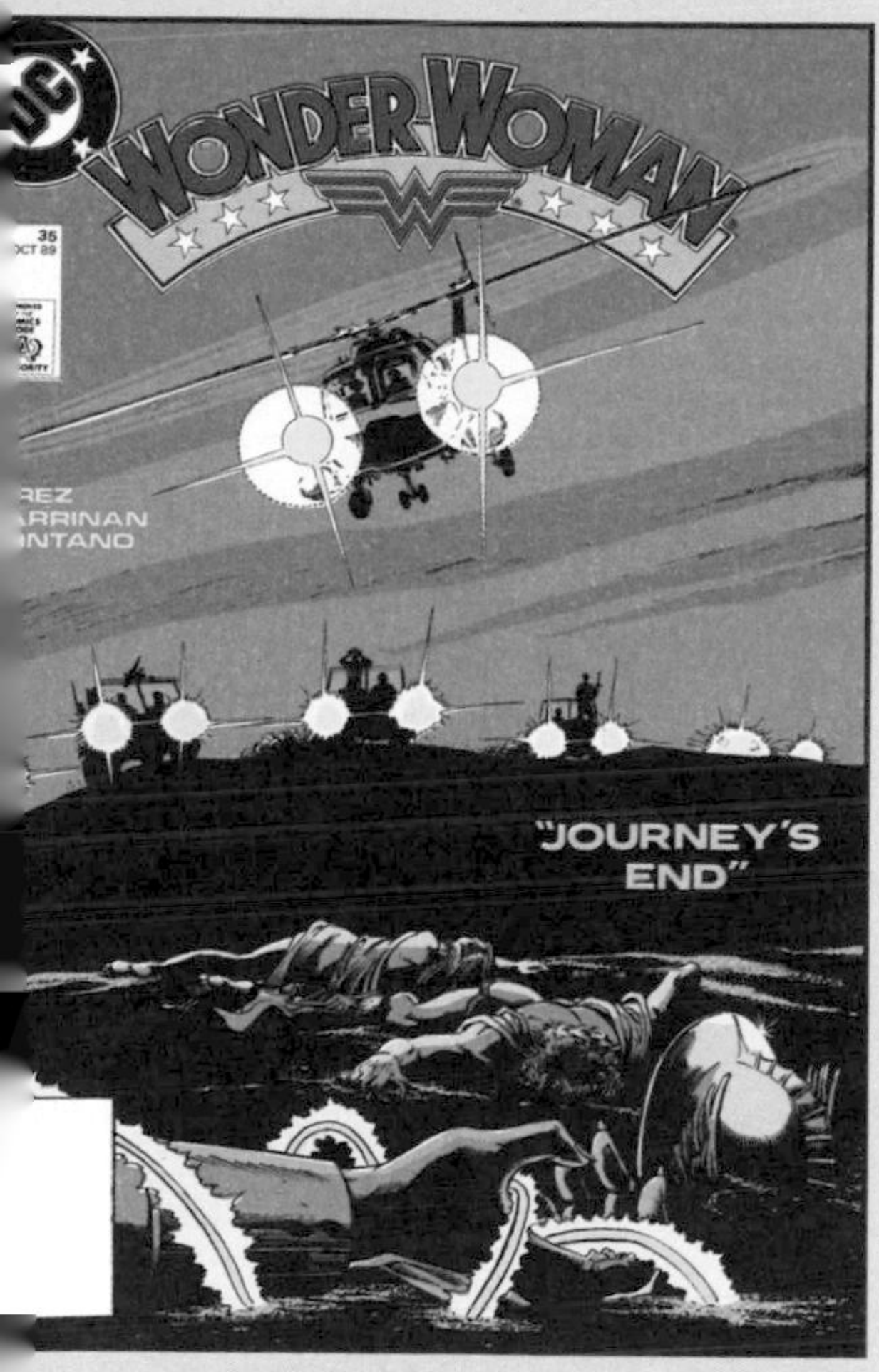
WONDER WOMAN
35
OCT 89
REZ
ARRINAN
NTANO
"JOURNEY'S END"

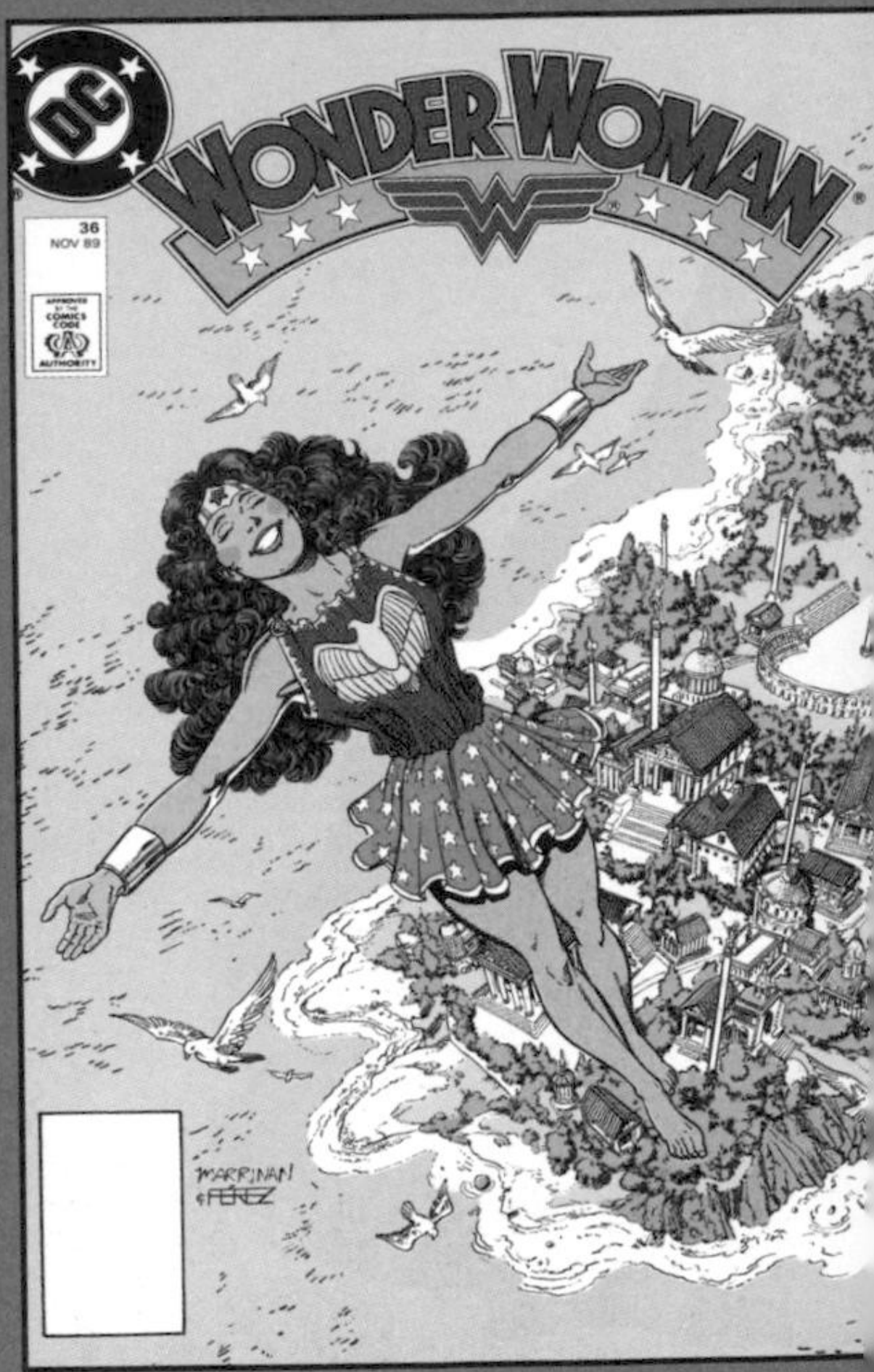
DC
WONDER WOMAN
36
NOV 89
APPROVED BY THE COMICS CODE AUTHORITY
MARRINAN
PÉREZ

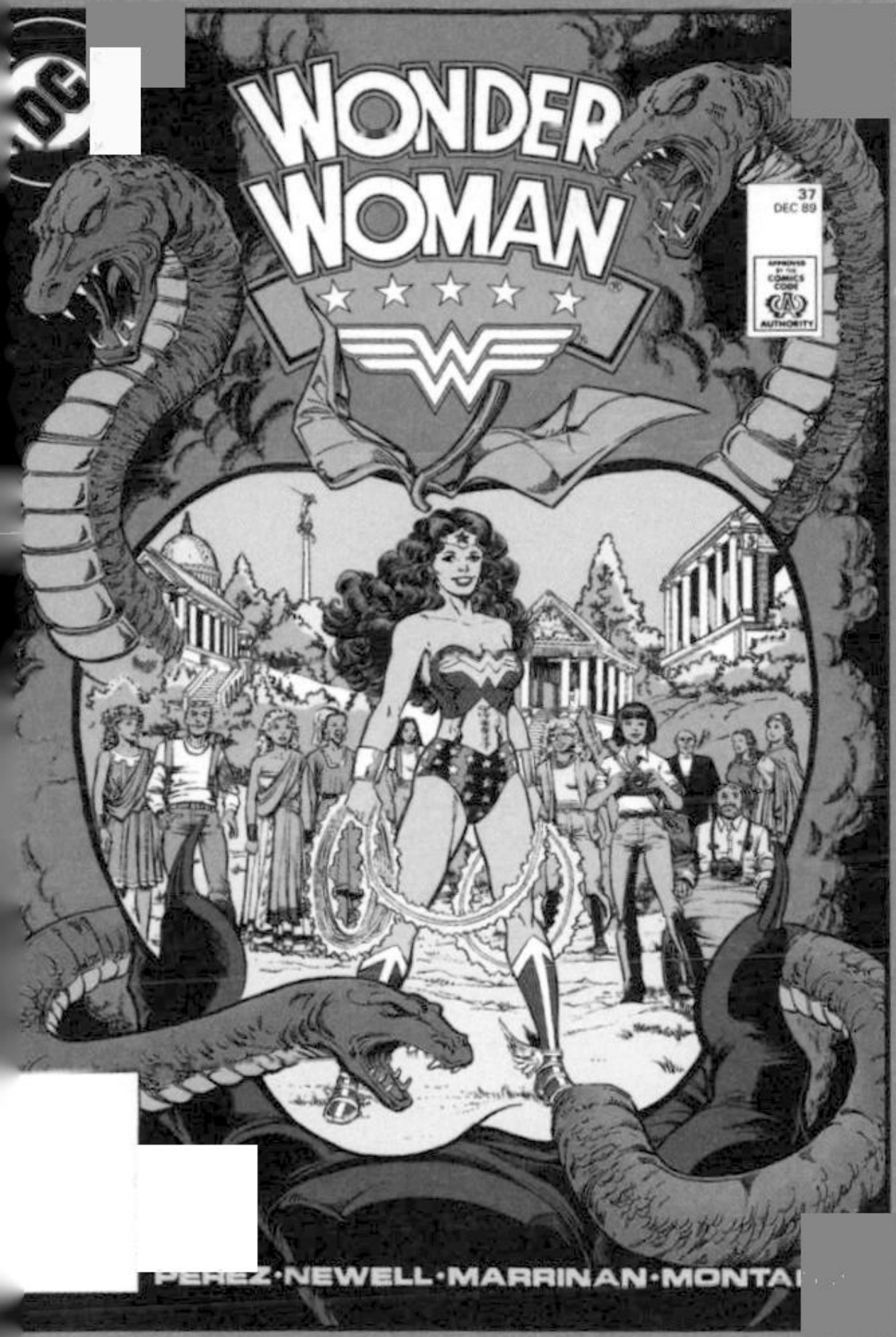
WONDER WOMAN
37
DEC 89
APPROVED BY THE COMICS CODE AUTHORITY
PEREZ·NEWELL·MARRINAN·MONTA

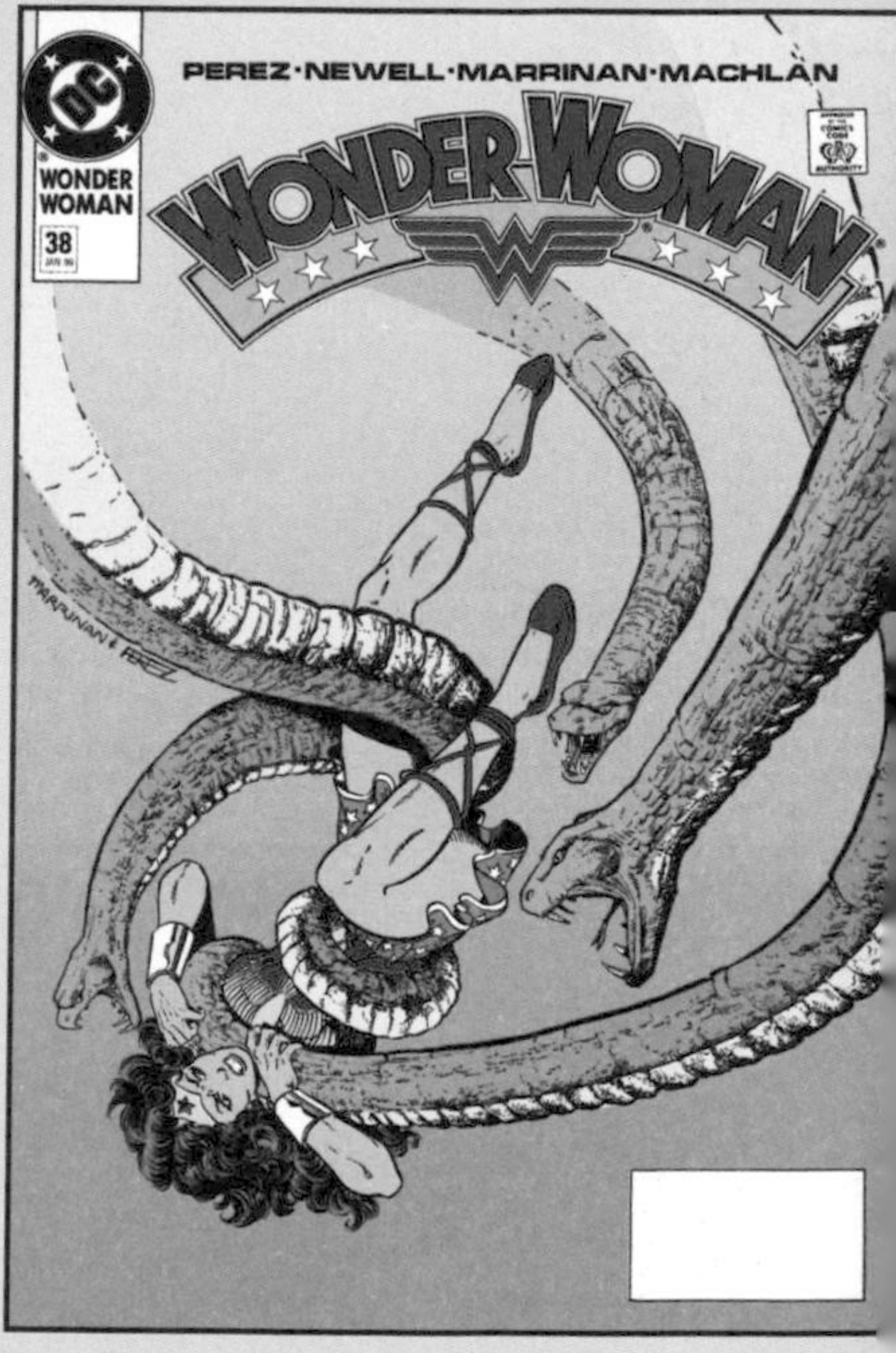
PEREZ·NEWELL·MARRINAN·MACHLAN
WONDER WOMAN
38
WONDER WOMAN
MARRINAN & PEREZ

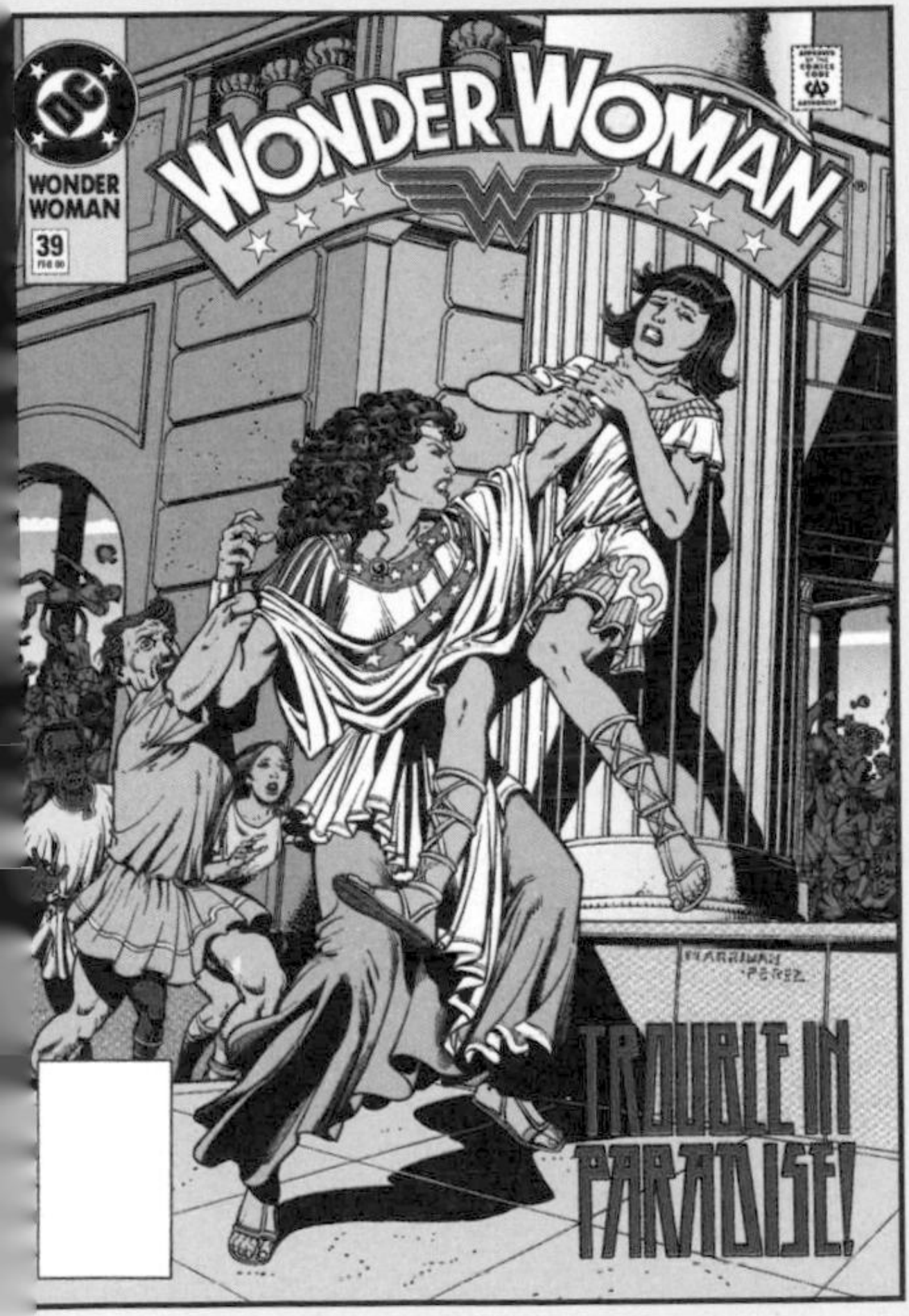
DC
WONDER WOMAN
39
WONDER WOMAN
TROUBLE IN PARADISE!

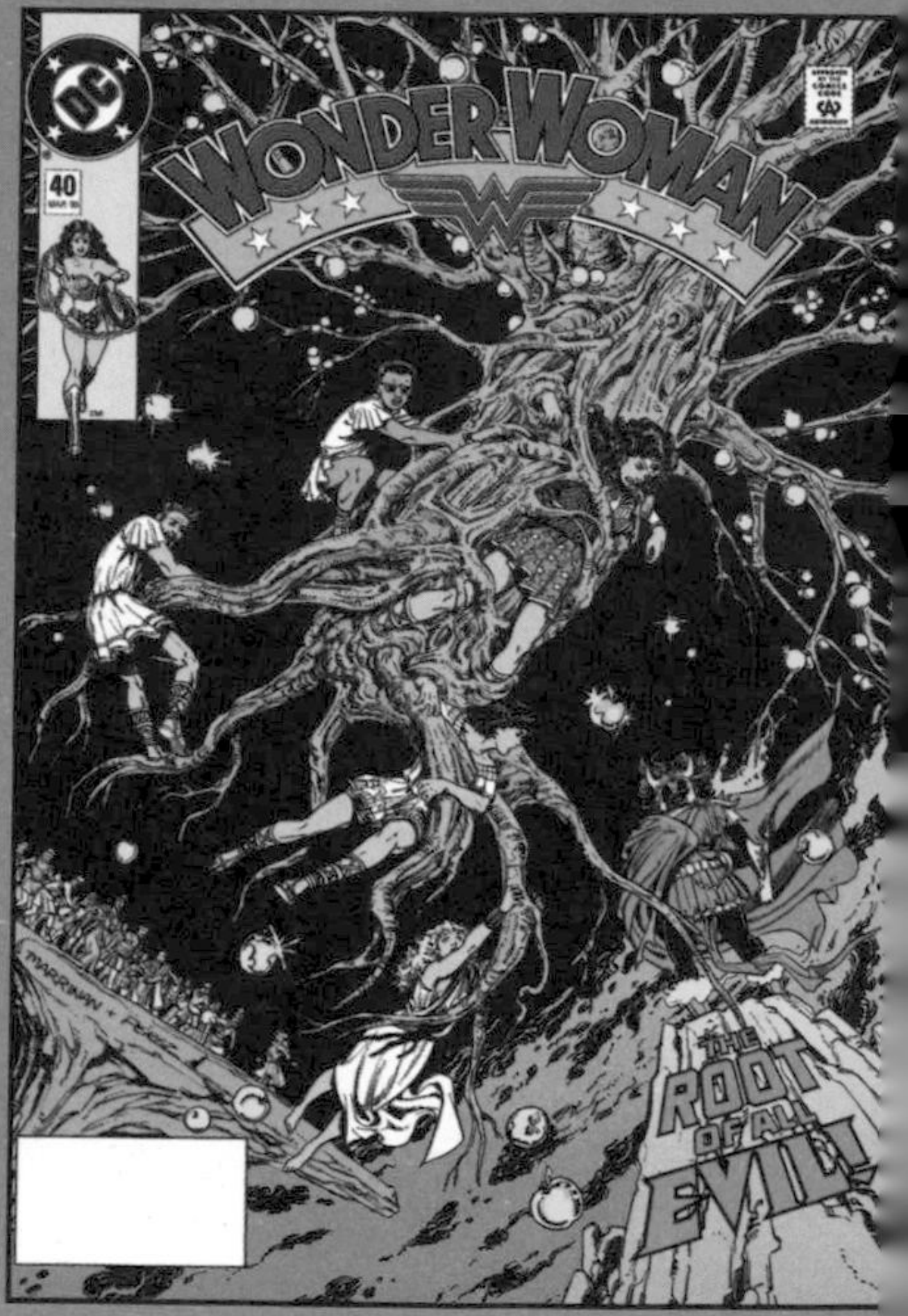
DC
40
WONDER WOMAN
THE ROOT OF ALL EVIL!

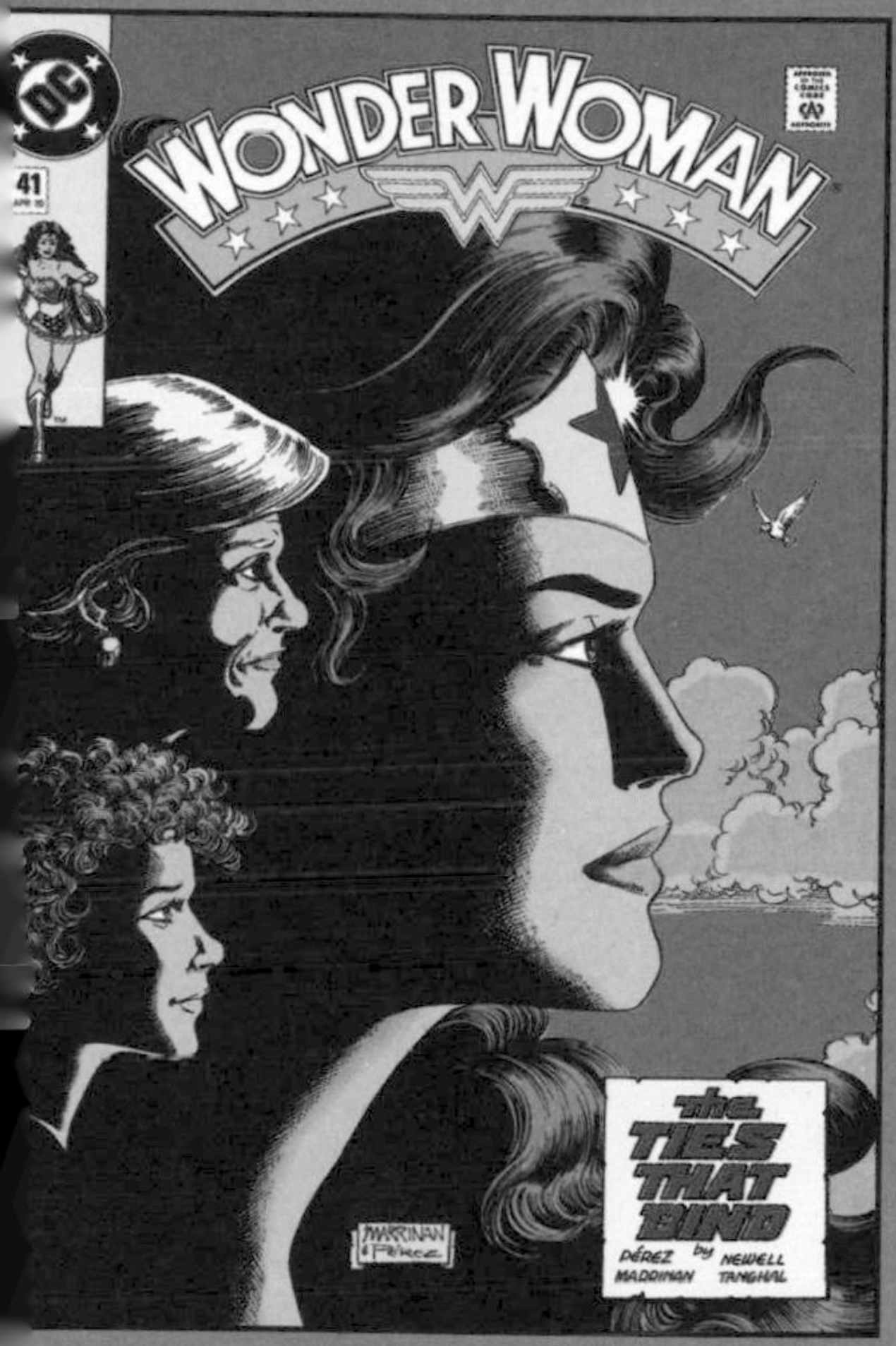
DC
WONDER WOMAN
41
the TIES THAT BIND
PÉREZ by NEWELL
MADDINAN TANGHAL
MARRINAN & PRINCE

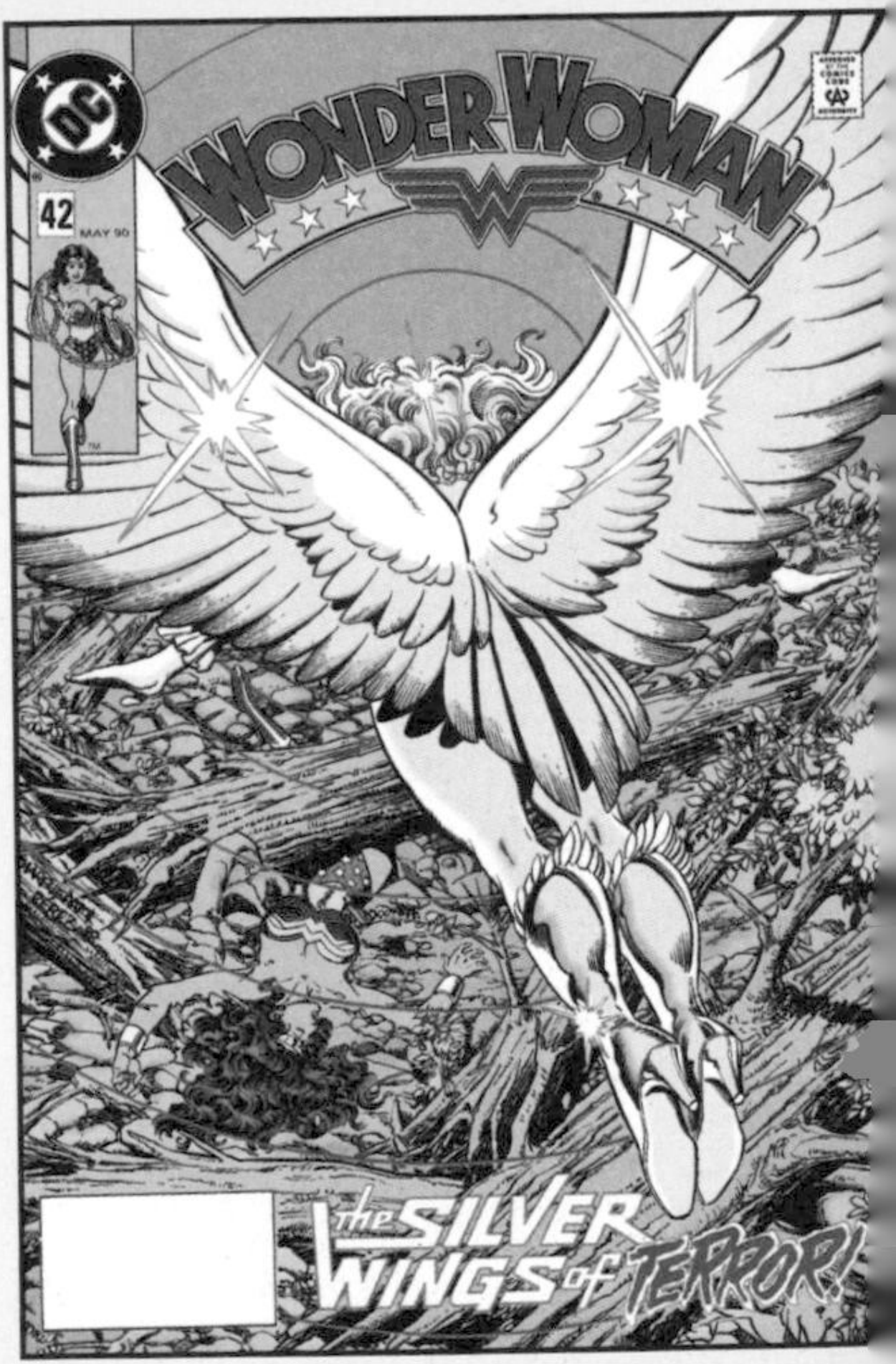
DC
WONDER WOMAN
42
MAY 90
the SILVER WINGS of TERROR!

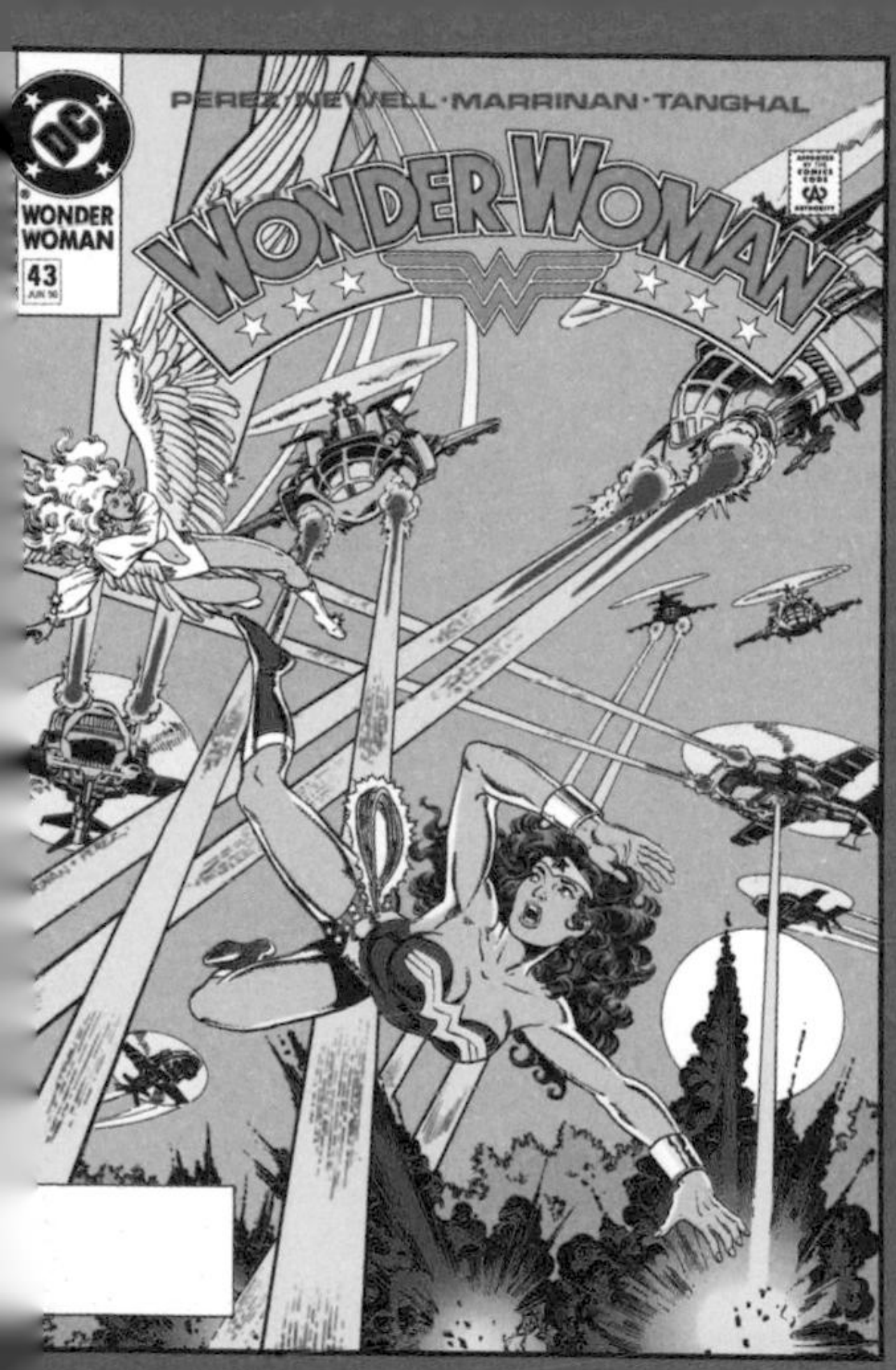
PEREZ · NEWELL · MARRINAN · TANGHAL
WONDER WOMAN
43
WONDER WOMAN

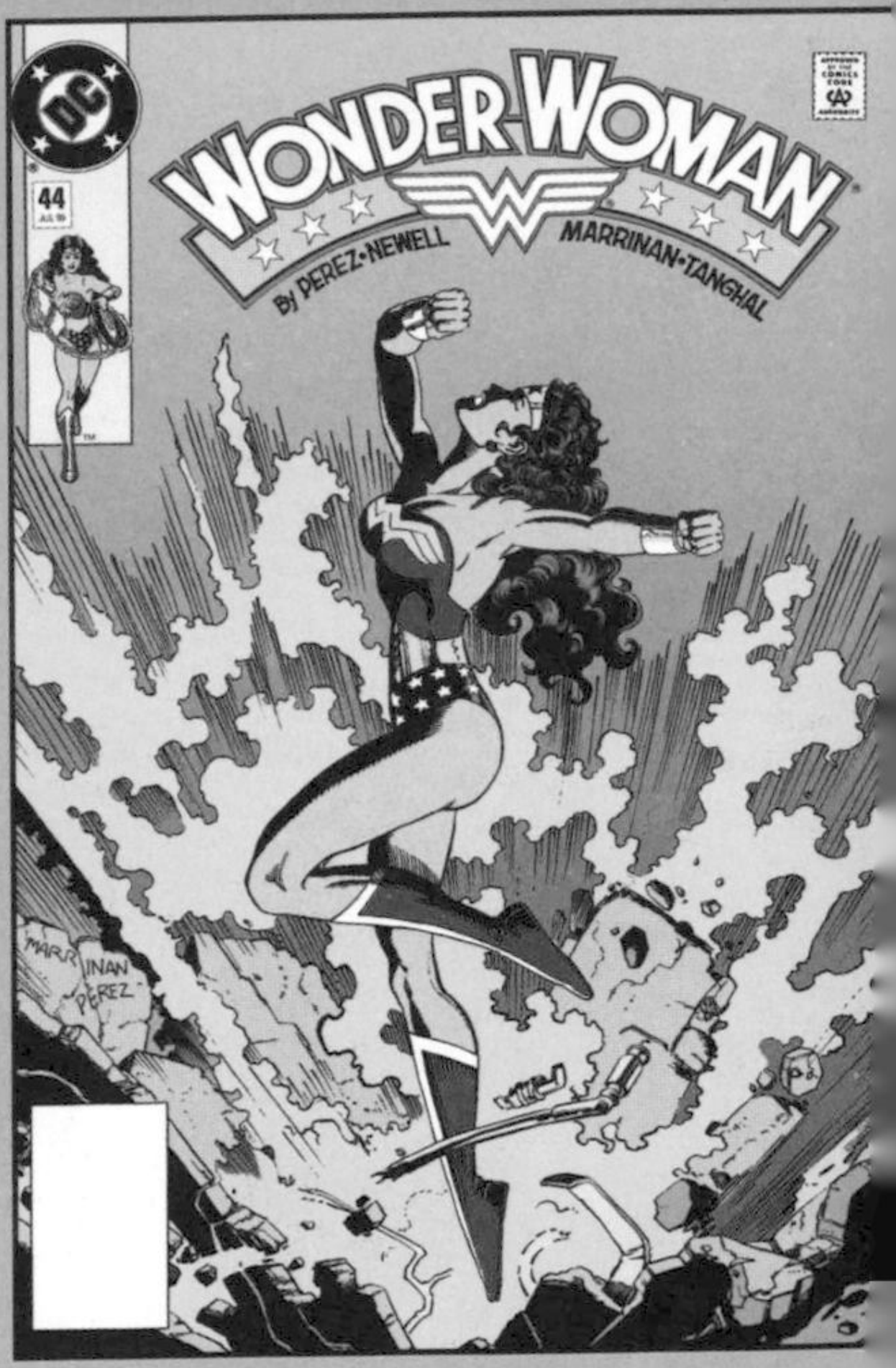
DC
44
WONDER WOMAN
BY PEREZ•NEWELL
MARRINAN•TANGHAL
MARRINAN
PEREZ

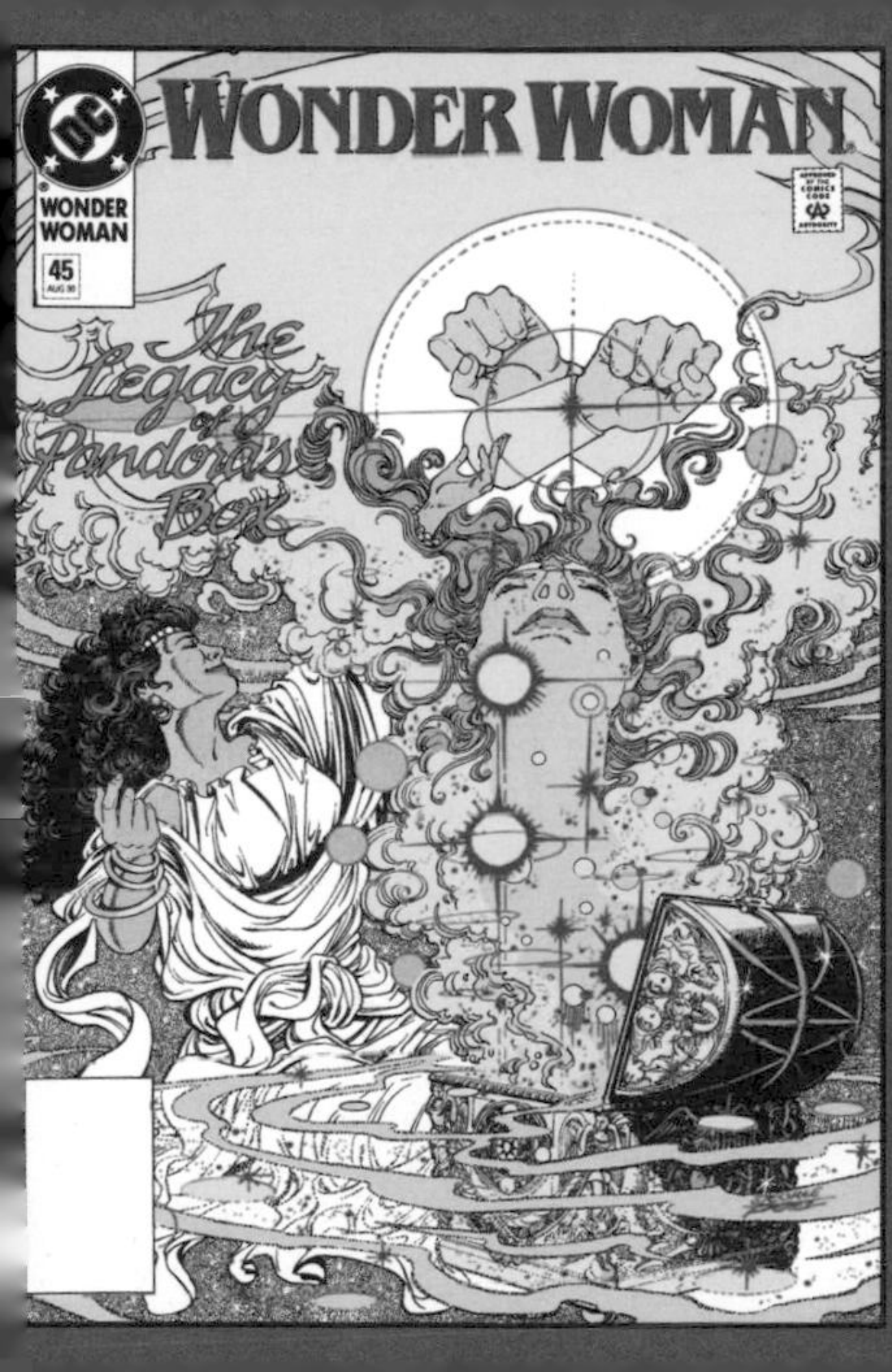
WONDER WOMAN
WONDER WOMAN
45
AUG 90
The Legacy of Pandora's Box

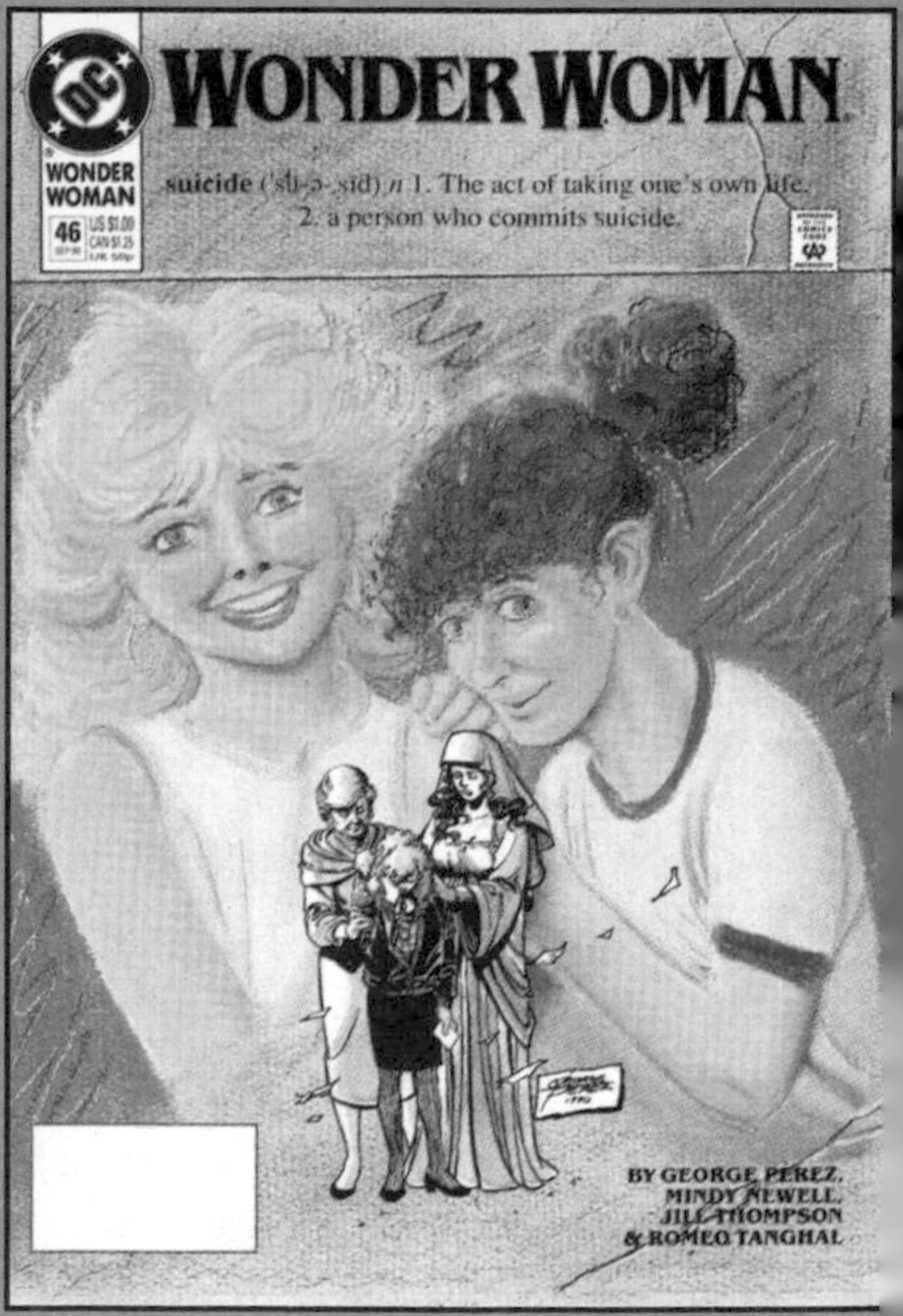
WONDER WOMAN
WONDER WOMAN
46
US $1.00
CAN $1.25
suicide ('sü-ə-,sīd) n 1. The act of taking one's own life.
2. a person who commits suicide.
BY GEORGE PEREZ,
MINDY NEWELL,
JILL THOMPSON
& ROMEO TANGHAL

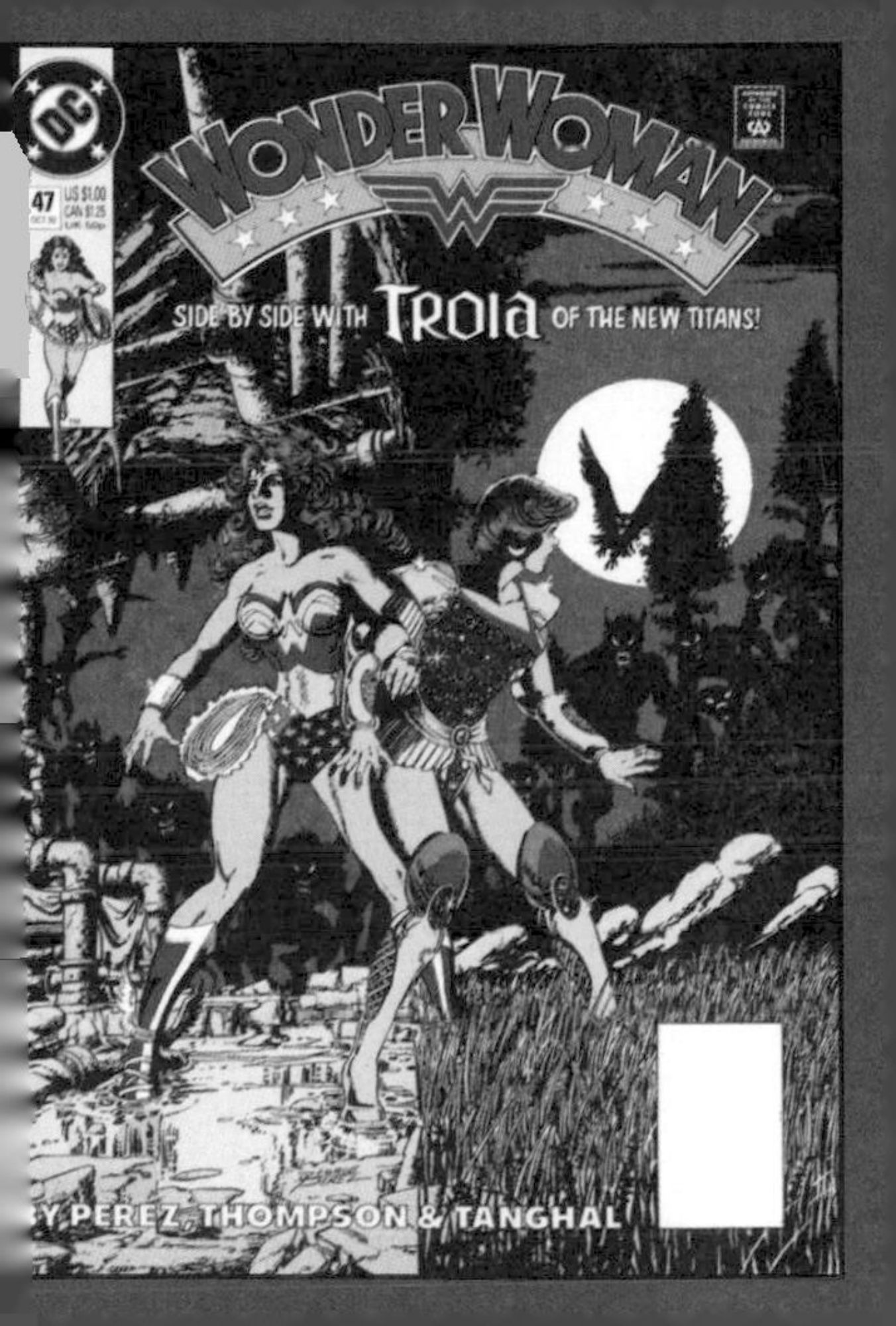
DC
47
US $1.00
CAN $1.25
WONDER WOMAN
SIDE BY SIDE WITH TROIA OF THE NEW TITANS!
Y PEREZ, THOMPSON & TANGHAL

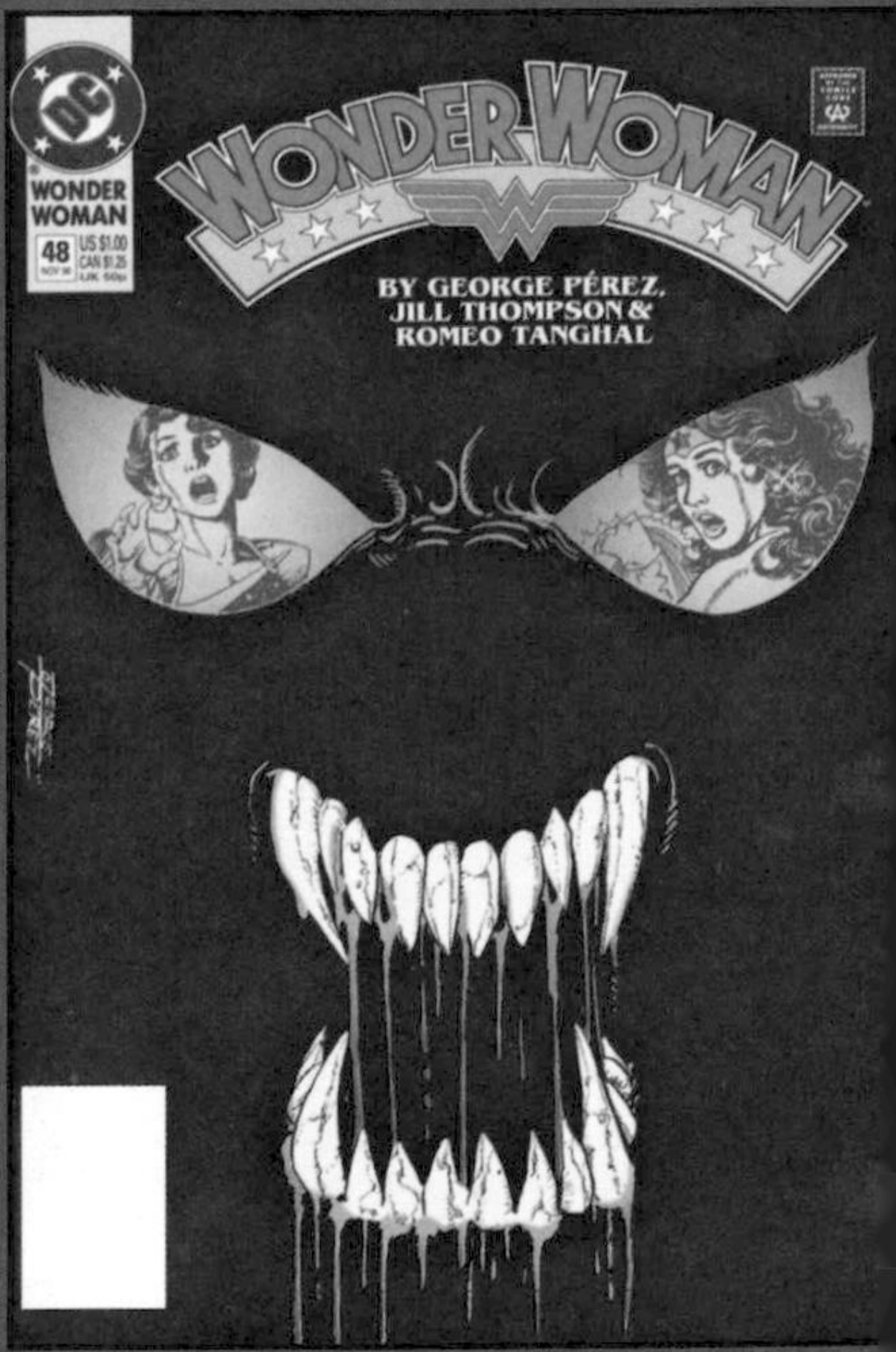
WONDER WOMAN
48
US $1.00
CAN $1.25
WONDER WOMAN
BY GEORGE PÉREZ, JILL THOMPSON & ROMEO TANGHAL

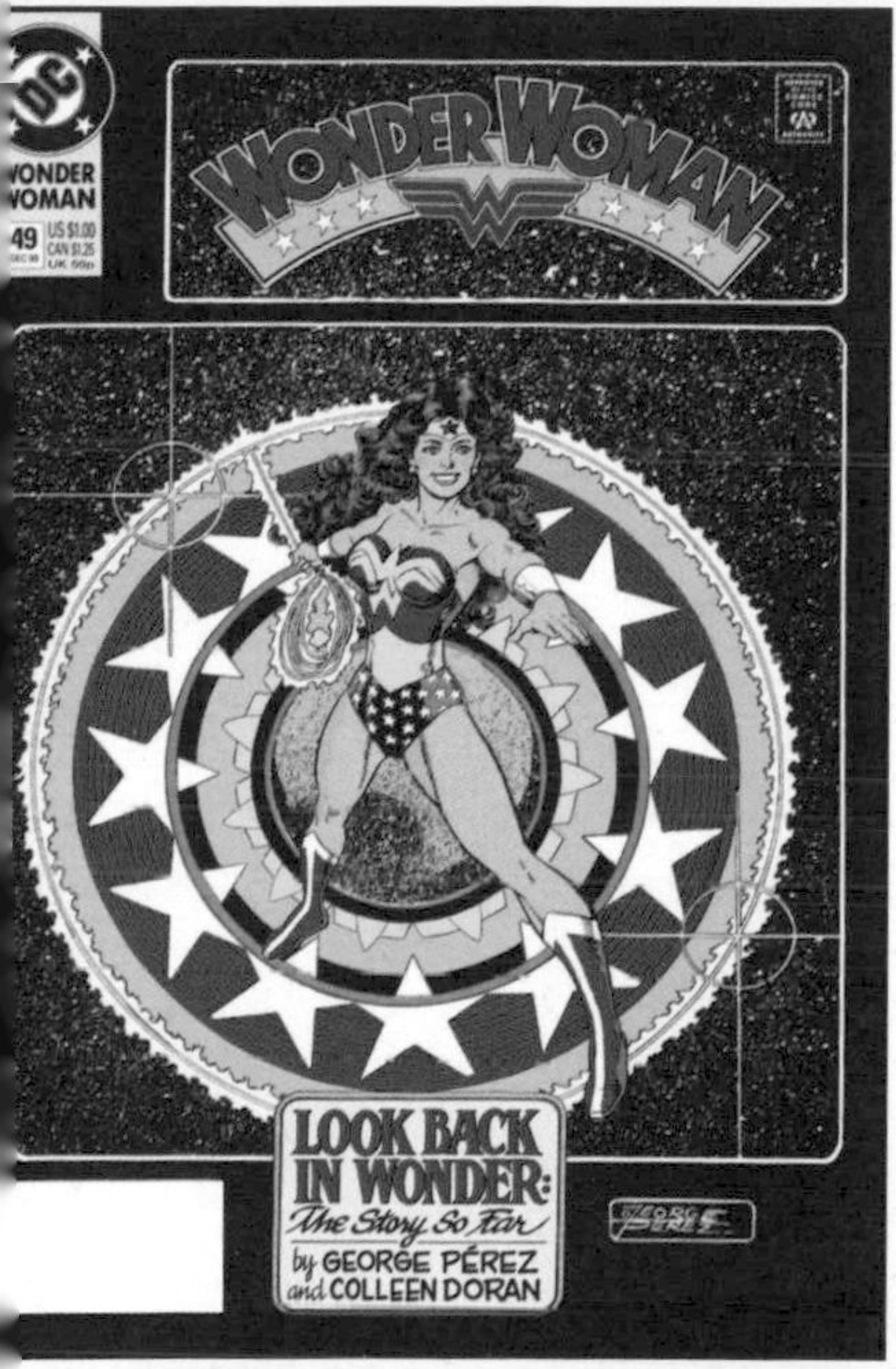
WONDER WOMAN
49
US $1.00
CAN $1.25
WONDER WOMAN
LOOK BACK IN WONDER:
The Story So Far
by GEORGE PÉREZ
and COLLEEN DORAN

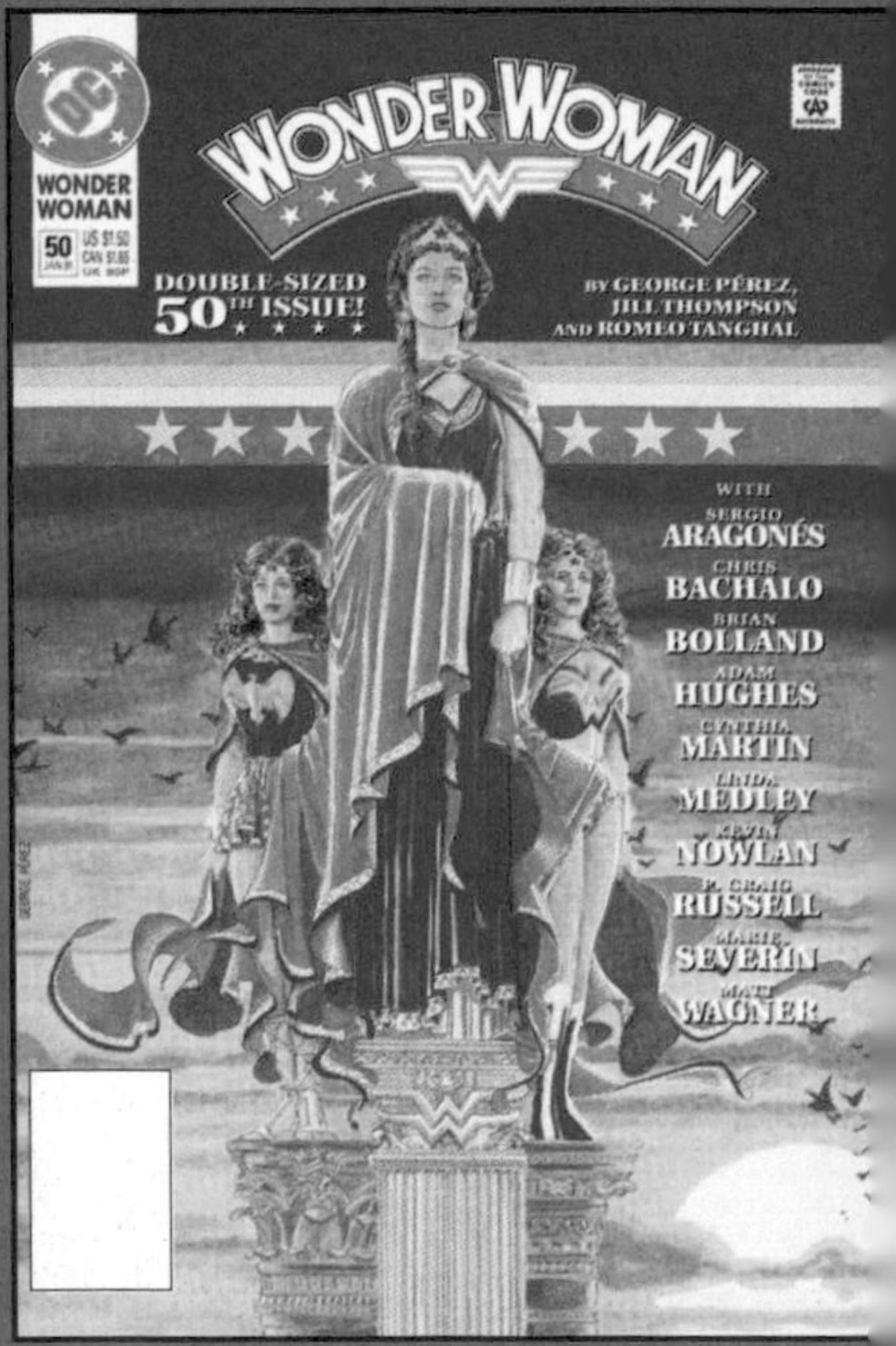
WONDER WOMAN
50
US $1.50
CAN $1.85
WONDER WOMAN
DOUBLE-SIZED 50TH ISSUE!
BY GEORGE PÉREZ, JILL THOMPSON AND ROMEO TANGHAL
WITH
SERGIO ARAGONÉS
CHRIS BACHALO
BRIAN BOLLAND
ADAM HUGHES
CYNTHIA MARTIN
LINDA MEDLEY
KEVIN NOWLAN
R. CRAIG RUSSELL
MARIE SEVERIN
MATT WAGNER

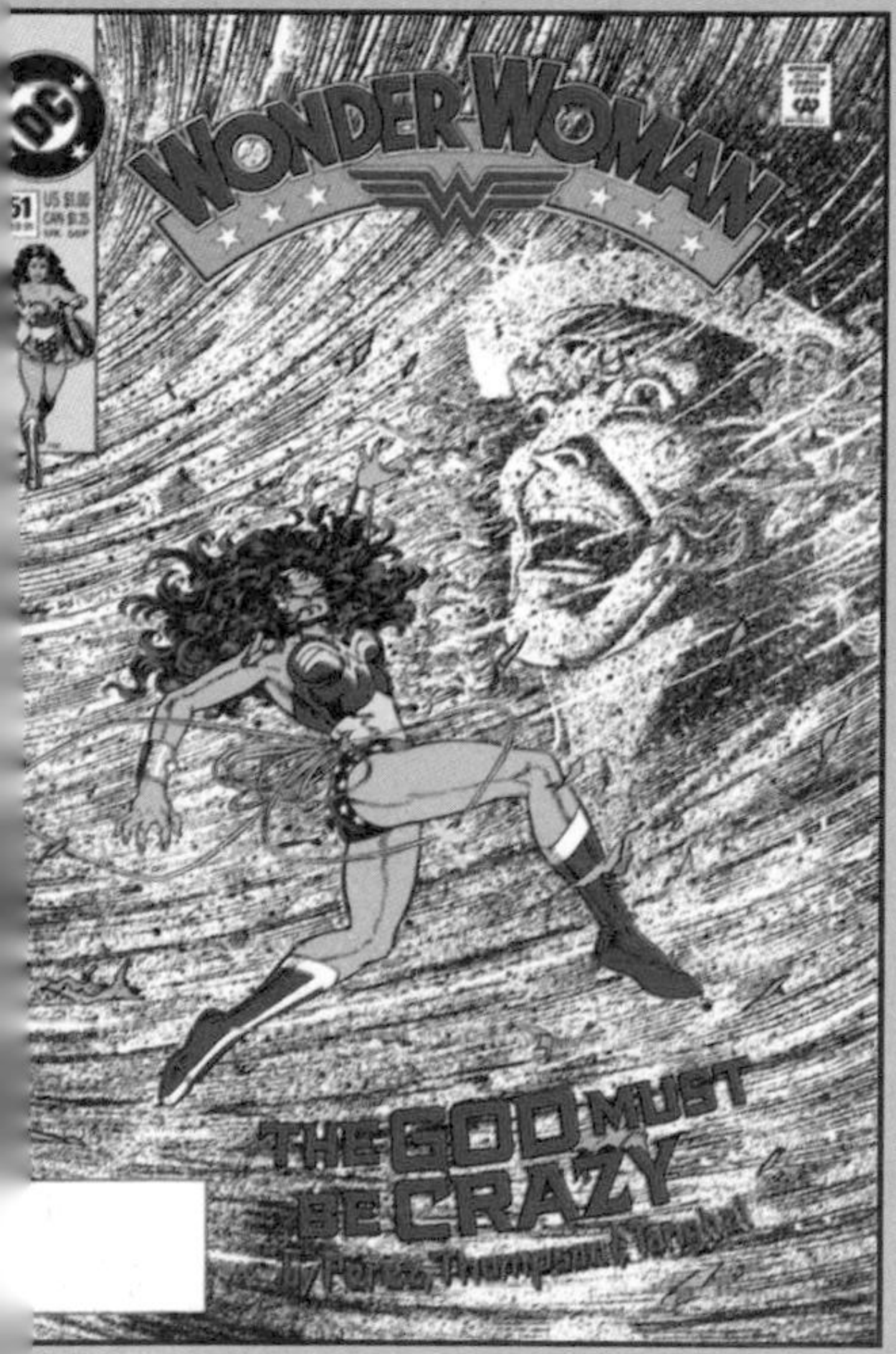
WONDER WOMAN
51
US $1.00
CAN $1.25
THE GOD MUST BE CRAZY

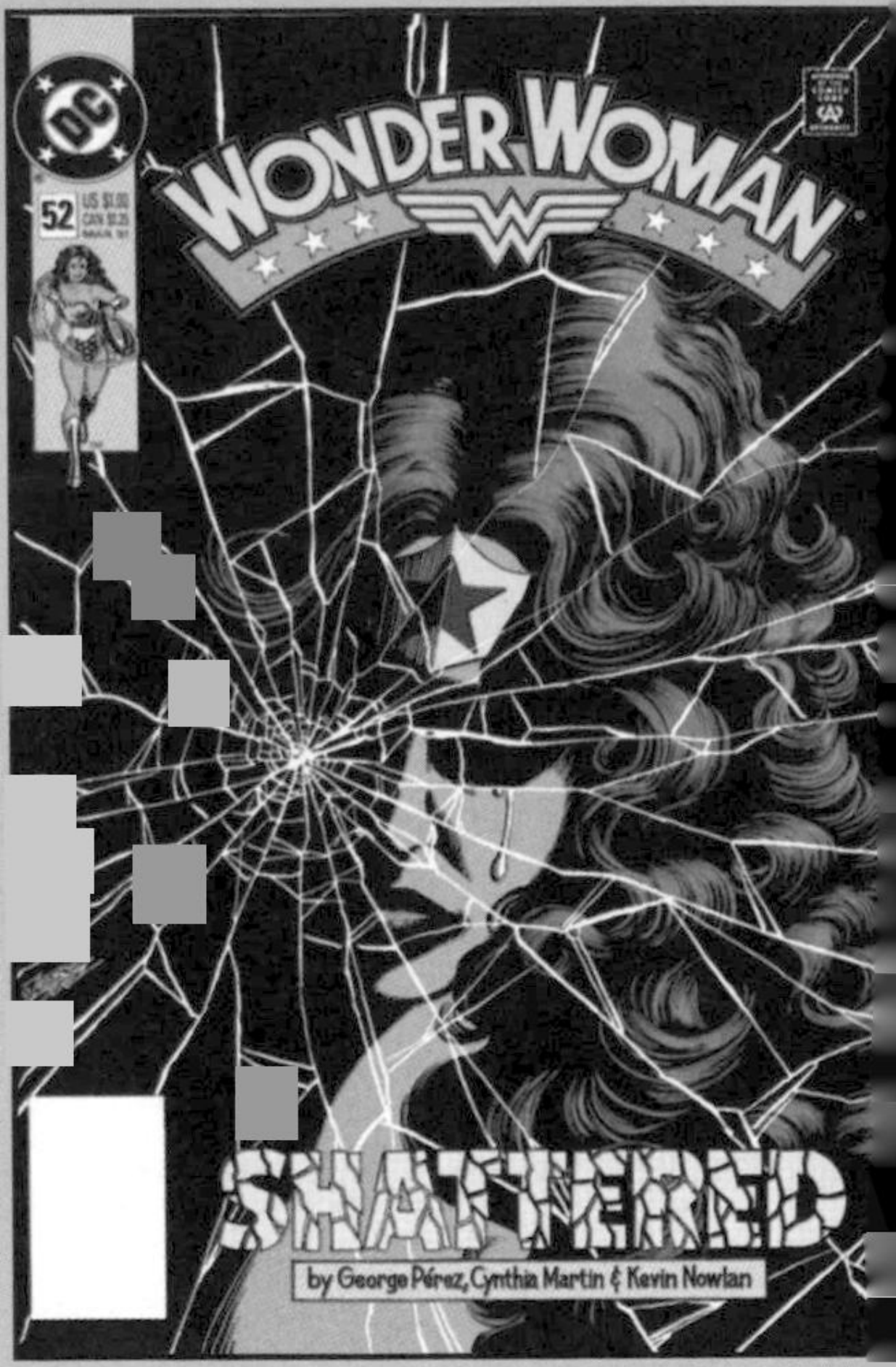
DC
52
US $1.00
WONDER WOMAN
SHATTERED
by George Pérez, Cynthia Martin & Kevin Nowlan

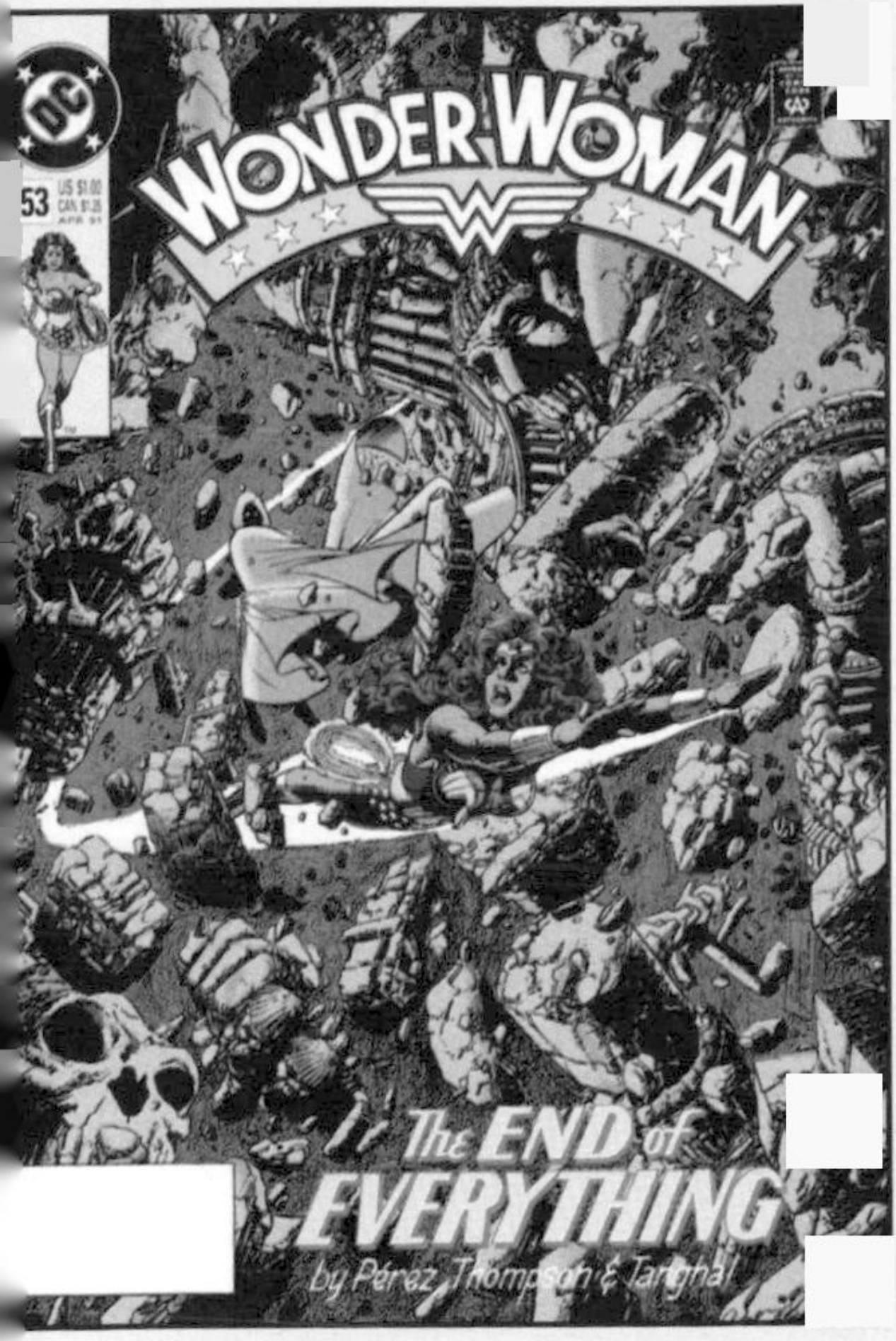
DC
53
US $1.00
CAN $1.25
WONDER WOMAN
The END of EVERYTHING
by Pérez, Thompson & Tanghal

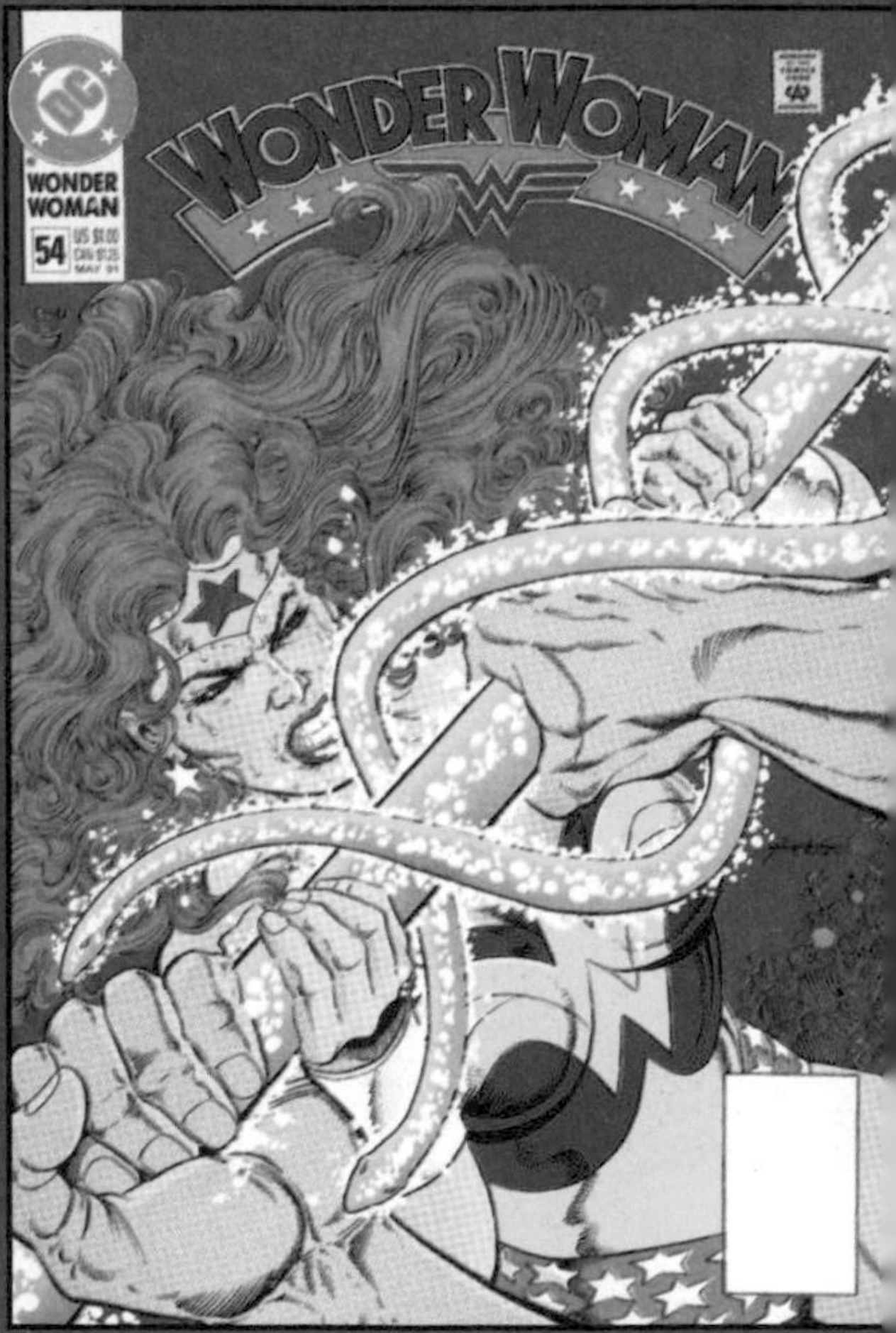
WONDER WOMAN
WONDER WOMAN
54

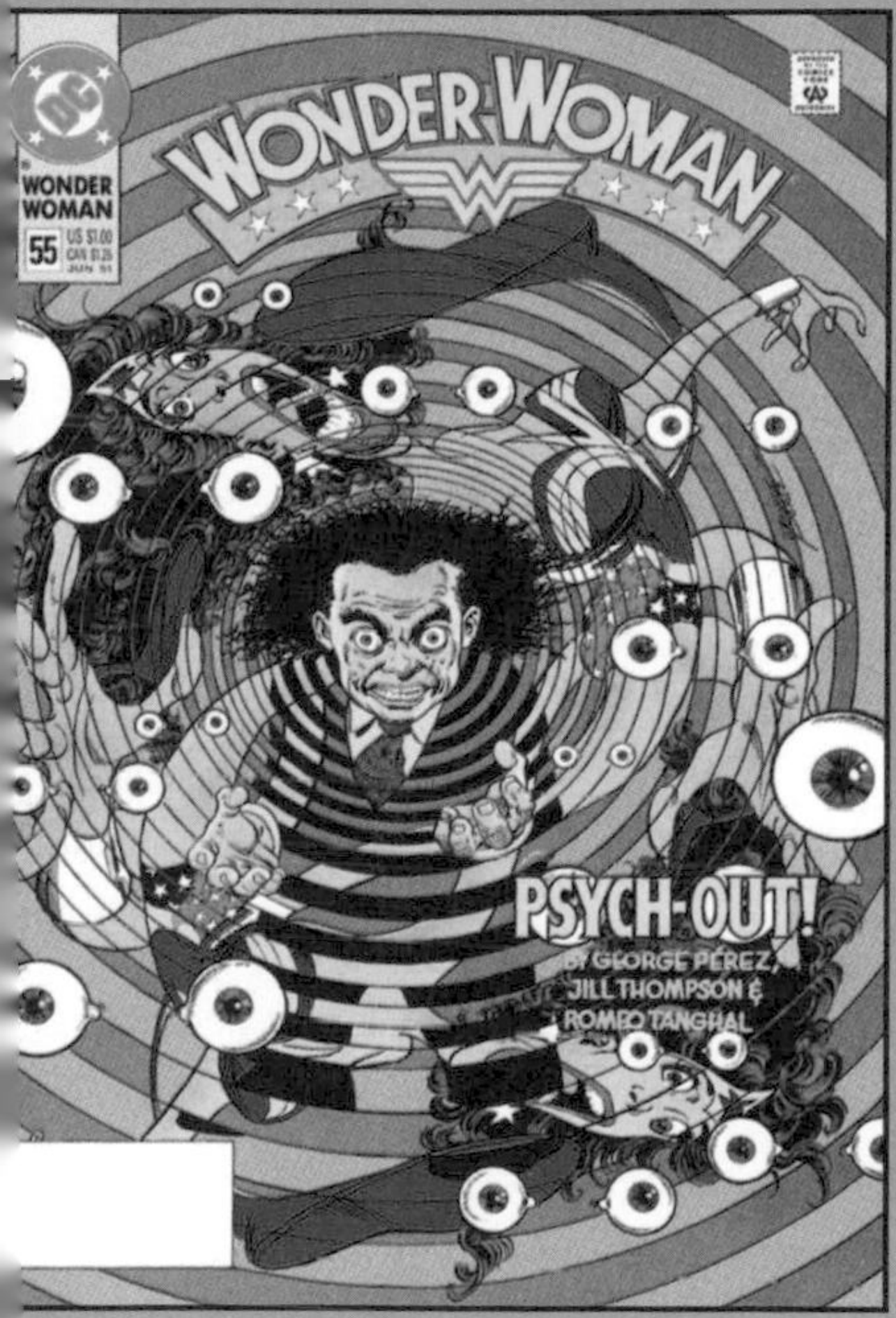
WONDER WOMAN
WONDER WOMAN
55
US $1.00
CAN $1.25
PSYCH-OUT!
BY GEORGE PÉREZ, JILL THOMPSON & ROMEO TANGHAL

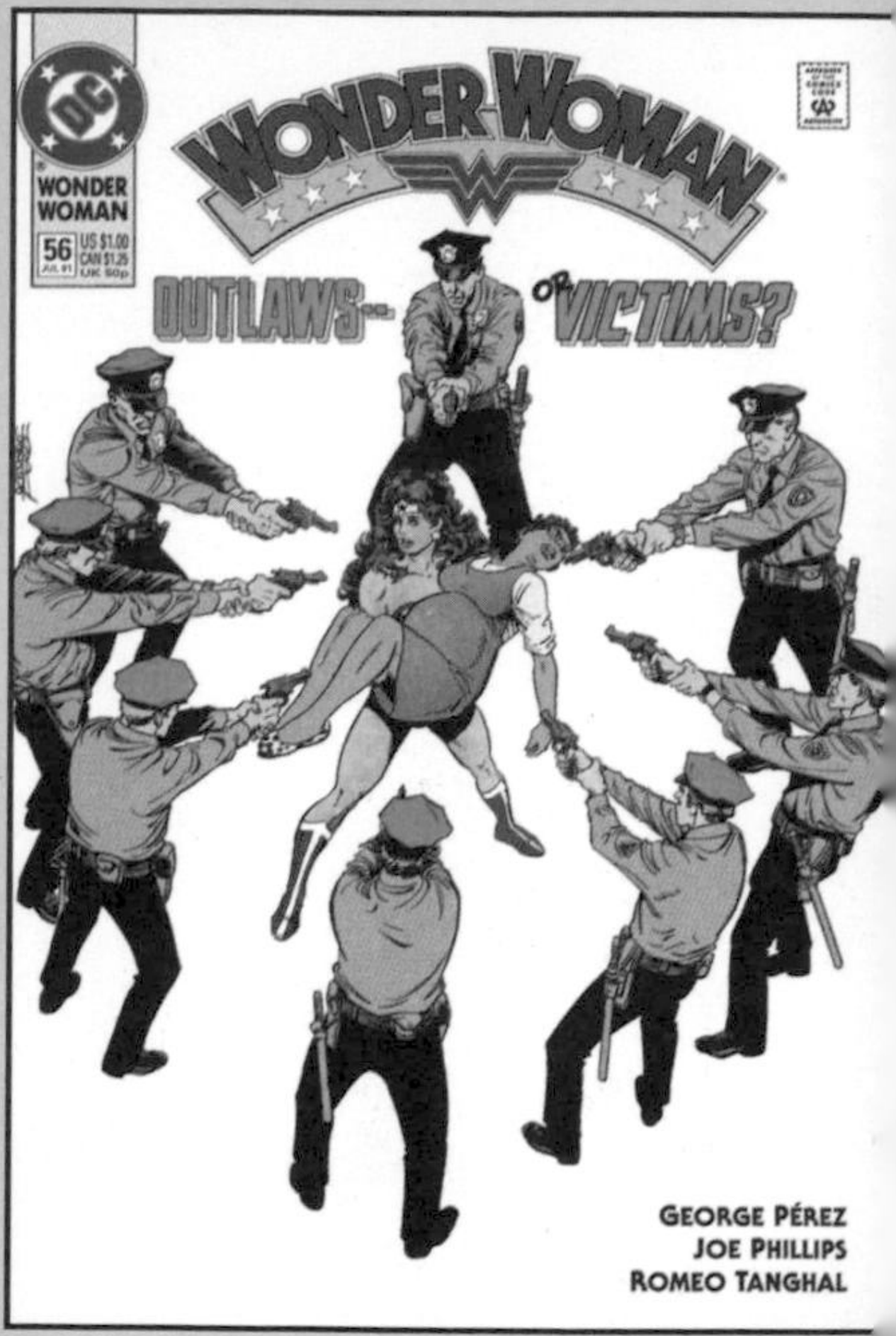
WONDER WOMAN
56
JUL 91
US $1.00
CAN $1.25
UK 60p
WONDER WOMAN
OUTLAWS— OR VICTIMS?
GEORGE PÉREZ
JOE PHILLIPS
ROMEO TANGHAL

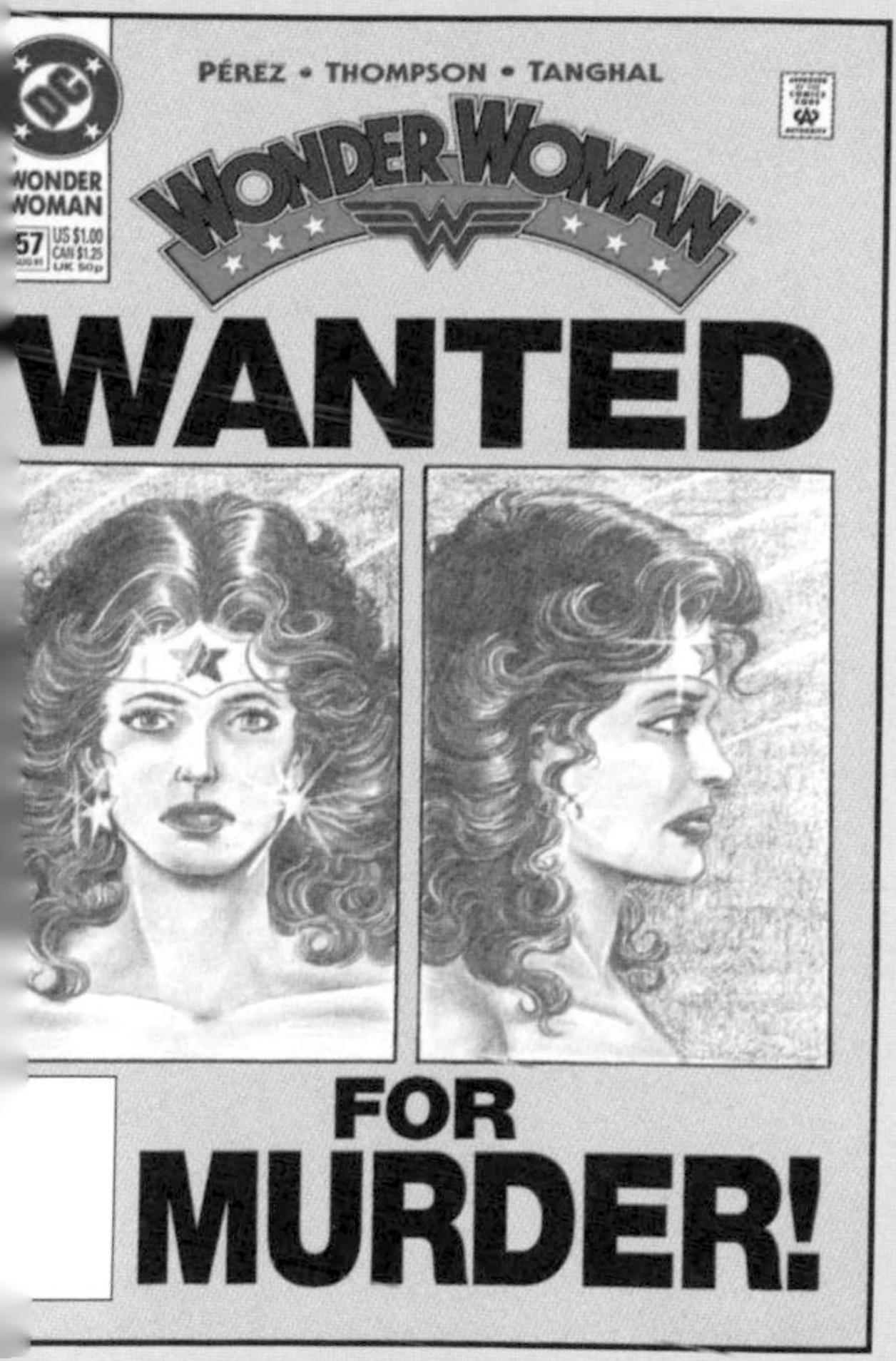
PÉREZ • THOMPSON • TANGHAL
WONDER WOMAN
57
US $1.00
CAN $1.25
UK 50p
WONDER WOMAN
WANTED
FOR
MURDER!

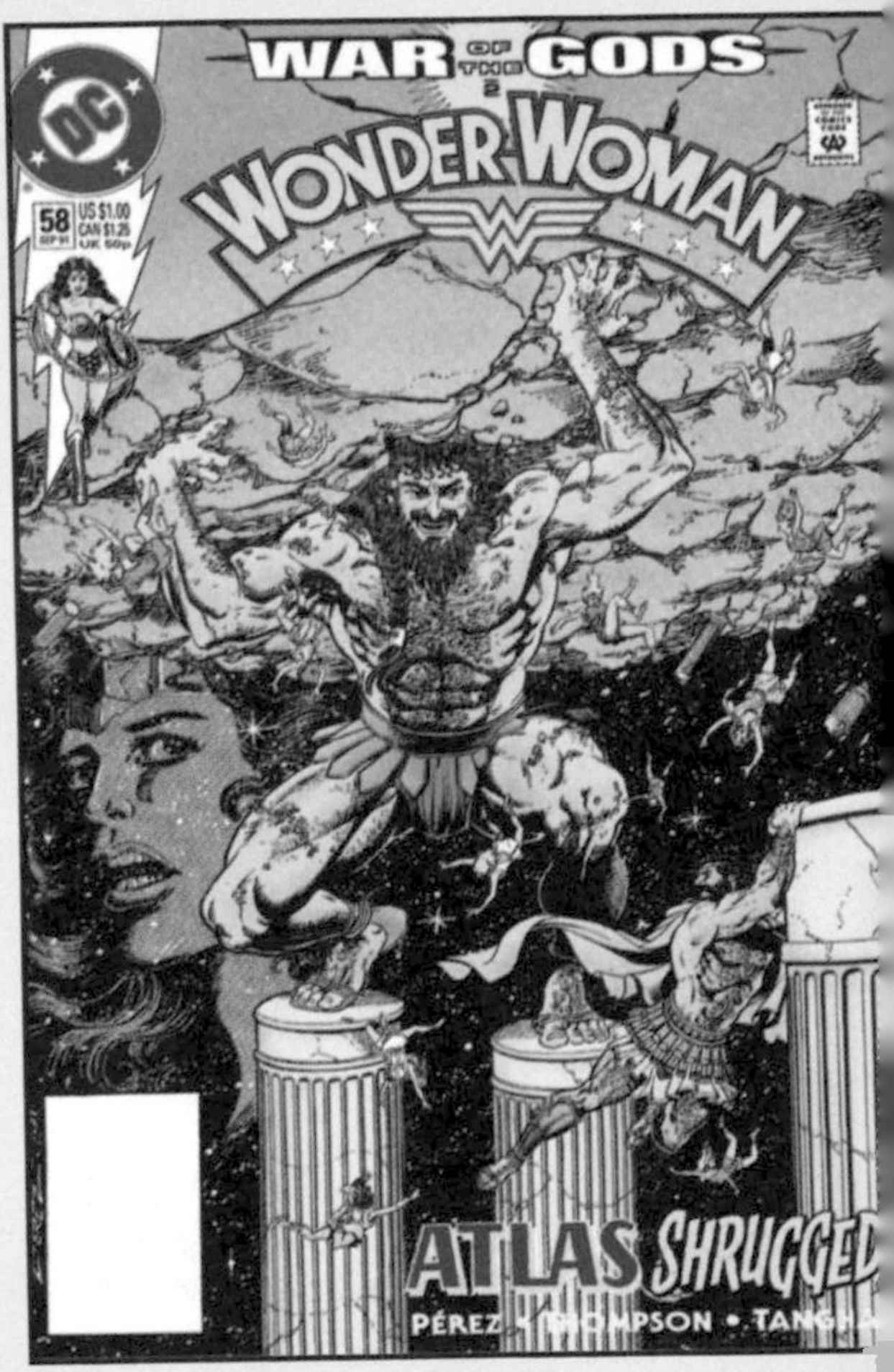
WAR OF THE GODS
2
DC
WONDER WOMAN
58
US $1.00
CAN $1.25
UK 60p
ATLAS SHRUGGED
PÉREZ • THOMPSON • TANGH

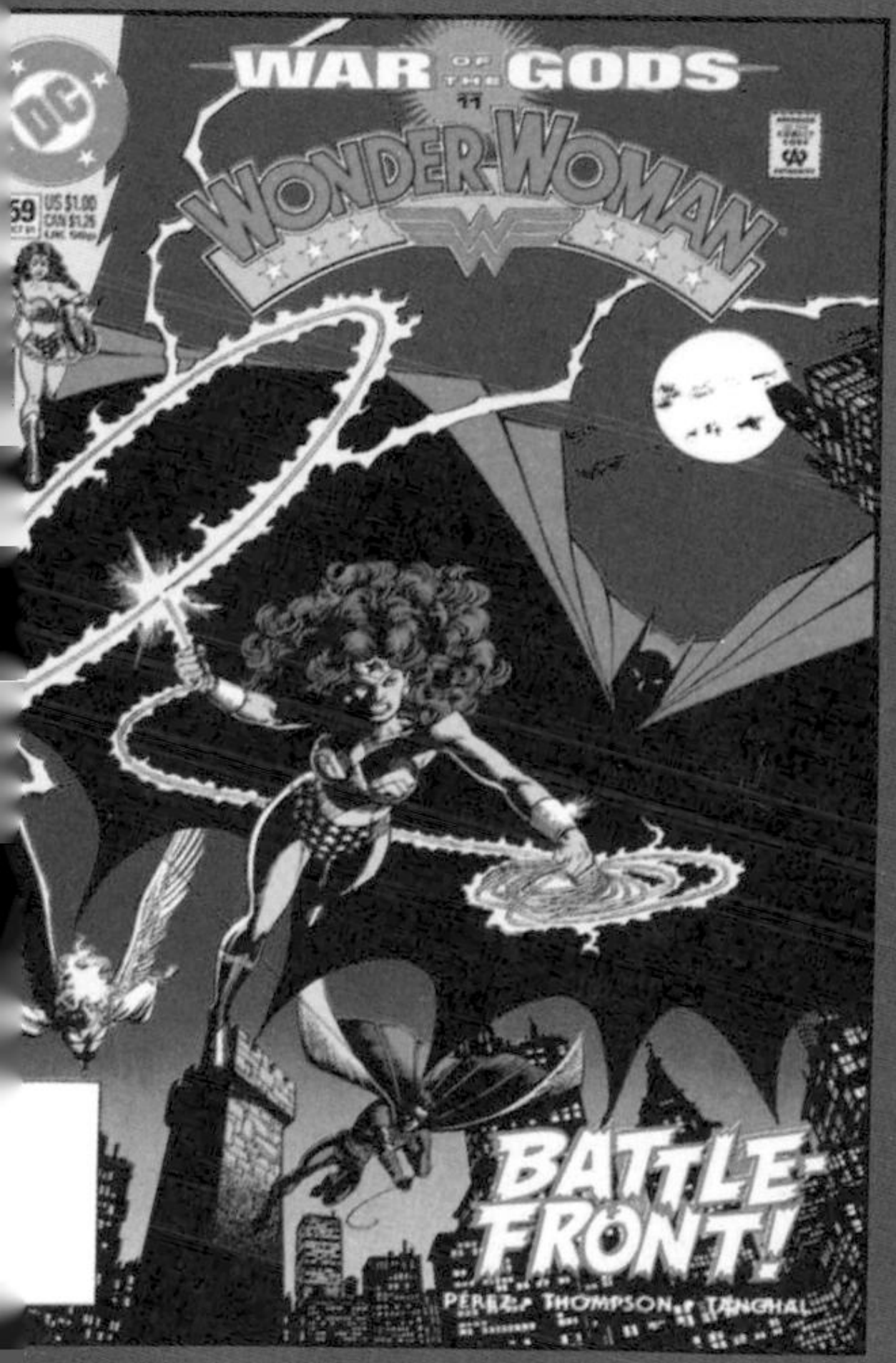
WAR OF THE GODS
WONDER WOMAN
59
US $1.00
CAN $1.25
BATTLE-FRONT!
PEREZ, THOMPSON, TANGHAL

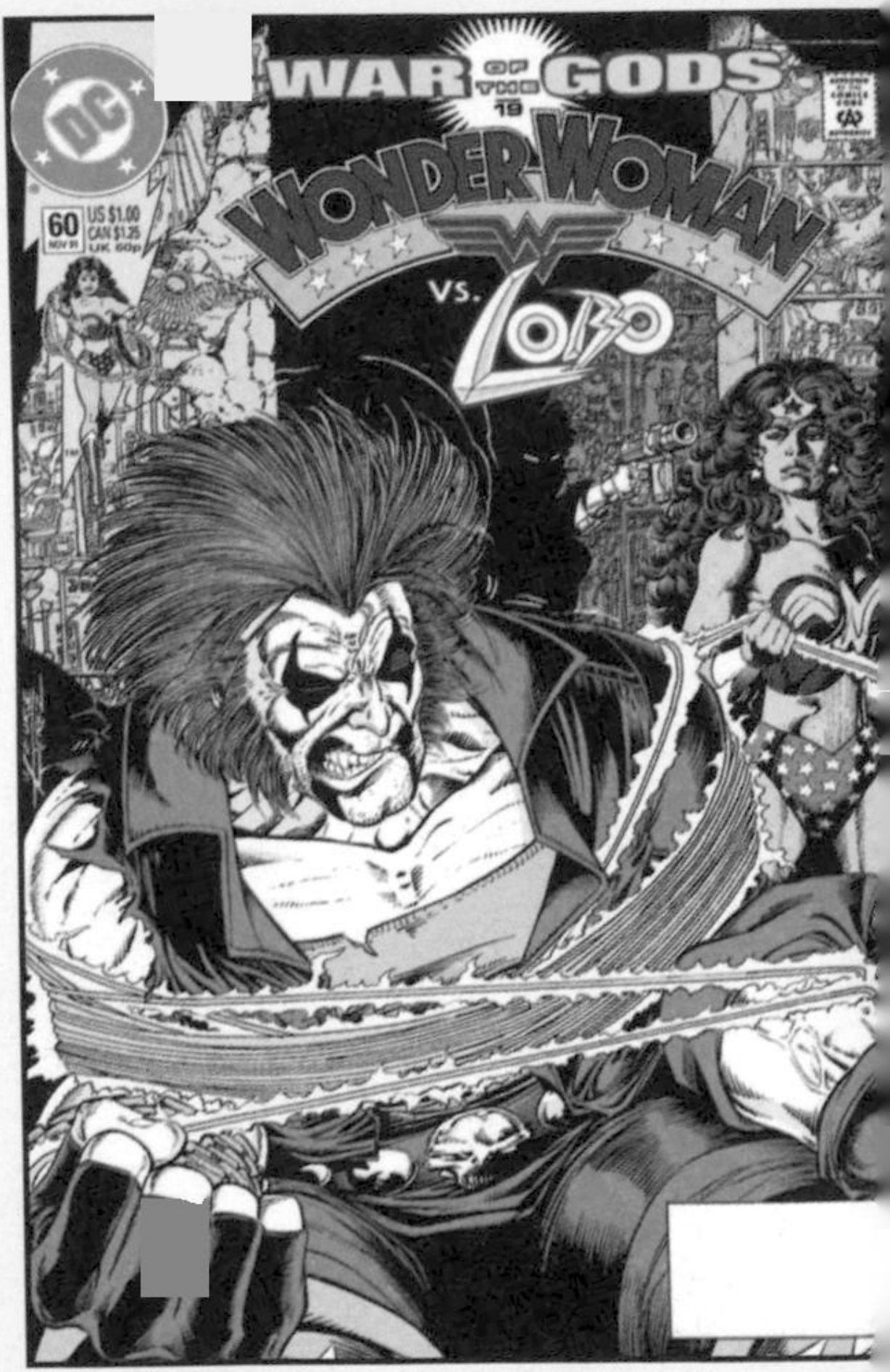
WAR OF THE GODS
19
WONDER WOMAN
VS.
LOBO
60
NOV 91
US $1.00
CAN $1.25
UK 60p

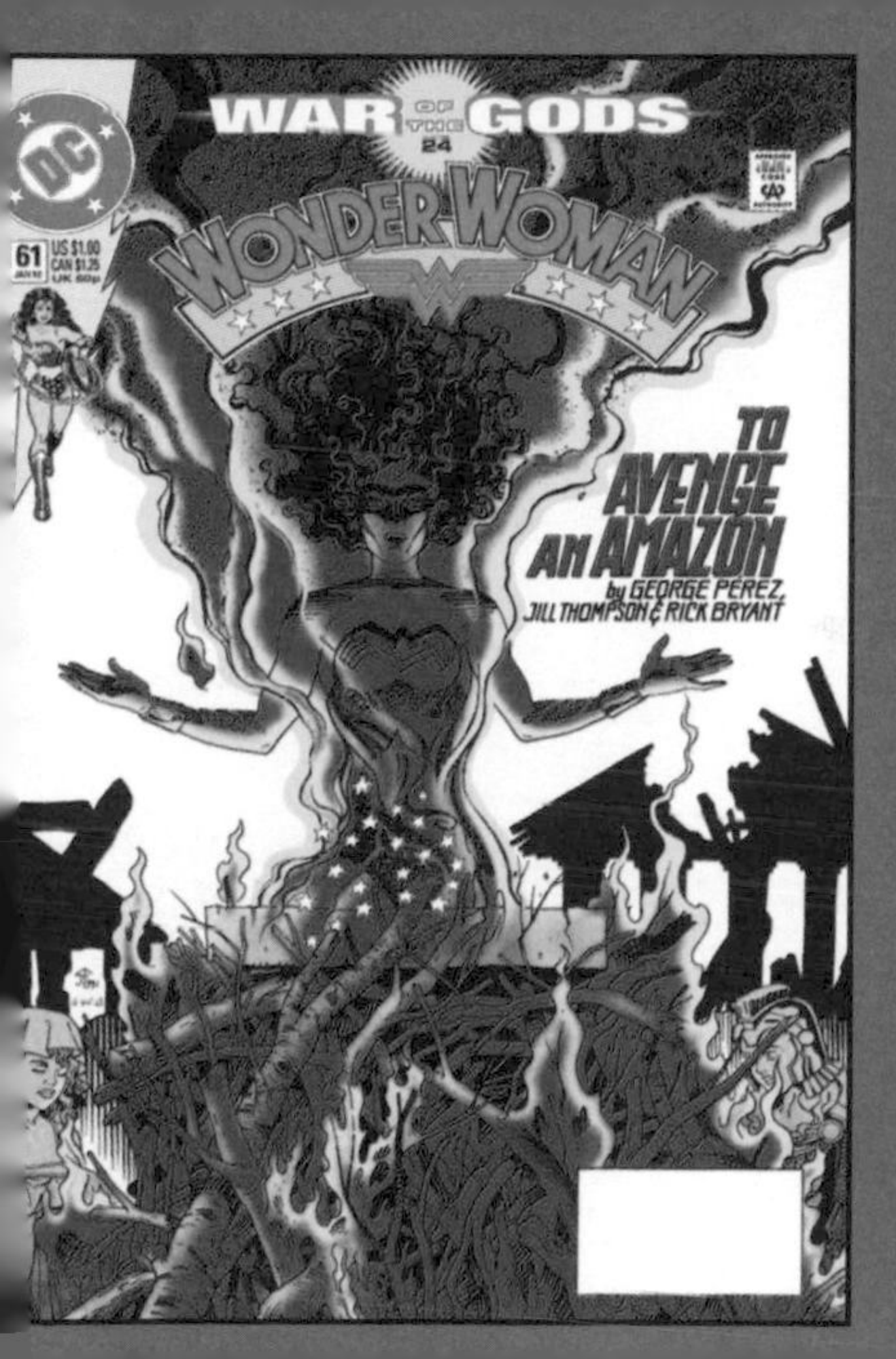
WAR OF THE GODS
24
DC
61
US $1.00
CAN $1.25
WONDER WOMAN
TO AVENGE AN AMAZON
by GEORGE PEREZ, JILL THOMPSON & RICK BRYANT

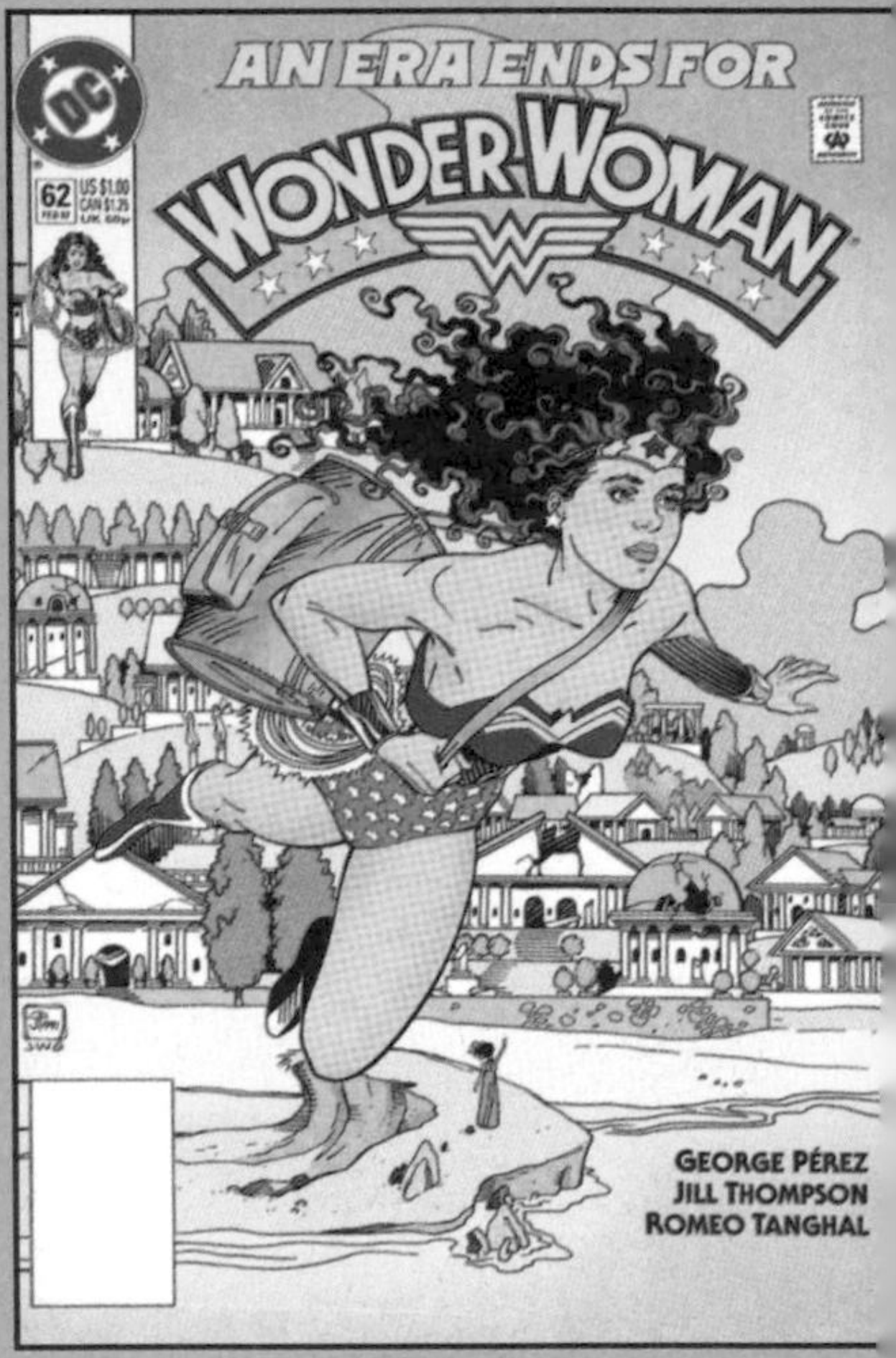
AN ERA ENDS FOR
WONDER WOMAN
62
US $1.00
CAN $1.25
GEORGE PÉREZ
JILL THOMPSON
ROMEO TANGHAL

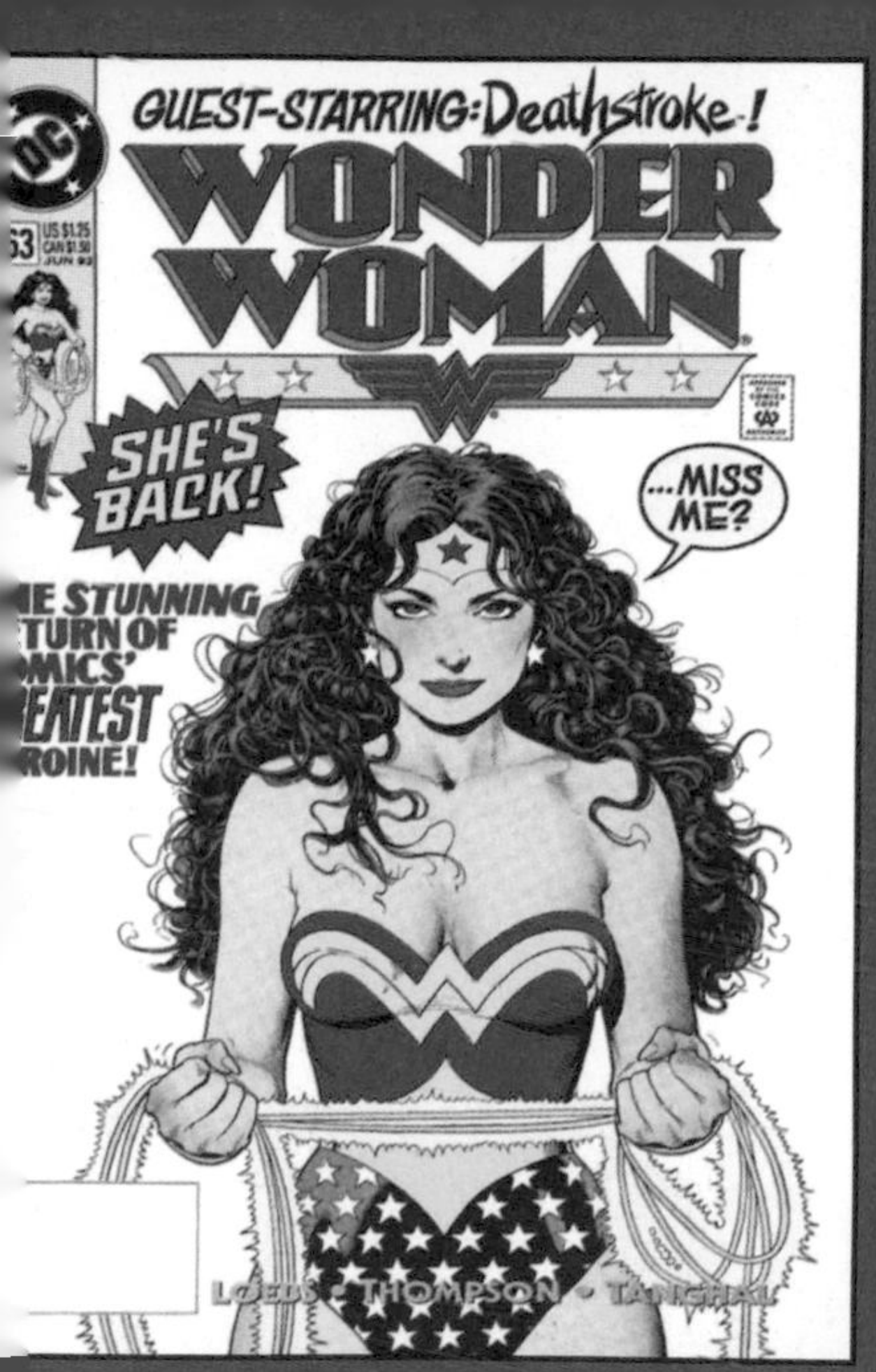
GUEST-STARRING: Deathstroke-!
WONDER WOMAN
63
US $1.25
CAN $1.50
JUN 93
SHE'S BACK!
...MISS ME?
E STUNNING
TURN OF
MICS'
EATEST
ROINE!
LOEBS • THOMPSON • TANIGUCHI

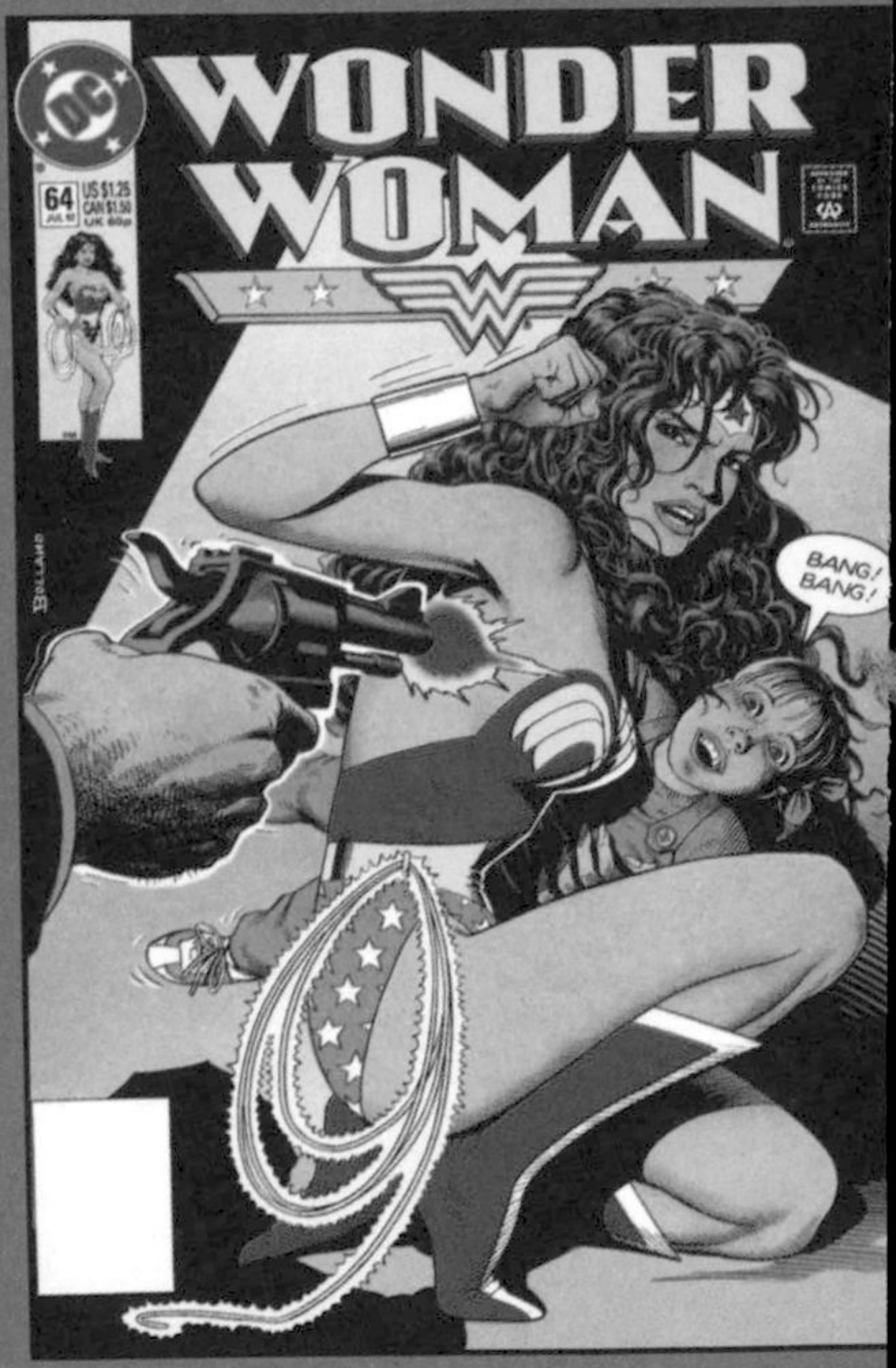
DC
WONDER WOMAN
64
JUL 92
US $1.25
CAN $1.50
U.K. 60p
BANG! BANG!

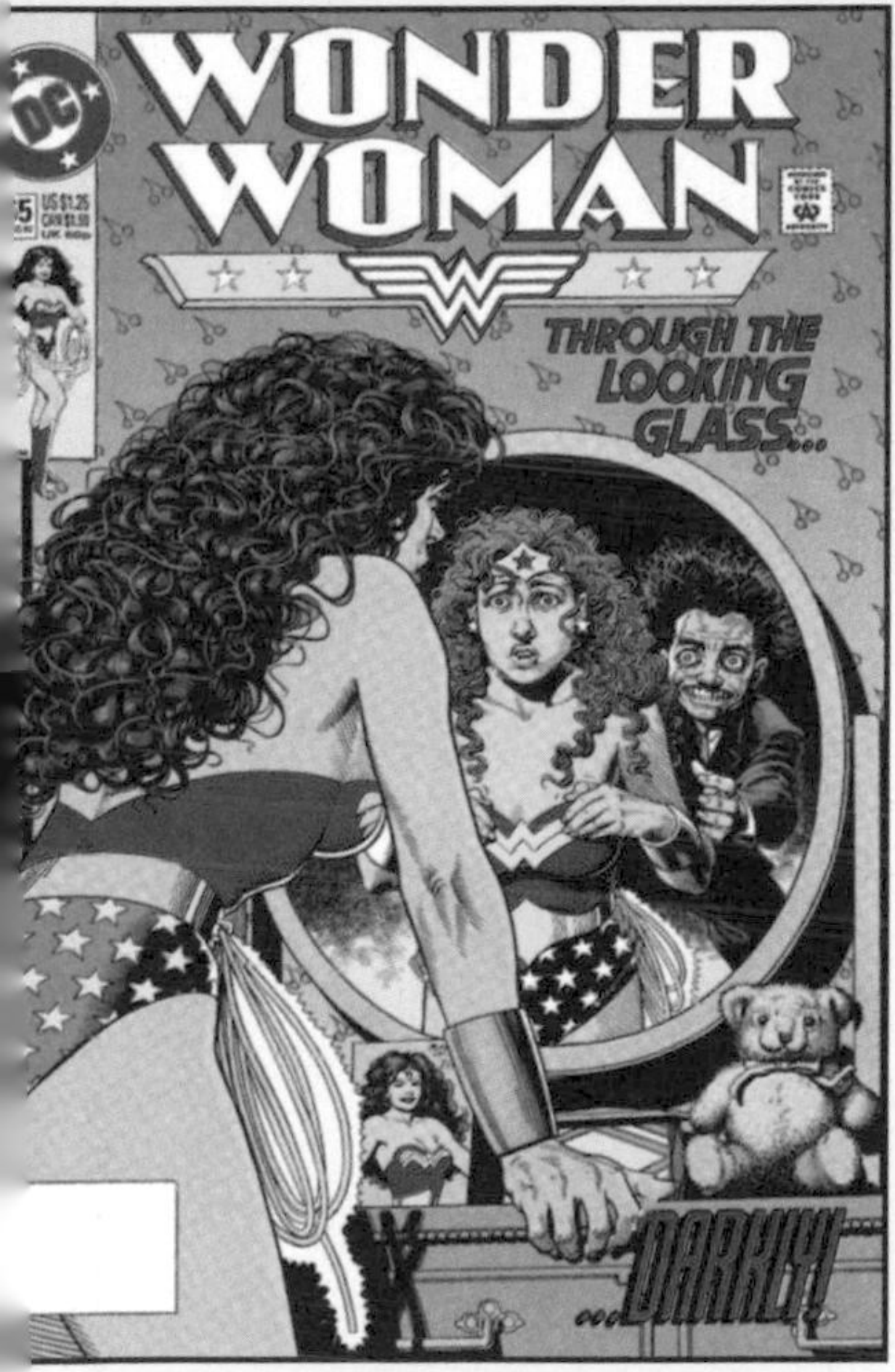
WONDER WOMAN
THROUGH THE LOOKING GLASS...
...DARKLY!

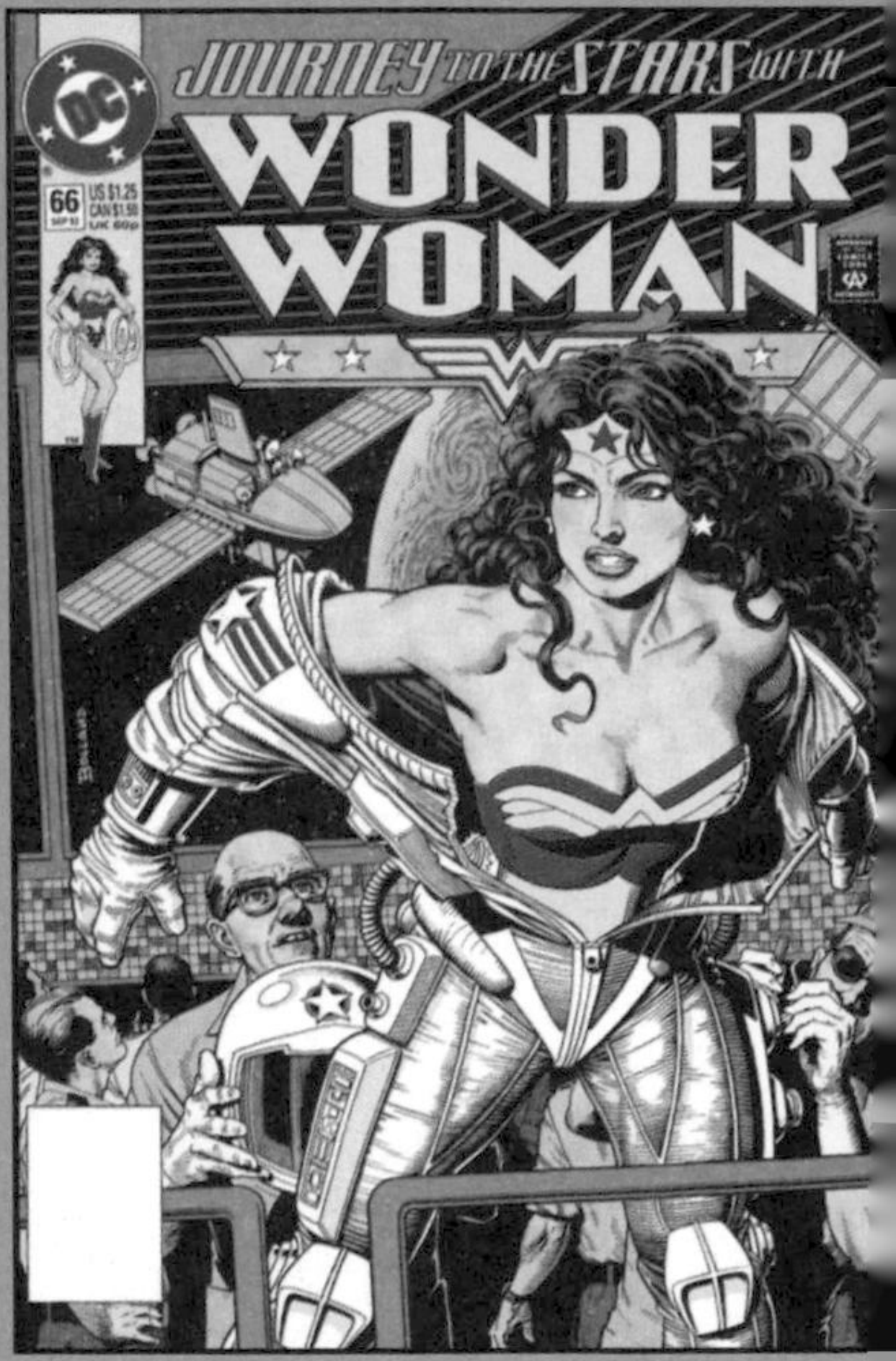
JOURNEY TO THE STARS WITH
WONDER WOMAN
DC
66
US $1.25
CAN $1.50
U.K. 60p

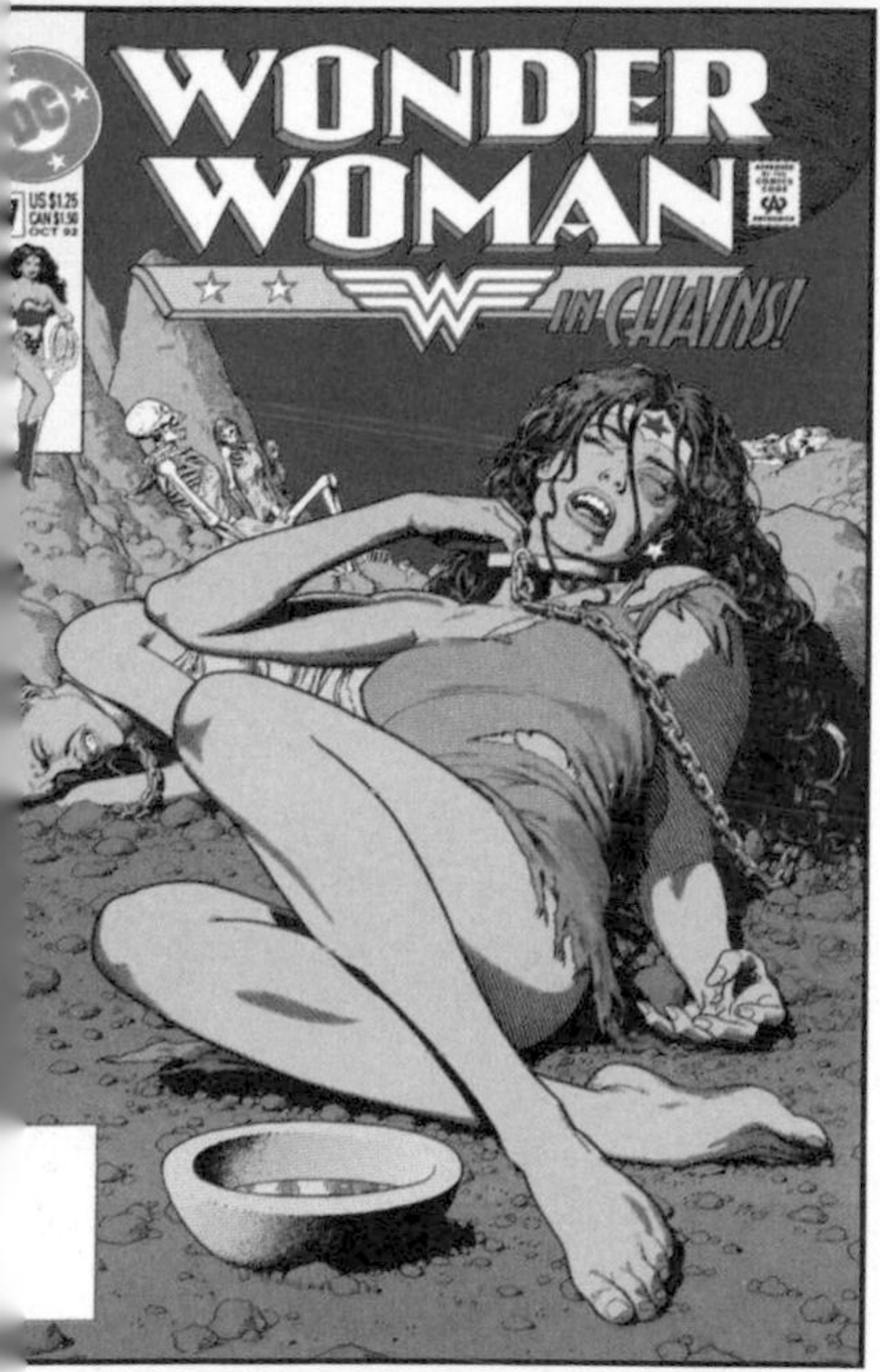
DC
WONDER WOMAN
IN CHAINS!
US $1.25
CAN $1.50
OCT 93

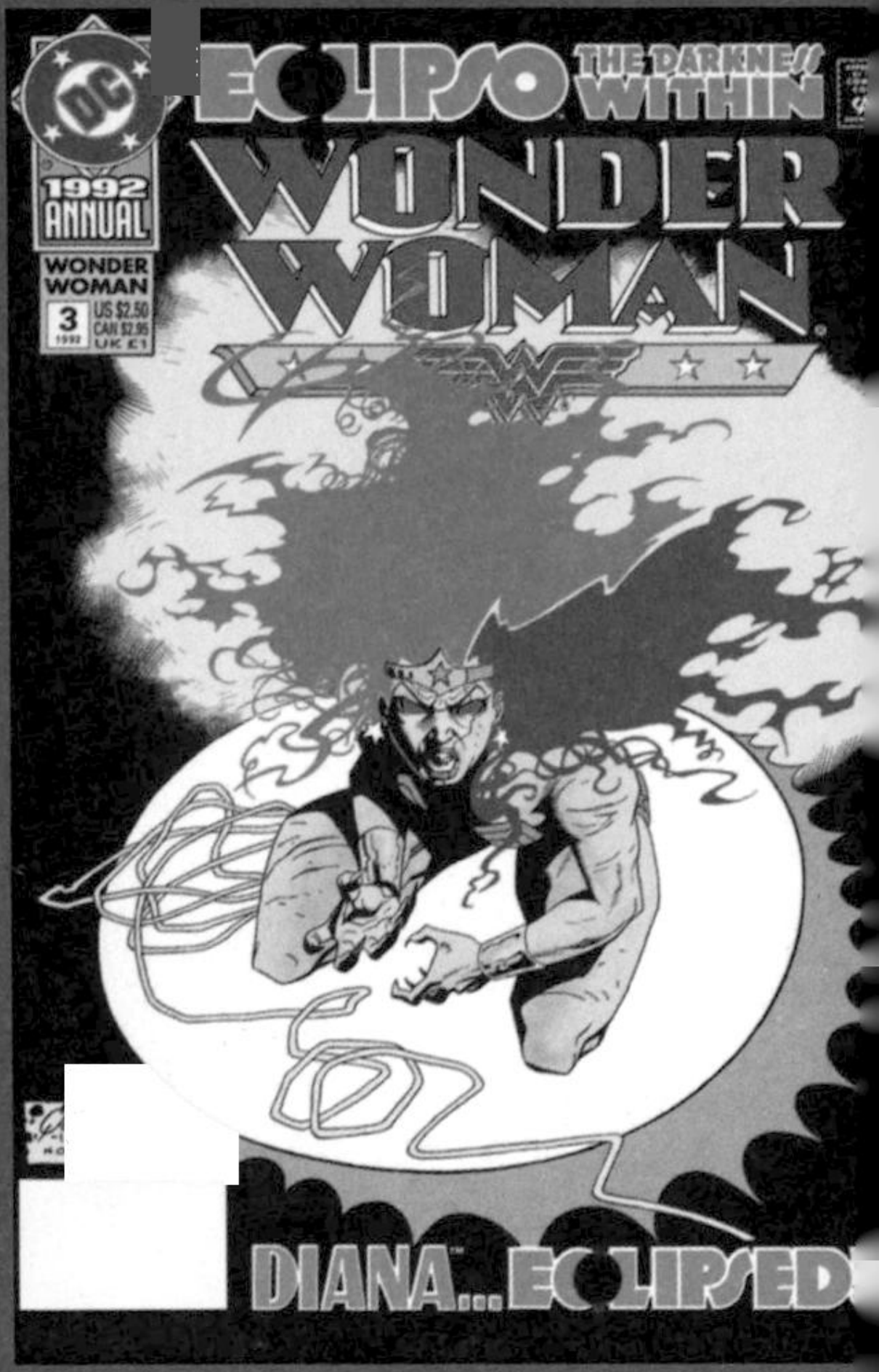
ECLIPSO THE DARKNESS WITHIN
WONDER WOMAN
1992 ANNUAL
WONDER WOMAN
3
1992
US $2.50
CAN $2.95
UK £1
DIANA...ECLIPSED

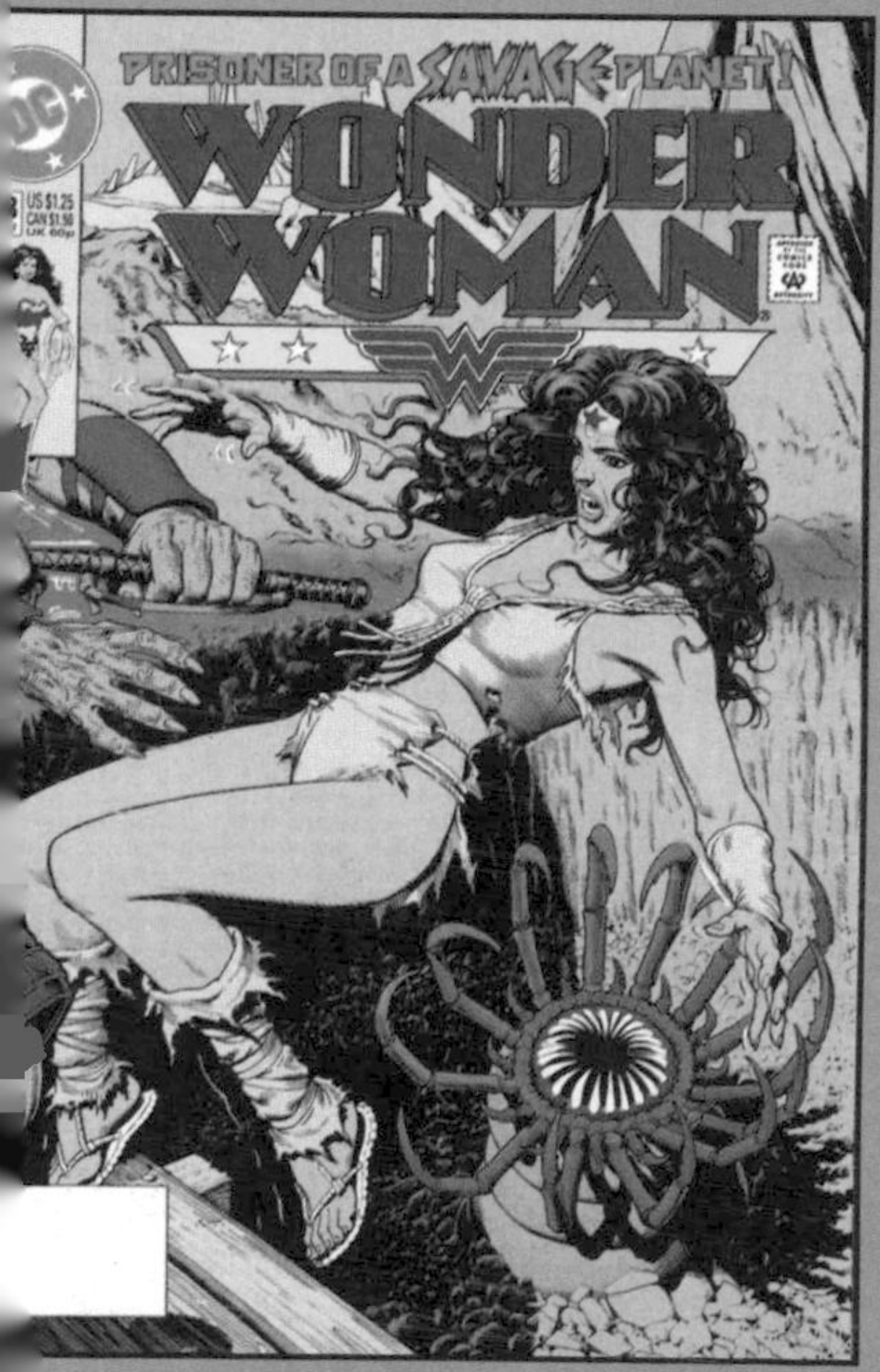
PRISONER OF A SAVAGE PLANET!
WONDER WOMAN
US $1.25
CAN $1.50

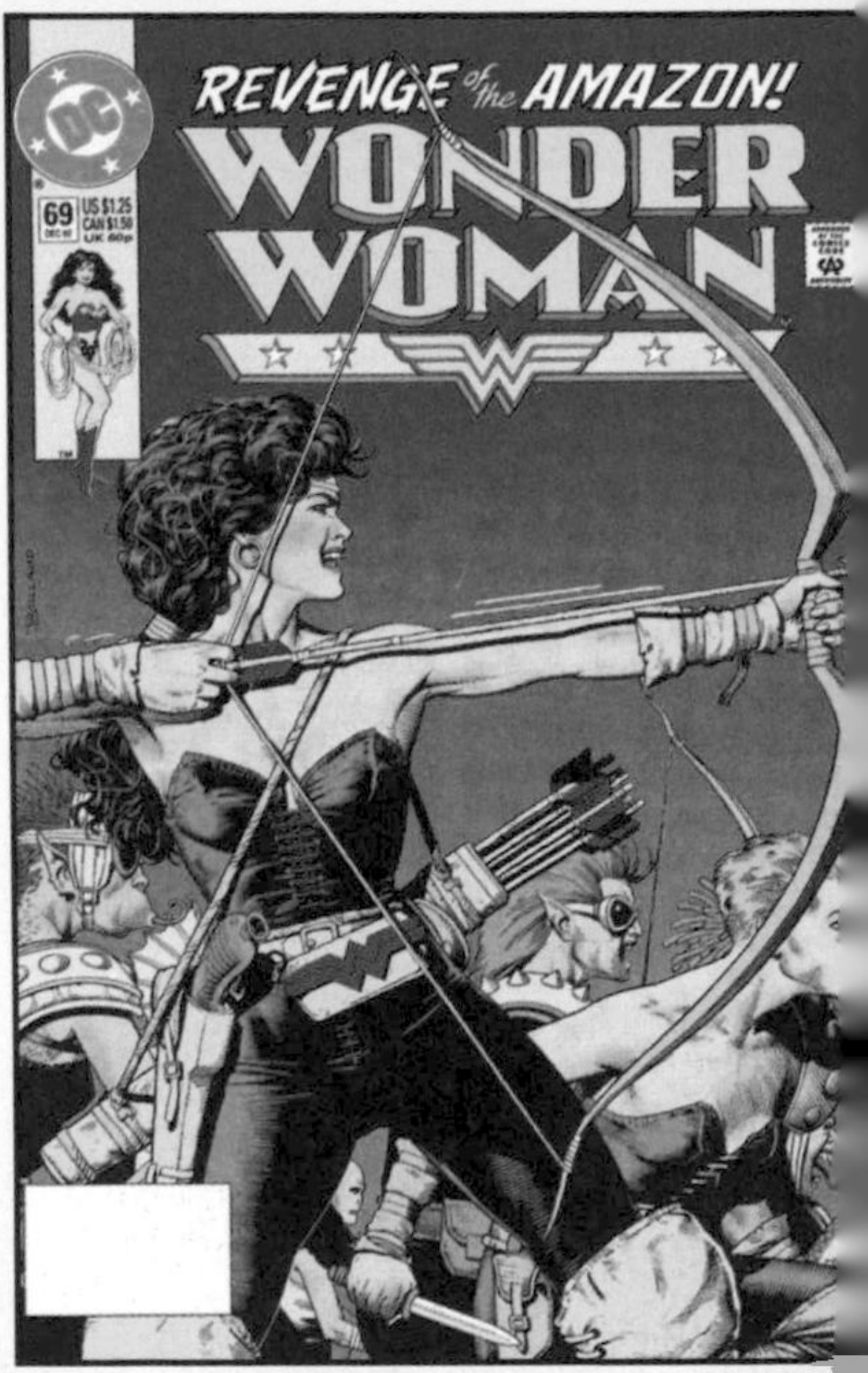
REVENGE of the AMAZON!
WONDER WOMAN
69
US $1.25
CAN $1.50
UK 60p

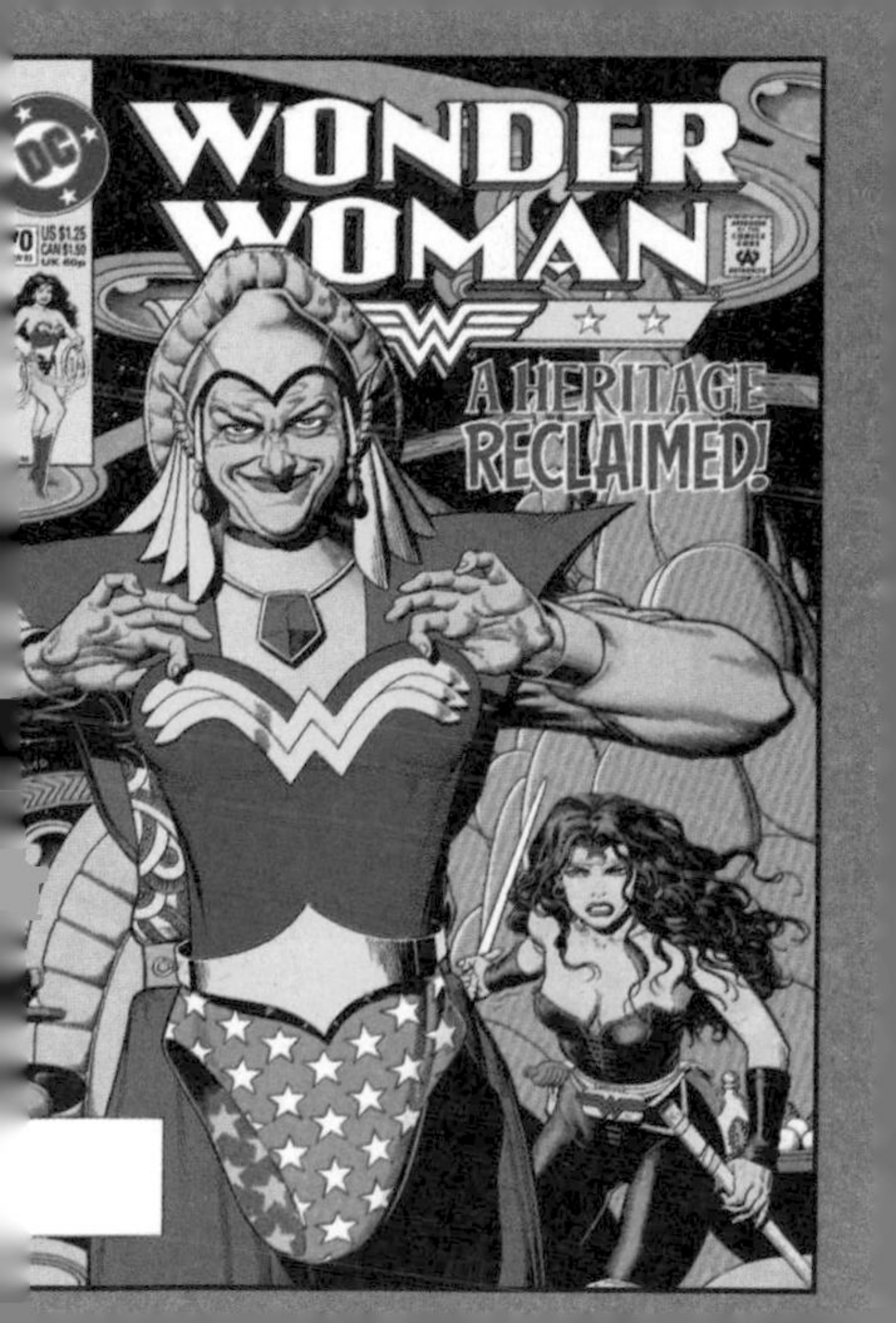
WONDER WOMAN
A HERITAGE RECLAIMED!
US $1.25
CAN $1.50

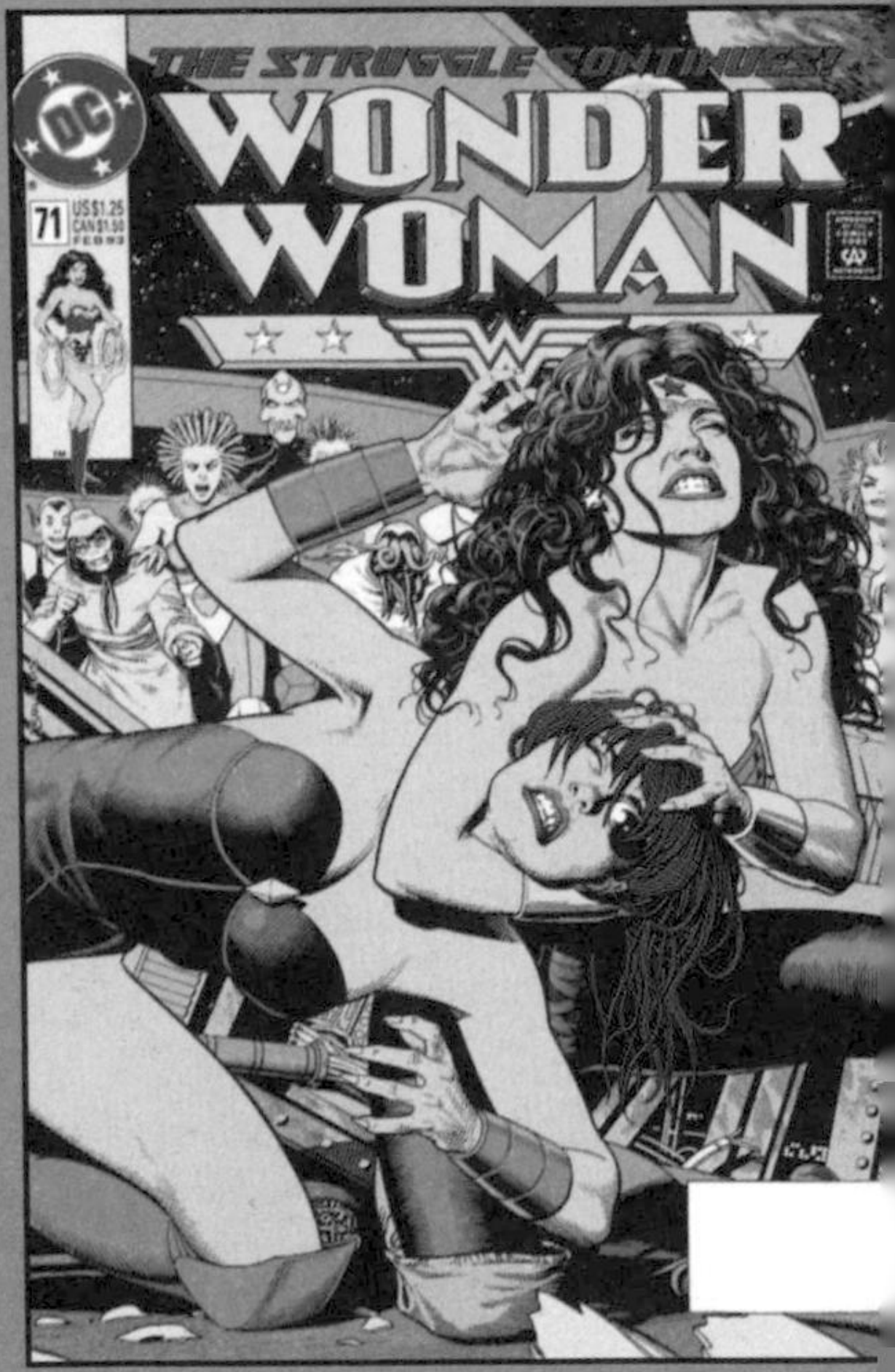
THE STRUGGLE CONTINUES!
DC
WONDER WOMAN
71
US $1.25
CAN $1.50

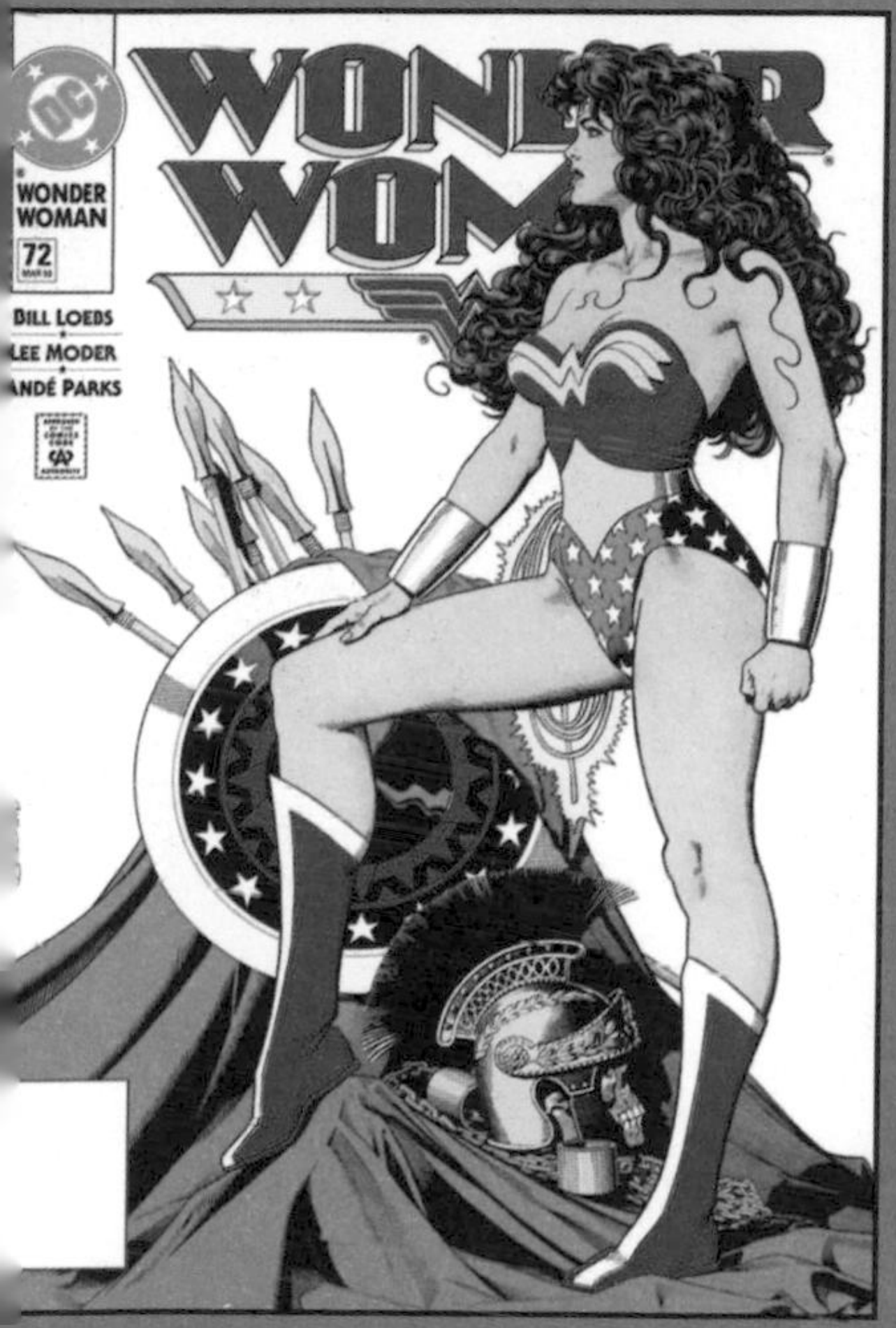
WONDER WOMAN
WONDER WOMAN
72
BILL LOEBS
LEE MODER
ANDÉ PARKS

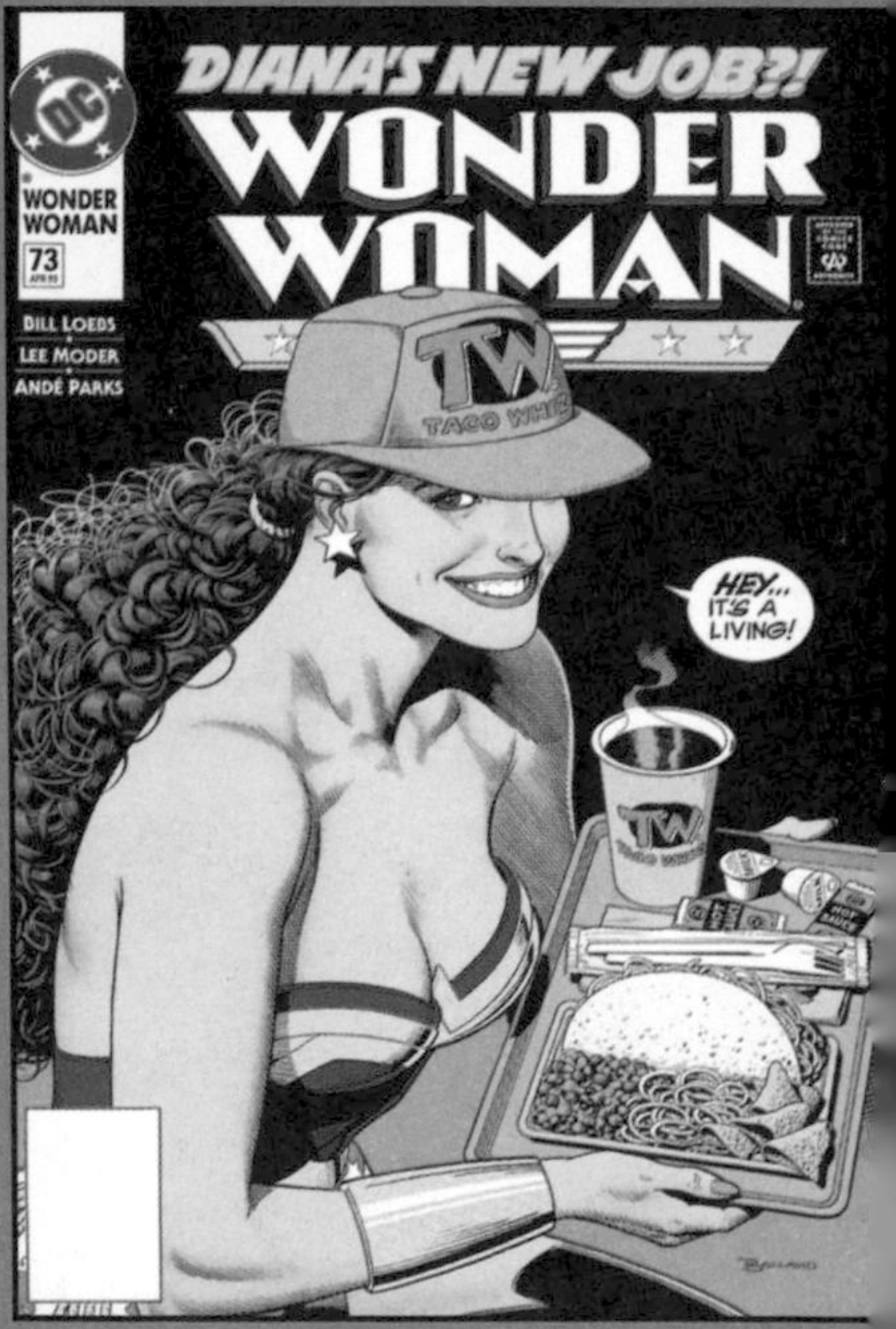
DIANA'S NEW JOB?!
WONDER WOMAN
WONDER WOMAN
73
BILL LOEBS
LEE MODER
ANDÉ PARKS
TW
TACO WHIZ
HEY... IT'S A LIVING!

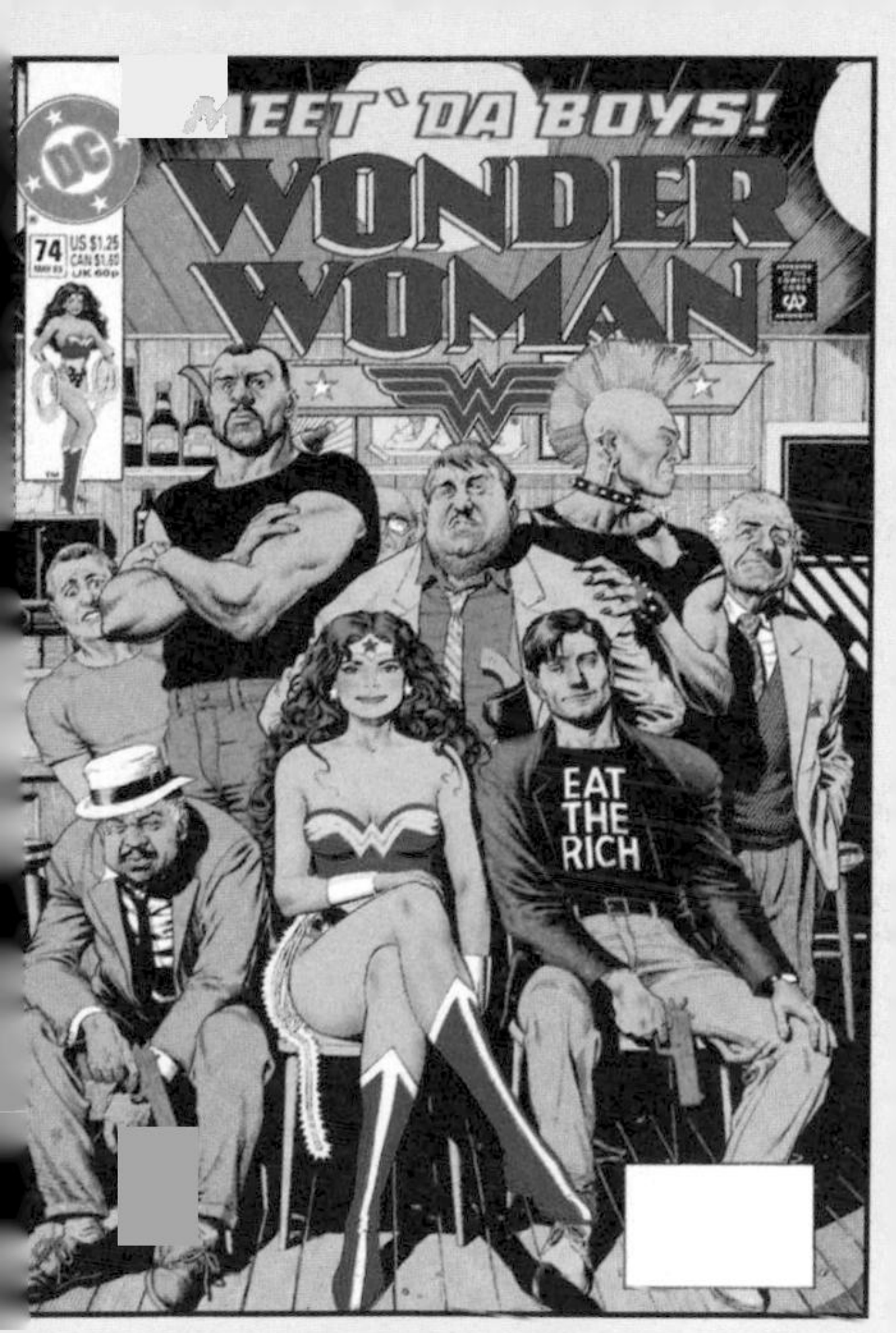
MEET 'DA BOYS!
WONDER WOMAN
DC
74
US $1.25
CAN $1.60
UK 60p
EAT THE RICH

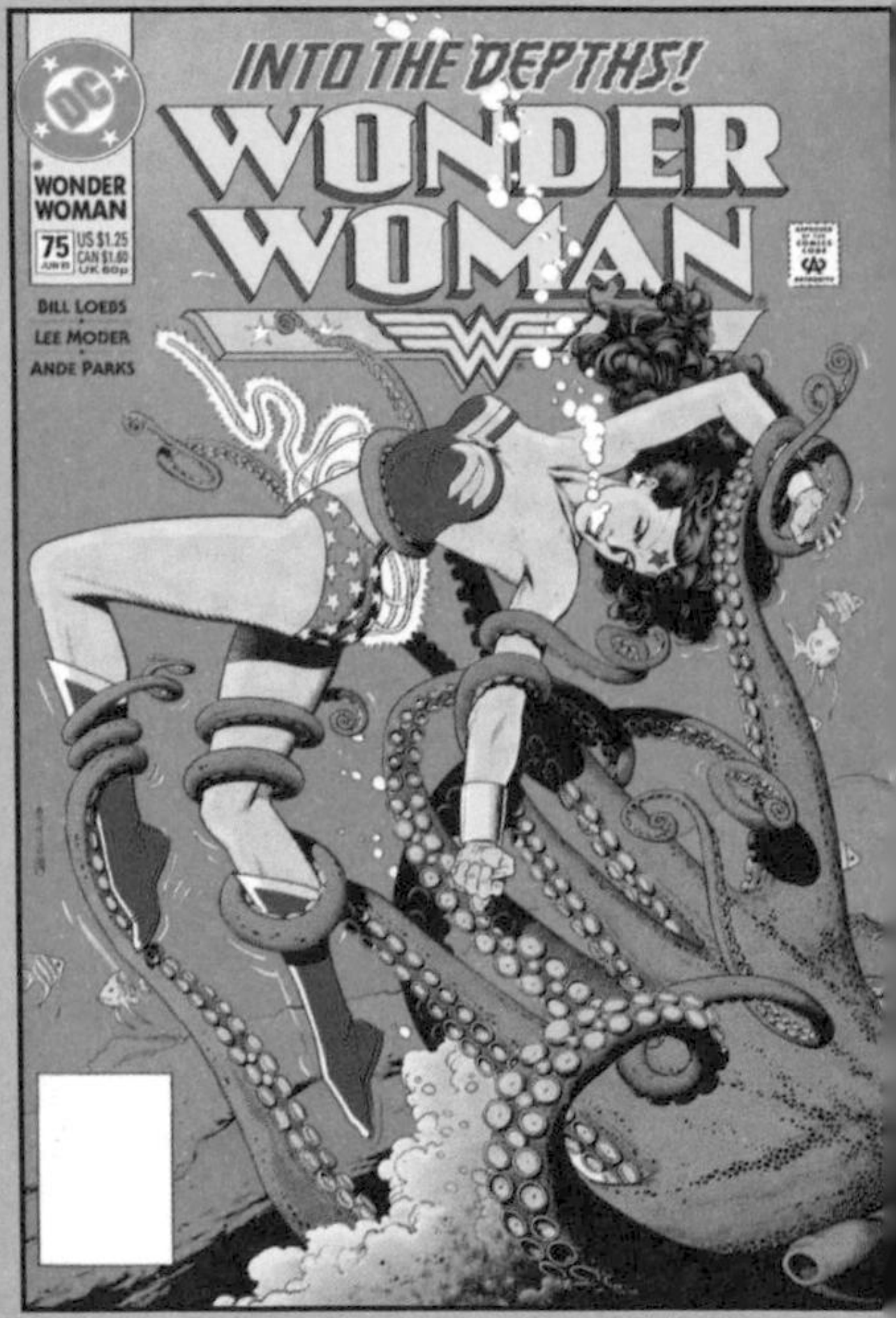
INTO THE DEPTHS!
WONDER WOMAN
WONDER WOMAN
75
JUN 93
US $1.25
CAN $1.60
UK 60p
BILL LOEBS
LEE MODER
ANDE PARKS

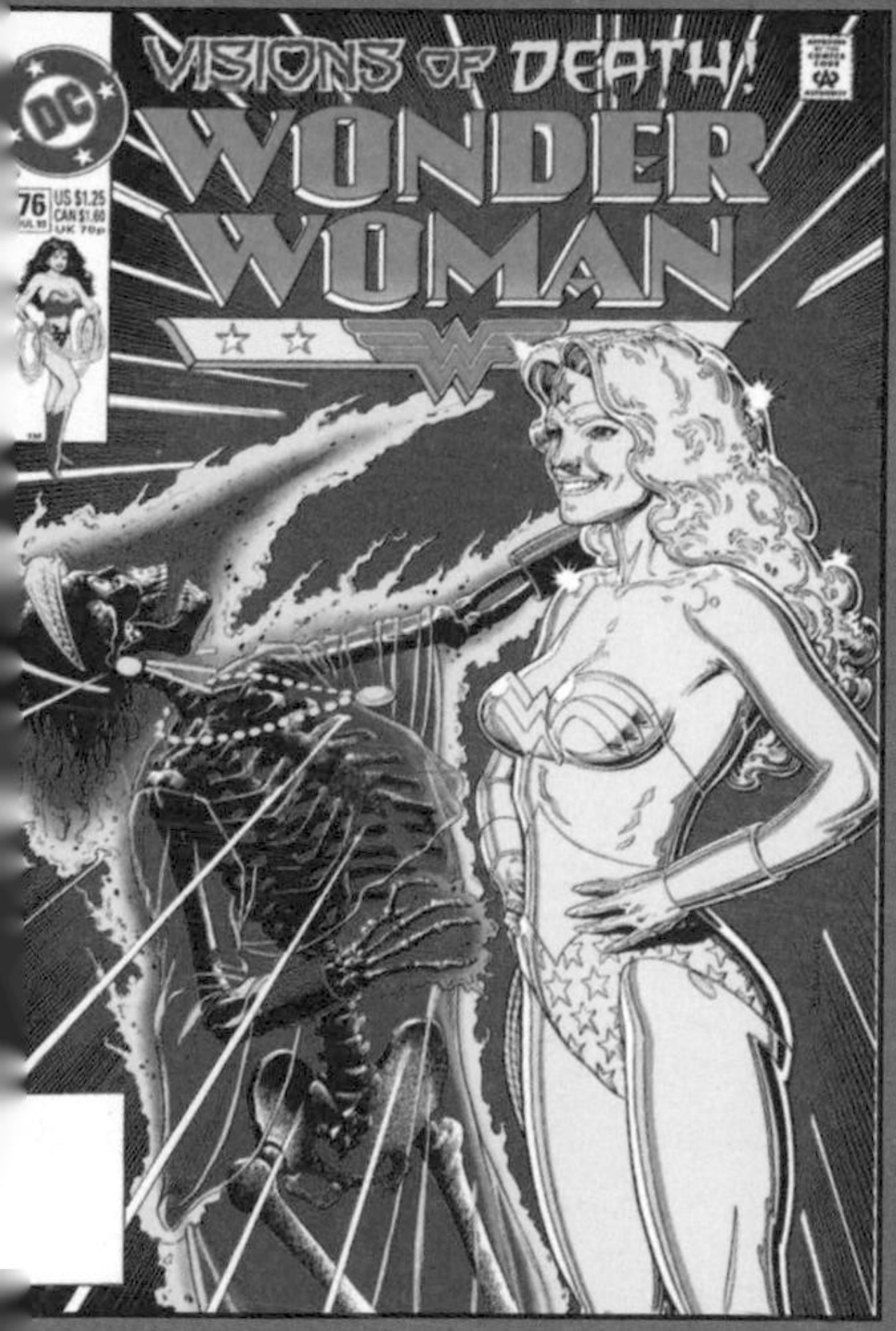
VISIONS OF DEATH!
WONDER WOMAN
DC
76
US $1.25
CAN $1.60
UK 70p

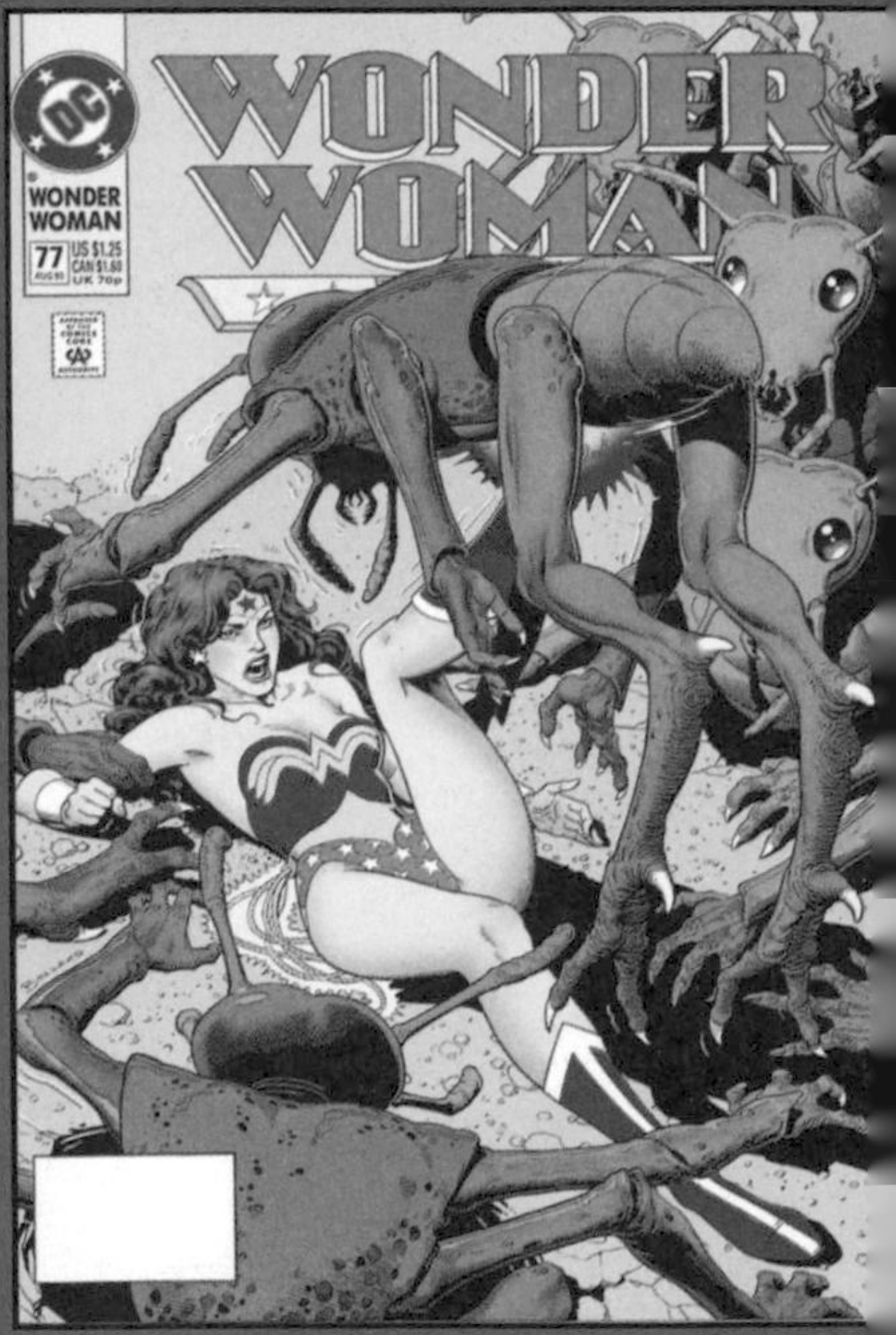
WONDER WOMAN
WONDER WOMAN
77
US $1.25
CAN $1.60
UK 70p

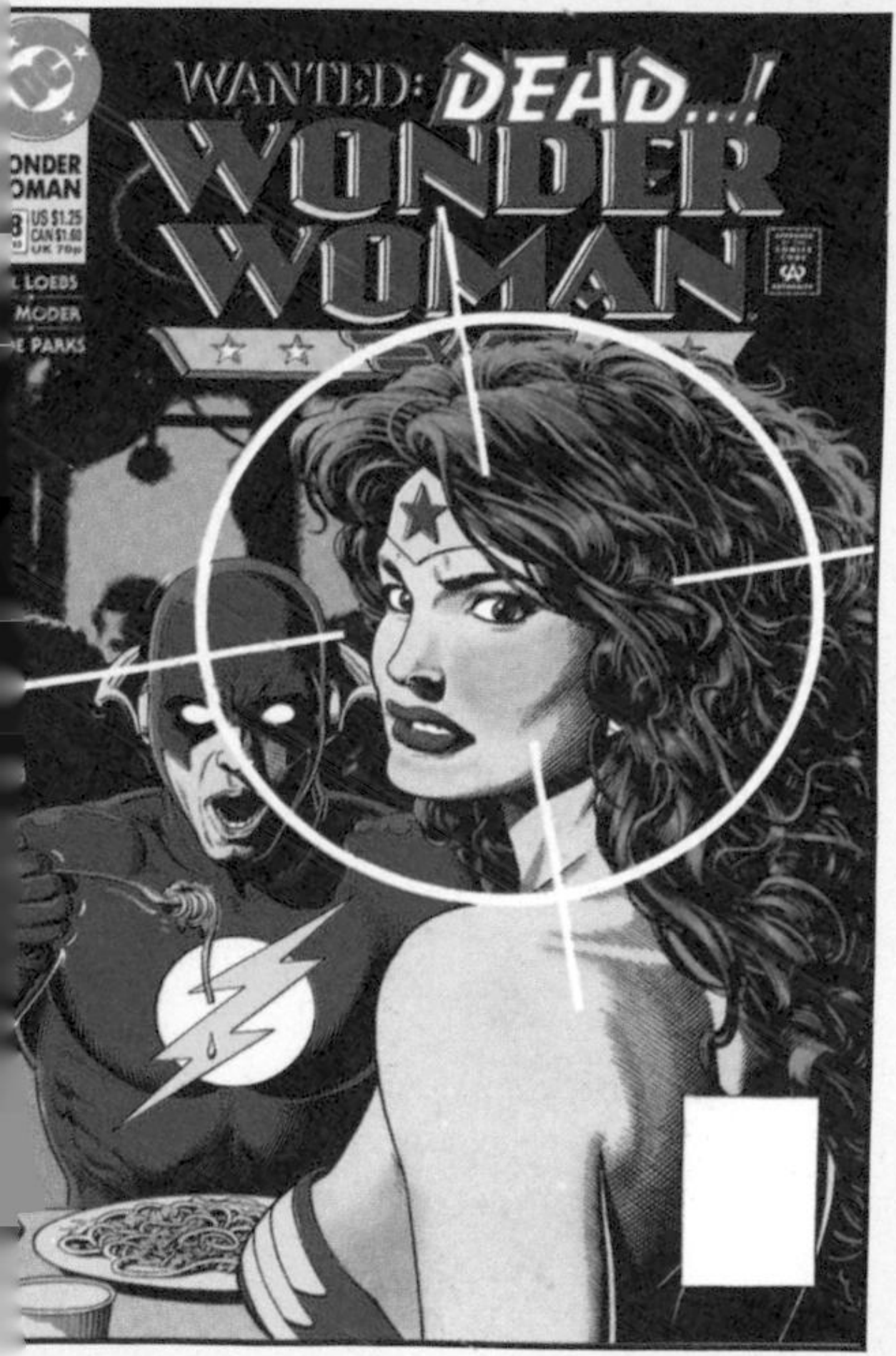
WANTED: DEAD...!
WONDER WOMAN
ONDER
OMAN
8
US $1.25
CAN $1.60
UK 70p
L LOEBS
MODER
E PARKS

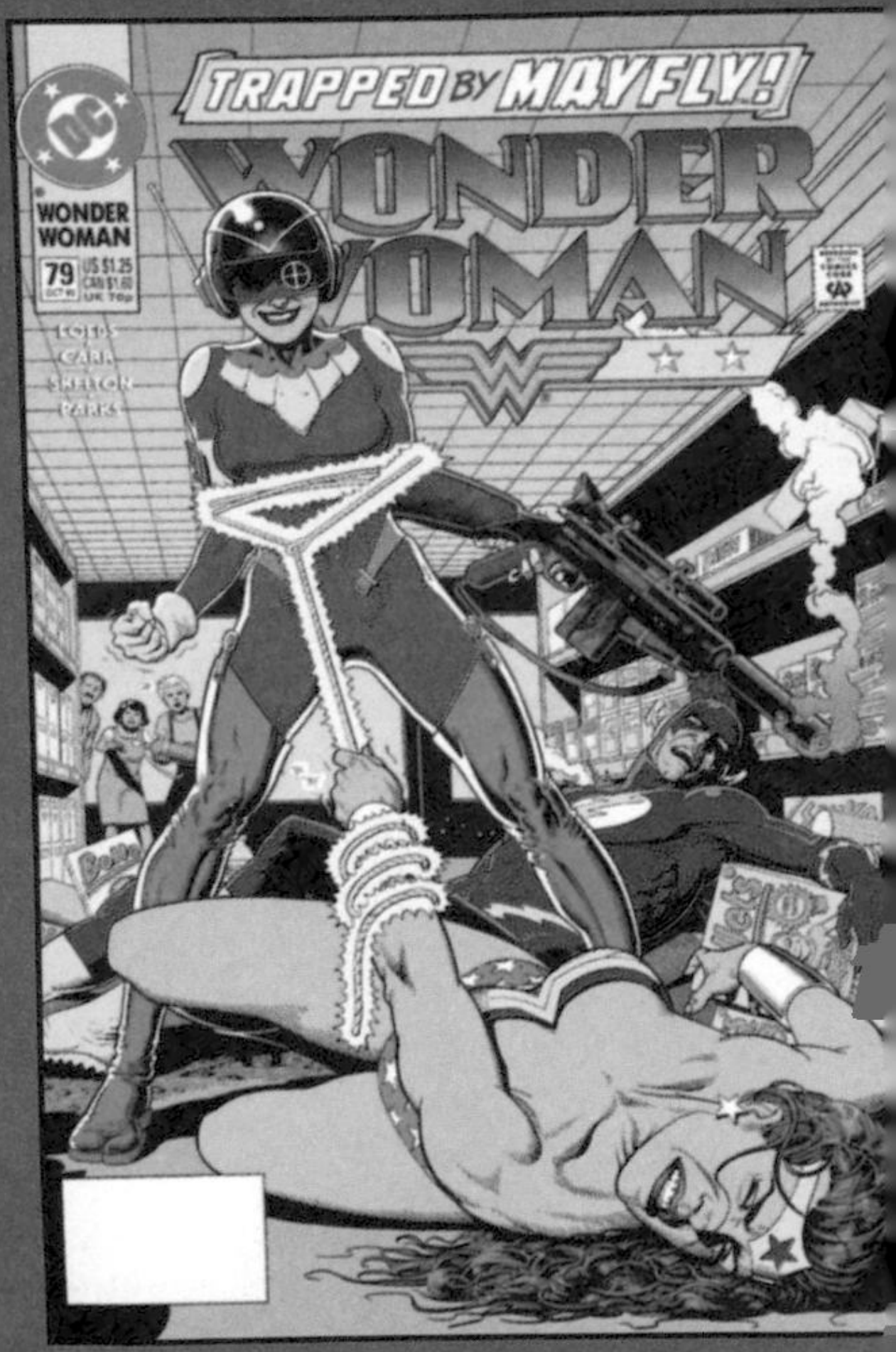
TRAPPED BY MAYFLY!
WONDER WOMAN
WONDER WOMAN
79
US $1.25
CAN $1.60
UK 70p
LOIS
CARL
SHEACOR
PARKS

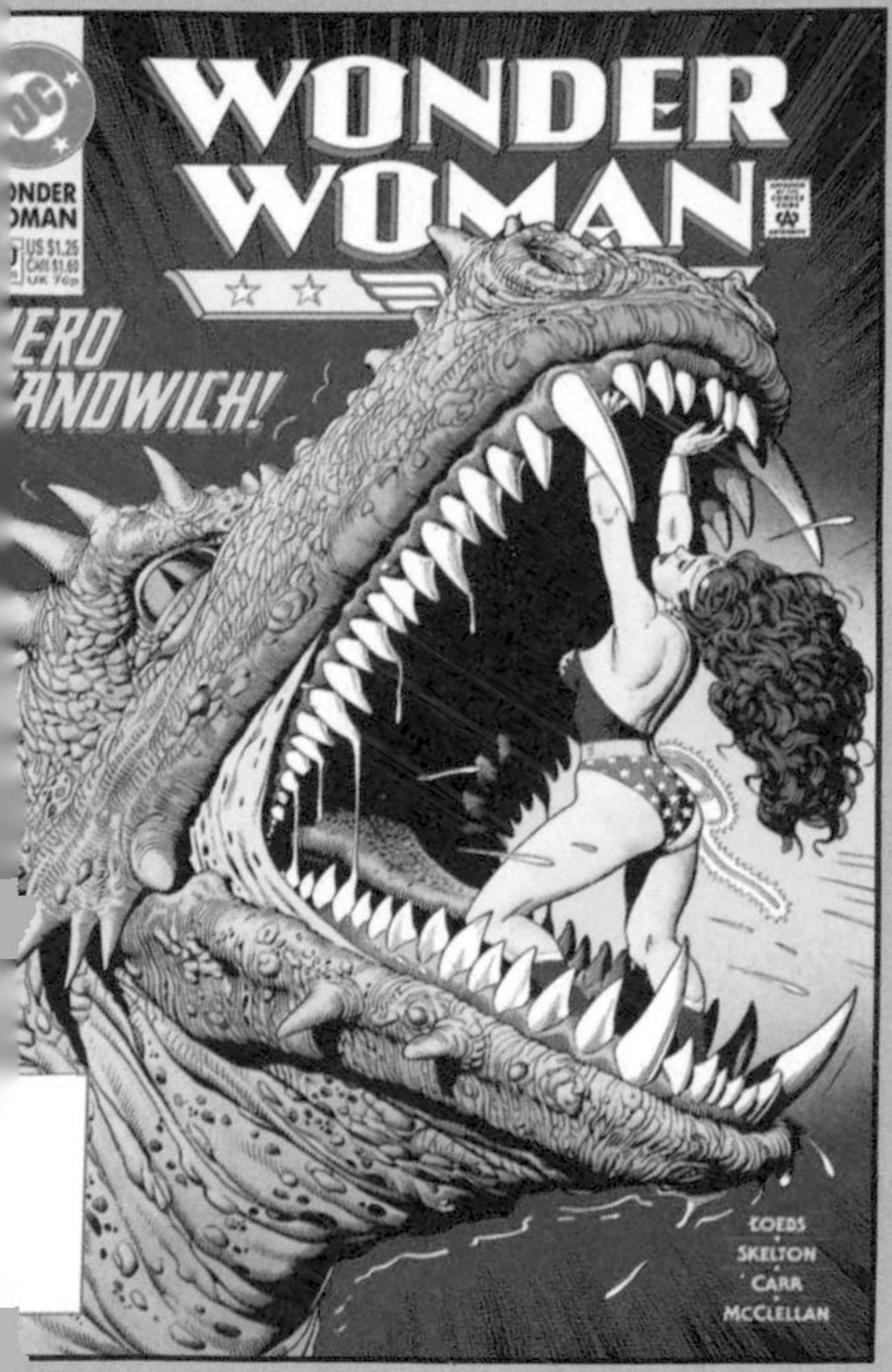
WONDER WOMAN
ONDER
OMAN
US $1.25
Can $1.60
UK 70p
ERO
ANDWICH!
EOEDS
SKELTON
CARR
McCLELLAN

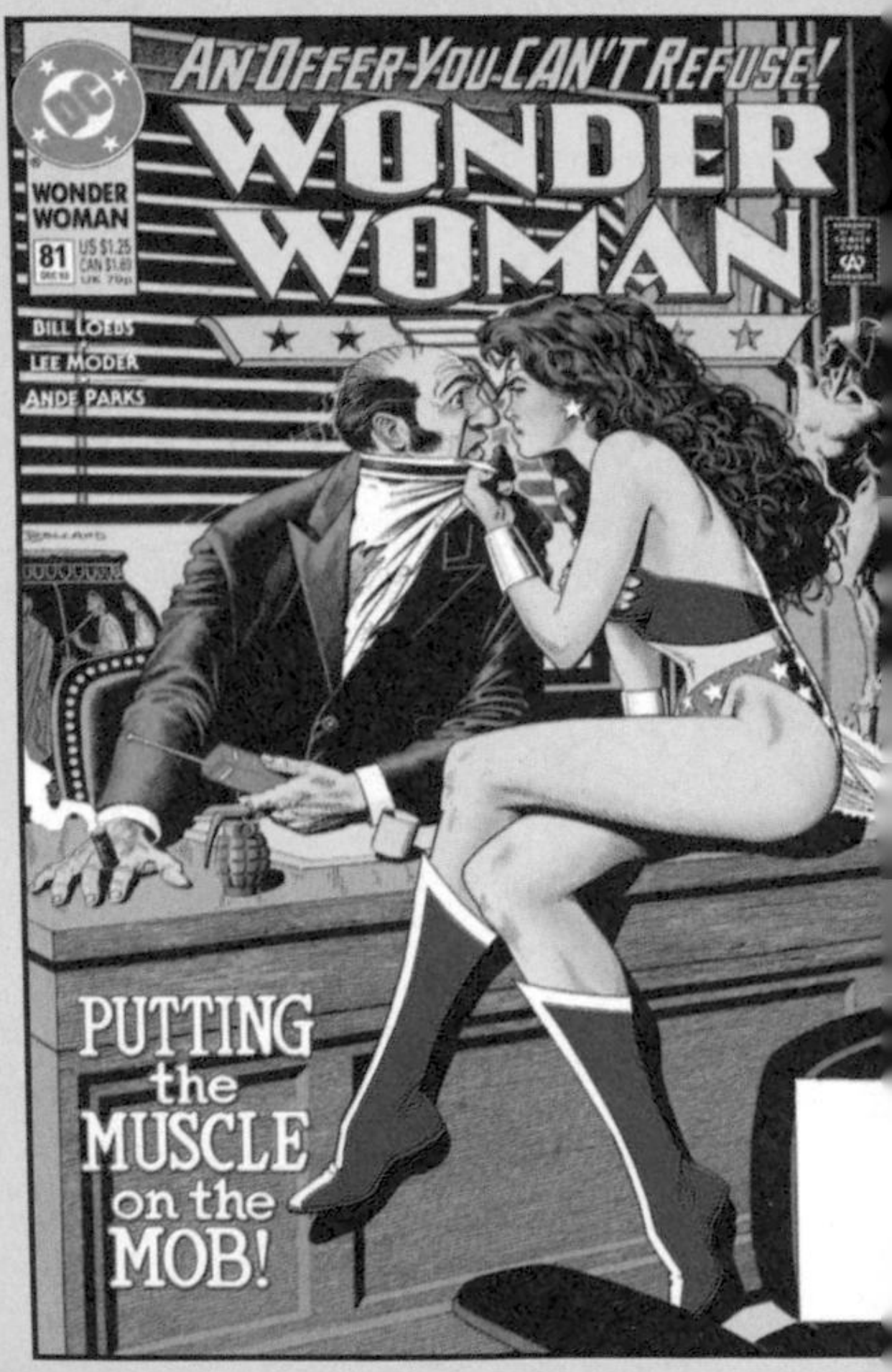
AN OFFER YOU CAN'T REFUSE!
WONDER WOMAN
WONDER WOMAN
81
US $1.25
CAN $1.60
BILL LOEBS
LEE MODER
ANDE PARKS
PUTTING the MUSCLE on the MOB!

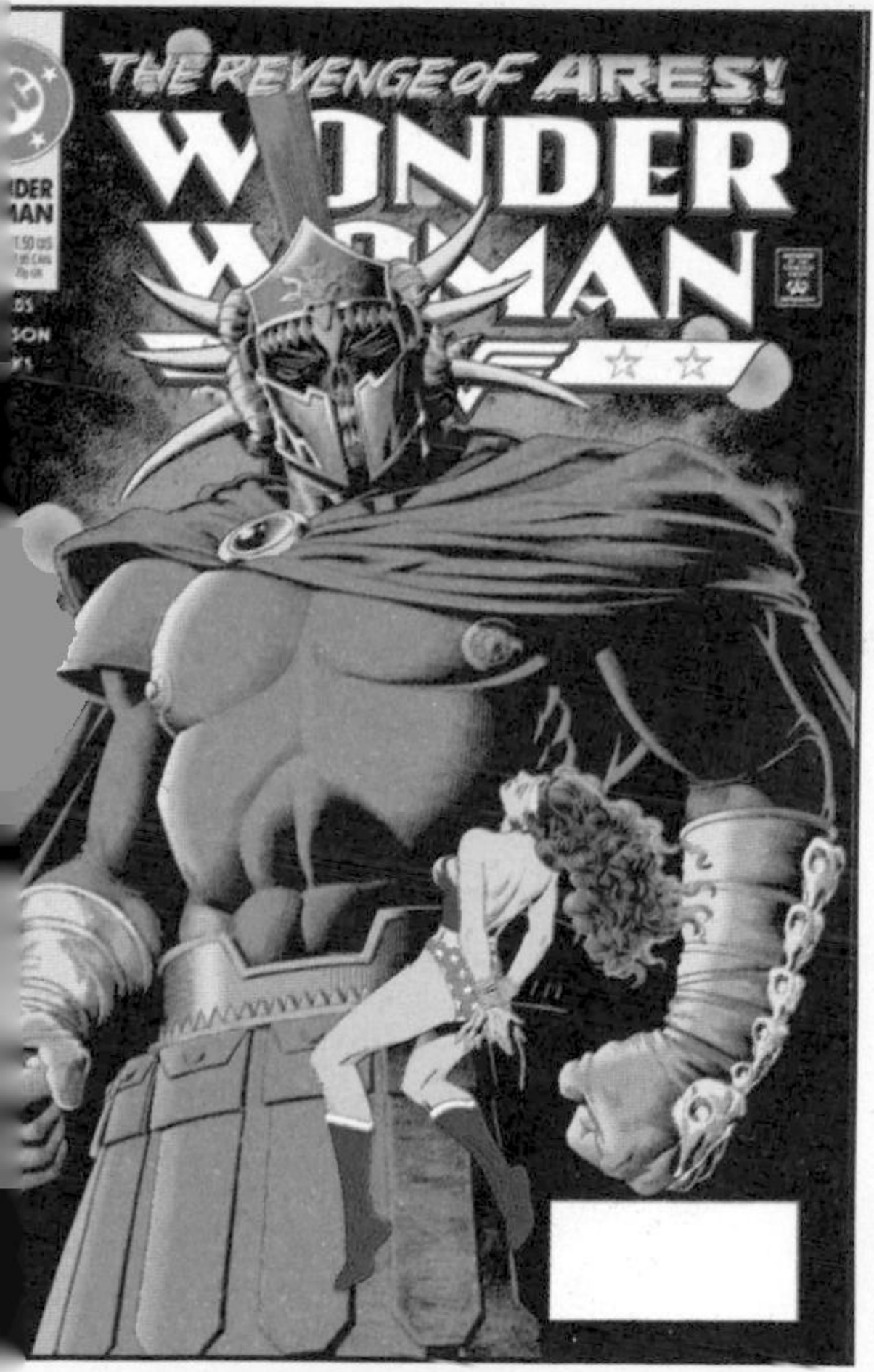
THE REVENGE OF ARES!
WONDER WOMAN

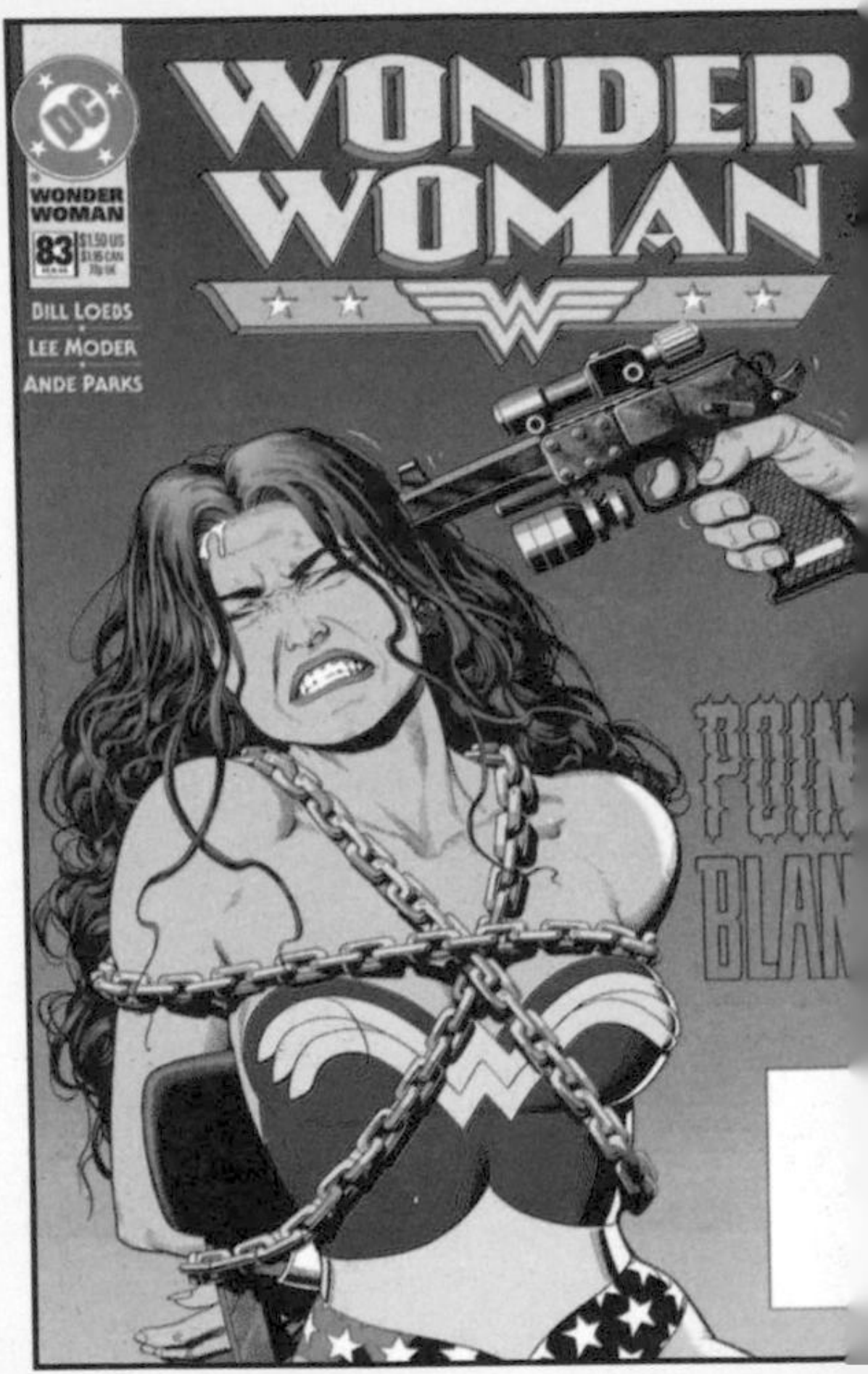
WONDER WOMAN
WONDER WOMAN
83
$1.50 US
$1.95 CAN
DILL LOEBS
LEE MODER
ANDE PARKS
POINT BLANK

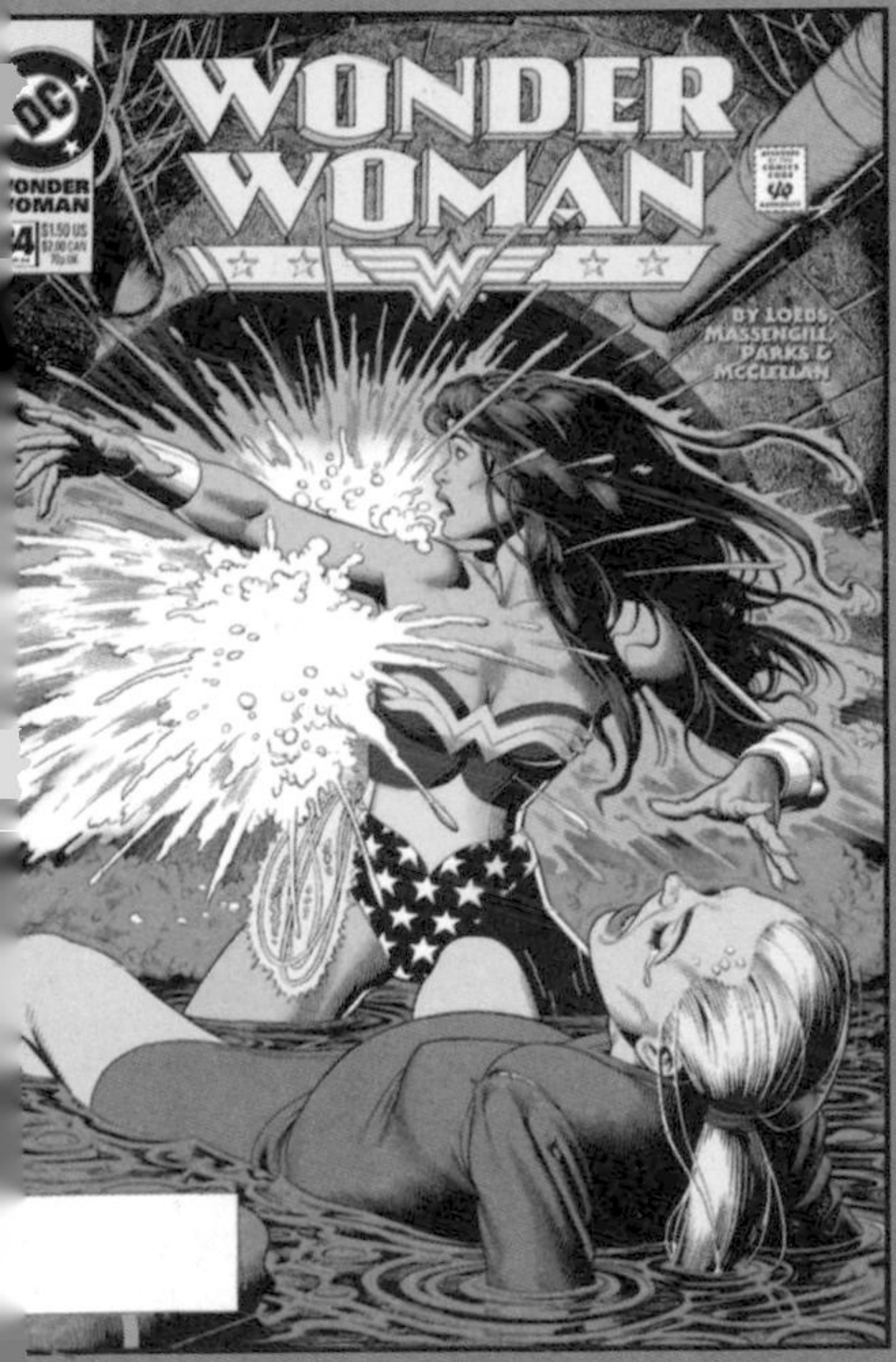
WONDER WOMAN
BY LOEBS, MASSENGILL, PARKS & MCCLELLAN
WONDER WOMAN
4
$1.50 US
$2.00 CAN

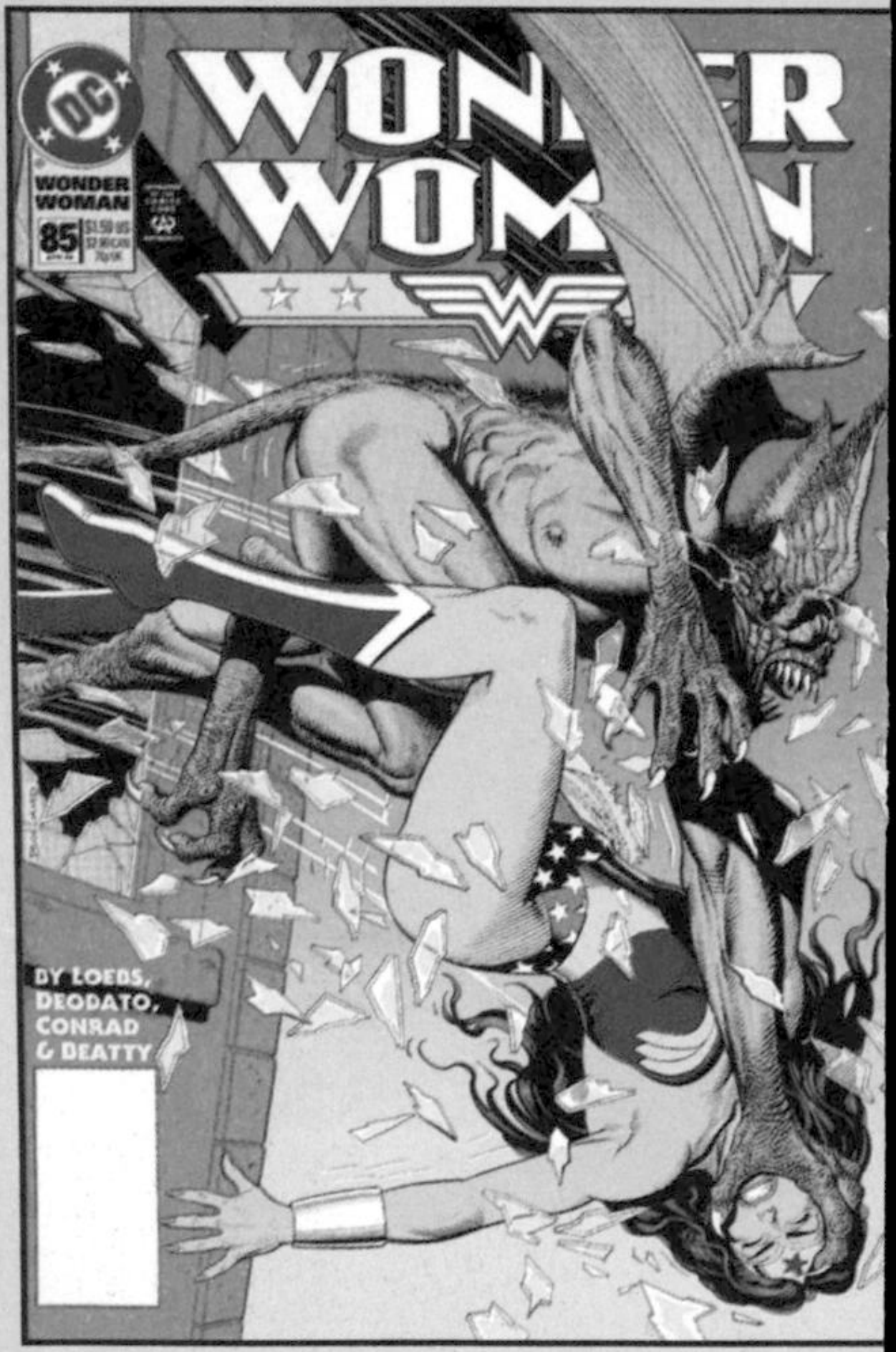
WONDER WOMAN
85
$1.50 US
BY LOEBS, DEODATO, CONRAD & BEATTY

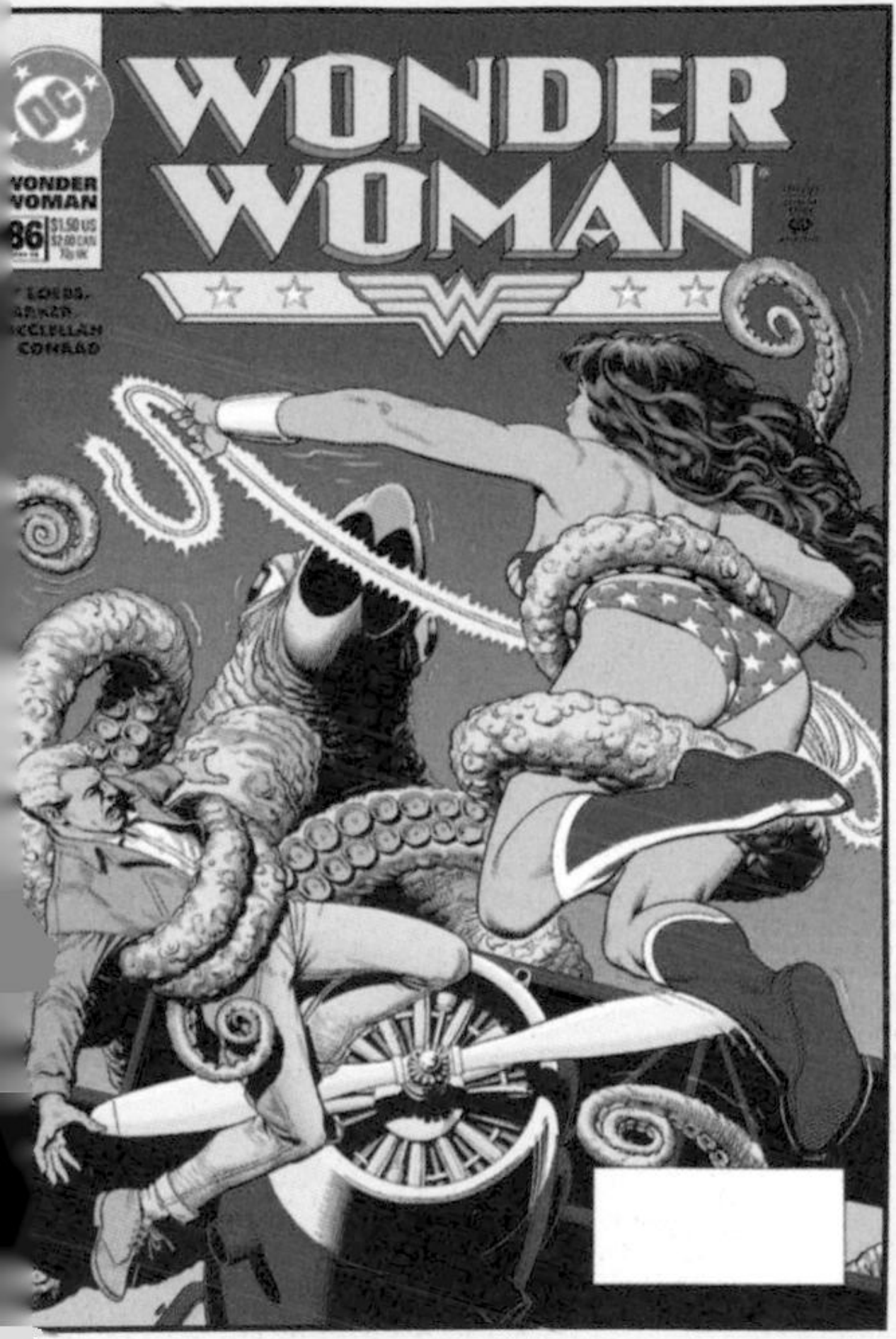
WONDER WOMAN
WONDER WOMAN
86
$1.50 US
$2.00 CAN
CONRAD

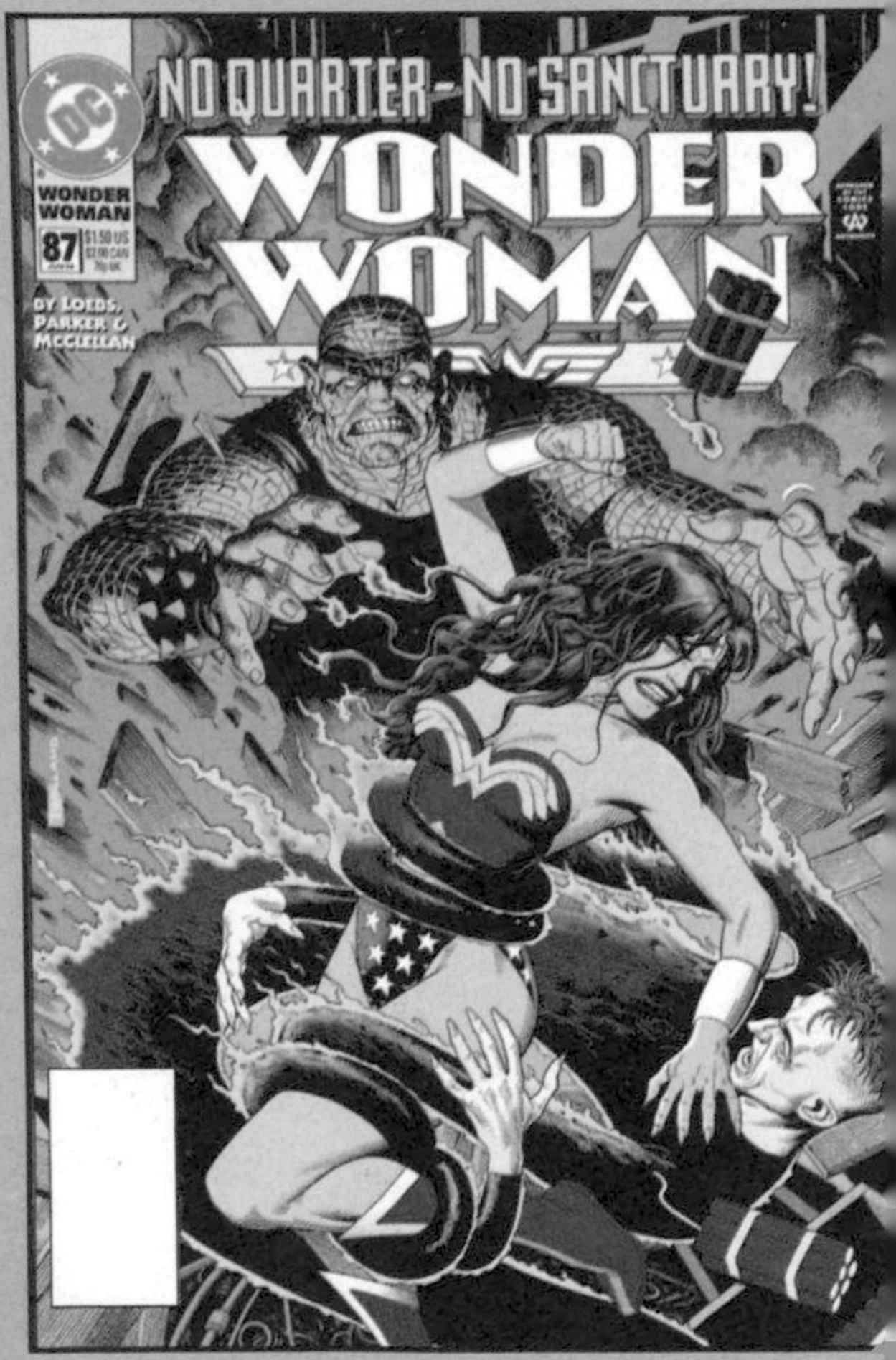
NO QUARTER - NO SANCTUARY!
WONDER WOMAN
WONDER WOMAN
87
$1.50 US
$2.00 CAN
BY LOEBS, PARKER & MCCLELLAN

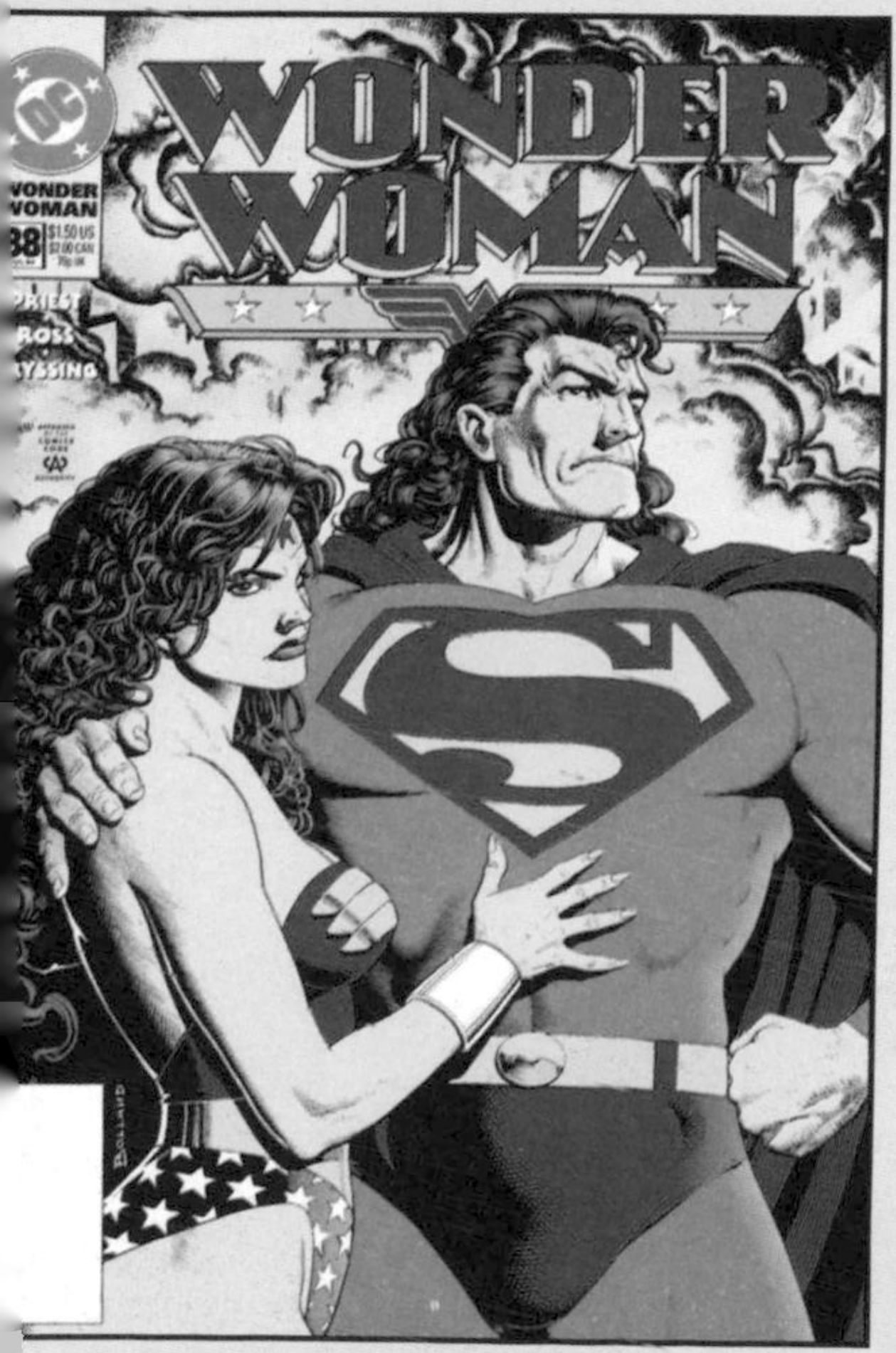
WONDER WOMAN
WONDER WOMAN
88
$1.50 US
$2.00 CAN
PRIEST
ROSS
LYSSING

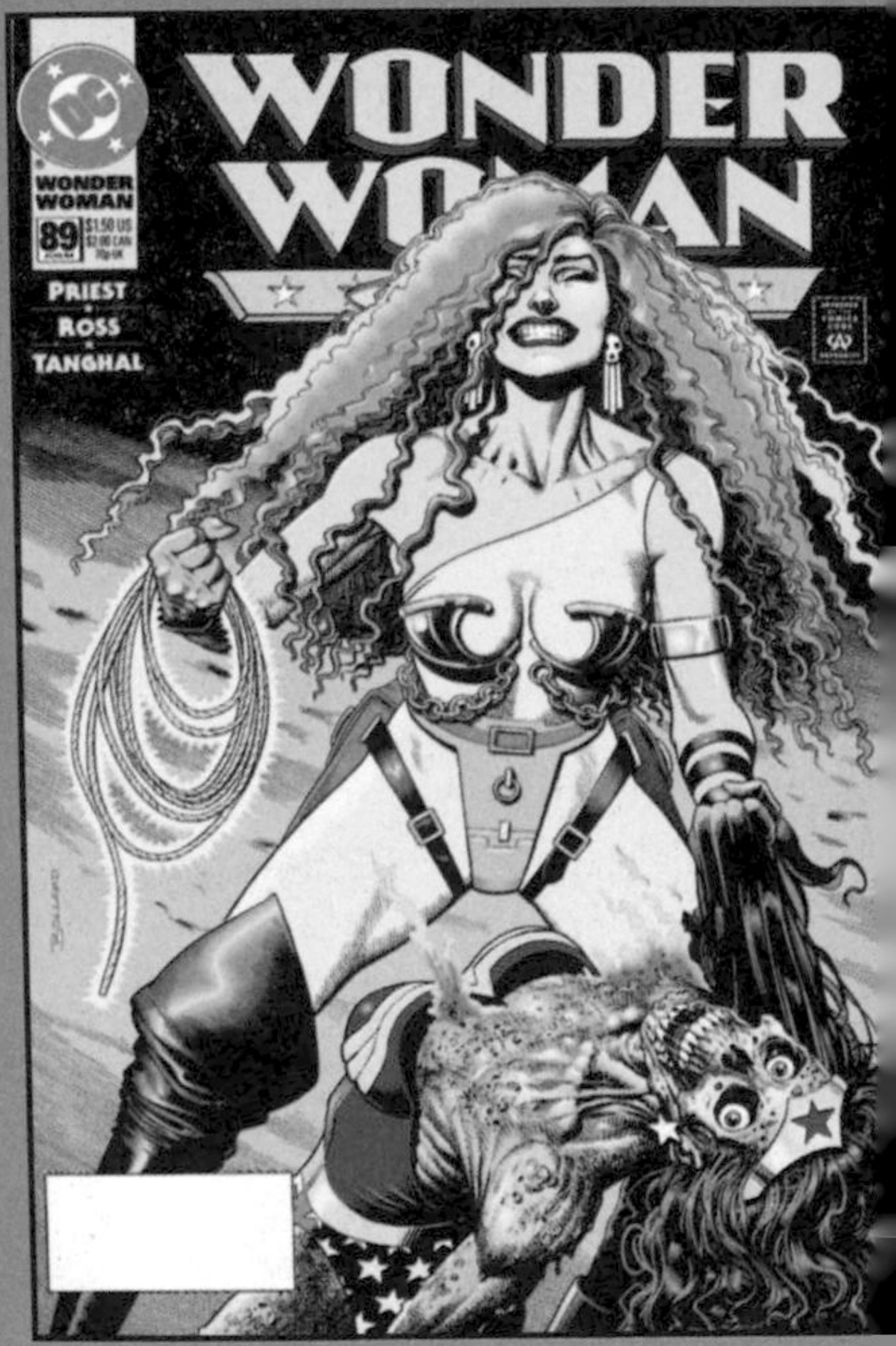
WONDER WOMAN
WONDER WOMAN
89
$1.50 US
$2.00 CAN
PRIEST
ROSS
TANGHAL

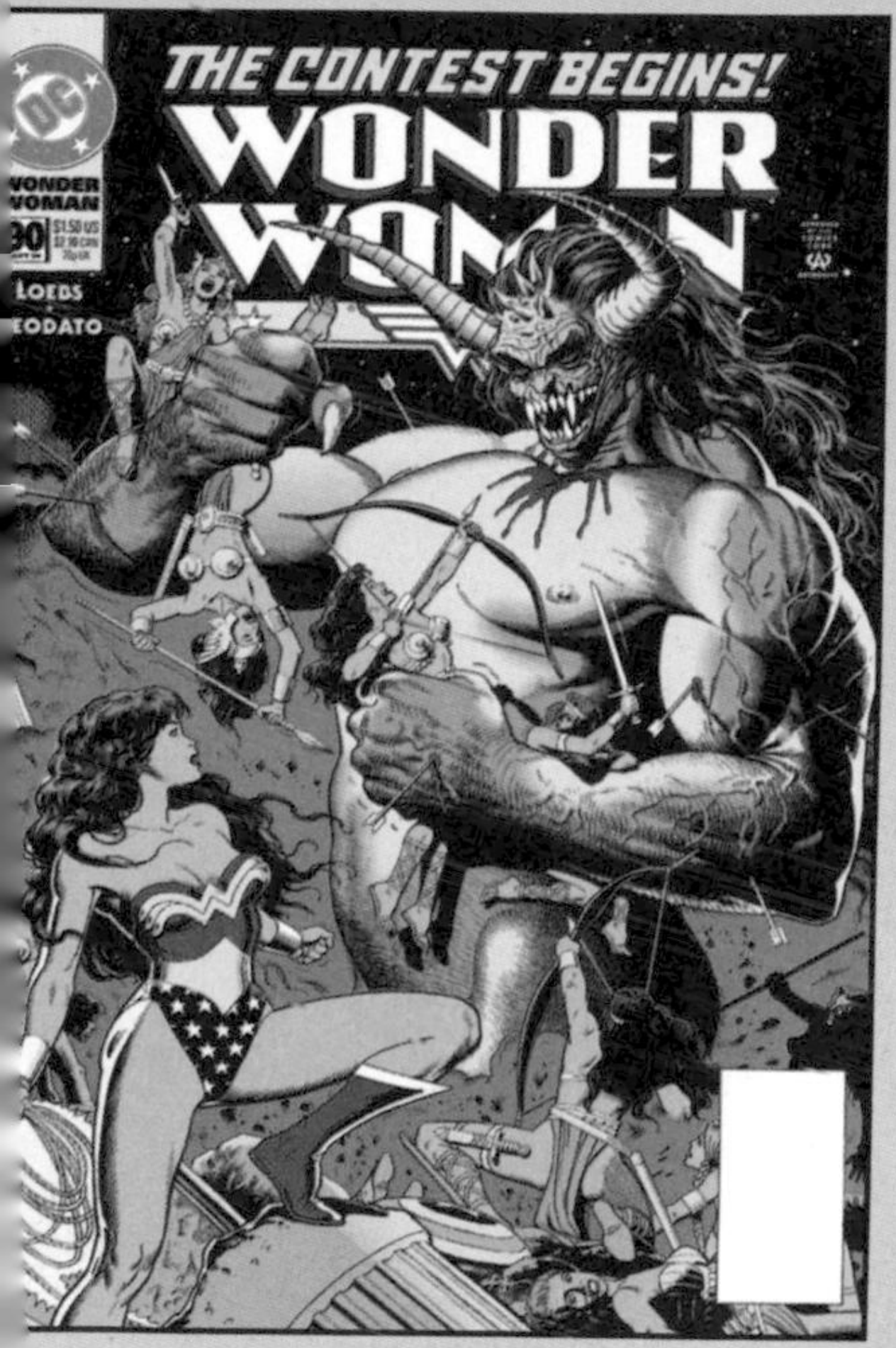
THE CONTEST BEGINS!
WONDER WOMAN
WONDER WOMAN
30
$1.50 US
LOEBS
EODATO

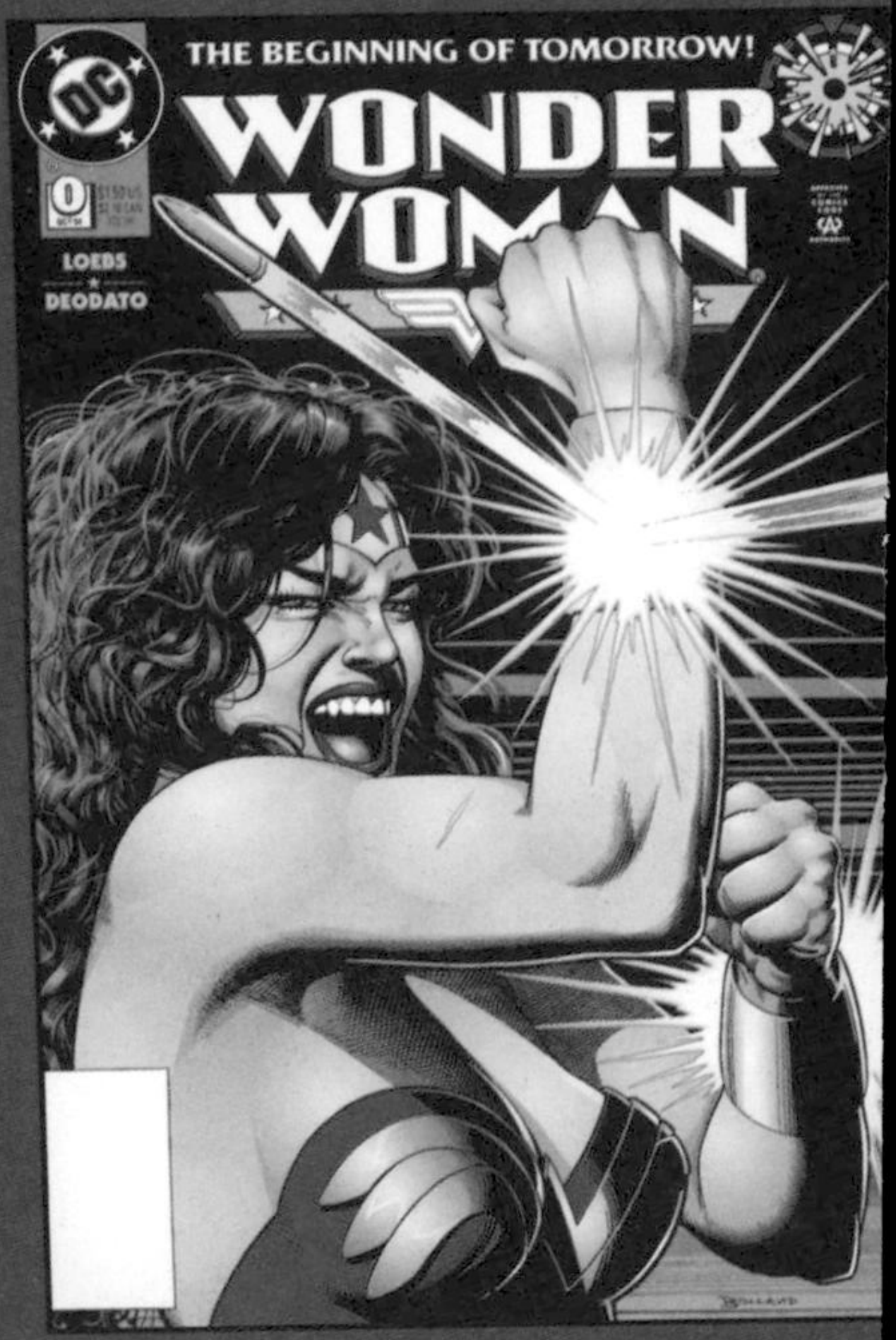
THE BEGINNING OF TOMORROW!
WONDER WOMAN
0
LOEBS
DEODATO

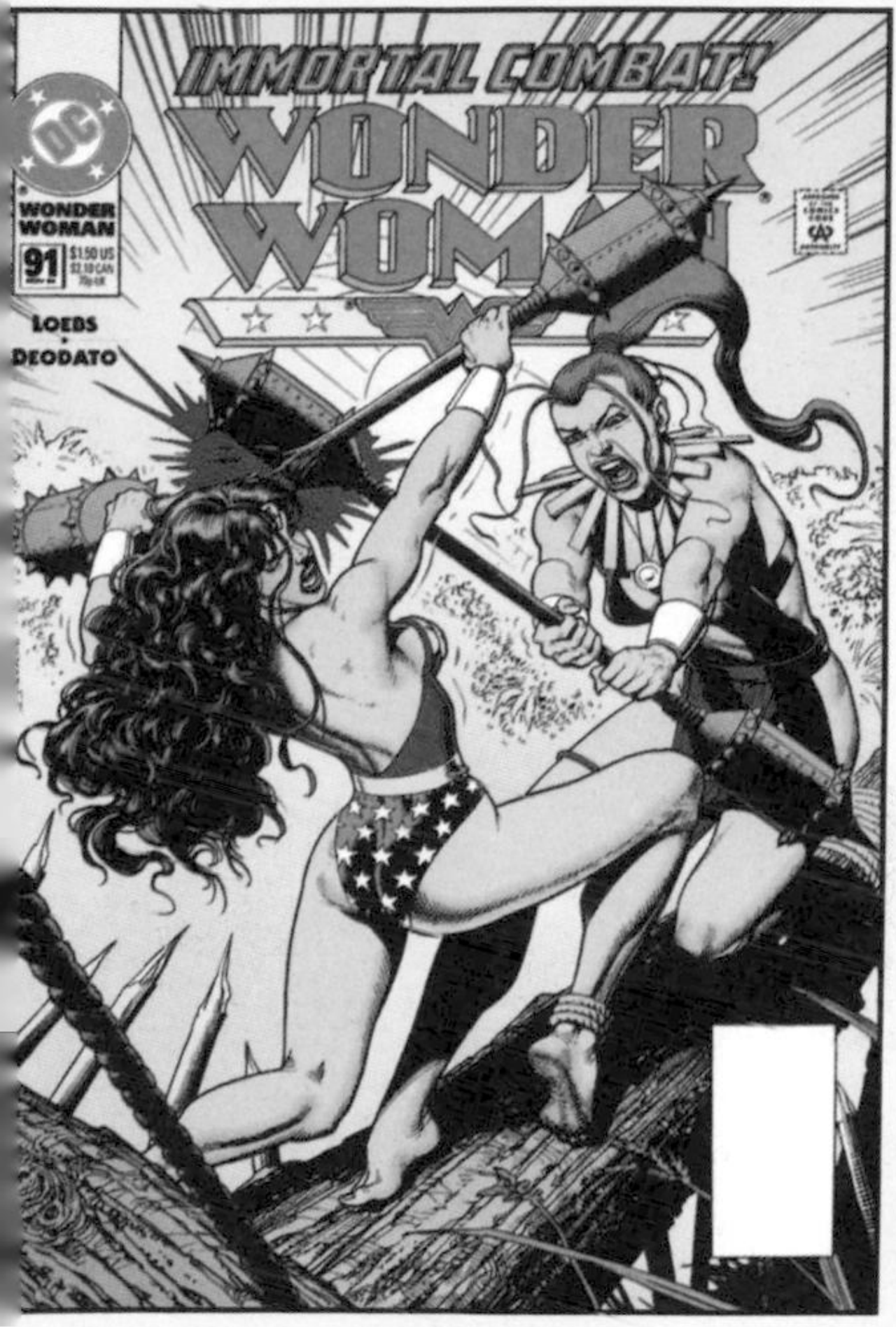
IMMORTAL COMBAT!
WONDER WOMAN
WONDER WOMAN
91
$1.50 US
$2.10 CAN
LOEBS
DEODATO

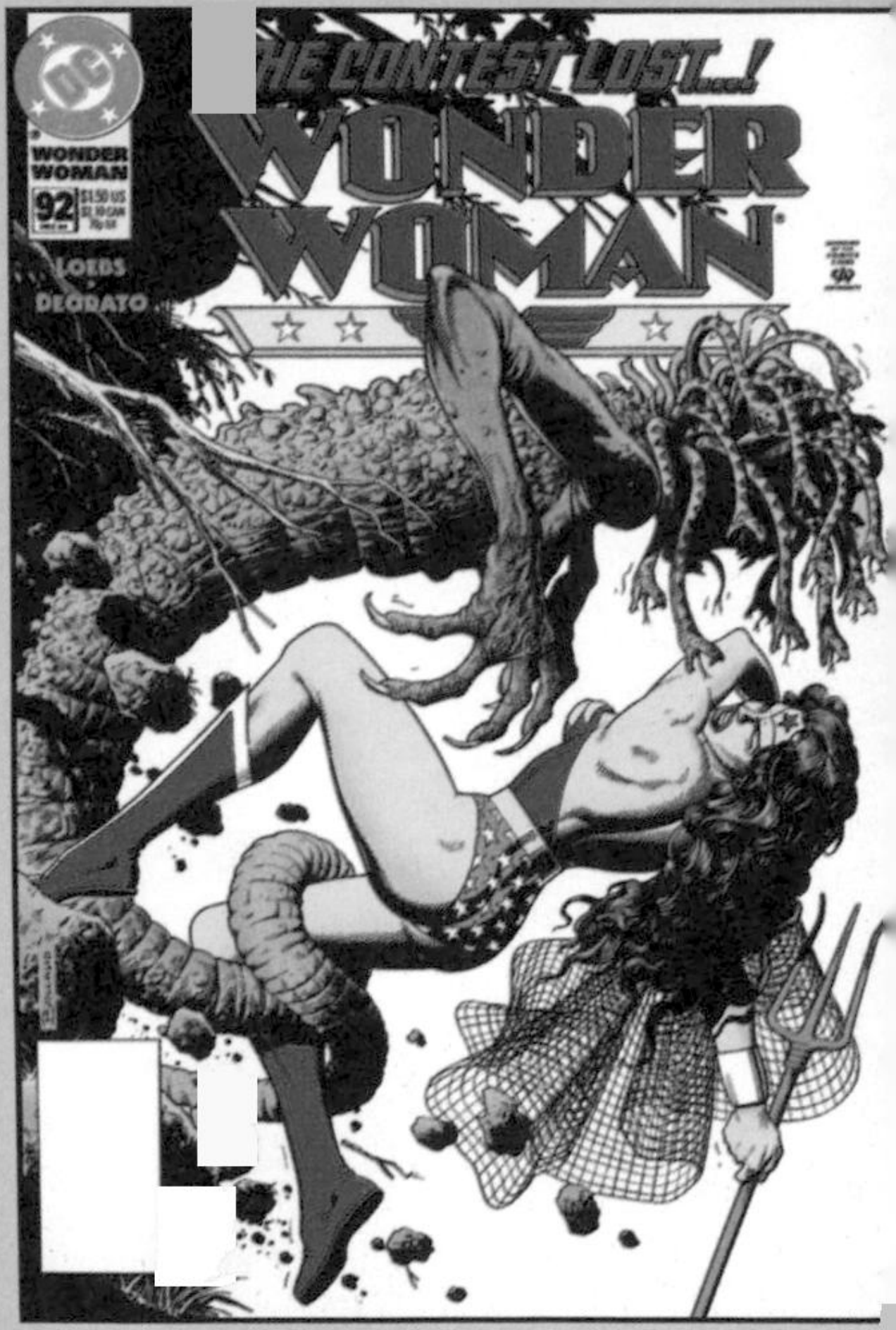
THE CONTEST LOST...!
WONDER WOMAN
WONDER WOMAN
92
$1.50 US
LOEBS
DEODATO

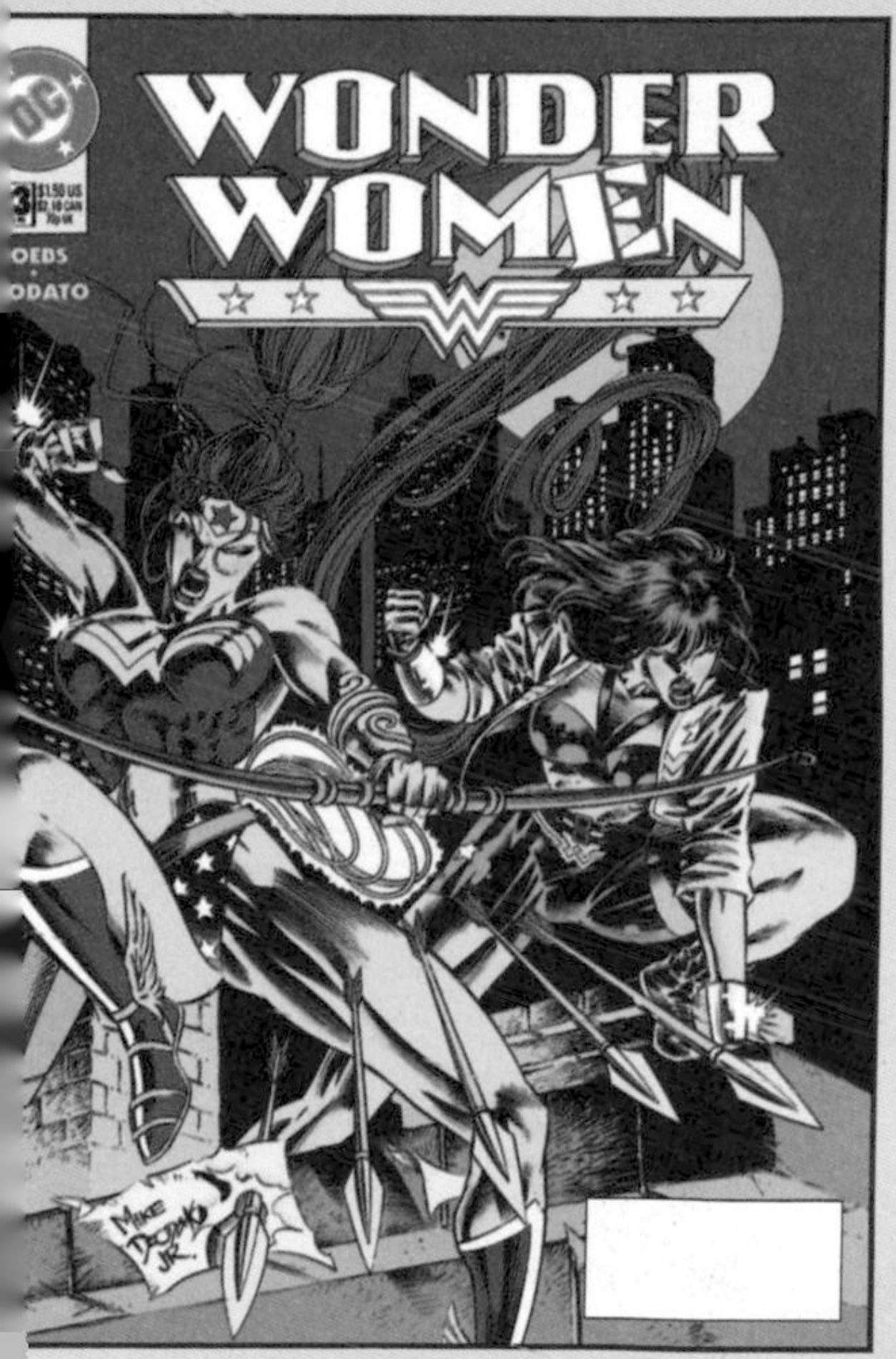
WONDER WOMEN
3
$1.50 US
$2.10 CAN
OEBS
ODATO
MIKE DEODATO JR.

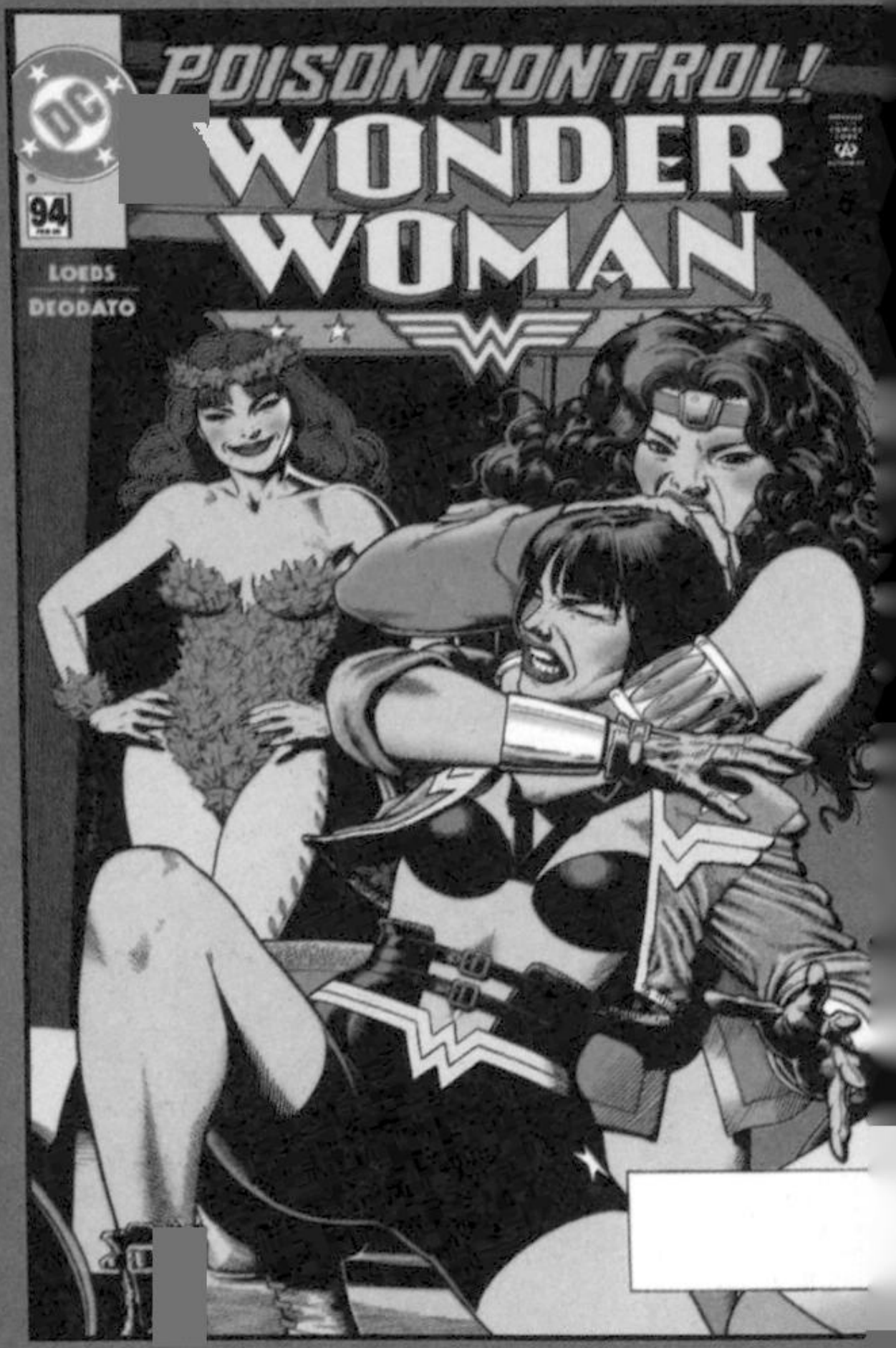
POISON CONTROL!
WONDER WOMAN
94
LOEBS
DEODATO

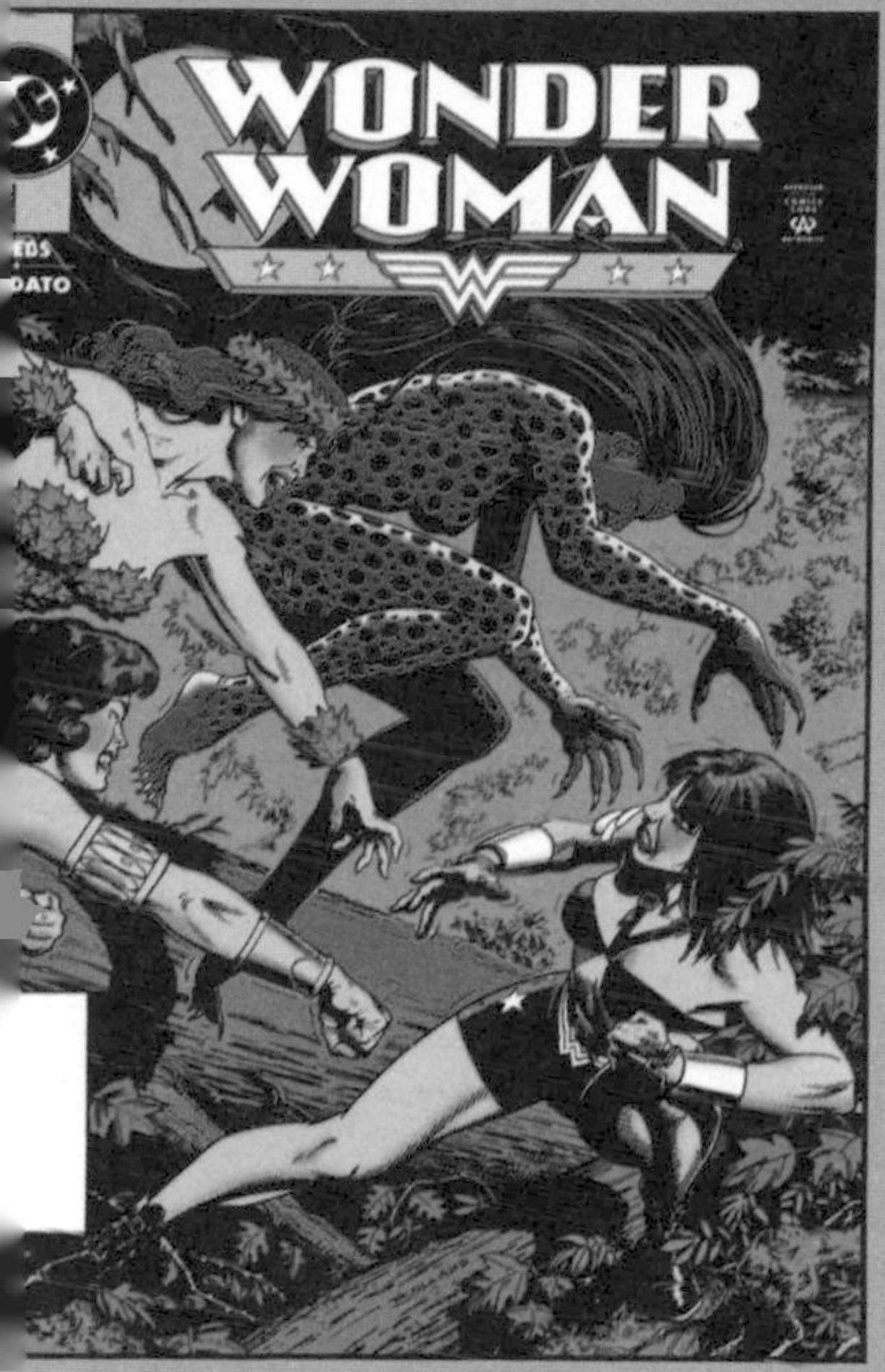
WONDER WOMAN
EDS
DATO

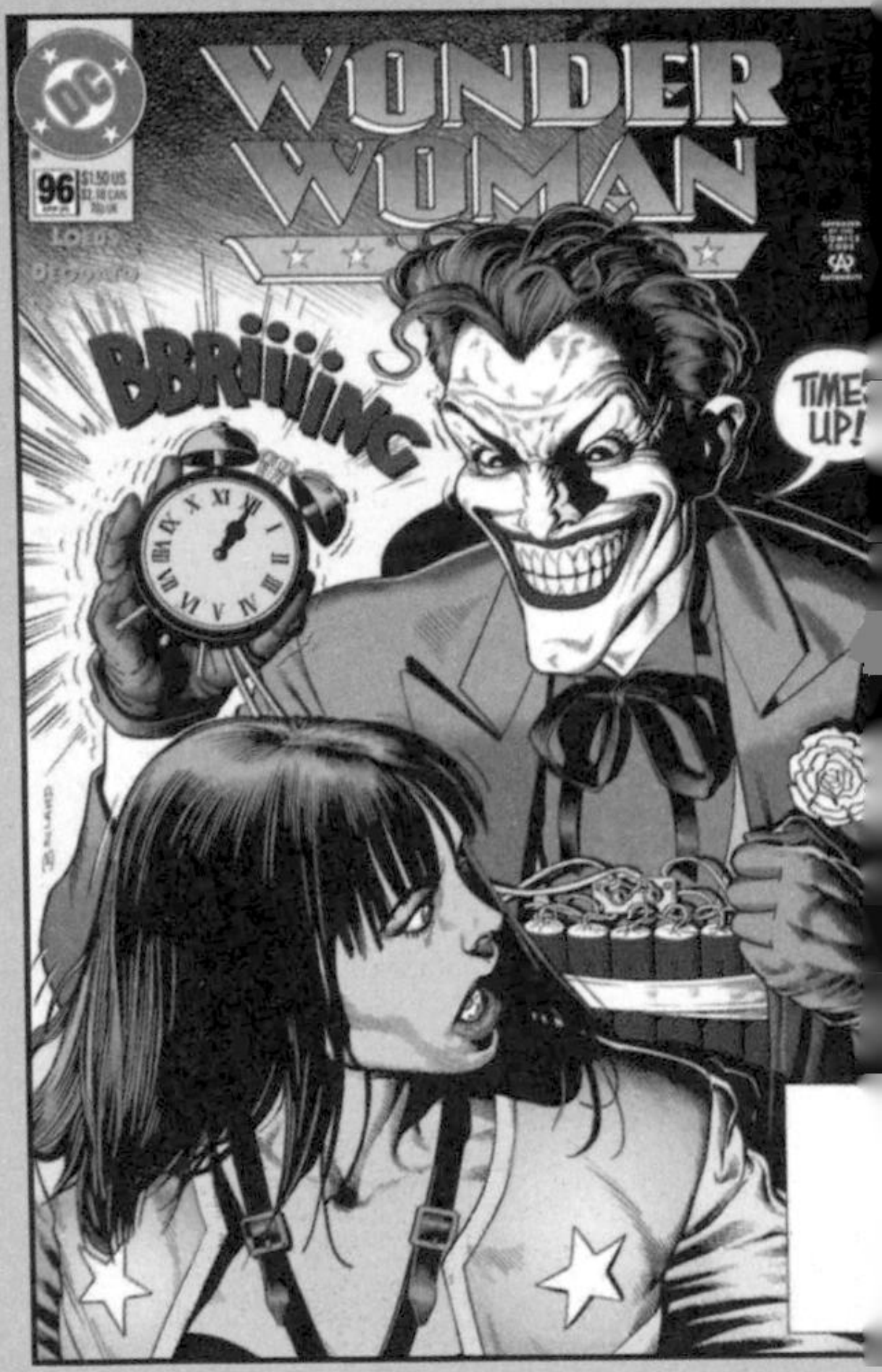
DC
96
$1.50 US
$2.10 CAN
WONDER WOMAN
BBRiiiiNG
TIME UP!

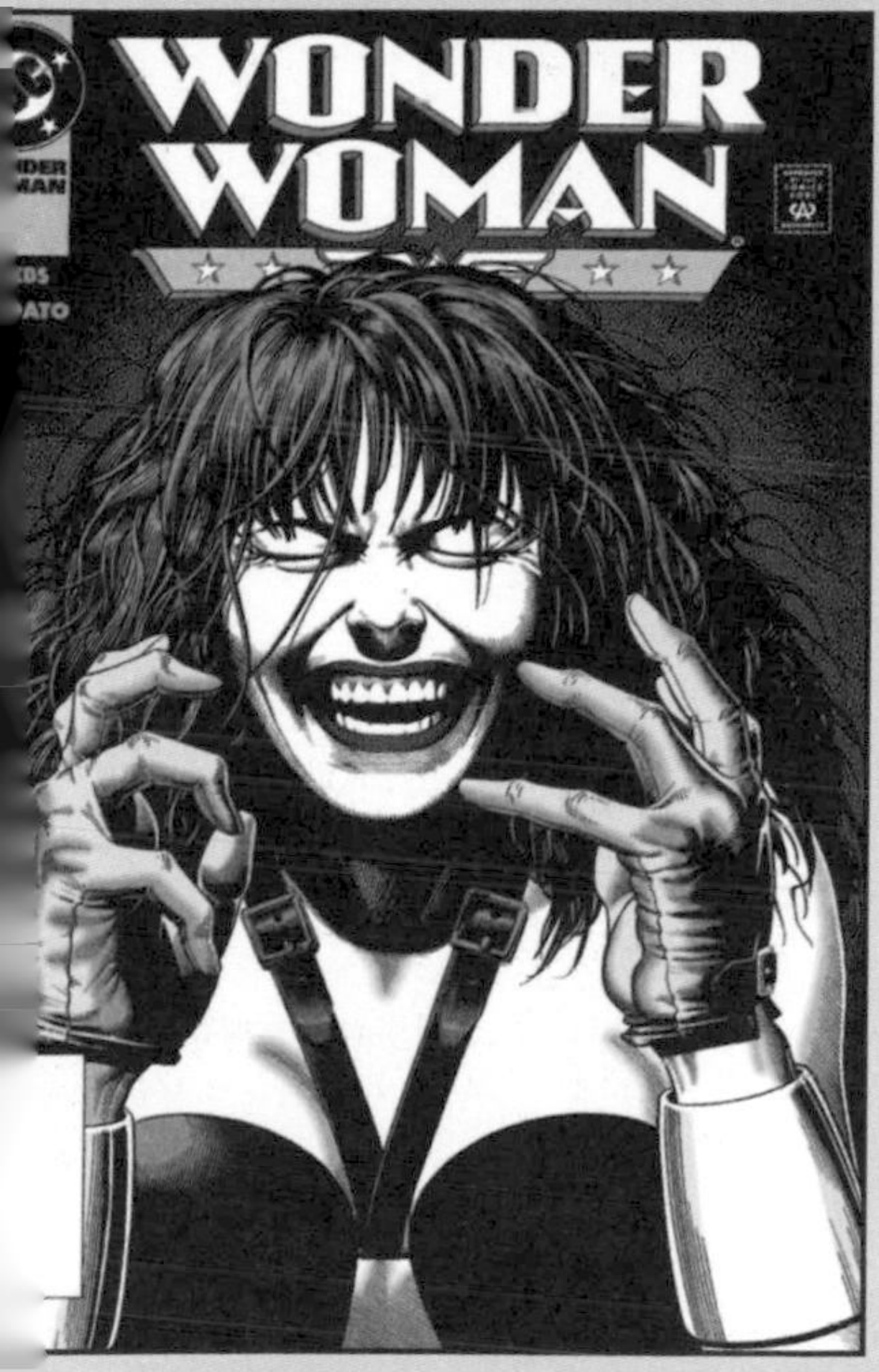
WONDER WOMAN

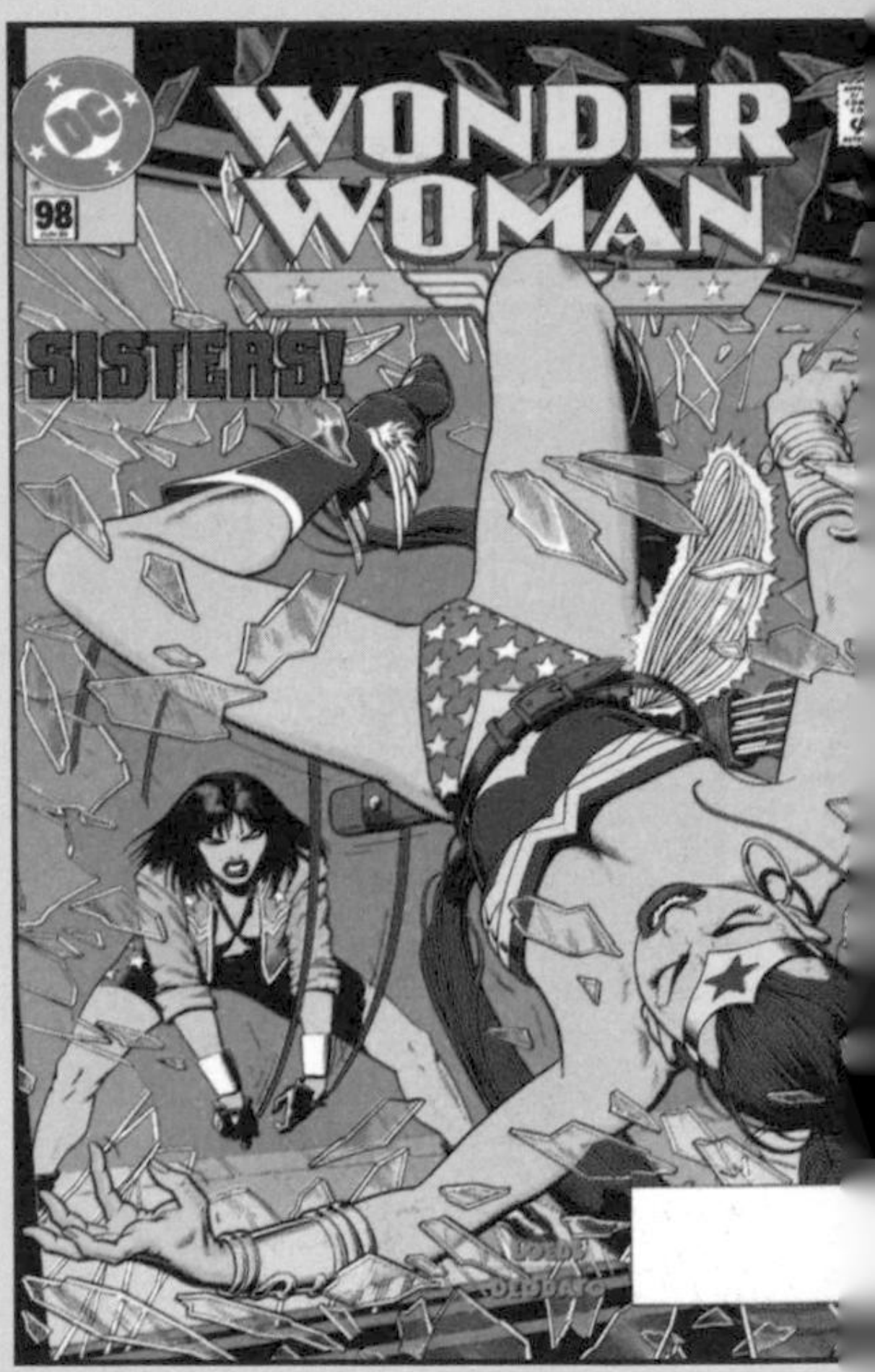
DC
98
WONDER WOMAN
SISTERS!

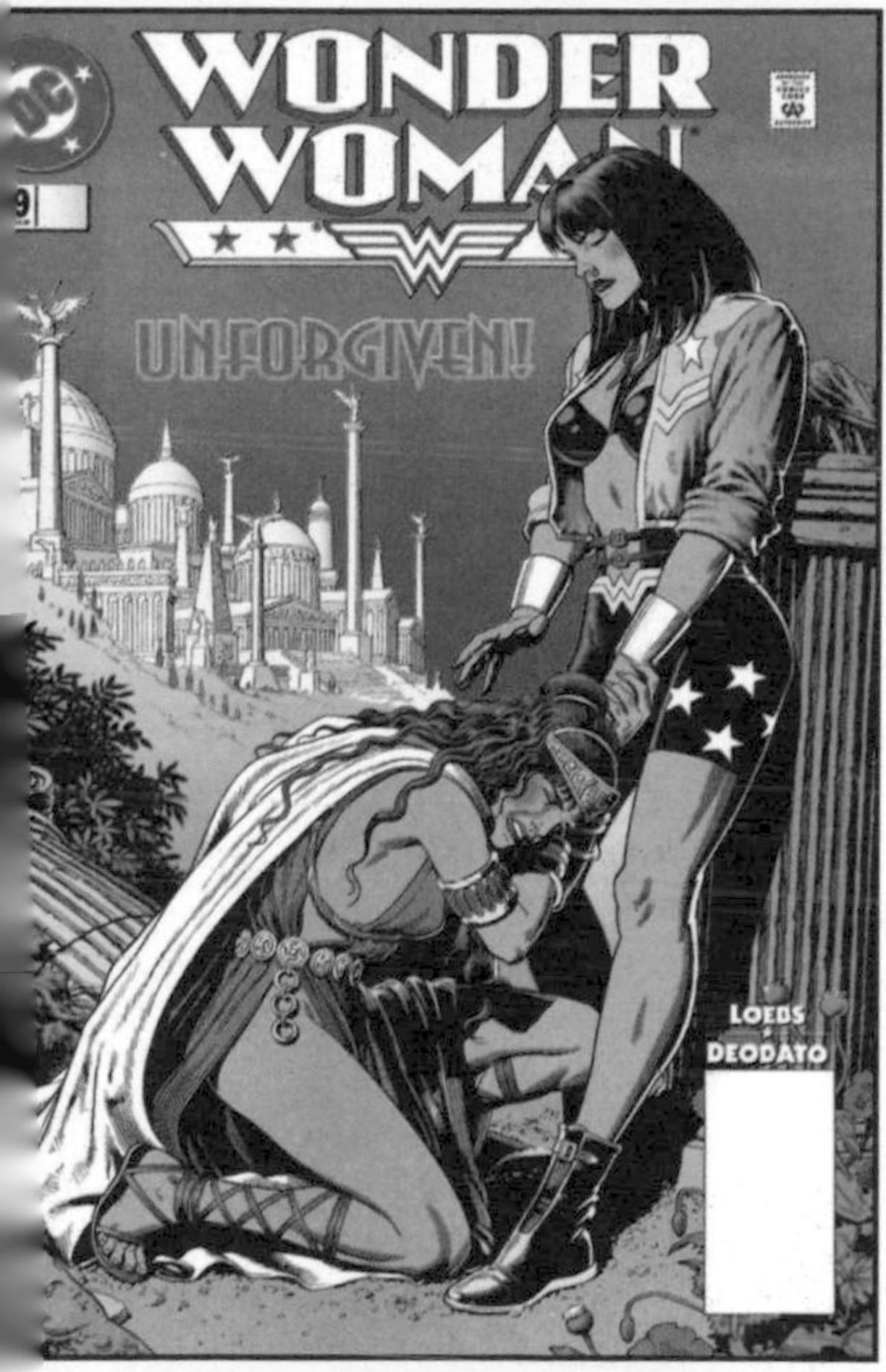
WONDER WOMAN
UNFORGIVEN!
LOEBS
DEODATO

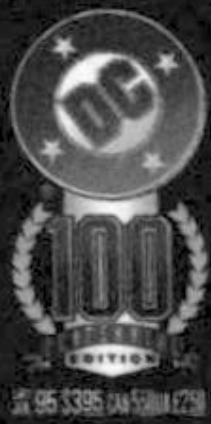

WONDER WOMAN

FALL OF AN AMAZON

BY WM MESSNER-LOEBS & MIKE DEODATO

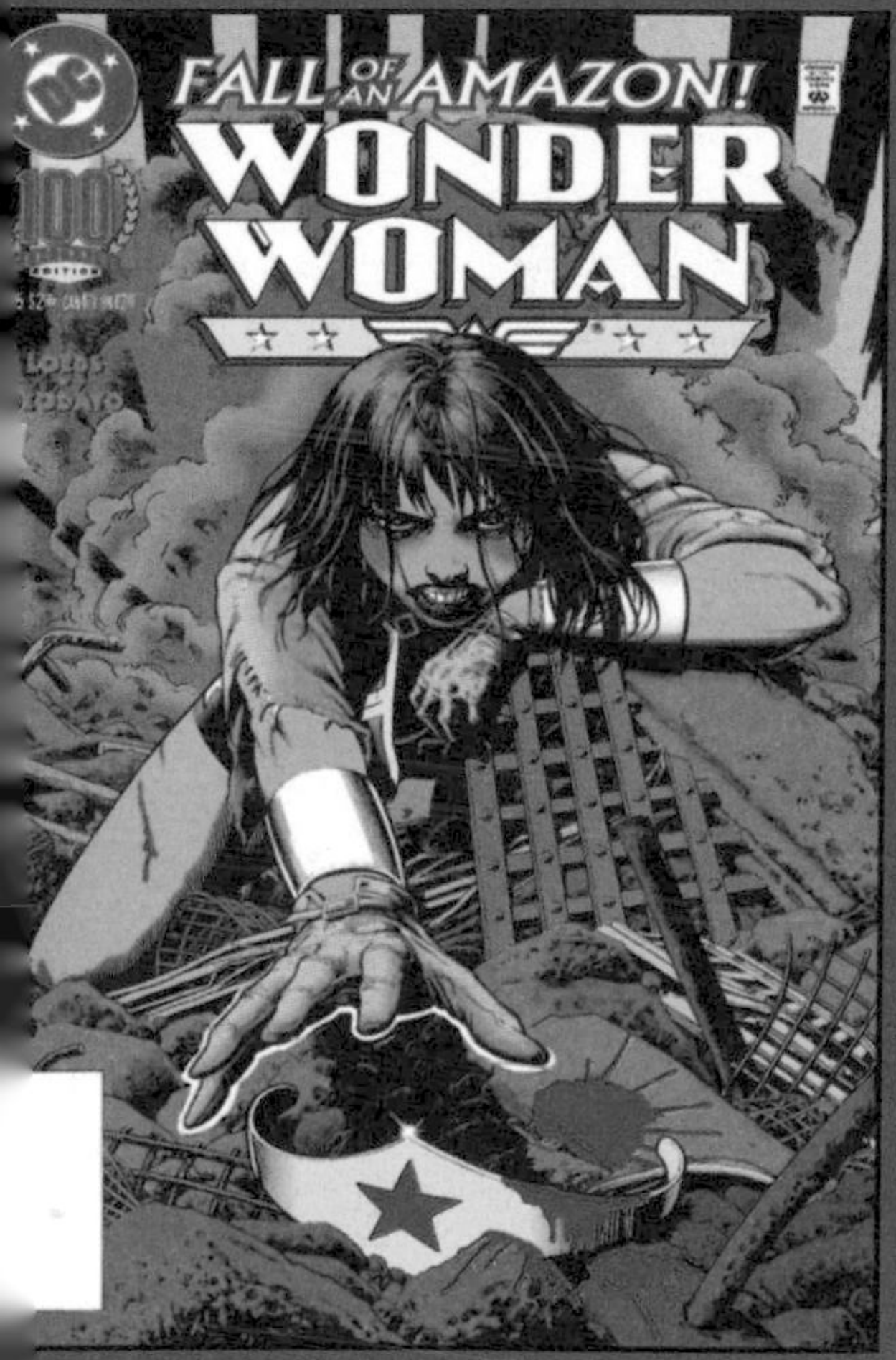
FALL OF AN AMAZON!
WONDER WOMAN
100

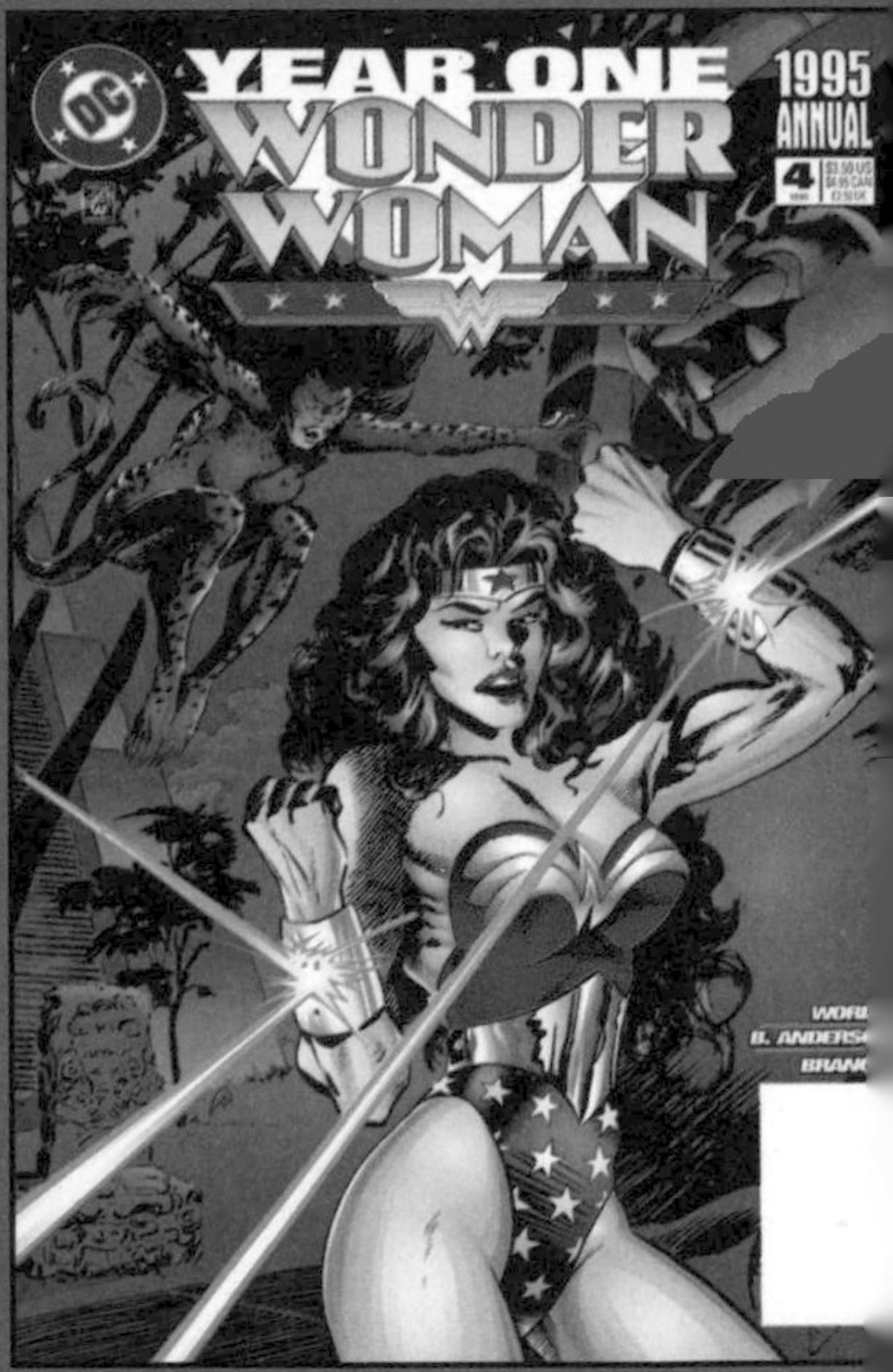
YEAR ONE
WONDER WOMAN
1995 ANNUAL
4

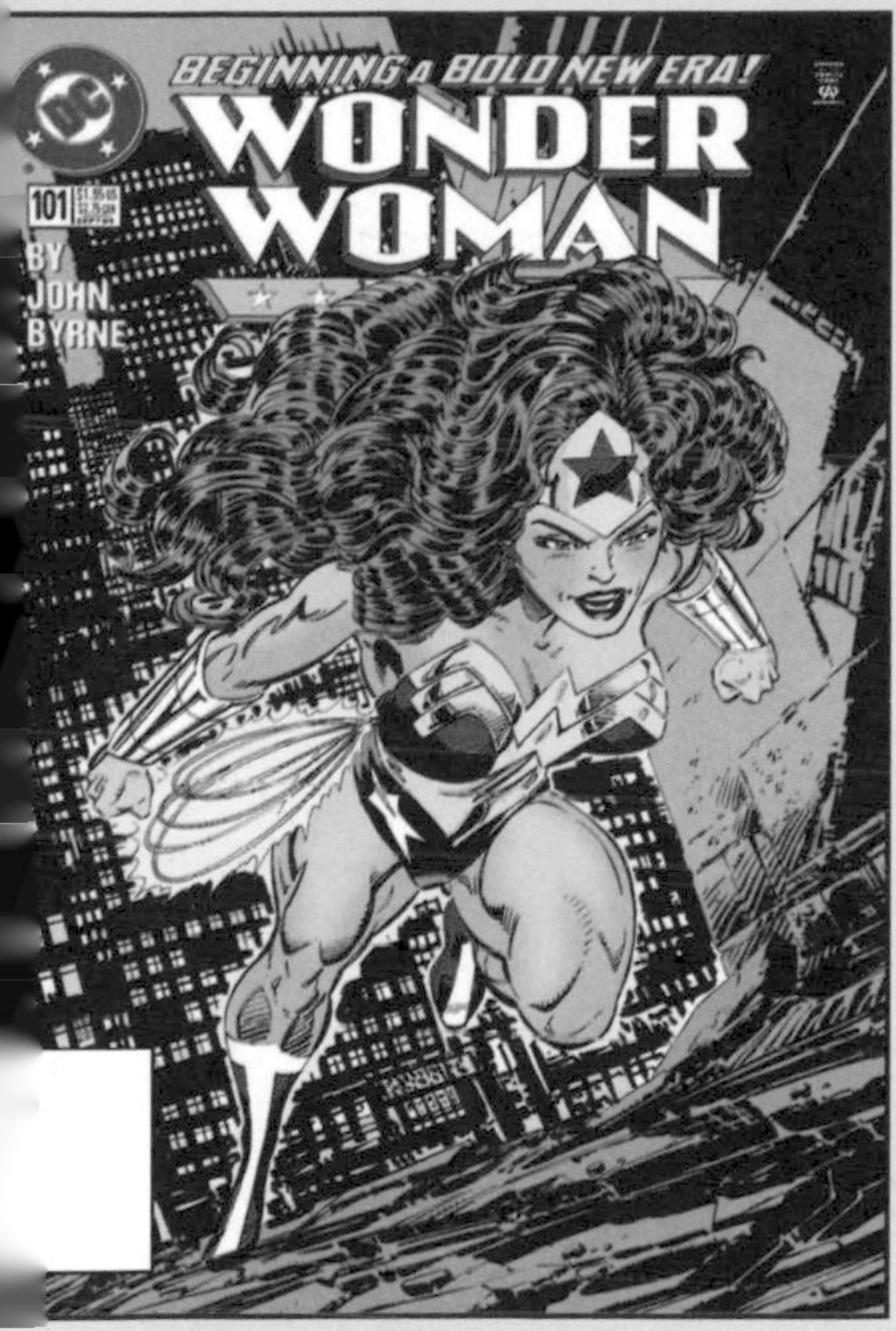
BEGINNING A BOLD NEW ERA!
WONDER WOMAN
101
BY JOHN BYRNE

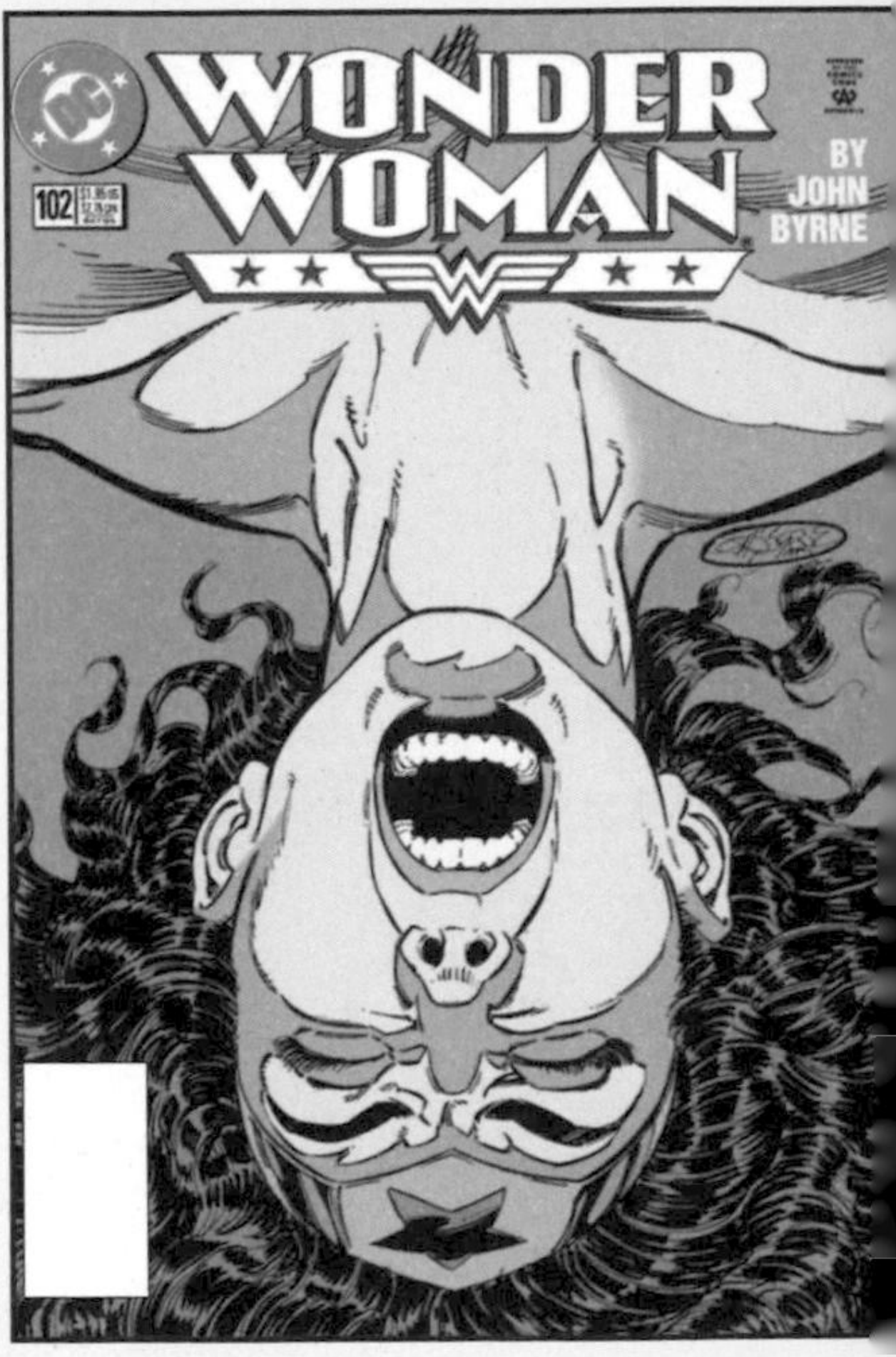
WONDER WOMAN
102
BY JOHN BYRNE

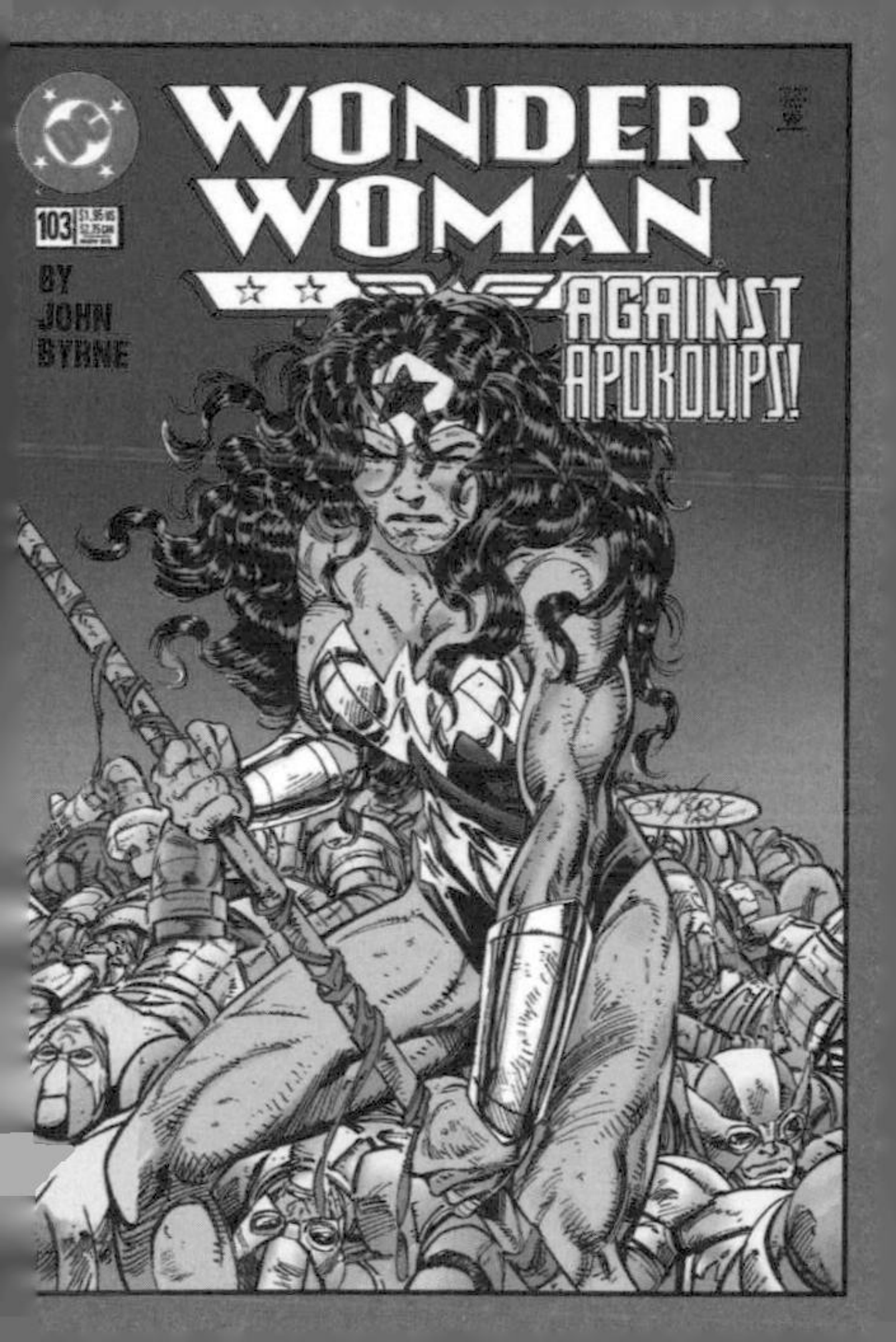
WONDER WOMAN
103
BY JOHN BYRNE
AGAINST APOKOLIPS!

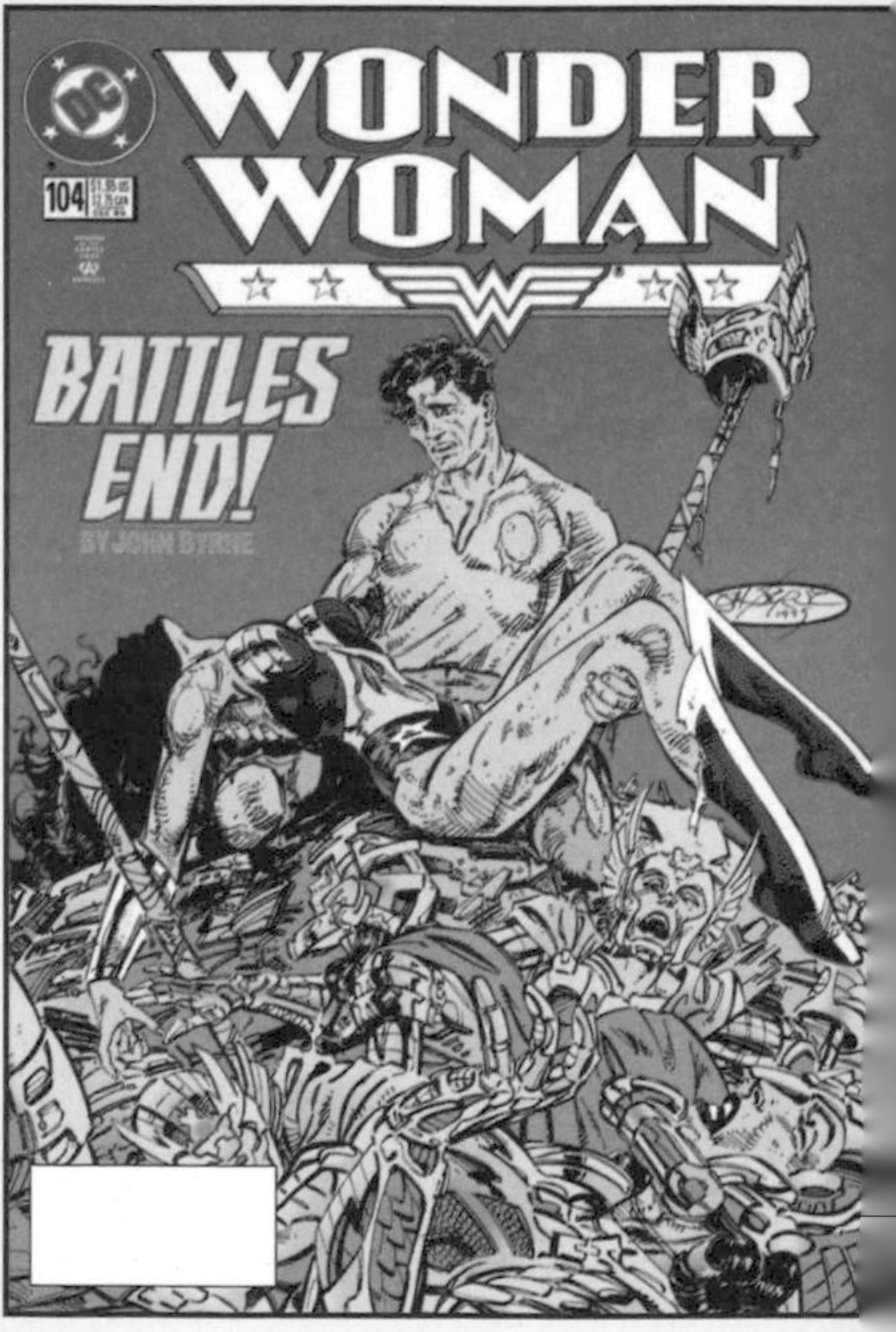
DC
WONDER WOMAN
104
BATTLES END!
BY JOHN BYRNE

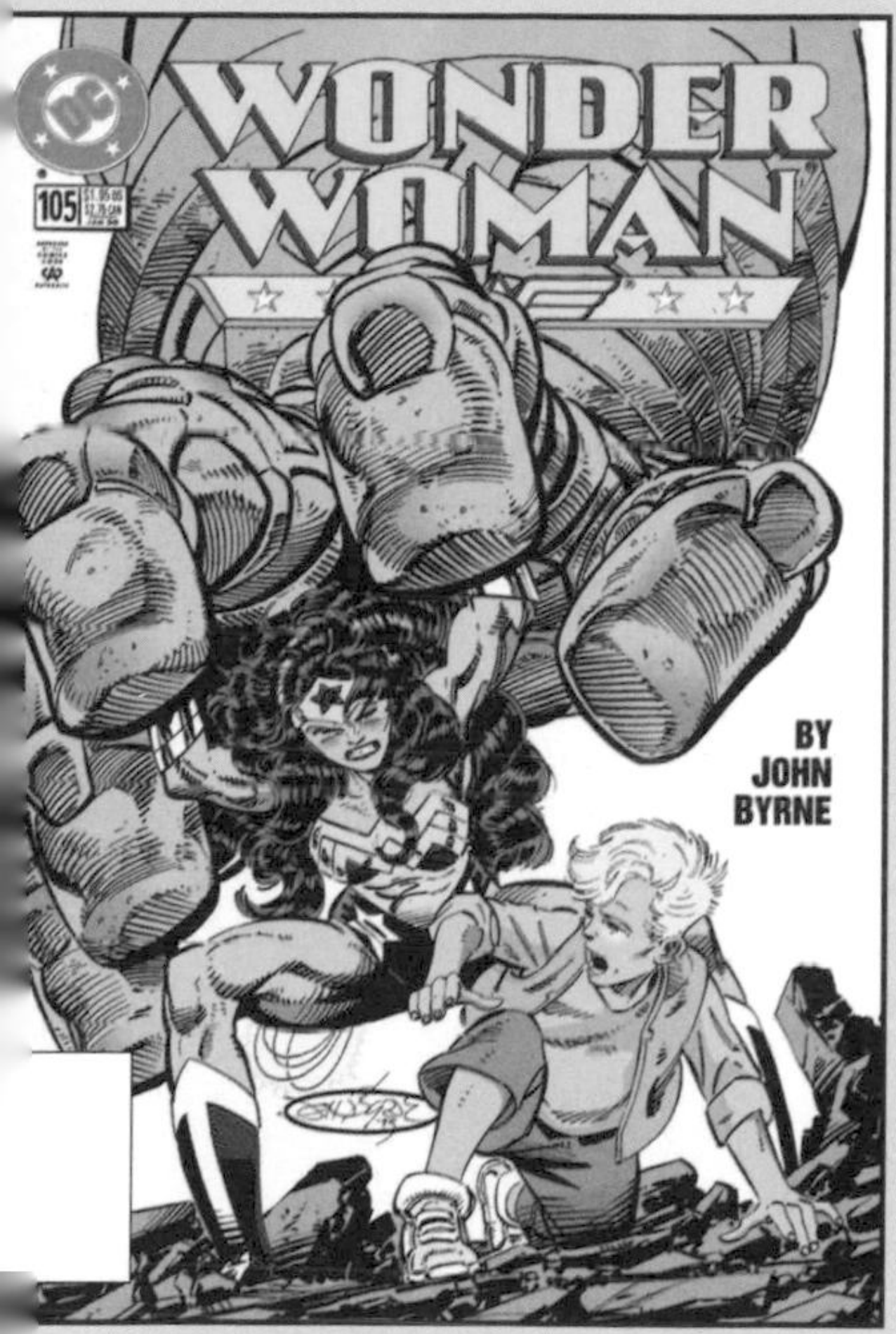
WONDER WOMAN
105
BY JOHN BYRNE

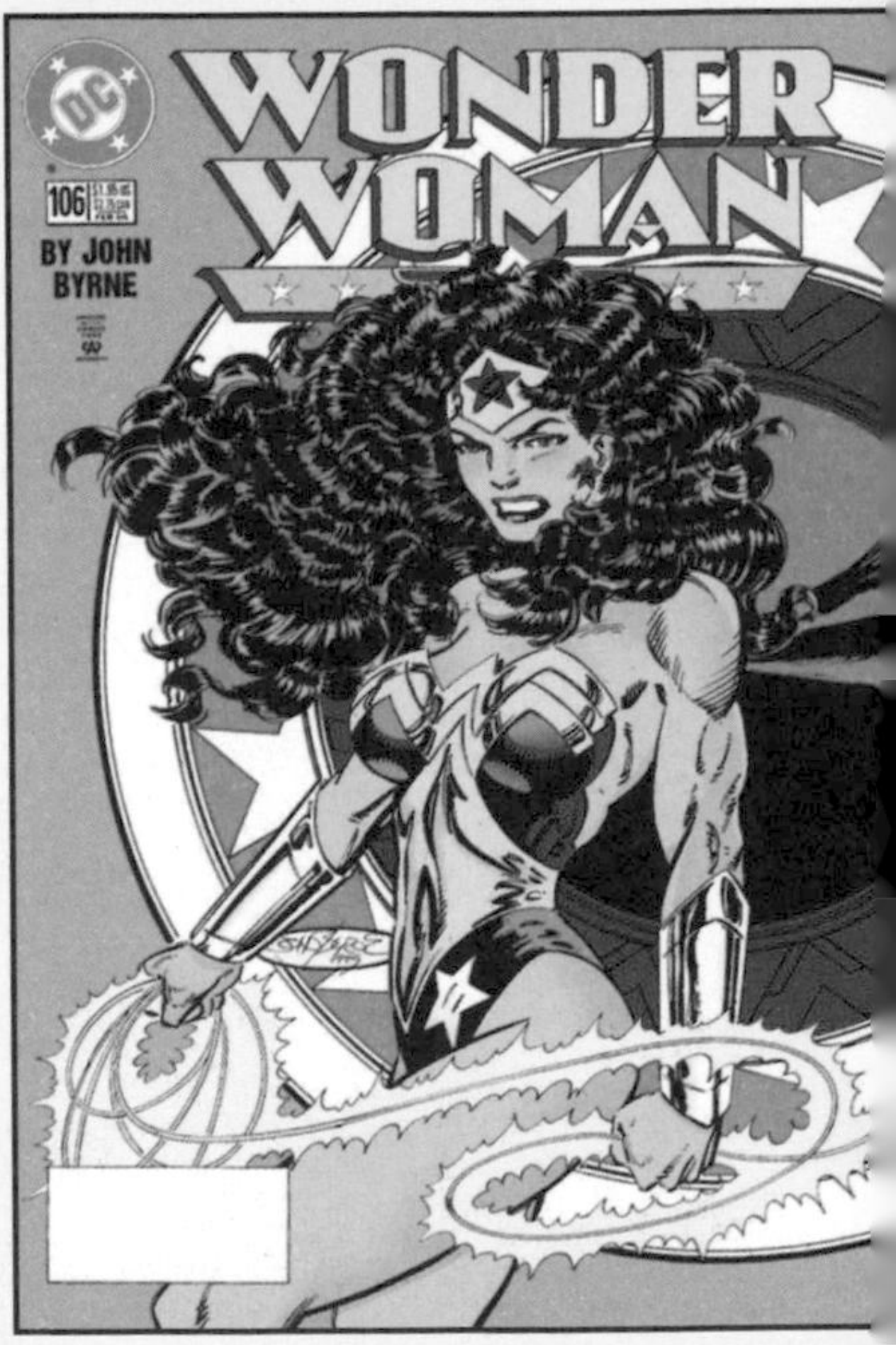
DC
WONDER WOMAN
106
BY JOHN BYRNE

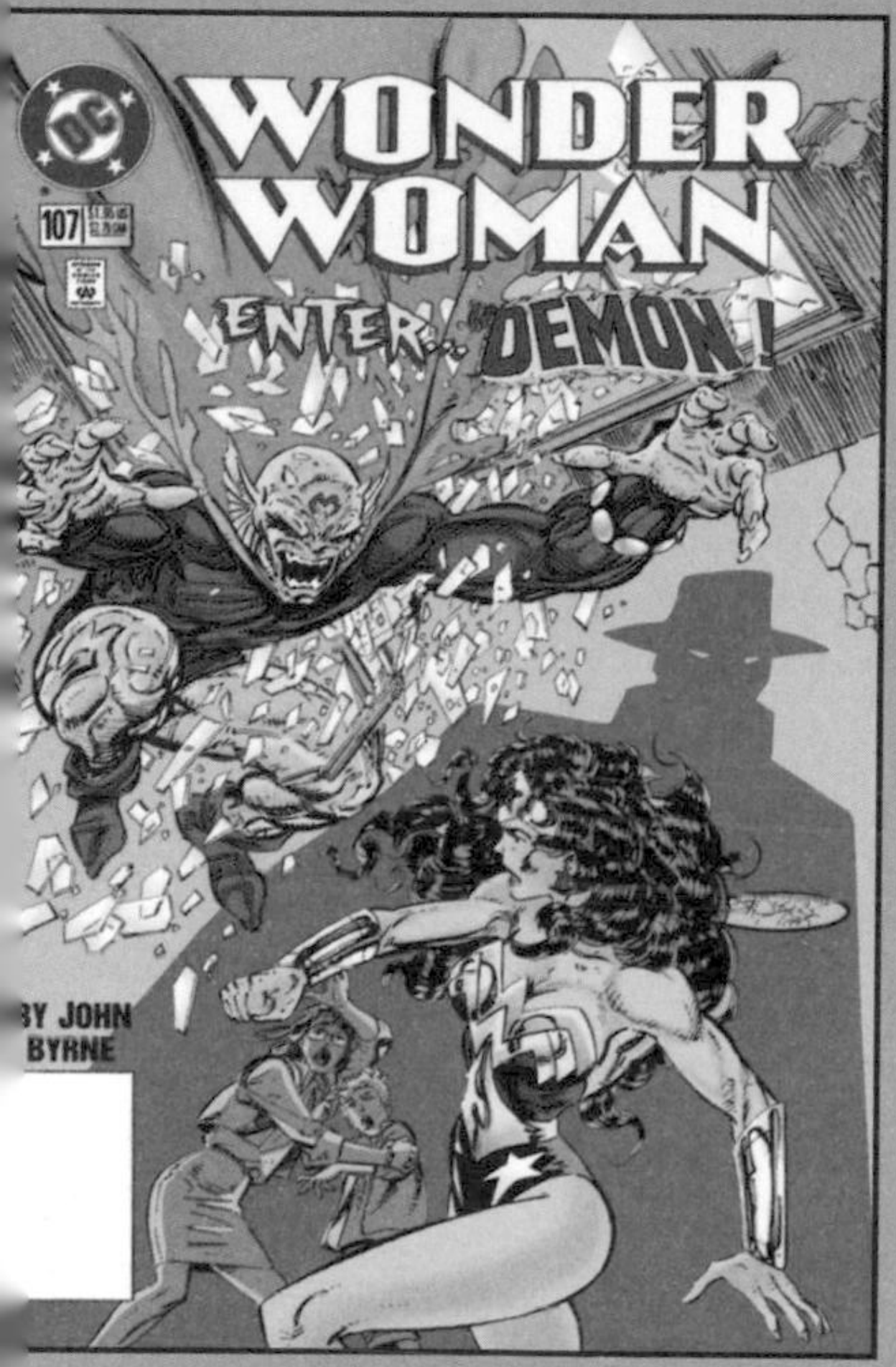
DC
WONDER WOMAN
107
ENTER... DEMON!
BY JOHN BYRNE

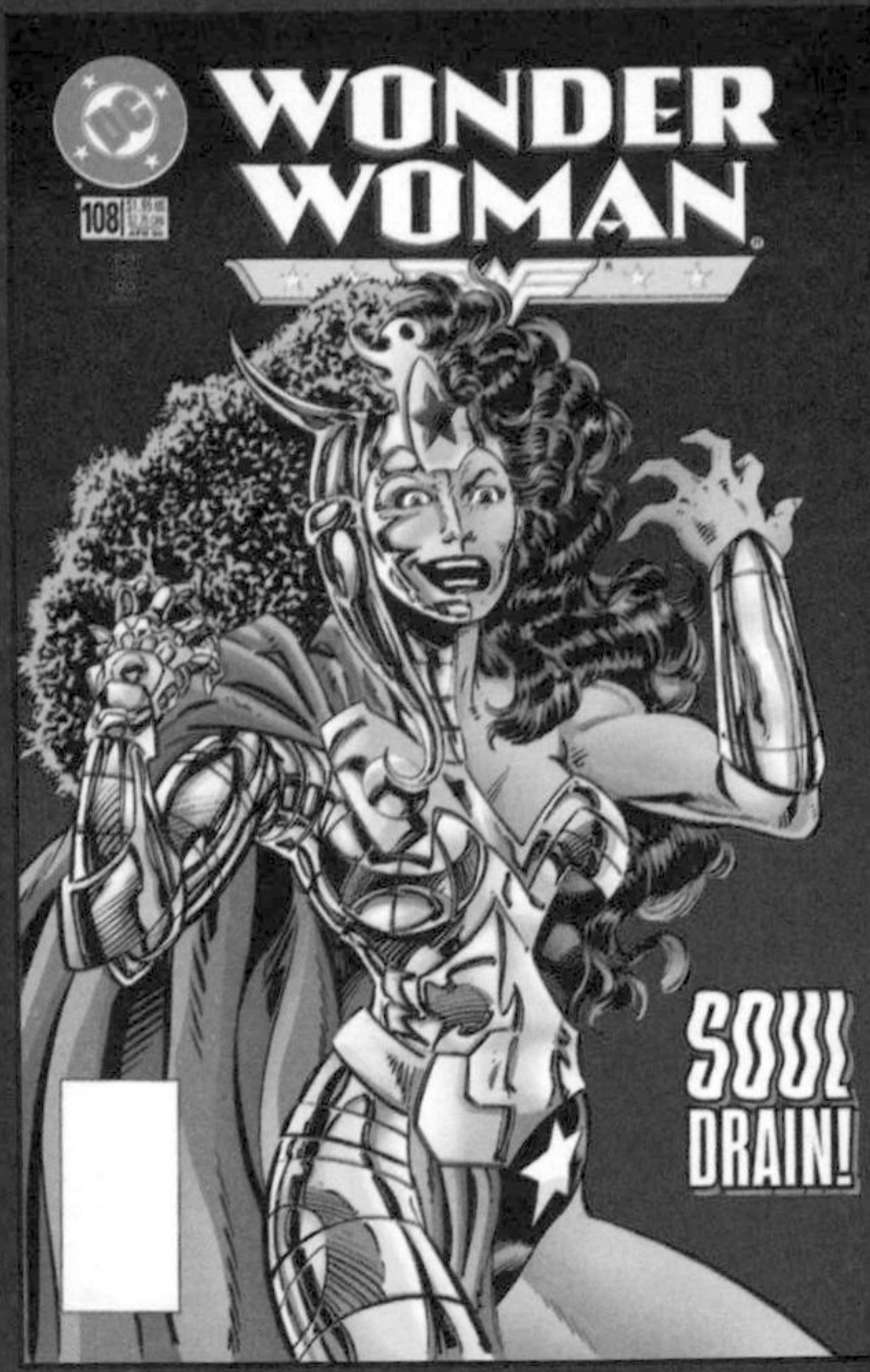
WONDER WOMAN
108
SOUL DRAIN!

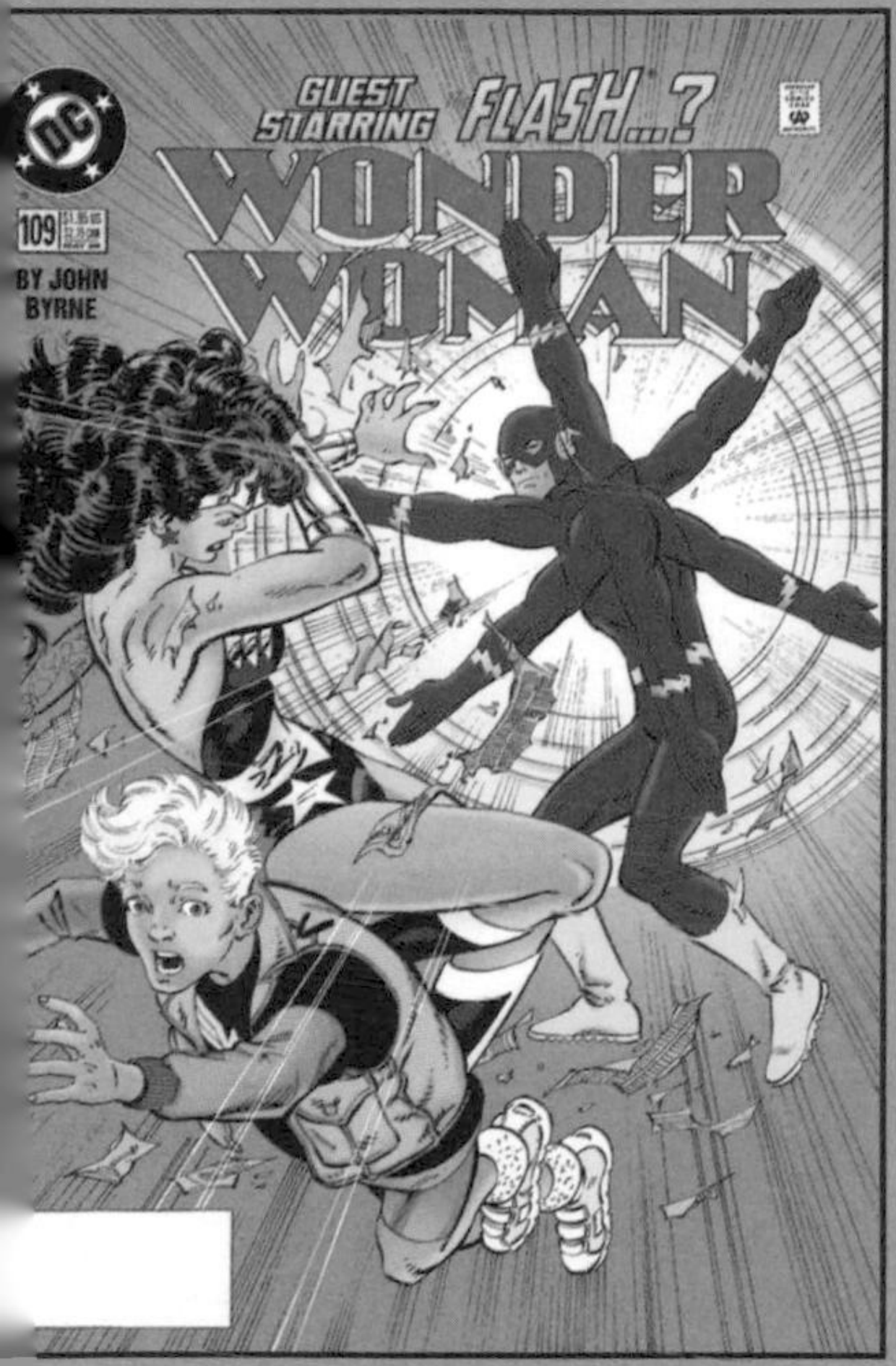
GUEST STARRING FLASH...?
WONDER WOMAN
109
BY JOHN BYRNE

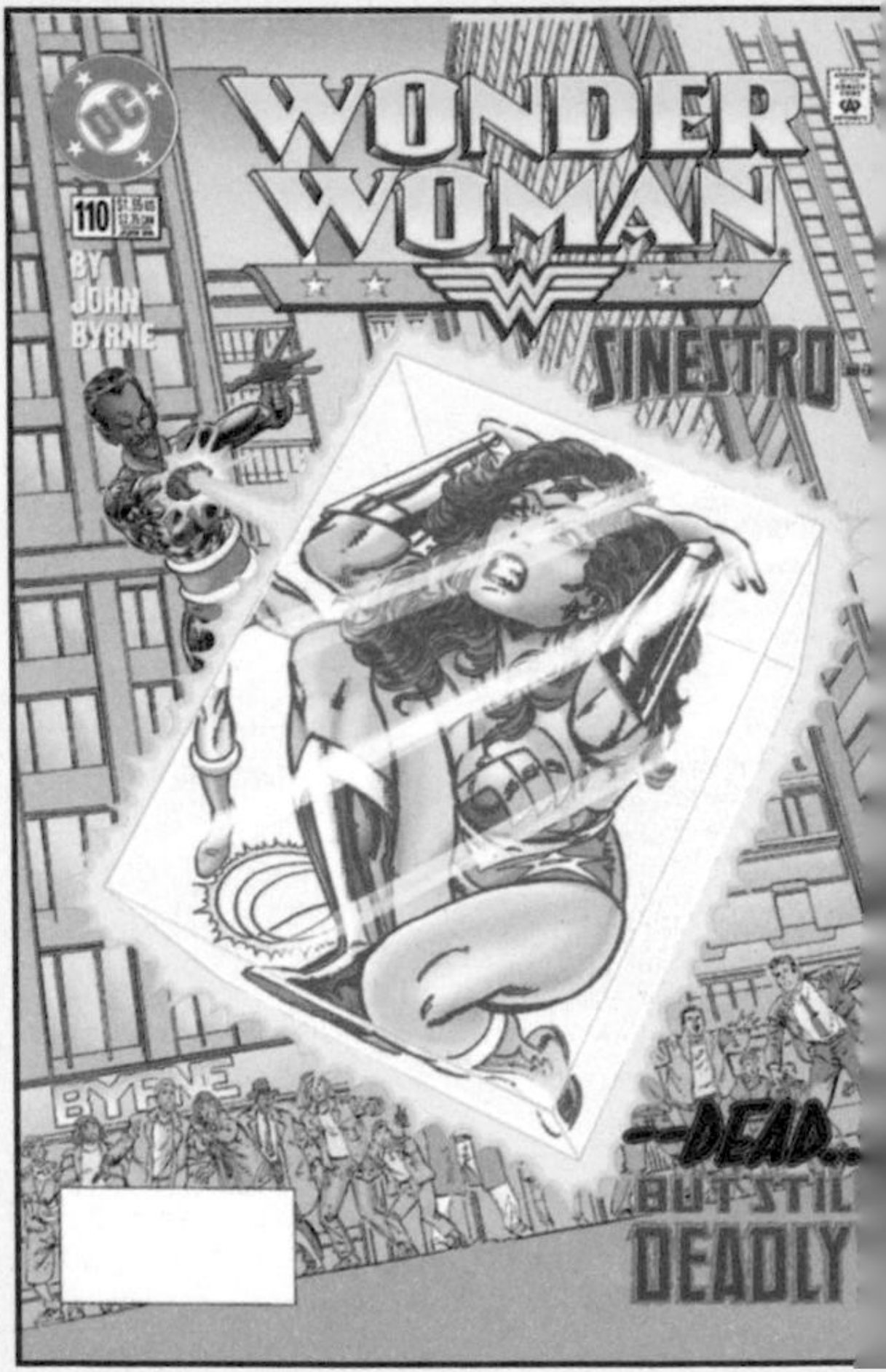
DC
110
BY JOHN BYRNE
WONDER WOMAN
SINESTRO
—DEAD...
BUT STIL
DEADLY

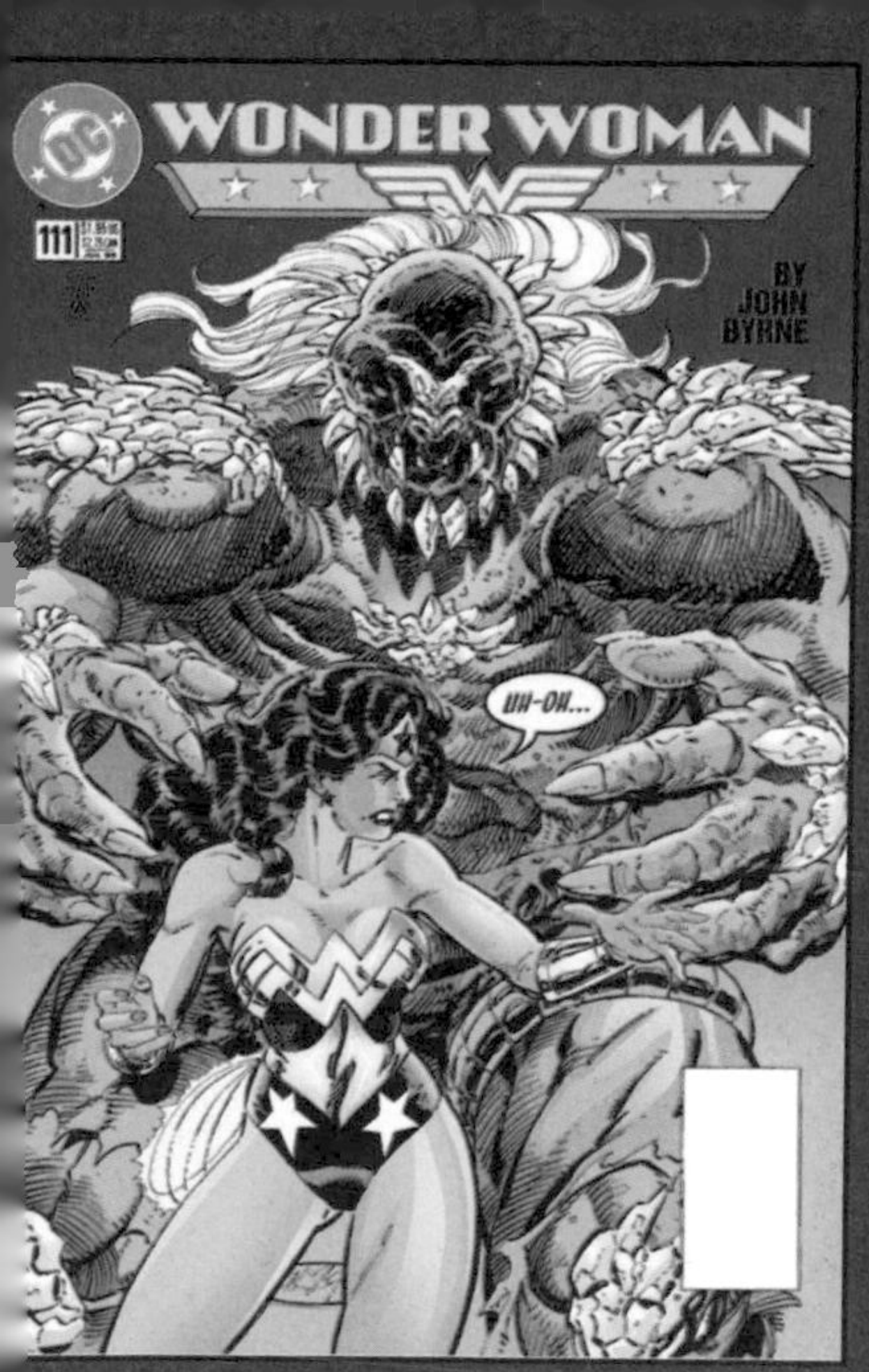
WONDER WOMAN
111
BY JOHN BYRNE
UH-OH...

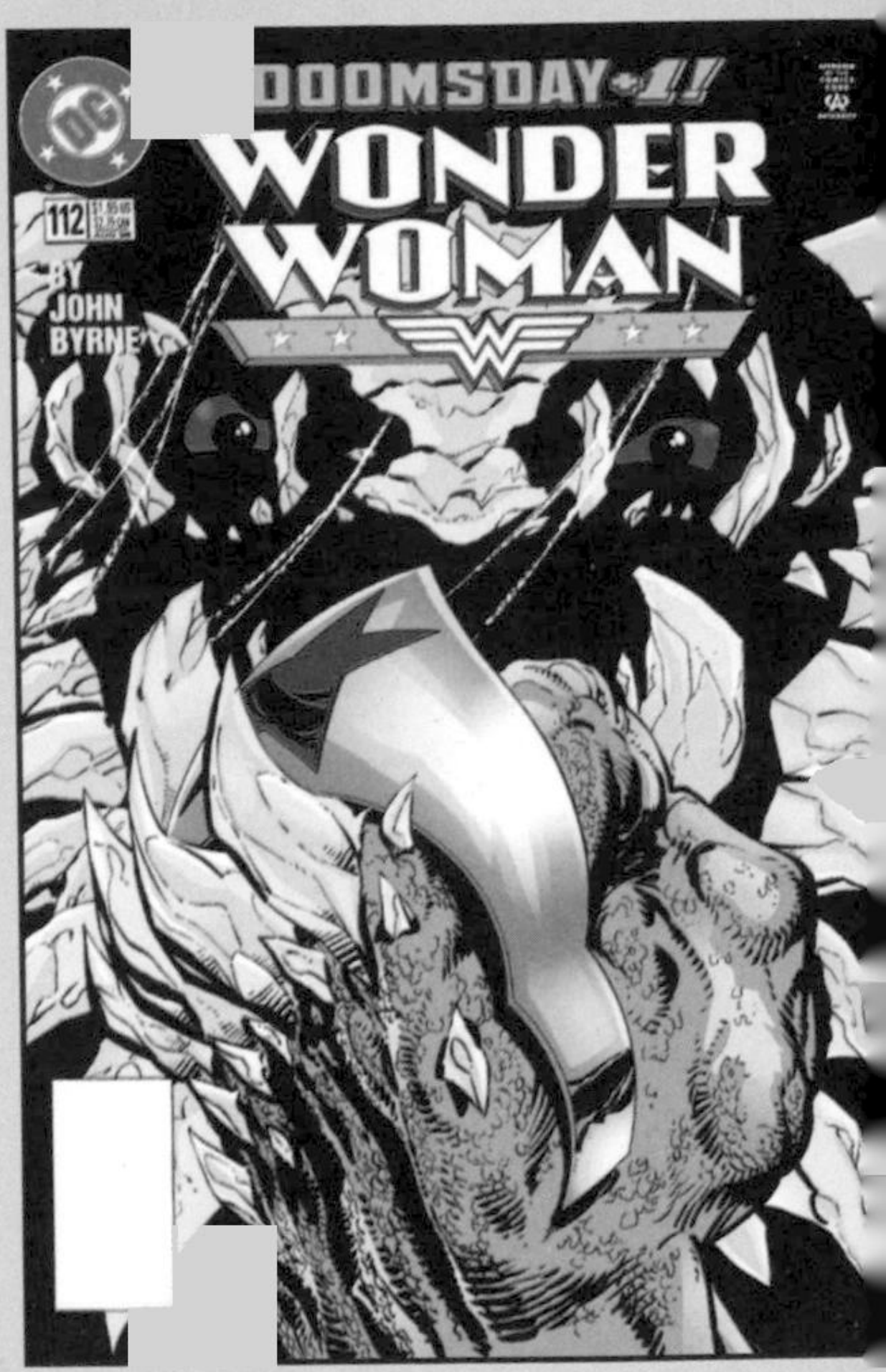
DOOMSDAY #1
WONDER WOMAN
112
BY JOHN BYRNE

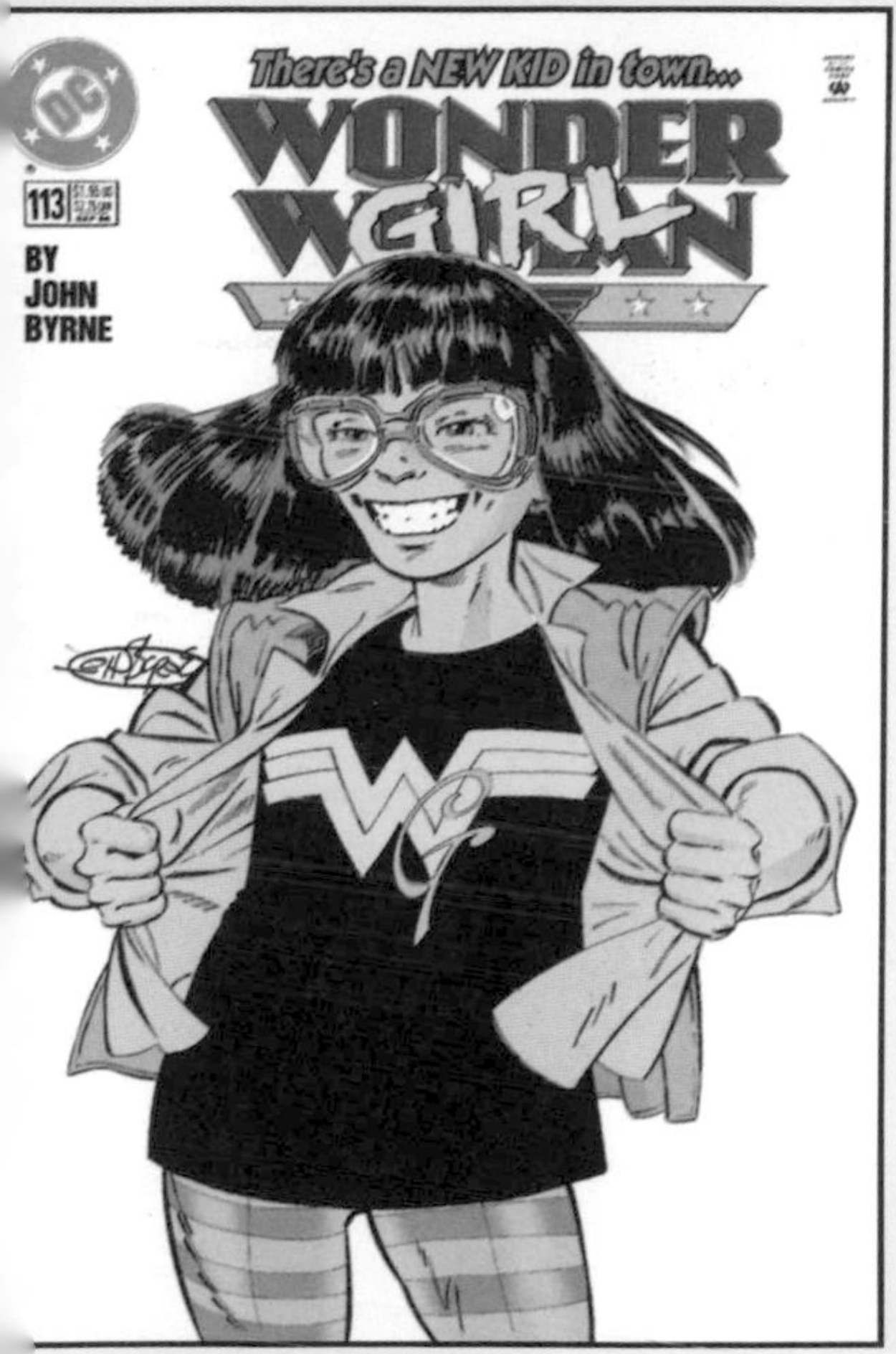
There's a NEW KID in town...
WONDER GIRL
113
BY JOHN BYRNE

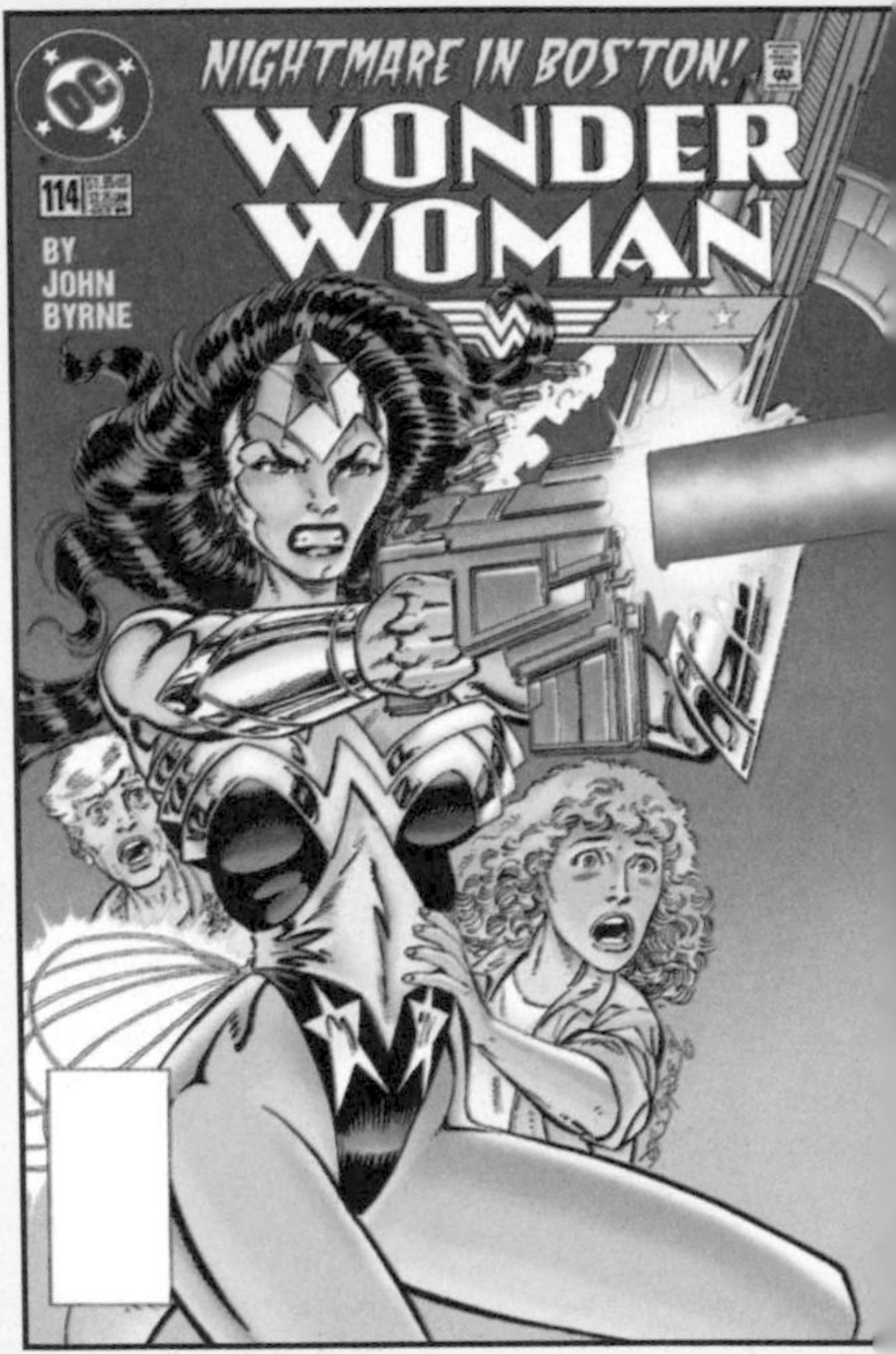
NIGHTMARE IN BOSTON!
WONDER WOMAN
114
BY JOHN BYRNE

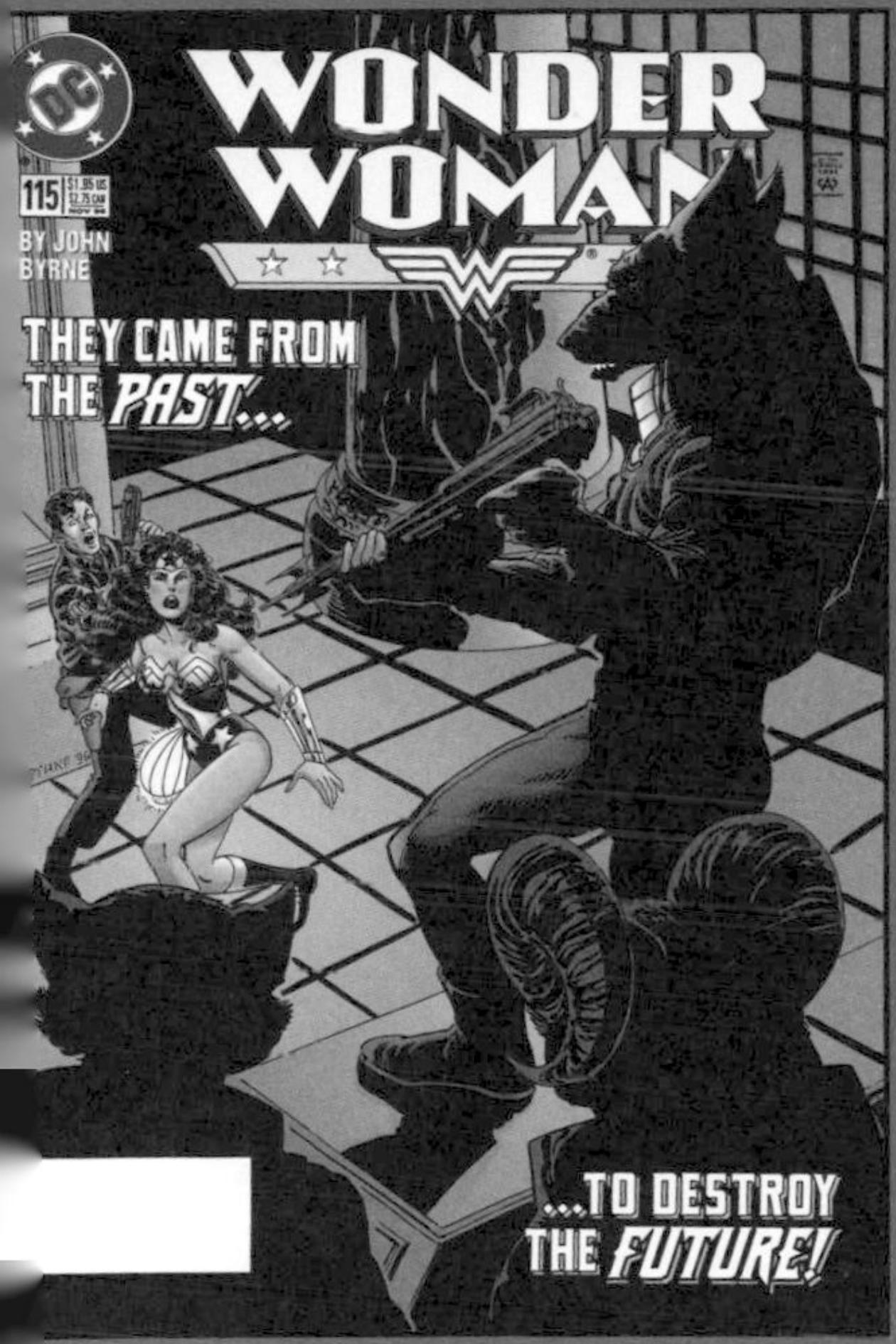
DC
WONDER WOMAN
115
$1.95 US
$2.75 CAN
BY JOHN BYRNE
THEY CAME FROM THE PAST...
...TO DESTROY THE FUTURE!

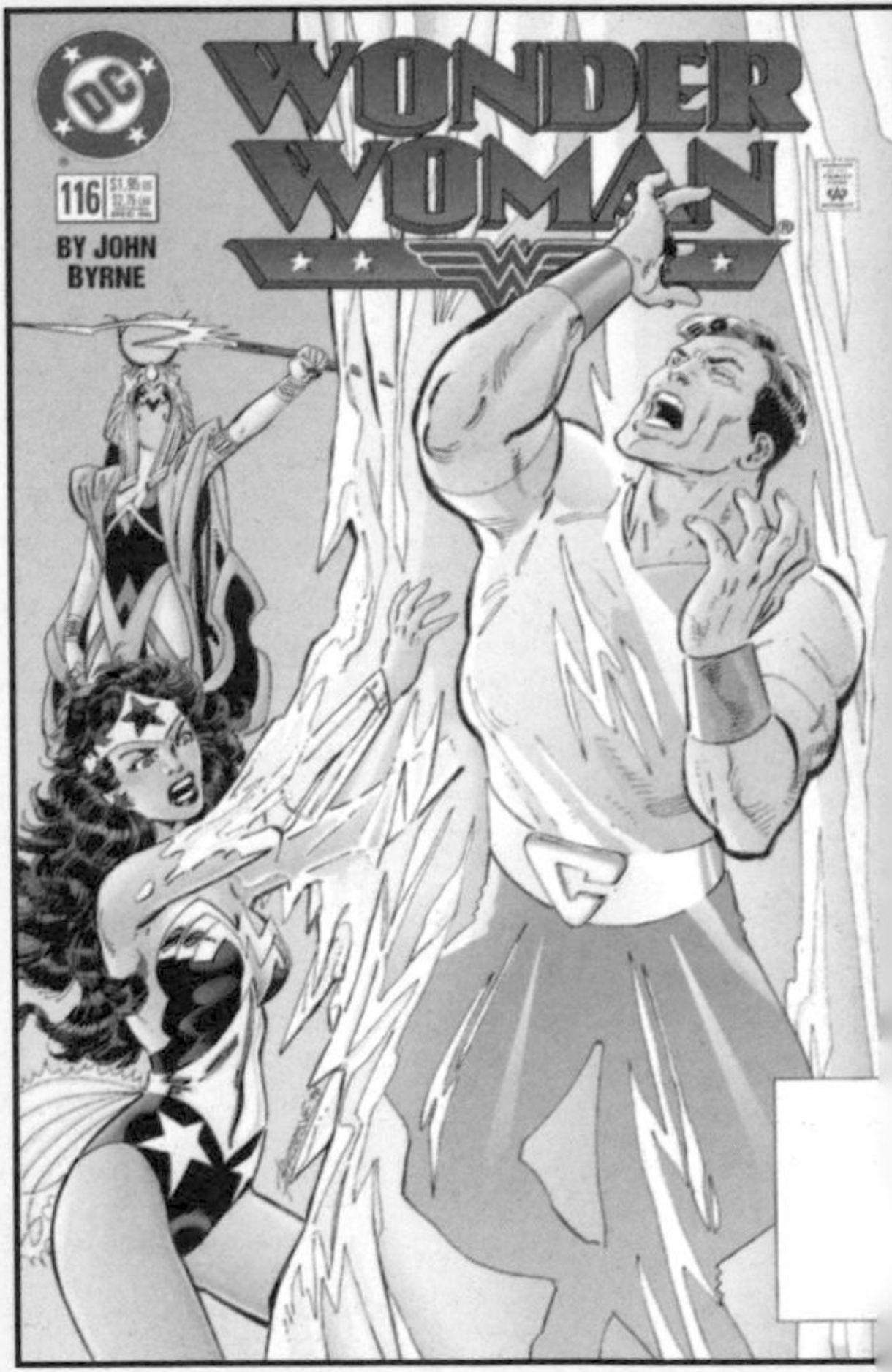
DC
WONDER WOMAN
116
BY JOHN BYRNE

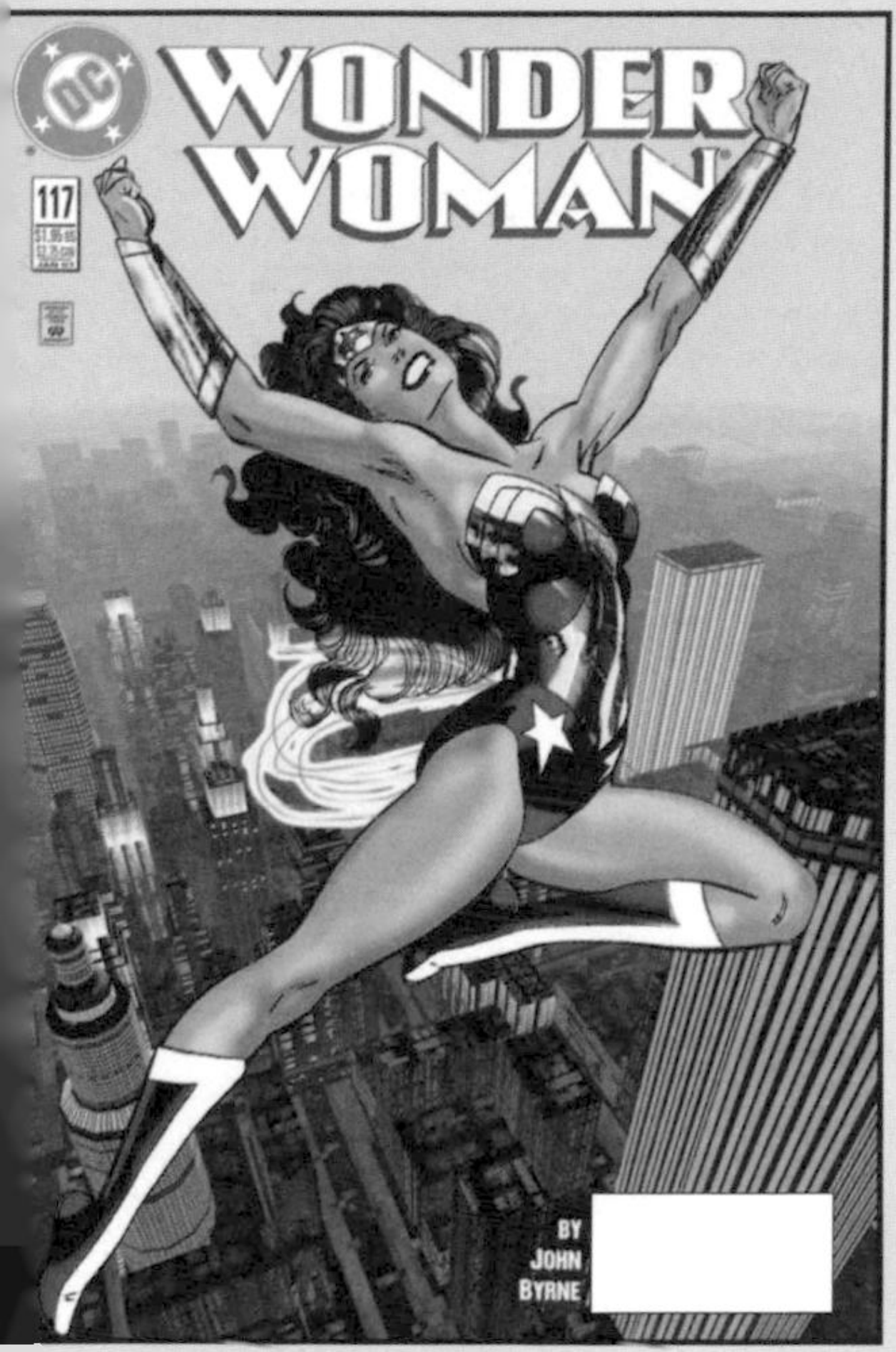
DC
WONDER WOMAN
117
BY JOHN BYRNE

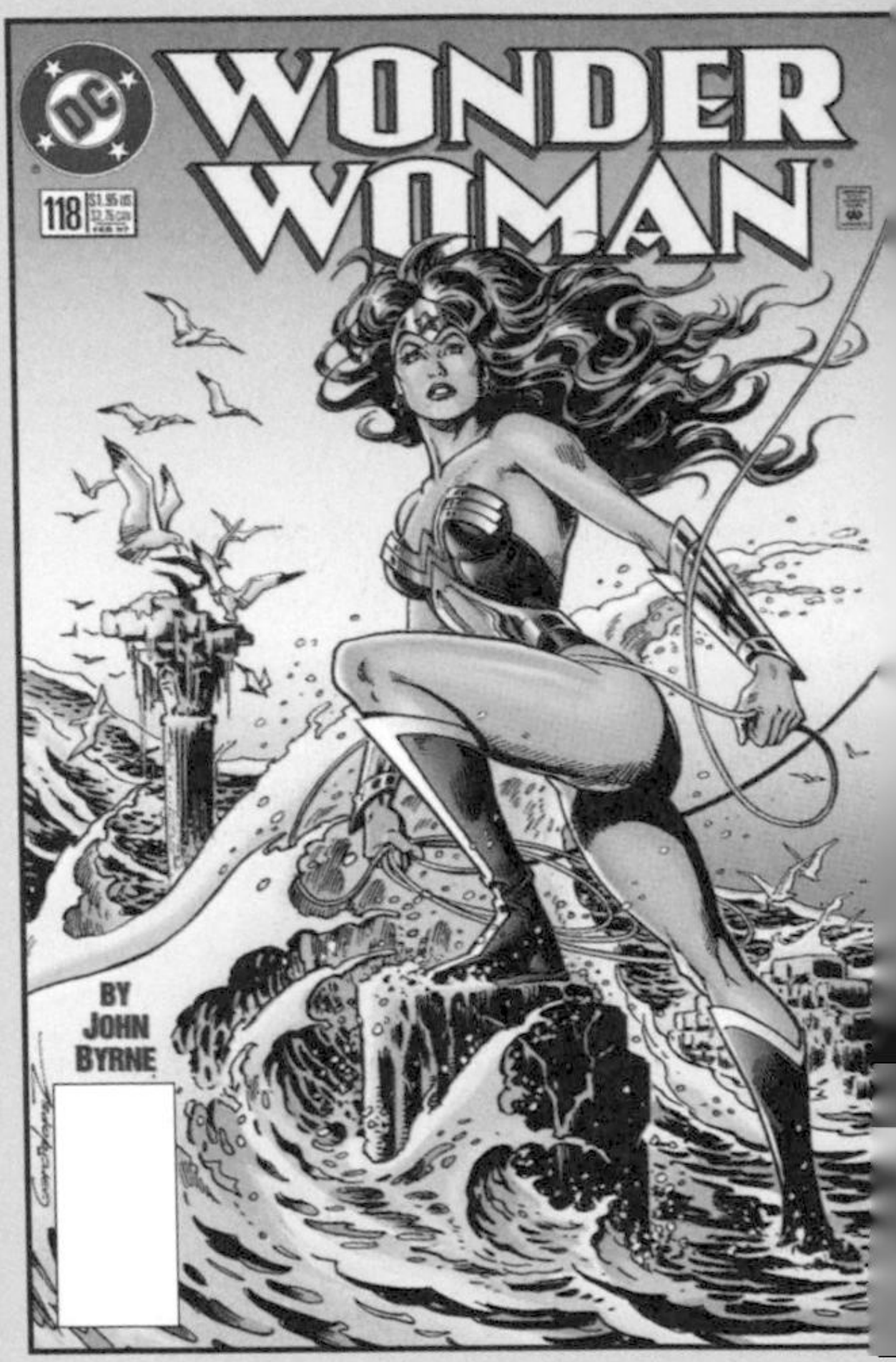
DC
WONDER WOMAN
118
BY JOHN BYRNE

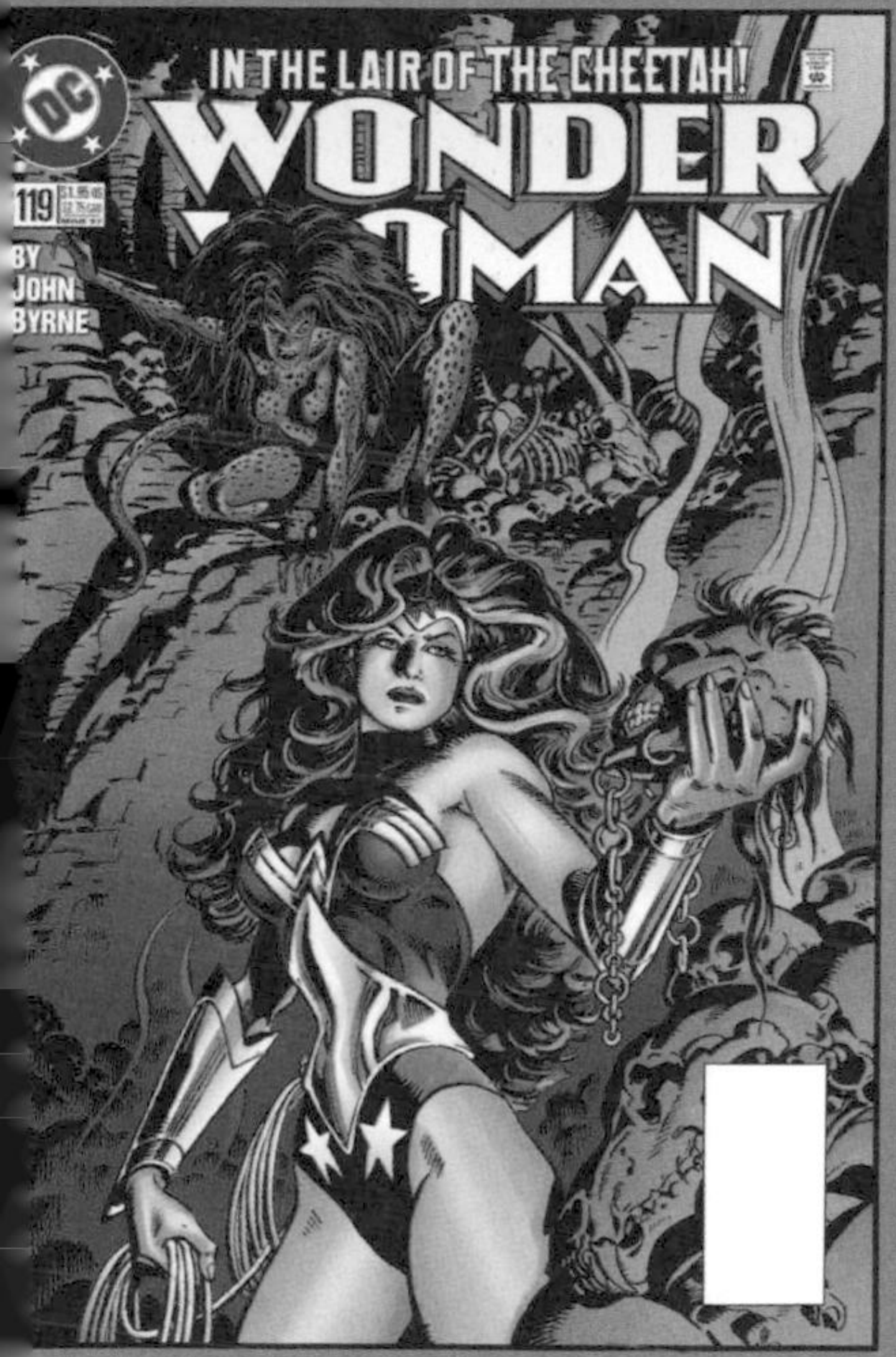
IN THE LAIR OF THE CHEETAH!
WONDER WOMAN
119
BY JOHN BYRNE

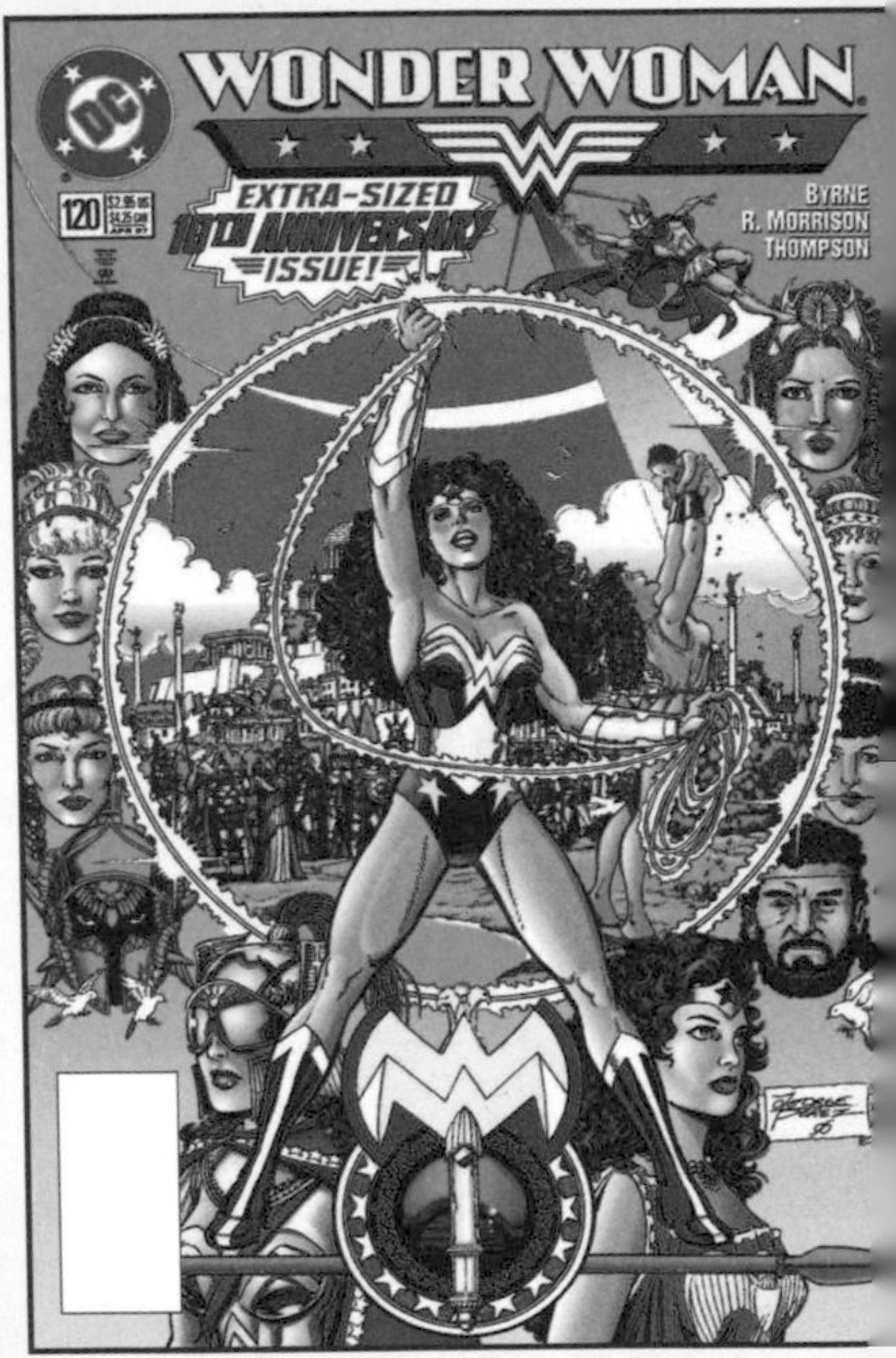
WONDER WOMAN
120
EXTRA-SIZED
10TH ANNIVERSARY
ISSUE!
BYRNE
R. MORRISON
THOMPSON

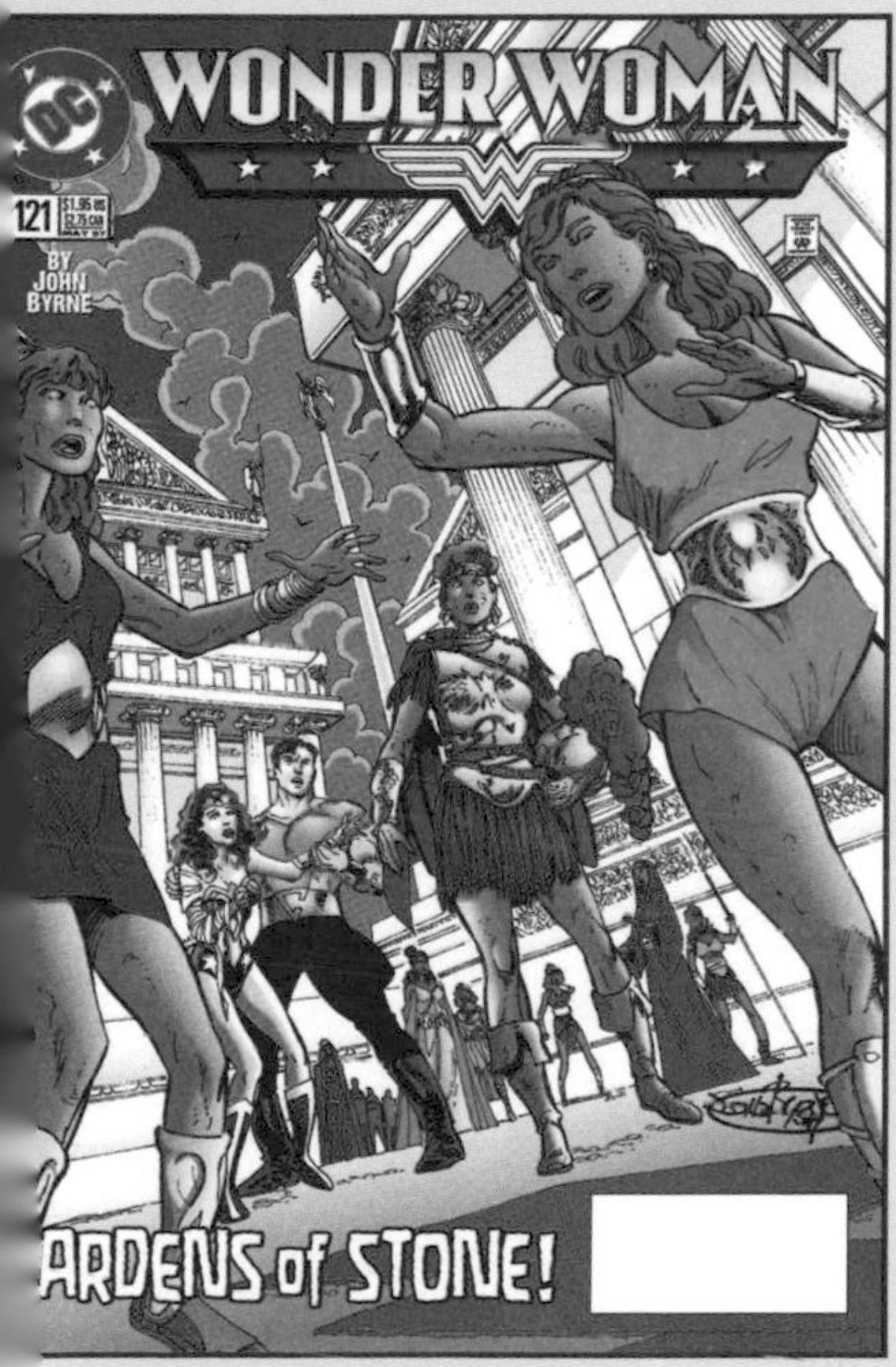
WONDER WOMAN
121
$1.95 US
$2.25 CAN
BY JOHN BYRNE
ARDENS of STONE!

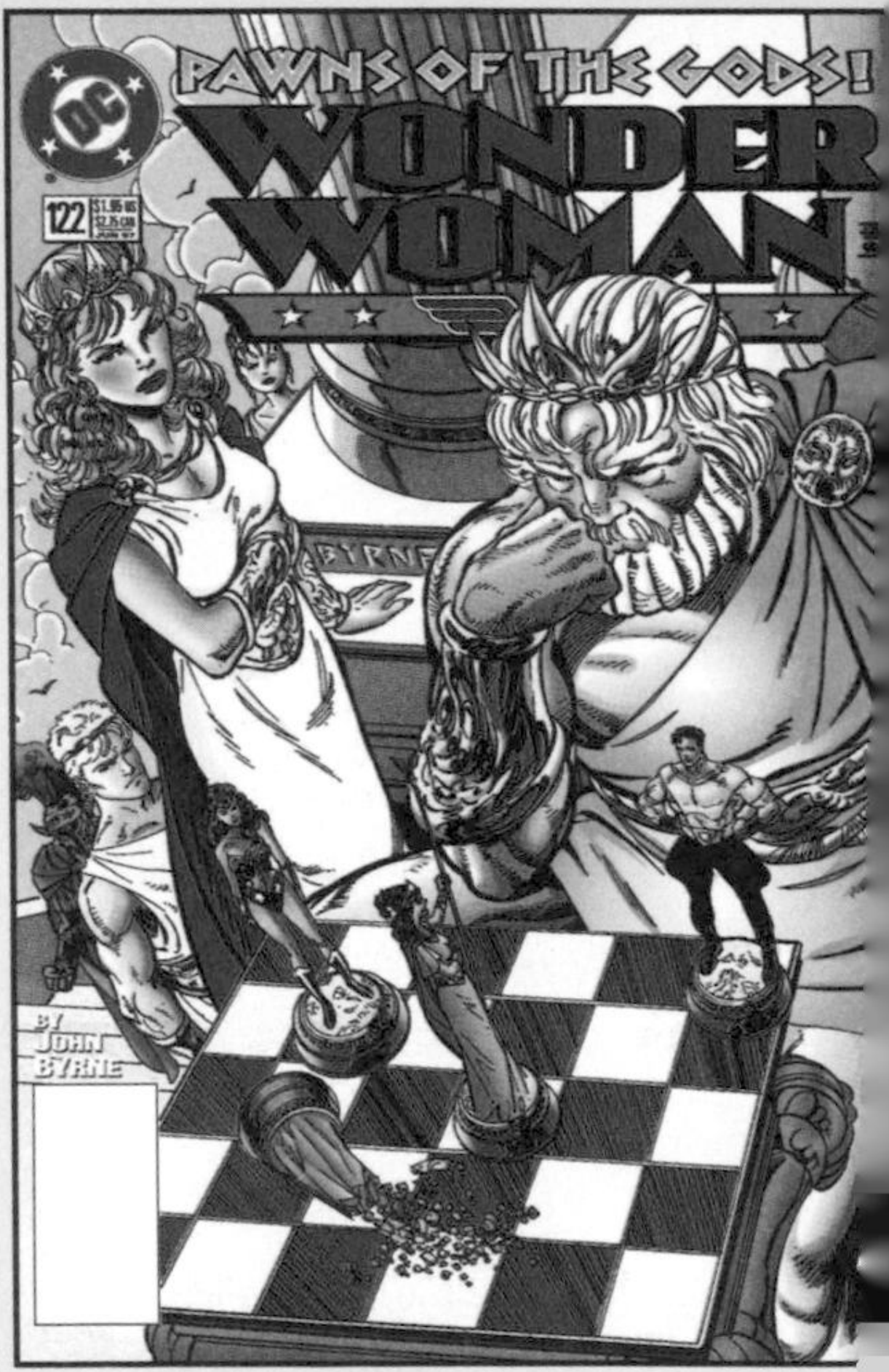
PAWNS OF THE GODS!
WONDER WOMAN
122
$1.95 US
$2.75 CAN
BYRNE
BY JOHN BYRNE

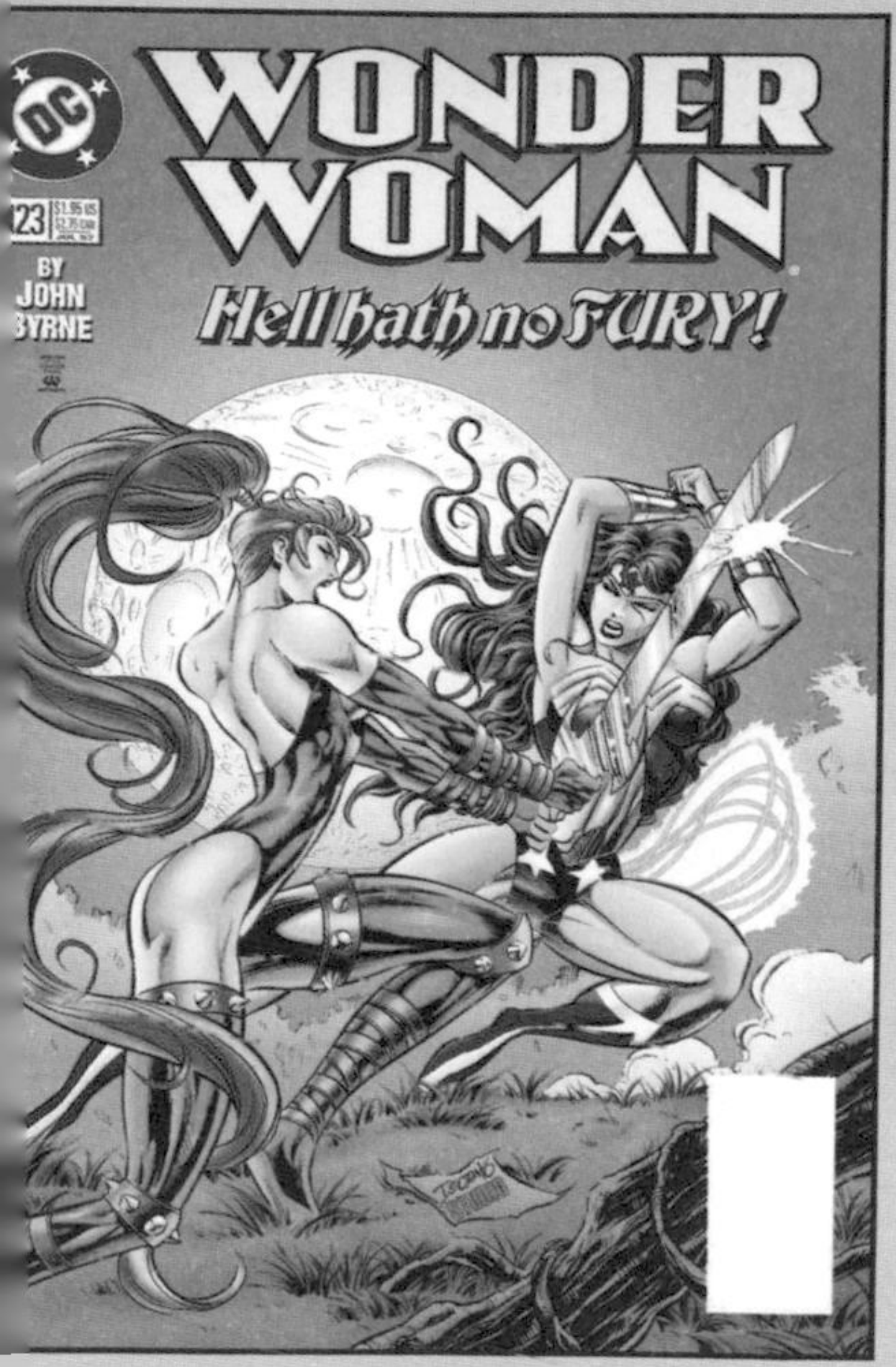
DC
WONDER WOMAN
23
$1.95 US
$2.25 CAN
BY JOHN BYRNE
Hell hath no FURY!

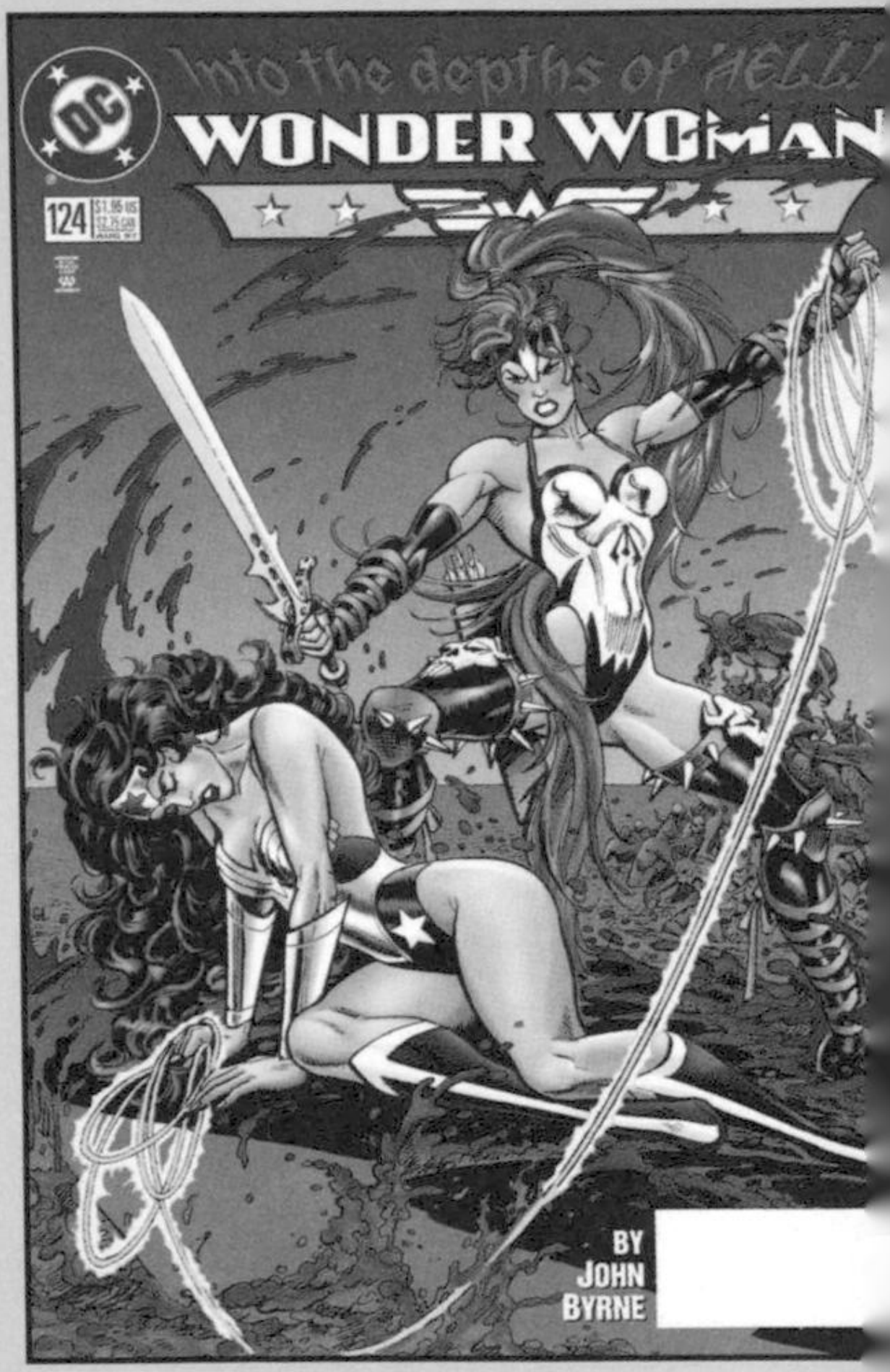
Into the depths of HELL!
WONDER WOMAN
124
$1.95 US
$2.25 CAN
BY
JOHN
BYRNE

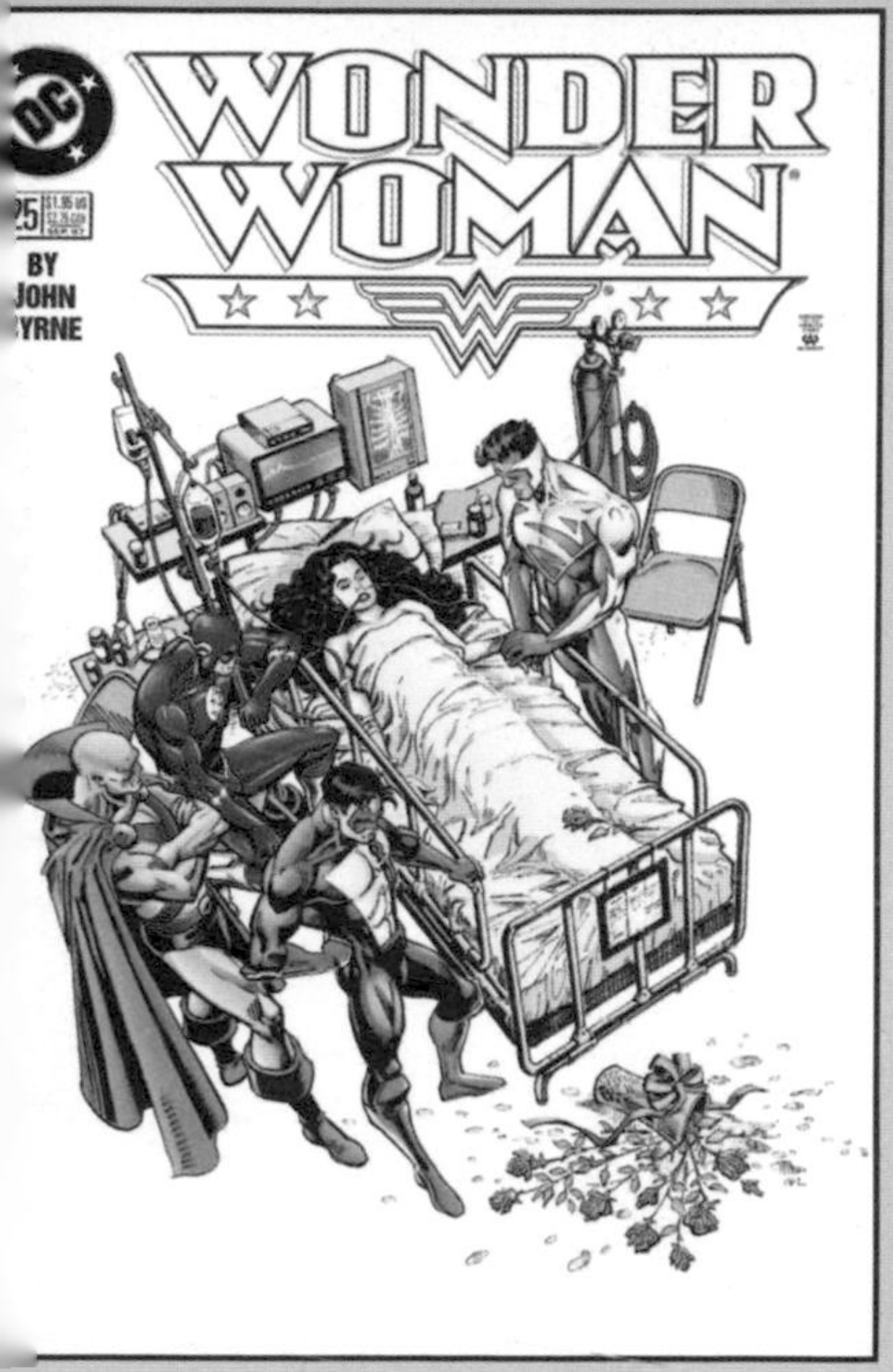
DC
WONDER WOMAN
25
BY
JOHN
YRNE

GENESIS
DAILY PLANET
126
METROPOLITAN NEWSPAPER SPECIAL ★★★★ EDITION Volume 1, Number 126

A WORLD WITHOUT WONDER WOMAN?

DIANA, PRINCESS OF THEMYSCIRA, STRUCK DOW

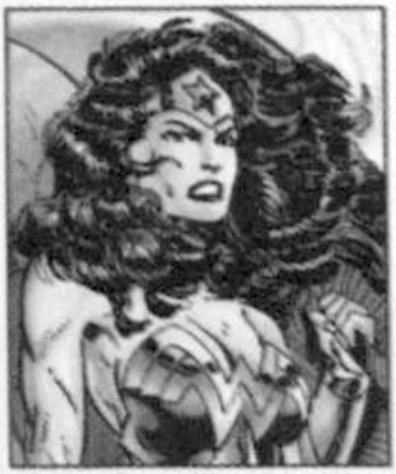

Princess Diana of Themyscira, in her heroic garb as Wonder Woman.

EXCLUSIVE TO THE PLANET

Story and Pictures by
JOHN BYRNE

(Gateway City) While details are still sketchy, sources in the Gateway City police have confirmed that Princess Diana of Themyscira, the Amazon heroine known as Wonder Woman, was struck down yesterday in a battle with an unknown foe in downtown Gateway.

Wonder Woman was brought to the emergency room of Gateway Memorial Hospital by companions who had, reportedly, taken part in the battle that caused her injuries. According to a doctor at the hospital, Wonder Woman is not suffering from any apparent wounds, but her condition is nonetheless listed as critical.

"Frankly, we're at a loss to explain exactly what her condition is," said Dr. W Chin. "From what we've been able to tain from her companions, Wonder W was the victim of an attack by a... called Neron who did no physical da to her per se, but who struck at her very This is, needless to say, unknown te to the medical profession. Pending f tests, all we can do is sustain her ph form and hope for answers."

Members of the JLA are reportedly ing vigil by Wonder Woman's bedsi

(Story continues 2nd page foll

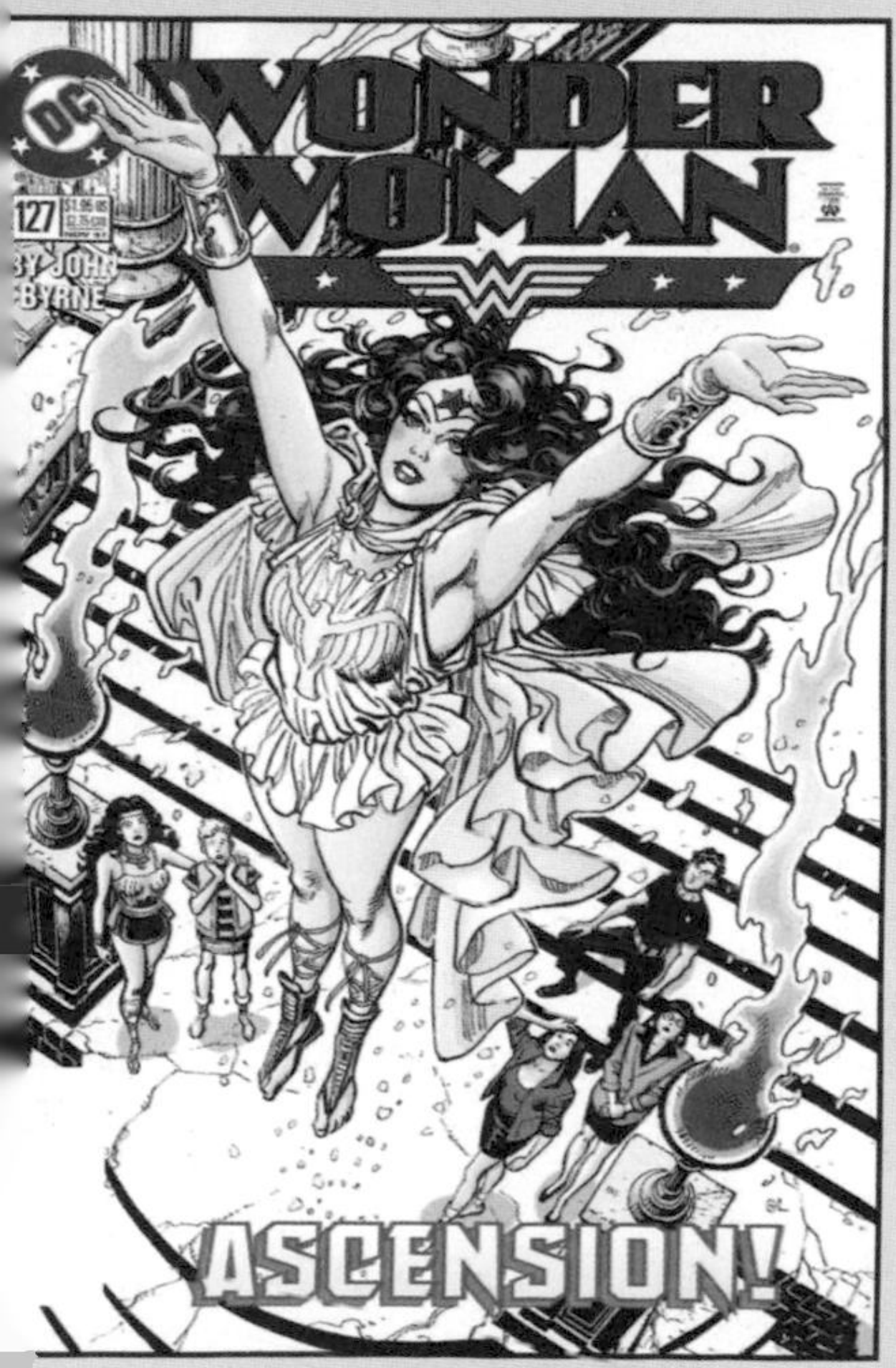
DC
WONDER WOMAN
127
BY JOHN BYRNE
ASCENSION!

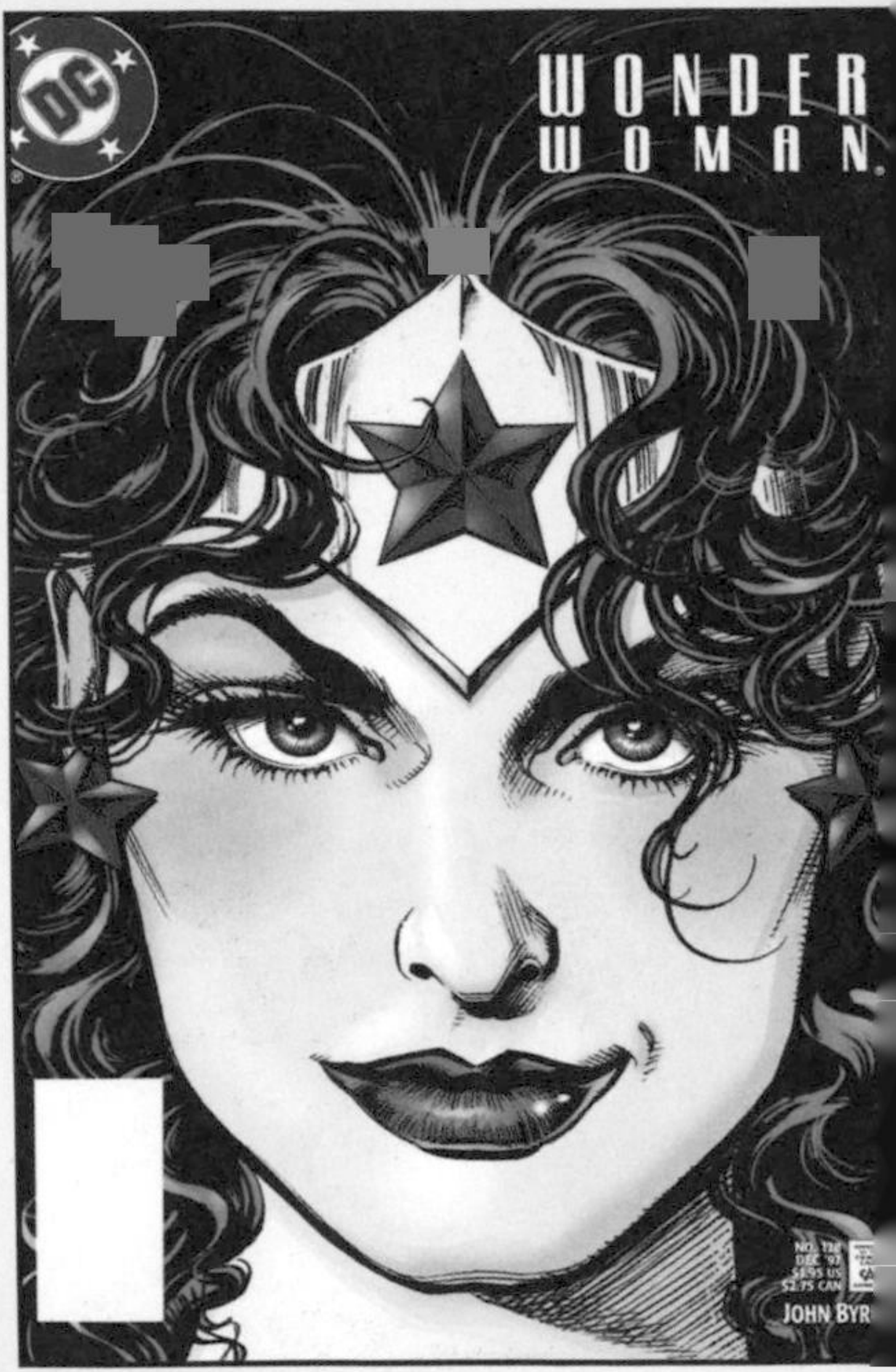
DC
WONDER
WOMAN.
DEC '97
$1.95 US
$2.75 CAN
JOHN BYR

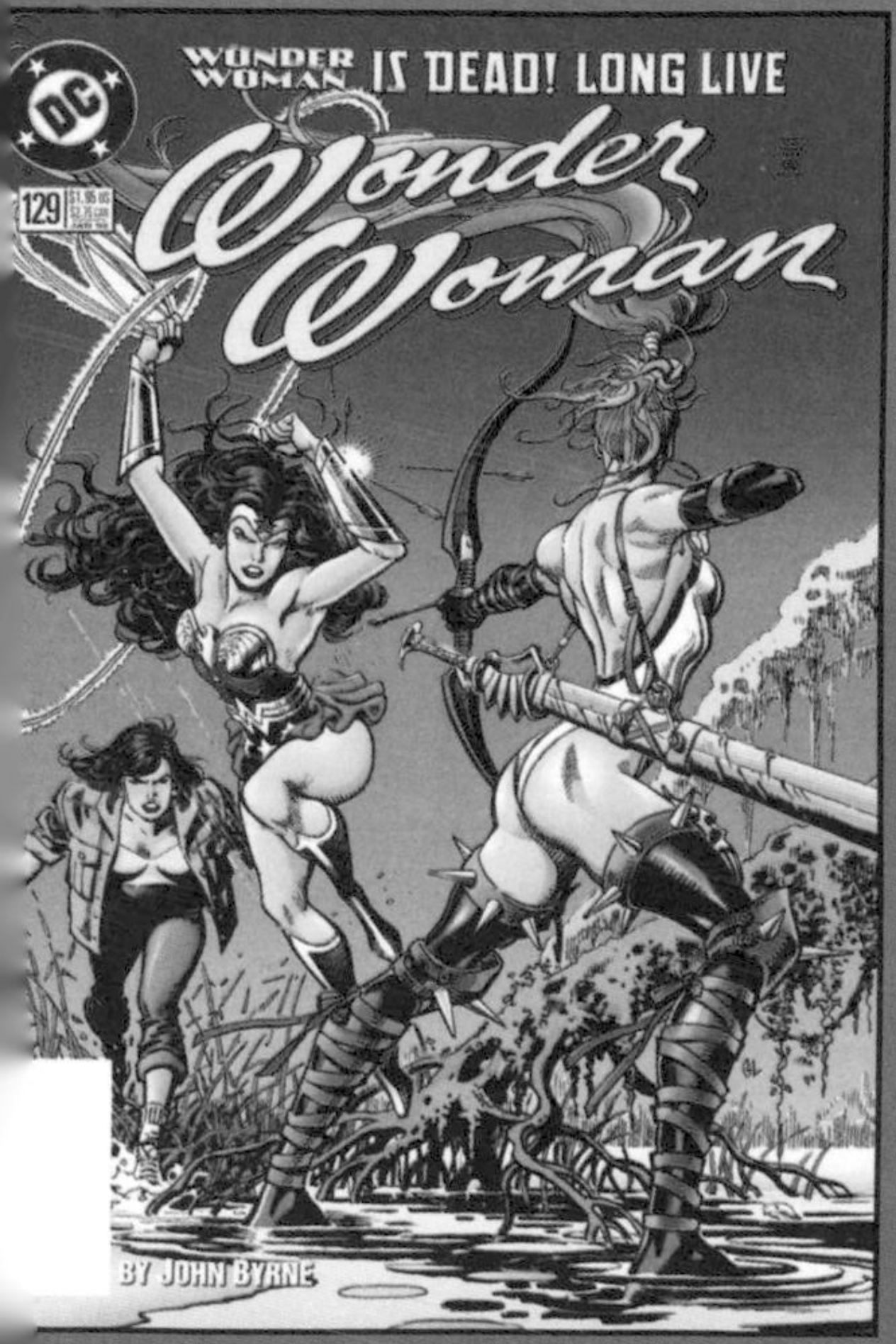
WONDER WOMAN IS DEAD! LONG LIVE
Wonder Woman
129
BY JOHN BYRNE

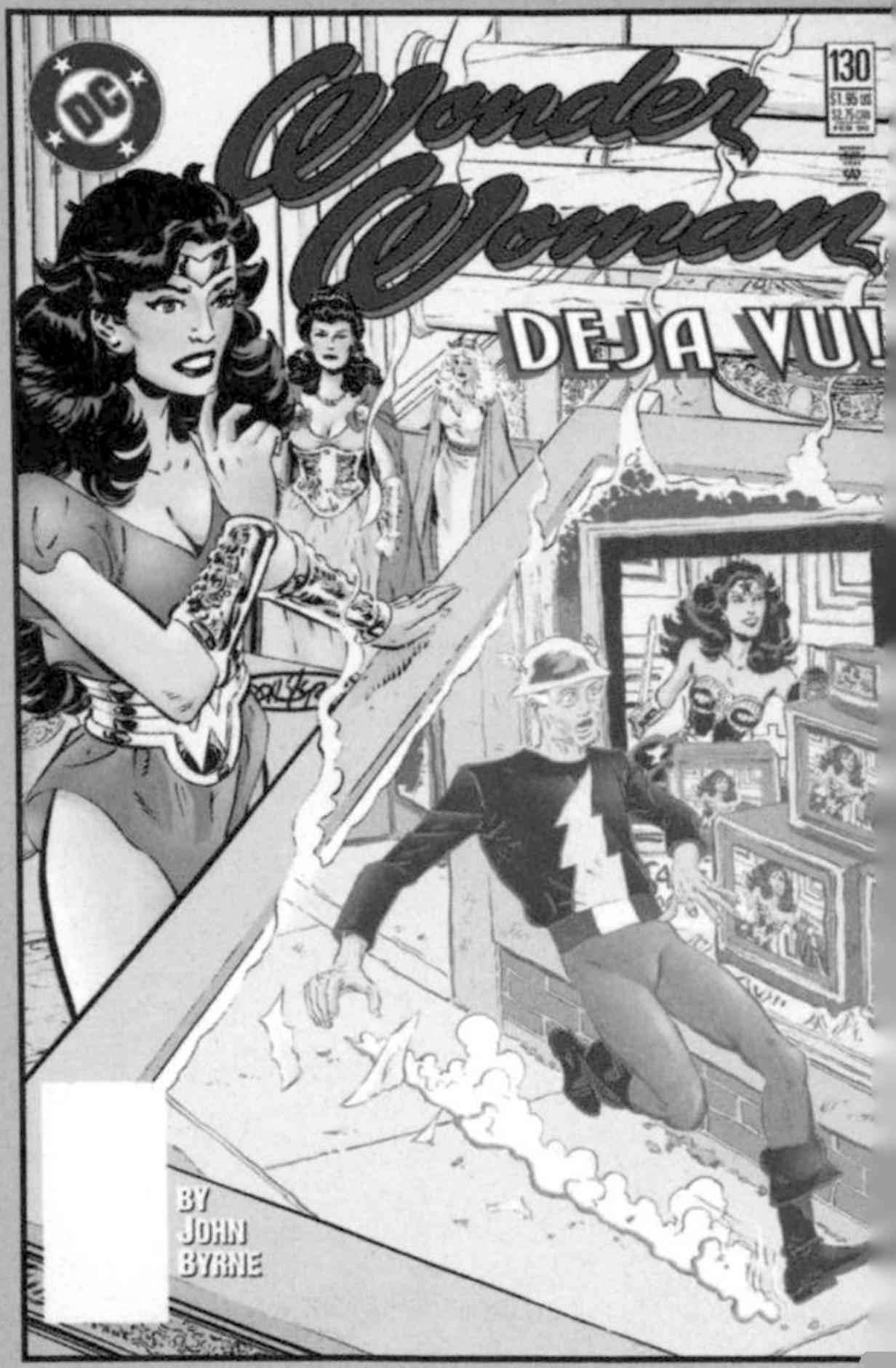
DC
Wonder Woman
130
$1.95 US
$2.75 CAN
DEJA VU!
BY
JOHN
BYRNE

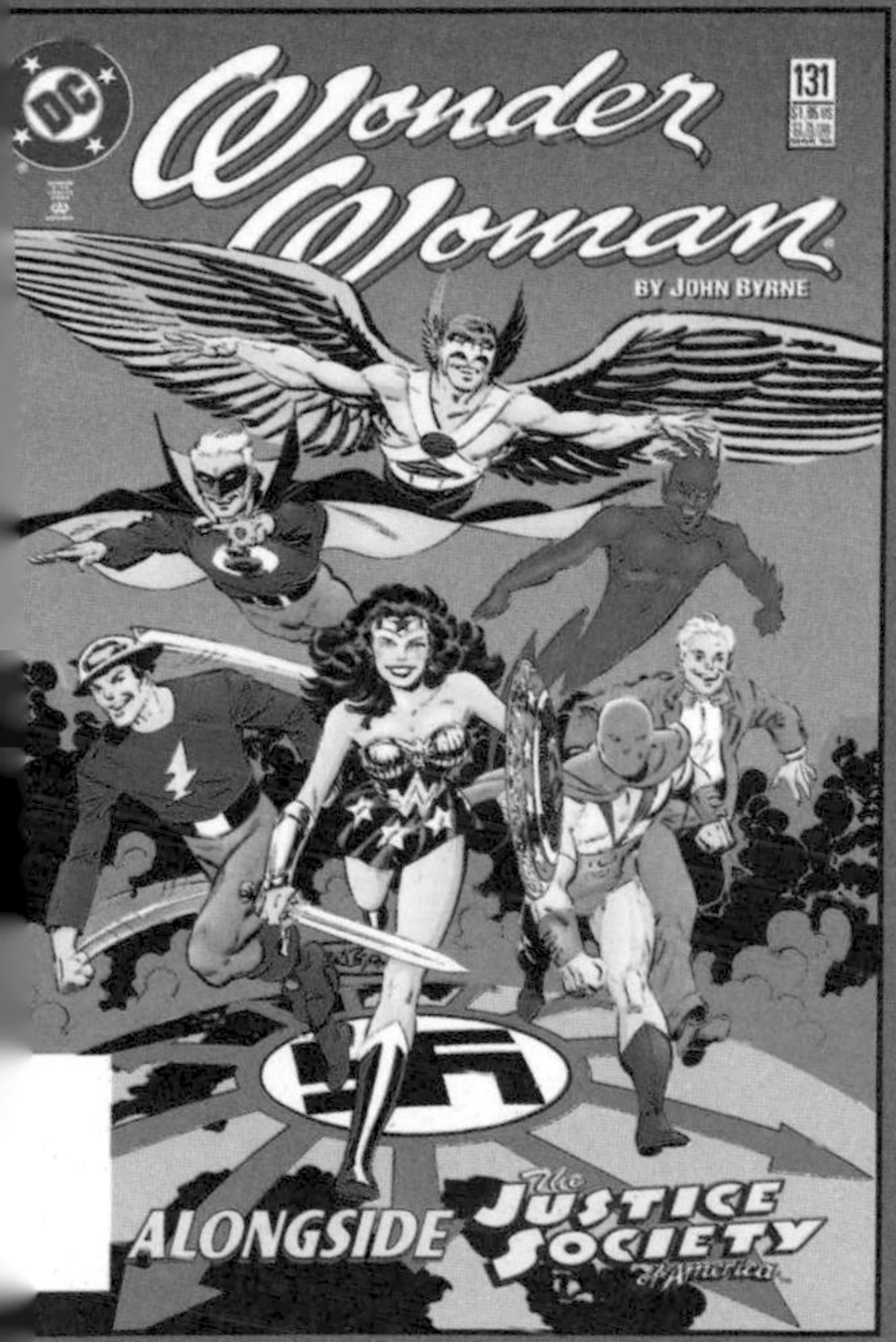
DC
Wonder Woman
131
BY JOHN BYRNE
ALONGSIDE The JUSTICE SOCIETY of America

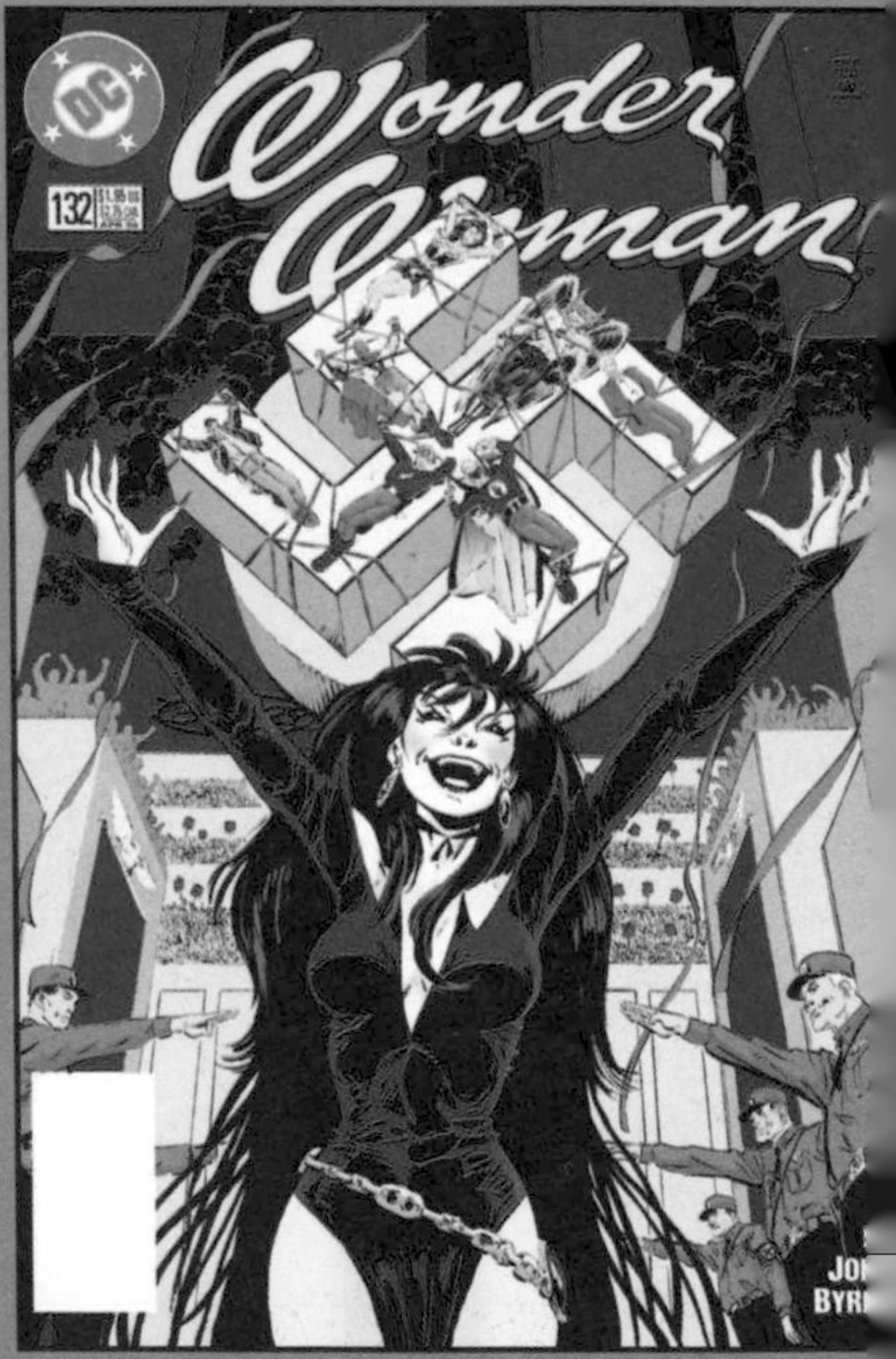
DC
Wonder Woman
132
JO
BYR

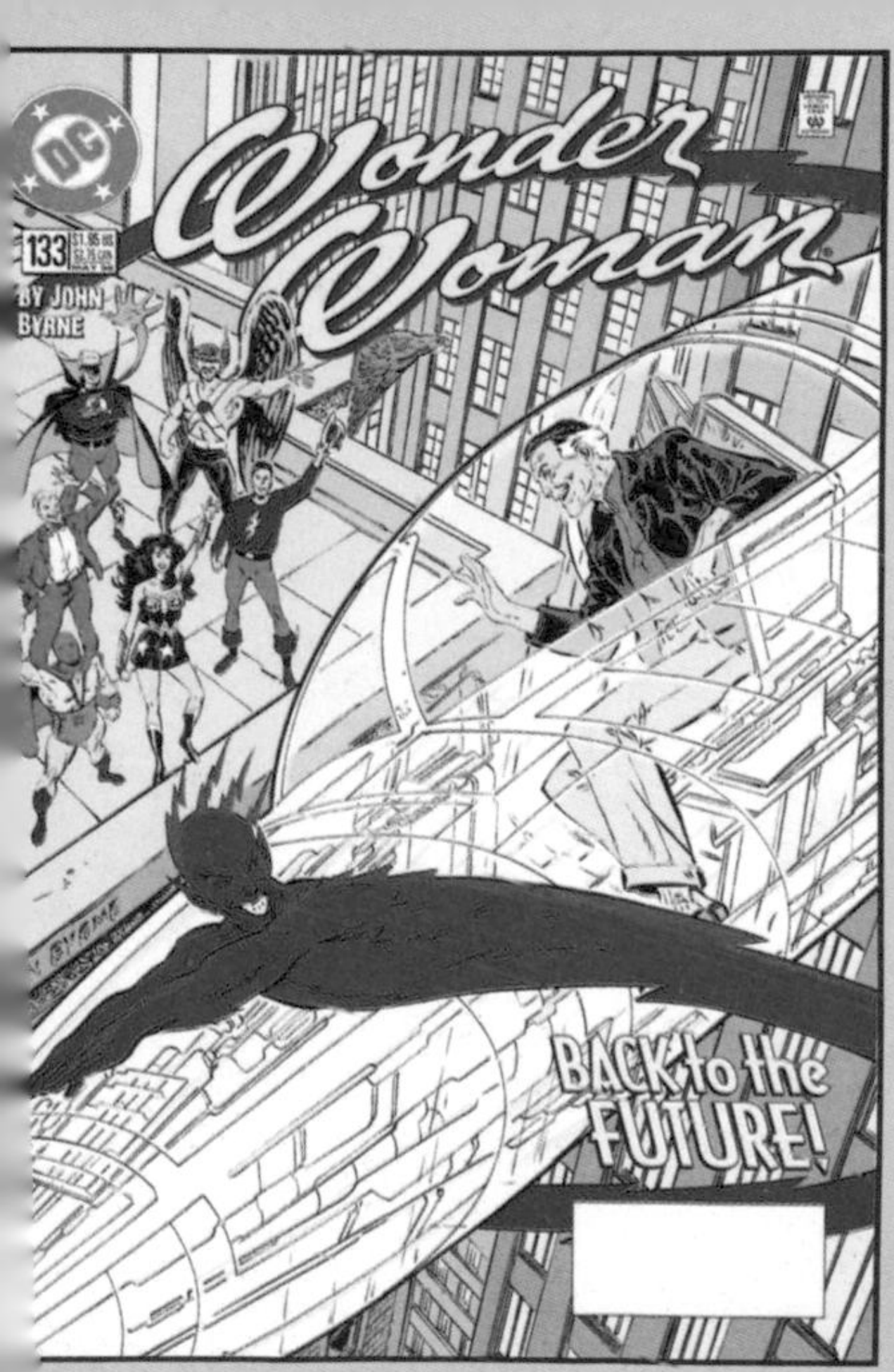
DC
Wonder Woman
133
BY JOHN BYRNE
BACK to the FUTURE!

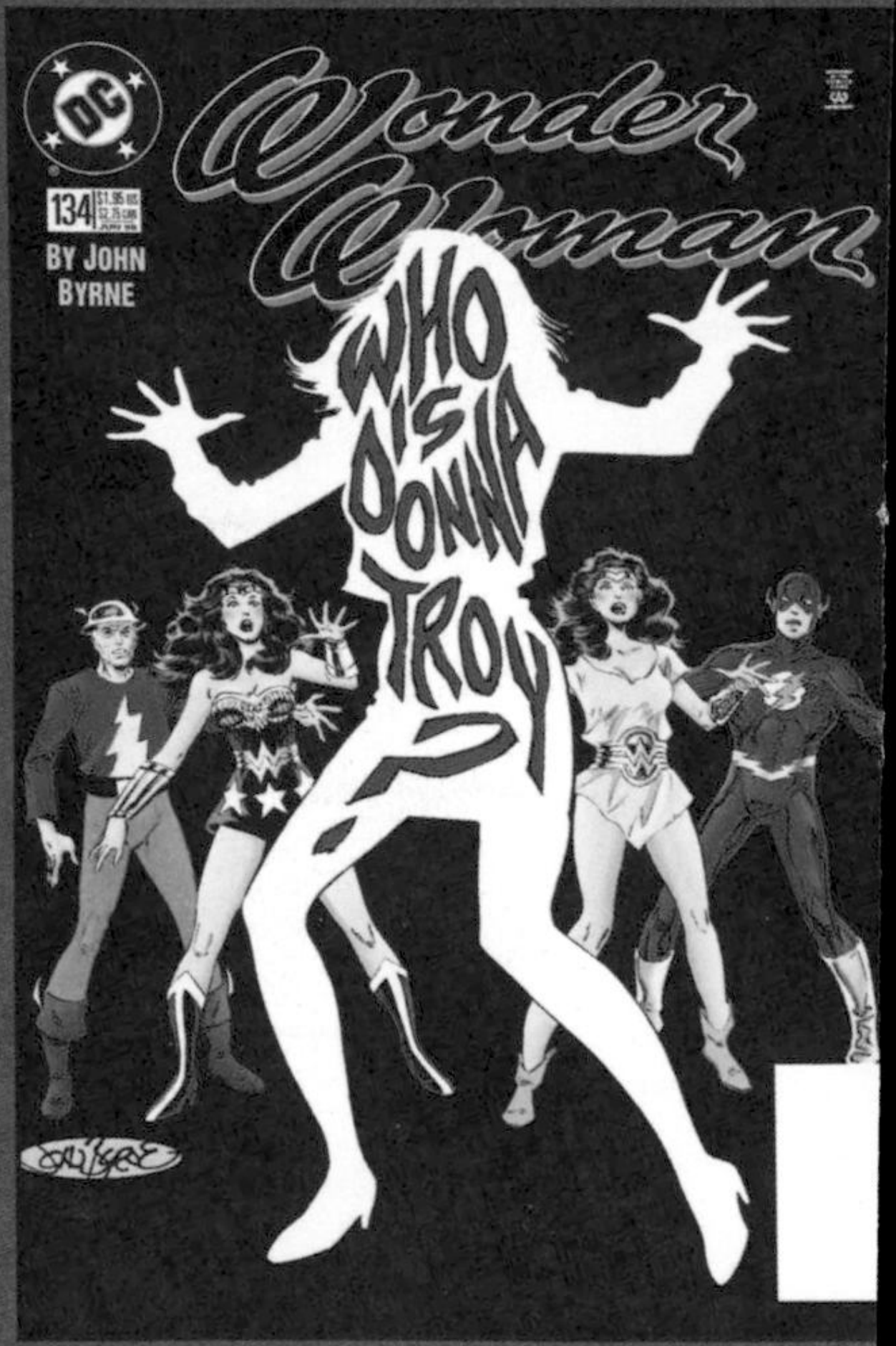
DC
Wonder Woman
134
$1.50 US
$2.25 CAN
BY JOHN BYRNE
WHO IS OONNA TROY

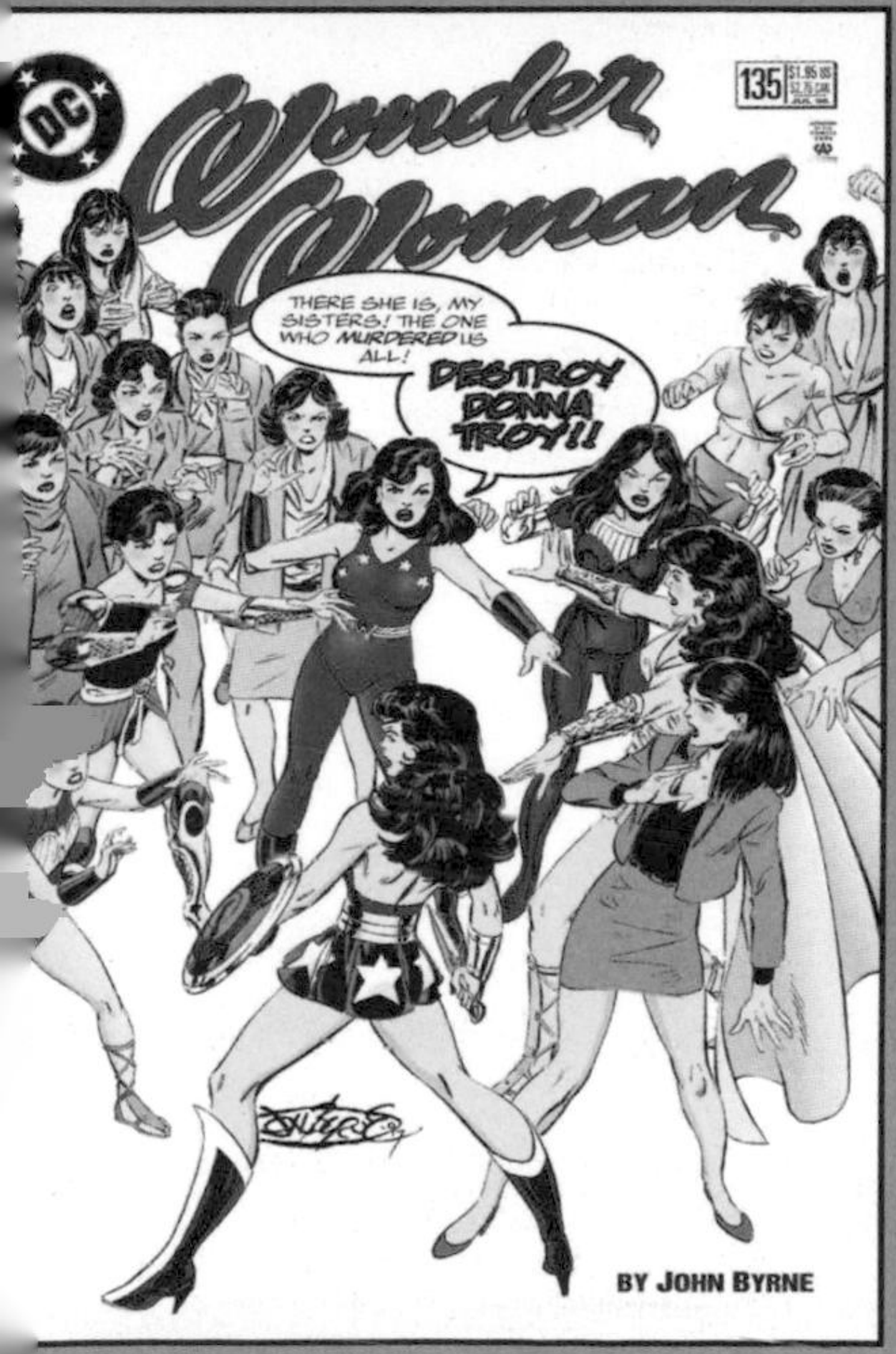
DC
Wonder Woman
135
$1.95 US
THERE SHE IS, MY SISTERS! THE ONE WHO MURDERED US ALL!
DESTROY DONNA TROY!!
BY JOHN BYRNE

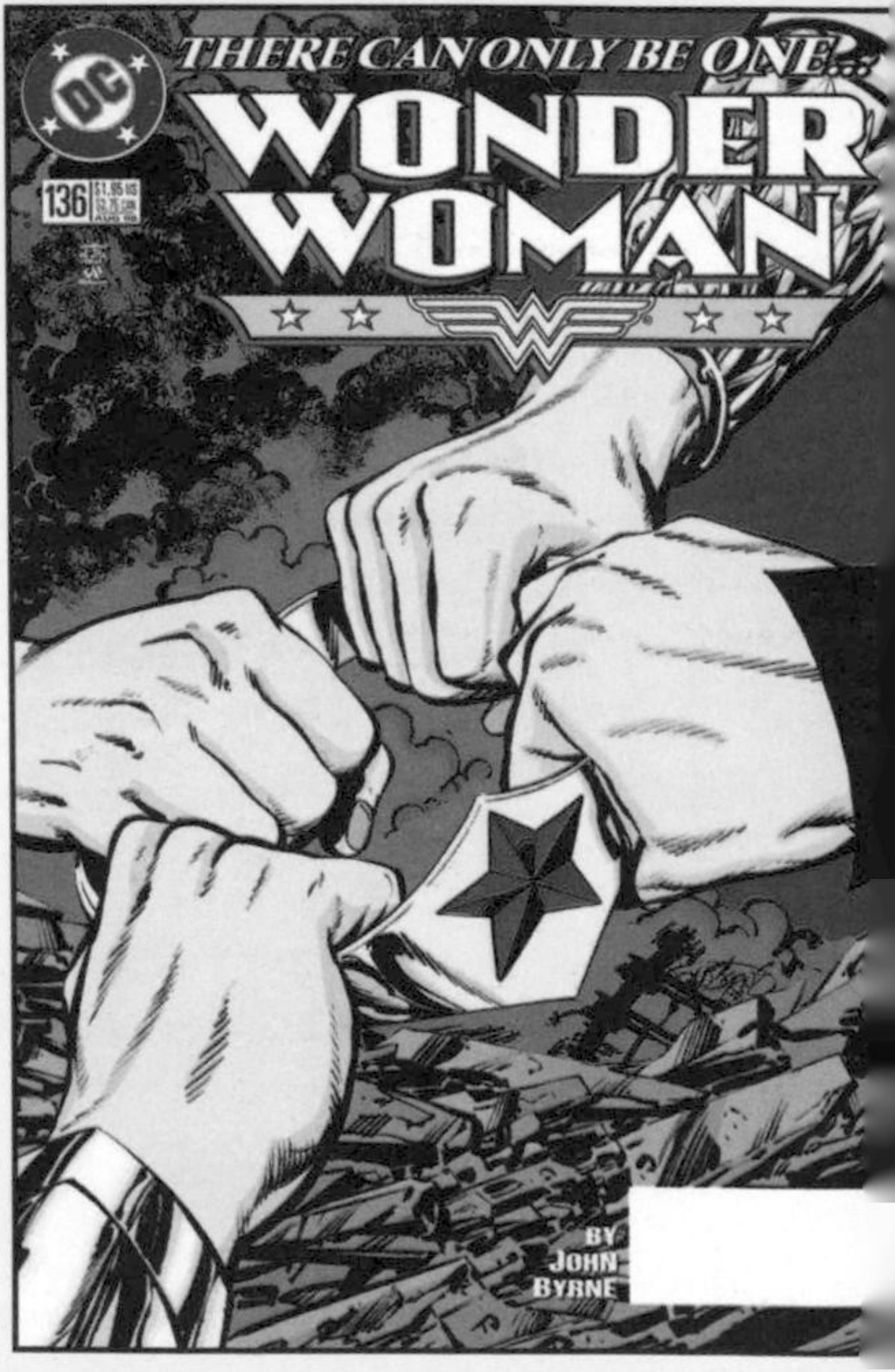
THERE CAN ONLY BE ONE...
DC
136
WONDER WOMAN
BY JOHN BYRNE

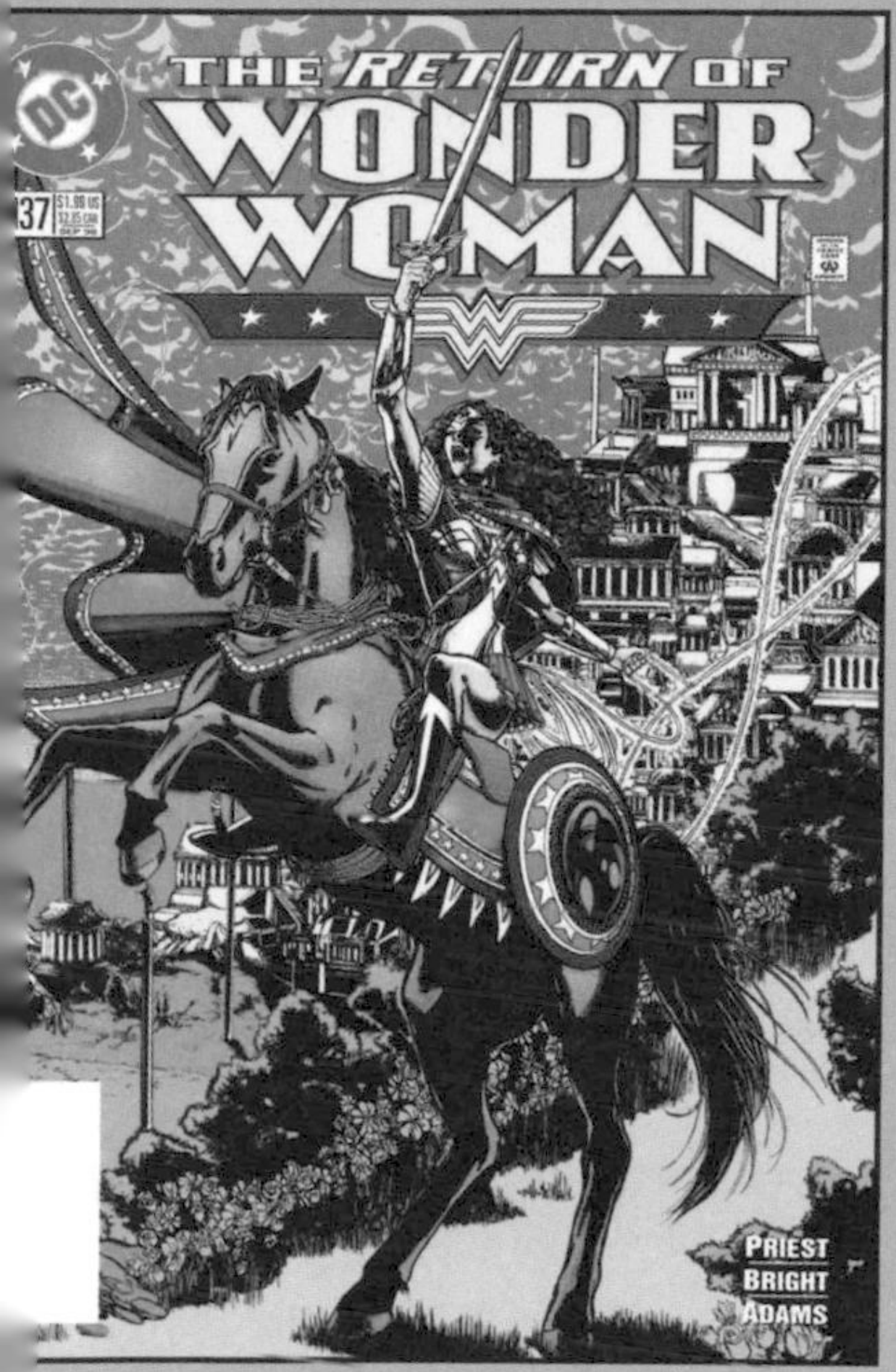
THE RETURN OF
WONDER WOMAN
37
$1.99 US
$2.25 CAN
PRIEST
BRIGHT
ADAMS

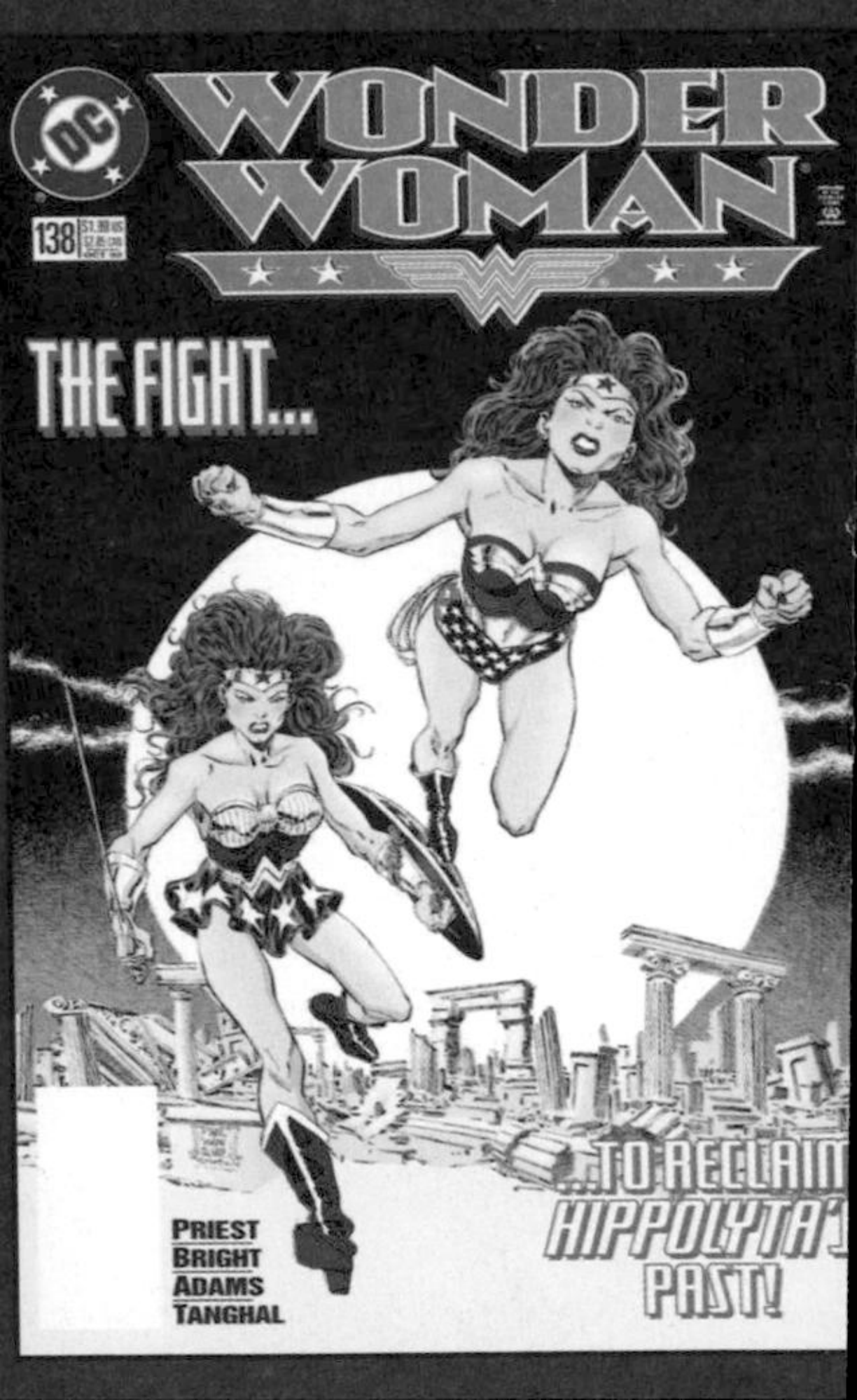
DC
WONDER WOMAN
138
THE FIGHT...
...TO RECLAIM HIPPOLYTA'S PAST!
PRIEST
BRIGHT
ADAMS
TANGHAL

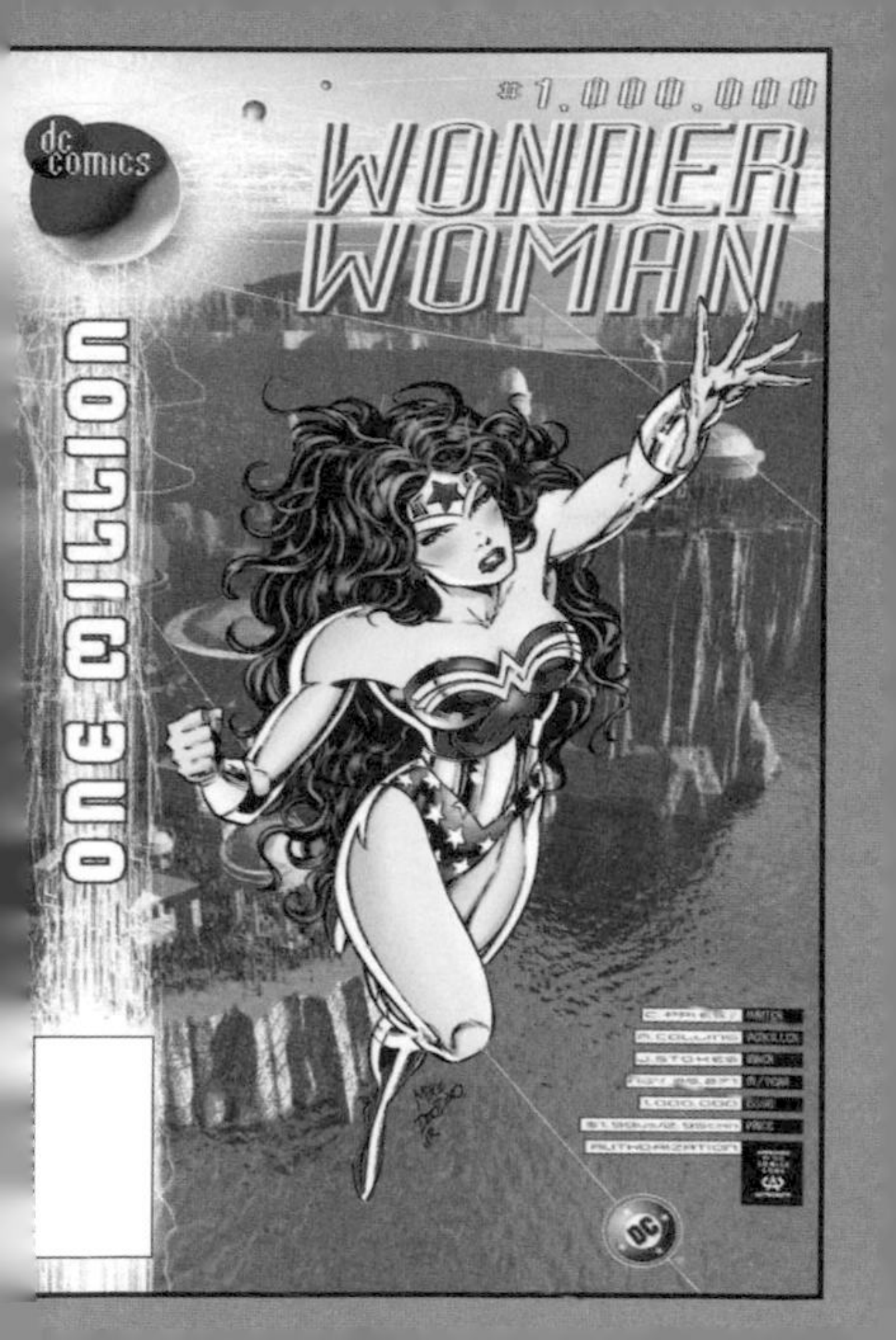
#1,000,000
dc comics
WONDER WOMAN
ONE MILLION
DC

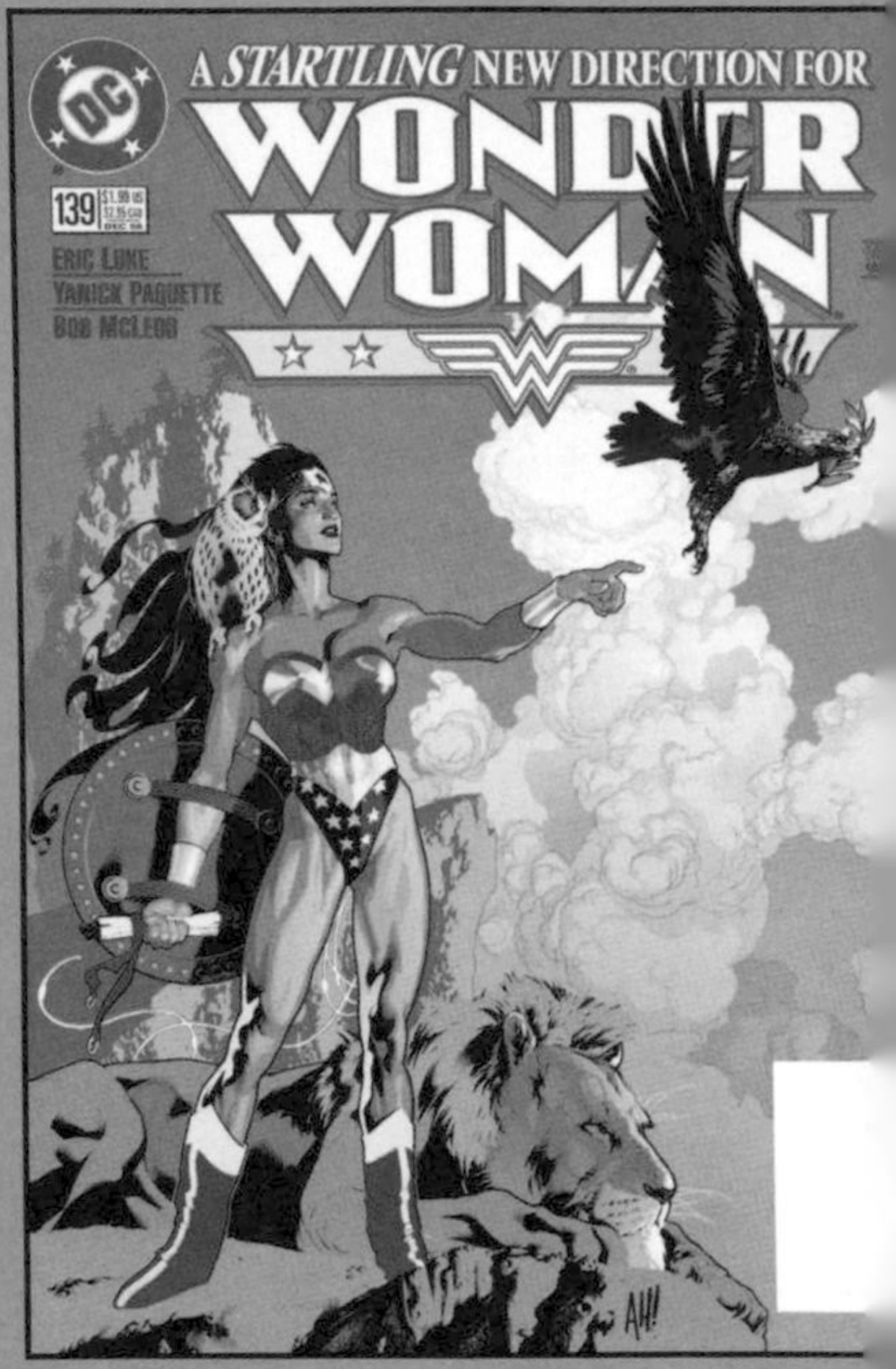
A STARTLING NEW DIRECTION FOR
WONDER WOMAN
139
$1.99 US
$2.95 CAN
ERIC LUKE
YANICK PAQUETTE
BOB MCLEOD
AH!

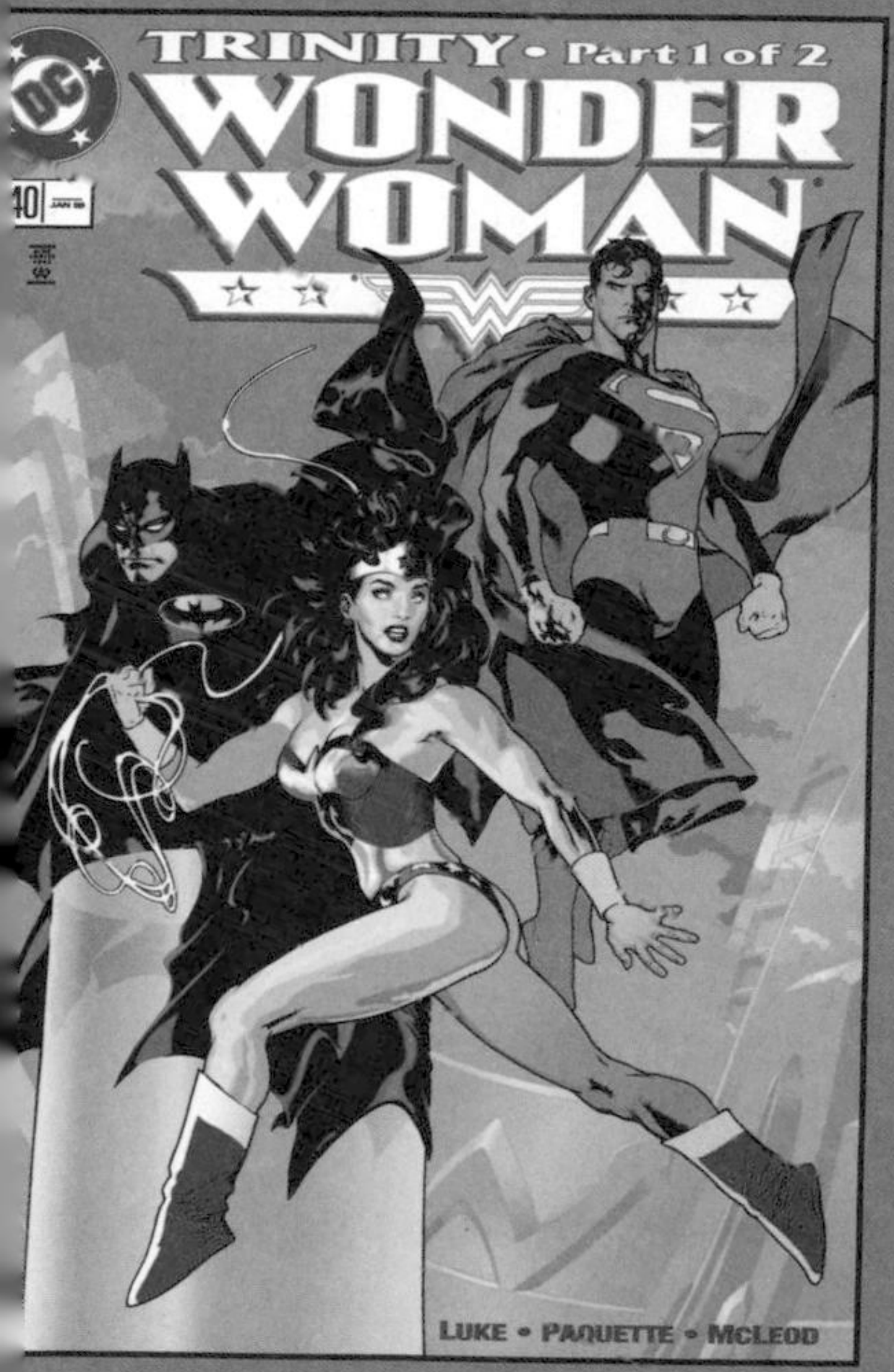
TRINITY • Part 1 of 2
WONDER WOMAN
10
LUKE • PAQUETTE • McLEOD

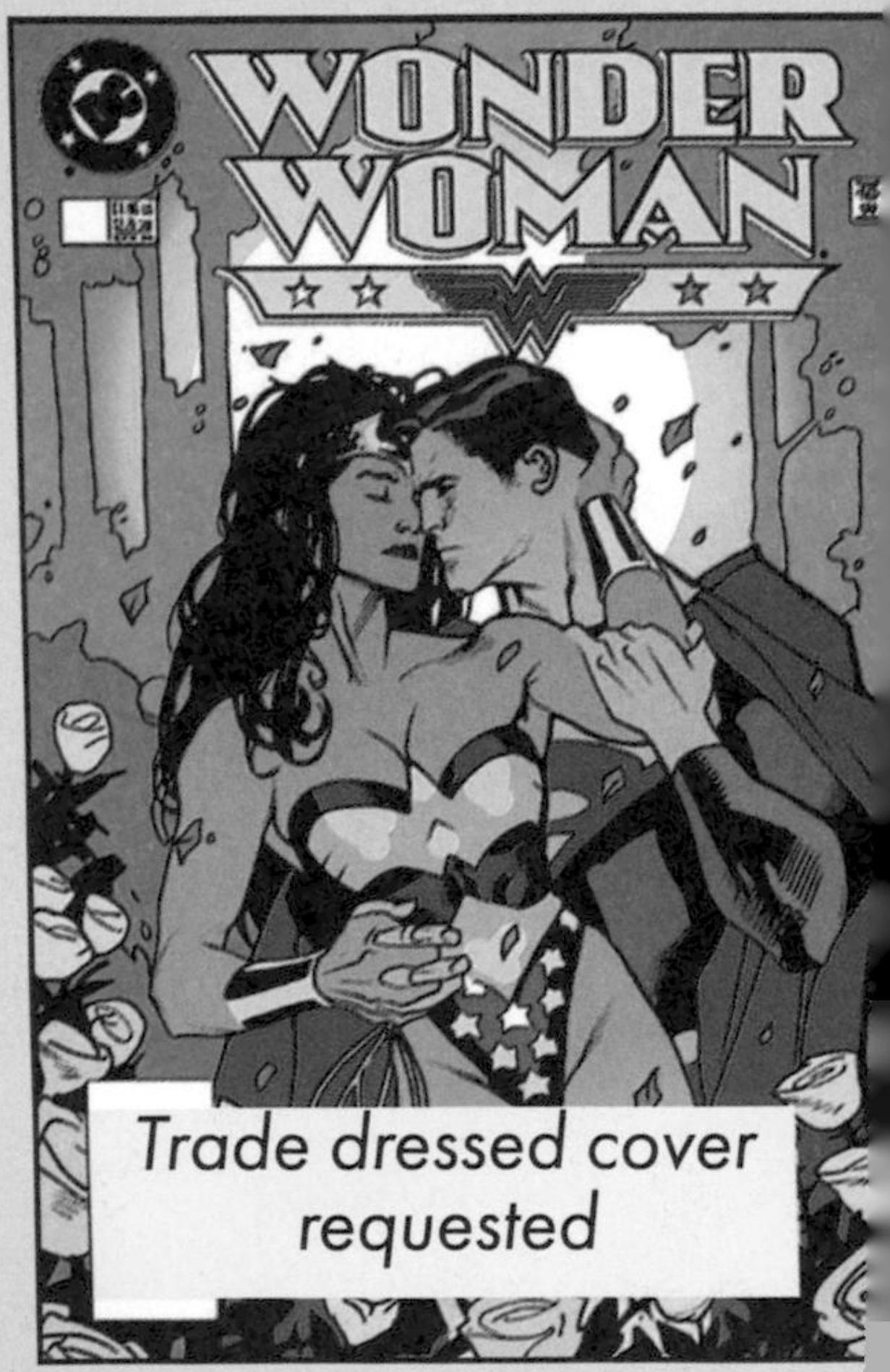

Trade dressed cover requested

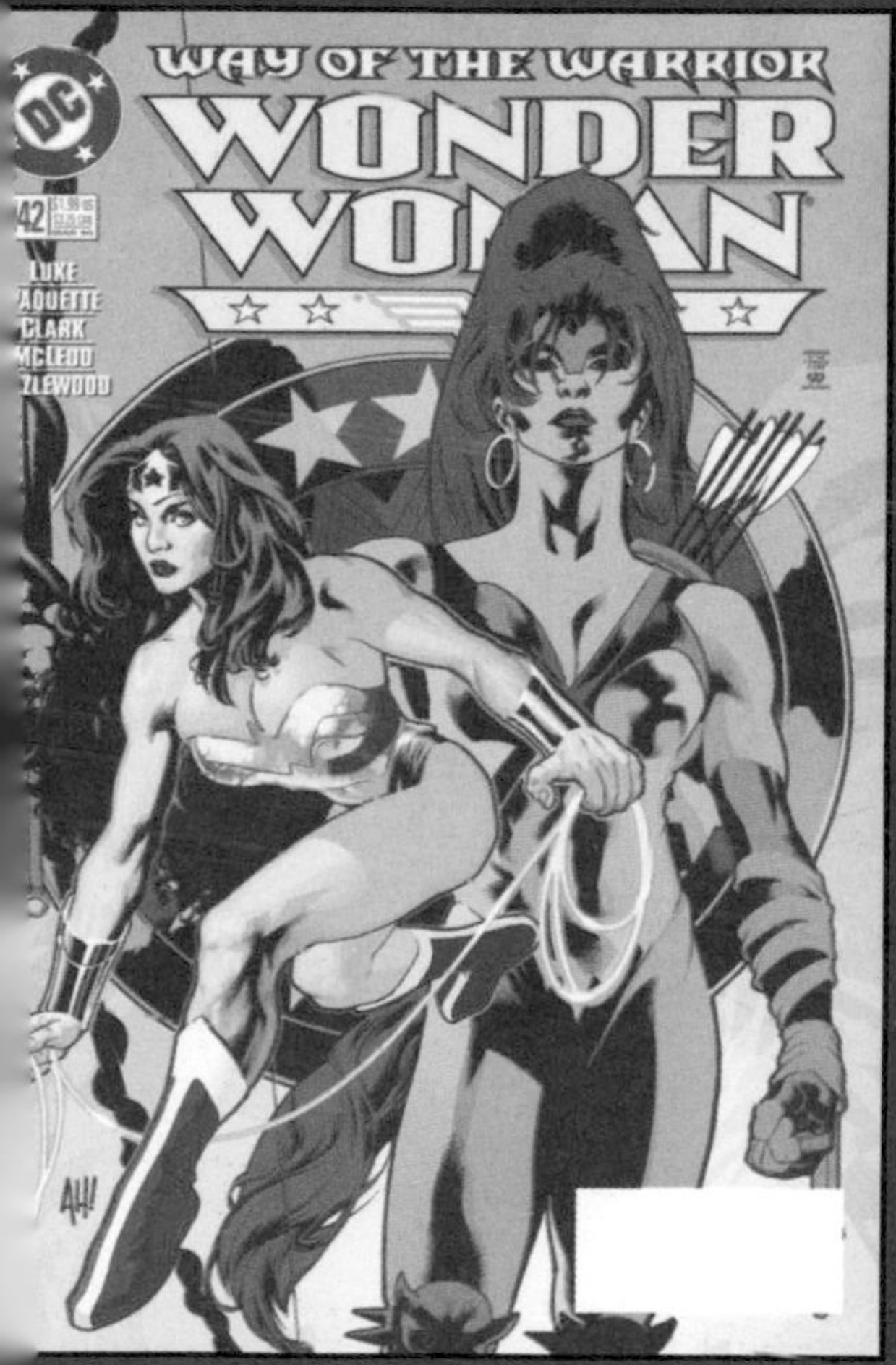
WAY OF THE WARRIOR
WONDER
WOMAN
DC
42
LUKE
AQUETTE
CLARK
MCLEOD
ZLEWOOD
AH!

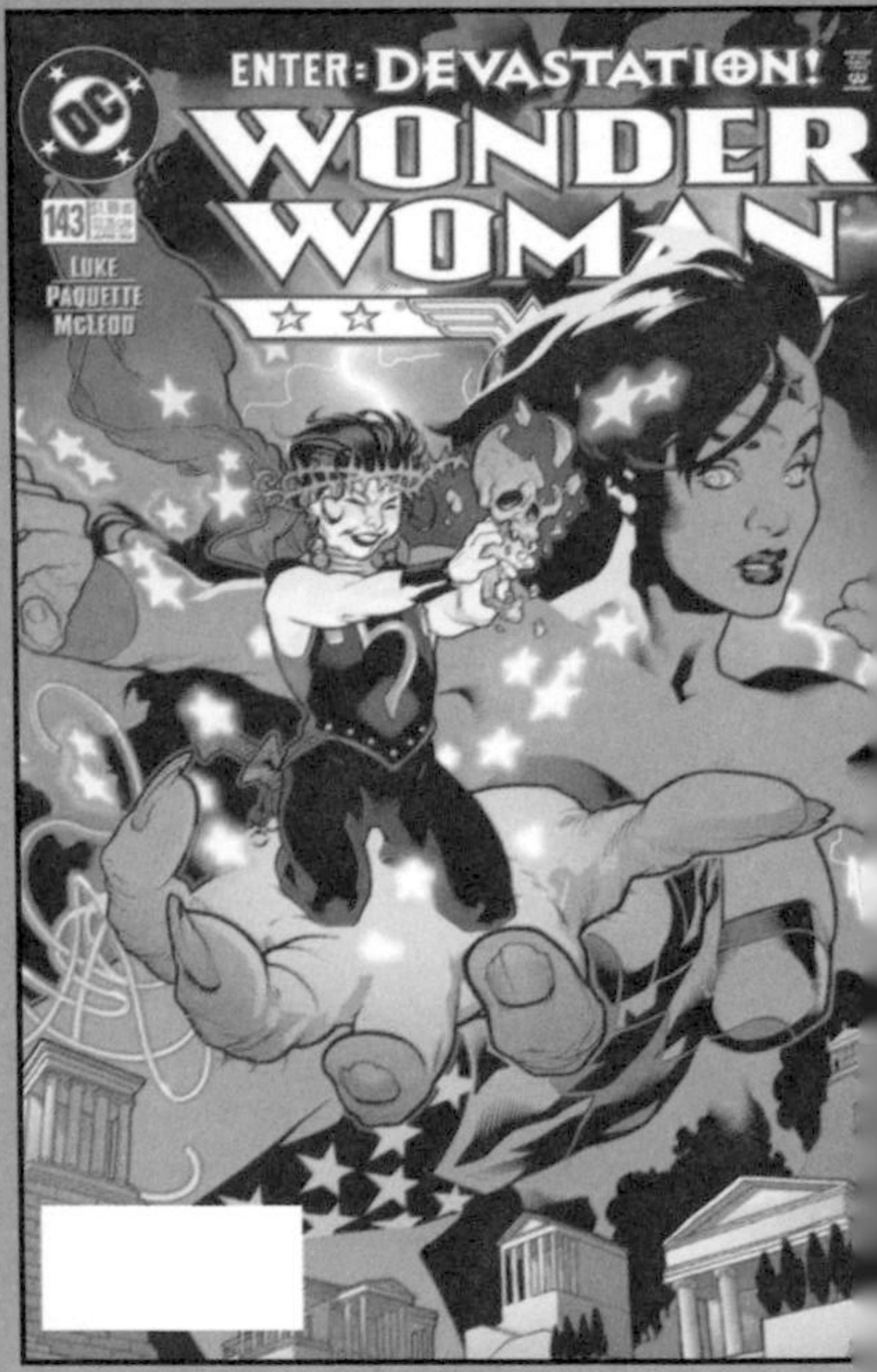
ENTER: DEVASTATION!
DC
WONDER WOMAN
143
LUKE
PAQUETTE
McLEOD

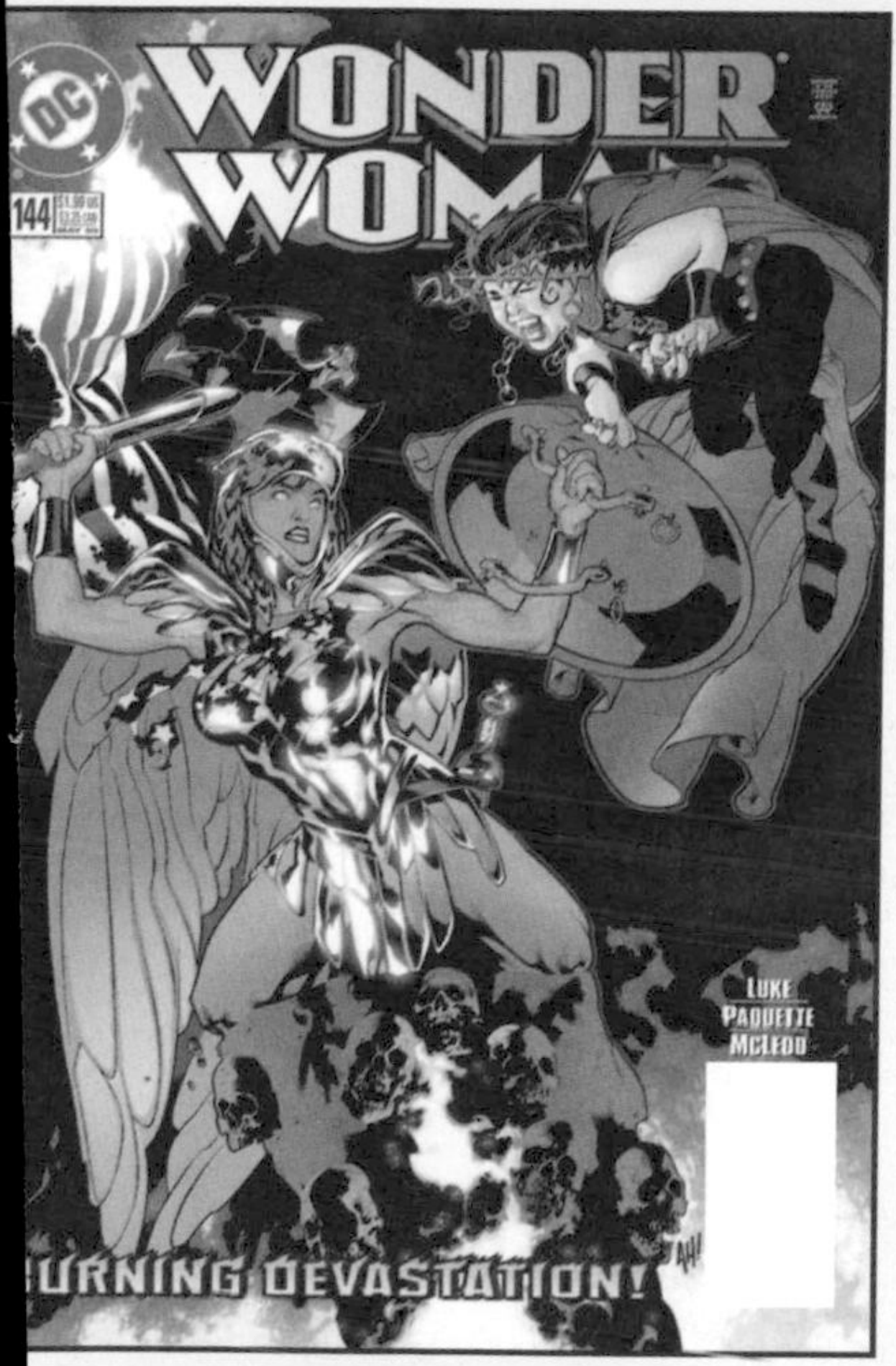
DC
WONDER WOMAN
144
LUKE
PADUETTE
McLEOD
URNING DEVASTATION!
AH!

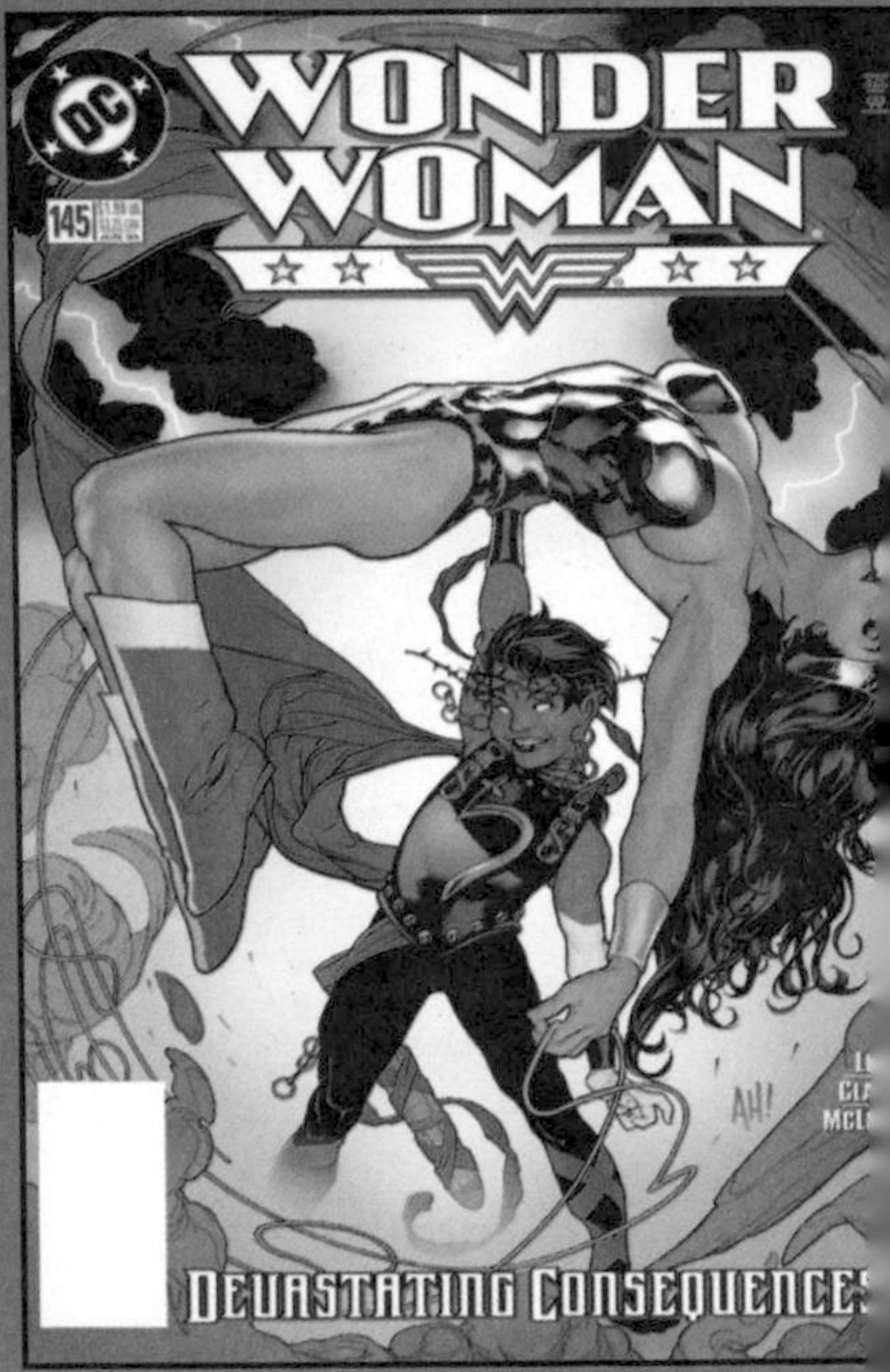
DC
WONDER WOMAN
145
AH!
DEVASTATING CONSEQUENCES

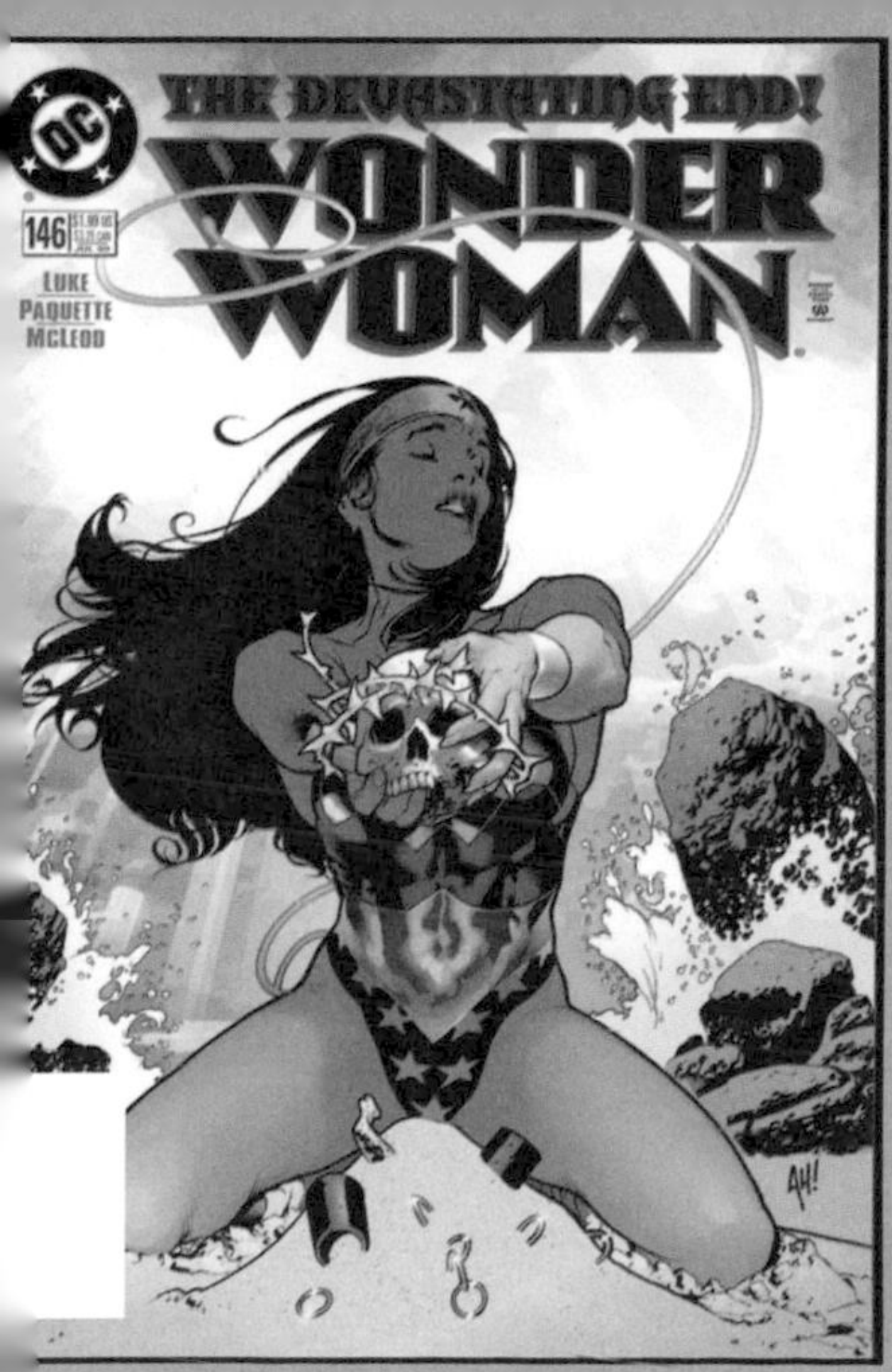
THE DEVASTATING END!
WONDER WOMAN
146
LUKE
PAQUETTE
MCLEOD
44!

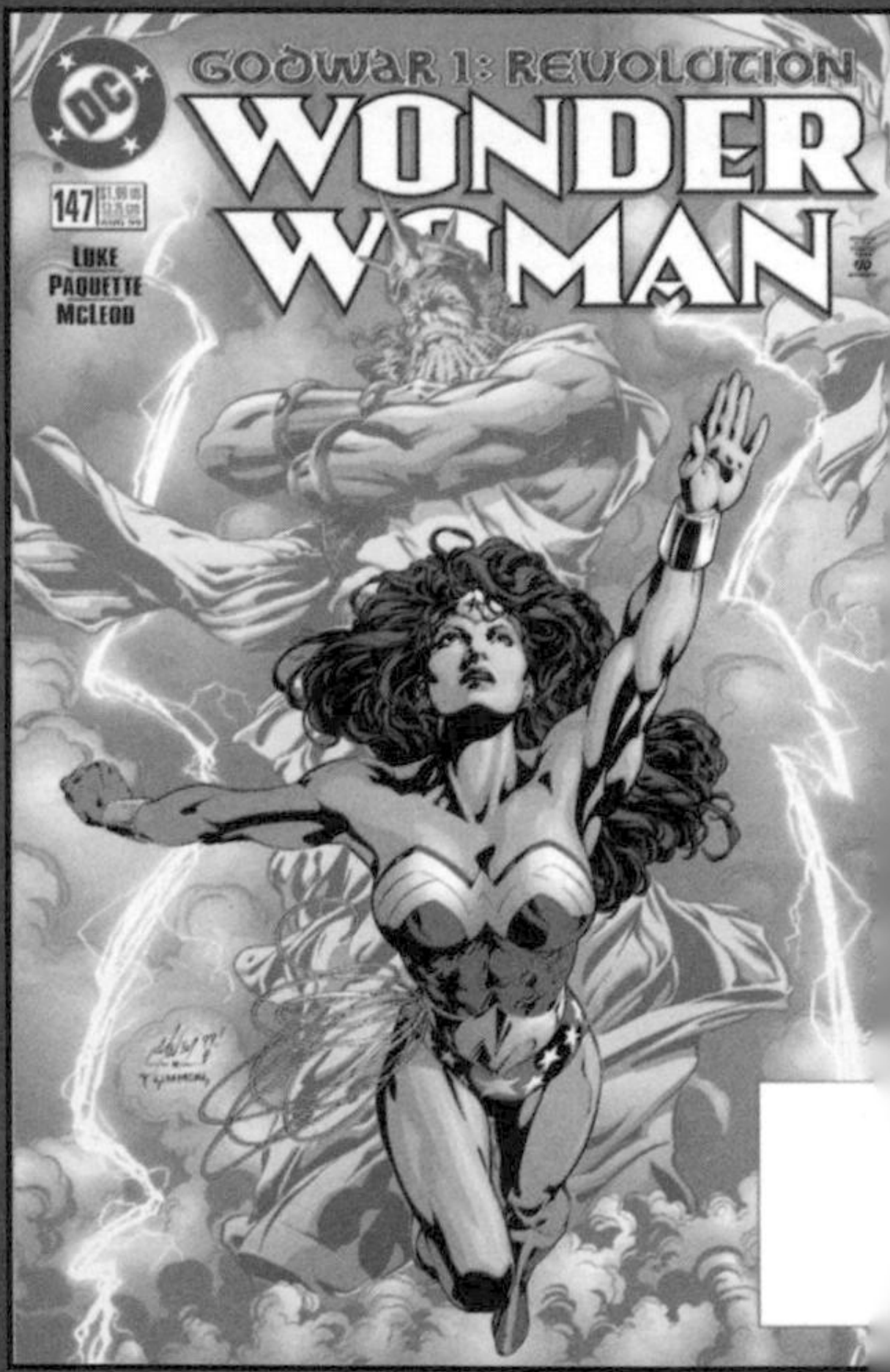
GODWAR 1: REVOLUTION
WONDER WOMAN
147
LUKE
PAQUETTE
McLEOD

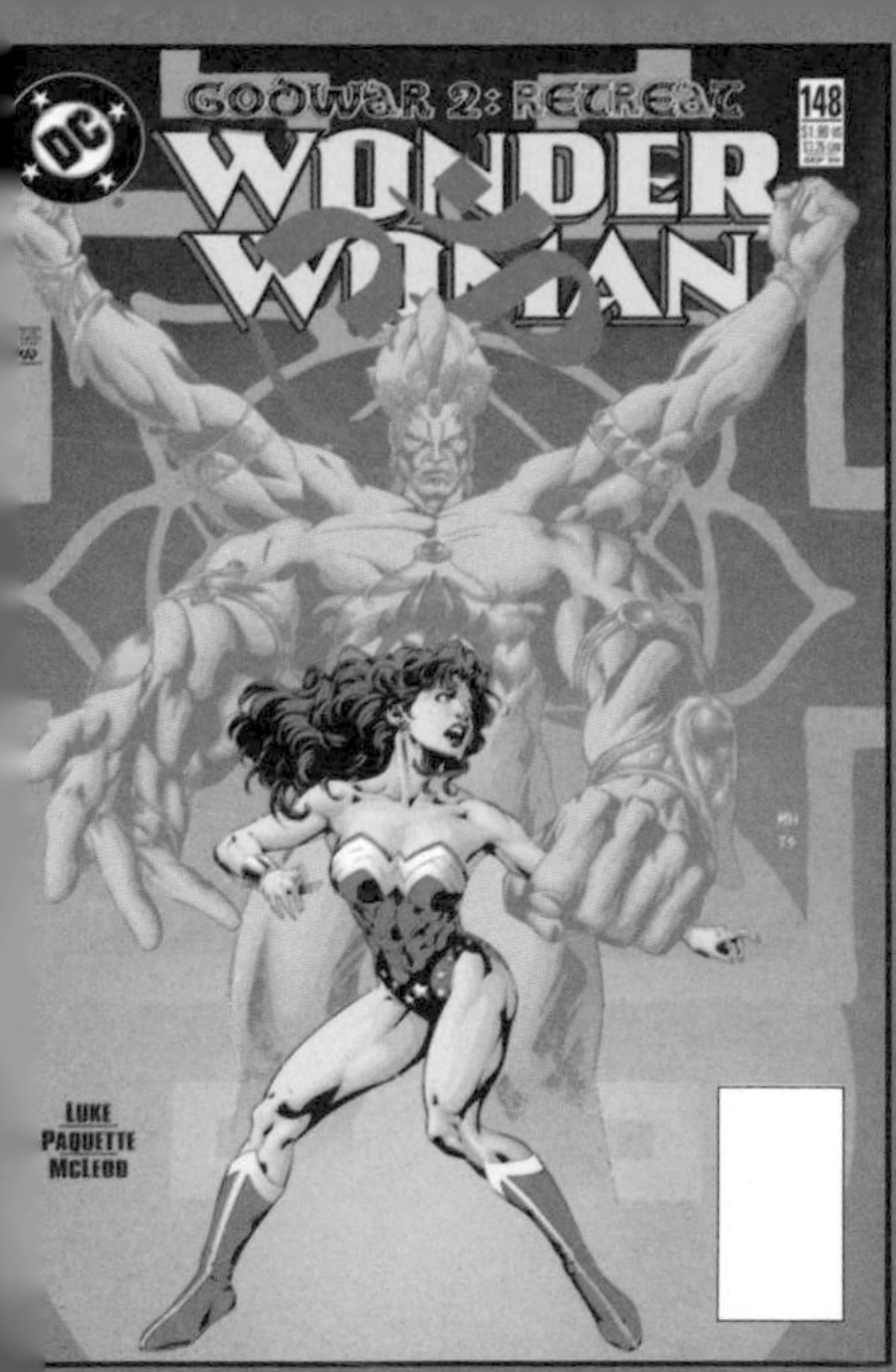
GOD WAR 2: RETREAT
148
WONDER WOMAN
LUKE
PAQUETTE
McLEOD

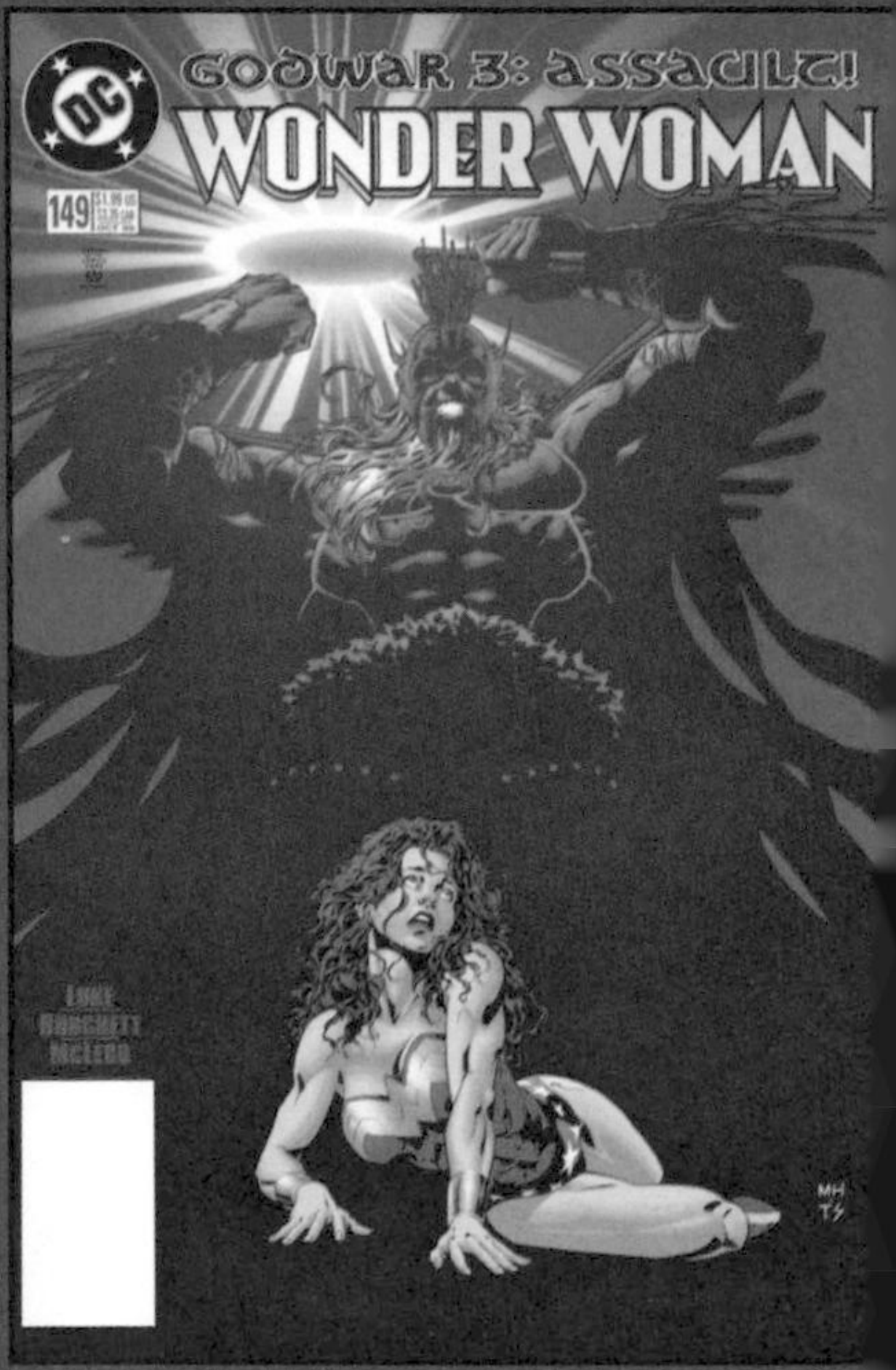
GODWAR 3: ASSAULT!
WONDER WOMAN
149
LUCIE
WOMACK
NICERO
MH
TS

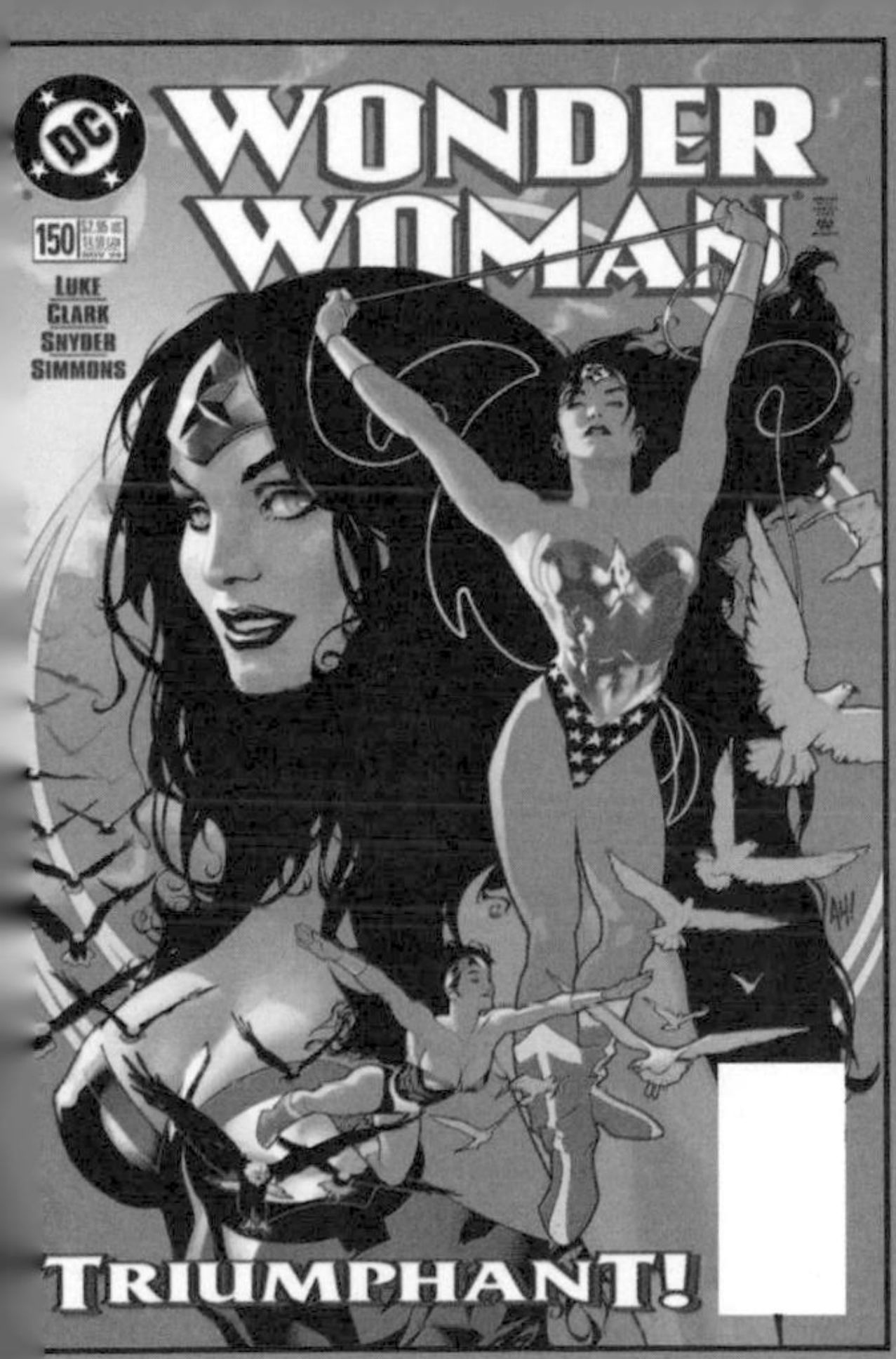
DC
WONDER WOMAN
150
LUKE
CLARK
SNYDER
SIMMONS
TRIUMPHANT!

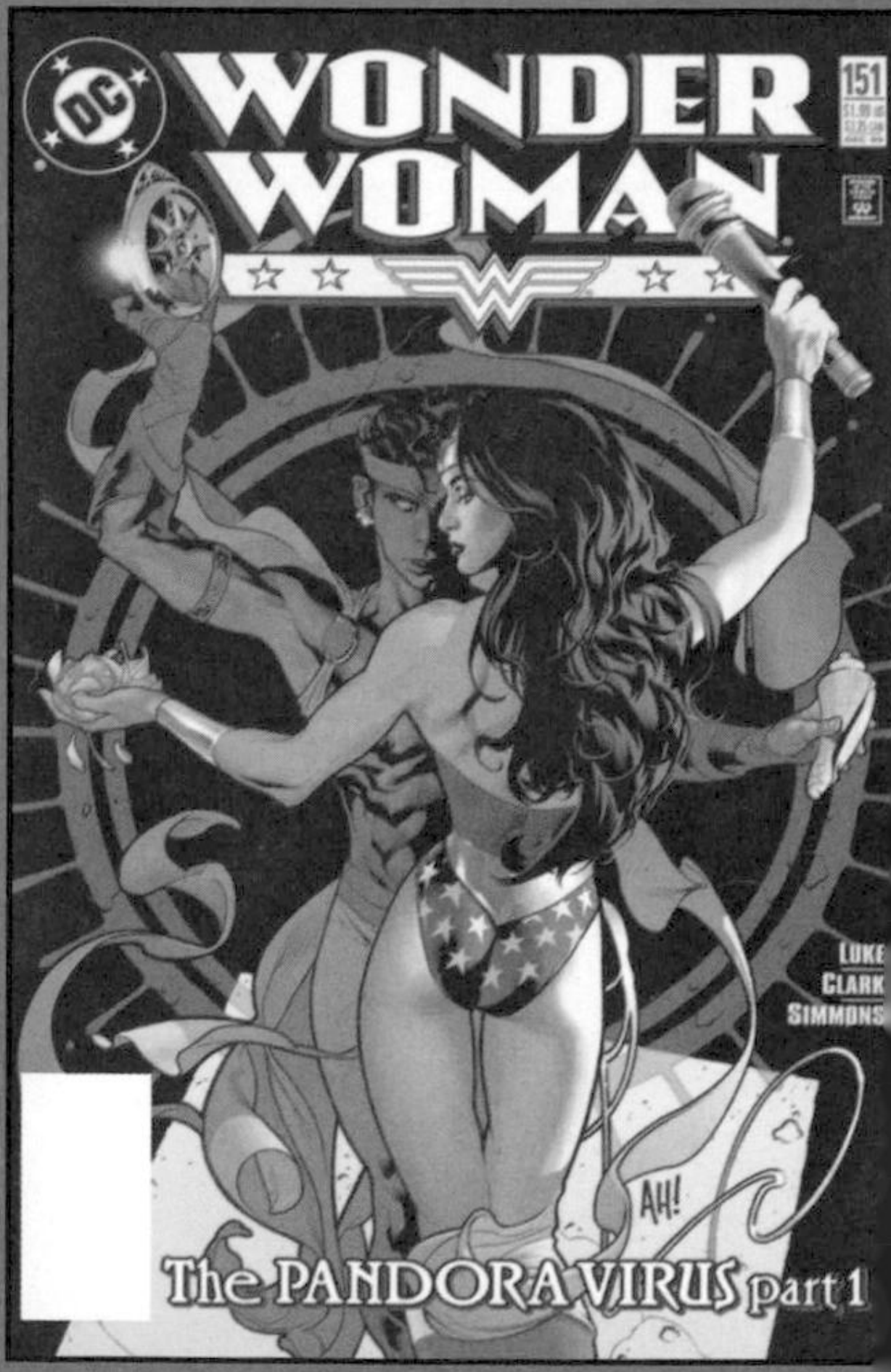
DC
WONDER WOMAN
151
LUKE
CLARK
SIMMONS
AH!
The PANDORA VIRUS part 1

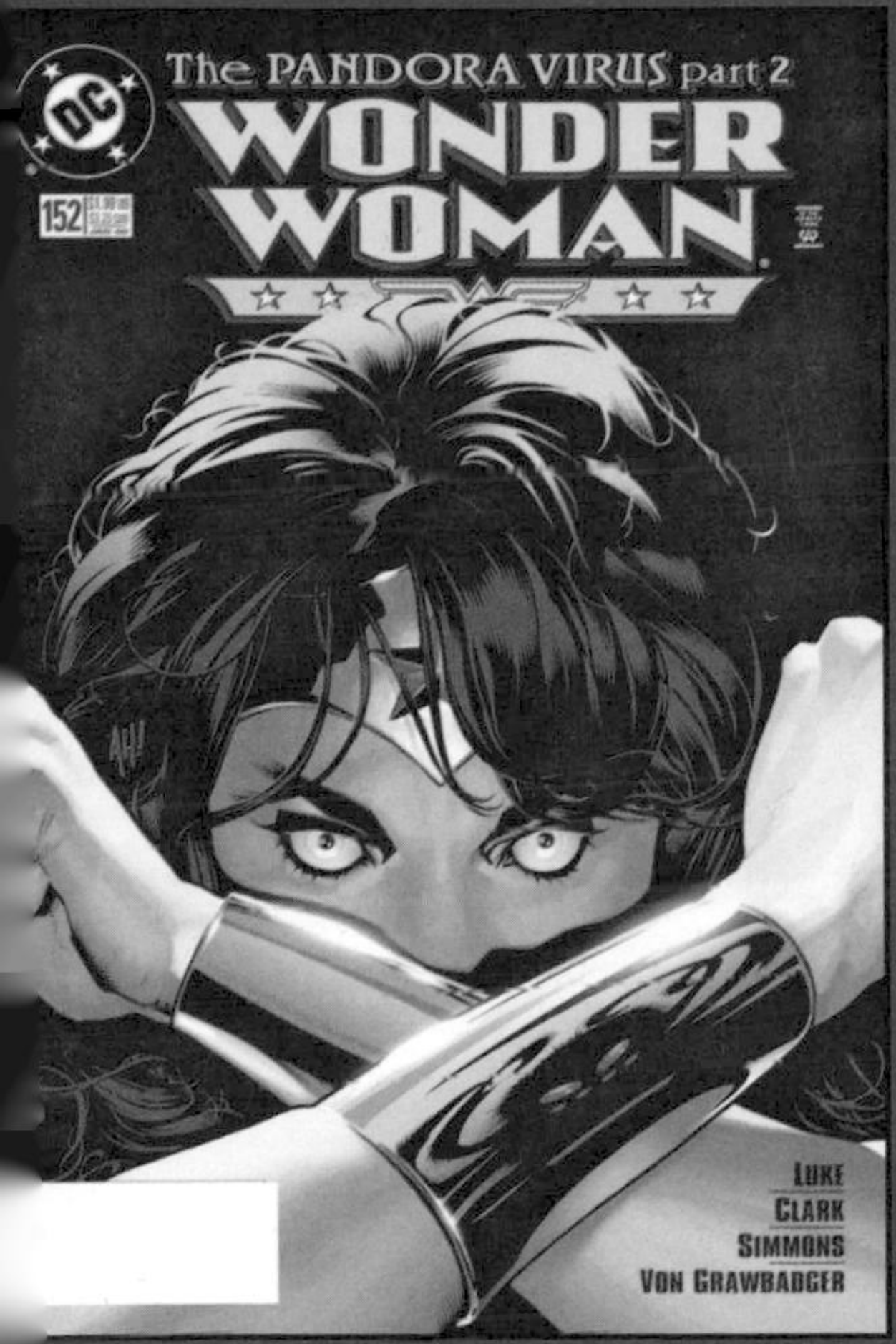
The PANDORA VIRUS part 2
DC
WONDER WOMAN
152
LUKE
CLARK
SIMMONS
VON GRAWBADGER

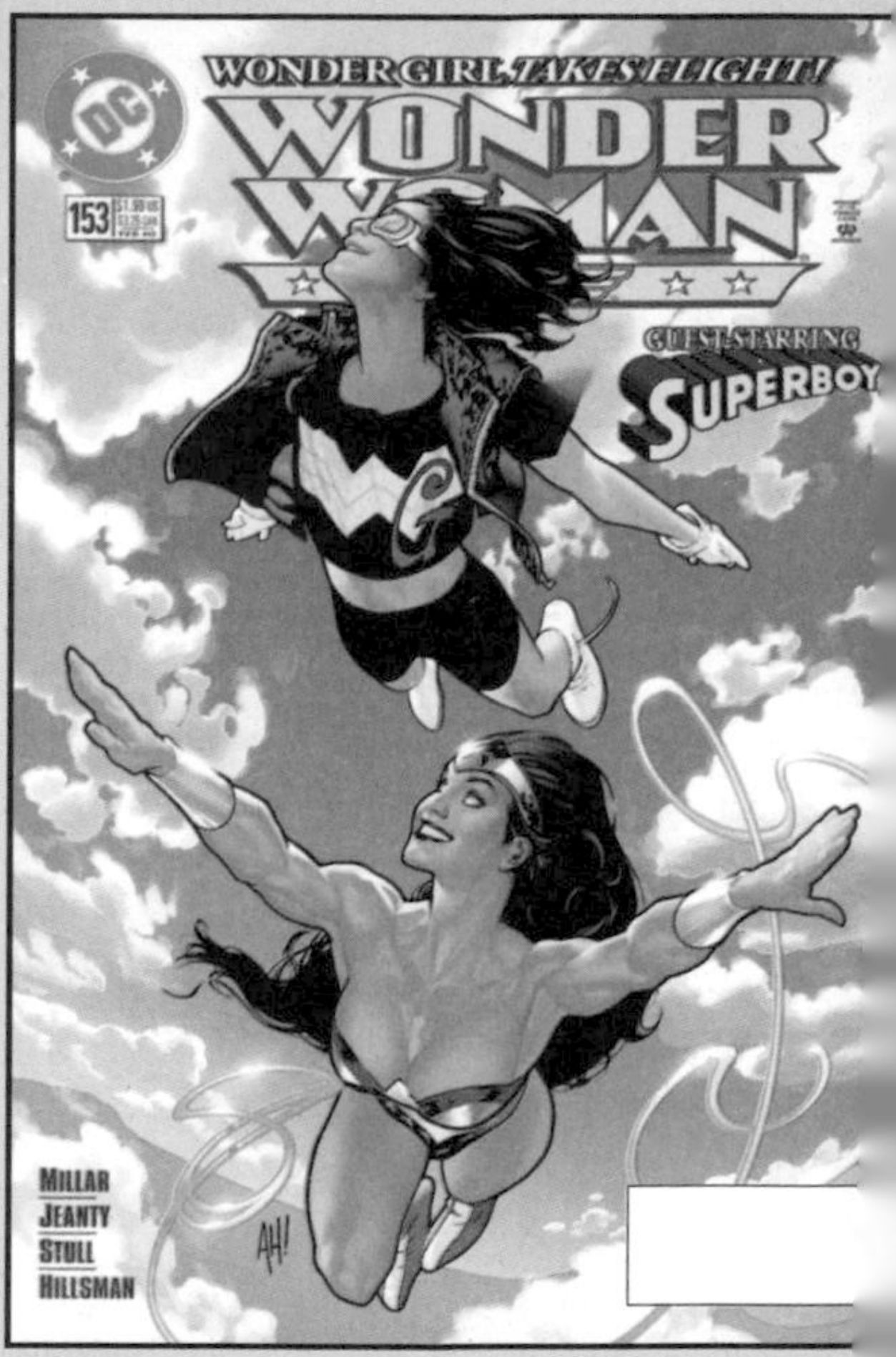
WONDER GIRL TAKES FLIGHT!
DC
WONDER WOMAN
153
GUEST-STARRING
SUPERBOY
MILLAR
JEANTY
STULL
HILLSMAN
AH!

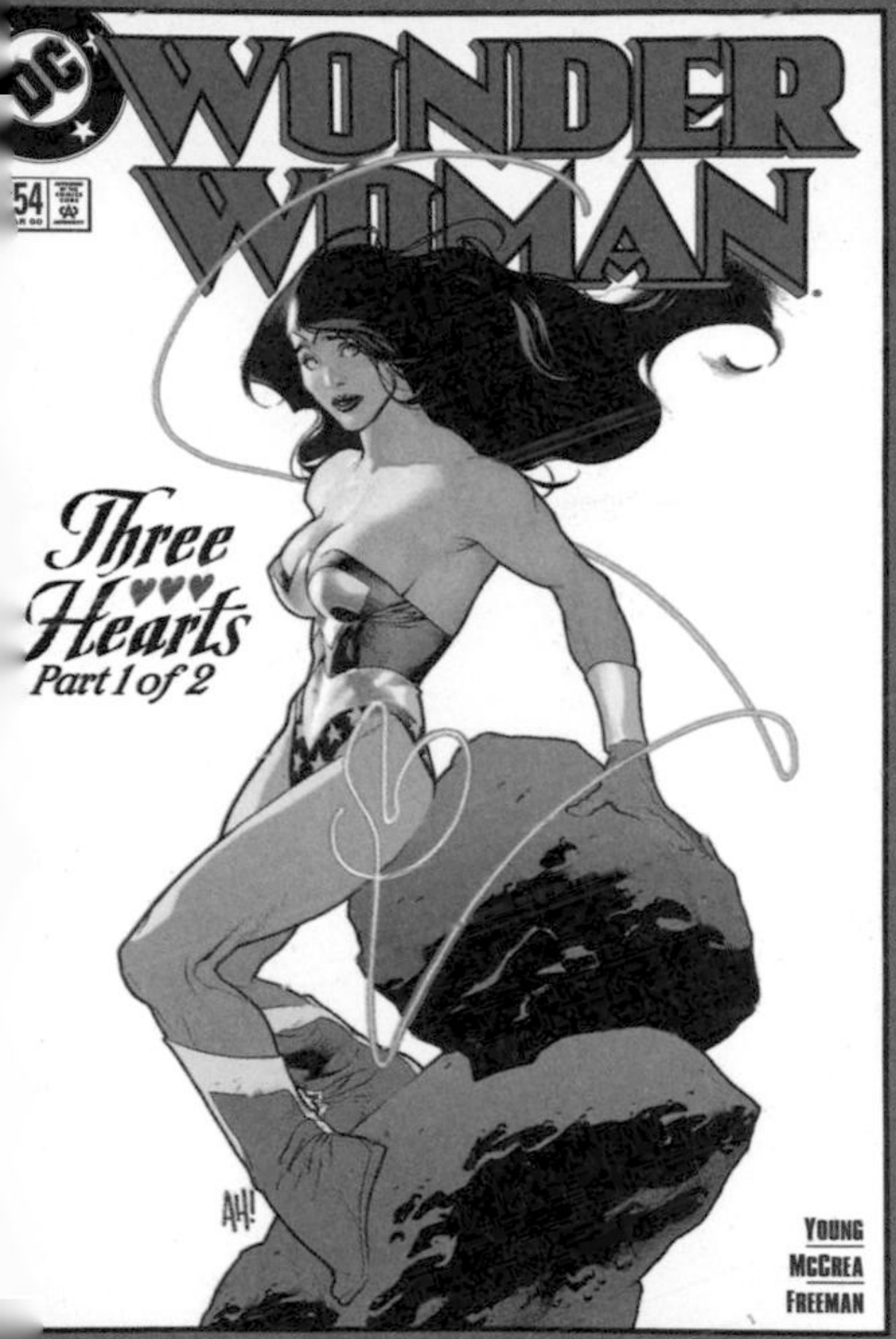
DC
WONDER WOMAN
54
Three Hearts
Part 1 of 2
AH!
YOUNG
McCREA
FREEMAN

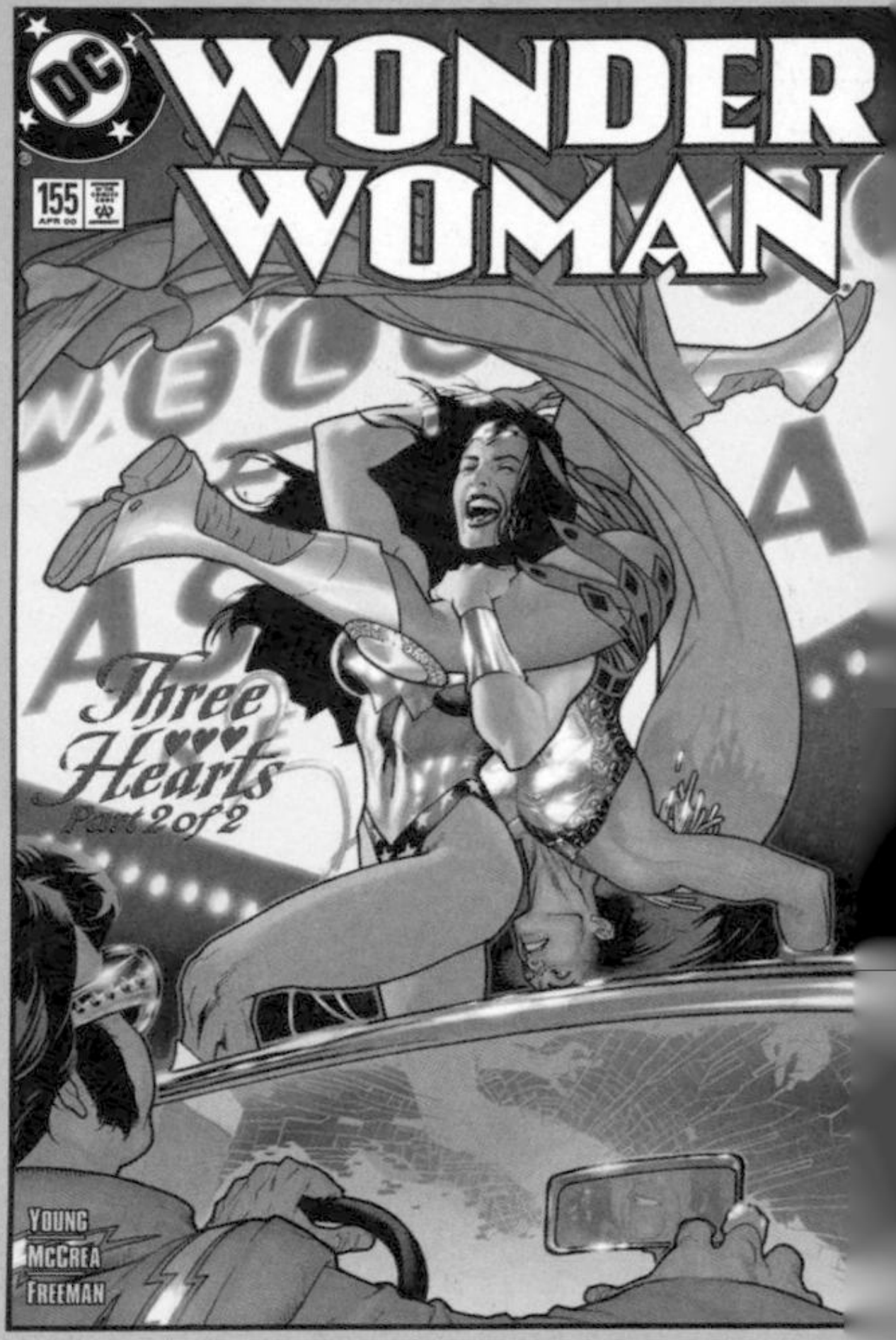
DC
WONDER WOMAN
155
APR 00
Three Hearts
Part 2 of 2
YOUNG
McCREA
FREEMAN

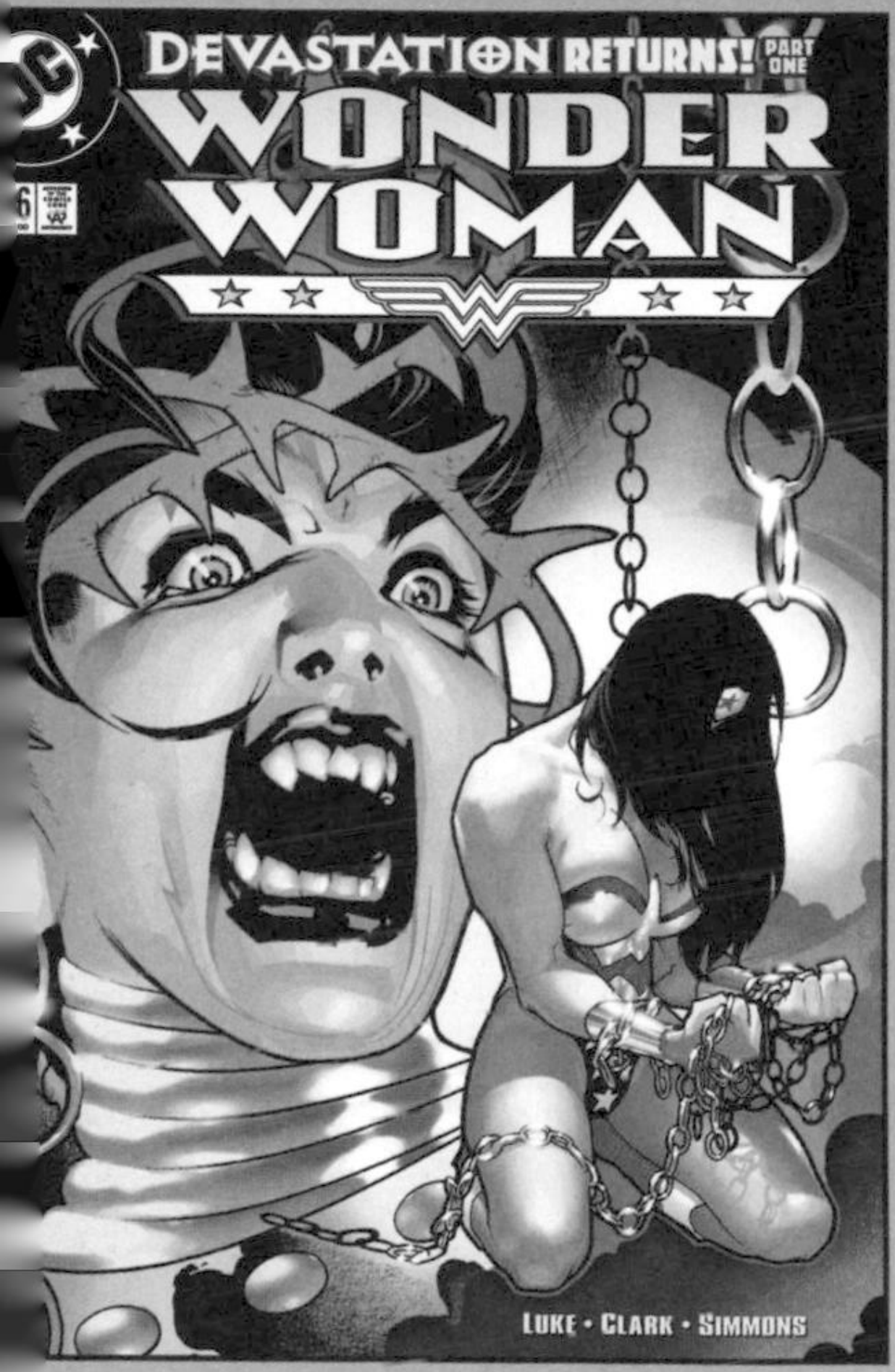
DC
DEVASTATION RETURNS! PART ONE
WONDER WOMAN
6
LUKE • CLARK • SIMMONS

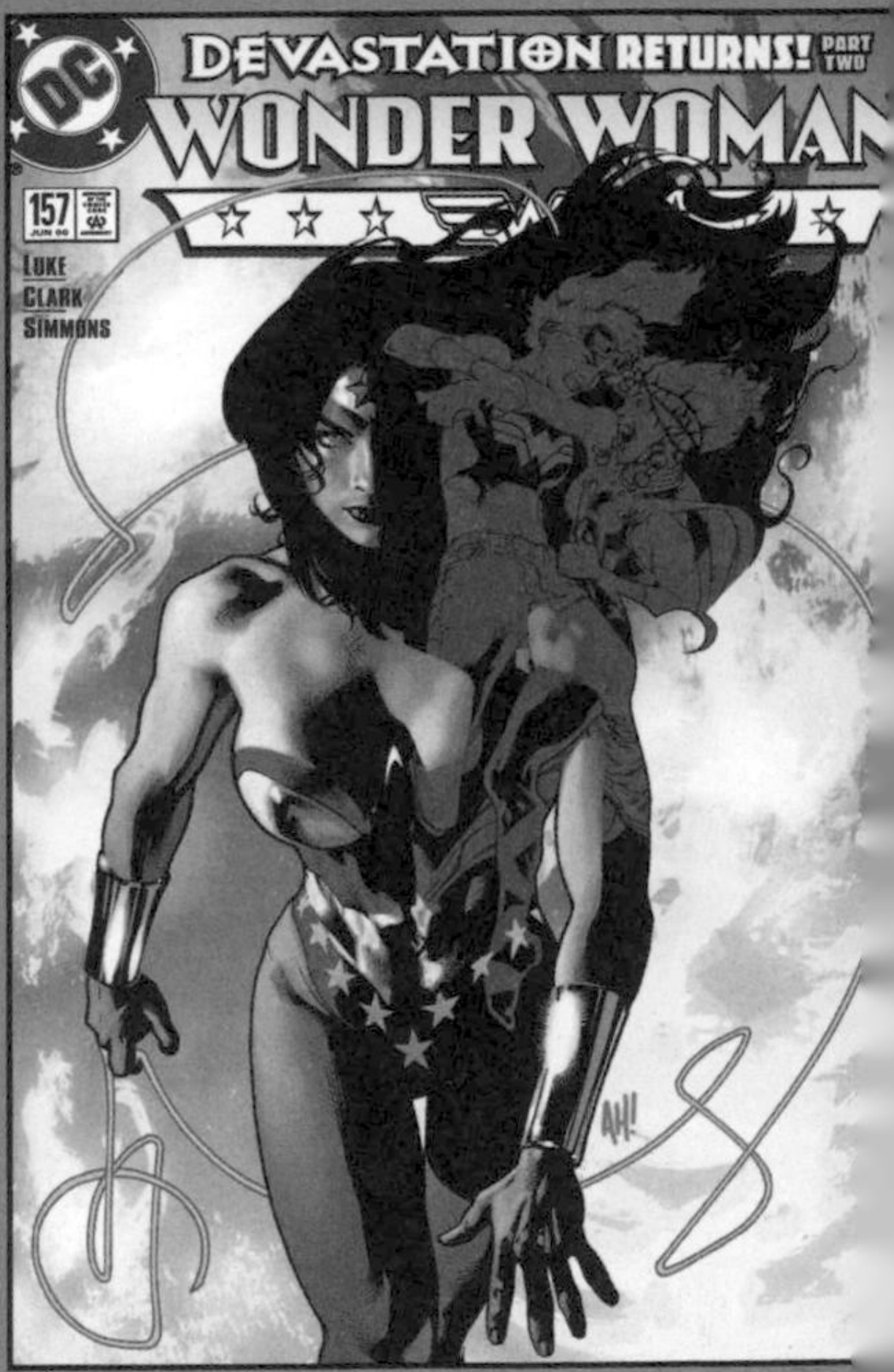
DC
DEVASTATION RETURNS! PART TWO
WONDER WOMAN
157
LUKE
CLARK
SIMMONS
AH!

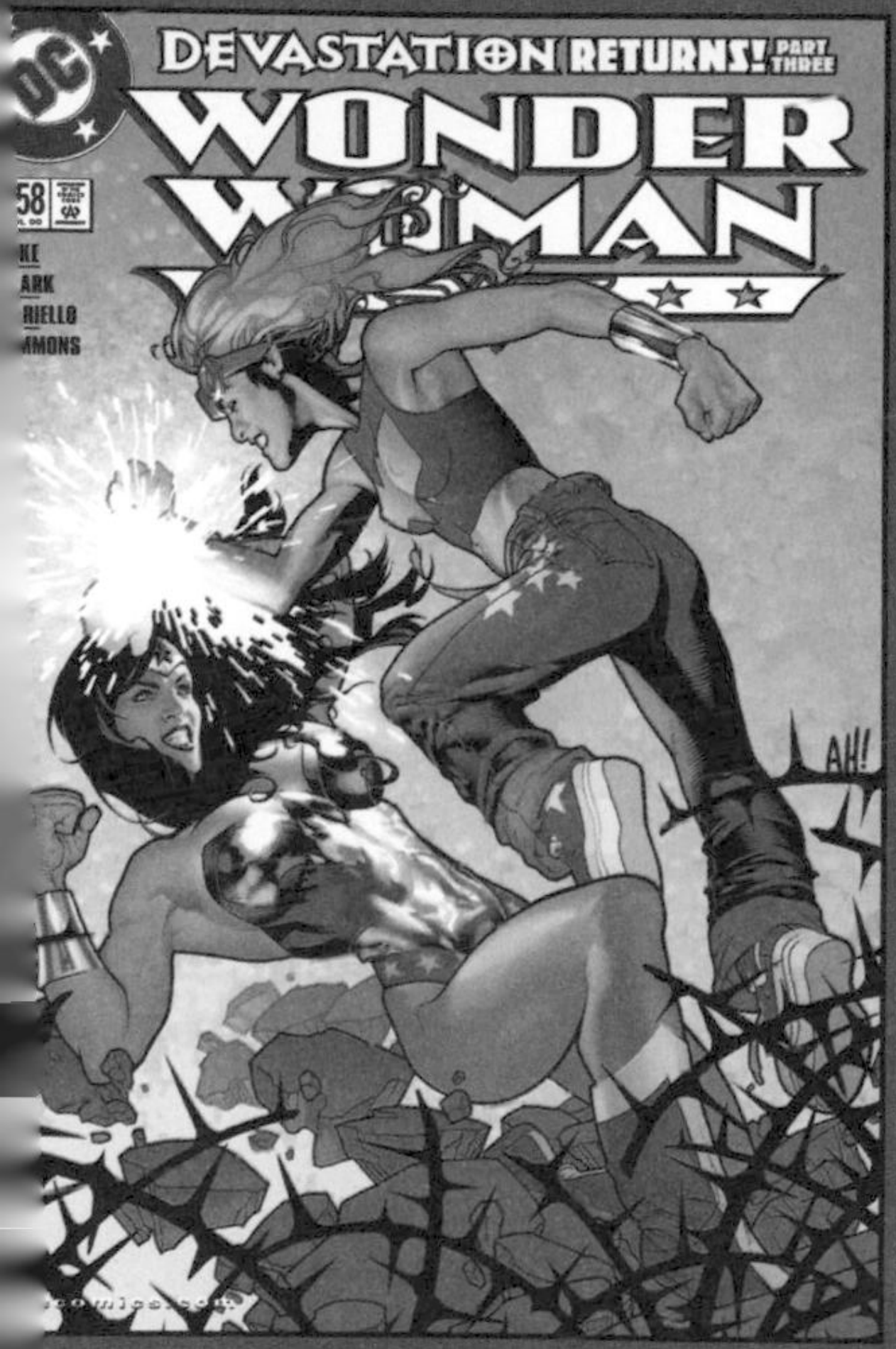
DC
DEVASTATION RETURNS! PART THREE
WONDER WOMAN
58
KE
ARK
RIELLO
MMONS
AH!

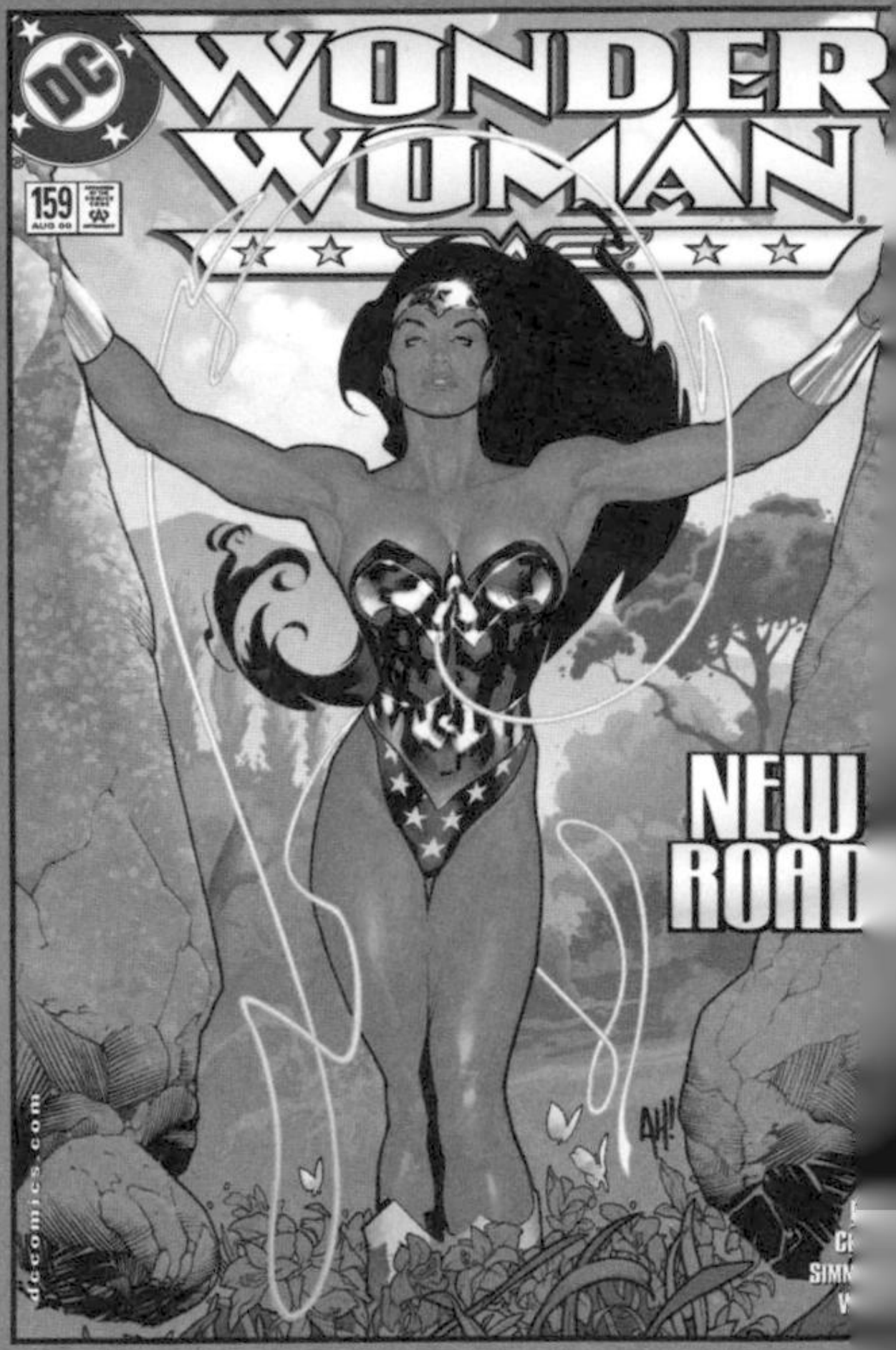
DC
WONDER WOMAN
159
AUG 00
NEW
ROAD
dccomics.com

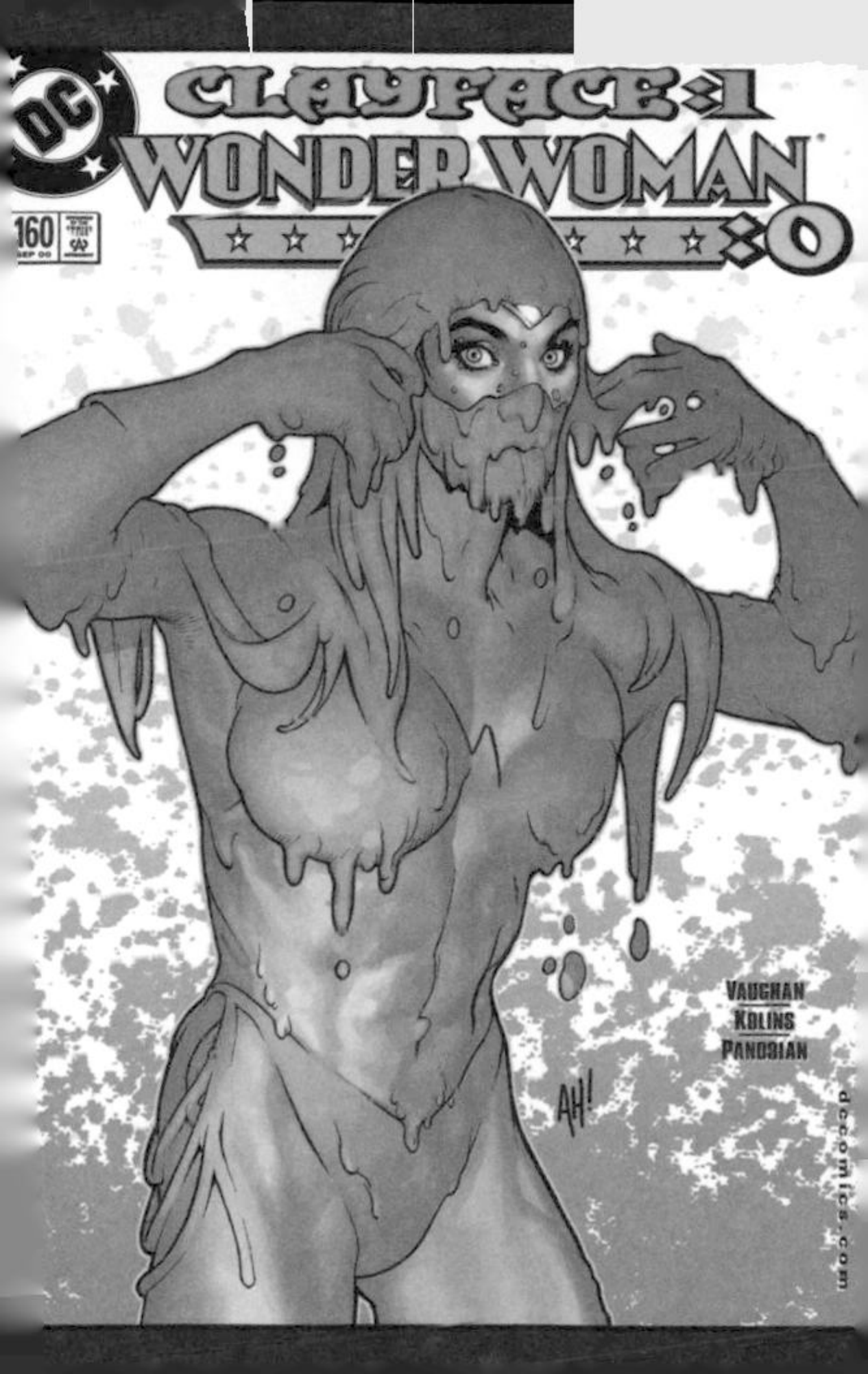
DC
CLAYFACE:1
WONDER WOMAN
80
160
SEP 00
VAUGHAN
KOLINS
PANOSIAN
AH!
dccomics.com

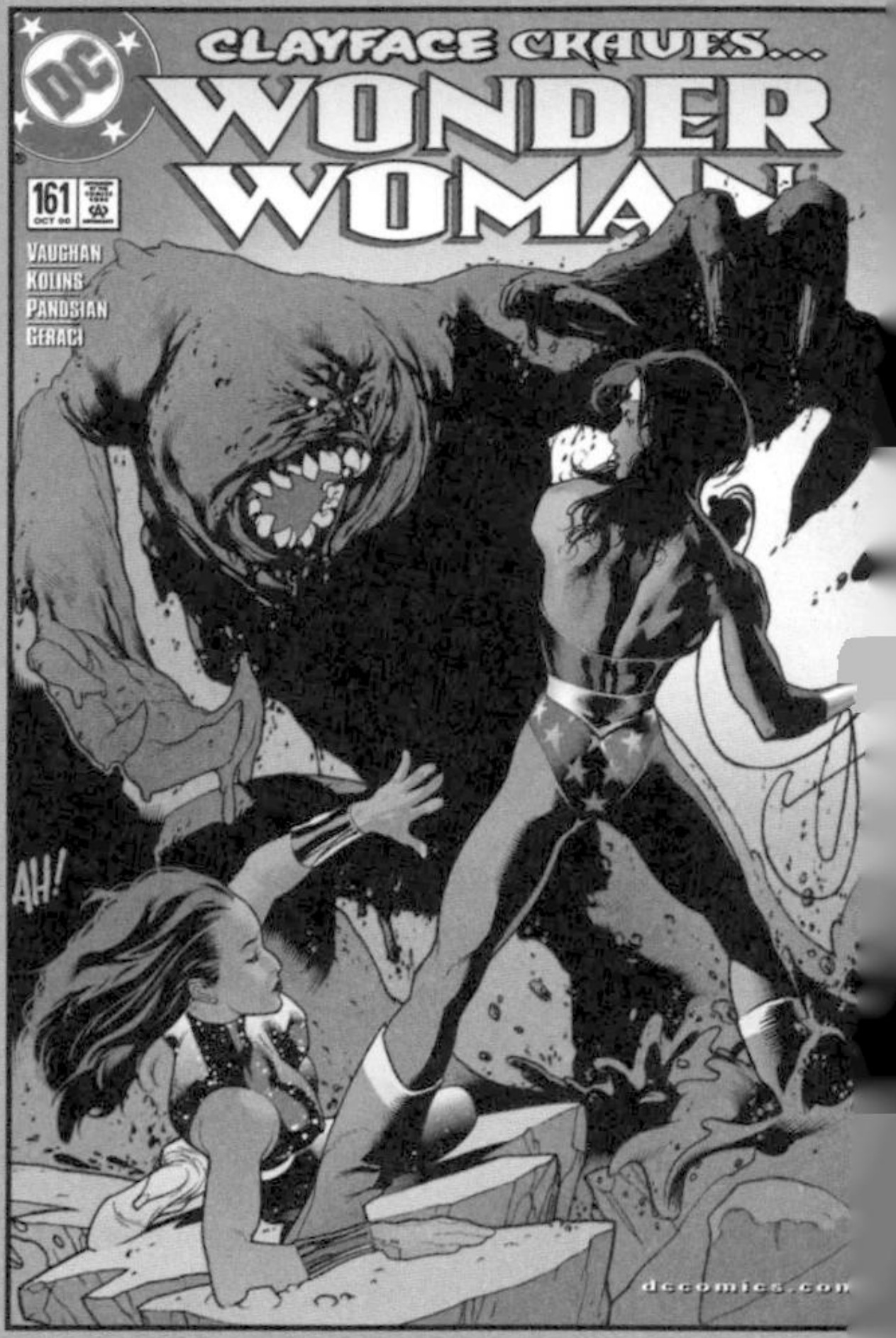
CLAYFACE CRAVES...
WONDER WOMAN
161
OCT 00
VAUGHAN
KOLINS
PANDSIAN
GERACI
AH!
dccomics.com

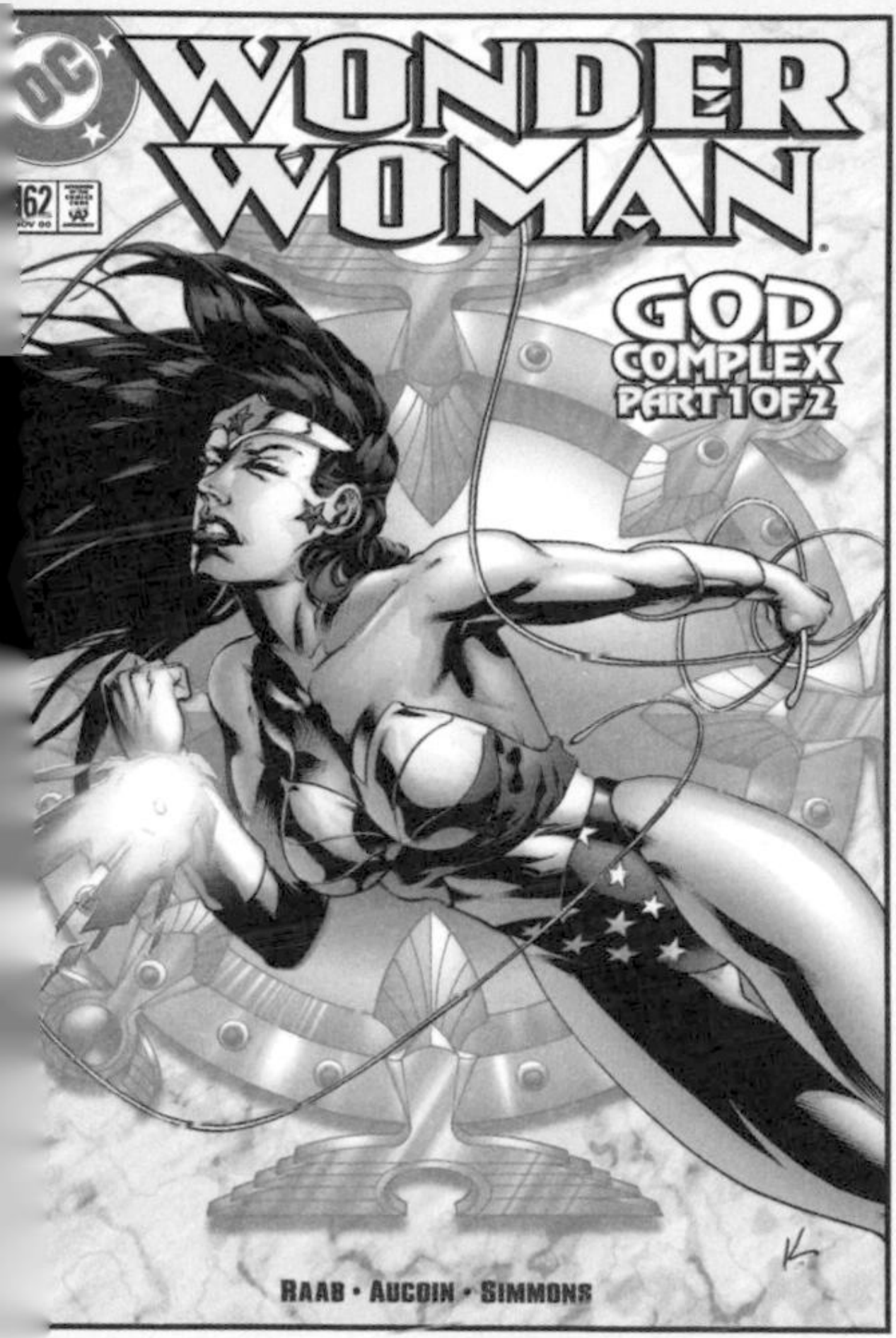
DC
WONDER WOMAN
162
GOD COMPLEX
PART 1 OF 2
RAAB • AUCOIN • SIMMONS

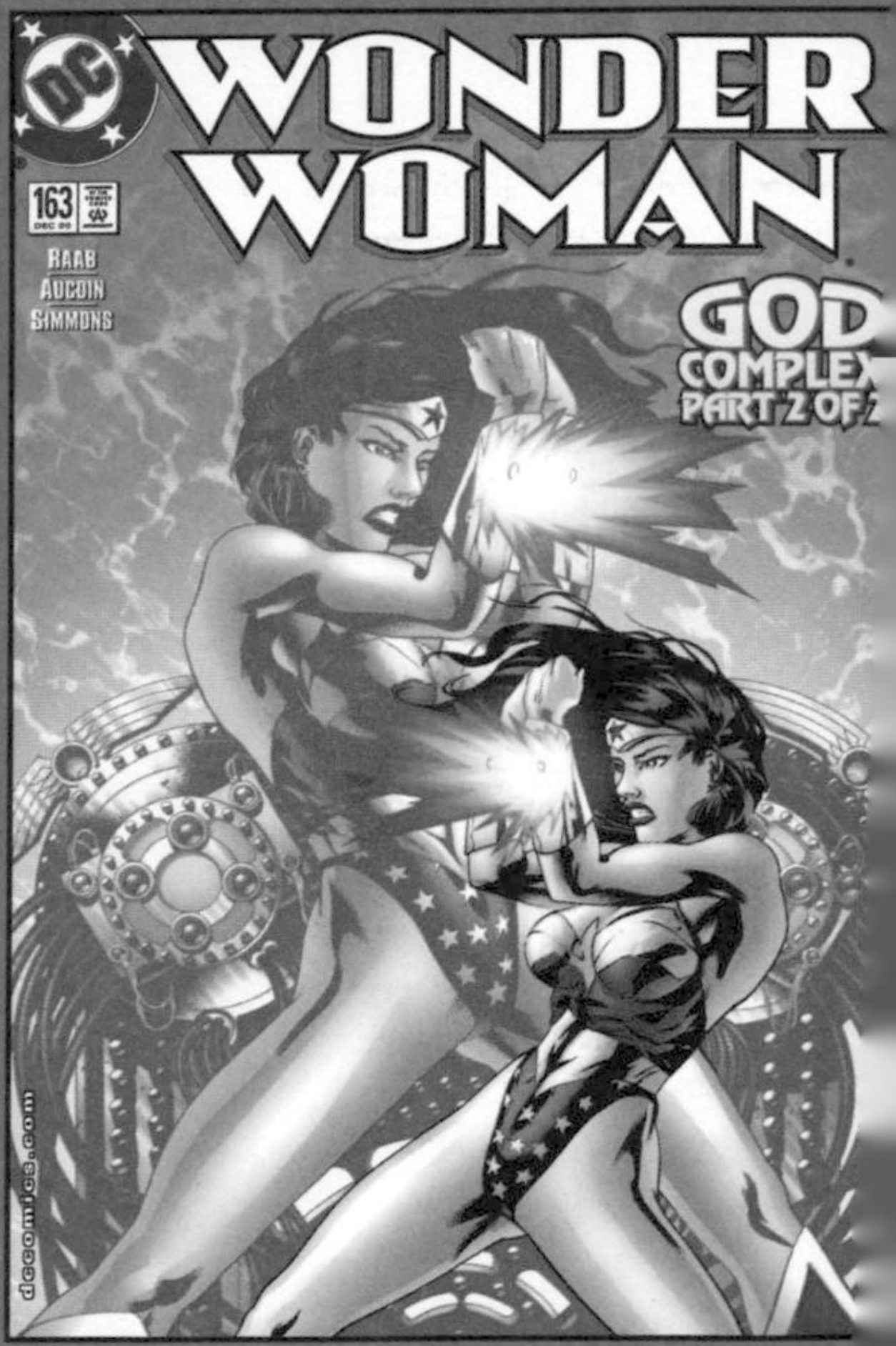
DC
WONDER WOMAN
163
RAAB
AUCOIN
SIMMONS
GOD COMPLEX
PART 2 OF 2
dccomics.com

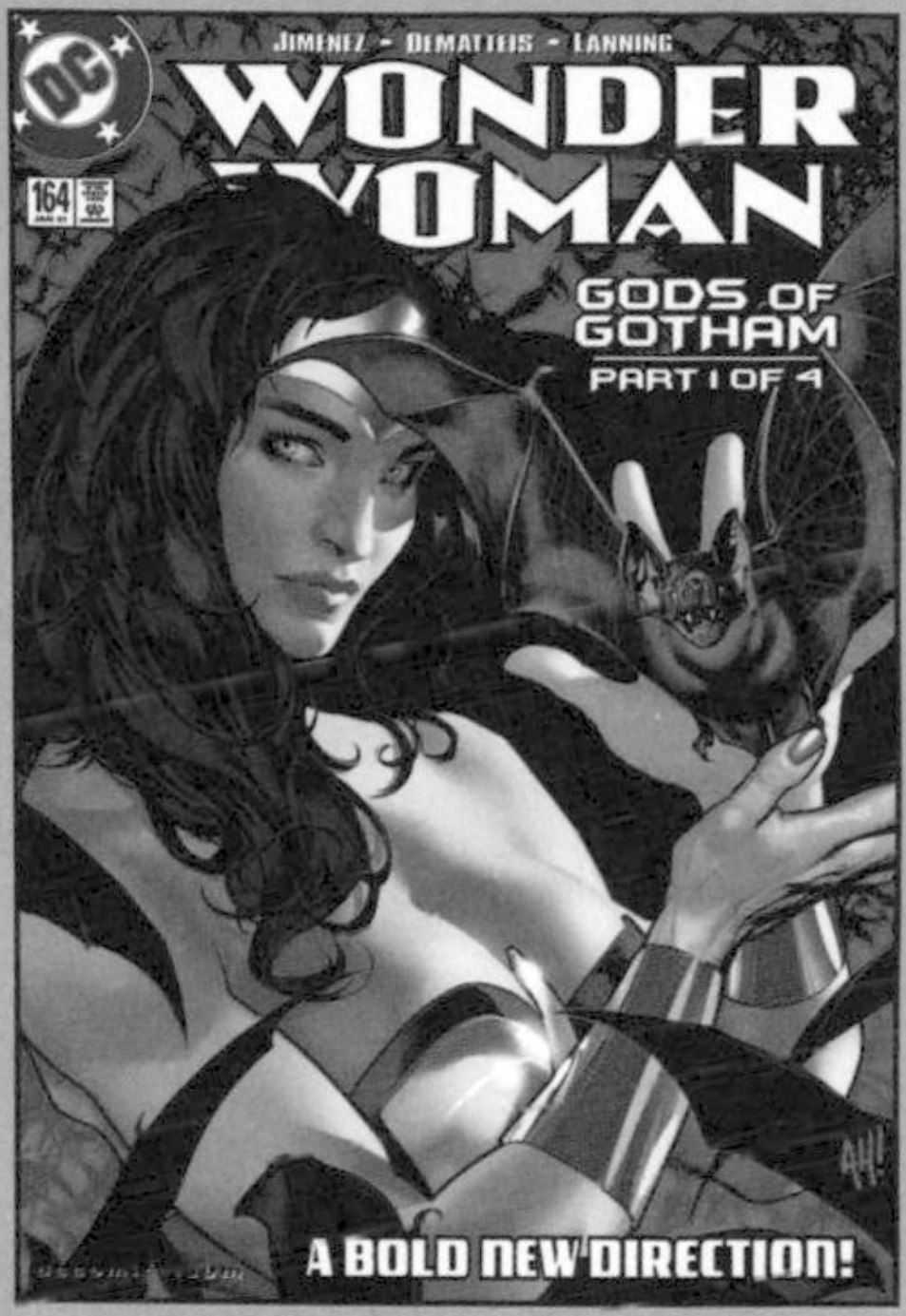

Wonder Woman (Vol. 2) #164

"Gods of Gotham" (issues #164 to #167), Wonder Woman travels to Gotham City to help Batman and his allies. This issue marks the beginning of writer-artist Phil Jimenez's *Wonder Woman* run.

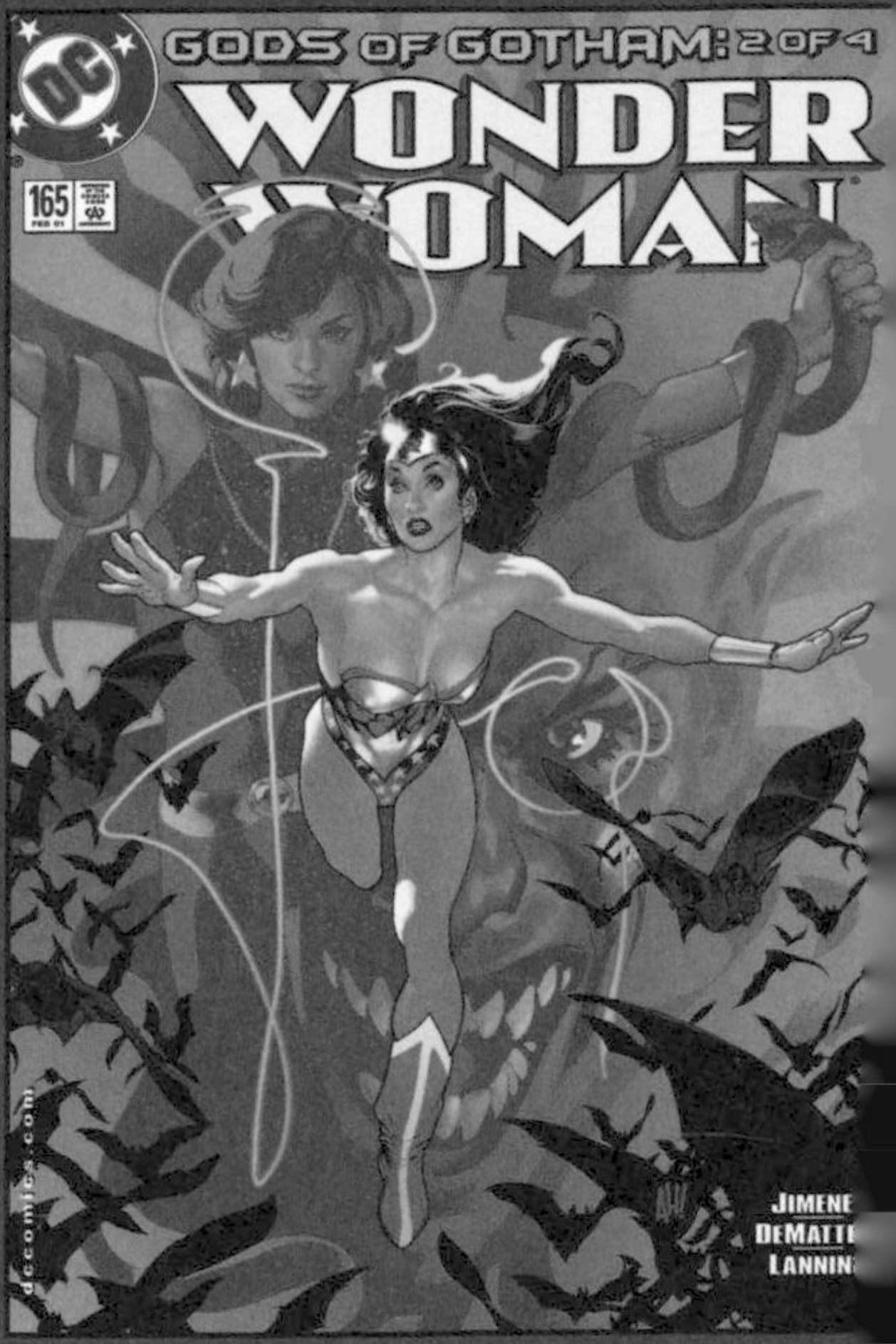
GODS OF GOTHAM: 2 OF 4
WONDER
165
JIMENE
DEMATTE
LANNIN
dccomics.com

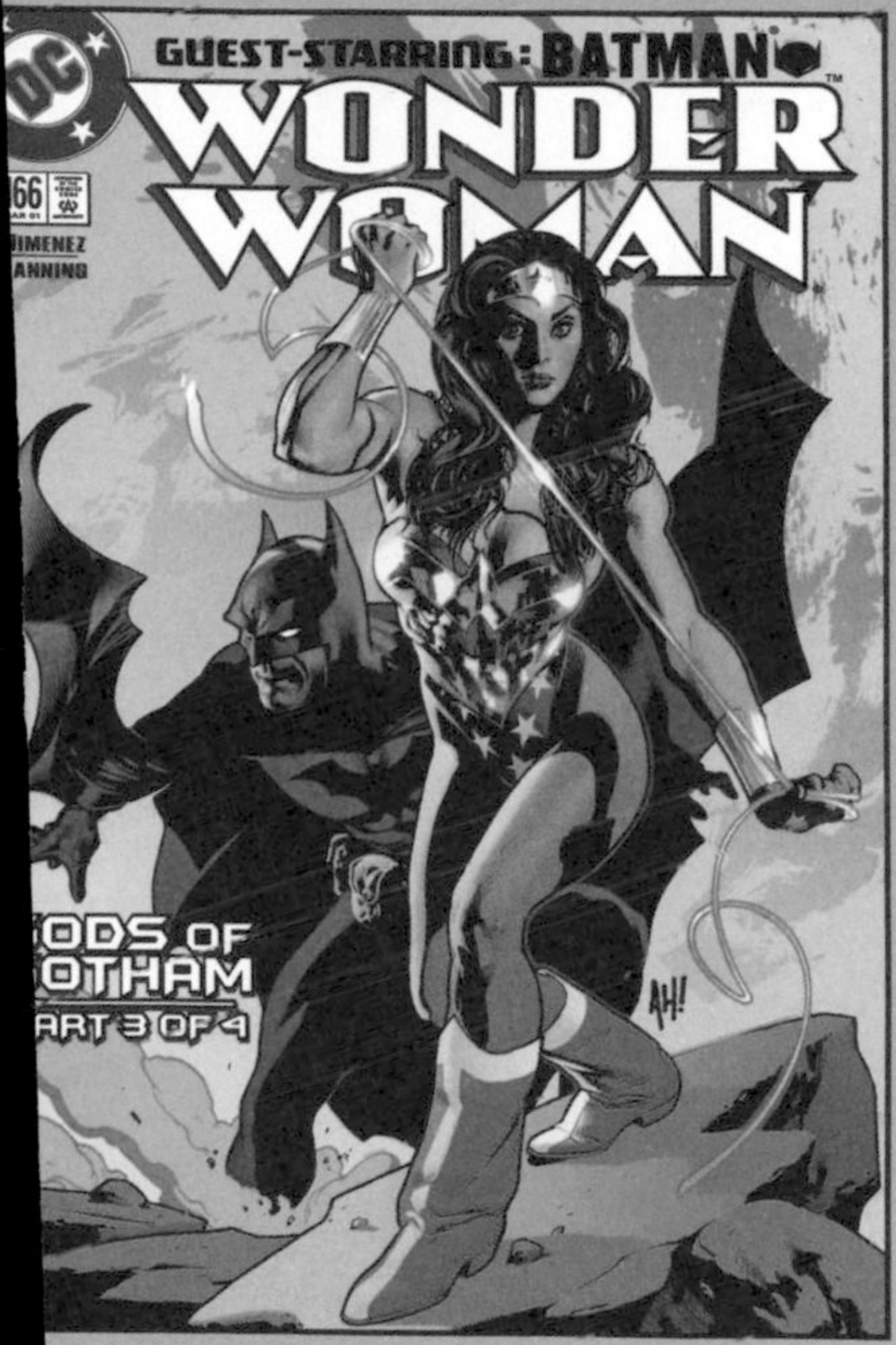
GUEST-STARRING: BATMAN
WONDER WOMAN
66
IMENEZ
ANNING
ODS OF
OTHAM
ART 3 OF 4
AH!

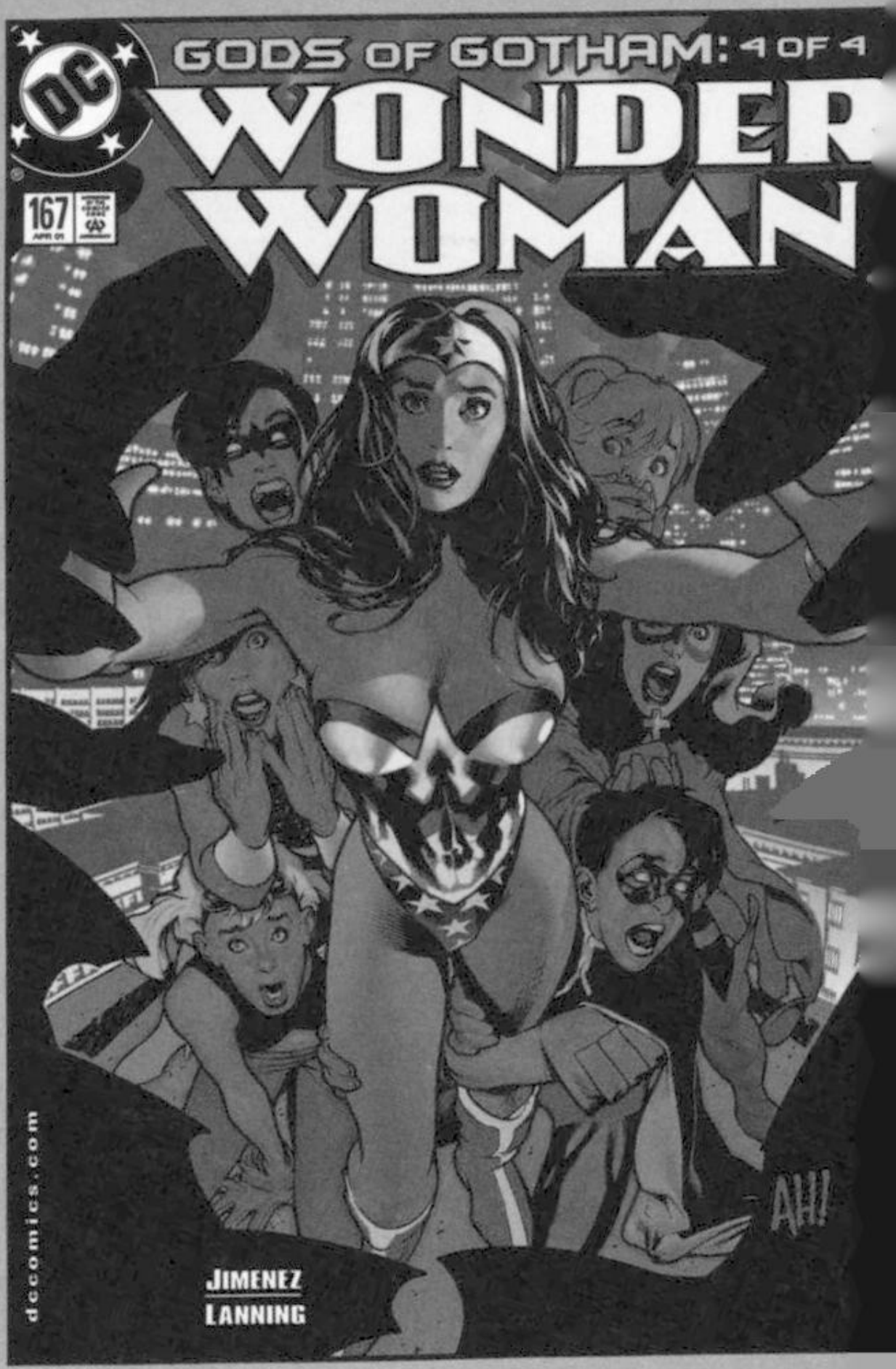
GODS OF GOTHAM: 4 OF 4
WONDER WOMAN
167
dccomics.com
JIMENEZ
LANNING
AH!

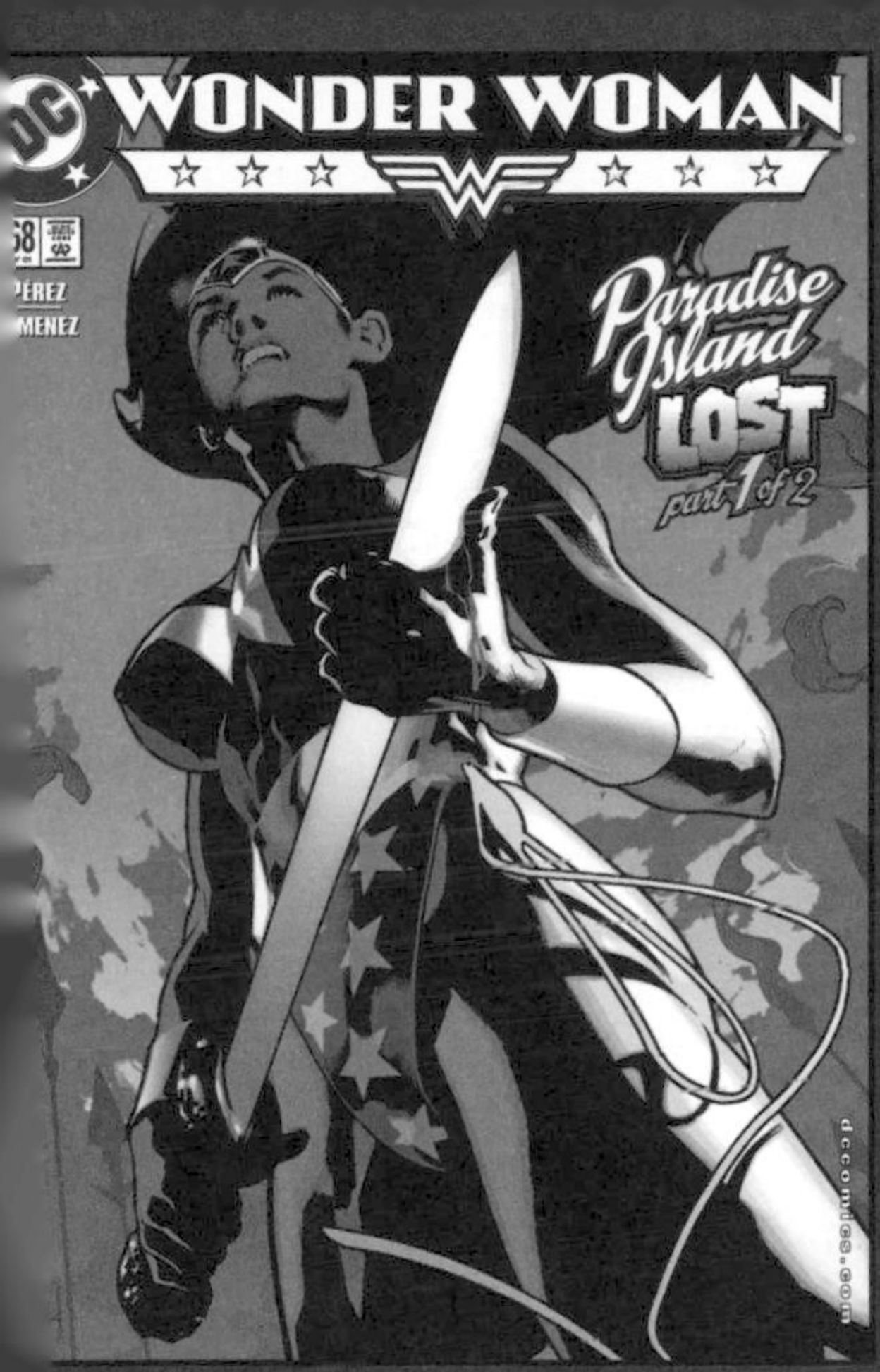
WONDER WOMAN
68
PEREZ
MENEZ
Paradise Island
LOST
part 1 of 2
dccomics.com

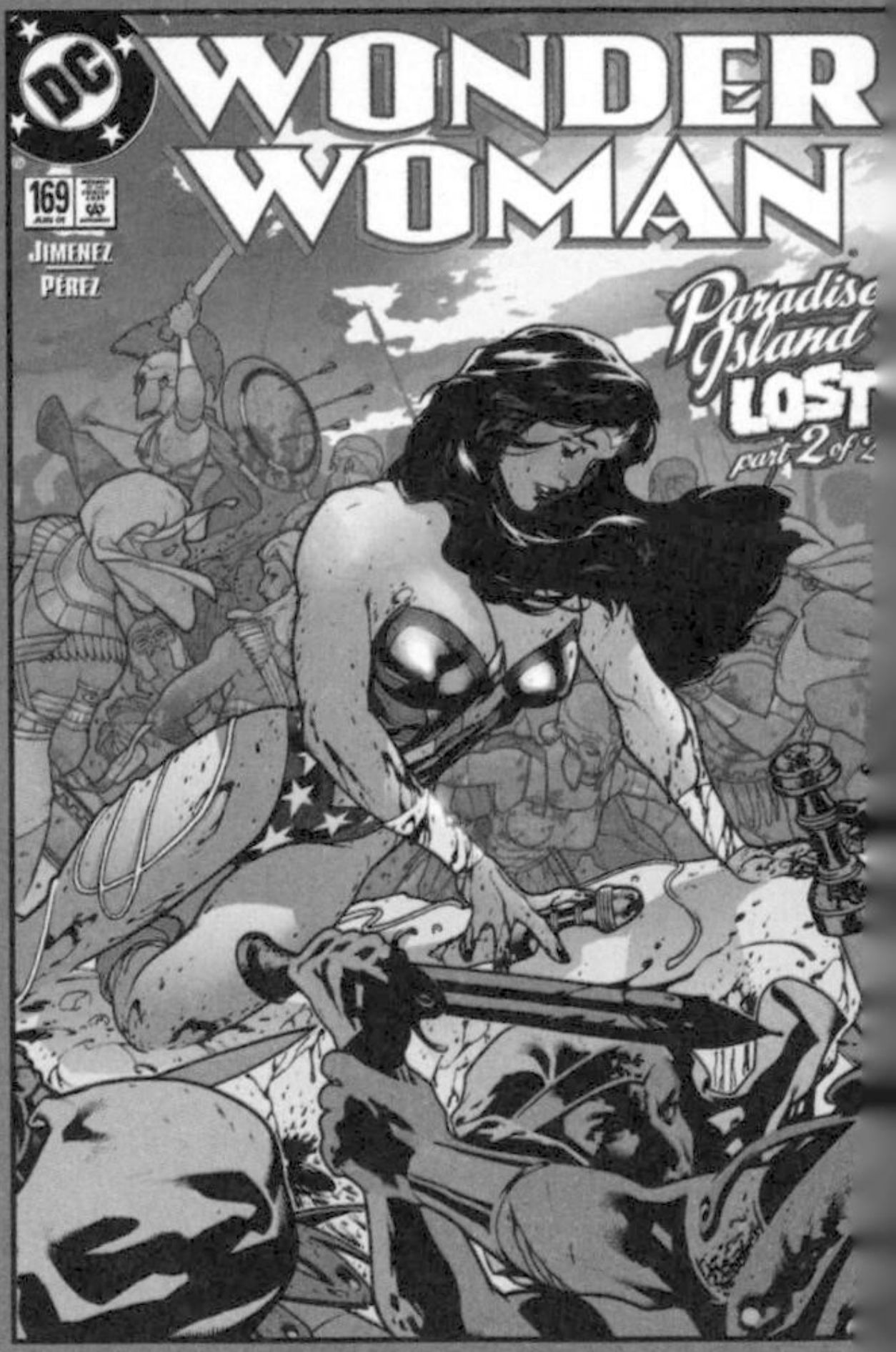
DC
WONDER WOMAN
169
JIMENEZ
PÉREZ
Paradise Island
LOST
part 2 of 2

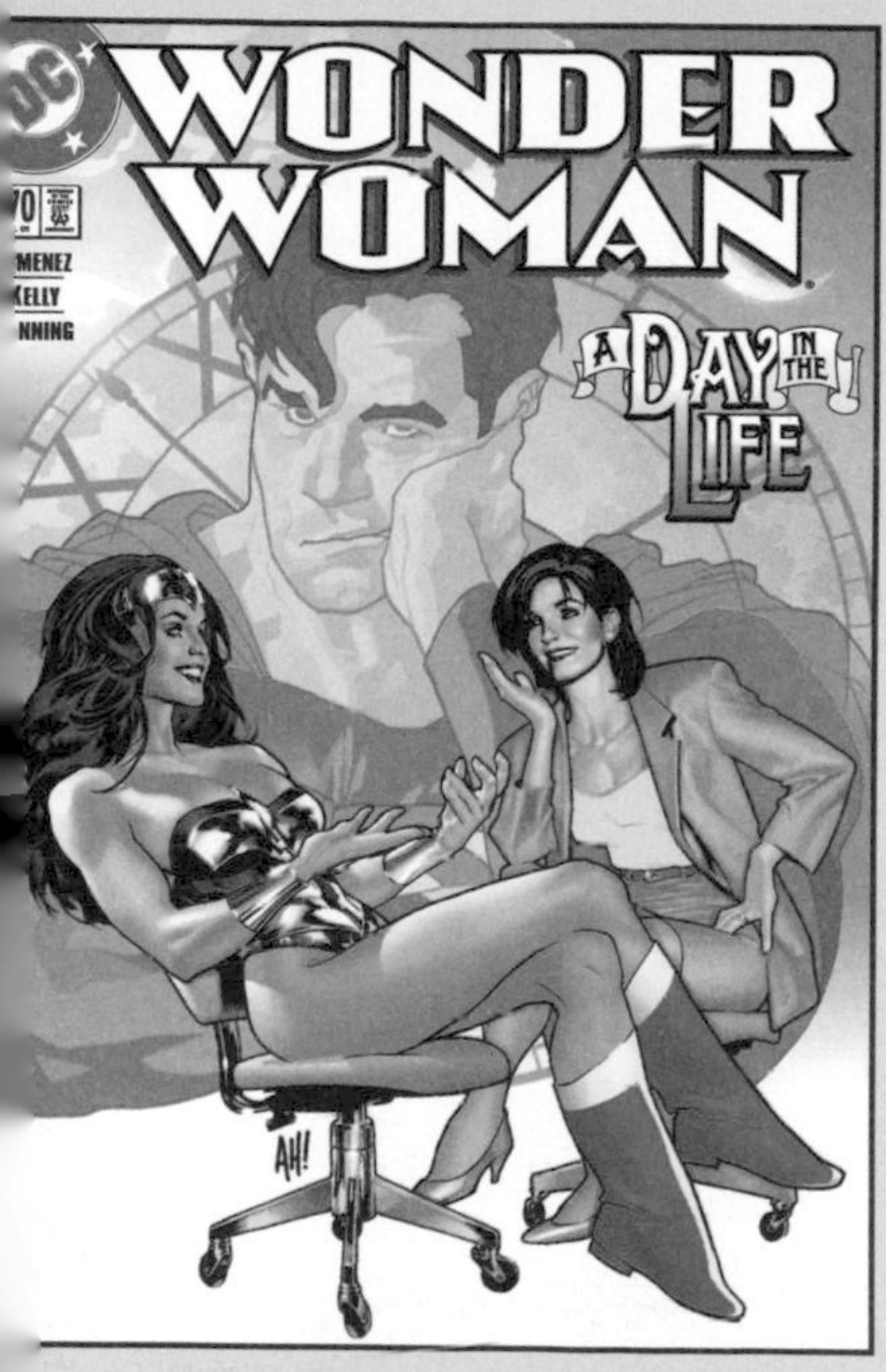
WONDER WOMAN
70
MENEZ
KELLY
NNING
A DAY IN THE LIFE
AH!

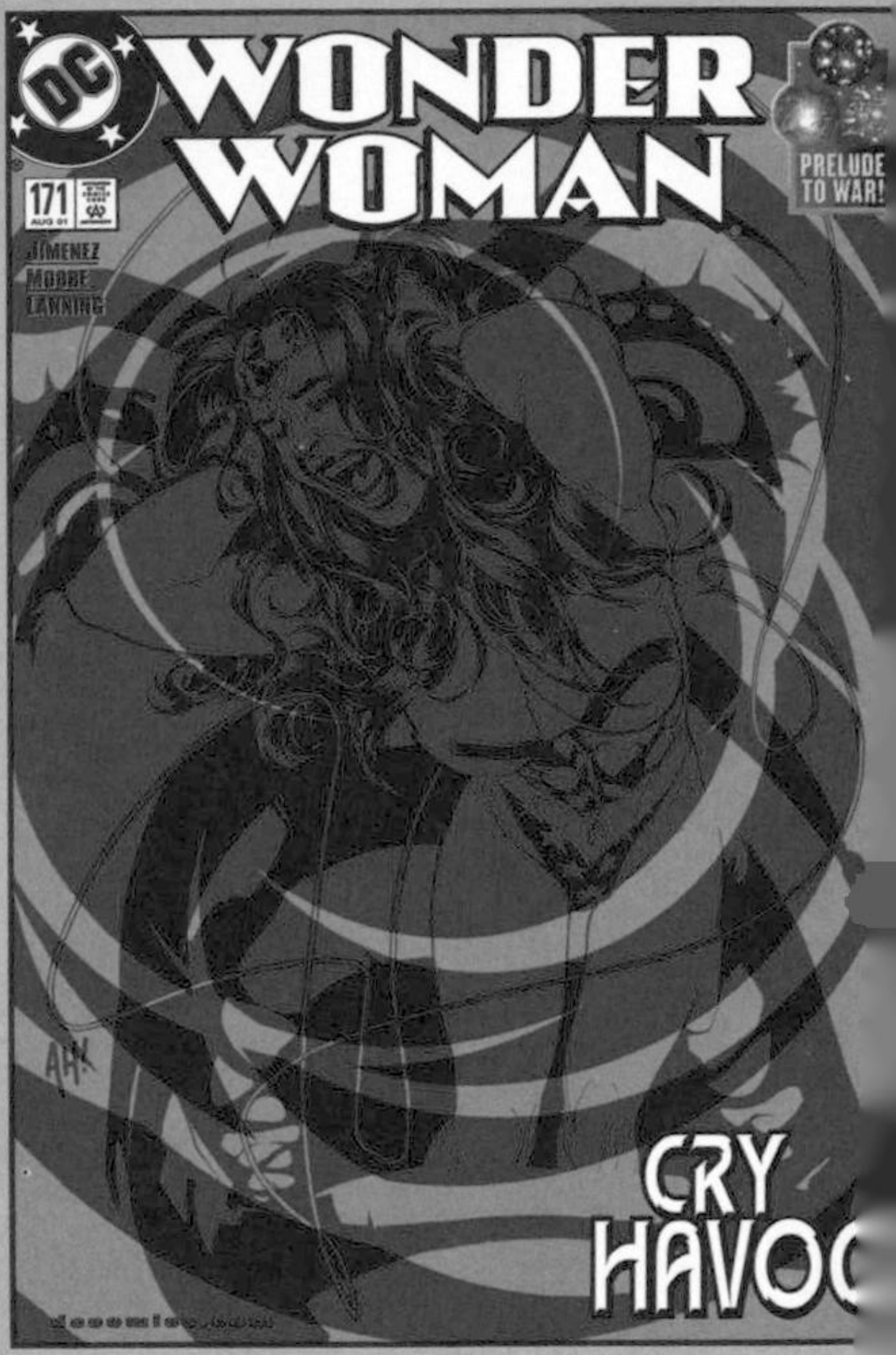
DC
WONDER WOMAN
171
AUG 01
JIMENEZ
MOORE
LANNING
PRELUDE TO WAR!
CRY HAVOC

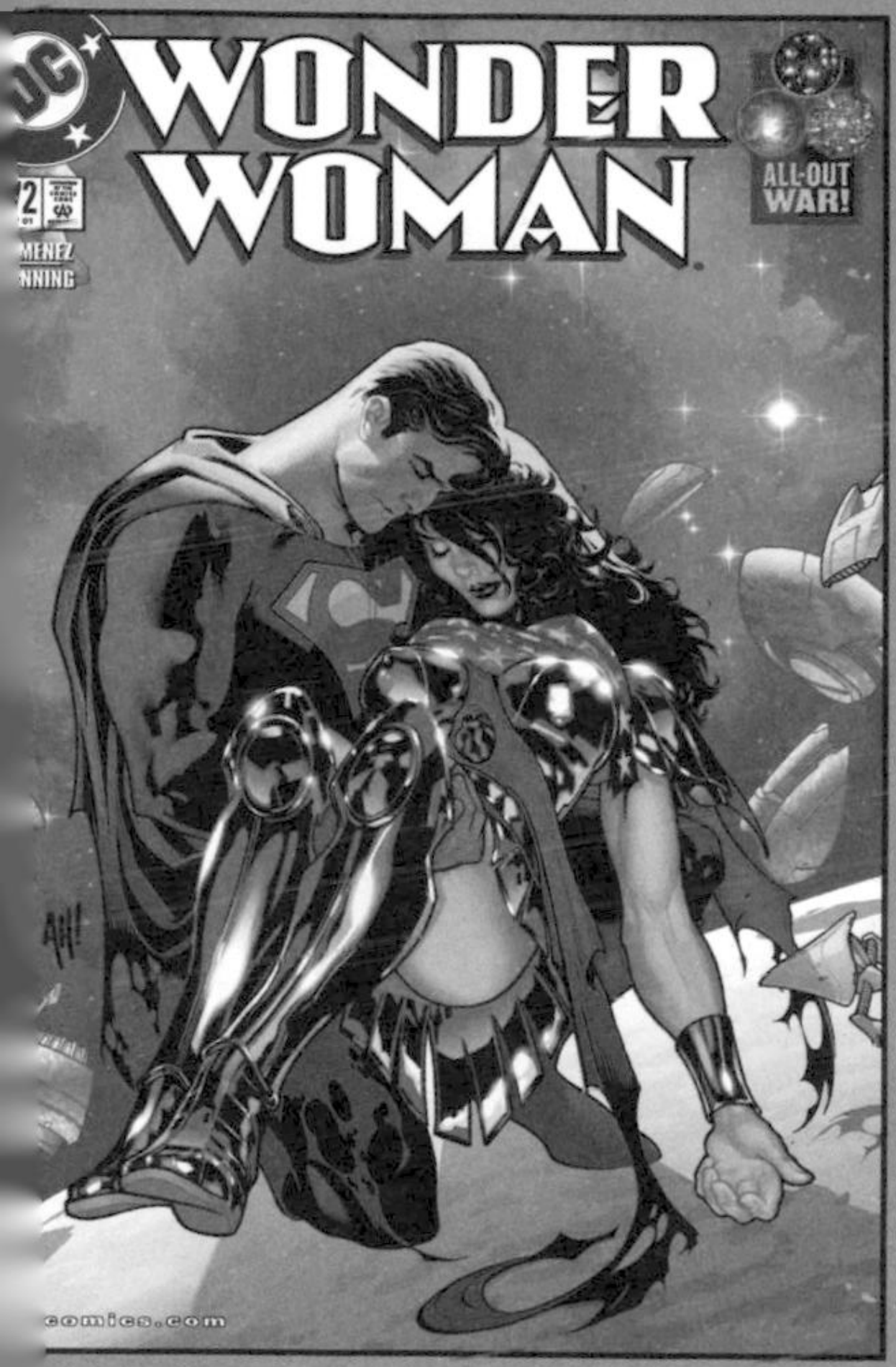
DC
WONDER WOMAN
ALL-OUT WAR!
MENEZ
NNING
AH!
comics.com

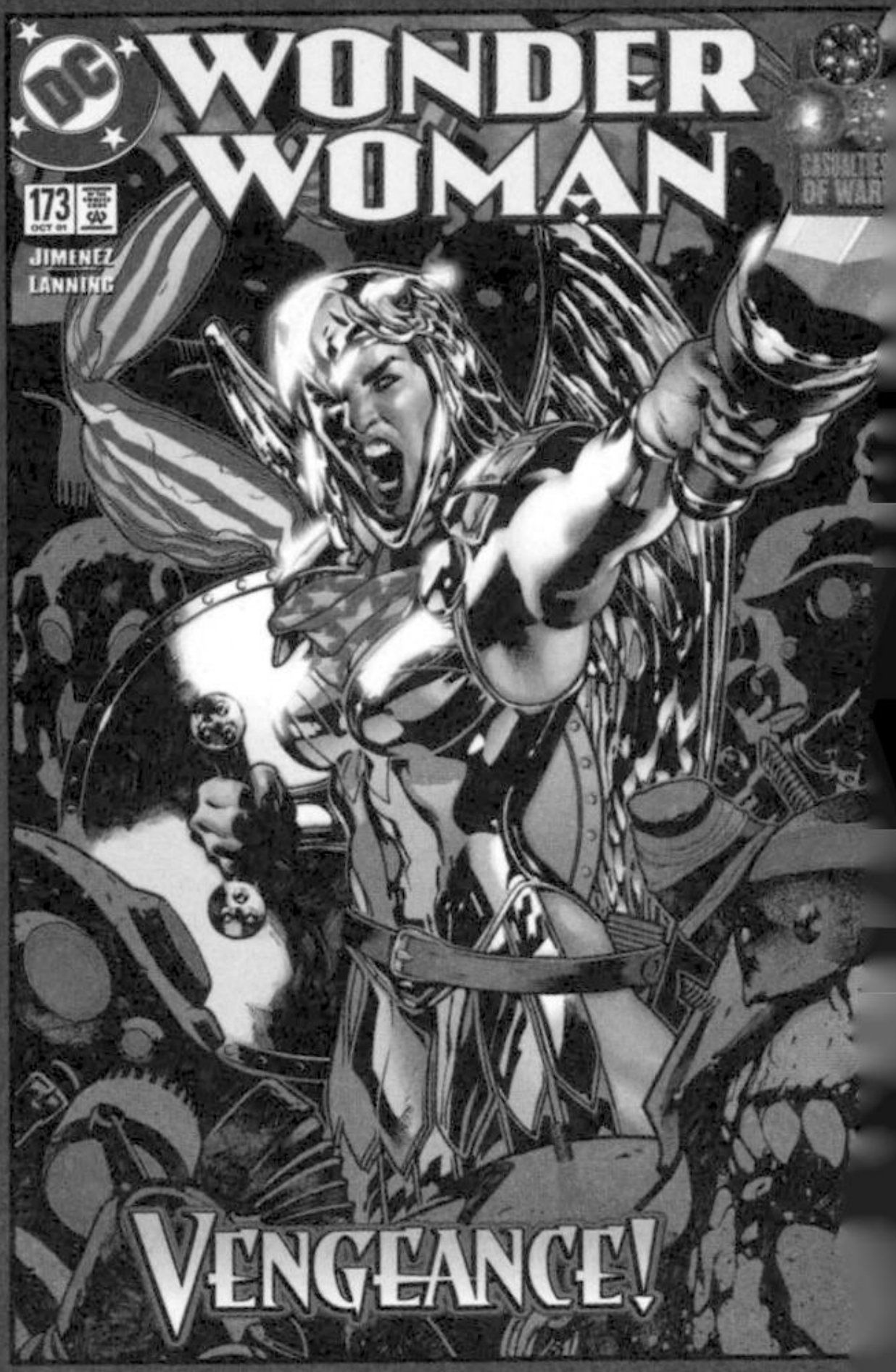
DC
WONDER WOMAN
173
OCT 01
JIMENEZ
LANNING
CASUALTIES OF WAR
VENGEANCE!

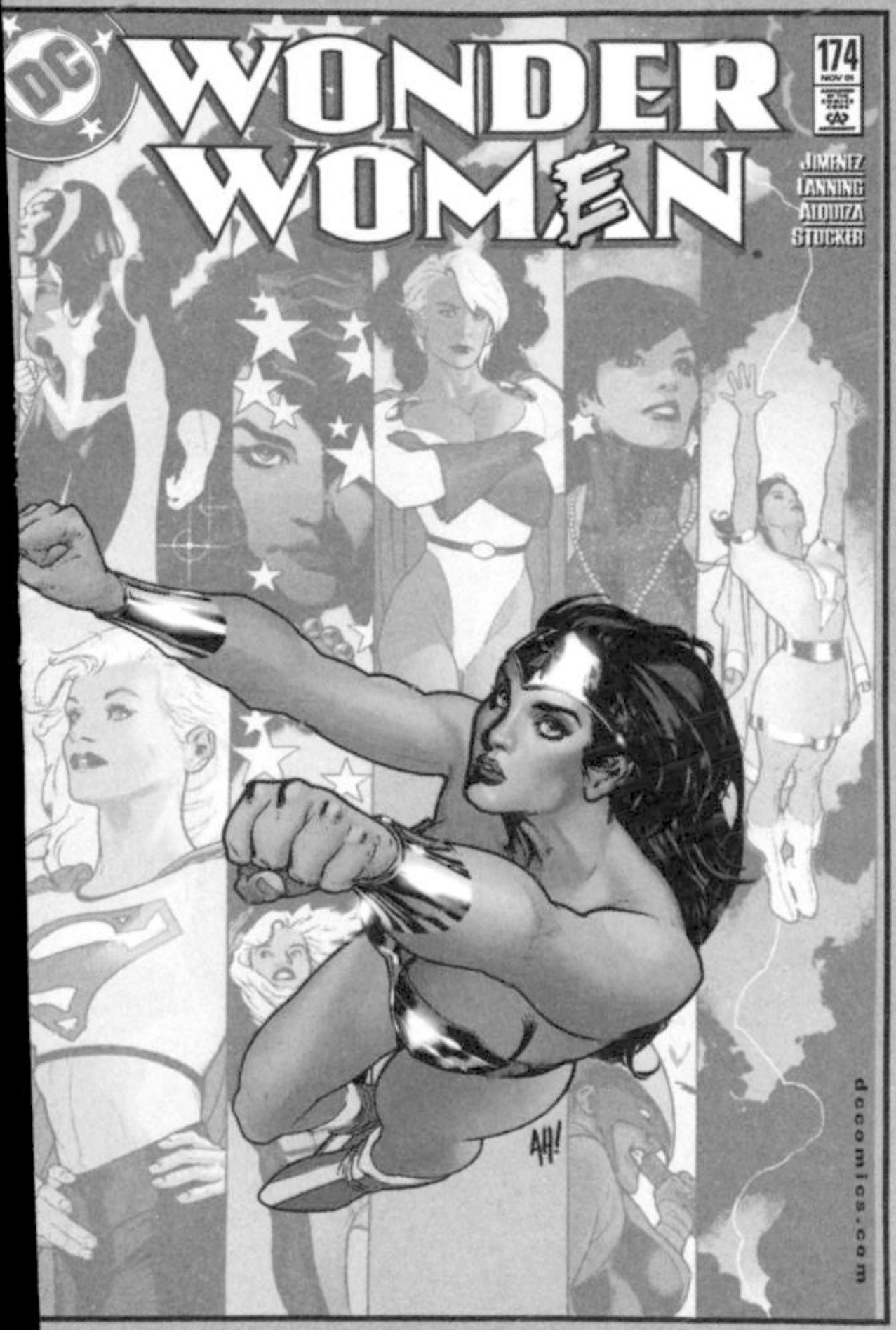
DC
WONDER WOMEN
174
NOV '01
JIMENEZ
LANNING
ALQUIZA
STUCKER
AH!
dccomics.com

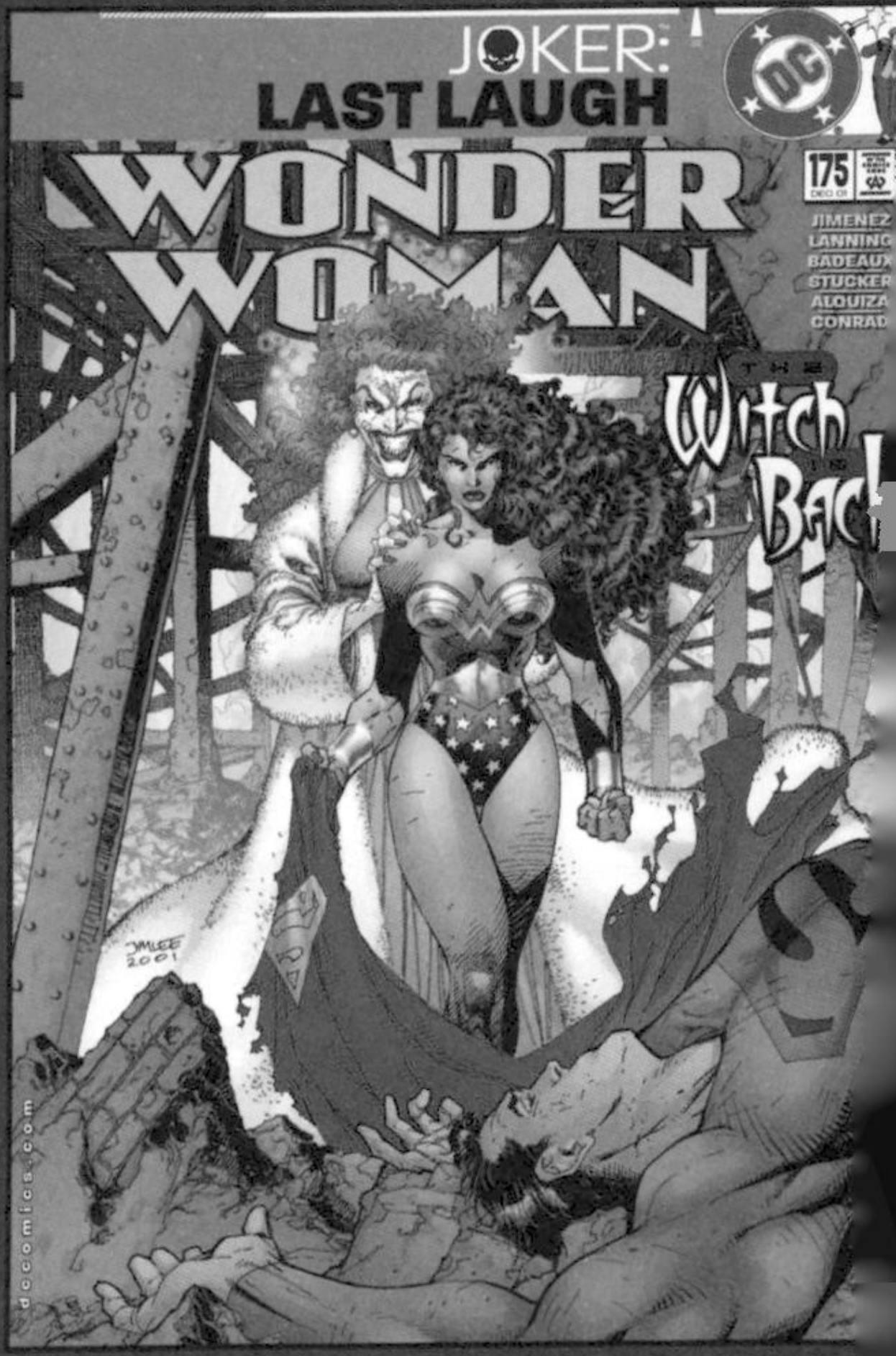
JOKER:
LAST LAUGH
WONDER WOMAN
175
DEC 01
JIMENEZ
LANNING
BADEAUX
STUCKER
ALQUIZA
CONRAD
THE
Witch
Back!
JMLEE
2001
dccomics.com

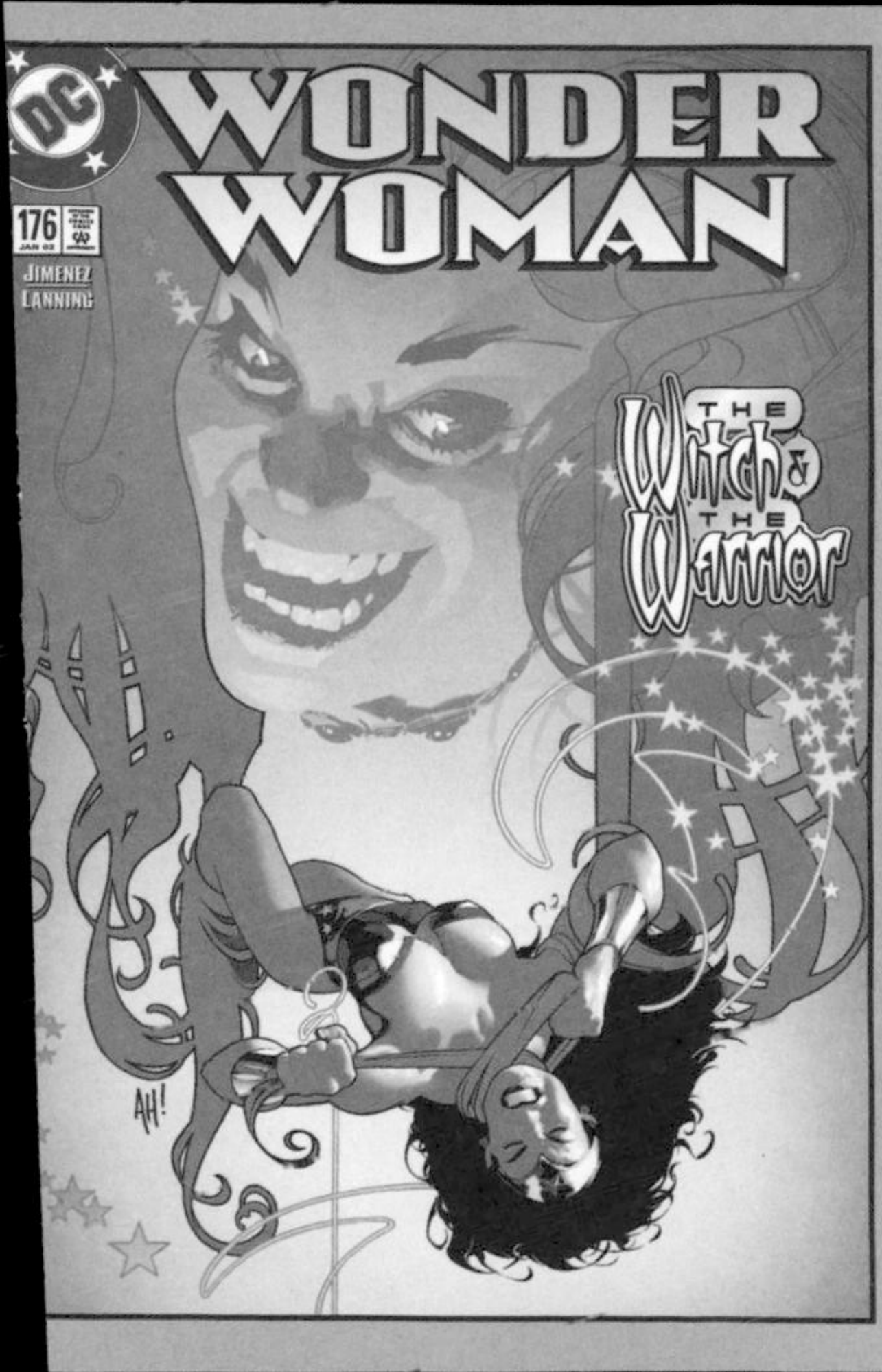
DC
WONDER WOMAN
176
JIMENEZ
LANNING
THE Witch & THE Warrior
AH!

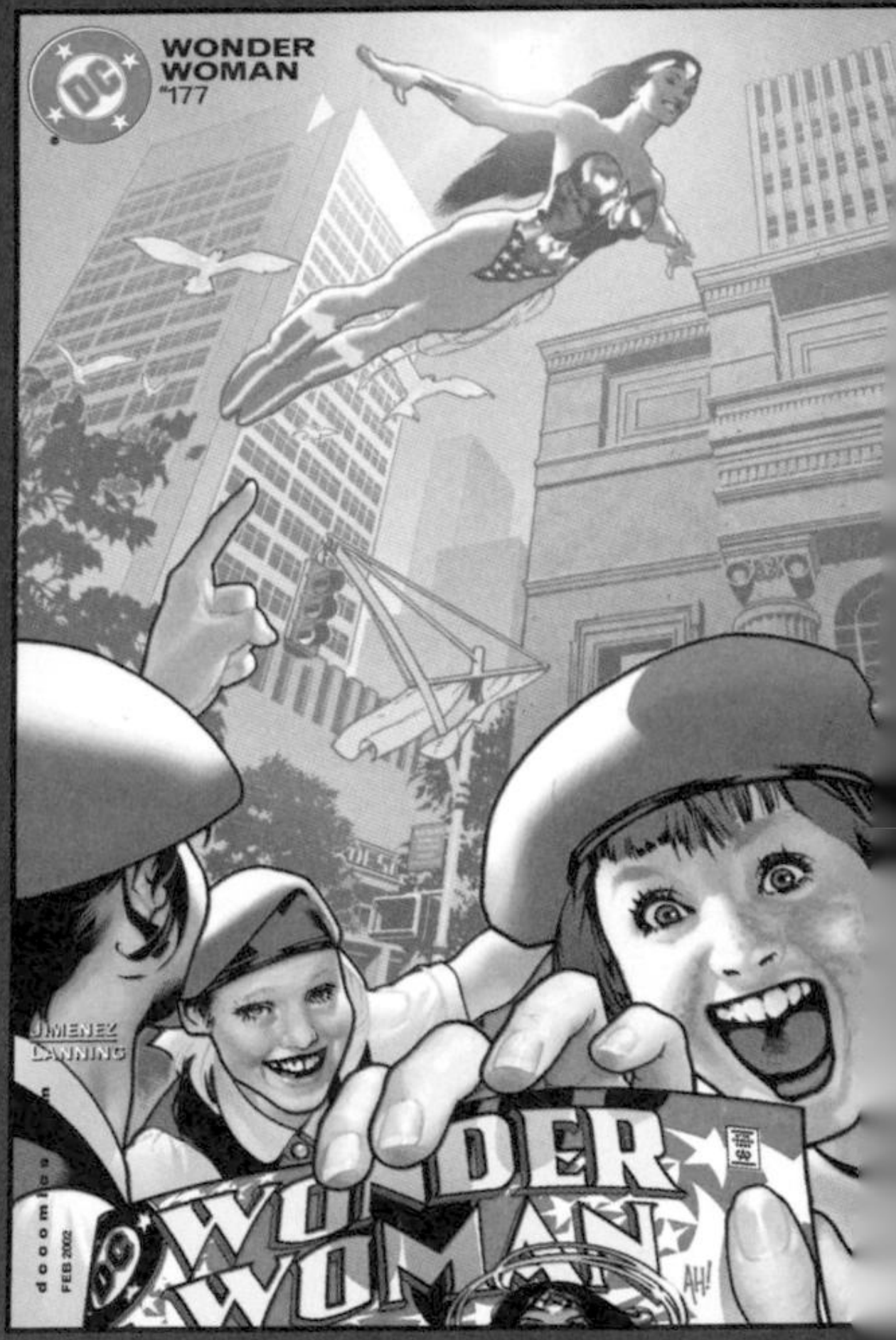
WONDER
WOMAN
#177
JIMENEZ
LANNING
WONDER
WOMAN
AH!
FEB 2002

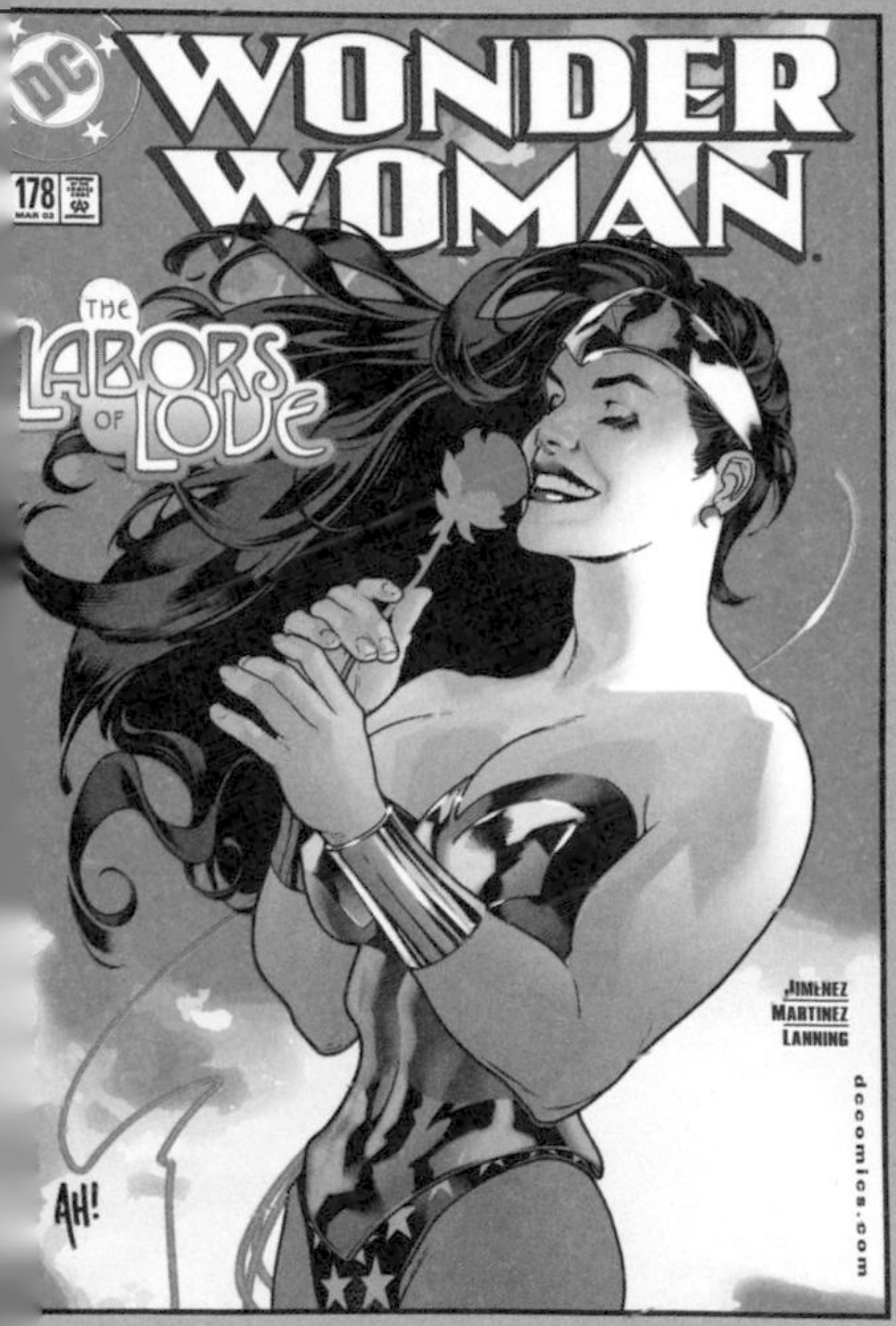
DC
WONDER WOMAN
178
THE LABORS OF LOVE
JIMENEZ
MARTINEZ
LANNING
AH!
dccomics.com

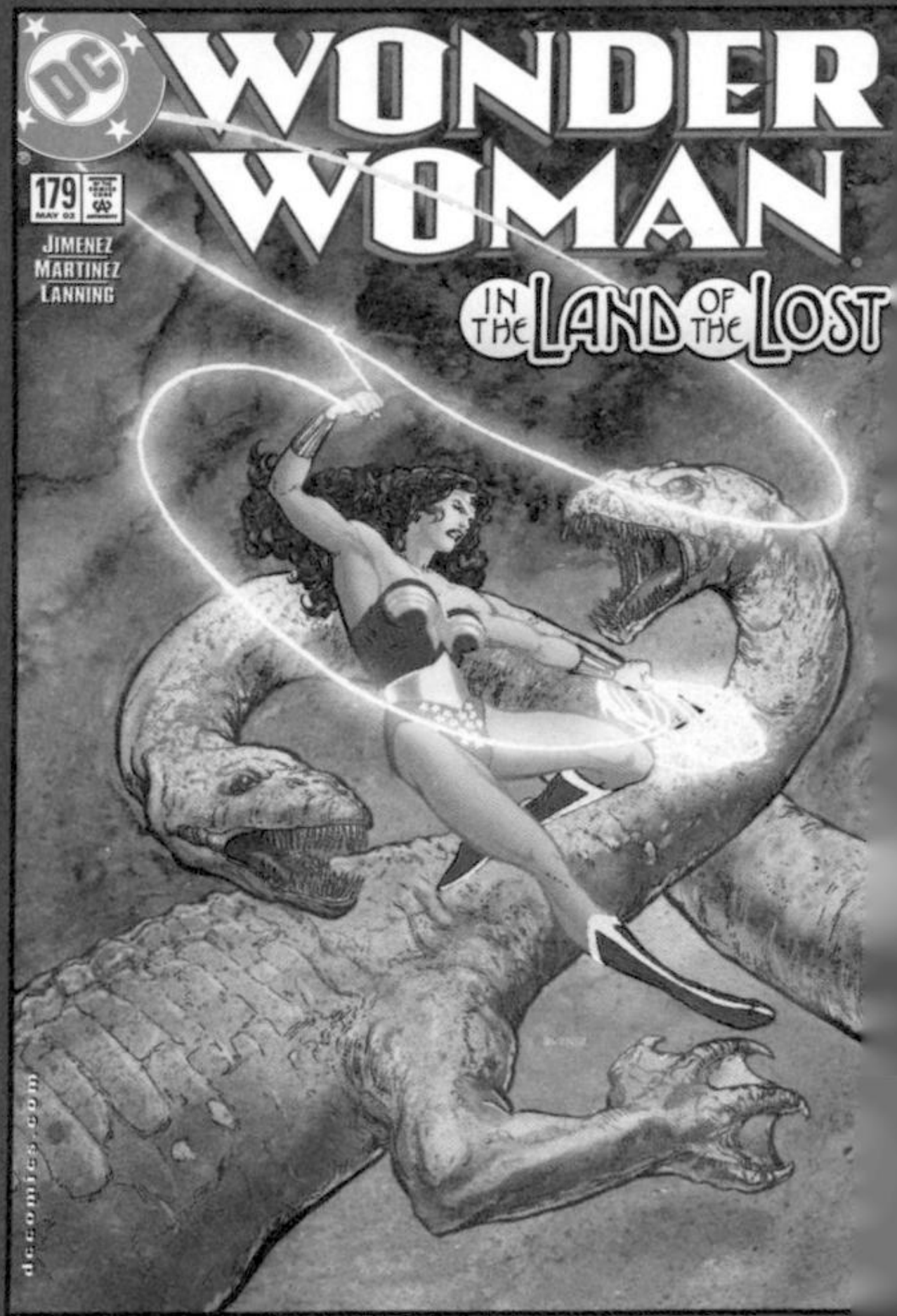
DC
WONDER WOMAN
179
MAY 03
JIMENEZ
MARTINEZ
LANNING
IN THE LAND OF THE LOST
dccomics.com

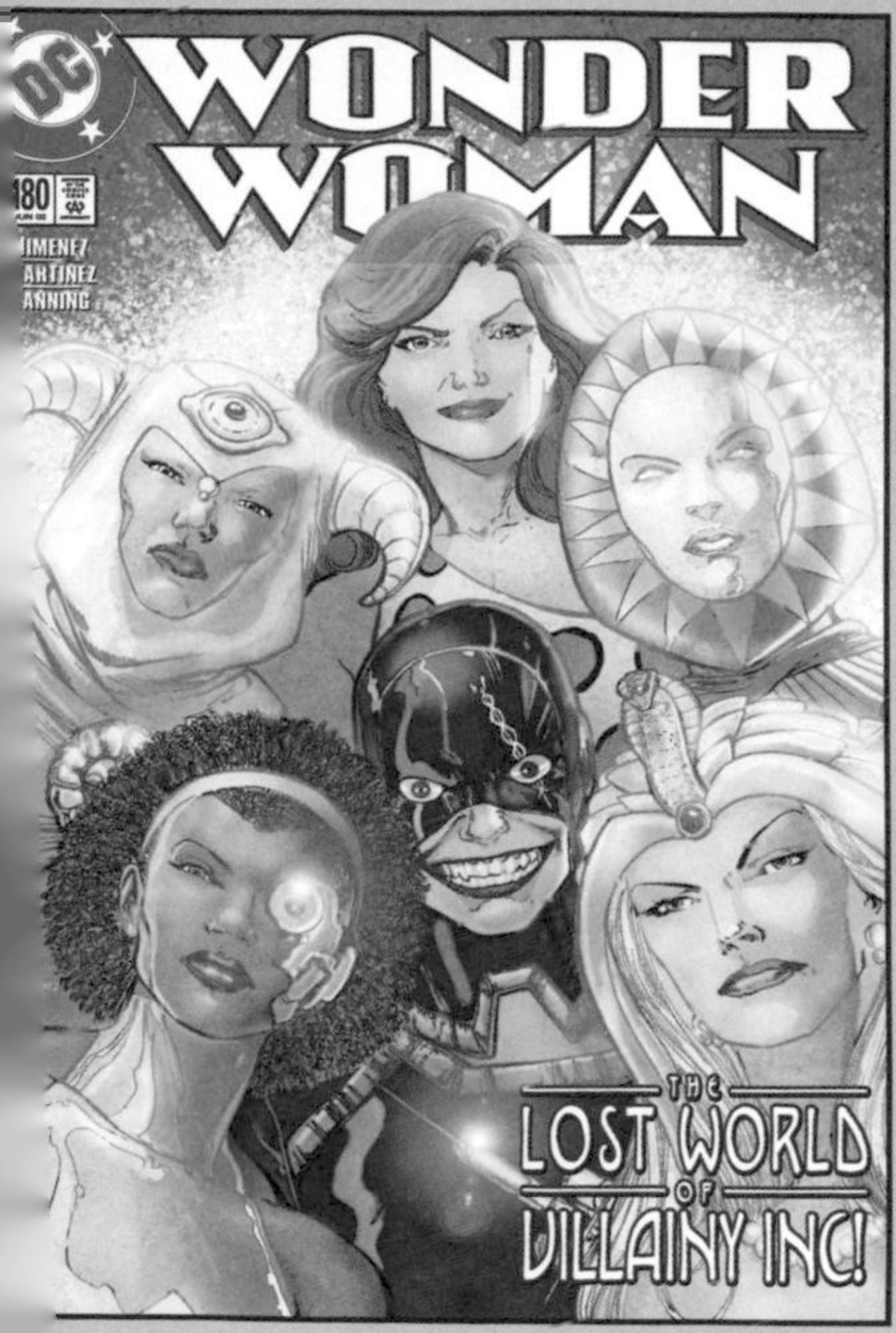
DC
WONDER WOMAN
180
IMENEZ
ARTINEZ
ANNING
THE LOST WORLD OF VILLAINY INC!

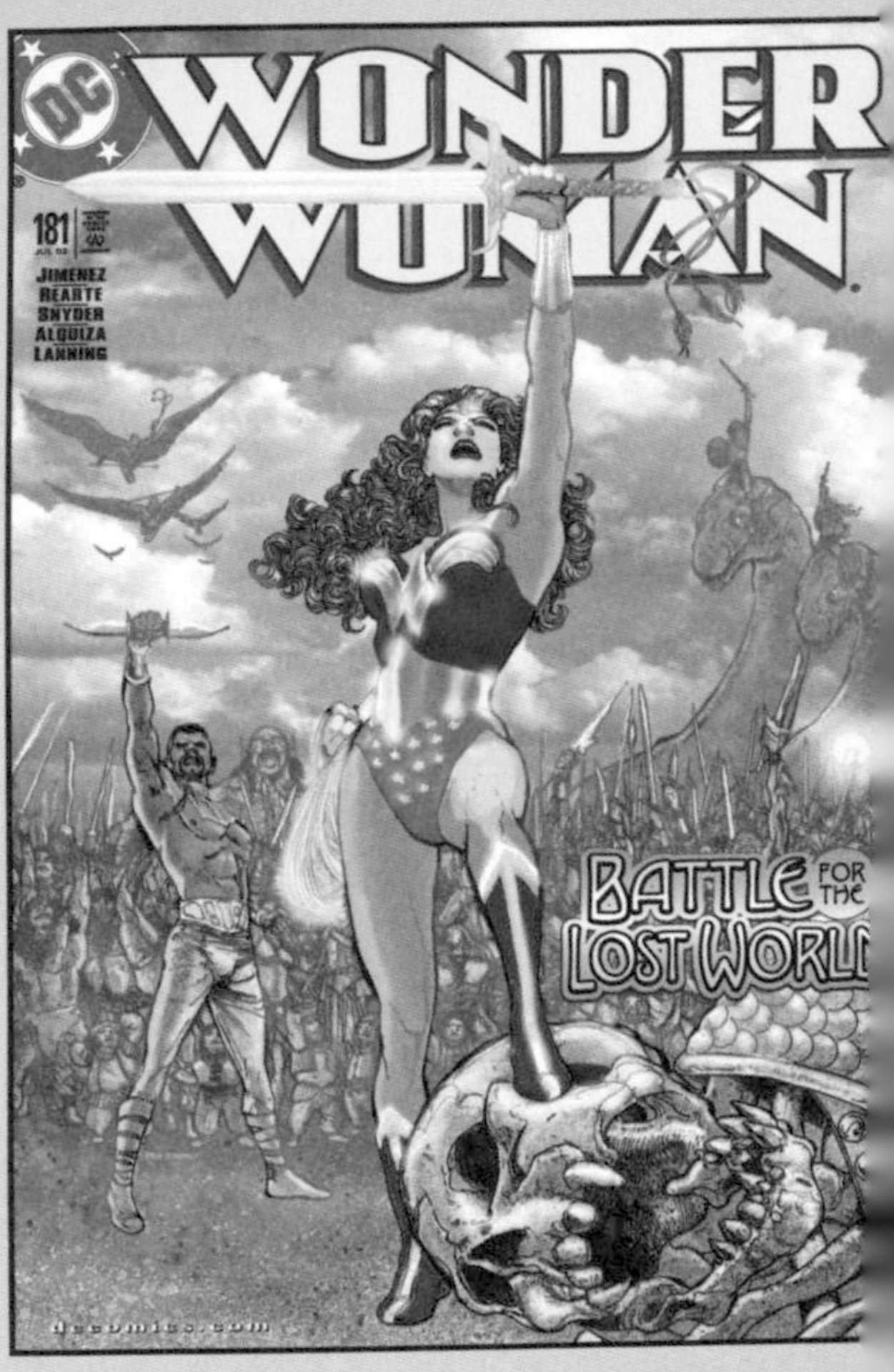
DC
WONDER WOMAN
181
JIMENEZ
REARTE
SNYDER
ALQUIZA
LANNING
BATTLE FOR THE LOST WORLD

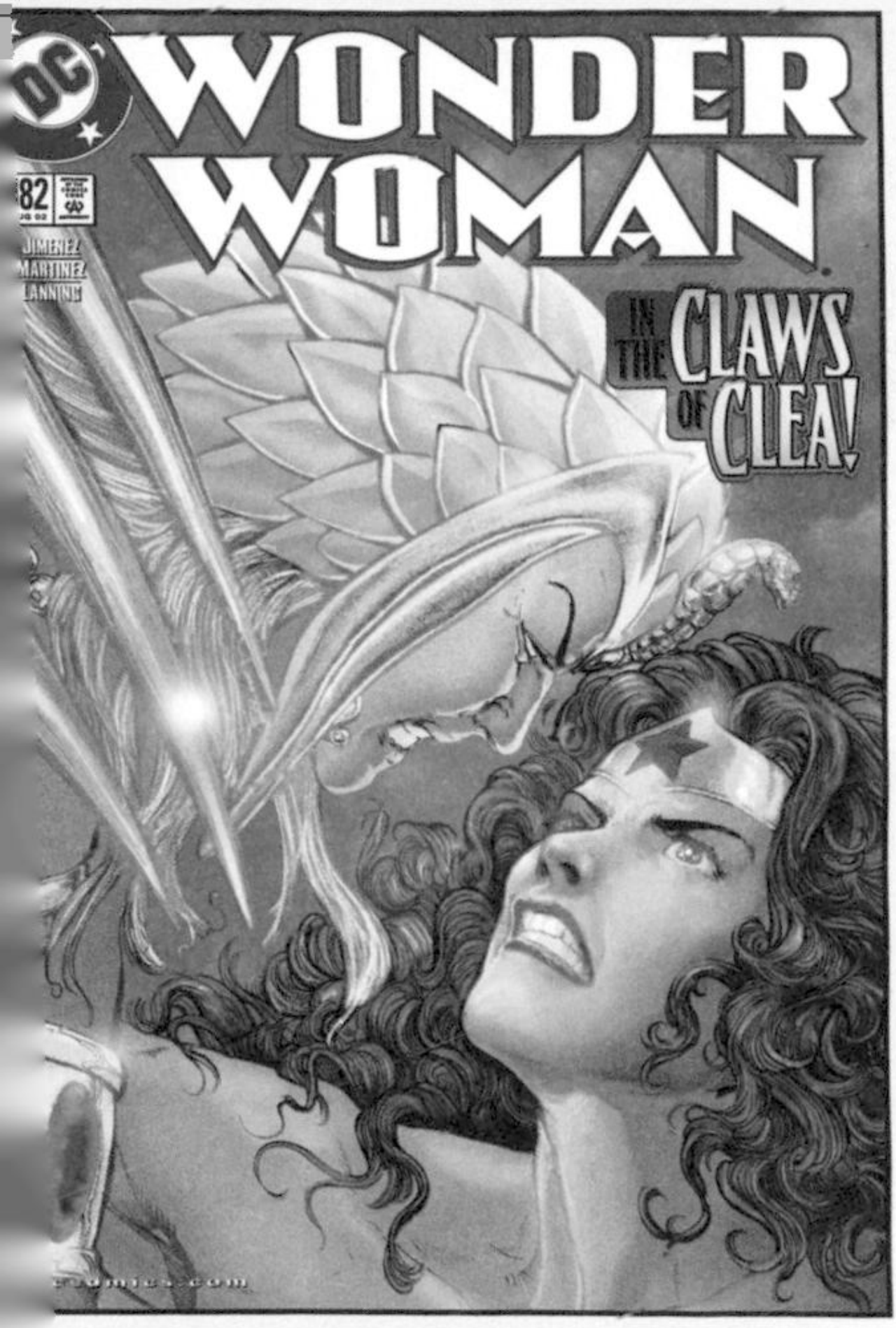
DC
WONDER WOMAN
82
JIMENEZ
MARTINEZ
LANNING
IN THE CLAWS OF CLEA!

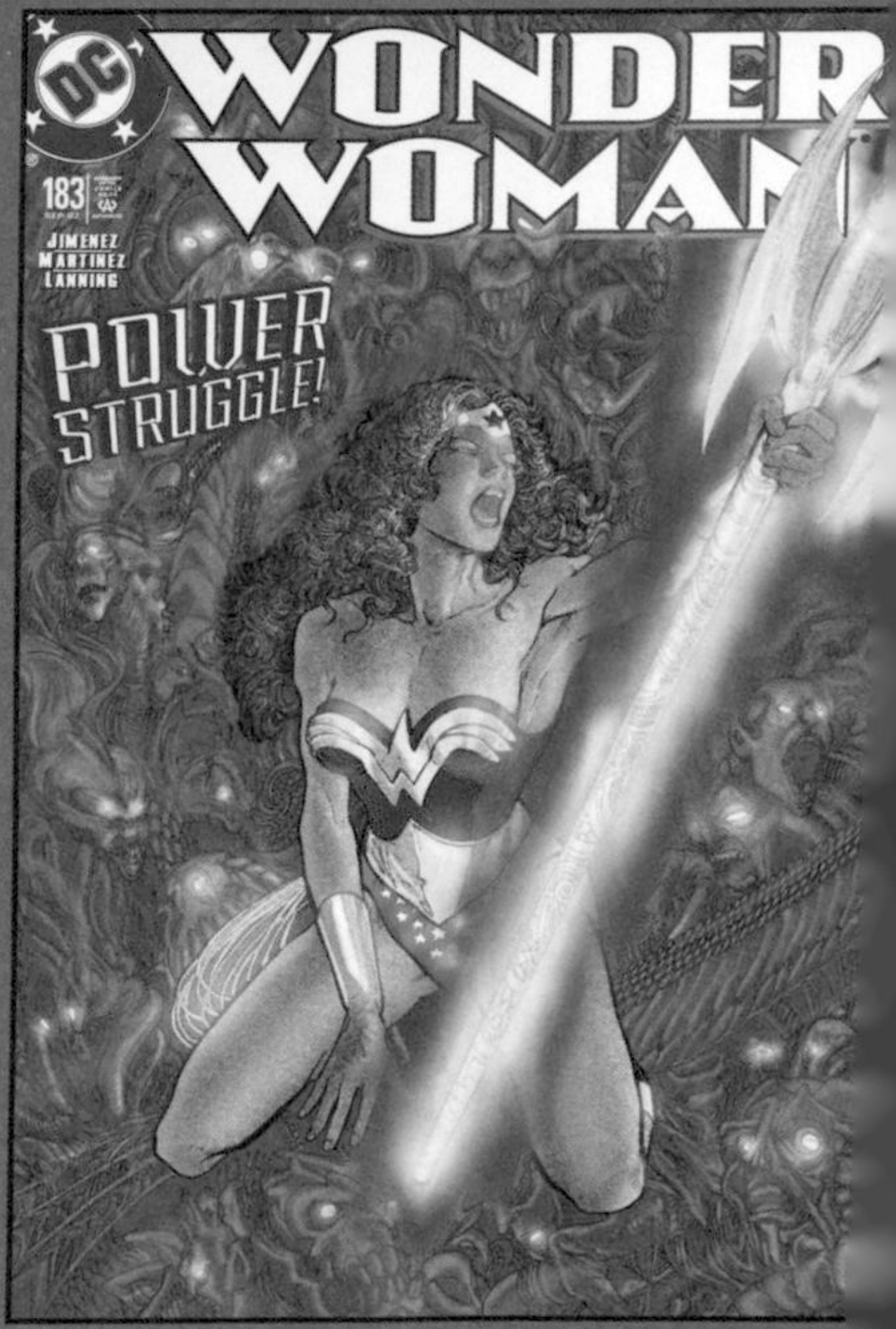
DC
WONDER WOMAN
183
JIMENEZ
MARTINEZ
LANNING
POWER STRUGGLE!

OCT. NO. 184

Wonder Woman

22½¢

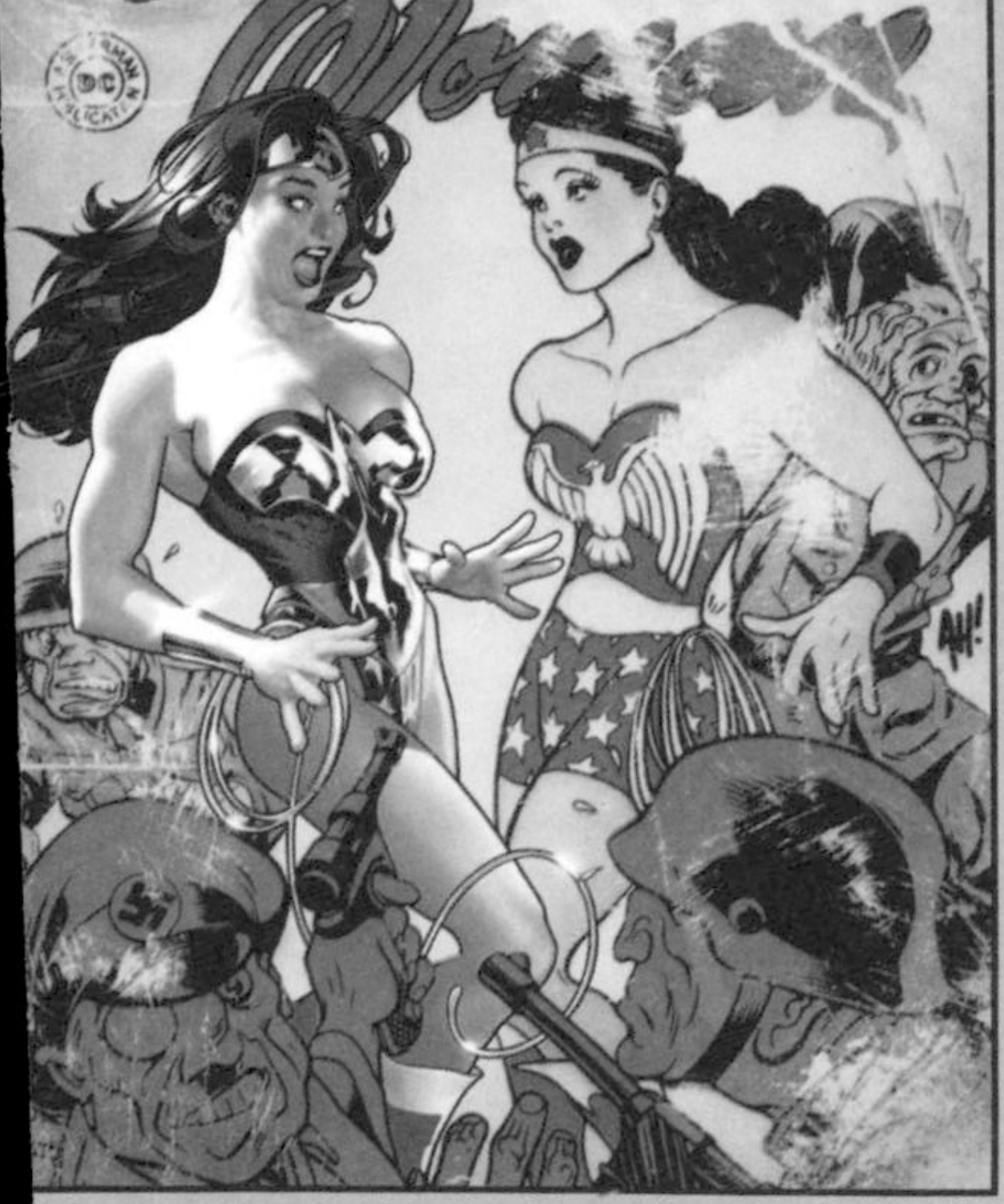

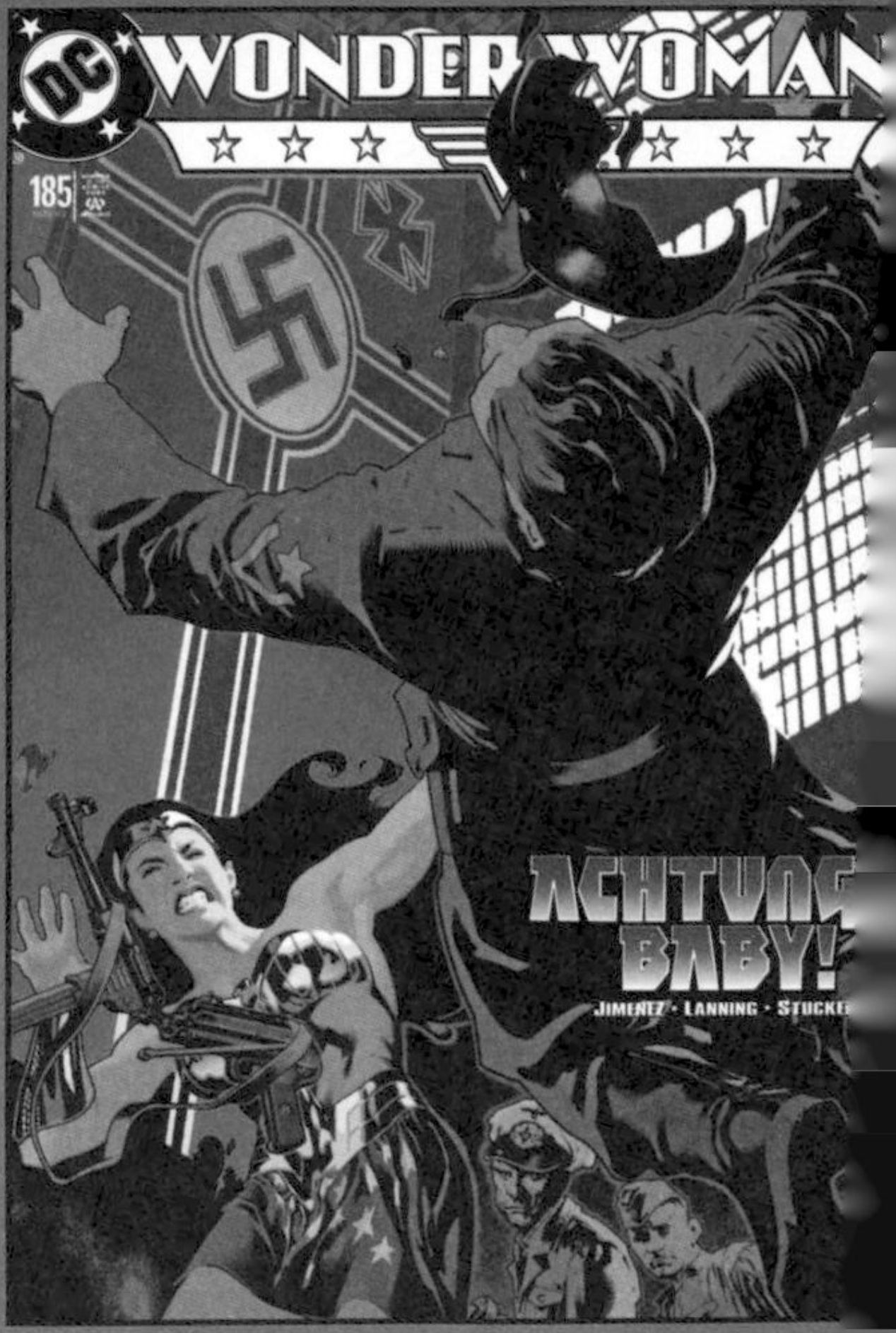
DC
WONDER WOMAN
185
ACHTUNG BABY!
JIMENEZ · LANNING · STUCKE

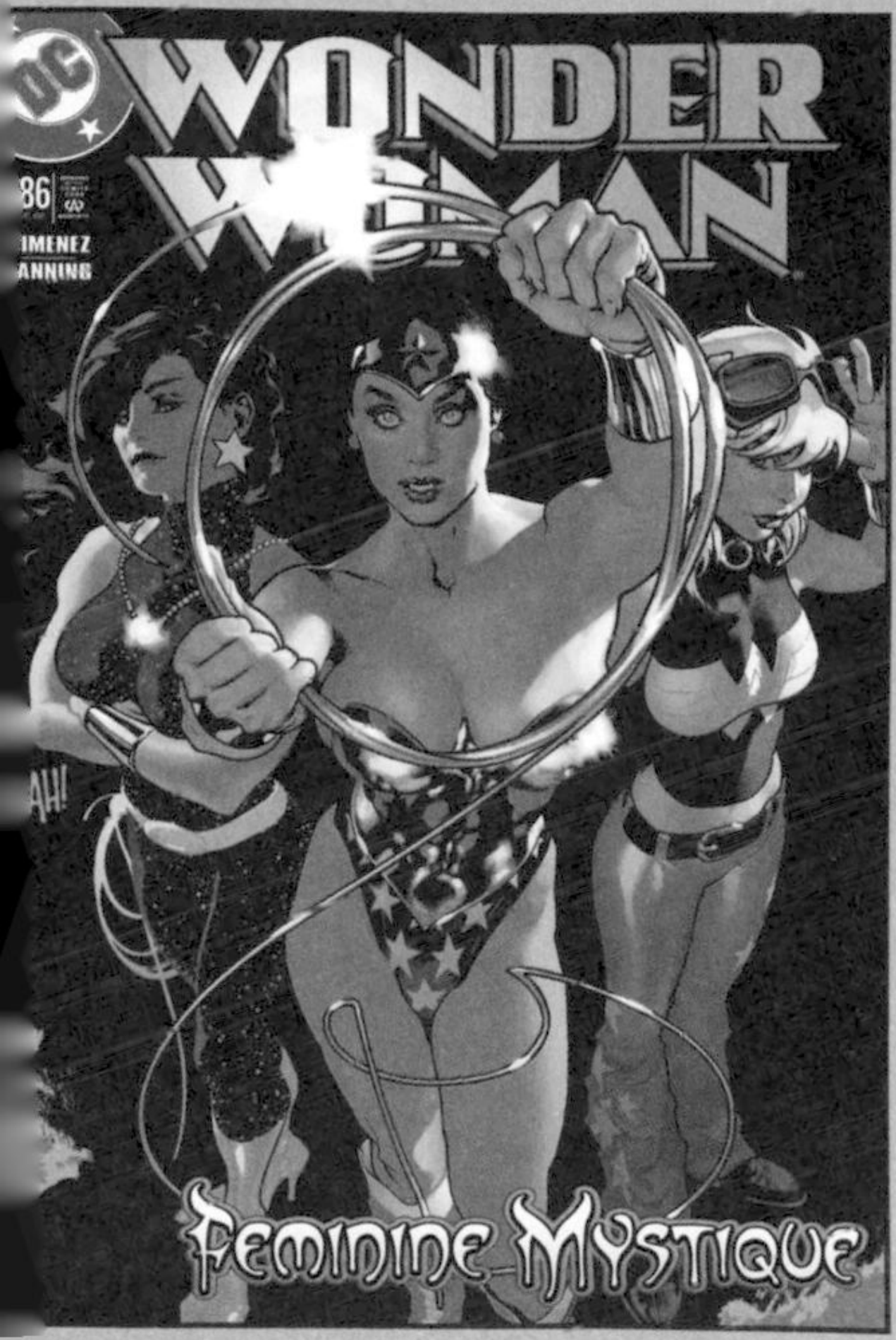
DC
WONDER WOMAN
86
IMENEZ
ANNING
AH!
Feminine Mystique

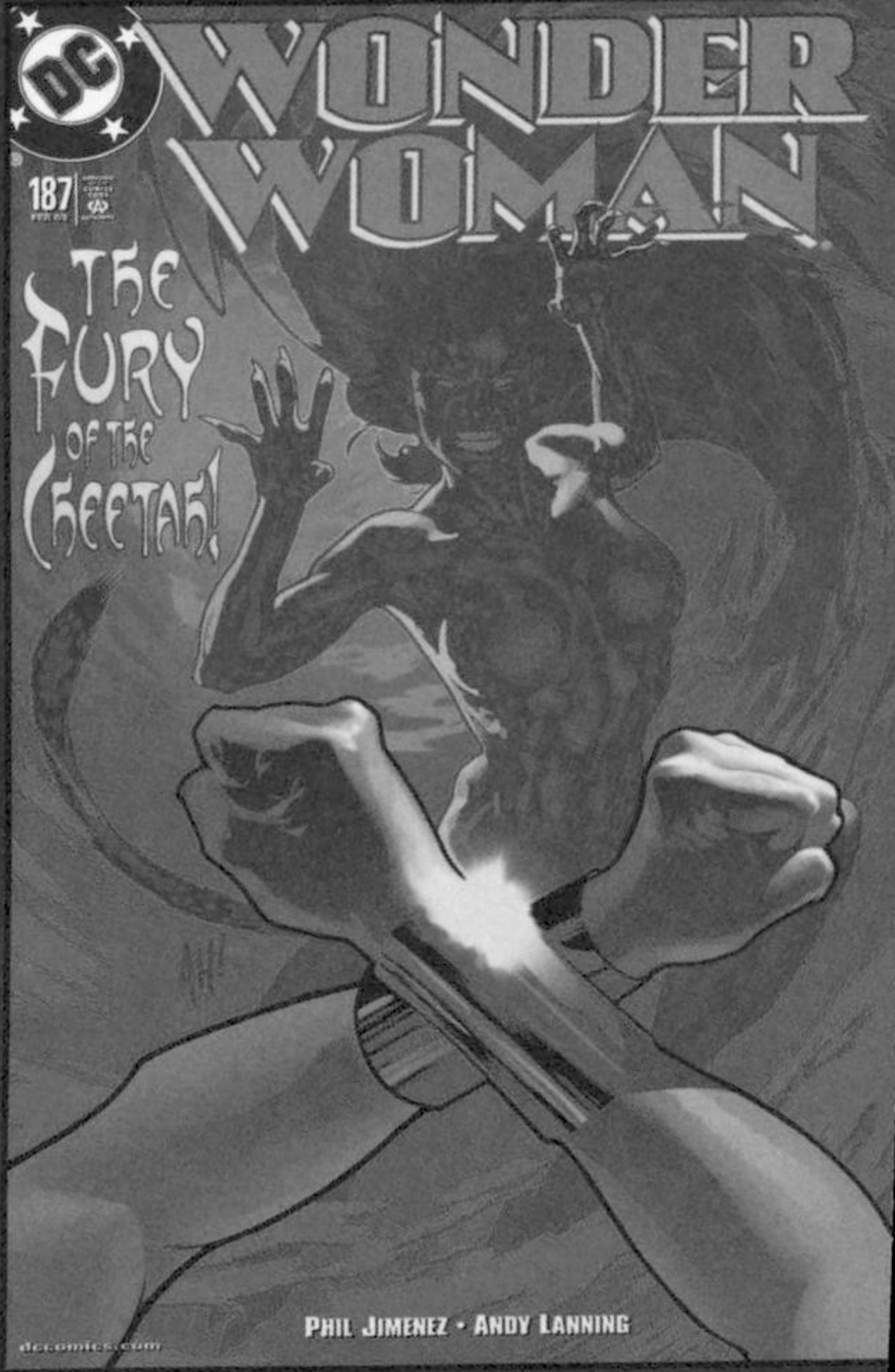
DC
WONDER WOMAN
187
THE FURY OF THE CHEETAH!
PHIL JIMENEZ • ANDY LANNING
dccomics.com

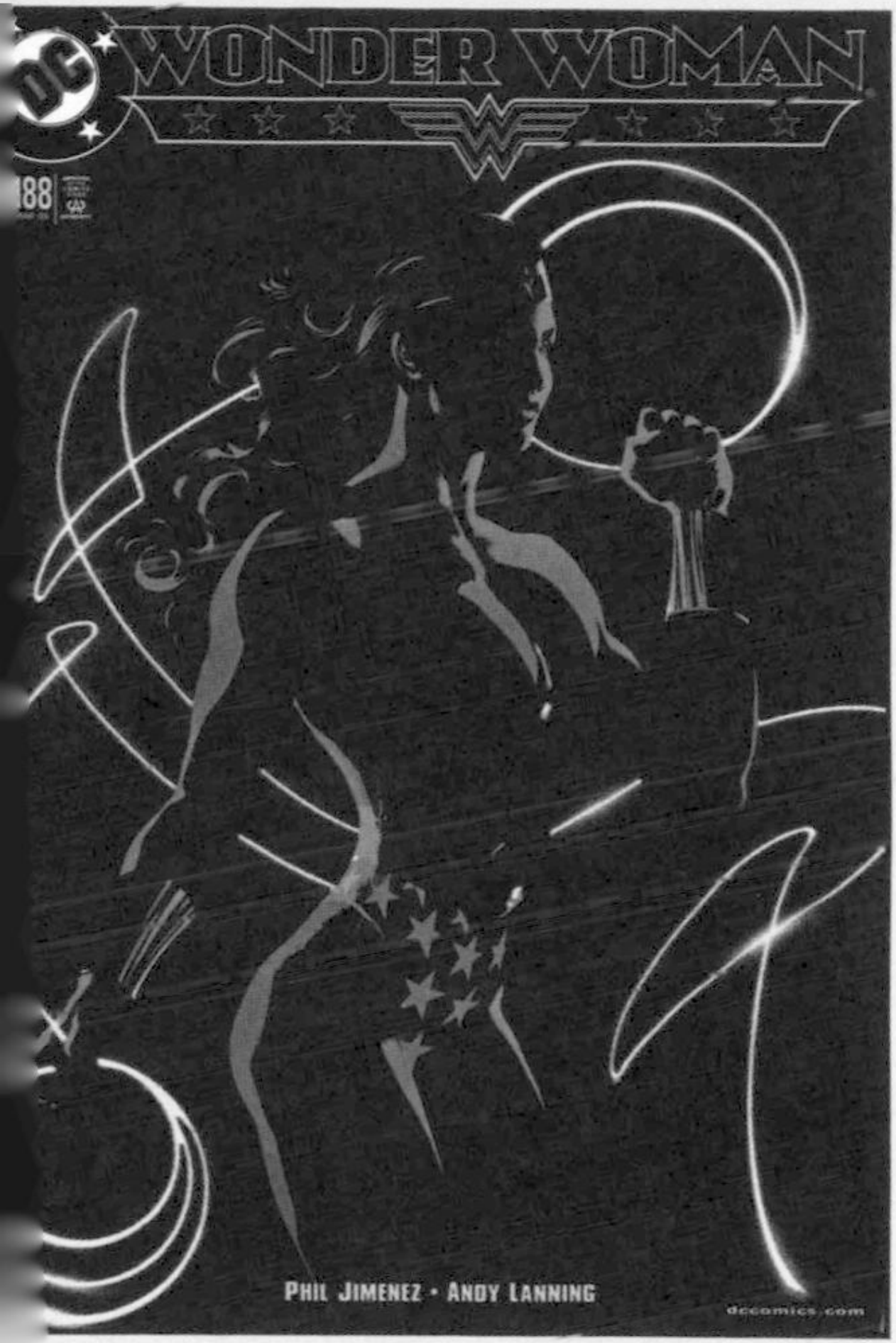
DC
WONDER WOMAN
188
PHIL JIMENEZ • ANDY LANNING
dccomics.com

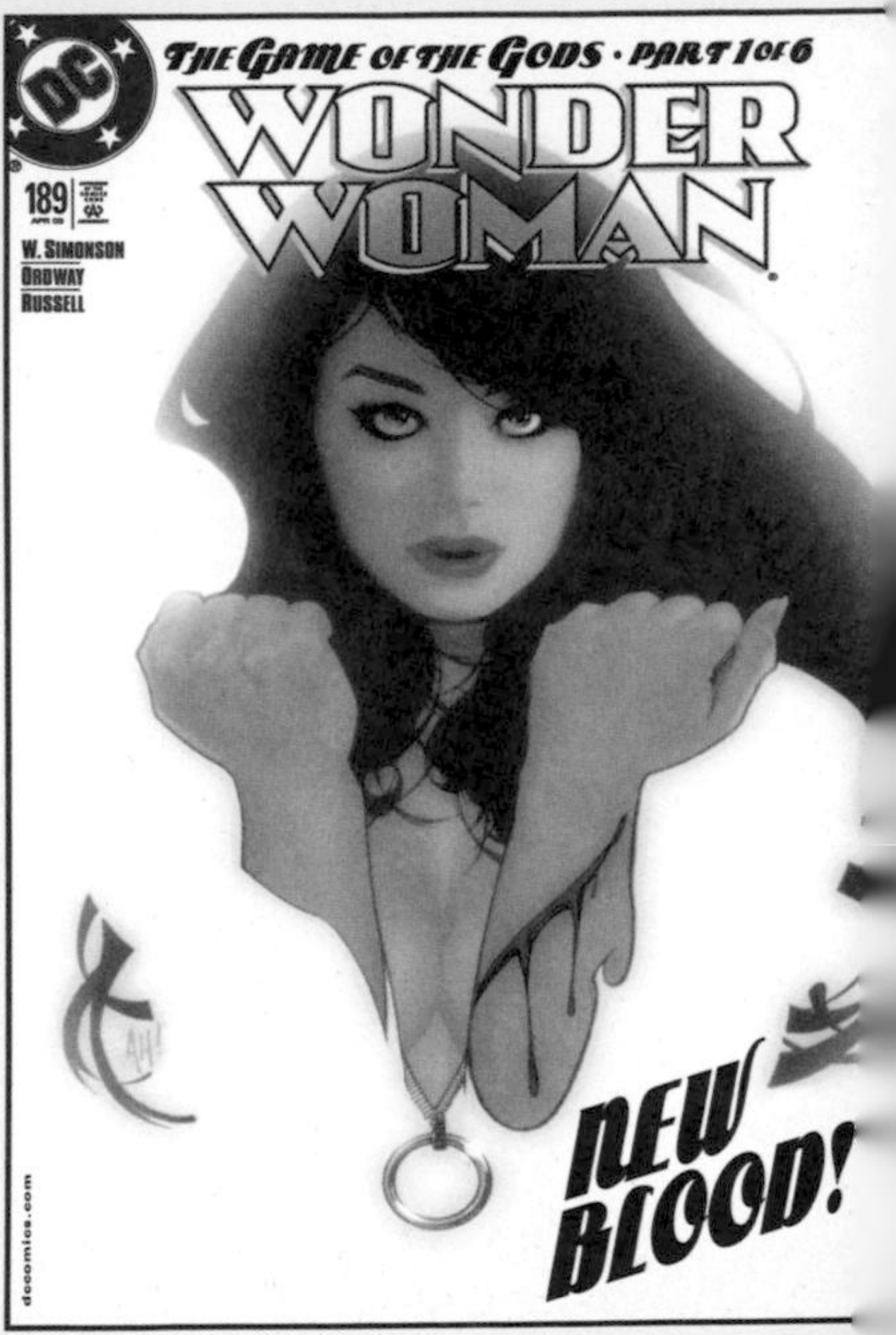
THE GAME OF THE GODS · PART 1 OF 6
WONDER WOMAN
189
W. SIMONSON
ORDWAY
RUSSELL
NEW BLOOD!
dccomics.com

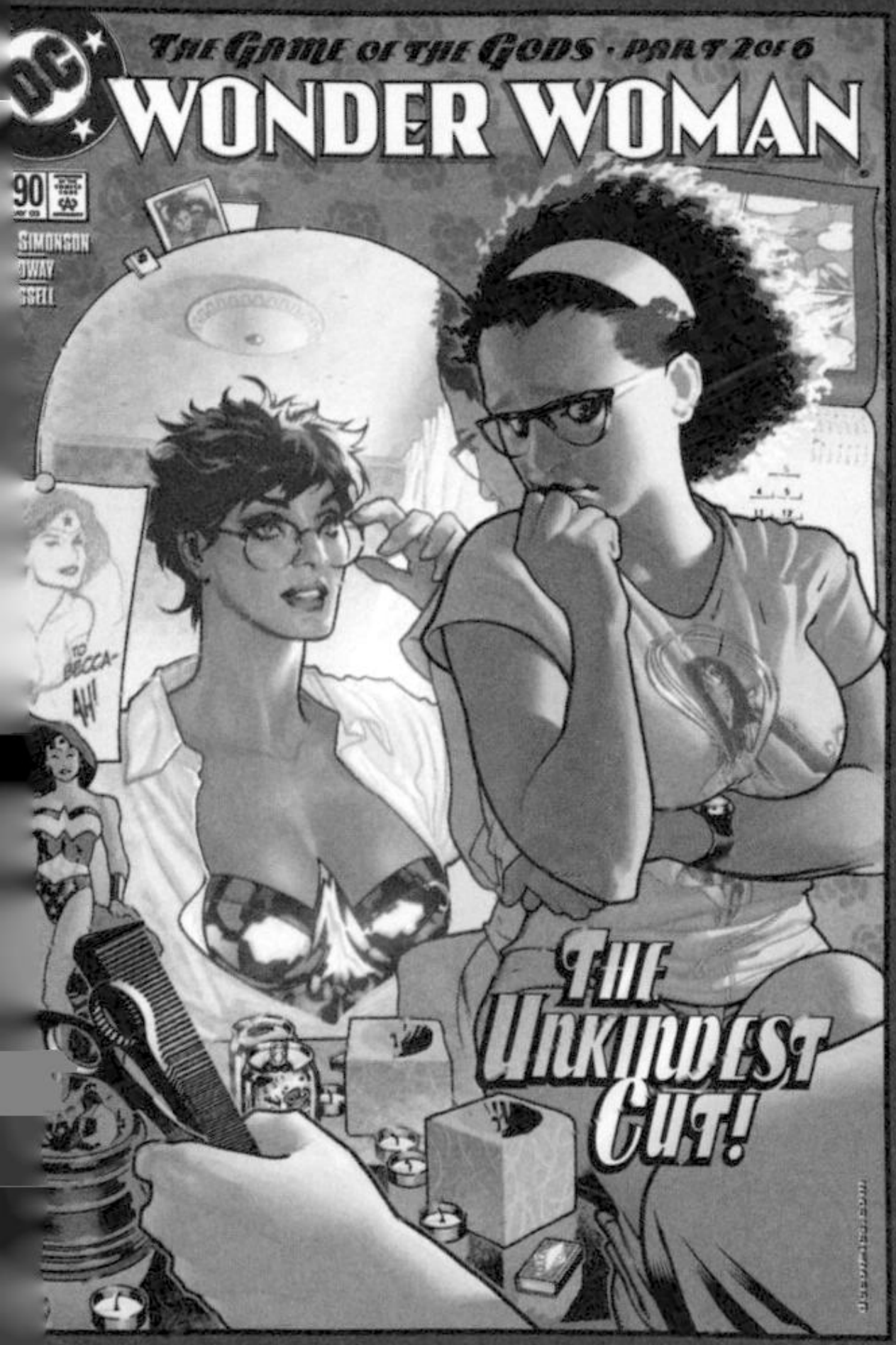
THE GAME OF THE GODS · PART 2 OF 6
WONDER WOMAN
90
SIMONSON
TO BECCA-
AH!
THE UNKINDEST CUT!

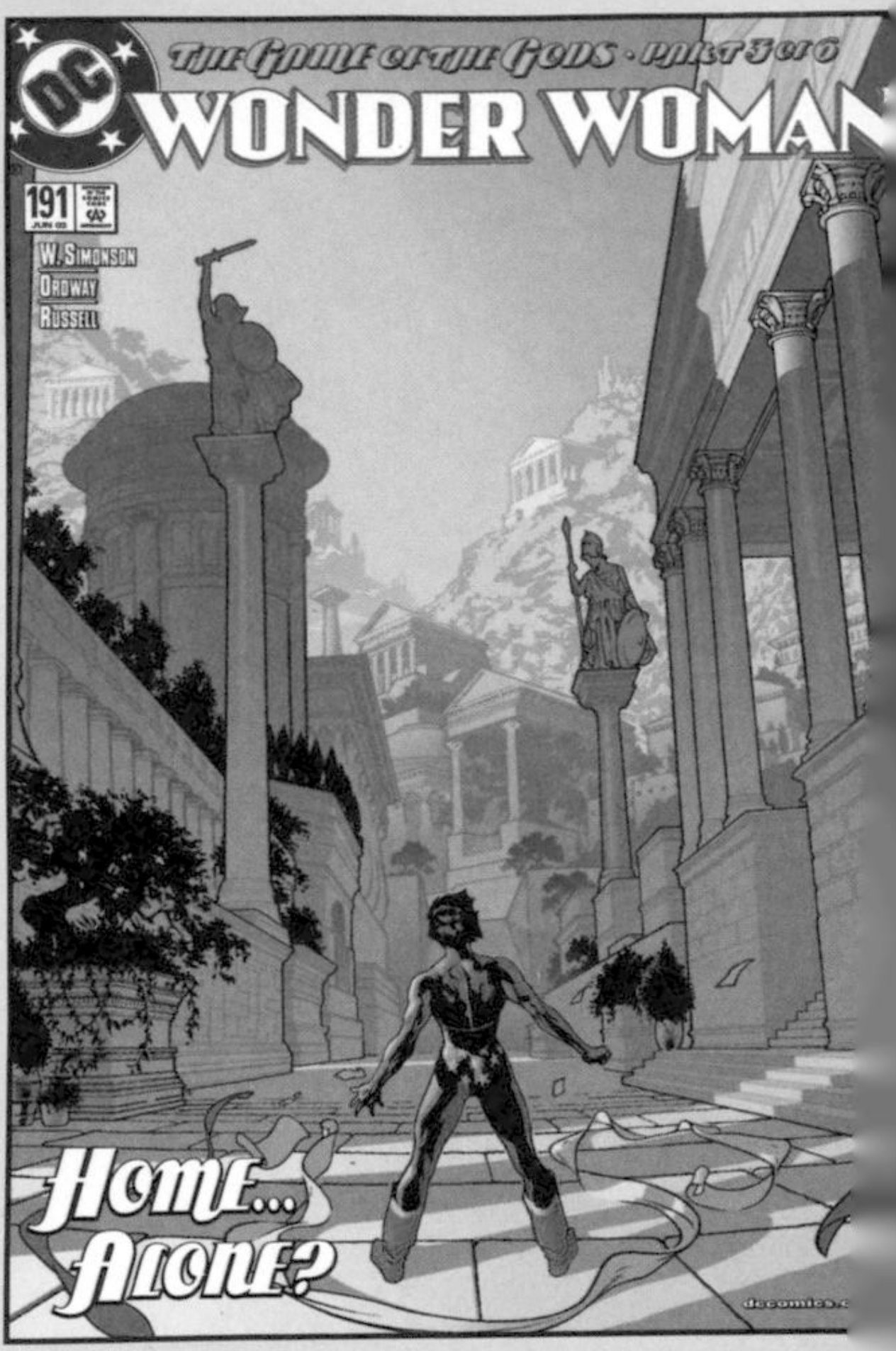
DC
THE GAME OF THE GODS · PART 3 OF 6
WONDER WOMAN
191
W. SIMONSON
ORDWAY
RUSSELL
HOME...
ALONE?

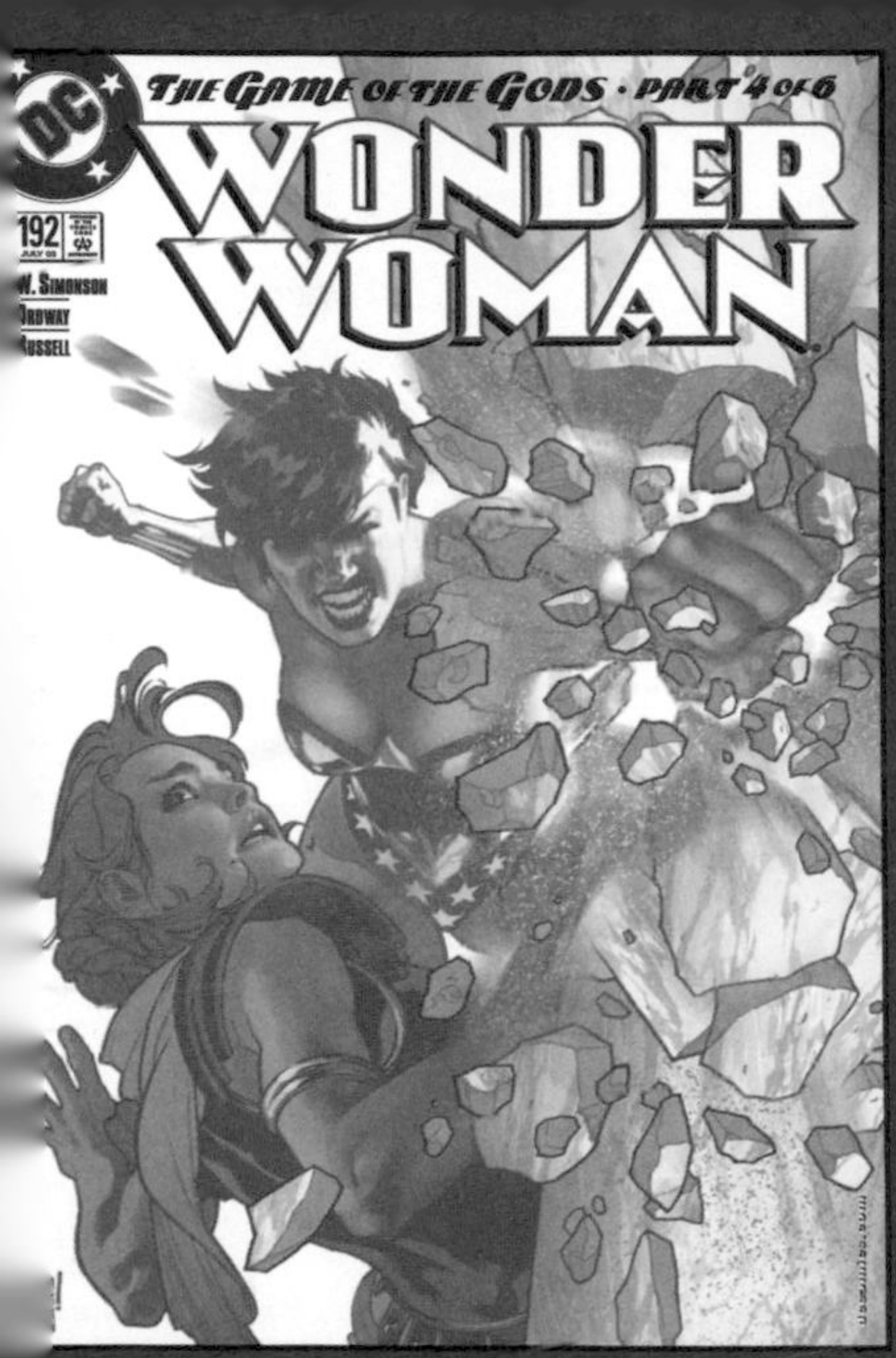
THE GAME OF THE GODS · PART 4 OF 6
WONDER WOMAN
192
JULY 03
W. SIMONSON
DRUWAY
RUSSELL

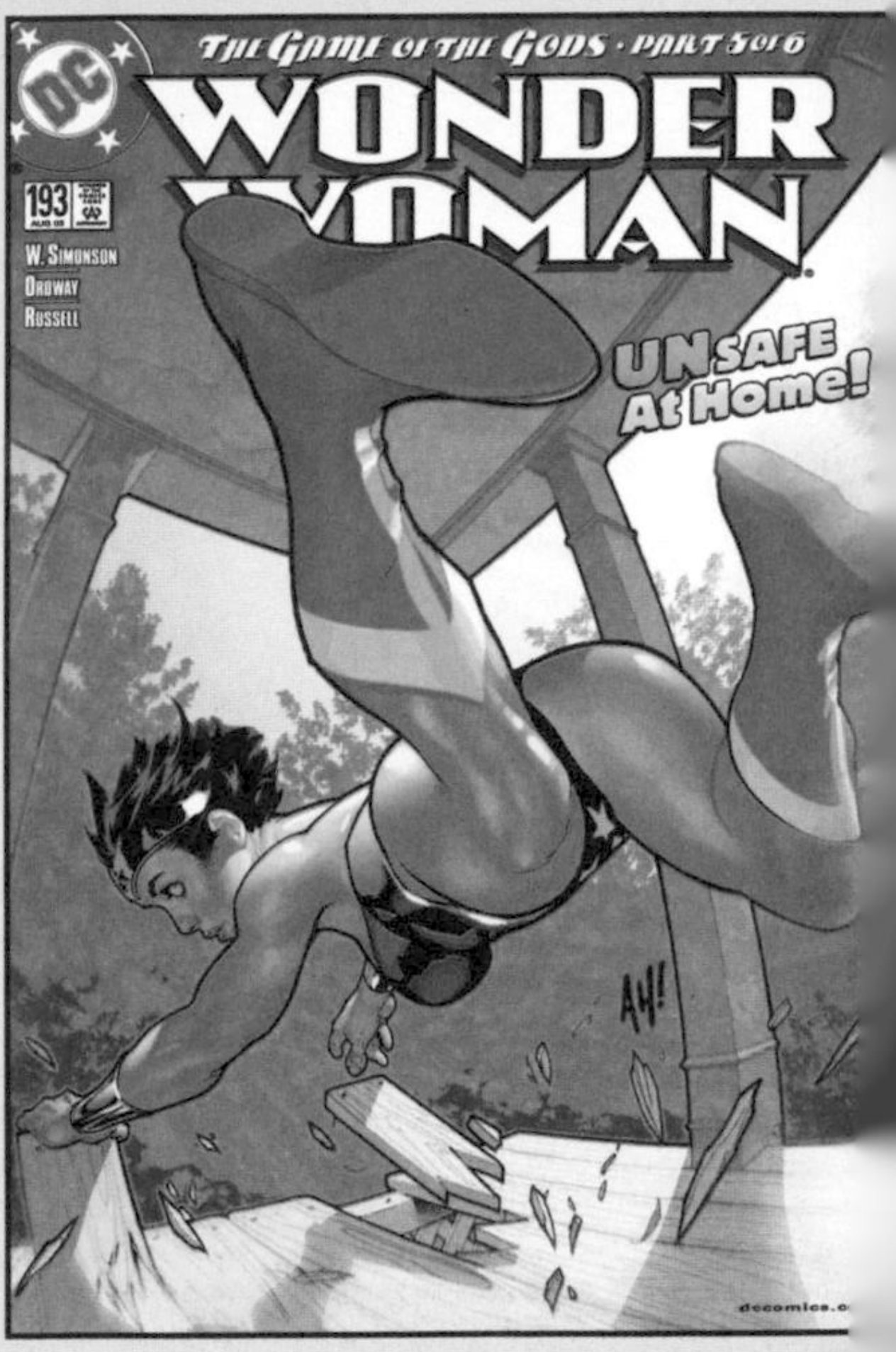
THE GAME OF THE GODS · PART 5 OF 6
DC
WONDER WOMAN
193
W. SIMONSON
DROWAY
RUSSELL
UNSAFE At Home!
AH!
dccomics.c

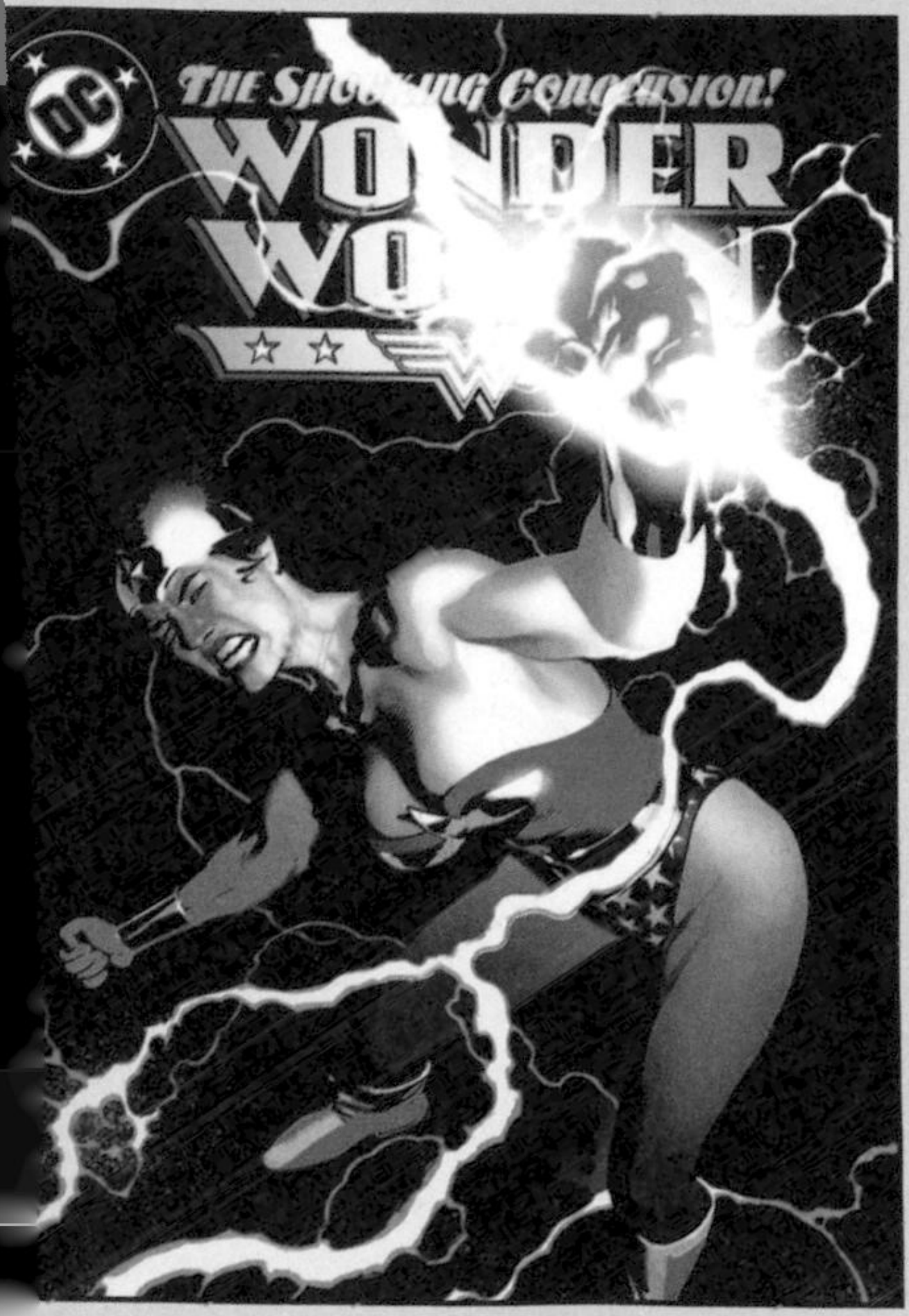
DC
THE SHOCKING CONCLUSION!
WONDER
WO

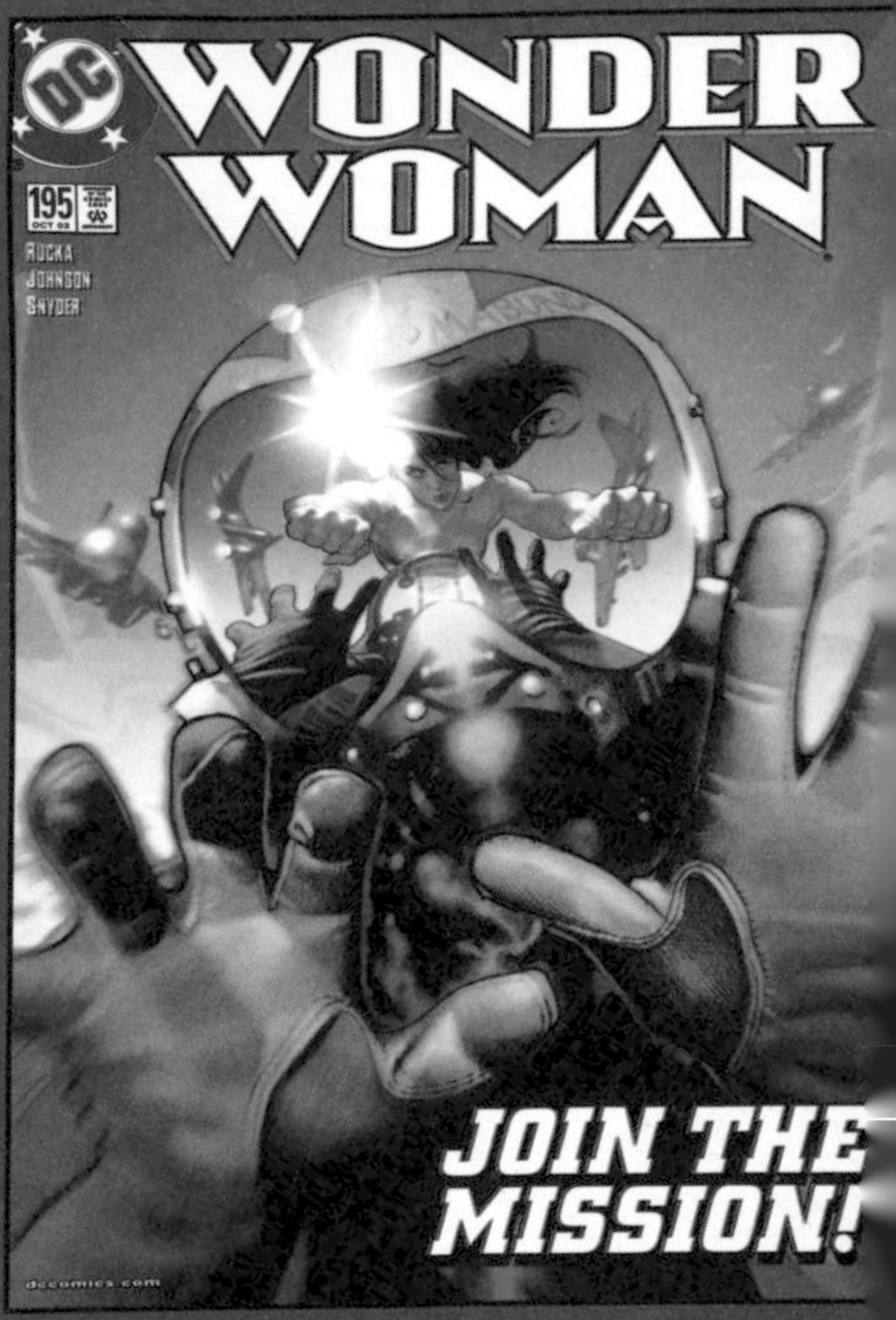
DC
WONDER WOMAN
195
OCT 03
ROCKA
JOHNSON
SNYDER
JOIN THE MISSION!
dccomics.com

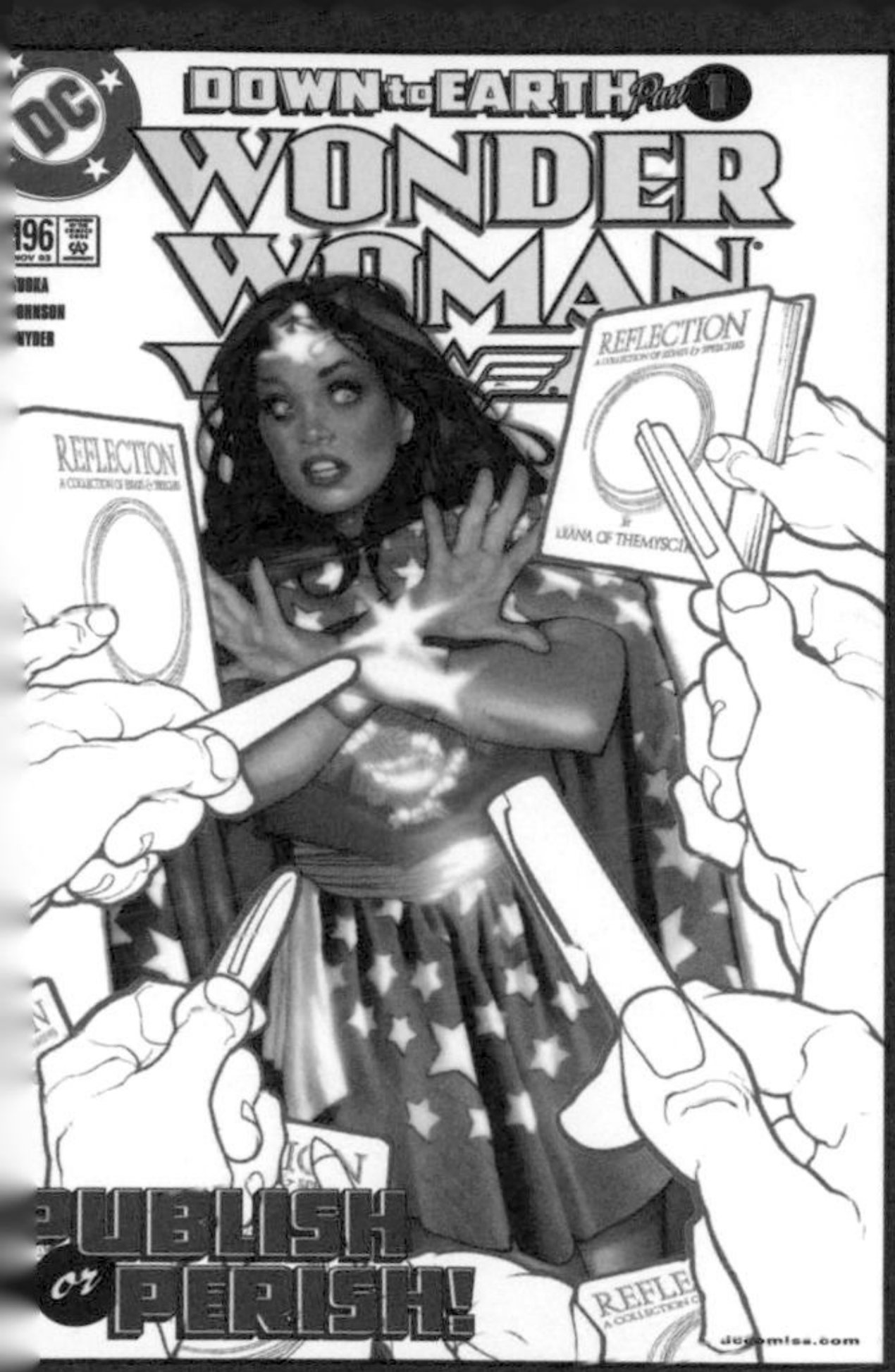
DOWN to EARTH Part 1
WONDER WOMAN
196
REFLECTION
REFLECTION
PUBLISH or PERISH!
dccomics.com

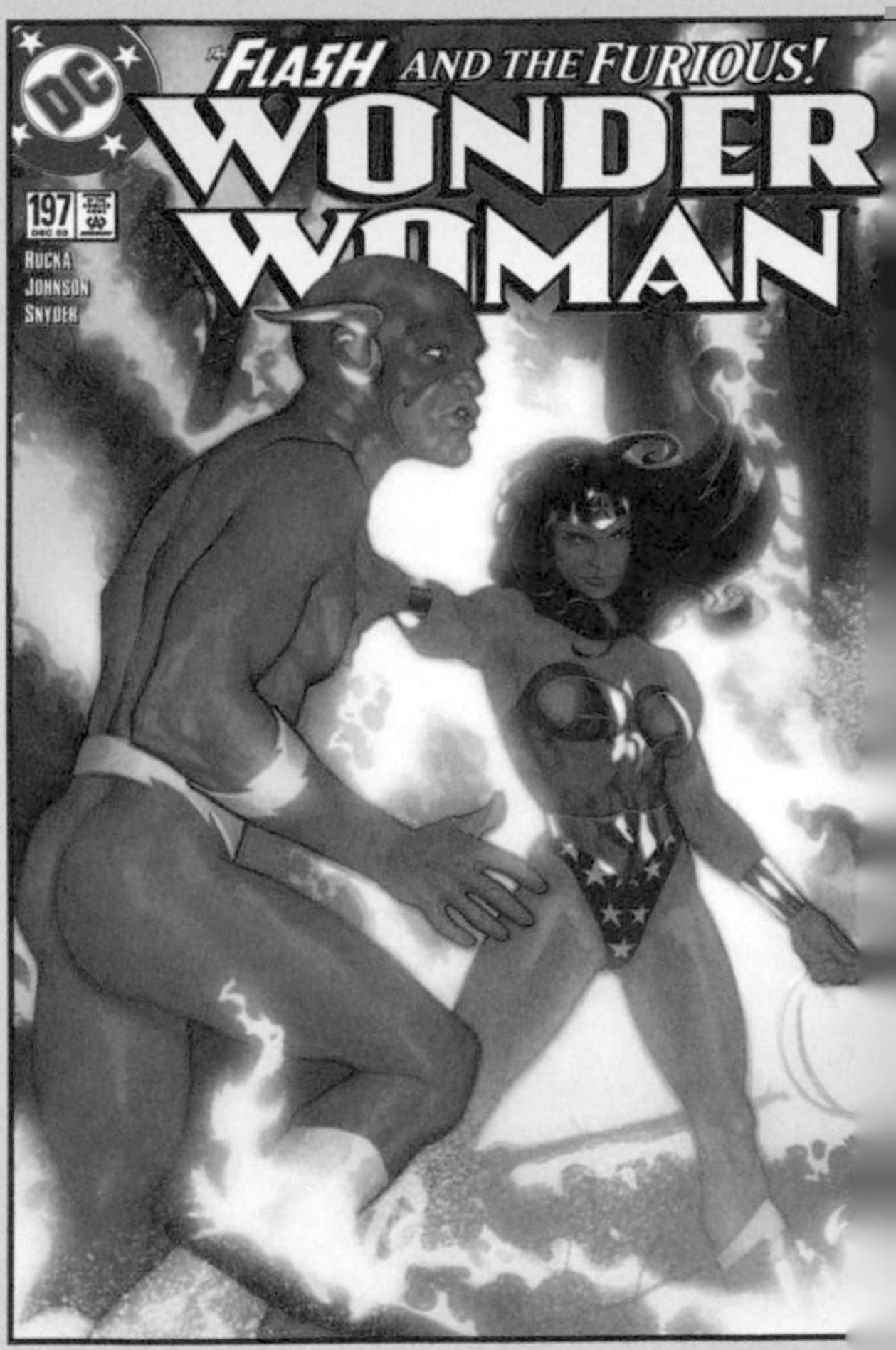
DC
The FLASH AND THE FURIOUS!
WONDER WOMAN
197
DEC 03
RUCKA
JOHNSON
SNYDER

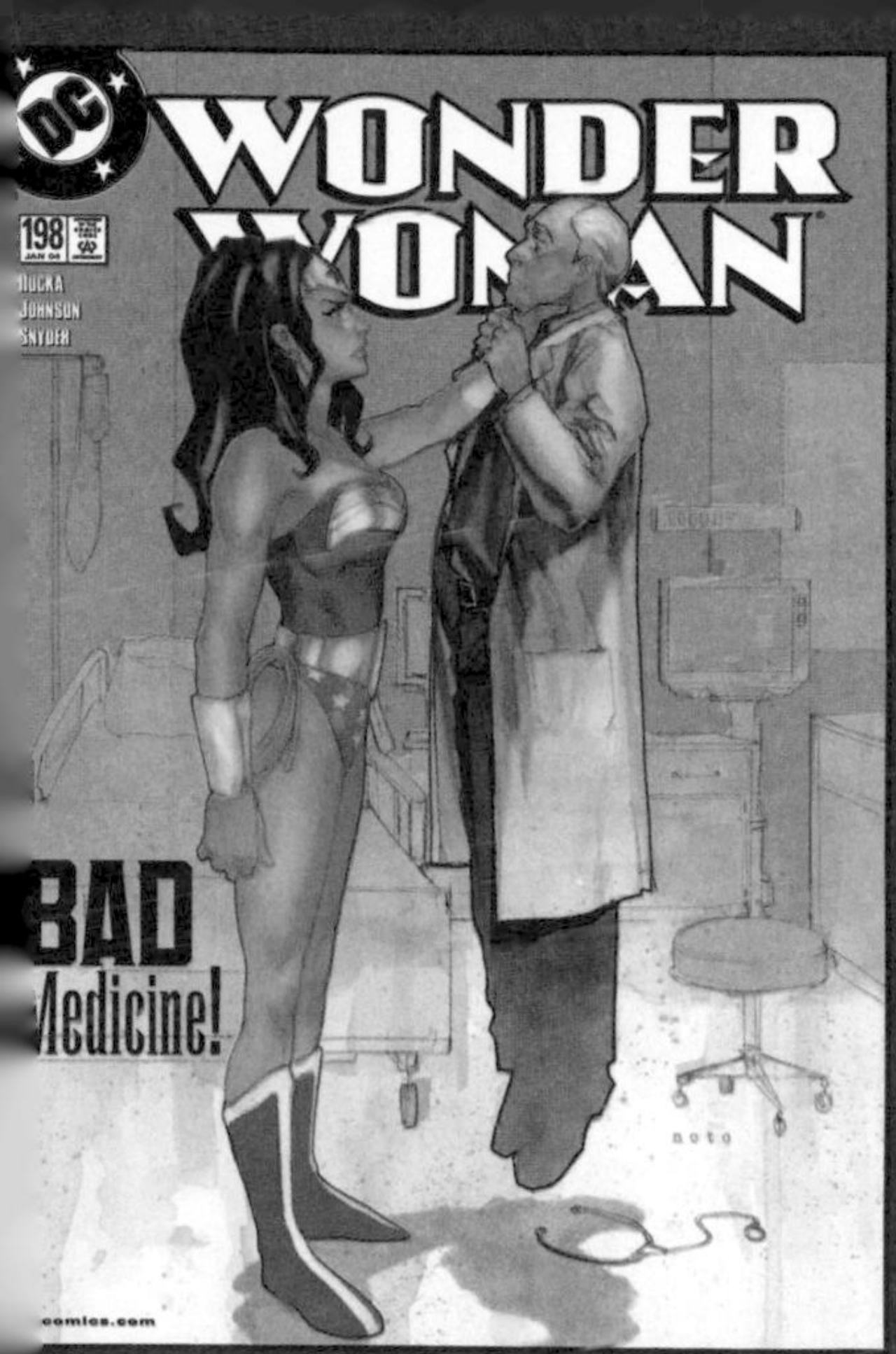
DC
WONDER WOMAN
198
JAN 04
BUCKA
JOHNSON
SNYDER
BAD
Medicine!
comics.com

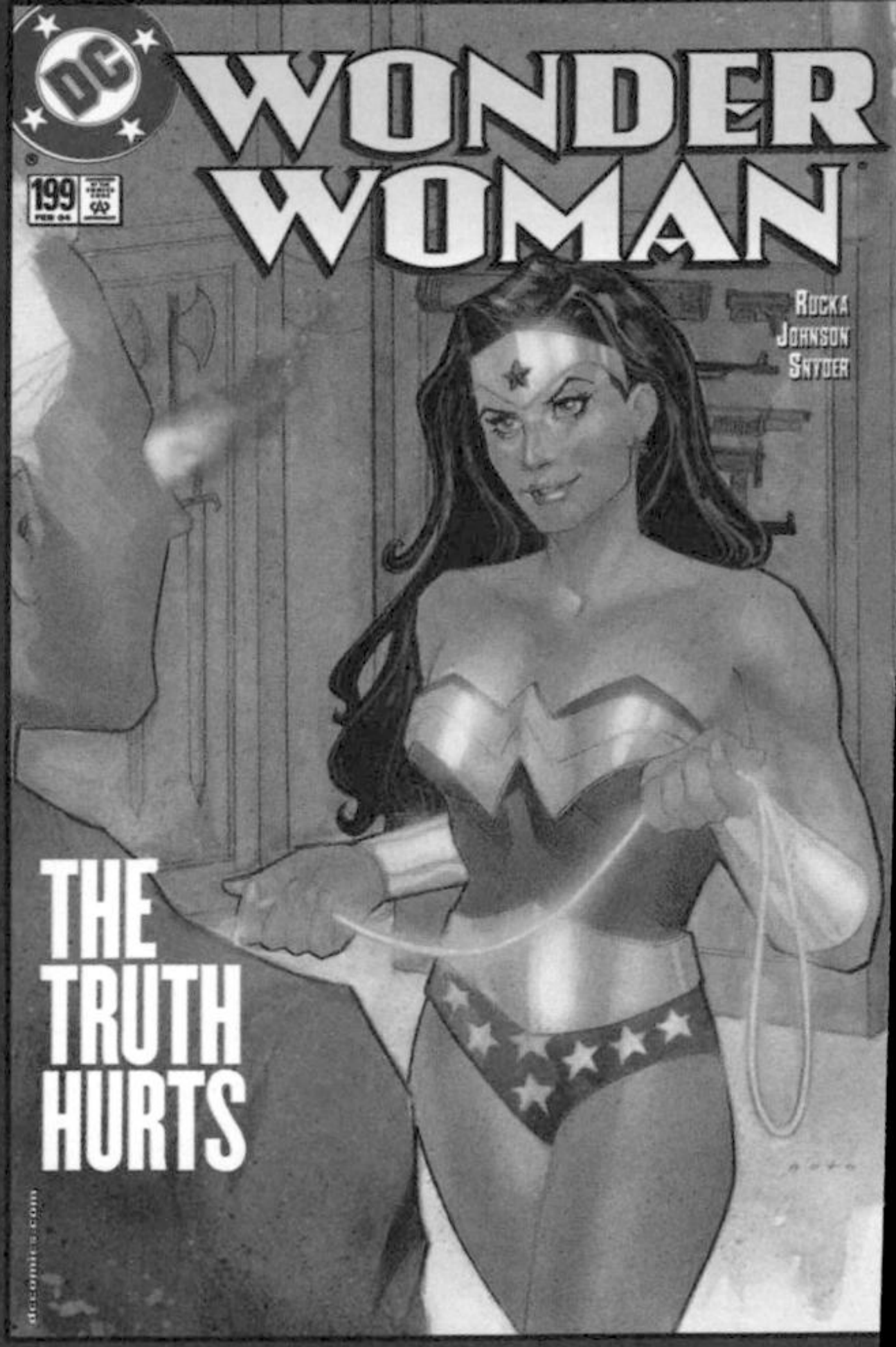
DC
WONDER WOMAN
199
ROCKA
JOHNSON
SNYDER
THE TRUTH HURTS

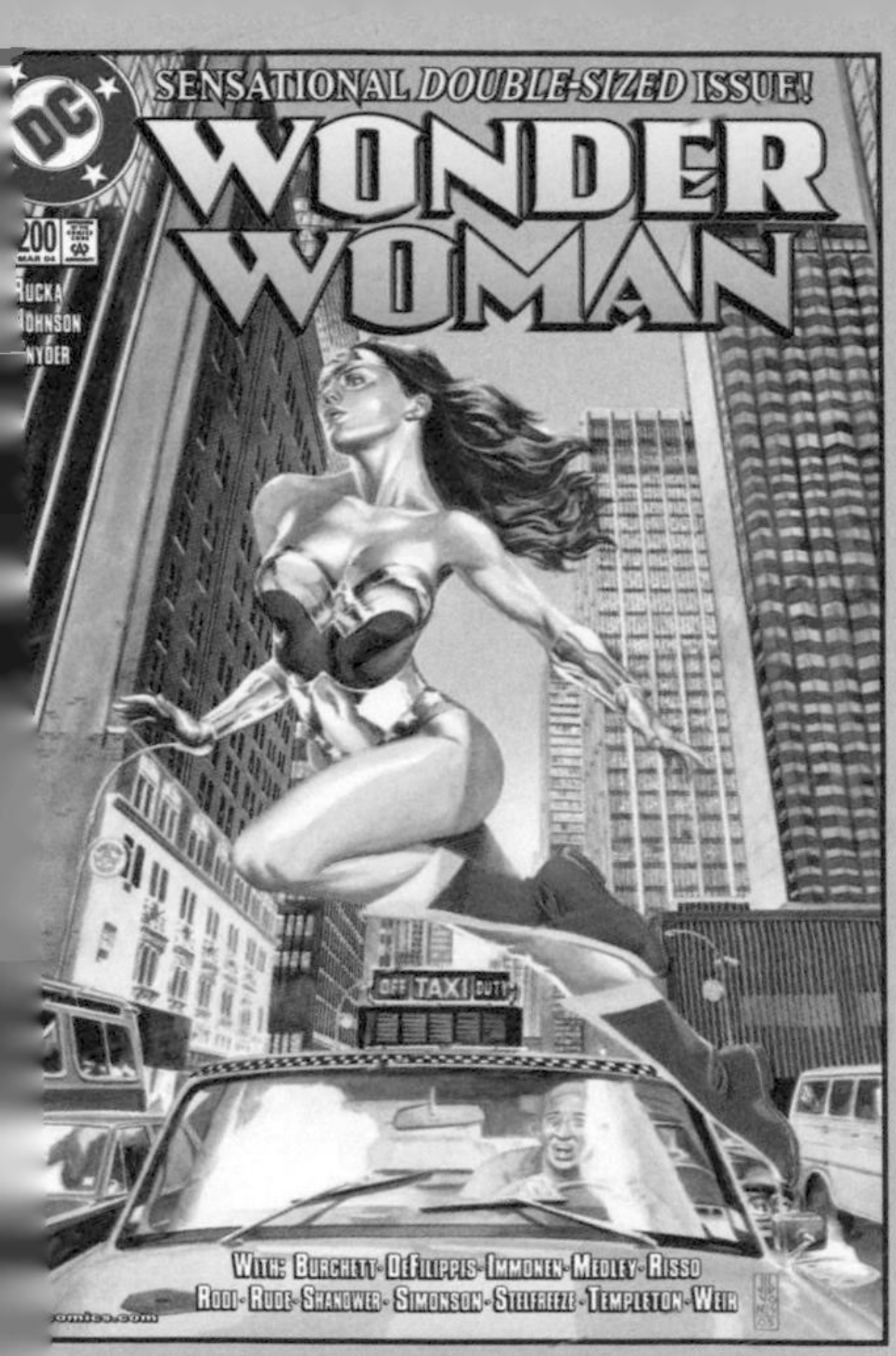
SENSATIONAL DOUBLE-SIZED ISSUE!
WONDER WOMAN
200
RUCKA
JOHNSON
NYDER
OFF TAXI DUTY
WITH: BURCHETT · DEFILIPPIS · IMMONEN · MEDLEY · RISSO
ROOI · RUDE · SHANOWER · SIMONSON · STELFREEZE · TEMPLETON · WEIR

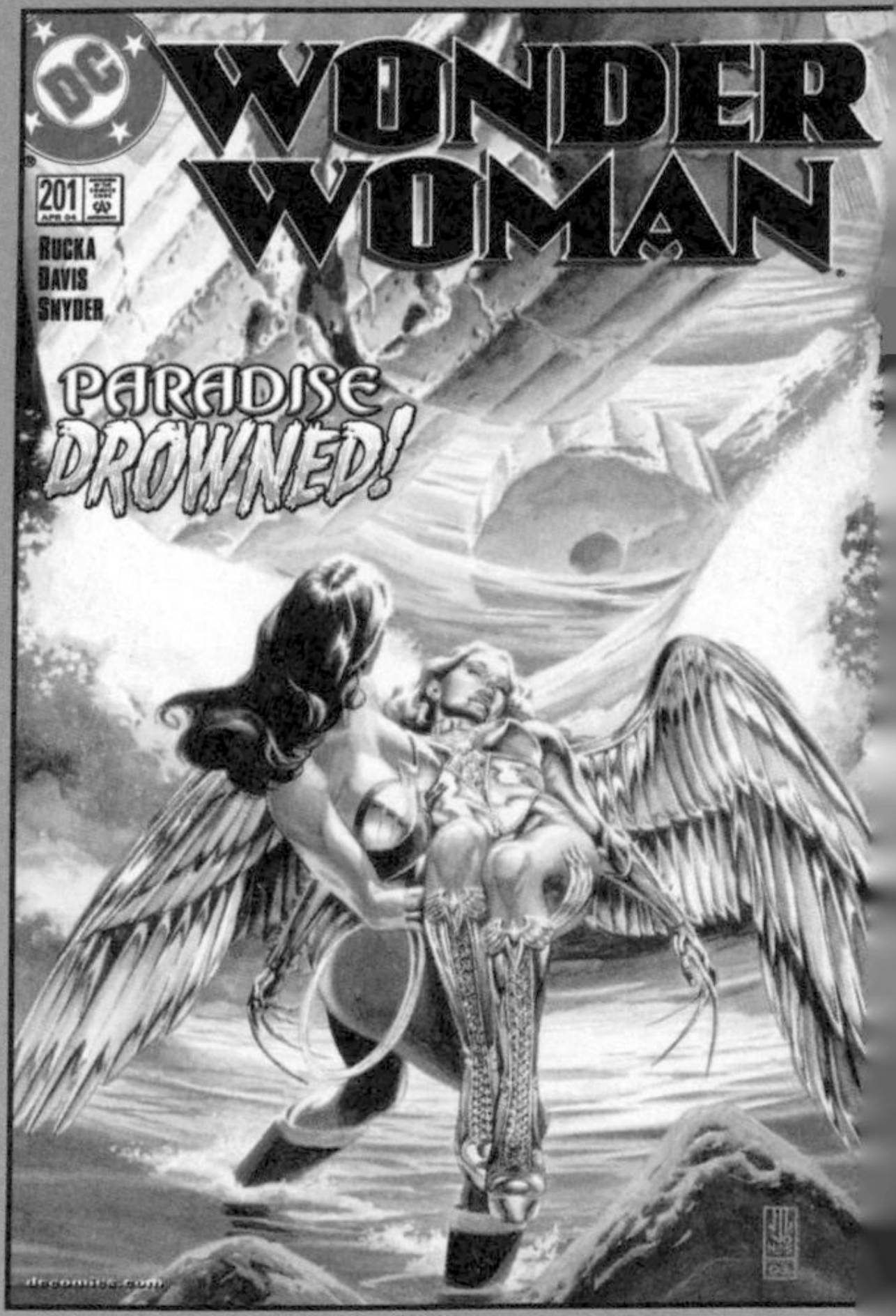
DC
WONDER WOMAN
201
RUCKA
DAVIS
SNYDER
PARADISE DROWNED!
dccomics.com

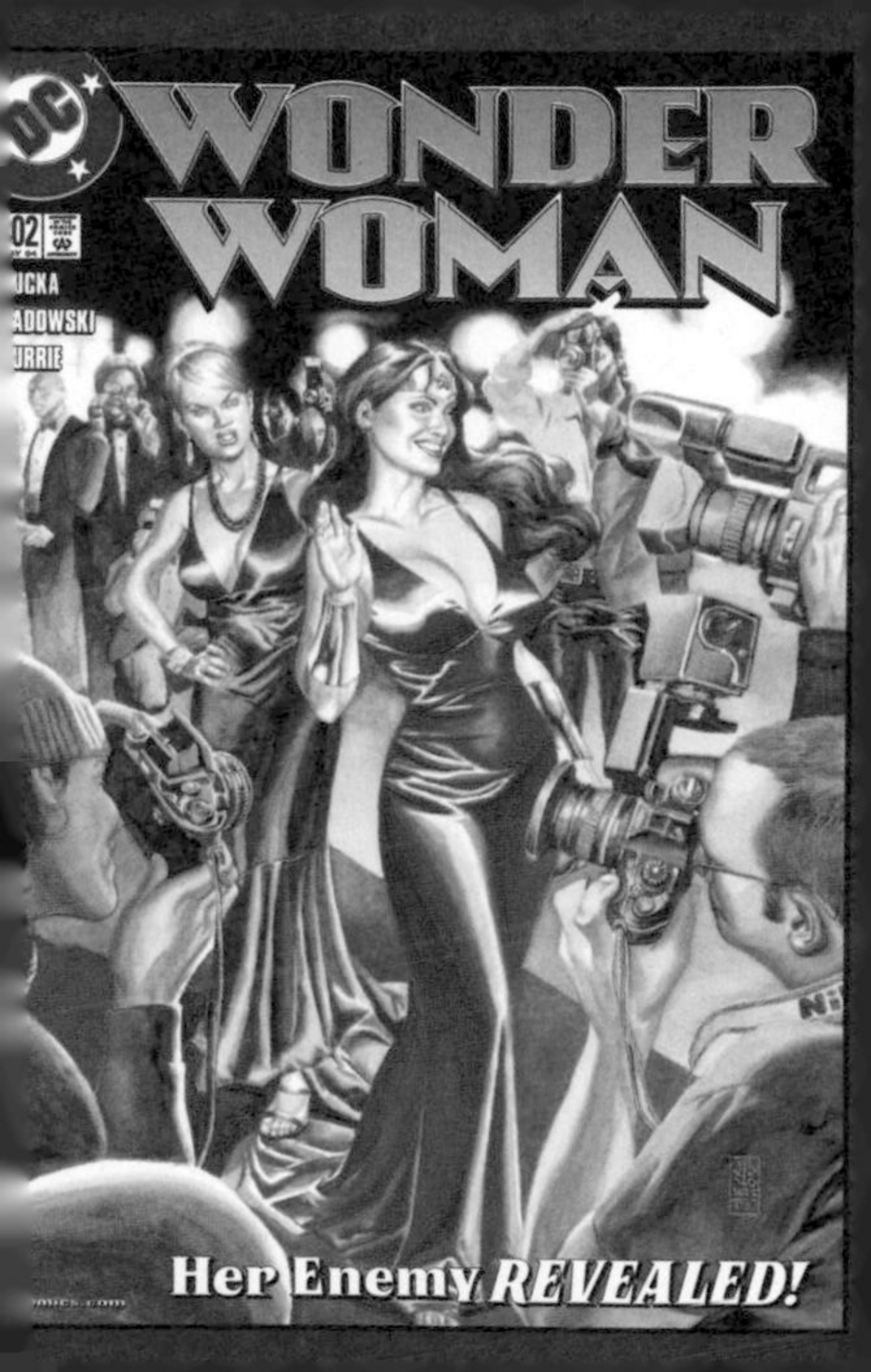
DC
WONDER WOMAN
02
UCKA
ADOWSKI
URRIE
Her Enemy REVEALED!

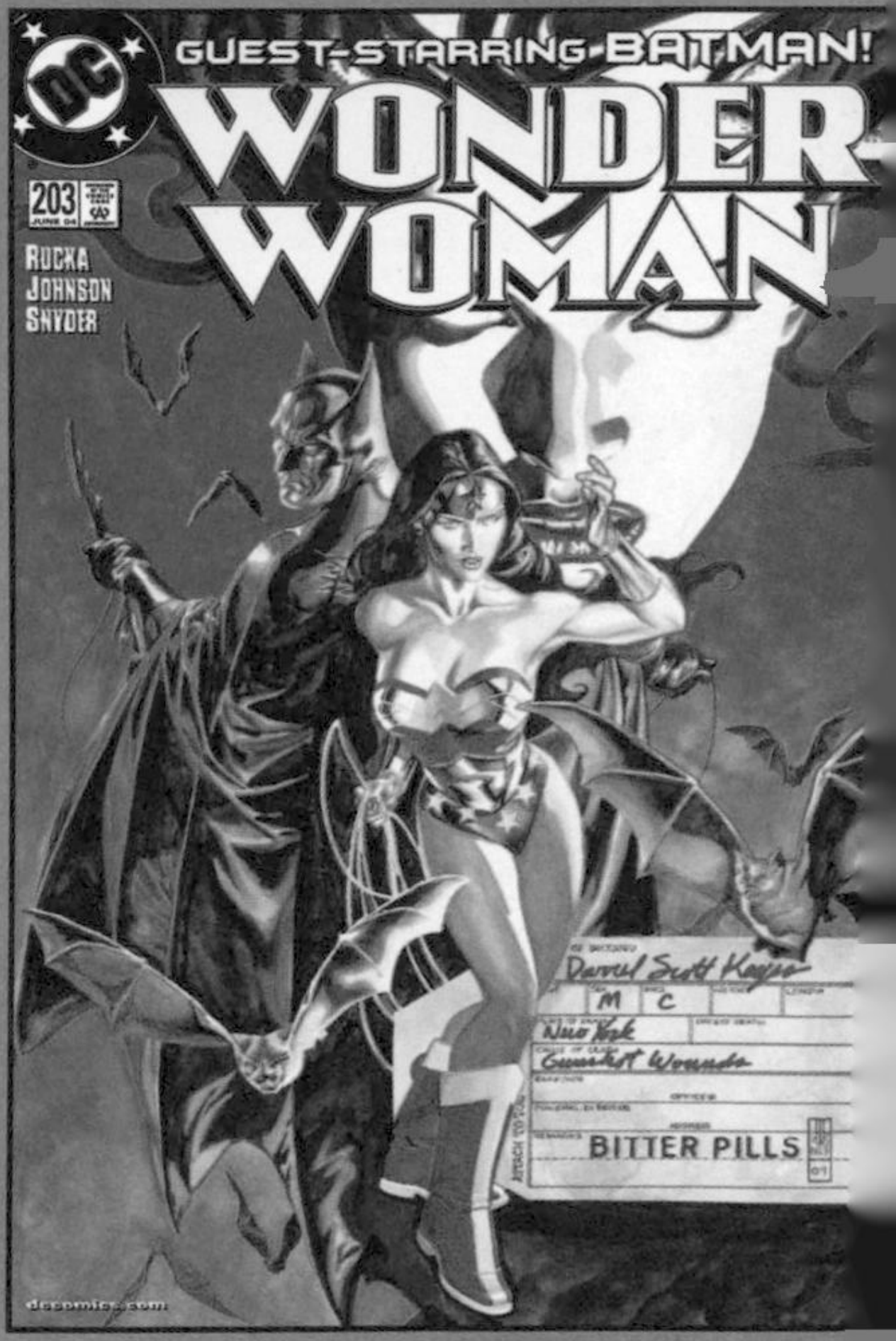
GUEST-STARRING-BATMAN!
DC
WONDER WOMAN
203
JUNE 04
RUCKA
JOHNSON
SNYDER
Darrel Scott Hayes
M
C
New York
Gunshot Wounds
BITTER PILLS
dccomics.com

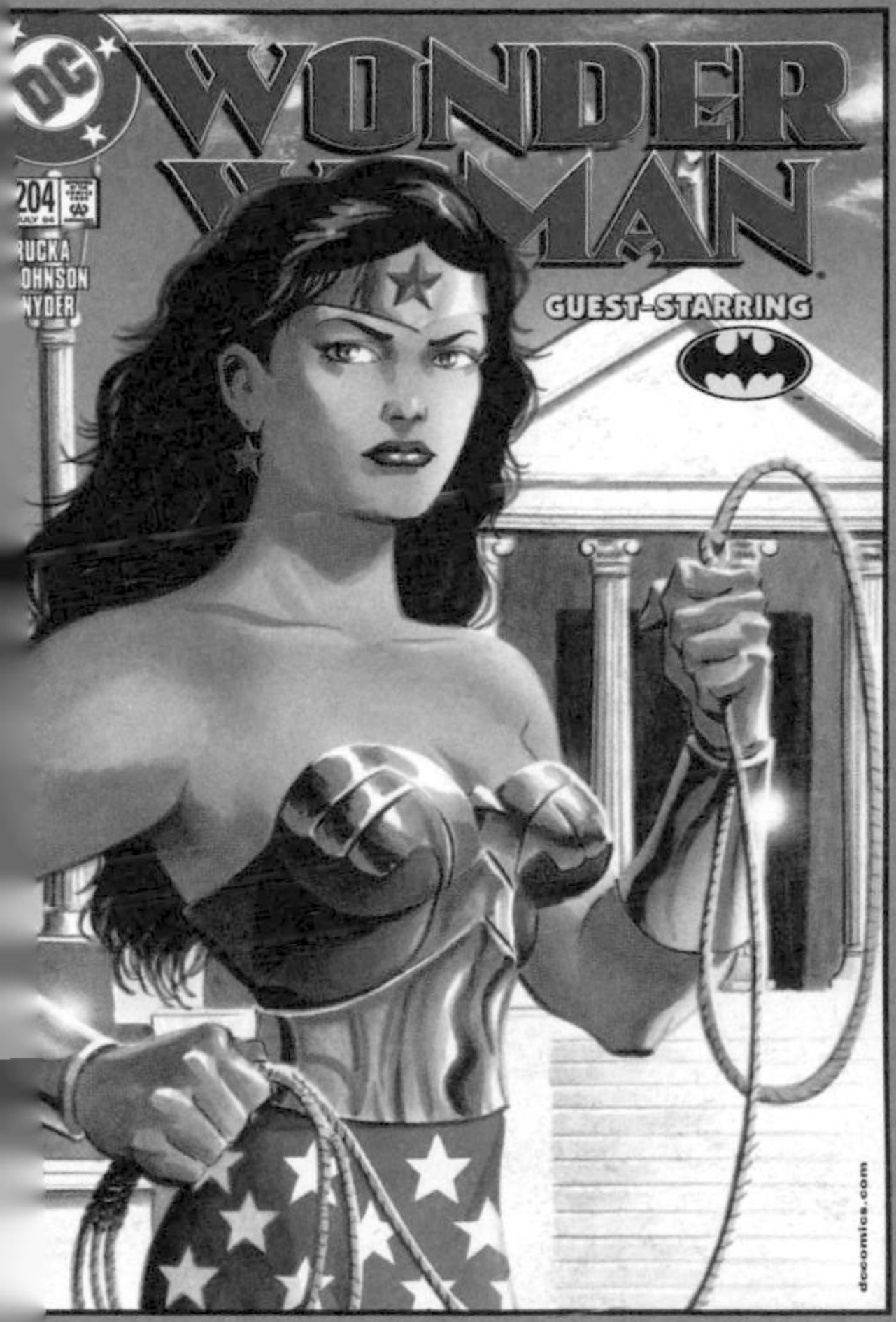
DC
WONDER WOMAN
204
RUCKA
OHNSON
NYDER
GUEST-STARRING
dccomics.com

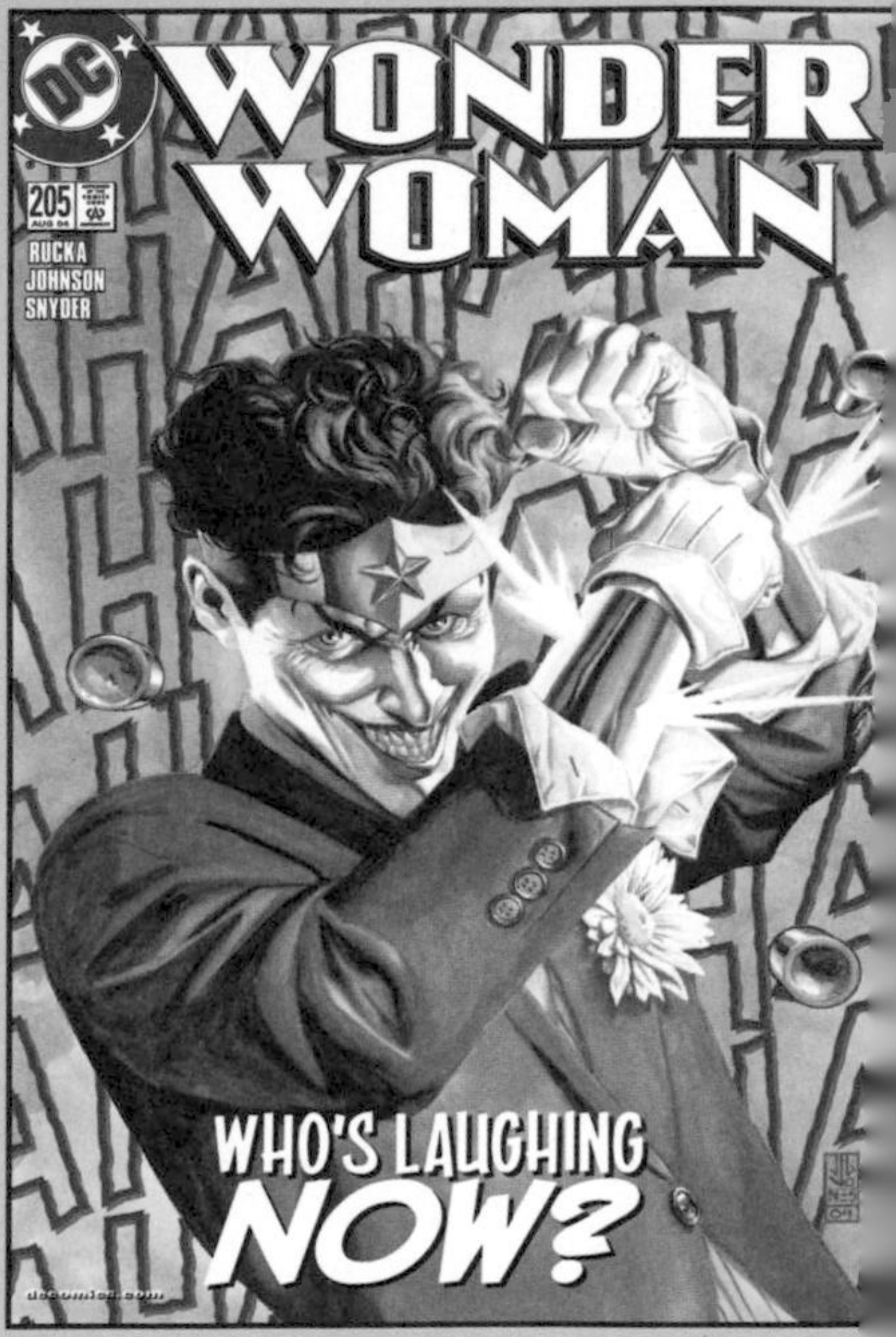
DC
WONDER WOMAN
205
AUG 06
RUCKA
JOHNSON
SNYDER
WHO'S LAUGHING
NOW?
dccomics.com

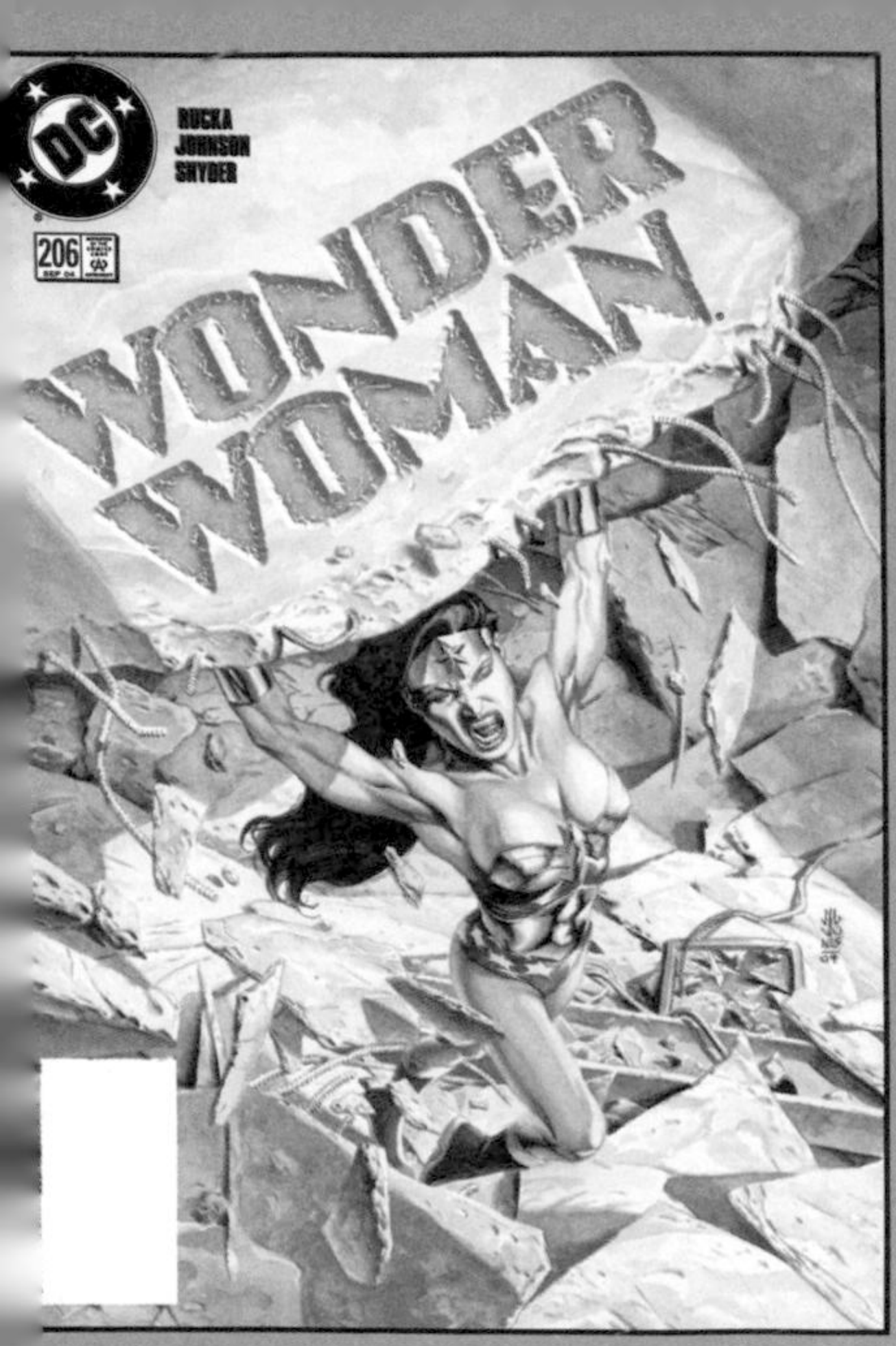
DC
RUCKA
JOHNSON
SNYDER
206
SEP 04
WONDER WOMAN

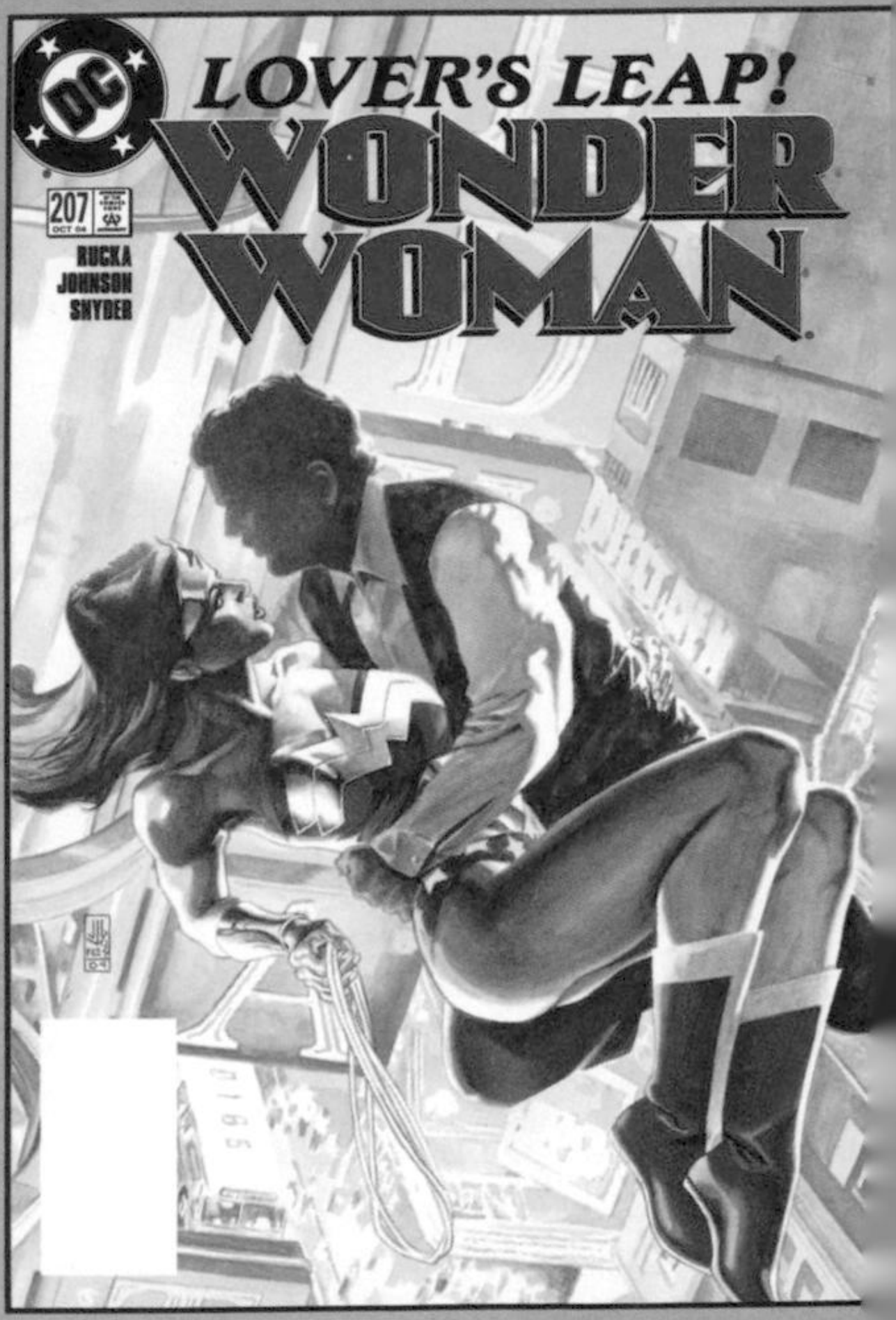
LOVER'S LEAP!
WONDER WOMAN
207
OCT 06
RUCKA
JOHNSON
SNYDER

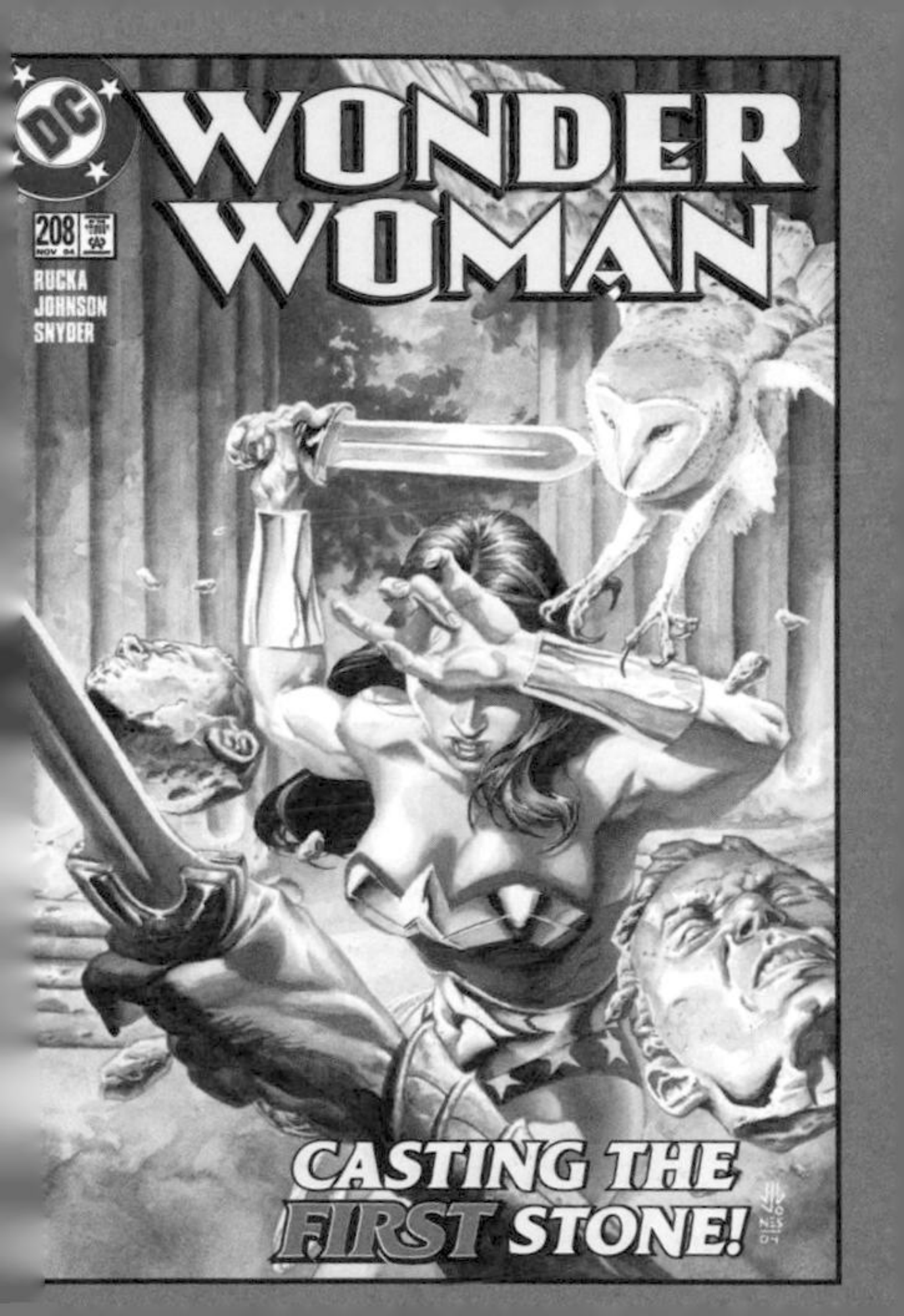
DC
WONDER WOMAN
208
NOV 84
RUCKA
JOHNSON
SNYDER
CASTING THE FIRST STONE!

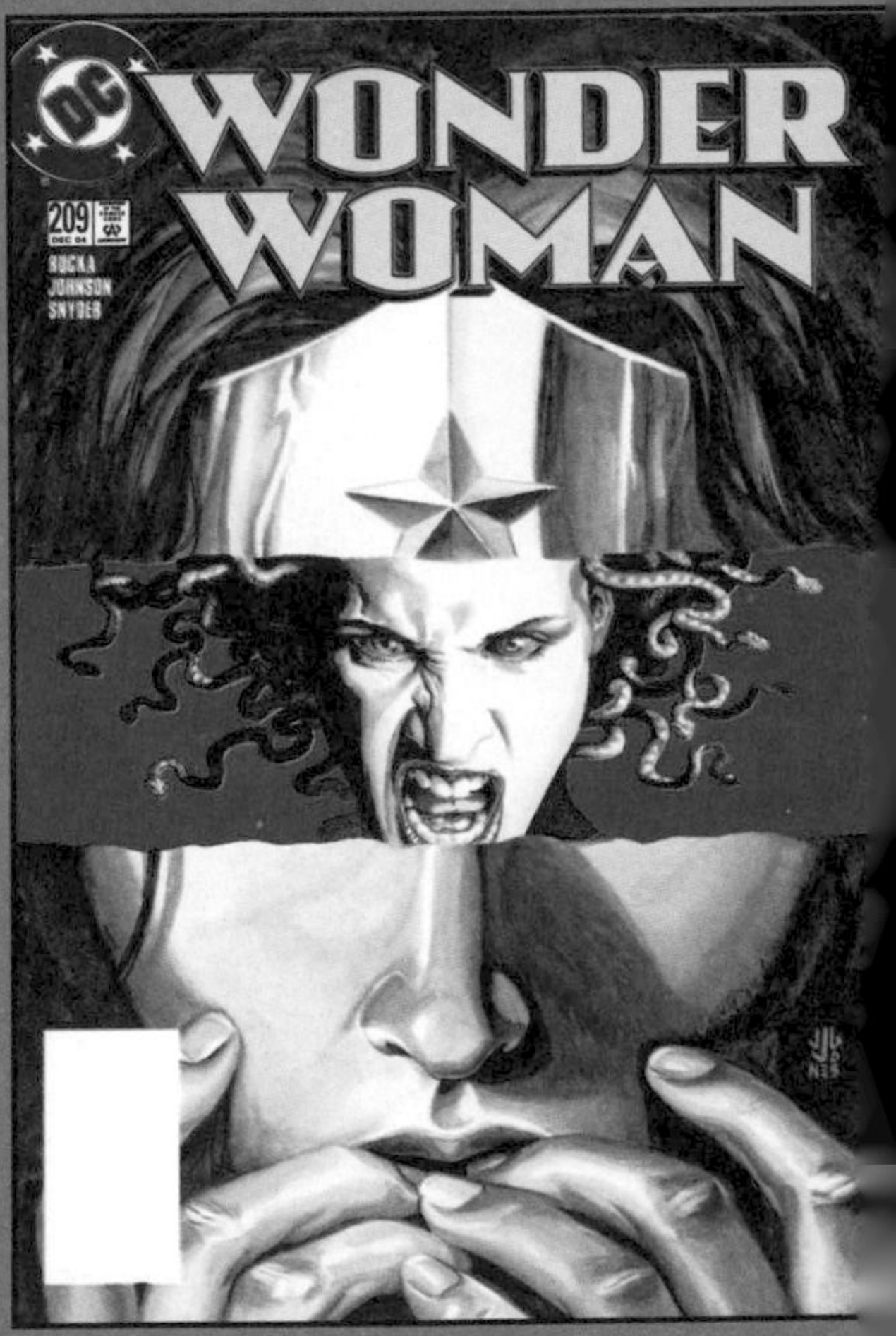
DC
WONDER WOMAN
209
DEC 04
BUCKA
JOHNSON
SNYDER

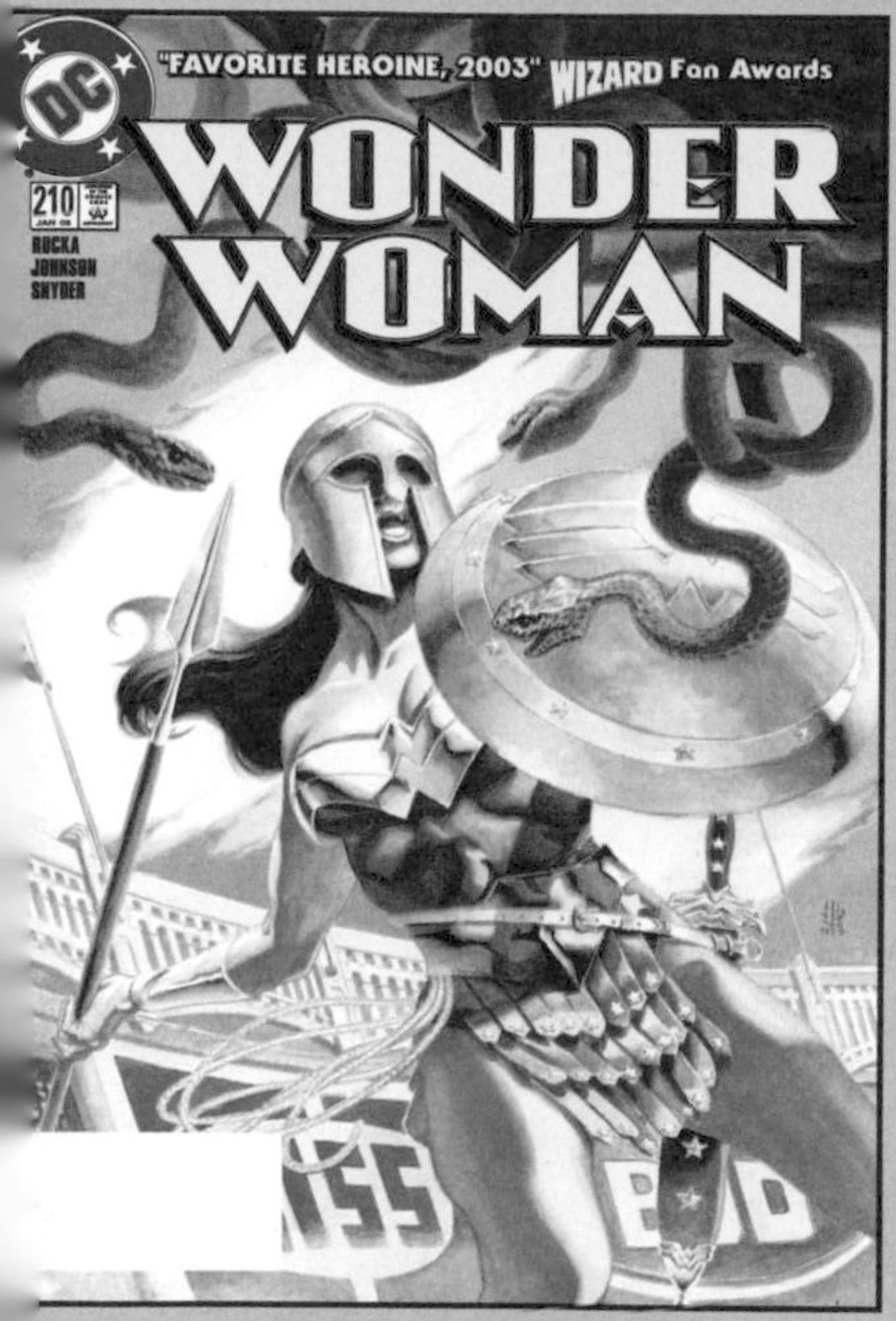
"FAVORITE HEROINE, 2003" WIZARD Fan Awards
DC
210
ROCKA
JOHNSON
SNYDER
WONDER WOMAN

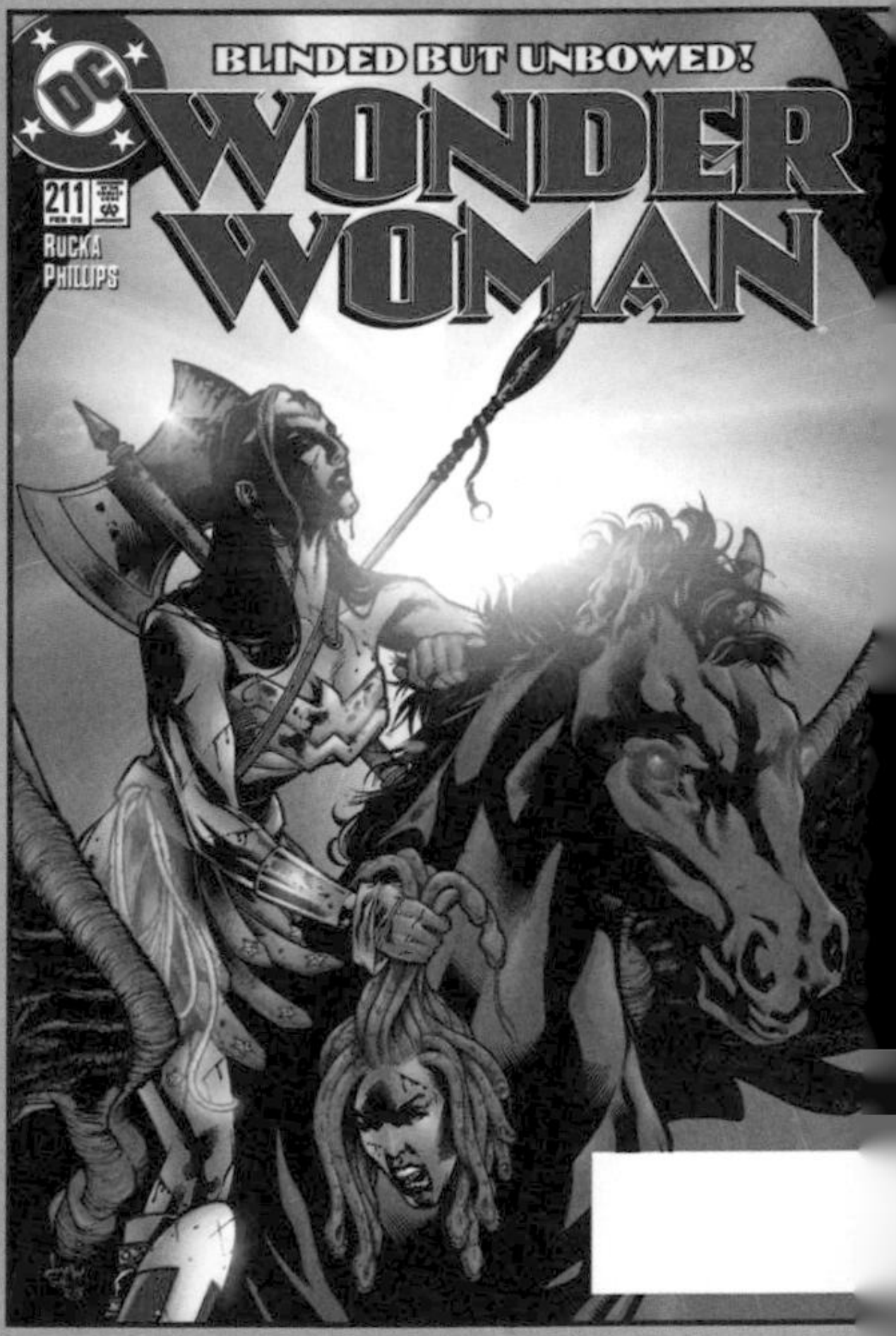
BLINDED BUT UNBOWED!
DC
WONDER WOMAN
211
RUCKA
PHILLIPS

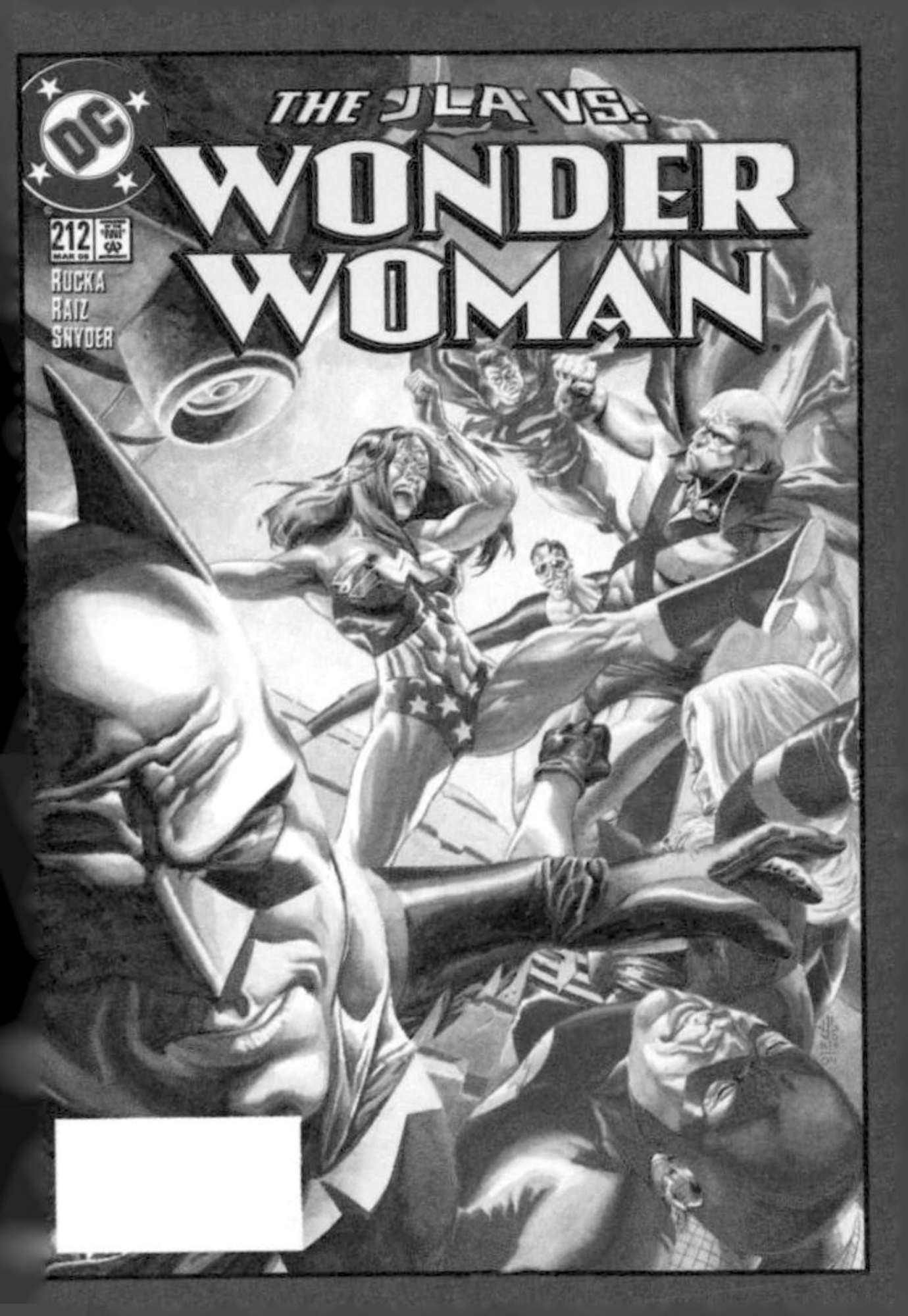
THE JLA VS.
WONDER WOMAN
212
RUCKA
RATZ
SNYDER

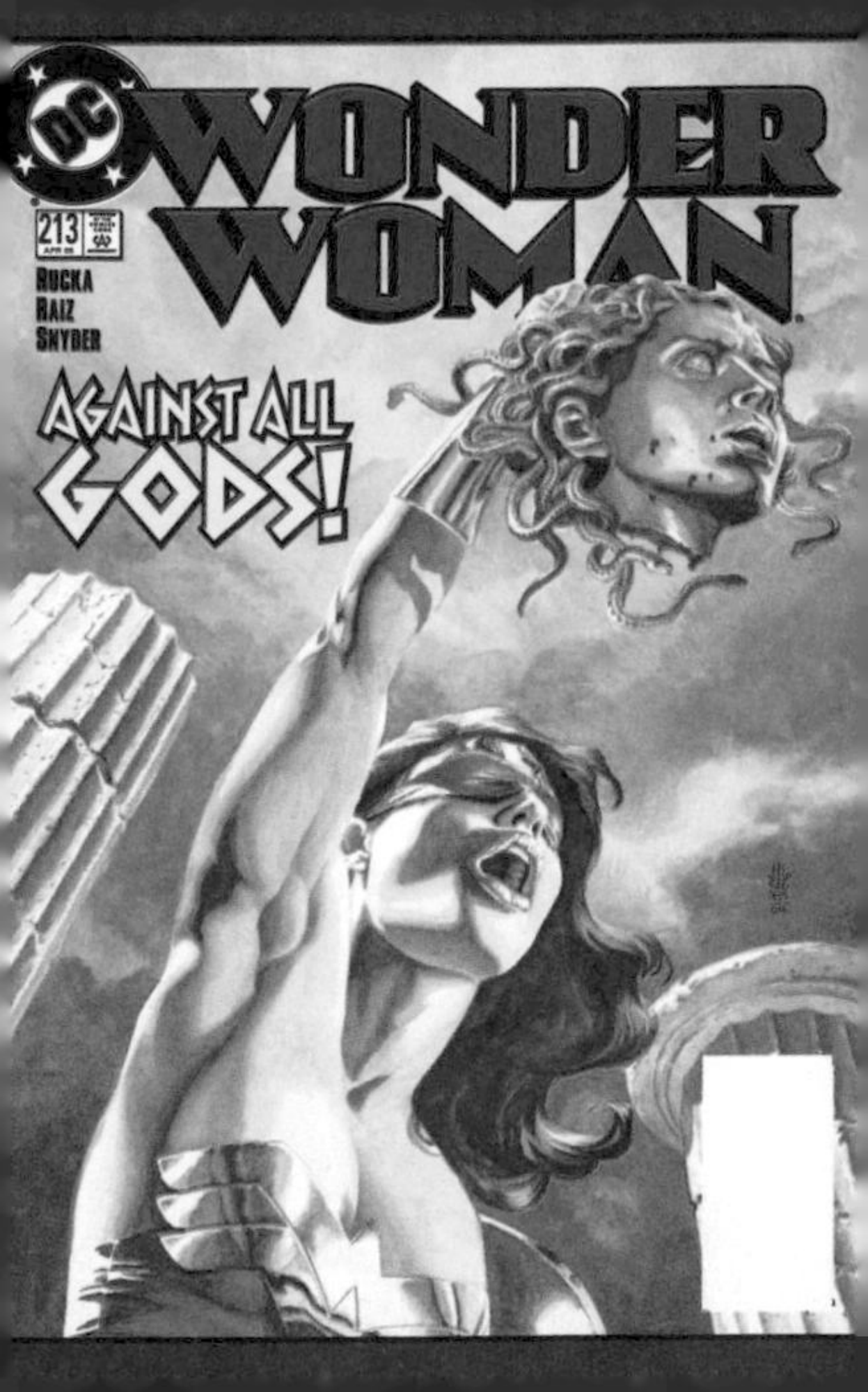
DC
WONDER WOMAN
213
RUCKA
RAIZ
SNYDER
AGAINST ALL GODS!

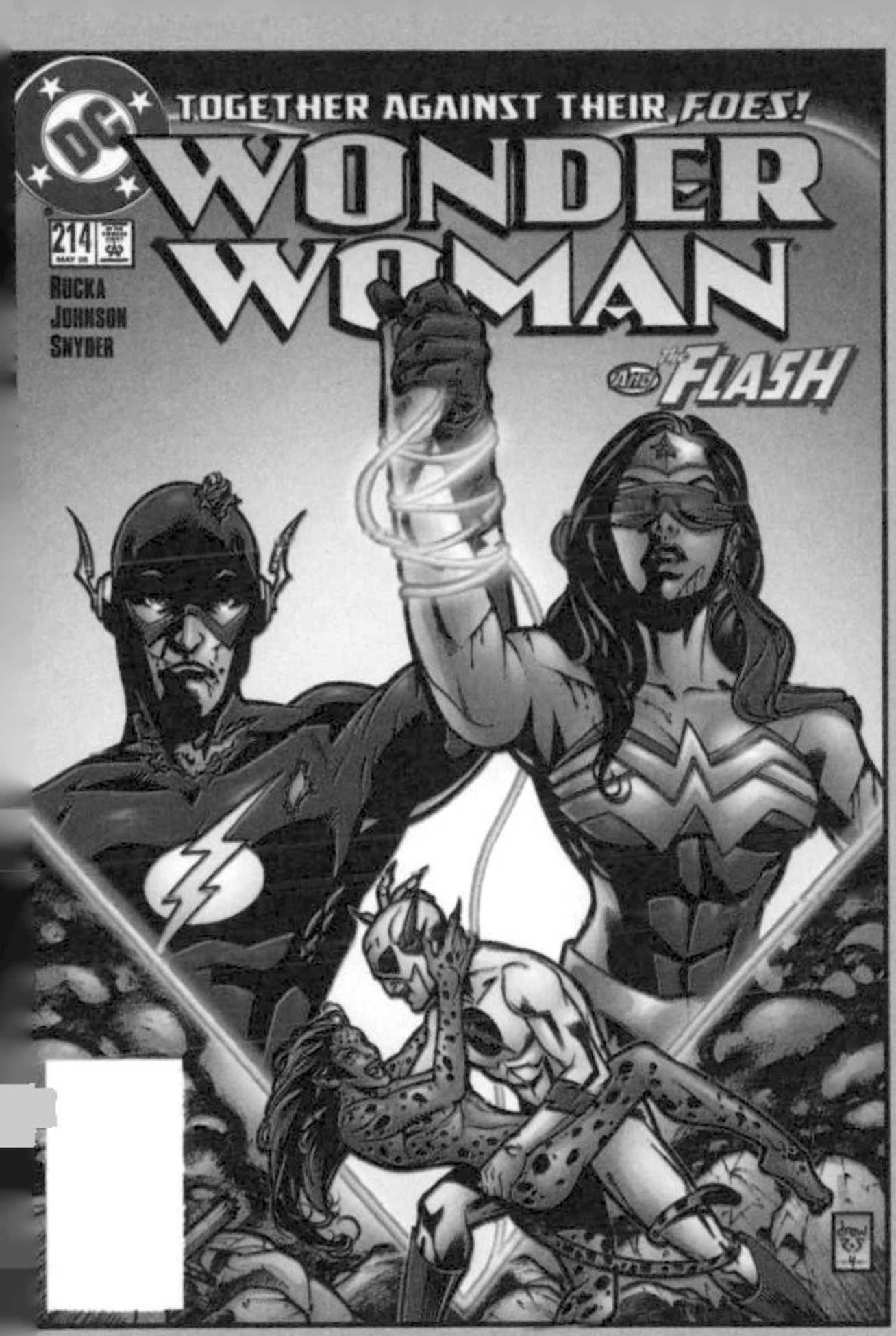
DC
TOGETHER AGAINST THEIR FOES!
WONDER WOMAN
214
RUCKA
JOHNSON
SNYDER
AND THE FLASH

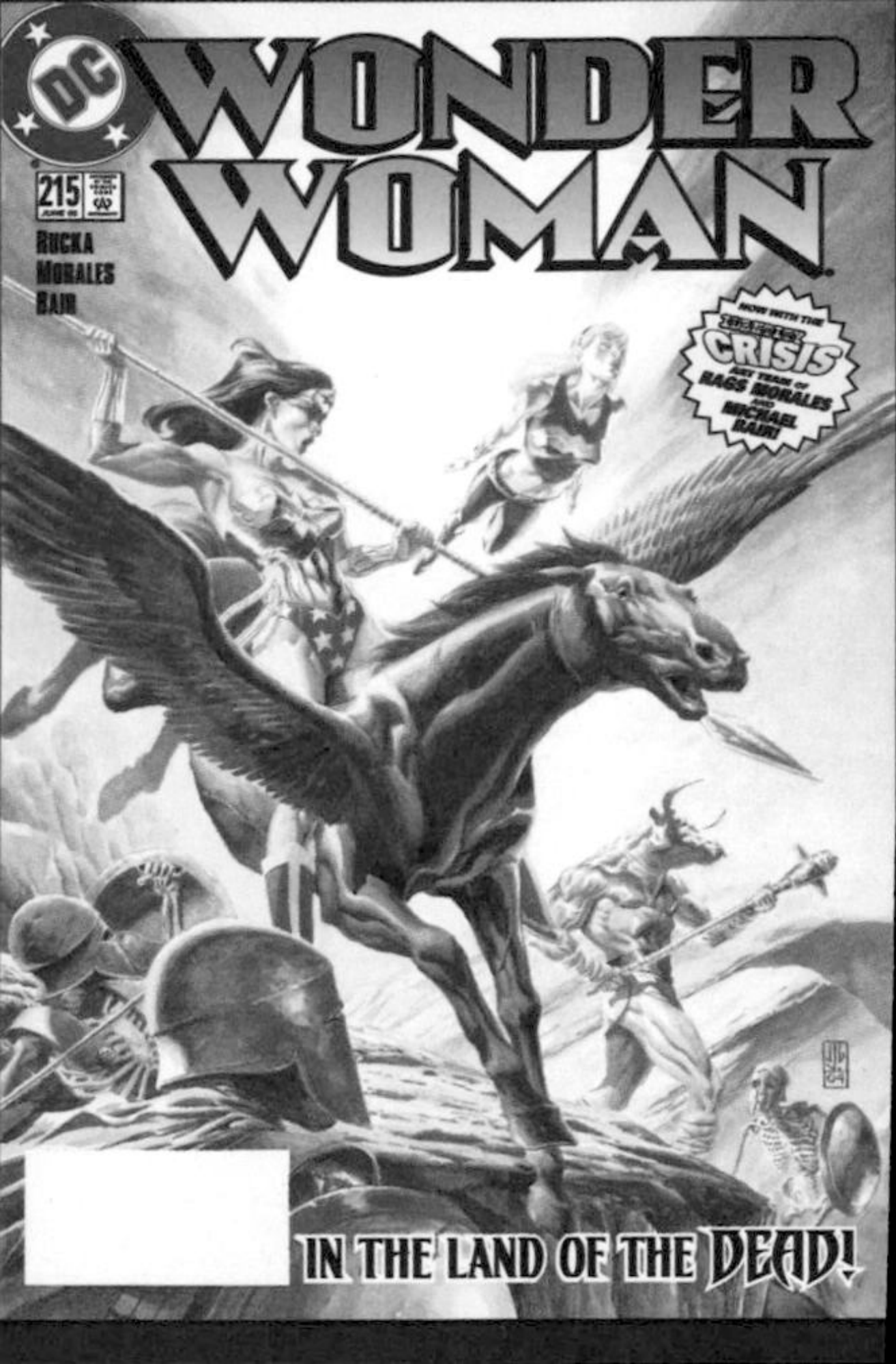
DC
WONDER WOMAN
215
RUCKA
MORALES
BAIR
NOW WITH THE
CRISIS
ART TEAM OF
RAGS MORALES
AND
MICHAEL BAIR!
IN THE LAND OF THE DEAD!

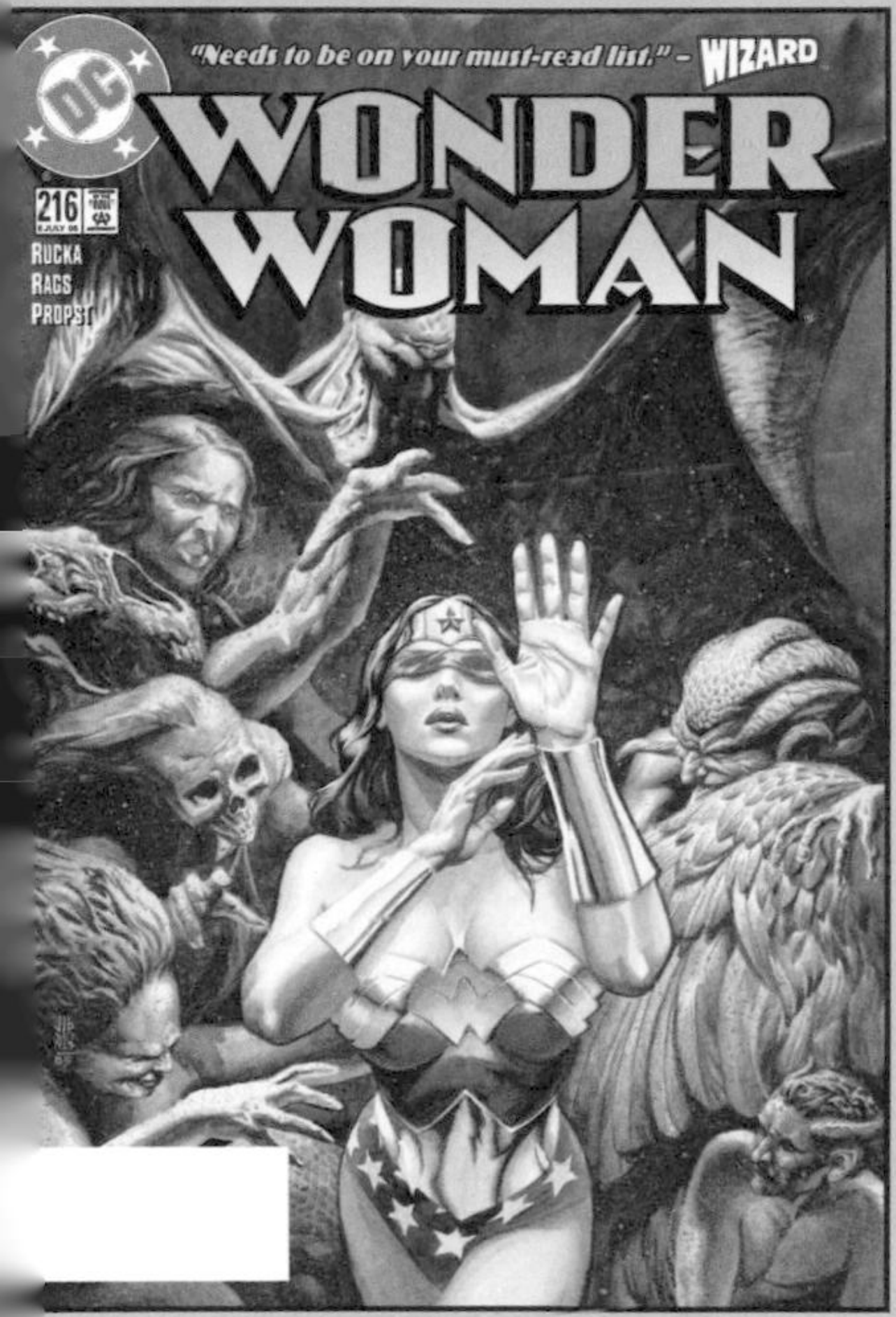
"Needs to be on your must-read list." - WIZARD
DC
WONDER WOMAN
216
RUCKA
RAGS
PROPST

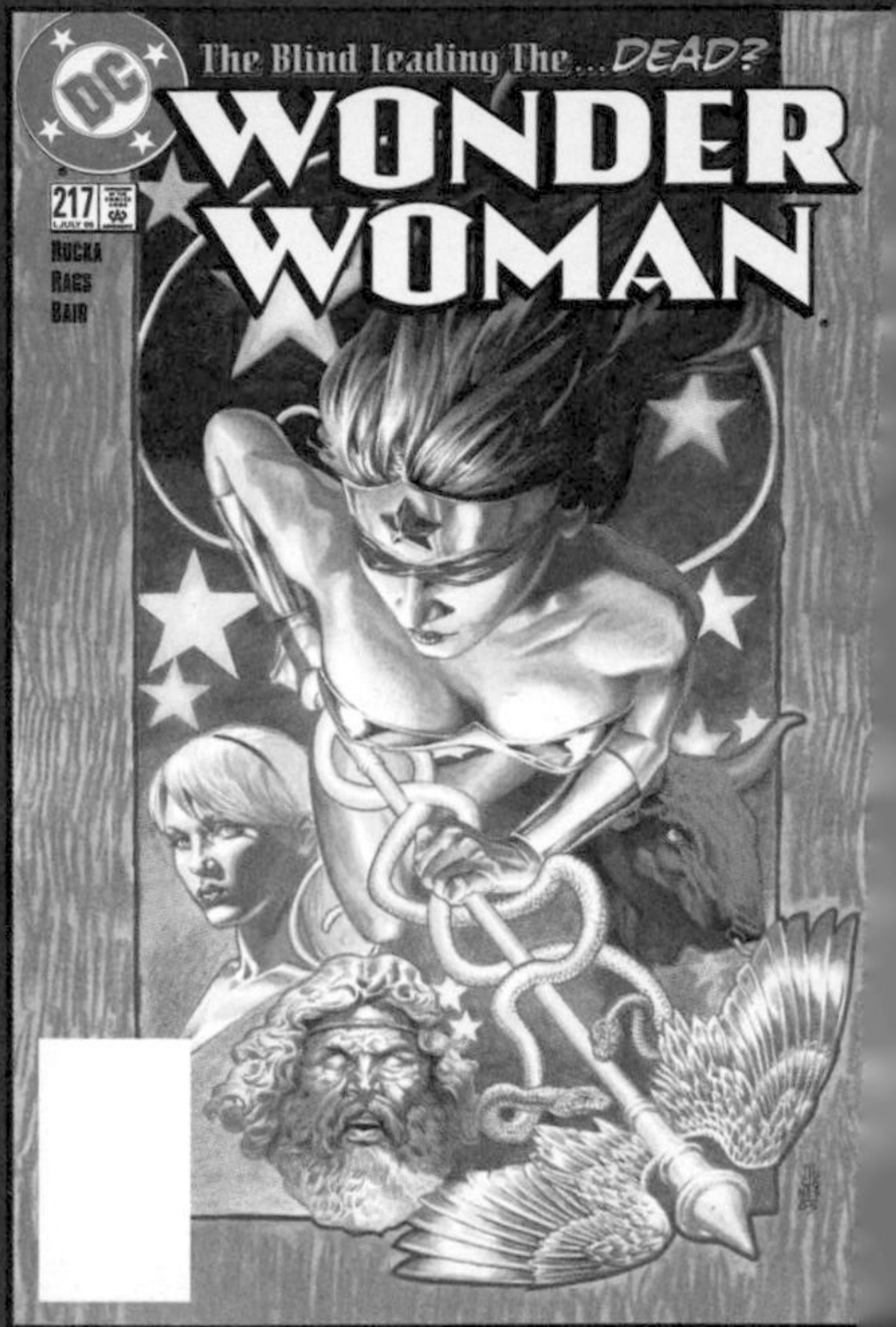
The Blind Leading The ... DEAD?
DC
WONDER WOMAN
217
JULY 05
HUCKA
RAGS
BAIR

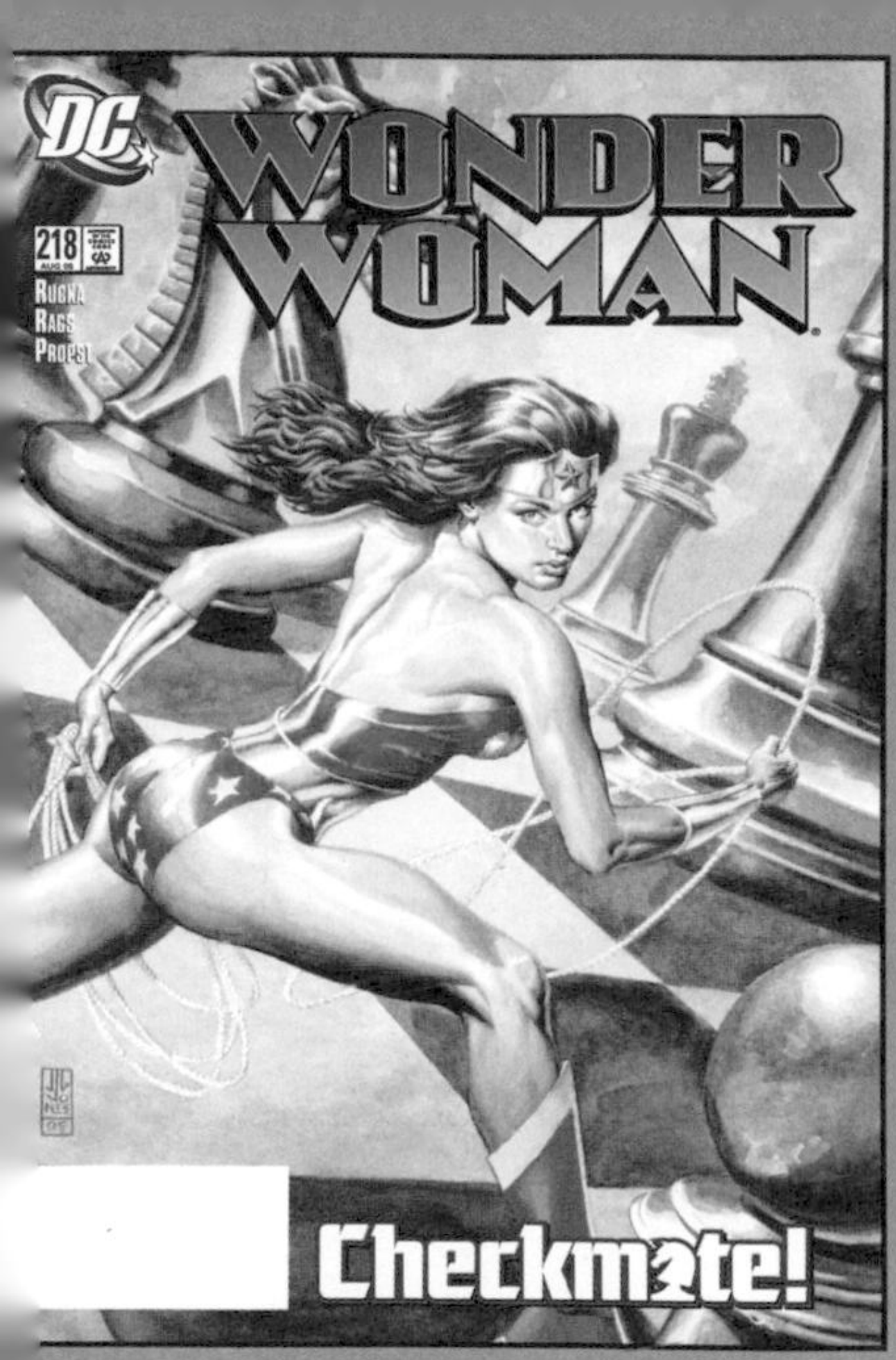
DC
WONDER WOMAN
218
RUGNA
RAGS
PROPST
Checkmate!

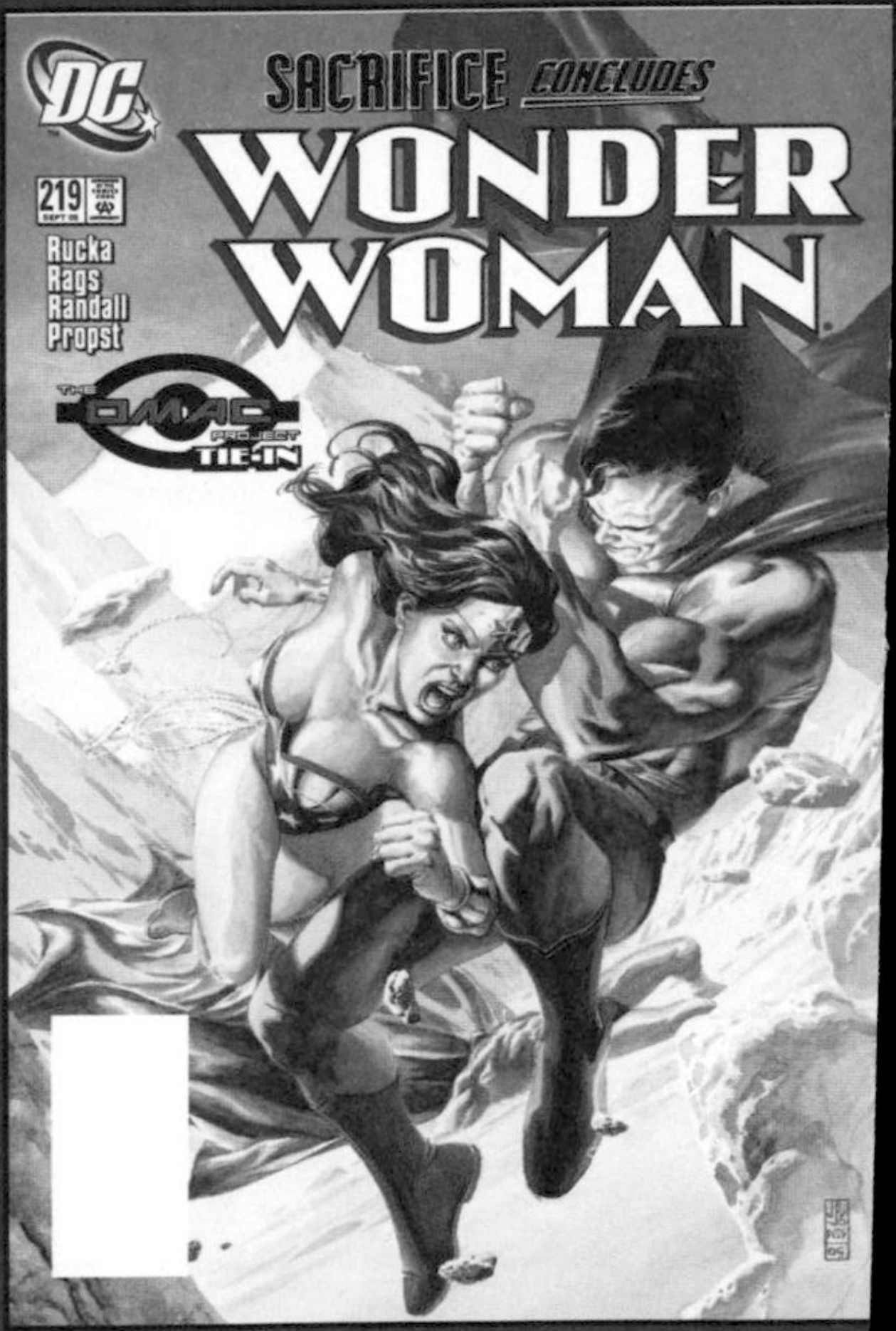
DC
SACRIFICE CONCLUDES
WONDER WOMAN
219
Rucka
Rags
Randall
Propst
THE OMAC PROJECT TIE-IN

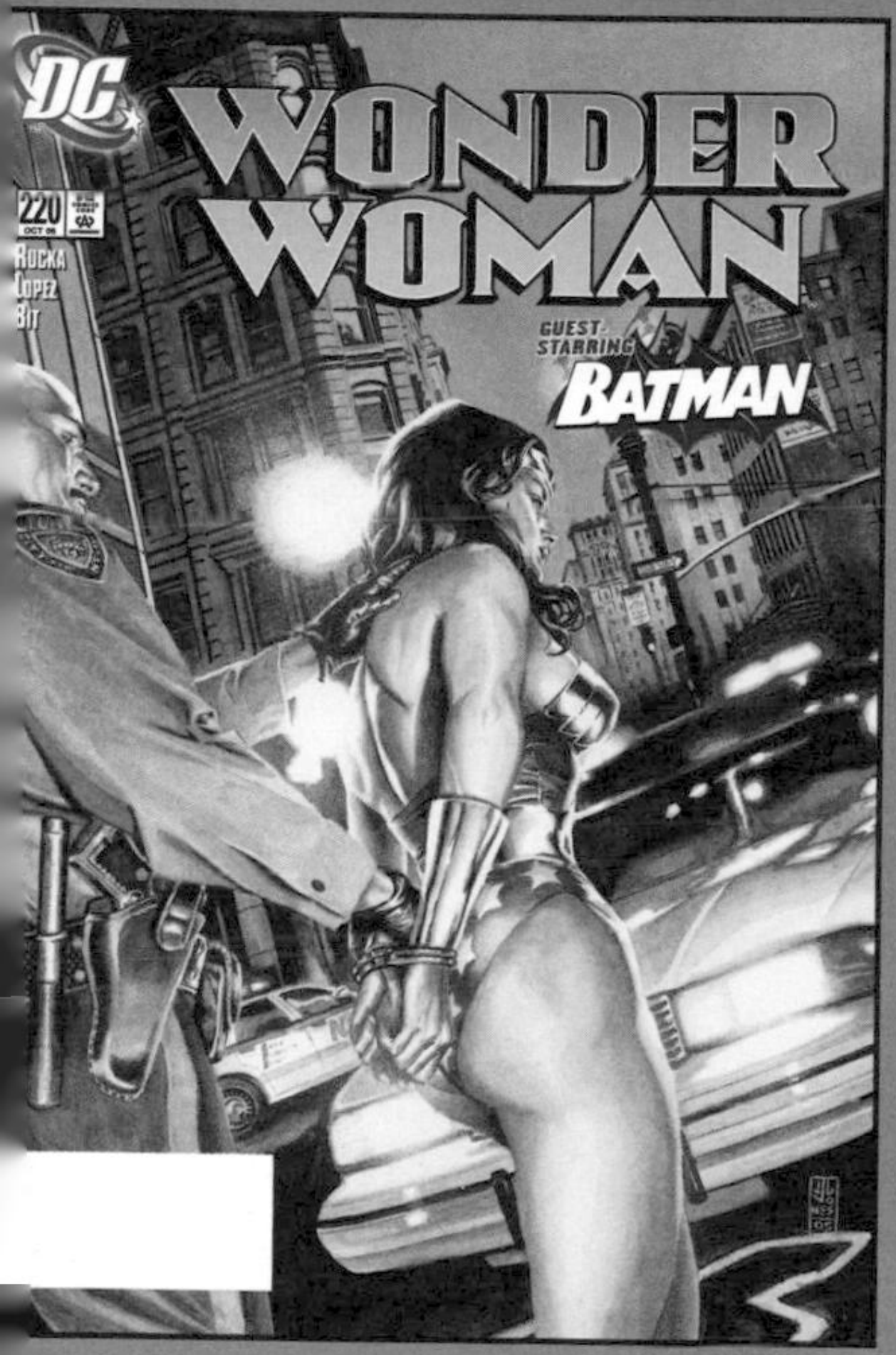
DC
WONDER WOMAN
220
OCT 06
ROCKA
LOPEZ
BIT
GUEST-STARRING
BATMAN

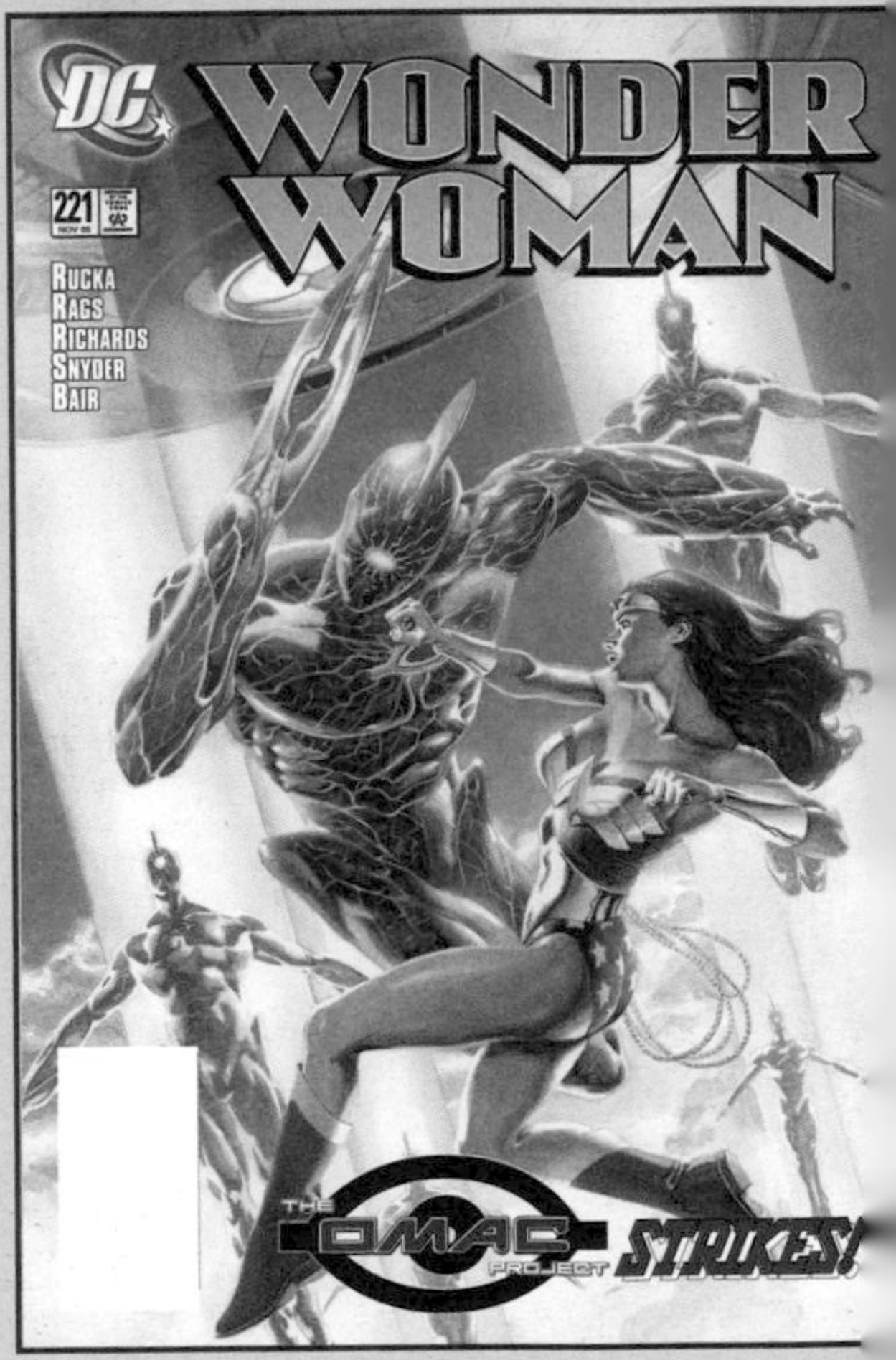
DC
WONDER WOMAN
221
NOV 05
RUCKA
RAGS
RICHARDS
SNYDER
BAIR
THE OMAC PROJECT STRIKES!

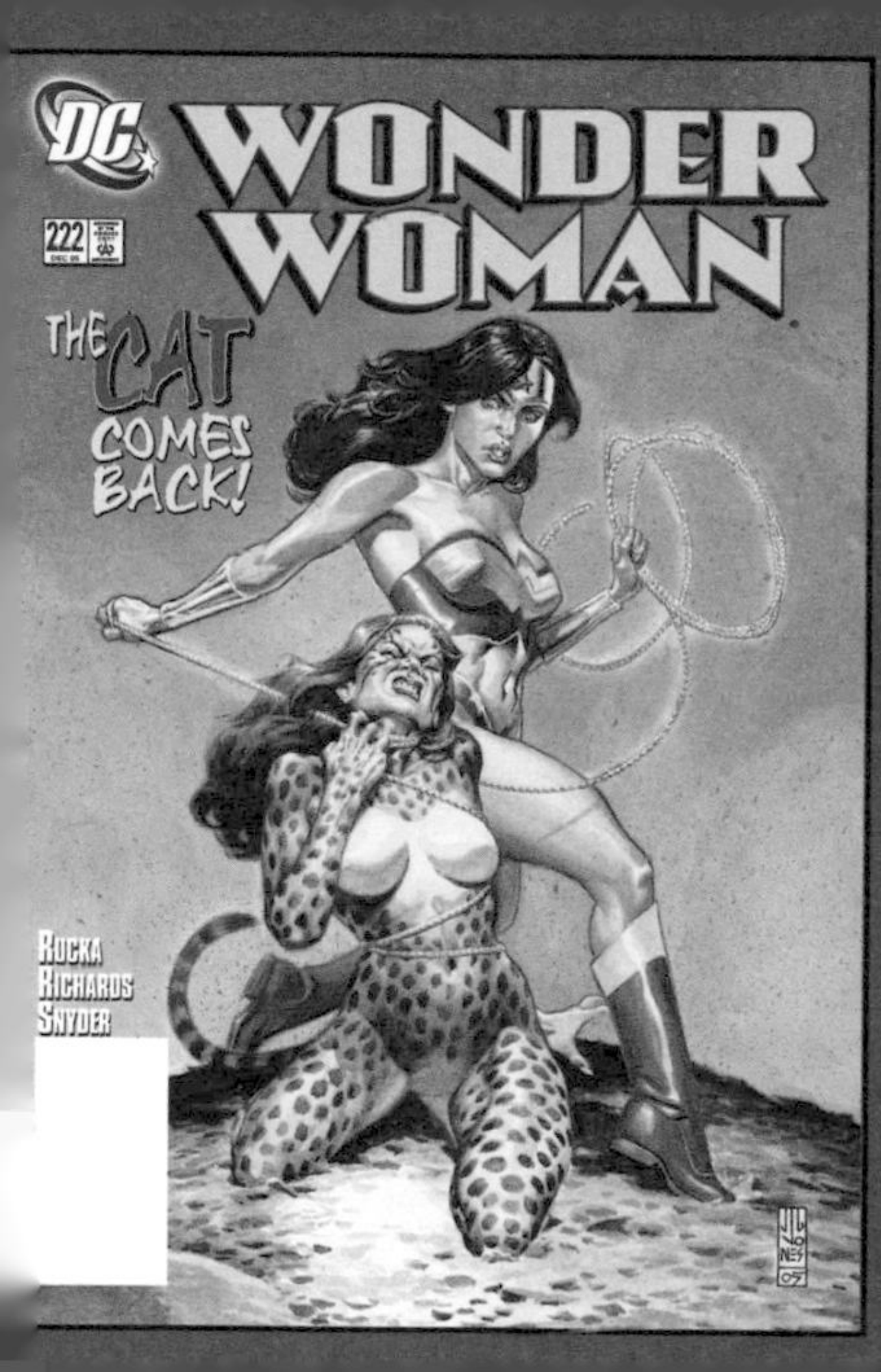
DC
WONDER WOMAN
222
THE CAT COMES BACK!
ROCKA
RICHARDS
SNYDER

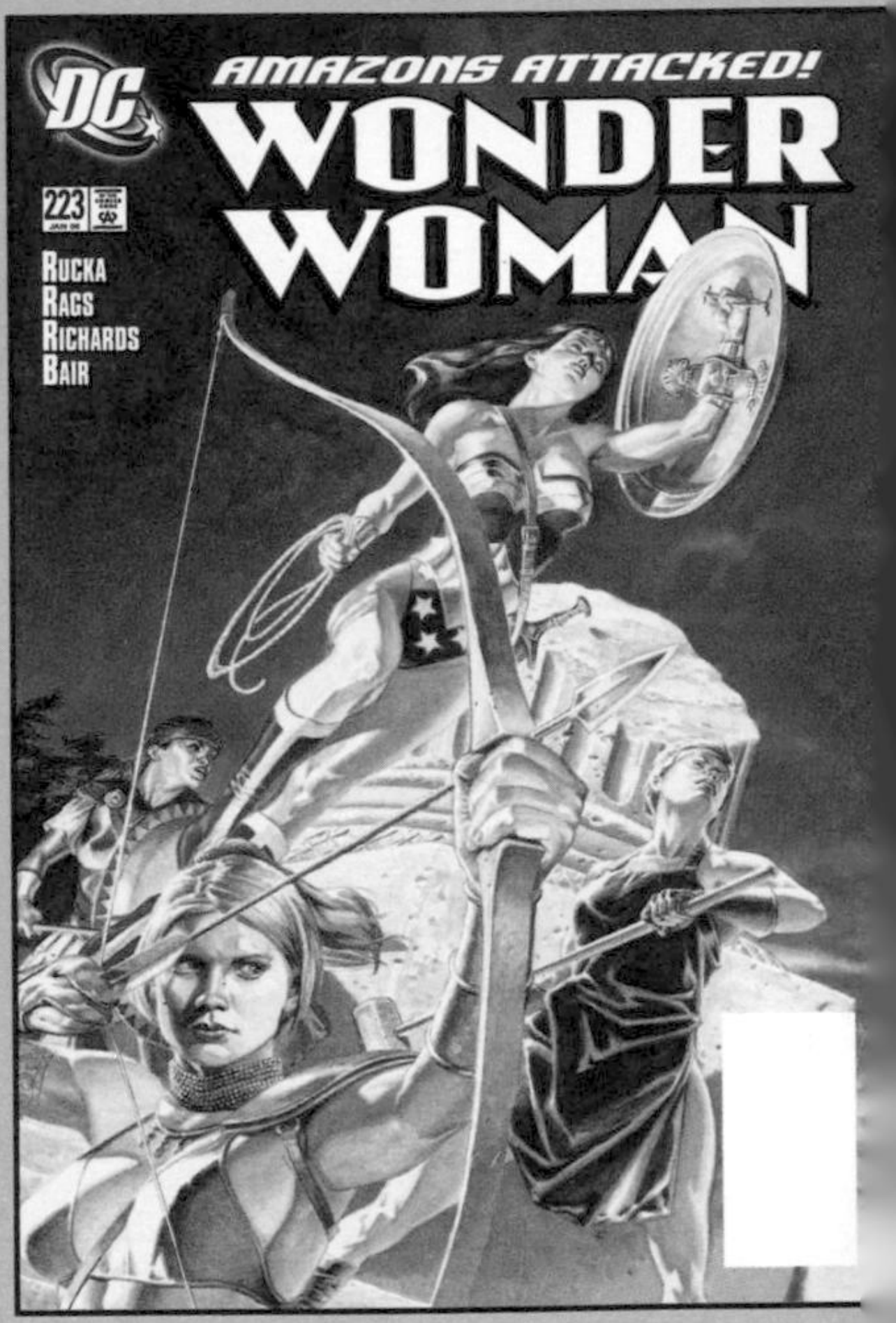
DC
AMAZONS ATTACKED!
WONDER WOMAN
223
RUCKA
RAGS
RICHARDS
BAIR

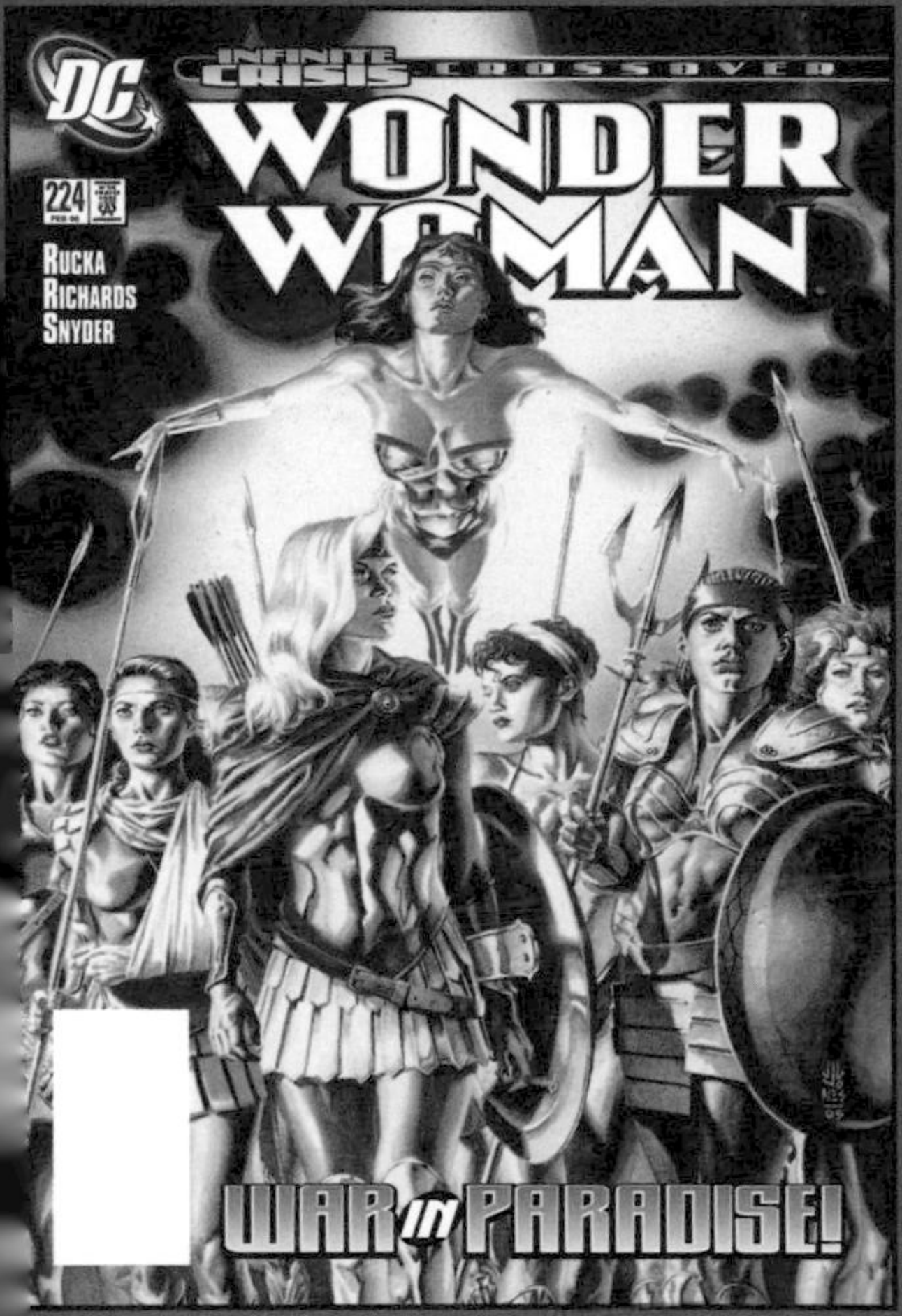
DC
INFINITE CRISIS CROSSOVER
WONDER WOMAN
224
RUCKA
RICHARDS
SNYDER
WAR IN PARADISE!

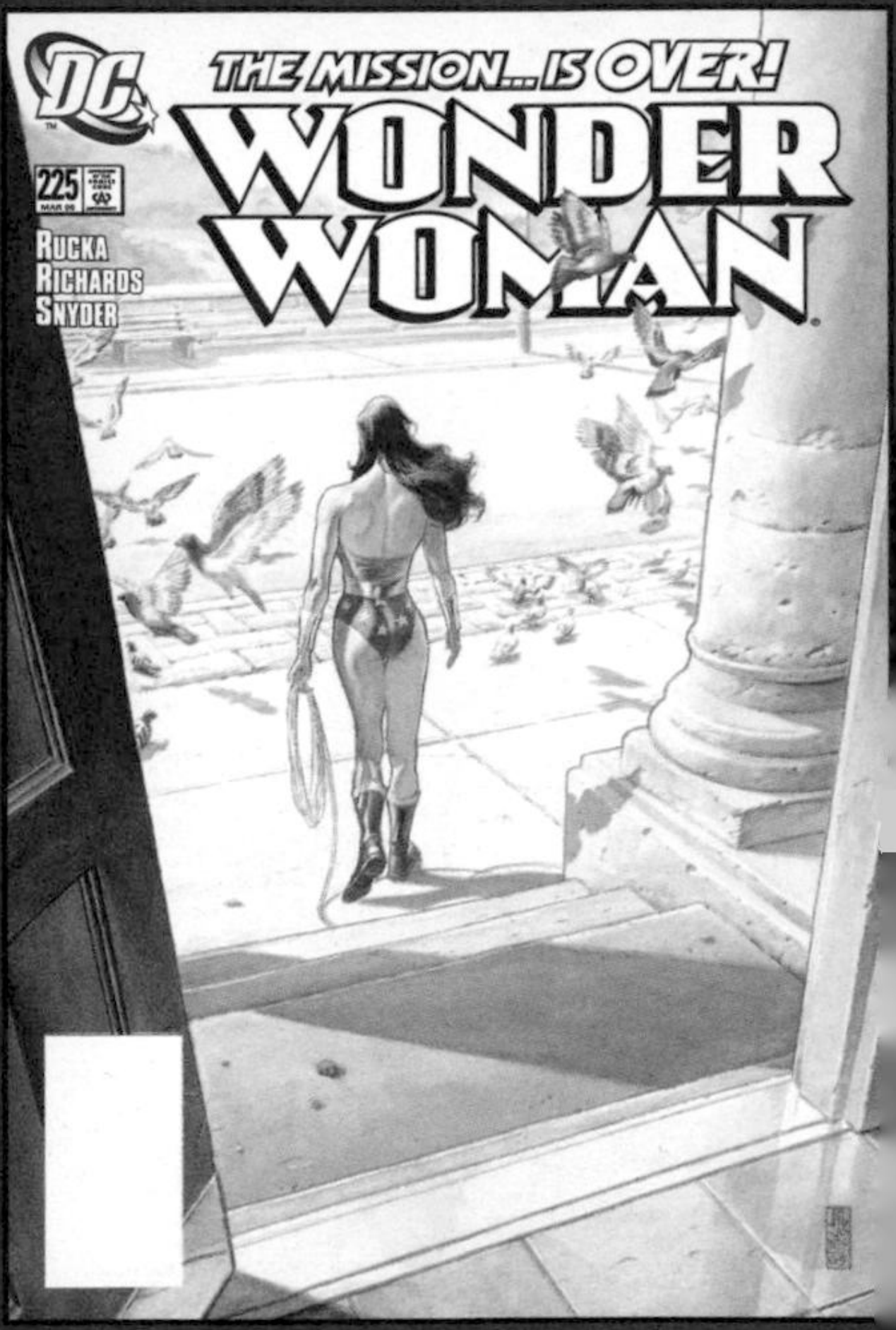
DC
THE MISSION... IS OVER!
WONDER WOMAN
225
RUCKA
RICHARDS
SNYDER

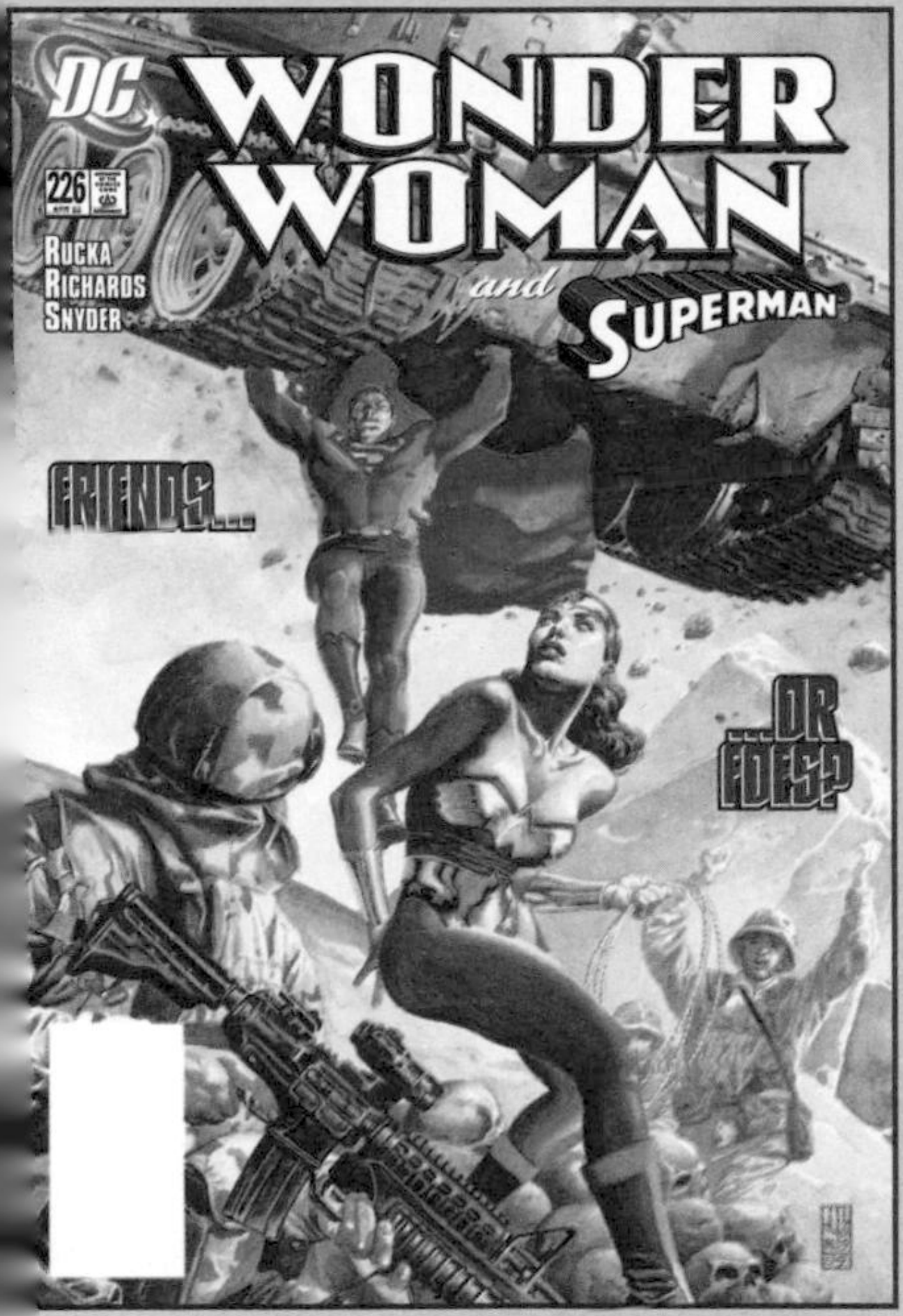
DC
WONDER WOMAN
226
RUCKA
RICHARDS
SNYDER
and
SUPERMAN
FRIENDS...
...OR FOES?

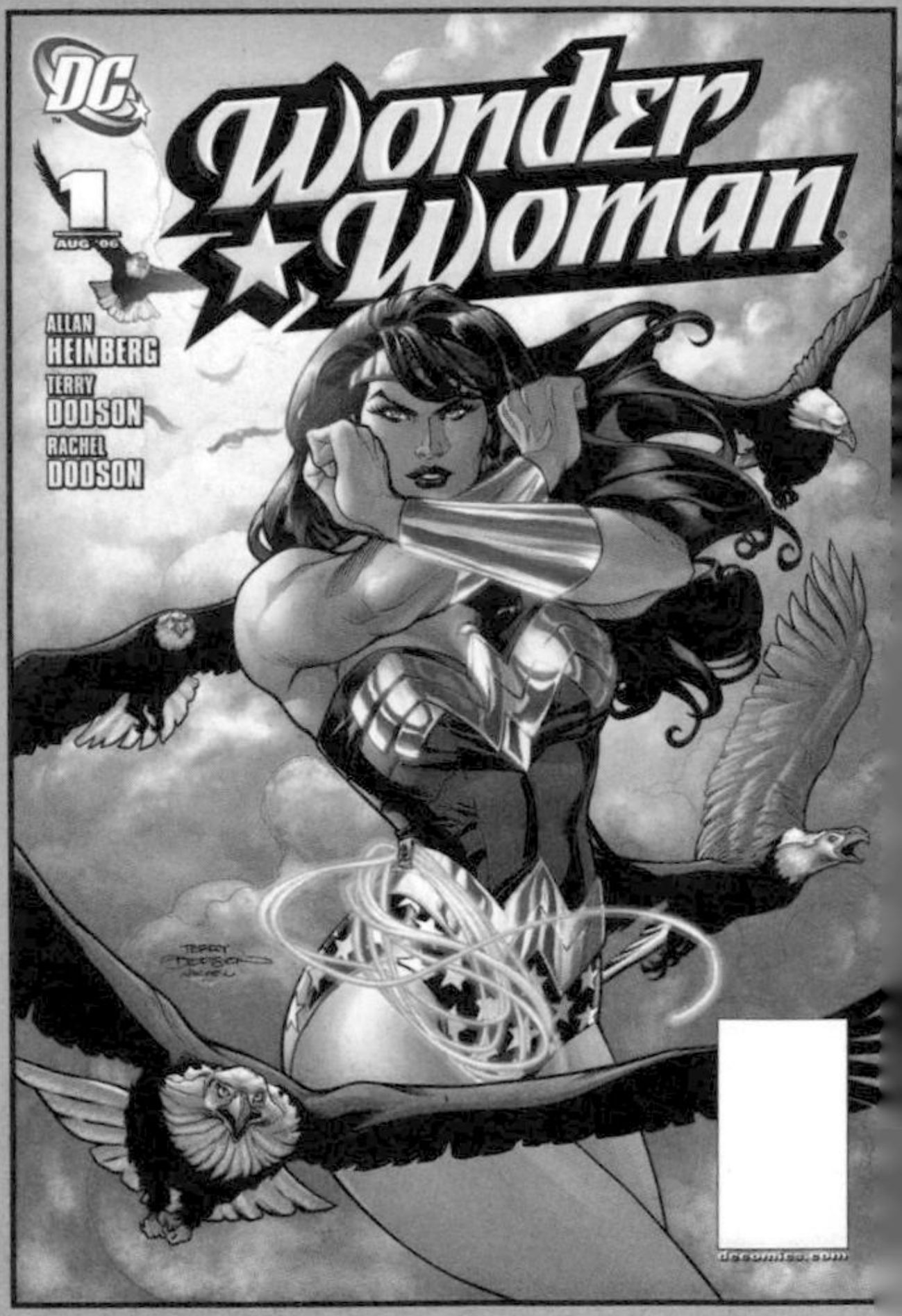
DC
Wonder Woman
1
AUG '06
ALLAN HEINBERG
TERRY DODSON
RACHEL DODSON
dccomics.com

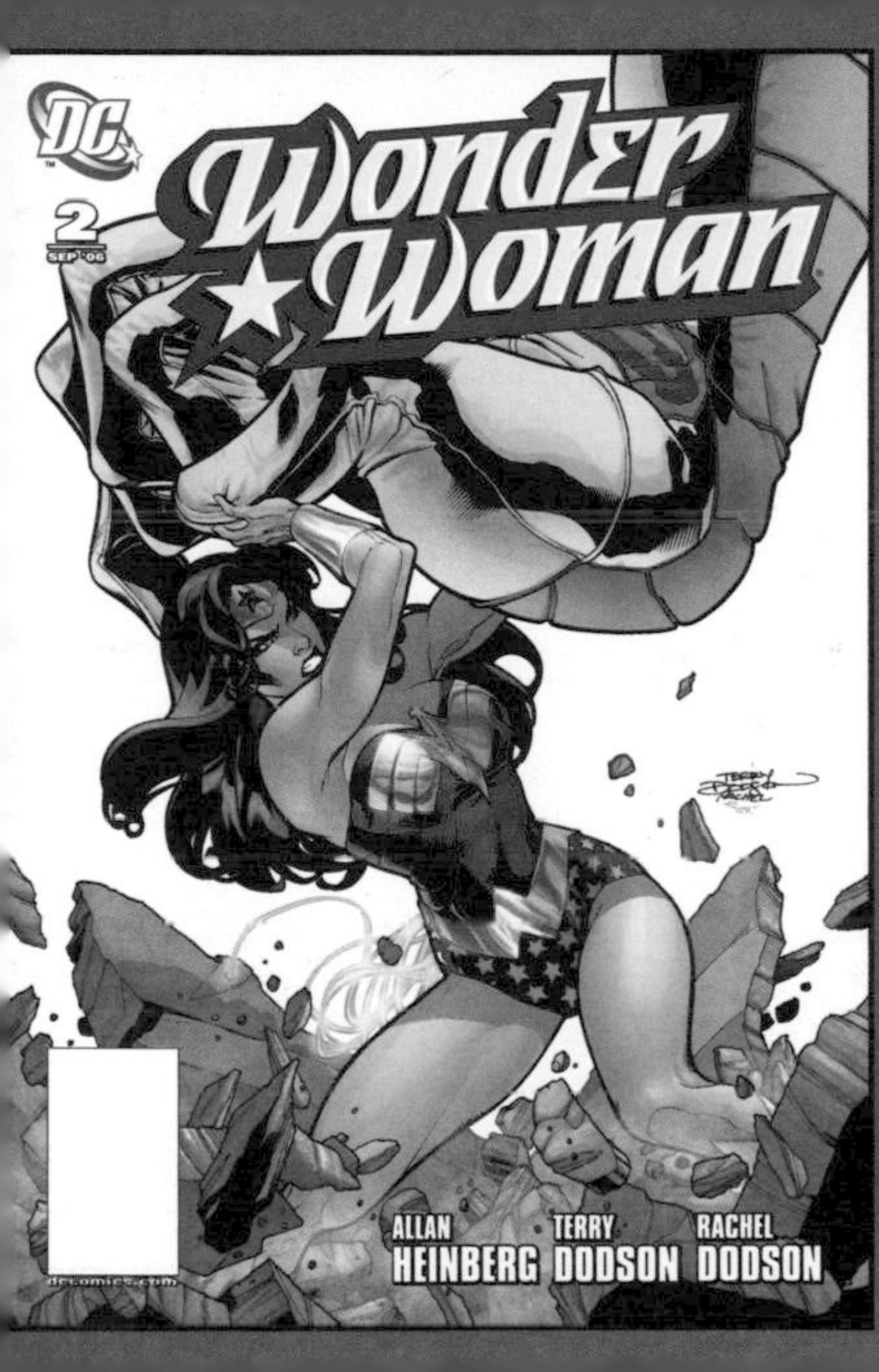
DC
Wonder Woman
2
SEP '06
ALLAN HEINBERG
TERRY DODSON
RACHEL DODSON
dccomics.com

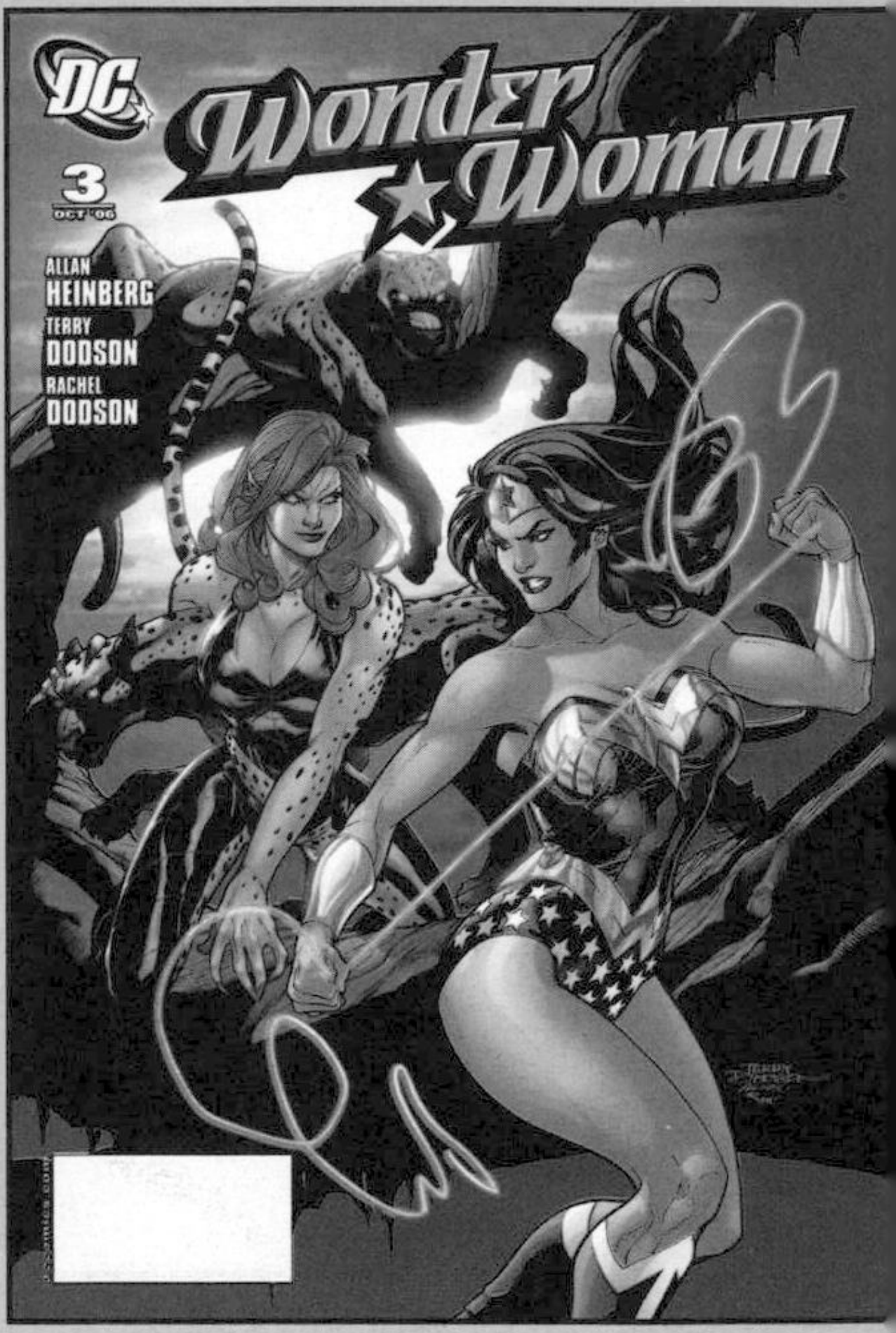
DC
Wonder Woman
3
OCT '06
ALLAN HEINBERG
TERRY DODSON
RACHEL DODSON

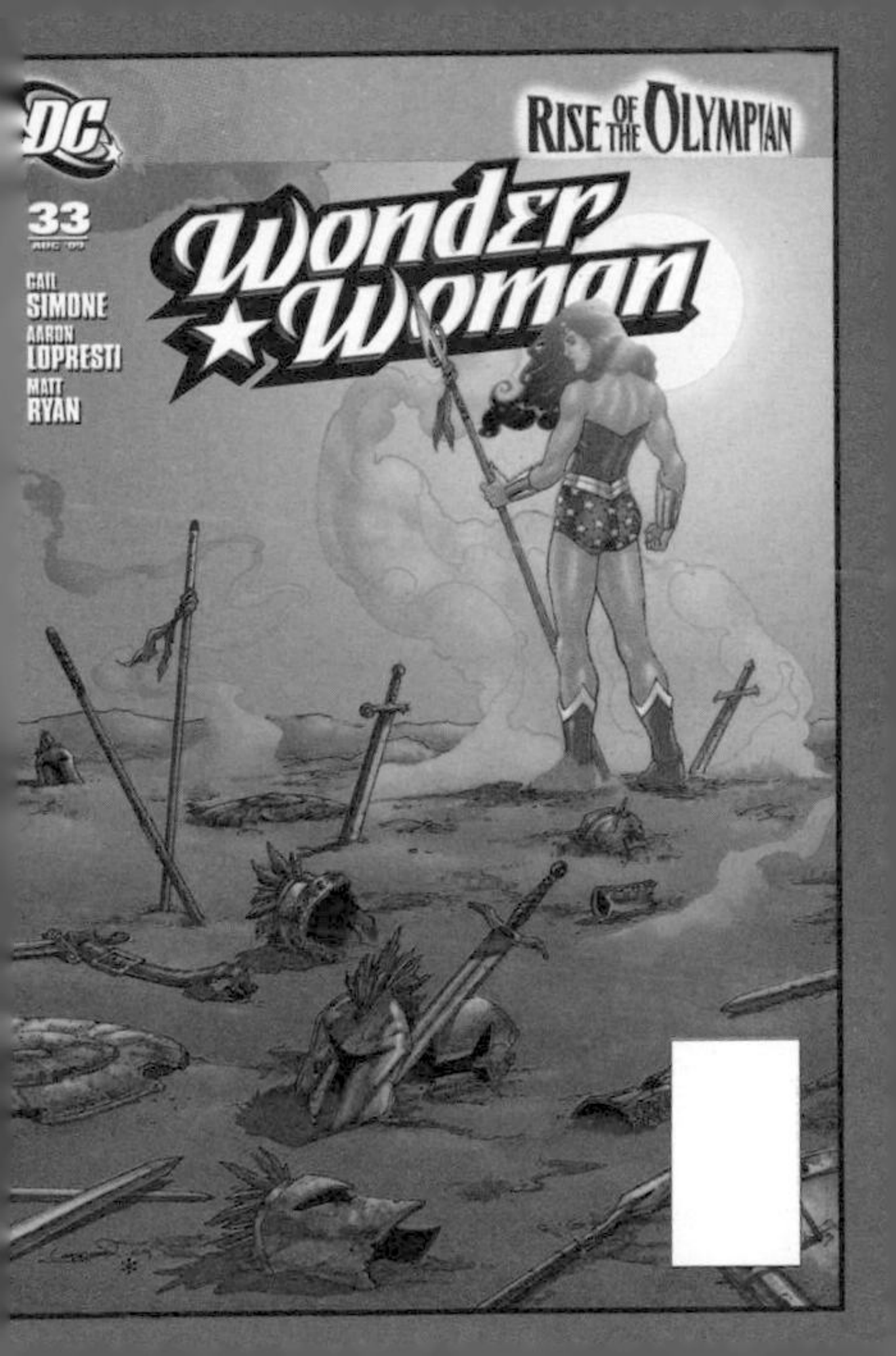
DC
RISE OF THE OLYMPIAN
33
Wonder Woman
GAIL SIMONE
AARON LOPRESTI
MATT RYAN

INSIGHT
EDITIONS

PO Box 3088
San Rafael, CA 94912
www.insighteditions.com

Find us on Facebook: www.facebook.com/InsightEditions

Follow us on Twitter: @insighteditions

WONDER WOMAN and all characters and elements © & ™ DC Comics.
WB SHIELD: ™ & © Warner Bros. Entertainment Inc. (s19)

INED41776

Wonder Woman was created by William Moulton Marston.

Published by Insight Editions, San Rafael, California, in 2019.
All rights reserved. No part of this book may be reproduced in any form without written permission from the publisher.

Library of Congress Cataloging-in-Publication Data available.

ISBN: 978-1-68383-485-4

Manufactured in China by Insight Editions

10 9 8 7 6 5 4 3 2 1